Latinas/os in the United States:
Changing the Face of América

Latinas/os in the United States:
Changing the Face of América

Edited by

Havidán Rodríguez
University of Delaware
Newark, Delaware

Rogelio Sáenz
Texas A&M University
College Station, Texas

Cecilia Menjívar
Arizona State University
Tempe, Arizona

With Forewords by

Clara E. Rodríguez

Douglas S. Massey

 Springer

Editors

Havidán Rodríguez
University of Delaware
Newark
Delaware

Rogelio Sáenz
Texas A&M University
College Station
Texas

Cecilia Menjívar
Arizona State University
Tempe
Arizona

ISBN-13: 978-0-387-71941-2   e-ISBN-13: 978-0-387-71943-6

Library of Congress Control Number: 2007929783

Printed on acid-free paper.

9 8 7 6 5 4 3 2 1

springer.com

*We dedicate this book to the millions of Latinas and Latinos who live
and work in the United States, and to the future generations who will continue
to change the face of América.*

Foreword

Clara E. Rodríguez

As is befitting a book on Latinas/os at the start of the 21st century, the chapters in this volume reflect the contemporary panorama of Latinas/os in the United States. Today, Latinas/os are the largest minority group. They accounted for 12.5% of the total U.S. population in the last decennial census; recent estimates showed the Hispanic population to be 41.3 million as of July 1, 2004, or 14% of the nation's total population.[1] However, this estimate does not include the 3.9 million residents of Puerto Rico, who are also U.S. citizens and would raise the total to 45.2 million.[2] This would make the U.S. population of Latinos the second-largest Spanish-origin population in the hemisphere, after Mexico.

The growth of this population since 1980 has been dramatic. Hispanics/Latinos grew more than seven times faster than the population of the nation as a whole, increasing by half, whereas the white (non-Hispanic) population increased by only 6% between 1980 and 1990 (U.S. Bureau of the Census, 1991, Table 1; U.S. Bureau of the Census, 1993, p. 2). In the 1990s, the Hispanic population increased 58%. Moreover, between 2003 and 2004, *one of every two* people added to the nation's population was Hispanic/Latino.[3] Consequently, not only are Latinos a substantial part of the U.S. population, but they account for half its population growth. However, such discussions of the Latino/Hispanic group often obscure the heterogeneous nature of the Latina/o population. Increasingly, Latinos are not just settling in very diverse parts of the country, but Latinas/os are also coming from many different countries. Intermarriage with non-Latinas/os and among different Latina/o national origin groups is also high and increasing. All of this makes for a very diverse population of Latinas/os playing an integral role in many aspects of American life.

Accordingly, all of the chapters in this volume reflect the contemporary panorama of Latinas/os in the United States. The chapters reflect the heterogeneity of Latinas/os and seek to include, to the degree possible, information not just on the three largest groups—Mexicans, Puerto Ricans, and Cubans—but also on smaller groups. In addition, the chapters incorporate a focus on public policy implications and views on future research agendas. This focus broadens the utility of this volume to many fields, not just in the social sciences (e.g., sociology, political science, economics, anthropology, history, geography, communications, and ethnic and racial studies) but also in the policy arena. This dimension of wide applicability is bolstered by the varied and talented contributors who reflect—as does the field of Latina/o Studies—a diversity of academic disciplines. This continues a long-standing tradition in the field of Latina/o Studies.

In addition to reflecting the current diversity of Latina/o America, another important reason to focus on Latina/o heterogeneity is to underscore how each group's mode of incorporation into the United States has influenced the group's geographic distribution, socioeconomic measures, lived experiences, and often their political orientations. It also provides an opportunity to reflect on the particular historical and geopolitical relationship that accompanies and has often influenced the migration and incorporation of different Caribbean and Latin American groups to the United States. For example, initially Mexicans became part of the United States as a result of military conquest and the Treaty of Guadalupe de Hidalgo in 1848. Puerto Ricans also became part of the United States and began to migrate to the states in substantial numbers as a result of another war, the 1898 Spanish American War. In the 20th century, the bulk of migrants from both countries arrived to fill labor shortages. In contrast, the initial waves of post-Castro Cubans arrived, fleeing a political regime that was ideologically at war with the United States. They were warmly accepted as political refugees, assisted in relocation, and given monthly allowances and other government assistance. They were seen to be predominantly skilled, upper class, white and supportive of democratic, capitalist (entrepreneurial) values and systems. Conversely, Mexicans and Puerto Ricans were tolerated because of labor shortages, but when such shortages disappeared, intolerance grew.

However, it is important to note that emphasizing the heterogeneity of the groups does not necessarily eliminate the commonalities that also exist between groups; nor does emphasizing heterogeneity mean that the diversity that exists within groups is ignored. For example, despite the ostensibly more welcoming mode of incorporation experienced by the early post-Castro immigrants, public attitudes began to shift as Cubans began to establish themselves in the United States and as less privileged Cubans (i.e., the Marielitos' migration) began to arrive. Difficulties were also experienced even by the early post-Castro immigrants. For example, the Peter Pan flights that brought young Cuban children to the Midwest did not prepare the children or the receiving community for the culture shock experienced. Also, for some Cubans, regardless of how much government assistance was provided or how well it was provided, living in the United States was not a positive experience. Finally, there had been an earlier pre-Castro community that included many members of the laboring or working classes, who shared geographic and occupational spaces as well as views and experiences with Puerto Ricans in the Northeast.

Another notable success of this volume is to expand the spectrum that has traditionally been used to examine Latinas/os in the United States. It does so, not just by focusing on the differences and commonalities of Latina/o groups but also by building upon earlier work in the field and introducing new areas of research. Of particular note is how the collected works provide updates on long-standing issues—for example, on new Latino destinations (Vásquez, Seales, & Friedmann Marquardt), demographic patterns (del Pinal), educational experiences (Vélez), labor market and labor force participation (Catanzarite & Trimble), and income, earnings, and poverty (Dávila, Mora, & Hales). Also, a number of the works take new twists or new views on such issues—for example, examining the issue of Latino incorporation in both local and transnational contexts (Courtney Smith). Others focus on relatively new fields—for example, examining the Latino demographic picture through children's eyes (Glick & Van Hook), how housing presents challenges to Latinos (Díaz McConnell), the health paradoxes among Latinos (Acevedo-Garcia & Bates), and two related and growing areas in the field: the media (Molina- Guzmán) and cultural production (Rodríguez).

Other contributions to this volume acknowledge the reality of new dimensions, as in "The Expanding Borders of Latino/as." The need for greater theoretical development is addressed by Ochoa, who focuses on cross-Latina/o relations in the United States, by Toro-Morn, who seeks to move beyond traditional conceptions of gendered dichotomies, and by González-Lopez and Vidal-Ortiz, who investigate a critical sociological perspective on sexuality. In addition, there are chapters that address political mobilization and participation (Geron & Michelson; Allen Gershon & Pantoja; Zlolniski). This is an area where we have seen only occasional and scattered works, despite its importance.

Finally, this volume also includes four chapters that address the future of important recurring issues: crime (Martínez), unions (Delgado), religion (De La Torre), and entrepreneurship (Valdez). In summary, this volume is a timely and important addition to the literature, for it addresses important theoretical and methodological issues that have not received sufficient attention in the past but that continue to surface when considering Latinas/os. The inclusion of both quantitative and qualitative in-depth analyses also makes this an exceptional volume that seeks to present a picture of the Latina/o community that is akin to a precious stone that sparkles from its numerous planes and angles.

NOTES

1. In this Foreword, I use the terms Hispanic and Latino because this is how the data I cite are gathered and presented.
2. Data on the most recent estimates of the Latino population are from http://www.census.gov/Press-Release/www/releases/archives/population/005164.html and http://www.census.gov/Press-Release/www/releases/archives/population/003153.html. Retrieved December 2, 2006.
3. Cited in http://www.census.gov/Press-Release/www/releases /archives/population/005164.html. Retrieved December 2, 2006.

Foreword

Douglas S. Massey

Latinos have been part of the American mosaic since 1848, when the Treaty of Guadalupe Hidalgo ceded the northern 40% of Mexico's territory to the United States. With its signing, some 50,000 Mexicans became U.S. citizens, and with the stroke of a pen, they were transformed from being a majority in their own country to a minority in an alien land. Thereafter, the Mexican-origin population expanded slowly through natural increase to reach around 150,000 by 1900. Before 1907, few Mexicans entered the country as immigrants, but in that year, the United States reached a "Gentlemen's Agreement" with Japan to end immigration from that country, and in response, U.S. employers began recruiting Mexicans. From just 1,400 immigrants in 1907, the inflow from Mexico grew rapidly to reach 6,600 in 1908 and 16,250 in 1909.

From 1910 to 1919, immigration from Mexico averaged around 17,000 persons per year and, once European immigration was curtailed by Congress, it mushroomed to 49,000 per year during the 1920s. By 1930, the Mexican immigrant population had reached 740,000, but the Great Depression had transformed Mexicans from wanted workers into unwanted guests, and mass deportation campaigns cut the immigrant population down to just 377,000 persons by 1940. With U.S. entry into the Second World War, however, Mexicans again became welcomed as workers and, in 1942, the Bracero Program was initiated to recruit Mexicans for short-term labor in the United States.

Although originally passed as a temporary wartime measure, this guest-worker program eventually lasted 22 years, and during its heyday in the late 1950s, it averaged 438,000 workers per year. Most braceros circulated back and forth across the border without settling, and after the termination of the Bracero Program in 1965, this circulation continued unofficially in the form of undocumented migration. From 1965 through 1985, millions of undocumented Mexicans came and went across the border, but the annual net increase was only around 150,000 per year, with around 59,000 legal immigrants arriving each year. Between immigration and natural increase, the Mexican-origin population grew to reach 13.5 million by 1990.

Although the United States acquired Puerto Rico in 1898, migrants only began arriving in large numbers on the mainland after the Second World War, when the economic transformation of the island displaced rural workers who took advantage of inexpensive flights to New York to occupy unskilled positions in its manufacturing and service sectors. By 1970, however, the outflow had largely come to a halt and the number of Puerto Ricans reached a rough annual balance that was slightly positive or negative depending on relative economic conditions on the island versus the mainland. By 1990, the number of mainland inhabitants who were of Puerto Rican origin stood at around 2.7 million.

During the 1970s, migration from the Spanish Caribbean came to be dominated by outflows from Cuba and the Dominican Republic, both of which were political in origin. The Castro Revolution of 1959 led to successive waves of emigration from Cuba, beginning with the political and economic elite in the 1960s, extending to the professional and middle classes in the 1970s, and moving on to the working classes during the 1980s. Emigration from the Dominican Republic began after U.S. occupation of the island in 1965 when American diplomats issued visas to former student agitators to leave the country in an effort to defuse a tense political situation. From small numbers during the 1960s, migration from the Dominican Republic grew to become the dominant outflow from the Caribbean by the 1980s. During this decade, the Cold War came to a head in a series of proxy confrontations between the United States and the Soviet Union in Central America, displacing large numbers of people from El Salvador, Guatemala, and Nicaragua, as well as from violence-torn Colombia.

The addition of Caribbean, Central American, and South American immigrants to the growing population of Mexicans yielded a sharp burst in the growth of the Latino population of the United States, which by 1990 had reached a total of 22.4 million persons, roughly 60% Mexican, 12% Puerto Rican, 5% Cuban, and 14% Central or South American. Given continued immigration and prevailing birth rates, it had become very clear to demographers that Latinos were on a trajectory to overtake African Americans as the nation's largest minority by around 2010.

In a variety of ways, however, the 1990s were a transformative decade, and when the results of the 2000 census were published, it quickly became clear that Latinos had already achieved this milestone. The militarization of the Mexico–U.S. border in the context of ongoing economic integration dramatically changed patterns of Mexican immigration that had prevailed for decades, bringing about an unexpected surge in population growth and a remarkable geographic diversification of the Latino population. In the 15 years from 1990 to 2005, the number of Latinos nearly doubled to 42.7 million, led by Mexicans, who increased their share to around two-thirds of the total. Whereas the vast majority of Latinos in 1990 could be found in just six states—California, New York, Texas, Florida, Illinois, and New Jersey—by 2005 they were present in significant numbers in virtually every state in the union, with the fastest growing populations being in states of the South and Midwest. During the 1990s, immigration from Latin America shifted from being a regional phenomenon affecting a handful of states into a national phenomenon affecting all 50 states. Moreover, a growing fraction of the new immigrants were in unauthorized status because the militarization of the Mexico–U.S. border had the perverse effect of reducing out-migration rather than lowering in-migration by undocumented migration.

The combination of rising numbers, growing geographic diversification, and mounting illegality combined to make Latin American immigration a controversial public issue and Latinos a lightening rod for popular discontent, a situation that was exacerbated by anti-foreign hysteria in the wake of September 11, 2001. In a context of confusing claims and counterclaims and strident but uninformed debate, a reliable book on Latinos represents a welcome and much needed contribution to public understanding. Never before in the nation's history have so many non-Hispanic blacks and whites been exposed to so many Latinos in so many places, and never before has such a huge amount of misinformation abounded.

This volume goes a long way toward setting the record straight by developing a factual portrait of contemporary Latinos in all their diversity. After considering the subtleties of Latino identity and how to measure it in actual populations, the volume's contributors apply the best methods of social science to the most accurate data available to construct a comprehensive demographic, social, economic, political, and cultural portrait not just of Latinos but also of the constituent national origin. The volume's factual results and balanced assessment of trends will prove an invaluable resource to citizens seeking to understand Latinos and their changing role in the population and society of the 21st-century United States.

Preface

This volume is about Latinas/os,[1] but what are Latinas/os? Who is this population that we cluster or lump together under the umbrella of Latinas/os or Hispanics? What is their historical background and culture? What are their demographic and socioeconomic characteristics? What language(s) do they speak? Where do they come from and where do they live? What are their levels of education? Where do they work? What are their religious, political, and sexual preferences? How do they identify themselves? How does U.S. society and the media view this growing population? What have been the demographic, social, economic, political, and cultural impacts that this population has had on the United States? What are the challenges and opportunities that this population confronts in the United States? How have and how will they continue to shape and change the face of América? There are no simple or easy answers to these questions. The answers depend on a number of diverse and complicated issues, such as the groups' cultural, historical, and political backgrounds, and on how these diverse groups arrived in the United States and how they were received (or not) by the host country, among many other factors. This volume aims to focus on, explore, and enhance our understanding of these issues.

WHO ARE THE LATINAS/OS IN THE UNITED STATES?

The National Research Council's (2006) report titled *Multiple Origins, Uncertain Destinies: Hispanics and the American Future* indicates that the Latina/o population in the United States is "characterized by a youthful age structure; a large number of foreign born, including many 'undocumented'; low levels of education; and disproportionate concentration in low-skill, low-wage jobs" (2006:3). However, although these characterizations and generalizations might be accurate, they tend to obscure and underscore the significant differences or heterogeneity that exists within and between the multiple groups that are lumped together under the Hispanic or Latina/o umbrella. Despite the fact that they are generally clustered together under the category of "Hispanics," important demographic and socioeconomic differences exist among these groups. Further, they also experience significant differences in terms of their historical and cultural backgrounds and their modes of integration into the United States, which, to a large extent, impacts their geographical distribution in this country and their employment patterns, educational levels, income, poverty, and even political affiliation, among other factors. This volume also seeks to explore these differences.

Latinas/os are a mosaic of people. They are Mexicans, Hondurans, Puerto Ricans, Argentineans, Cubans, Salvadorans, Dominicans, Panamanians, Guatemalans, Nicaraguans, Peruvians, Costa Ricans, Bolivians, Chileans, Colombians, and Venezuelans, and we can go on with an extensive list of Latina/o subgroups. They are also black, white, *trigueño/a, café con leche*, or some combination thereof; Latinas/os are a rainbow of colors and they have different racial preferences. For example, whereas Cubans overwhelmingly (84.5%) identified themselves as "white" in the 2000 U.S. Census about three-fifths (58.6%) of Dominicans, 45% of Mexicans, and 38% of Puerto Ricans self-identified as "others," as did more than half of Salvadorans and Guatemalans and one-third of Nicaraguans.

Latinas/os are (mostly) Catholics, Protestants, Jewish, and Islamic, but there are also atheists, *Santeros/as*, and *Curanderos/as* (see De La Torre in this volume). Many have relatively high and increasing levels of education but, nevertheless, lack of education and elevated high school attrition rates (some of the highest in the country) remain critical issues. The chapter on education by Velez will document the critical challenges and the opportunities for Latinas/os in the educational arena. Latinas/os in the United States have high levels of labor force participation and have experienced rapid economic mobility and yet unemployment and dead-end and low-wage jobs dominate the occupations that Latinas/os occupy, as documented by Dávila and colleagues.

Latinas/os or persons of "Spanish" descent were part of this land before the United States of America came into being.[2] Others were born and raised in the United States, and yet others are fairly recent arrivals. Latinas/os are also U.S. citizens, resident "aliens," and there are those who are "undocumented" or find themselves in "in-between" legal statuses (Menjívar, 2006). They speak only English, only Spanish, while some are bilingual, some prefer *Spanglish*, and yet others might speak one or several Mayan languages, Garifuna, or languages other than Spanish. Again, language patterns and preferences vary, quite significantly, by Latino-origin group (Saenz, 2004).

Some Latina/o groups were very well received by the U.S government and integrated *fairly well* into the U.S. economy and society while others were rejected and continue to experience significant discrimination and racism in this country. It is noteworthy that, as highlighted by Golash-Boza (2006:29), Latinas/os who experience discrimination are less likely to identify themselves as "Americans" and are more likely to identify themselves as "Latina/o" or "Hispanic." This presents an important predicament: In order for Latinas/os to become fully integrated into the fabric of the U.S. society, problems associated with racism and discrimination need to be addressed and alleviated.

Stereotypes regarding the Latina/o population in the United States seem to prevail in our public discourse, are promulgated by the media, and go mainly unchallenged throughout our educational system. Golash-Boza indicates that Latina/o-based stereotypes portrayed in the United States are similar to those used for African Americans: "Latinos/as are seen as less intelligent, more prone to be on welfare, and more likely to be involved in drugs or other criminal activities than whites or Asians" (2006:28). This volume will address some of these stereotypes and will provide empirical evidence to debunk such myths.

Latinas/os have become part of the U.S. population as a result of annexation, invasion, or military conquest; as a result of political or religious persecution in their home countries; because they were fleeing communism or other types of oppressive political systems; or because they were searching for opportunities to improve their lives and that of their families and they came to this country in search of the "American dream." Previous research shows that the mode of integration into the United States is an important determinant of a group's socioeconomic well-being. In this context, the experiences of Mexicans, Puerto Ricans, Dominicans, Cubans, Nicaraguans, and Salvadorans, among others, are very different and have significant implications for these groups. The different modes of integration into the United States have had an important impact on the subgroups' abilities to adapt to the receiving country and on their eventual economic success or lack thereof. Moreover, these diverse backgrounds, experiences, and modes of incorporation have, to a large extent, shaped the integration, growth, and development of the Latina/o population in the United States and they have impacted how the U.S. government and its population welcomes (or not) and views these diverse groups of Latina/o immigrants.

This volume will explore and expand on the aforementioned issues and will present a portrait of Latinas/os in this country; it seeks to educate and increase our awareness regarding the diversity or heterogeneity that exists among the Latina/o population and to carefully examine the social, economic, demographic, and cultural impacts and contributions that this ever-increasing population has had and will continue to have in the United States.

THE GROWTH OF THE LATINA/O POPULATION

As a result of rapid migration from Latin America and the Caribbean and relatively high levels of fertility, the Latina/o population in the United States has experienced significant and rapid growth during the past decades, particularly since the 1960s. Consequently, Latinas/os have become the largest minority group, surpassing the African American population in the United States. The 2000 U.S. Census shows that Latinas/os constituted 12.5% of the U.S. population, compared to 12.1% for African Americans. The 2005 American Community Survey (ACS) shows that the Latina/o population represented 14.5% of the U.S. population compared to under 3% in 1950 (Lee & Edmonston 2005). The Latina/o population will continue to experience rapid growth and it is estimated that by 2030, given current demographic trends, this group could constitute about one-fourth of the U.S. population (National Research Council, 2006). It is noteworthy, however, that some Latina/o groups are experiencing more rapid growth than others. For example, according to Rumbaut (2006, Table 2-1), from 1990 to 2000, the fastest growing Latina/o population subgroups were Hondurans, which experienced a population growth of about 166% during this decade, followed by Venezuelans (157%), Costa Ricans (134%), Guatemalans (118%), Ecuadorians (116%), Mexicans (115%), Paraguayans (101%), and Dominicans (100%). It is important to note that with the exception of Mexican Americans (with a population of about 9.2 million in 2000), these groups are relatively small in terms of their total population size and almost all of their growth during this 10-year period was due to immigration. On the other hand, Cubans and Puerto Ricans experienced much lower rates of growth from 1990 to 2000, 18% and 22%, respectively (see Rumbaut, 2006); these two groups, especially Cubans, are increasingly becoming an aging (elderly) population as a consequence of low levels of fertility (see del Pinal in this volume).

According to population estimates from the 2005 ACS, Mexican Americans, primarily concentrated in the southwestern United States, accounted for about 64% of Latinas/os compared to 9% for Puerto Ricans (primarily located in the Northeast, not including the 3.9 million Puerto Ricans residing on the Island), 3.5% for Cubans (primarily concentrated in Florida), 3% for Salvadorans (with a heavy concentration in the Northeast and West/Southwest), 2.7% for Dominicans (with very large concentrations in the Northeast), 1.8% for Guatemalans, 1.7% for Colombians, and 14.3% for "other" Latinas/os (with a significant presence in the Southwest and in the Northeast).

Despite the concentration of these groups in particular geographical areas, many of them have experienced significant geographical dispersion throughout this country. Indeed, over the last couple of decades, Latinas/os have increasingly moved to areas of the country that have not had this population in the past—places that have been designated "Latina/o new destinations."

For example, the documentary "Estamos Aquí" (We Are Here) examines the growth of the Guatemalan population in Georgetown, Delaware. The film provides a critical and thought-provoking overview of the Guatemalan migratory movement (over 2,000 miles) and the experiences of these Guatemalan groups both in their home countries and in Georgetown. These migrants left their "patria" as a consequence of about 36 years of civil war, political instability, extreme poverty, and lack of economic opportunities; they eventually came to Sussex County, Delaware (the "birthplace of the broiler industry") to work, primarily, in the poultry industry (e.g., Perdue Farms). "Estamos Aquí" "explores how the influx of Guatemalan immigrants, legal and illegal, to Georgetown, Delaware has impacted [the] state, as well as how immigration in general has figured into the national political agenda."[3] In some ways, the experiences of these Guatemalan immigrants are also a reflection of the *journey* and the social and economic experiences of millions of Latina/o immigrants that continuously arrive in the United States.

The increasing Latina/o population has important social, cultural, and political implications for the United States and for the Latina/o population itself. Not only are they growing, but their origins are now more varied. The United States recognized the importance of the increasing Latina/o population when, for the first time in U.S. history, the 1980 Census included a question to obtain a count of the population of "Hispanic" descent. For those who selected the "Hispanic" category, they were asked to identify their ethnic background (e.g., Mexican American, Puerto Rican, Cuban, and "other" Spanish/Hispanic/Latino).

The economic power of U.S. Latinas/os has been recognized at all levels. It is estimated that in 2000, the buying power of Latinas/os was about $440 billion. According to the University of Georgia's Selig Center, by 2008 the purchasing power of Latinas/os will approximate $1 trillion. These figures, however, can be misleading and might obscure the high levels of inequality and extreme poverty experienced by many Latina/o subgroups in the United States. As we will document in this volume, poverty continues to be widespread among the Latina/o population and varies quite significantly among the different subgroups that fall within this category.

The political power of Latinas/os (despite their relative low participation in electoral politics) has also been recognized by politicians who have attempted to develop campaigns specifically aimed at Latina/o subgroups, with commercials and even politicians trying to address these groups in their "native" tongue (e.g., Spanish); some have been quite successful in their endeavors. For example, we should note that from the 2000 to the 2004 presidential elections, President George W. Bush experienced a significant increase in the number of Latinas/os voting for his candidacy as President of the United States, an increase of 9%, which was higher than any other ethnic/racial group. Nevertheless, during the 2004 elections, we also observed significant differences in political preferences and actual voting behavior among the different Latina/o subgroups.

Despite the aforementioned results for the 2004 U.S. presidential elections, the Latina/o population tends to predominantly affiliate themselves with the Democratic Party, with the notable exception of Cubans, who tend to vote Republican. As will be documented in this volume, the political power, electoral participation, and activism of Latinas/os in this country is becoming more visible in U.S. politics. The political mobilization or activism of Latinas/os has, more recently, been fueled by stringent and even more restrictive immigration policies (particularly following the terrorist attacks of September 11, 2001). For example, there are new federal mandates aimed at "tightening" the border and providing more stringent enforcement of "illegal" immigration for the sake of enhancing "national security," including the deployment of the National Guard and building a fence in the border[4] between Mexico and the United States, the targeting of "undocumented" immigrants as "criminal aliens," and the English-only movement that has spread throughout the United States. Further, anti-immigrant laws or ordinances have been emerging throughout the country, especially in small towns or local cities, aimed at preventing "undocumented" immigrants from renting apartments; fining companies that hire and landlords that rent to "illegal" immigrants; allowing police to "ticket" anyone who is not able to prove that they are U.S. residents, or passing voters' initiatives to keep immigrants from voting (even though they are already prohibited by law to vote), not allowing immigrants to obtain a drivers license, or even to obtain medical care.

In 2006, the city of Hazleton, Pennsylvania, which has been one of the leaders in the battle against "illegal" immigrants, approved what seemed to be one of the most restrictive ordinances of its kind in the United States, imposing fines of up to $1,000 to landlords who rent to "illegal" immigrants, denying business permits to corporations who employ "undocumented" immigrants, and making English the official language. Elsmere, Delaware soon followed suit and attempted to implement similar restrictions, to the extent that *The News Journal* (Delaware's primary newspaper, October 21, 2006) reported: "Elsmere: a wonderful place to live…unless you are Mexican." In Pahrump, Nevada, an ordinance was passed that made it illegal to have a foreign nation's flag flying higher than the U.S. flag or standing alone; this was primarily a result of the increasing Mexican population and the home country flags that were emerging throughout the city.

Similar types of local anti-immigrant (or anti-Latina/o) initiatives have emerged in many parts of the country, including California, Nevada, Utah, Louisiana, Montana, Pennsylvania, Colorado, Texas, and Georgia.[5] The consequences of these types of anti-immigrant (particularly anti-Latina/o) initiatives is that all Latina/o subgroups have been negatively impacted and the "burden of proof" falls on the Latina/o population; that is, individuals are "undocumented" immigrants unless able to prove otherwise (guilty unless proven innocent). Many of the aforementioned ordinances have been challenged by the Latina/o community and supporters of civil rights, and, in some cases, they have been blocked by federal judges. For example, on July 26, 2007, a federal judge ruled that the city of Hazleton's anti-immigration law was "unconstitutional." Moreover, this has also resulted in increasing activism and political mobilization, bringing to the forefront the political power of the Latina/o population. This was made evident quite recently during the Spring 2006 marches around the country demanding the protection of immigrant rights and a just immigration law reform, events that were spearheaded by Latinas/os and multiple Latina/o organizations. The section of this volume titled "Political Mobilization and Participation Among Latinas/os" will highlight and explore these and related issues.

It is also important to note that the Latina/o population stands out in a number of ways from previous generations of immigrants to the United States from different countries and cultural backgrounds. As mentioned previously, the Latina/o population continues to experience unprecedented growth and will continue to do so in the foreseeable future. It already constitutes the largest minority group in the nation and will represent about one-fourth of the total U.S. population by 2030. Although experiencing geographic dispersion, Latinas/os remain concentrated in certain social and economic sectors or regions of the country, which has resulted in important and increasing economic and political visibility and the preservation of cultural expressions. They have come and continue to arrive in the United States in a historical period in which technological, transportation, and communication advancements and innovations have transformed our ability to communicate and stay connected with loved loves; this has facilitated and encouraged close connections and frequent interactions with their home countries (although this is impacted by socioeconomic factors as well). Moreover, in a variety of Latin American countries, politicians, seeking the support and votes of those who have left their countries, have rallied to allow these emigrants to vote in local elections. Also, some Latin American governments have taken a proactive role (albeit with limited success) in working with the U.S. government to call for the protection of immigrant workers and residents from their home countries living in the United States.

Finally, Latinas/os in this country continue to be an important source of income or revenue for their families left behind and for their home countries. The national economies of many Latin American and Caribbean countries depend heavily on the remittances from their nationals in the United States. For example, remittances have far outpaced revenue from coffee exports in Guatemala, El Salvador, and Nicaragua; as well as in Honduras and Panama, relative to the banana export industry. In these countries, remittances tend to be at least three times greater than tourism revenues (see Agunias, 2006). These factors not only shape the interactions and connectedness of Latinas/os to their home countries but they also impact their integration and adaptation to the American society.

WHY A NEW BOOK ON THE LATINA/O EXPERIENCE IN THE UNITED STATES?

Important differences exist among the different Latina/o subgroups in terms of their ethnic and racial identities, religious beliefs, interracial marriages, sexual preferences, health status, and language patterns, among others.[6] Further, how Latinas/os identify themselves and their incorporation into the United States is, to a large extent, determined by a number of historical, cultural, social, political, and economic factors. However, we continue to lump all of these groups together under the category of "Hispanics" or "Latinas/os" without paying special attention to the heterogeneity or diversity that exists among the different national groups. Moreover, an overwhelming number of books, articles, and research initiatives on the Latina/o population generally tend to focus on and emphasize the differences among the three largest subgroups (e.g., Mexicans, Puerto Ricans, and Cubans) while clustering the other Latina/o subgroups into the "other" category, thus masking or ignoring important and significant cultural, demographic, and socioeconomic differences that exist between these groups.

This volume is unique compared to extant volumes that have focused on the Latina/o population in that it is multidisciplinary in its focus and it covers a range of topics and issues in an attempt to provide a holistic or comprehensive overview on Latinas/os in the United States. Most importantly, we seek to explore and discuss the diversity that exists within the Latina/o population and to uncover and examine the different pieces that form part of this collage or medley of people. Most researchers or scholars who write about, conduct research, or focus on Latinas/os in this country tend to present or develop their substantive or theoretical arguments based on their academic and disciplinary backgrounds as well as their methodological expertise, thus ignoring other elements, disciplines, and research informed by other methods that might bring important ideas to their corresponding analyses. This volume brings together different academic disciplines and perspectives in order to enhance our understanding of the Latina/o population in the United States. To our knowledge, there has been no systematic effort to generate a publication that uses a multidisciplinary framework to provide a detailed overview and comparative analysis of the different Latina/o subgroups in this country and their experiences, including (but not limited to) their historical, cultural, political, demographic, economic, and religious experiences. This volume is an important step in that direction.

We attempt to present a holistic perspective on Latinas/os in the United States, taking into account their divergent backgrounds, modes of integration, and their experiences in this country. The authors of the different chapters included in this volume address important theoretical and methodological issues related to the study of Latinas/os and present in-depth analyses (both quantitative and qualitative) of substantive issues relevant to this population, including migration; demographic patterns and processes; education; labor force participation; income and poverty; housing; health; religion and religiosity; political participation and activism; the politics of identity; gender, sex roles, and feminism; sexuality; Latinas/os in the media; and cultural production, among other topics and issues. We attempt to provide a comprehensive portrait of the diverse subgroups that comprise the Latina/o population and their impact on the U.S. economy and society.

All of the contributors were asked to address the complexities and the heterogeneity of the different Latina/o groups. This task or request was easier said than done. In some thematic areas, very little information, data, and research exists that go beyond the "big three" (e.g., Mexicans, Puerto Ricans, and Cubans). For many authors, this was indeed a challenge, but many prevailed and were able to develop excellent discussions that highlighted the diversity that exists within the Latina/o population. We also asked the authors to explore the political and public policy implications of the issues, topics, and findings presented in their thematic areas. For example, authors were *strongly encouraged* to think, critically and creatively, about the implications and impact of the research and the findings presented in their respective chapters, particularly as they relate to the increasing Latina/o population in the United States.

Finally, all authors were asked to provide recommendations regarding areas for future research, focusing on critical areas and issues that merit further study and exploration. What are the next steps? What are the remaining gaps? What issues merit further attention/research? We hope that these recommendations will serve as an impetus and encouragement that will engage scholars and researchers interested in topics related to Latinas/os in the United States and will provide an opportunity for further dialogue and collaboration across disciplines. In addition, our expectation is that the areas for future research on the Latina/o population, identified throughout this volume, will impact the funding priorities of federal agencies, such as the National Science Foundation and the National Institutes of Health, among others, as well as private and nonprofit research foundations.

BOOK FORMAT AND STRUCTURE

The volume is divided into seven sections focusing on the following thematic areas: theoretical and methodological issues related to research on the Latina/o population; immigration and Latina/o incorporation; the social demography of Latinas/os; schooling, work, and income; Latina/o culture; redefining borders; and political mobilization and participation among Latinas/os. Although the editors worked to ensure that all of the chapters were a "good fit" for the thematic sections in which they were included, at times these might appear to be arbitrary decisions, as the chapters and the topics discussed could have very well fitted in a number of these sections.

It is also noteworthy that in the long journey that resulted in this volume, we lost (due to a variety of factors) and could not include a number of issues/chapters that we thought were important for this contribution, including chapters focusing on citizenship and naturalization, U.S. immigration policy and its impact on the Latina/o population, race and racial stratification in the United States, the politics of language, sports in the Latina/o and the American context, intraethnic and interethnic relationships, the 1.5 and 2.0 Latina/o generations, and the public sociology of Latinas/os. However, one of the advantages of a volume of this nature is that although we do not have chapters exclusively focusing on these particular issues, the majority of these topics permeate through many, if not all, of the chapters included in this volume. Many of the topics discussed in the different chapters require a careful examination and discussion of race and racism, interethnic relations, immigration policy, and citizenship and naturalization; topics that are critical to any subject matter focusing on the Latina/o population in the United States.

CLOSING REMARKS

This volume focuses on the Latina/o experience in the United States; it highlights the accomplishments, problems, challenges, and opportunities for change that Latinas/os confront, as well as their contributions to the U.S. society. The contributing authors have generated important and provocative discussions that emphasize the heterogeneity that characterizes Latina/o subgroups, public policy implications, and areas for future research. As such, this work goes beyond the traditional approach of only focusing on the largest Latina/o groups in the United States (e.g., Mexicans, Puerto Ricans, and Cubans). Furthermore, this volume has a multidisciplinary focus, which includes the collaboration and contributions of distinguished scholars and researchers (as well as rising scholars) from a diverse number of academic areas, including sociology, political sciences, economics, demography, history, religious studies, anthropology, ethnic studies, criminal justice, and health, among other areas.

Participating authors were able to focus on and compare/contrast the Latina/o subgroups and their experiences in the United States in their particular substantive areas. They highlight the difficulties and challenges that this population is confronting in the United States and provide public policy recommendations in order to enhance the educational, employment, and economic opportunities for this population. We hope that this volume will have an important impact in our understanding of the Latina/o experiences and their significant and positive contributions to this country. In conclusion, let us not forget that the Latina/o population is here to stay and that it has had and will continue to have an important impact on our society. As the beginnings of the 21st century clearly show, Latinas and Latinos have changed and will continue to change the face of América.

Havidán Rodríguez
University of Delaware
Rogelio Sáenz
Texas A&M University
Cecilia Menjívar
Arizona State University

NOTES

1. Throughout this volume, we will use the terms "Latinas/os" and "Hispanics" interchangeably to denote the population of Hispanic, Latin American, or Caribbean descent that reside in the United States.
2. The population of Spanish heritage has resided in what we call today the United States since the 16th century (see del Pinal & Singer, 1997).

3. For additional information, visit www.ServiamMedia.org; Retrieved January 31, 2007. "Estamos Aquí" is a production of Serviam Media, a nonprofit media organization.
4. It is important to note that it has been the Republican Party, under the leadership of President George W. Bush, that has spearheaded these policies along the U.S.–Mexico border. This is the same Republican Party of former President Ronald Reagan, who, in an internationally acclaimed speech in West Berlin, Germany (June 12, 1987 at the Brandenburg Gate), indicated:
    Behind me stands a wall that encircles the free sectors of this city, part of a vast system of barriers that divides the entire continent of Europe. From the Baltic, south, those barriers cut across Germany in a gash of barbed wire, concrete, dog runs, and guard towers. Farther south, there may be no visible, no obvious wall. But there remain armed guards and checkpoints all the same—still a restriction on the right to travel, still an instrument to impose upon ordinary men and women the will of a totalitarian state. Yet it is here in Berlin where the wall emerges most clearly; here, cutting across your city, where the news photo and the television screen have imprinted this brutal division of a continent upon the mind of the world. Standing before the Brandenburg Gate, every man is a German, separated from his fellow men. Every man is a Berliner, forced to look upon a scar … Today I say: As long as the gate is closed, as long as this scar of a wall is permitted to stand, it is not the German question alone that remains open, but the question of freedom for all mankind … General Secretary Gorbachev, if you seek peace, if you seek prosperity for the Soviet Union and Eastern Europe, if you seek liberalization: Come here to this gate! Mr. Gorbachev, open this gate! *Mr. Gorbachev, tear down this wall!* (our emphasis; retrieved January 21, 2007; http://www.reaganfoundation.org/reagan/speeches/wall.asp).
5. According to a report in *The News Journal*, over 100 municipalities in 27 states have considered laws targeted at "illegal" immigrants; the report indicates that "35 towns have approved illegal-immigrant laws, 35 have defeated them and 35 others have ordinances pending" (January 21, 2007: A14).
6. Although these Latina/o subgroups are quite heterogeneous, they do share and, some would argue, are unified by similar social, cultural, and economic experiences, thus contributing to a "common" Latina/o or Hispanic identity.

REFERENCES

Agunias, D. (2006). Remittance Trends in Central America. *Migration Information Source*. Retrieved January 31, 2007; http://www.migrationinformation.org/Feature/display.cfm?id=393

del Pinal, J., & Singer, A. (1997). Generations of Diversity: Latinos in the United States. *Population Bulletin*, *52*(3). Washington, DC: Population Reference Bureau.

Golash-Boza, T. (2006). Dropping the Hyphen? Becoming Latino(a)-American through Racialized Assimilation. *Social Forces*, *85*(1), 27–56.

Lee, S. M., & Edmonston, B. (2005). New Marriages, New Families: U.S. Racial and Hispanic Intermarriage. *Population Bulletin*, *60*(2). Washington, DC: The Population Reference Bureau.

Menjívar, C. (2006). Liminal Legality: Salvadoran and Guatemalan Immigrants' Lives in the United States. *American Journal of Sociology*, *111*(4), 999–1037.

National Research Council. (2006). *Multiple Origins, Uncertain Destinies: Hispanics and the American Future*. Panel on Hispanics in the United States. In M. Tienda & F. Mitchell (Eds.). Committee on Population, Division of Behavioral and Social Sciences and Education. Washington, DC: The National Academies Press.

Rumbaut, R. G. (2006). The Making of a People. In Marta Tienda & Faith Mitchell (Eds.), *Multiple Origins, Uncertain Destinies: Hispanics and the Future of America*. Panel on Hispanics in the United States (pp. 16–65). Committee on Population, Division of Behavioral and Social Sciences and Education. Washington, DC: The National Academies Press.

Saenz, R. (2004). *Latinos and the Changing Face of America*. The American People Series, Census 2000. New York: Russell Sage Foundation and Population Reference Bureau.

Acknowledgments

Editing this volume was a long journey that allowed us to interact with many colleagues and friends from throughout the United States, with individuals from different academic and research backgrounds, from diverse areas of expertise, and with very strong scholarly commitments to the Latina/Latino population in the United States. As is always the case with edited volumes, it was a difficult and complex matter to determine the correct mix of chapters, topics, and people that would result in a contribution that significantly impacts or transforms our knowledge and understanding of a particular subject area and that debunks the myths and fallacies associated with a particular racial, ethnic, or underrepresented group. However, we are confident that we have achieved the appropriate mix and balance.

The contributors of this volume have thought long and hard about the Latina/o population in the United States—their struggles, challenges, success stories, and contributions, as well as the implications for our society. The authors were asked to engage in an important discussion about a number of topics and issues that are critical to our understanding of the Latina/o population in América. Some authors were pushed very (some would argue too) hard to think about the causes, consequences, and implications of the heterogeneity that exists among our Latina/o population. It was a long but interesting and provocative (albeit at times difficult) discussion. Working with such a distinguished and diverse group of professionals can be a challenging but a very important, engaging, and productive endeavor. To all our colleagues who made this journey possible and who contributed to this volume, we want to say "muchas gracias." Thank you for your time, your ideas, your thoughts, and for putting up with all of the comments, changes, and recommendations provided by the reviewers.

Many other people made important contributions to our deliberations, provided interesting ideas and recommendations, and, at times, were our sounding boards. Their help and cooperation in this process is also greatly appreciated. Melanie Scriptunas, a graduate student in the Department of English at the University of Delaware, carefully reviewed all of the chapters and provided important and critical feedback. Thanks Melanie! Our appreciation also goes to Dr. Stephen A. Bernhardt, the Andrew Kirkpatrick Professor of Writing and Chairperson of the Department of English at the University of Delaware. He provided the necessary assistance to allow Melanie to work with us in developing this project. There are also many people at Springer who were instrumental in helping us develop this project; special thanks go to Teresa M. Krauss and Katie Chabalko, at the Springer Social and Behavioral Sciences Division, for their feedback and support in this process.

Finally, we would like to express our most sincere appreciation and gratitude to our "familias," who have been patient and supportive, have endured our long hours at the office, in front of the computer monitor, and our frequent travels, and have served as catalysts for the work that we do. Many sacrifices have been made here and in our home countries that have contributed to our formation and development; without our "familias," our lives and our world views would have been very different.

Contents

SECTION C. THE SOCIAL DEMOGRAPHY OF LATINAS/OS

SECTION D. SCHOOLING, WORK, AND INCOME AMONG LATINAS/OS

SECTION E. LATINA/O CULTURE

Contributors

Dolores Acevedo-Garcia, Associate Professor of Society, Human Development and Health, Harvard School of Public Health. Her research focuses on the social determinants of racial/ethnic disparities in health, and the social policies that might contribute to reduce such disparities.

Lisa M. Bates, Robert Wood Johnson Health & Society Scholar with the Institute for Social and Economic Research and Policy and the Department of Epidemiology at Columbia University, New York, New York. She is trained as a social epidemiologist and her research focuses on social inequalities, immigrant adaptation, and health.

Lisa Catanzarite, Associate Professor, Department of Sociology, Washington State University. Catanzarite's research centers on labor market inequality by race, ethnicity, gender, and immigration.

Alberto Dávila, Professor of Economics, V.F. "Doc" and Gertrude Neuhaus Chair for Entrepreneurship, and Department Chair, Department of Economics and Finance, The University of Texas—Pan American. His research focuses on Hispanic labor markets, the economics of language, the economics of the U.S.-Mexico border, and immigration.

Miguel A. De La Torre, Director of Iliff's Justice & Peace Institute and Associate Professor of Social Ethics, Iliff School of Theology. He has published over 11 books, including the award-winning *Reading the Bible from the Margins*, *Santería: The Beliefs and Rituals of a Growing Religion in America,* and *Doing Christian Ethics from the Margins*. His most recent work is *A Lily among the Thorns: Imagining a New Christian Sexuality.*

Héctor L. Delgado, Professor of Sociology, University of La Verne. He is the author of *New Immigrants, Old Unions: Organizing Undocumented Workers in Los Angeles* (Temple University Press, 1993) and several articles on unions, immigrants, and race and ethnicity.

Jorge del Pinal, formerly Assistant Division Chief for Special Population Statistics, Population Division, U.S. Census Bureau. His research focuses on the population dynamics of Latinos and on immigration.

Elisa Facio, Associate Professor, Department of Ethnic Studies, University of Colorado, Boulder. She is the author of *Understanding Older Chicanas*. Her research focuses on Chicana feminisms and knowledges, age, aging and generations, transnational studies, and Cuban sex workers.

Kim Geron, California Department of Political Science, State University East Bay. His most recent publication is *Latino Political Power* (Lynne Rienner Publications, 2005).

Sarah Allen Gershon, doctoral candidate, Department of Political Science, Arizona State University. Her research focuses on media and politics, as well as race, ethnicity, and gender.

Jennifer E. Glick, Associate Professor of Sociology, School of Social and Family Dynamics and Center for Population Dynamics, Arizona State University. Her research focuses on adaptation of immigrants to the United States, family and household structure of immigrants and the academic trajectories of immigrant children from diverse national origins.

Gloria González-López, Assistant Professor, Department of Sociology, The University of Texas at Austin. Her most recent book is *Erotic Journeys: Mexican Immigrants and Their Sex Lives* (University of California Press, 2005). Her research focuses on sexuality and gender with Mexican populations in both countries, the United States and Mexico.

Brian Gratton, Professor, Department of History, and Affiliate Faculty, Center for Latin American Research, Arizona State University. Research interests include refugees, immigration policy, and Latino immigrants in the United States and Europe. http://www.asu.edu/clas/history/FundedProjects/.

Myron P. Gutmann, Director, Inter-university Consortium for Political and Social Research, Professor of History, and Research Professor, Population Studies Center, University of Michigan. His research focuses on the demographic history of the western United States and on the relationship among population, agriculture, and environment.

Isabel Molina Guzmán, Assistant professor of Communications, Institute of Communications Research, and affiliate of the Latina/o Studies Program and Gender and Women's Studies Program, University of Illinois Champaign-Urbana. Her research examining media discourses of Latinidad and its intersectionality with gender, sexuality, race, and ethnicity has appeared in journals such as *Critical Studies in Media Communication* and *Latino Studies*.

Alma D. Hales, Ph.D. student in International Business, College of Business Administration, The University of Texas—Pan American. Her research interests include Hispanic labor markets and the economics of language and education.

Marie Friedmann Marquardt, Department of Religious Studies, Agnes Scott College. Her research focuses on religion among Latino immigrants to the U.S. Southeast, and she is co-author, with Manuel A. Vásquez, of *Globalizing the Sacred: Religion across the Americas* (Rutgers University Press, 2003).

Ramiro Martinez, Jr., Associate Professor of Criminal Justice, Florida International University. He is the author of *Latino Homicide: Immigration, Violence and Community*, editor of *Immigration and Crime: Race, Ethnicity, and Violence*. He is a recent recipient of the Florida International University Faculty Award for Excellence in Research.

Douglas S. Massey, Henry G. Bryant Professor of Sociology and Public Affairs, Princeton University. His most recent book is *Categorically Unequal: The American Stratification System* (Russell Sage Foundation, 2007).

Eileen Diaz McConnell, Department of Transborder Chicana/o and Latina/o Studies, Tempe, Arizona State University. Professor McConnell's research interests include racial/ethnic inequality in U.S. housing outcomes, Latina/o demography, and Latina/o experiences in nontraditional areas of the United States.

Cecilia Menjívar, Associate Professor of Sociology, School of Social and Family Dynamics, Arizona State University. Her areas of research include social networks, family, gender relations, religion, and the church among Latin American-origin immigrants in the United States as well as in Central America.

Melissa R. Michelson, Department of Political Science, California State University East Bay. Her research focuses on Latino immigrant political incorporation and minority political mobilization.

Marie T. Mora, Professor of Economics, Department of Economics and Finance, The University of Texas—Pan American. Her research focuses on Hispanic labor markets, the economics of the U.S.-Mexico border, and the economics of language. She is currently on the editorial board of *Social Science Quarterly* and is the President of The American Society of Hispanic Economists.

Gilda L. Ochoa, Associate Professor of Sociology and Chicana/o Studies, Pomona College. She is the author of *Becoming Neighbors in a Mexican American Community: Power, Conflict, and Solidarity* (University of Texas Press, 2004) and co-editor of *Latino Los Angeles: Transformations, Communities, and Activism* (University of Arizona Press, 2005).

Adrian D. Pantoja, Associate Professor of Political Studies and Chicano Studies, Pitzer College, a member of the Claremont Colleges. Professor Pantoja has published widely in the fields of Latino political behavior, immigration, and ethnic and racial politics.

Ana Patricia Rodríguez, Associate Professor, Department of Spanish and Portuguese, School of Languages, Literatures, and Cultures, University of Maryland, College Park. Her research focuses on U.S. Latina/o and Central American literary and cultural production, popular culture, diaspora, and transnational migration.

Clara E. Rodríguez, Professor, Department of Sociology & Anthropology, Fordham University. Lincoln Center, New York City. Her most recent book on Latinas/os is *Heroes, Lovers and Others: The Story of Latinos in Hollywood* (Smithsonian Books, 2004).

Havidán Rodríguez, Vice Provost for Academic Affairs and International Programs, Professor of Sociology, and Core Faculty Member at the Disaster Research Center, University of Delaware. His areas of interest include vulnerability, income inequality, and disasters. He is the co-editor (with E.L. Quarantelli and R.R. Dynes) of the *Handbook of Disaster Research* (Springer, 2006).

Nestor Rodriguez, Professor and Chair in the Department of Sociology, University of Houston. He served as the Joseph S. Werlin Scholar in Latin American/Hispanic Studies at the University of Houston during 2004-2006. His research focuses on political relations, international migration, and urban development.

Rogelio Sáenz, Professor of Sociology, Texas A&M University. His research focuses on the demography of Latinas/os, social inequality, and immigration.

Chad E. Seales, Ph.D. candidate, Religious Studies, University of North Carolina at Chapel Hill. His research focuses on religion and labor in the American South.

Denise A. Segura, Professor, Department of Sociology, University of California, Santa Barbara. She is co-editor, with Patricia Zavella, of *Women and Migration in the U.S.-Mexico Borderlands: An Anthology* (Duke University Press, 2007).

Emily Skop, Assistant Professor, Department of Geography and Environmental Studies, University of Colorado at Colorado Springs. Her research interests include international migration processes, the social and spatial constructions of racial/ethnic/gender identities, and urbanization, segregation, and inequality in the contexts of the United States and Latin America.

Robert Courtney Smith, Associate Professor of Sociology, Immigration Studies and Public Affairs, Baruch College and the Graduate Center, City University of New York (CUNY). He is the author of *Mexican New York: Transnational Worlds of New Immigrants* (California, 2006). He is also the winner of the 2006 W.I. Thomas and Florian Zaniecki Prize and Vice President, Co-founder, of the Mexican Educational Foundation of New York.

Maura I. Toro-Morn, Professor of Sociology, Department of Sociology and Anthropology, Director of Latin American and Latino Studies Program, Illinois State University. She is the author of numerous articles on the class and gender dimensions of Puerto Rican migration to Chicago, gender in the Puerto Rican experience, and gender during the Special Period in Cuba. She edited *Migration and Immigration: A Global View* (Greenwood, 2004) with Marixsa Alicea. Her most recent work addresses the gendered dimensions of global migrations.

Lindsey Trimble, Graduate Student, Department of Sociology, Washington State University. Her research focuses on stratification within the labor market and on immigration.

Zulema Valdez, Assistant Professor of Sociology, Texas A&M University. Her research examines how group membership (race & ethnicity, class, gender) affects socioeconomic outcomes in advanced capitalism. Currently, she is investigating how ethnic and racial minority business owners mobilize economic and noneconomic resources to start and maintain their businesses in Houston, Texas.

Jennifer Van Hook, Professor of sociology, Bowling Green State University. A demographer with research interests in immigration, with particular attention focused on the incorporation and settlement patterns of immigrants and their children. She has conducted research on multiple outcomes related to immigrant incorporation, including welfare receipt, child poverty, food insecurity, child obesity, and school outcomes.

Manuel A. Vasquez, Associate professor of Religion and Latin American Studies at the University of Florida, Gainesville. He is co-director of the project entitled "Latin American Immigrants in the New South: Religion and the Politics of Encounter," which is supported by the Ford Foundation.

William Velez, Professor, Department of Sociology, University of Wisconsin-Milwaukee. His scholarship is broadly focused on educational and urban issues with specialized research interests in Latino urban populations.

Salvador Vidal-Ortiz, American University, Washington DC. His areas of research include racialization, race and ethnic studies, gender and sexuality scholarship, and auto-ethnography and feminist experiential writing. He is working on his first book analyzing the concept of "sexual minorities" in U.S. Santería practice.

Christian Zlolniski, Department of Sociology and Anthropology, and Center for Mexican American Studies, University of Texas at Arlington. A social anthropologist specialized in globalization and transnational labor migration, he is the author of *Janitors, Street Vendors and Activists: The Lives of Mexican Immigrants in Silicon Valley* (University of California Press, 2006). He is currently participating in an interdisciplinary collaborative research on economic development and labor migration in Baja California, Mexico.

THEORETICAL AND METHODOLOGICAL ISSUES OF LATINA/O RESEARCH

CHAPTER 1

Theoretical and Methodological Issues of Latina/o Research

NESTOR RODRÍGUEZ

INTRODUCTION

Latino research has expanded dramatically since the 1980s. It has developed across the traditional social science disciplines and expanded into other fields, drawn by the rapidly growing Latino population. In contrast to studies of other populations, such as Irish studies, Latino studies is less easily defined by social and cultural boundaries. Indeed, as discussed in this chapter, Latino boundaries are fluid, not fixed, from the perspectives of objective and subjective indicators.

This chapter addresses several issues concerning the development of Latino social science in the United States. These issues concern the change in theoretical and empirical approaches, the definition of Latino, the nature of Latino social change, conceptualizations of Latino social incorporation, and the limitations of the institutional base of Latino research. The chapter concludes with brief comments on future Latino research. The discussion is developed with broad strokes, given the size limitation of the exercise. What is presented is what the author considers to be the salient patterns, admittedly from a sociological perspective, and others might reach different conclusions. A challenge in attempting an overview of Latino research is to determine the boundaries of the field. For expediency in this limited exercise, Latino research refers to studies on Latin American-origin people in the United States. Latinas and Latinos have undertaken much of this research, and members of other groups have contributed to this field of research as well.

BACKGROUND: THEORETICAL AND EMPIRICAL APPROACHES

Researchers have conducted studies of the Latino population in the United States since before World War II (e.g., Chenault, 1938; Gamio, 1931), but it was primarily in the 1960s and early 1970s when the first phase of Latino research took off mainly from the perspectives of Mexican American and Puerto Rican studies (e.g., Galarza, Gallegos, & Samora,1969; Maldonado-Denis, 1972). These two focuses did not share a unified identity as Latino studies, but they often shared a theoretical framework based on conflict. This framework came in the forms of internal colonialism, imperialism, dependency, racism, and mode of production analysis (e.g., Acuña, 1972; Bonilla & Girling, 1973). The main theoretical proposition of the conflict perspective was that the inferior political and economic conditions of these two groups were the results of U.S. capitalist exploitation and racist oppression. Similar to Marx's (1867/1967) writing about unrestrained, class exploitation in the developing capitalist division of labor, Chicano, Puerto Rican, and other researchers (e.g., Blauner, 1972), highlighted the structures of oppression in periods of intense racial and ethnic subordination. At times, Chicano and Puerto Rican researchers related the conditions of oppression they studied to the larger structures of imperialism and colonialism that third-world populations suffered abroad.[1]

The theoretical units of analysis of these early Latino researchers involved mainly the points of contact between Latinos and the "dominant group," which became a code term for whites (non-Hispanic). No work illustrated this theoretical focus better than *Occupied America* by Acuña (1972). Chicano struggles in the educational, labor, and political arenas became the basis for theorizing about Chicano development, or the development of the underdevelopment of this population. In a similar vein, Puerto Rican struggles for equal access to institutional resources on the U.S. mainland or for independence in Puerto Rico became the backdrop to theorize about conditions of economic and political inequality in that population (Bonilla & Girling, 1973; Maldonado-Denis, 1972).

In this first phase of Latino studies, it was possible to theorize about the whole of the Chicano or Puerto Rican population because these populations were much smaller and less differentiated than the whole of the Latino population today.[2] Moreover, immigration was a major driving force of Latino population growth only for the smaller groups (e.g., Central/South Americans, Cubans, Dominicans, and other Caribbean Latinos). The lack of social mobility among Chicanos and Puerto Ricans, the largest groups of the Latino population, could not be explained as a function of immigrant clustering in the lower strata, because immigration levels were low.[3] For the early Latino conflict theorists, the explanation existed in the conditions of oppression (e.g., Garcia, 1974; Maldonado-Denis, 1972).

The large immigration waves of Latinos starting in the 1980s caused a major shift—a second phase – in the theoretical focus of Latino research. The racial perspective of white oppression of the 1960s and 1970s lost currency, and given the methodological sophistication of the field, quantitative analyses increasingly formed the basis of theory, in the form of statistical models, to explain empirical associations in Latino populations (e.g., Borjas & Tienda, 1985; Melendez, Rodriguez, & Figueroa, 1991). In this change, the macrotheory of Latino development receded to the background, with notable exceptions.[4] The shift also involved paying greater attention to Latino immigration, which now formed a major source of Latino growth (e.g., Chavez, 1992; Portes & Bach, 1985). If, in the pre-1980s period, Latino studies swung far into grand theories of Latino development, in the post-1980s it swung far into descriptive and causal analysis.

Latino heterogeneity produced by immigration created much ethnographic interest in exploring the new Latino national-origin groups and subgroups from Central and South America and from the Caribbean (e.g., Cordero-Guzmán, Smith, & Grosfoguel, 2001; Hagan, 1994; Mahler, 1995; Suárez-Orozco & Páez, 2002). However, this research was conducted often without theorizing much about the development of these groups within the larger United States-dominated regional system. With the lessening of theories to explain past social development or to predict future ones, Latino research became more concerned with explaining the what and how of Latino development, especially of new immigrant groups, and less concerned with theorizing about the why of this development. One exception has been Latina studies, which has continually theorized about the unequal conditions of Latinas from the perspective of gender relations and patriarchal dominance (Garcia & Garcia, 1997).

A consequence of the diminishment of theory is the inability to explain the basis of transitions in Latino development. For example, did the new wave of Latino immigration that started in the late 1970s and early 1980s represent a new developmental logic or the geographical extension of an old one? Actually, the question can be asked from either a U.S. or Latin American perspective. From the U.S. perspective, for example, Central American immigration is associated with social disruptions in Central America in the late 1970s and early 1980s, but from a Central American perspective, long-distance migration to the United States appears as a geographical extension of *historical patterns* of labor migration (Hamilton & Chinchilla, 1991). It would not be far-fetched to argue that these historical patterns were bound to reach the United States once the means of communication and transportation advanced—with or without the influences of social turmoil.

The complete answer to the question, of course, necessitates going beyond a single U.S. or Latin American perspective and taking into account new regional developments between the United States and Latin America. Failing to take these developments into consideration can lead to ironic research conclusions. For example, new, low-income immigrants are seen as forming a subordinate class in U.S. labor markets, whereas throughout many Latin American home countries, they form an upwardly mobile, new rich category (Hagan, 1994; Smith, 2006). An investigation of their economic status should take into account both conditions.

DEFINITION OF LATINO

Undoubtedly, the absence of a broad theory to explain Latino development is partly the result of the Latino term itself. Latino research implies the existence of a Latino population, but membership and identity in this population are not well defined beyond having a Latin American origin. Even this criterion is debatable for some groups. It is questionable that there is a Pan-Latino identity among the Latino people in terms of having a shared sense of common culture or community. For example, for many in the second, third, or older generation of Mexican Americans, "Latino" refers to persons who have close ties to Latin America. In Texas, the preferred ethnic group identity of many second or older Mexican American generations is "Hispanic," not "Latino" (Mindiola, Niemann, & Rodriguez, 2002). Although many Mexican Americans express solidarity with Mexican and Central American immigrants, many also have expressed restrictionist views toward these Latinos, and some have even taken political action to limit the involvement of non-Mexican Latinos in Mexican American neighborhoods (Rodriguez & Urrutia-Rojas, 1990). In an insightful essay, Torres-Saillant (2002) argued that Latino researchers have yet to recognize the significance of race and other social factors in existent intra-Latino borders.

Indigenous immigrants from Latin America, who collectively reach almost 200,000, also demonstrate the fuzziness of the Latino identity boundary (U.S. Census Bureau, 2003). With their pre-Columbian origins, some of these immigrants maintain social distances in some arenas from Latinos in the United States (Burns, 2000). Many of these immigrants adopt the Spanish language, but with distinctive indigenous mannerisms. In the ancestral worldviews of some indigenous cultures, the very concepts of "Latin America" and "Latino" belong to the world of outsiders. From perspectives such as these, the idea of the existence of a Latino people is not well grounded in social reality. This is not to deny that in special moments (such as in international competitions) many Latin Americans share a Latino identity, but to illustrate the fact that in any given moment, the shared definition of Latino can vary, causing fluctuations in the boundaries of Latino identities.

A challenge of Latino research is how to capture the simultaneous bonding and divisive influence of Latino identity. For example, how far do social networks and social capital formations extend among different national identity groups or among subgroups of the same national identity? Research in places of worship has demonstrated the coalescing power of religious institutions on different national identities (Ebaugh & Chafetz, 2000), but, as other research has shown, religious institutions also have been settings of intra-Latino divisiveness, especially among new immigrants (Hagan, 1994). Many questions remain as to how intra-Latino identity issues develop in other social institutions (economic, educational, political, recreational, etc.). One problem in answering these questions is that only a few studies have explored patterns of *intra*group relations beyond comparisons of group profiles (e.g., Gutierrez, 1995).

Latino research methodologies that seek to explore the uniting and dividing aspects of Latino identity have to traverse through a theoretical sampling grid of national origin, race, ethnicity, and class along one dimension and Latino identity as an independent and then dependent variable on a second dimension. This theoretical sampling frame gets more complicated when one considers that a third dimension is the presence of "Latino" as identity and/or practice. There is a fourth dimension to consider; that is, what are the particular internal and external circumstances that bring a sense of being Latina or Latino to the surface, either as identity or practice, in ways that increase unity or division among Latinos? An example is helpful to illustrate this question: On the undocumented migration northward, unaccompanied Central American youth of different nationalities sometimes bond closely to survive the dangerous journey; on the other hand, Latinas and Latinos working as U.S. Border Patrol agents lay in wait on the U.S. southern border ready to apprehend them and other unauthorized entrants.

There is also an overarching gender question regarding the definition of Latino. How does gender affect the matrix of all of the above-listed dimensional variables? To give one example, how do work environments where men concentrate in large workplaces and women in smaller ones, including individual households where they work as domestics, affect the working class-based reproduction of Latino identity and practice? While Latino men occupy the summit of Latino patriarchy, it is safe to argue that Latinas generally play a more crucial role in the social reproduction of Latino cultures through their roles in the socialization of children and the administration of household activities, including the culturally loaded activities of worship and food preparation (Willams, 1990). A gender-oriented investigation of Latino cultural reproduction has yet to be fully implemented.

Finally, another issue related to attributes of researchers in Latino research involves the lack of an exploration of how the very language of research affects findings, especially the interpretation of findings. This question is in tune with the claim that the researcher is a variable in the research process (Sjoberg & Nett, 1968). In a nutshell, the question is whether English-dominant researchers of Spanish-speaking Latinos suffer a compromise in research validity due to cultural differences. This question goes beyond the issue of competent technical translations (such as backward translations of questionnaire items) to the issue of the association of worldviews with cultures.

This issue is about the sociology of social scientists, about which Gouldner (1970) had much to say in his discussion of world hypotheses and domain assumptions as background influences. Are English-dominant researchers bringing to the field sets of world hypotheses and domain assumptions different from those of the Spanish-speaking Latinos they study? This question is not meant to imply the existence of a linguistic determinism of worldviews, but to raise the point that the whole world does not think alike and thus it is logical to posit hypotheses regarding the effects of different cultural backgrounds on the interpretation of Latino social experiences. As Sjoberg and Nett (1968) explained, social scientists should be aware of the special problems of cross-cultural research and examine the social forces that might produce biases in their investigations. Adhering to the principles of the scientific method of research alone is not a sufficient safeguard against biases, because the listing of hypotheses draws from basic assumptions of relations among social units.

It is important to note that for Latino researchers, the Latino research enterprise can involve a component of intercultural negotiation even within the self. Some Latino researchers experience continual negotiations within the self as they shift from one social world to another in the course of their Latino research. For instance, some Latino researchers will immerse themselves in lengthy, detailed interviews of Latino refugees who have experienced or witnessed atrocities and then moments later return to their campuses to follow the university routine of classes and meetings. This shifting between roles requires an ongoing negotiation within the self to balance one's reactions to the inhumanity of one world with the banality of another. The high drama of one world and the sharp contrast between the two undoubtedly lead some Latino researchers to bifurcate their self-identity as a negotiated coping mechanism.

ASSUMPTIONS OF SOCIAL CHANGE AND SOCIAL INCORPORATION

Latino population growth since the 1980s is one of the focal points of the dynamism of U.S. society. More than just becoming the largest minority group in the United States, in many ways Latinos are restructuring the social landscapes in the areas where they settle. Yet, Latino research has not adequately analyzed the underlying social forces of this development. Traditionally, discussions of social development have been narrated from perspectives of human agency or impersonal structures, and these discussions have generated considerable debate (e.g., see Giddens, 1979). As academic as these debates might appear, it is fruitful to keep their principles in mind to appreciate better the limits of what we know about the driving forces of Latino development.

Some studies have explicitly framed aspects of Latino development (e.g., immigration) from the perspective of human agency, casting Latinas and Latinos as social actors driven by intended pursuits (e.g., Rodriguez, 1996). Many other studies appear to make this assumption as well, but only implicitly, as they focus mainly on empirical correlations using individual units of analysis (e.g., Greenlees & Saenz, 1999). Quantitative studies of this nature might include a host of contextual variables, but, ultimately, agency is implied in the final dependent outcomes. The causality of action in these studies is not what individuals are caused to do (structuralism), but what they must rationally do (agency) in a given set of empirical circumstances. In qualitative studies, agency is closer to the surface. Social actors, as subjects, think, talk, plan, and execute, as reported in these studies (e.g., see Hondagneu-Sotelo, 2001; Menjívar, 2000).

Yet, in moments of policy formulation, studies that regard only the agency component of the population under study might play into the hands of those who wish to restrict the population. The present movement to restrict immigration, especially unauthorized immigration, is a case in point. Restriction advocates are mustering the nativist sentiments of the day through their depictions of unauthorized migrants as deviant social actors (Dougherty, 2004). In this policy debate there is little discussion of how larger social forces, such as regional economic restructuring, are reconfiguring human economic relations across international boundaries. Even sympathizers of unauthorized migrants remain landlocked at the agency level of discussion when they present their sympathetic arguments in terms of net positive effects of unauthorized workers or in terms of humanitarian values. By not highlighting macrorelations that underpin the development of international migration—authorized *and* unauthorized—Latino research indirectly cedes the policy podium to the restrictionist movement.

The issue is not that Latino research needs to return to the days of rigid structuralism in search of a logic "out there," but to consider the underlying, *human-made* circumstances (e.g., neo-liberalism) that shape the conditions under which foreign-born Latinos and their families attempt to make a living. The theoretical and empirical challenge here is to cast Latino development, including the aspect of unauthorized immigration, as a current of historical, social change and not simply as the aggregate outcome of individual decisions.

For scientific purposes alone, there is a need to put Latino research in a larger frame than the social-problems perspective promoted by the state through its conceptualization of Latino deviant subgroups (such as "illegal aliens," "drug users," "school drop-outs," etc.). Research that stays grounded on state conceptualizations of Latino deviance might miss more central features of Latino development. In other words, the problematic Latino conditions that the state defines through its enforcement agendas and through research fundings might not be the sources that will direct Latino development in the long term. This is not to imply that state-directed research does not eventually yield findings useful for intervention (e.g., Lopez, Roosa, Tein, & Dinh, 2004), but rather that this research might remain locked in a social-problems perspective with no way out to a larger theoretical and empirical path.

In the second phase of Latino research, little explicit attention has been given to how state policies affect Latino development, in spite of the fact that across many spheres the state plays a significant role in this development (and by no means a neutral one).[5] Conflict theories of Latino development in phase one of Latino studies placed a central focus on state actions to subordinate or control Latino populations, but in later years, Latino research seems to have changed concepts of the state to contextual variables. For example, studies of Latino access to health care sometimes implicitly consider the mediating role of the state by measuring the status variable of U.S. citizen and non-U.S. citizen (e.g., Freeman & Lethbridge-Cejku, 2006). There are notable exceptions, such as Calavita (1992), but, for the most part, what we know about the role of the state in Latino development comes more from implicit deductions rather than from explicit inferences. Immigration is a key field for researching state actions affecting Latino development because the state plays an exclusive role in legally admitting or excluding foreign-born Latinos, who are a major source of Latino growth. Yet, researchers of Latino immigration have yet to develop a full-blown theory of the role of the state in Latino migration to the United States beyond case studies of specific immigration policies. In many ways, at federal and local levels, the state affects the larger trends of Latino development, such as in the spheres of education, health, and economic development.

Latino research still appears unclear as to the nature of Latino social incorporation. In other words, what are the larger substantive patterns of Latino participation in U.S. society? Two opposing perspectives compete to answer this question. One perspective argues that Latinos and other minorities are continuing the historical process of assimilation, although into a mainstream changed by immigrants (Alba & Nee, 2003). The opposing perspective argues that Latinos not only are not assimilating but also are incapable of assimilating given their different non-European origins and value systems (Huntington, 2004). Indeed, according to the latter perspectives, Latinos endanger the very survival of U.S. society, as it is known today.

Undoubtedly, addressing the nature of Latino social incorporation is one of the most difficult challenges facing Latino research because of the great variety of Latino groups and experiences. The groups and experiences range from U.S.-born Latinos who have completely integrated into white society and culture to foreign-born Latinos who live in traditional barrios and maintain strong ties to their countries of origin. The larger question, however, is not whether Latinos are assimilating, but what does assimilation mean today in the context of increasingly diverse social environments, in which the white population is losing (if not already lost) its role as the referent group? Given the prevalence of Latino ethnic enclaves and segmented forms of assimilation (Portes & Rumbaut, 1996), is it valid to conclude that Latinos have developed enduring, alternative paths to participation in the social structure? Certainly for many Latino youth in inner-city environments, these conditions constitute competing avenues of adaptation, even for some second- and third-generation youth (Valenzuela, 1999).

Some studies have characterized the adaptation of immigrant populations as different forms of assimilation or acculturation (e.g., Portes & Rumbaut, 2001, chap. 3), but it is not clear what the substance of this assimilation or acculturation is. Are the end results of these processes what Gordon (1964) envisioned in his model of multistage assimilation (i.e., assimilation into a [non-Hispanic] white society)? Or are the end results significantly different from Gordon's prediction because the mainstream has changed significantly?

It is logical to assume that in settings where Latinos and other populations of color constitute the majority of the population (such as in the five largest cities) whites are becoming less significant standards of assimilation and acculturation. In these settings, first-generation Latino immigrants might be experiencing levels of assimilation and acculturation as they increasingly become English dominant and take on mainstream institutional roles (teachers, lawyers, health care workers, etc.), but many might not be making the attitudinal and identity transitions as completely as assimilation theorists predicted. Still, for older generations of Latinos, a Latino identity might linger in a latent state and reemerge under particular circumstances. Identity is typically considered to be a micro-level formation within contexts of primary groups and significant others (Mead, 1934). Yet, changes in the larger social environment can influence the development of collective identities, which can nourish the individual self-concept (Stryker, Owens, & White, 2000). From this perspective, the question of what the substance of assimilation is becomes more meaningful as Latino social environments become more salient. The challenge for Latino research is to go beyond check-off measures of identity and to try to assess the occurrences of identity from the perspective of social situations. Underlying this challenge is the assumption that identity is not a hard and fixed self-designation, but a fluctuating self-perception that increases or decreases the weight given to individual qualities (gender, race, nationality, ethnicity, occupation, etc.) according to changing social conditions.

Conditions of binationalism found among Latinos also raise questions concerning the significance of social incorporation among Latinos. The established models of assimilation in U.S. society did not address how activity in two (or more) societies can affect assimilation. Indeed, Gordon's assimilation model seems to limit assimilation to a one-dimensional plane with his claim that assimilating individuals develop a sense of peoplehood "based exclusively on [the] host society" (1967:71). Yet, millions of Latinos maintain active binational lives, as do a proportion of second-generation Latinos. What is missing from Latino research is a greater understanding of how binational existence affects conditions of assimilation. Does continuing attachment to the home country subtract from social incorporation to the host society, or does it add to this process? It is likely that the answer varies by class, as higher-class immigrants might be better able than lower-class immigrants to transfer formal institutional resources from the home country to the United States, but a complete understanding of this phenomenon requires a focused study.

INSTITUTIONAL LIMITATIONS OF LATINO RESEARCH

The institutional base of Latino research has been mainly the U.S. academy. A question for the future of Latino research is whether this institutional foundation is sufficient or whether increased collaboration with researchers in Latin America will enhance the power of Latino research, as the U.S. Latino population becomes more international. The answer to this question will affect the answers to the questions of the theoretical and methodological issues of Latino research.

With some exceptions, the institutional base of U.S. social science has remained strongly attached to assumptions of the order perspective (Ross, 1991). In sociology, the European origins of social theory assumed a continuing social order, such as in the works of Durkheim and Weber, even if at times the social order experienced major transformations (e.g., industrialization and in the rise of Protestantism). Even Karl Marx, the great conflict theorist, derived his concepts of class conflict from an order perspective of the economic relations of production.[6] Talcott Parsons, a major purveyor in the United States of the European classical order orientation, placed the order perspective firmly in his theory of the social system (Parsons, 1951).

As Sjoberg and Vaughan (1971) have explicated, implicit in the European origins of Western sociology is the primacy of the nation-state as an empirical and moral unit of analysis. From Durkheim to Weber, the nation-state looms as the foundation of society. In the United States, several founders of U.S. sociology, such as Parsons, explicitly or implicitly used the nation-state is a central unit of analysis in their sociological conceptualizations (Sjoberg & Vaughan, 1971). More often than not, the order perspective and the primacy of the nation-state as a unit of analysis are passed on to new generations of students of U.S. social science.

Given the particular exigencies and popular responses in Latin American societies (e.g., Eckstein, 2001; Winn, 2006) it is logical to conclude that Latin American populations in general have followed a less stable course than U.S. society in the post-World War II era.[7] This is not simply an observation of high-profile social unrest, but of fluidity, discontinuities, and transitions in the everyday lives of millions of poor Latin Americans who struggle in the periphery of their societies (see, Kowarick, 1994; Lomnitz, 1977; Winn, 2006).[8] For many Latin Americans, it is a life of survival in simultaneous premodern, modern, and postmodern hybrid forms (García Canclini, 1995; also see Portes & Hoffman, 2003)—in sharp contrast with the assumptions of the order perspective in which individual progress is propelled by the rationalism of modernity. Given the major penetrations of Latin American populations in U.S. society, a challenge for Latino research is to investigate how Latino newcomers live in the incongruities of the social forms they bring and the ones they encounter in their settlement *and how their adaptations reverberate throughout the larger social structure*. Social science offers the qualitative and quantitative methods to measure the attitudinal and behavioral traits of these adaptations, but it might require additional methods from the humanities and phenomenology to investigate the inner-sensate-based drives to succeed in the social and individual campaigns of adaptation.

Researchers of Latino immigration have already established the limitations of the nation-state as a unit of analysis and responded with the methodological concepts of binational or transnational units (e.g., Glick Schiller, Basch, & Blanc, 1992). This is a distancing from the state-direct conceptualization of "national" units in which geographical lines literally divide populations. Latin American expansion into the United States is not occurring by a shift of geographical lines but by a change of social and cultural boundaries, with and without authorization. This development necessitates a multidimensional research approach that takes into account not only how Latino social relations transcend geographical spaces (binationalism or transnationalism) but also how they expand across Latino and U.S. social spaces in the same settings. The challenge is more than measuring conditions of acculturation or assimilation. Similar to studies of linguistic code switching among Latinos (e.g., Aguirre, 1988), Latino research needs to reach for a better understanding of how Latino newcomers and their descendents combine internal and external social forms and worldviews to operate in their multilayered social–spatial environments. The issue is not to dispense with the nation-state as a unit of analysis but to investigate how the coexistence of different social spaces simultaneously produces opportunities and limitations for many Latinas and Latinos.[9]

FUTURE OF LATINO STUDIES

Two present-day developments are having major impacts on the future of Latino studies. One development is the changing demography of the Latino population and the second is the growing intellectual and methodological sophistication of Latino researchers. Of the many characteristics of the changing Latino demography in the United States, two of the most salient are the large growth of the population and the large proportion of first-generation immigrants.

The Latino population reached 42 million in 2005 and is projected to reach over 100 million by 2050 (U.S. Census Bureau, 2004, 2006). Latinos now constitute the majority or the largest proportion of the population in some of the largest U.S. cities. Although they will be less than 50% of the population even through mid-century, in significant ways they no longer fit the model of an isolated minority. A research issue that large Latino population growth is creating in many settings is how to explore the effects of Latino social identities (gender, race, national origin, etc.) in U.S. milieus of increasing social pluralism, which includes nationalities from Africa, Asia, the Middle East, and other world regions. This will require exploring how new social relations in restructured environments affect Latino development across different arenas. For example, do the new linkages of Asian capital and Latino labor in small businesses across U.S. cities affect the established patterns of Latino social incorporation? If yes, in which meaningful ways, across which domains (social, cultural, political, etc.), and how do the new conditions promote or limit Latino development?

Because Latino immigrants constitute 45% of the Latino population (U.S. Census Bureau, 2006), their presence requires a greater attention to transnational developments in order to understand fully the dynamism of the Latino population in the United States. Latino immigrants provide many bidirectional influences between U.S. and Latin American settings (e.g., Levitt, 2001; Smith, 2006). Directly or indirectly, they have influenced policy and institutional developments in local, national, and international arenas far beyond the economic sphere in which they are commonly perceived by policy makers. They are also major agents of socialization for the second generation they produce. Over the past two decades, immigrants have played major functions in the social reproduction of Latino communities and institutional cultures, but the effects of this influence have yet to be fully explored.

In the 1990s, Latino studies began a third phase characterized by enhanced intellectual and research sophistication. The phase partly involves a strengthening of poststructuralist, critical theory and analysis and a deepening of the perspectives of women, gender, and sexuality beyond the traditional empiricism of social science (Anzaldúa, 1990; Yosso, 2005). Drawing partly from postmodernism and postcolonial theory, and with precursors that extend back several decades, these critical perspectives criticize one-dimensional approaches of past research and earlier Latino intellectual traditions. This evolving phase includes a plethora of humanist and historical subfields, such as critical literary theory, critical race theory, cultural studies, Latina feminist studies, and Latino/a gay/lesbian studies, which delve deeply into Latina and Latino subjective experiences (e.g., Yarbo-Bejarano, 1999; Alarcón, 1993). These evolving poststructuralist perspectives represent the growing involvement of Latinos in larger intellectual genres, albeit from a Latina or Latino standpoint.

Poststructuralism plays a significant role in the evolving third phase of Latino studies, but not a defining one. Indeed, a key characteristic of the emerging phase seems to be the absence of a dominant theoretical or methodological paradigm. A variety of empirical and humanist perspectives are generating studies and conceptualizations of Latinos at various levels. Yet, the original research questions raised by Latina and Latino scholars in the 1960s continue to frame the Latino research enterprise; that is, what is the significance of the Latino population within the larger social context and what is the meaning of this significance for Latina and Latino individuals?

ACKNOWLEDGMENTS

Gratitude is owed to the Werlin family for providing research support and to Andy Gordon, Tatcho Mindiola, Charles Munnell, and Maria Theresa Hernandez for their comments on drafts of this chapter.

NOTES

1. "As my research progressed, I became convinced that the experience of Chicanos in the United States parallels that of other third-world peoples who have suffered under the colonialism of technologically superior nations" (Acuña, 1972:iii).
2. In 1960, the number of Mexicans and Puerto Ricans in the United States, who accounted for most Latinos, was about 13% of the 35.3 million Latinos in 2000 (Grebler, Moore, & Guzman, 1970; U.S. Census Bureau, 2001). By 1969, the Latino population reached 26% of the Latino population in 2000 (U.S. Census Bureau, 1971, Table 30).
3. In 1969, the reported foreign-born rates of the 9.2 million Latinos for selected Latino groups were as follows (U.S. Census Bureau, 1971: Table 30): Mexicans, 17.1%; Puerto Ricans, 0.5%; Cubans, 82.5%; and Central and South Americans, 63.7%. Mexicans and Puerto Ricans accounted for 71% of the total Latino population, and Cubans and Central/South Americans accounted for 12%. "Others" accounted for the remainder.
4. The notable exceptions include works such as Gómez-Quiñones (1990), Almaguer (1994), and Gonzalez & Fernandez (2003). The point is not that the grand conflict theory of Latino development has vanished, but that it is no longer the dominant frame of Latino research as it was in phase one of Latino studies.
5. This is not the place to engage in a full discussion regarding the definition of the state. Suffice for the moment to say that, in theory, in the democratic system of U.S. society, the state represents the political will of the people and is materialized in the bureaucratic apparatus that implements it or contracts for its discharge. At times, a large variance exists between the will of popular sectors and state actions.

6. The tone of orderly development is clear in Marx's characterization of social development: "In the social production of their life, men enter into definite relations that are indispensable and independent of their will, relations of production *which correspond to a definite stage of development* [italics added] of their material productive forces" (1867/1969:503).

7. This is not meant to imply that the problems of Latin Americans are completely of their own making. For discussions of how the United States has played a systematic role in supporting Latin American state repression, see Menjívar & Rodriguez (2005).

8. According to the Population Reference Bureau (2006), 24% of the Latin American/Caribbean population lived on less than US$2.00 per day, measured in 1993 purchasing power parity (PPP) rates. Three countries in Central America, a major region of U.S.-bound emigration, had particularly high percentages: Nicaragua, 80%; El Salvador, 41%; Honduras, 44%. The Population Reference Bureau does not list the rates for all the countries in the region. A report by Portes & Hoffman (2003) on Latin American class structures finds that income inequality is increasing in the region.

9. There are works that give us insights into how this works out; for example, see M. P. Smith (2001) and R. C. Smith (2006).

REFERENCES

Acuña, Rodolfo. (1972). *Occupied America: The Chicano's Struggle Toward Liberation*. San Francisco: Canfield Press.

Aguirre, A. (1988). Code Switching, Intuitive Knowledge, and the Bilingual Classroom. In H. Garcia & R. Chavez (Eds.), *Ethnolinguistic Issues in Education* (pp. 28–38). Lubbock, TX: Texas Tech University.

Alarcón, Norma. (1993). *Chicana Critical Issues*. Berkeley, CA: Third Woman Press.

Alba, Richard, & Nee, Victor. (2003). *Remaking the American Mainstream: Assimilation and Contemporary Immigration*. Cambridge, MA: Harvard University Press.

Almaguer, Tomas. (1994). *Racial Fault Lines*. Berkeley: University of California Press.

Anzaldúa, Gloria. (1990). *Haciendo Caras/Making Face, Making Soul: Creative and Critical Perspectives by Women of Color*. San Francisco: Aunt Lute Press.

Blauner, Robert. (1972). *Racial Opression in America*. New York: Harper & Row.

Bonilla, F., & Girling, R. (Eds.). (1973). *Structures of Dependency*. Stanford, CA: Stanford Institute of Politics.

Borjas, George J., & Tienda, Marta (Eds.). (1985). *Hispanics in the U.S. Economy*. Orlando, FL: Academic Press.

Burns, Allen. (2000). Indiantown, Florida: The Maya Diaspora and Applied Anthropology. In James Loucky & Marilyn M. Moors (Eds.), *The Maya Diaspora: Guatemalan Roots, New American Lives* (pp. 152–171). Philadelphia: Temple University Press.

Calavita, Kitty. (1992). *Inside the State: The Bracero Program, Immigration, and the I.N.S.* New York: Routledge.

Chavez, Leo. (1992). *Shadowed Lives: Undocumented Immigrants in American Society*. Fort Worth, TX: Harcourt, Brace, Jovanovich College Publishers.

Chenault, Lawrence. (1938). *The Puerto Rican Migrant in New York City*. New York: Russell & Russell.

Cordero-Guzmán, Héctor, Smith, Robert C., & Grosfoguel, Ramón. (2001). *Migration, Transnationalization, and Race in a Changing New York*. Philadelphia: Temple University Press.

Dougherty, Jon E. (2004). *Illegals: The Immigrant Threat Posed by Our Unsecured U.S.-Mexico Border*. Nashville, TN: WND Books.

Ebaugh, Helen Rose, & Chafetz, Janet Saltzman. (2000). *Religion and the New Immigrants: Continuities and Adaptations in Immigrant Congregations*. Walnut Creek, CA: AltaMira Press.

Eckstein, Barbara (Ed.). (2001). *Power and Popular Protest: Latin American Social Movements*. Berkeley: University of California Press.

Freeman, Gulnur, & Lethbridge-Cejku, Margaret. (2006). Access to Health Care Among Hispanic or Latino Women: United States, 2000–2002. *Advanced Data from Vital and Health Statistics, 368*, Hyattsville, MD: National Center for Health Statistics.

Galarza, Ernesto, Gallegos, Herman, & Samora, Julian. (1969). *Mexican-Americans in the Southwest*. Santa Barbara, CA: McNally and Loftin.

Gamio, Manuel. (1931). *The Mexican Immigrant, His Life Story*. Chicago: University of Chicago Press.

Garcia, Alma, & Garcia, Mario (Eds.). (1997). *Chicana Feminist Thought: The Basic Historical Writings*. New York: Routledge.

Garcia, F. Chris (Ed.). (1974). *La Causa Política: A Chicano Politics Reader*. Notre Dame, IN: University of Notre Dame Press.

García Canclini, Néstor. (1995). *Hybrid Cultures: Strategies for Entering and Leaving Modernity*. Minneapolis: University of Minnesota Press.

Giddens, Anthony. (1979). *Central Problems in Social Theory: Action, Structure, and Contradictions in Social Analysis*. Berkeley: University of California Press.

Glick Schiller, Nina, Basch, Linda, & Blanc, Cristina Szanton (Eds.). (1992). *Towards a Transnational Perspective on Migration*. New York: New York Academy of Sciences.

Gómez-Quiñones, Juan. (1990). *Chicano Politics: Reality and Promise, 1940–1990*. Albuquerque: University of New Mexico Press.

Gonzalez, Gilbert G., & Fernandez, Raul A. (2003). *A Century of Chicano History: Empire, Nations, and Migration*. New York: Routledge.

Gordon, Milton. (1964). *Assimilation in American Life: The Role of Race, Religion, and National Origins*. New York: Oxford University Press.

Gouldner, Alvin Ward. (1970). *The Coming Crisis of Western Sociology*. New York: Basic Books.

Grebler, Leo, Moore, Joan W., & Guzman, Ralph C. (1970). *The Mexican-American People: The Nation's Second Largest Minority*. New York: The Free Press.

Greenlees, Clyde S., & Saenz, Rogelio. (1999). Determinants of Employment of Recently Arrived Mexican Wives. *International Migration Review*, *33*(2), 354–377.

Gutíerrez, David. (1995). *Walls and Mirrors: Mexican Americans, Mexican Immigrants, and the Politics of Ethnicity*. Berkeley: University of California Press.

Hagan, Jacqueline Maria. (1994). *Deciding to be Legal: A Maya Community in Houston*. Philadelphia: Temple University Press.

Hamilton, Nora, & Chinchilla, Norma Stoltz. (1991). Central American Migration: A Framework for Analysis. *Latin American Research Review*, *26*(1), 75–110.

Hondagneu-Sotelo, Pierrette. (2001). *Doméstica: Immigrant Workers Cleaning and Caring in the Shadows of Affluence*. Berkeley: University of California Press.

Huntington, Samuel P. (2004). *Who Are We? The Challenges to America's National Identity*. New York: Simon & Schuster.

Kowarick, Lucio. (1994). *Social Struggles and the City: The Case of São Paulo*. New York: Monthly Review Press.

Levitt, Peggy. (2001). *The Transnational Villagers*. Berkeley: University of California Press.

Lomnitz, Larissa A. (1977). *Networks and Marginality: Life in a Mexican Shantytown*. New York: Academic Press.

Lopez, Vera A., Roosa, Mark W., Tein, Jenn-Yun, & Dinh, Khanh T. (2004). Accounting for Anglo-Hispanic Differences in School Misbehavior. *Journal of Ethnicity in Criminal Justice*, *2*(1/2), 27–46.

Mahler, Sarah J. (1995). *American Dreaming: Immigrant Life on the Margins*. Princeton, NJ: Princeton University Press.

Maldonado-Denis, Manuel. (1972). *Puerto Rico: A Socio-historic Interpretation*. New York: Random House.

Marx, Karl. (1967). *Capital, Volume 1: A Critique of Political Economy*. New York: International Publishers. (Original work published 1867)

Mead, George Herbert. (1934). *Mind, Self & Society from the Standpoint of a Social Behaviorist*. Chicago: University of Chicago Press.

Melendez, Edwin, Rodriguez, Clara, & Figueroa, Janis Barry (Eds.). (1991). *Hispanics in the Labor Force: Issues and Policies*. New York: Plenum Press.

Menjívar, Cecilia. (2000). *Fragmented Ties: Salvadoran Immigrant Networks in America*. Berkeley: University of California Press.

Menjívar, Cecilia, & Rodríguez, Nestor (Eds.). (2005). *When States Kill: Latin America, the U.S. and Technologies of Terror*. Austin: University of Texas Press.

Mindiola, Tatcho, Jr., Niemann, Yolanda Flores, & Rodriguez, Nestor. (2002). *Black–Brown Relations and Stereotypes*. Austin: University of Texas Press.

Parsons, Talcott. (1951). *The Social System*. Glencoe, IL: Free Press.

Population Reference Bureau. (2006). *2006 World Population Data Sheet*. Retrieved October 26, 2006, from www.prb.org.

Portes, Alejandro, & Bach, Robert L. (1985). *Latin Journey: Cuban and Mexican Immigrants in the United States*. Berkeley: University of California Press.

Portes, Alejandro, & Hoffman, Kelly. (2003). Latin American Class Structures: Their Compostion and Change During the Neoliberal Era. *Latin American Research Review*, *38*(1), 41–82.

Portes, Alejandro, & Rumbaut, Rubén G. (1996). *Immigrant America: A Portrait*. Berkeley: University of California Press.

Portes, Alejandro, & Rumbaut, Rubén G. (2001). *Ethnicities: Children of Immigrants in America*. Berkeley: University of California Press.

Rodriguez, Nestor. (1996). The Battle for the Border: Notes on Autonomous Migration, Transnational Communities and the State. *Social Justice, 23*(3), 21–37.

Rodriguez, Nestor P., & Urrutia-Rojas, Ximena. (1990). Impact of Recent Refugee Migration to Texas: A Comparison of Southeast Asian and Central American Newcomers. In Wayne H. Holtzman & Thomas H. Bornemann (Eds.), *Mental Health of Immigrants and Refugees* (pp. 263–278). Austin, TX: Hogg Foundation.

Ross, Dorothy. (1991). *The Origins of American Social Science*. Cambridge: Cambridge University Press.

Sjoberg, Gideon, & Nett, Roger. (1968). *A Methodology for Social Research*. New York: Harper & Row.

Sjoberg, Gideon, & Ted R. Vaughan. (1971). The Sociology of Ethics and the Ethics of Sociologists. In Edward & Tiryakian (Eds.), *The Phenomenology of Sociology* (pp. 259–276). Newyork: Appleton-Century-Crofts.

Smith, Michael Peter. (2001). *Transnational Urbanism: Locating Globalization*. Malden, MA: Blackwell Publishers.

Smith, Robert Courtney. (2006). *Mexican New York: Transnatonal Lives of New Immigrants*. Berkeley: University of California Press.

Stryker, Sheldon, Owens, Timothy J., & White, Robert W. (Eds.). (2000). *Self, Identity, and Social Movements*. Minneapolis: University of Minnesota Press.

Suárez-Orozco, Marcelo, & Páez, Mariela M. (2002). *Latinos: Remaking America*. Berkeley: University of California Press.

Torres-Saillant, Silvio. (2002). Problematic Paradigms: Racial Diversity and Corporate Identity in the Latino Community. In Marcelo Suárez-Orozco & Mariela M. Páez (Eds.), *Latinos: Remaking America* (pp. 435–455). Berkeley: University of California Press.

U.S. Census Bureau. (1971). *Statistical Abstract of the United States: 1971*, 92nd ed. Washington D.C.: Government Printing Office.

U.S. Census Bureau. (2001). *2000 Census of Population* (Census 2000 Summary File 3 (SF 3), custom tables). Retrieved October 26, 2006, from http://factfinder.census. gov/.

U.S. Census Bureau. (2003). 2000 Census of the Population. Five percent public-use microdata file. Machine-readable data file. Produced and distributed by the U.S. Bureau of the Census.

U.S. Census Bureau. (2004). U.S. Interim Projections by Age, Sex, Race, and Hispanic Origin. Retrieved October 26, 2006, from http://www.census.gov/ipc/www/usinterimproj/.

U.S. Census Bureau. (2006). 2005 American Community Survey, Custom Tables. Retrieved October 26, 2006, from http://factfinder.census.gov/.

Valenzuela, Angela. (1999). *Subtractive Schooling: U.S. –Mexican Youth and the Politics of Caring*. Albany: State University of New York Press.

Williams, Norma. (1990). *The Mexican American Family: Tradition and Change*. Dix Hills, NY: General Hall.

Winn, Peter. (2006). *Americas: The Changing Face of Latin America and the Caribbean*. Berkeley: University of California Press.

Yarbo-Bejarano, Yvonne. (1999). Sexuality and Chicana/o Studies: Towards a Theoretical Paradigm for the Twenty-First Century. *Cultural Studies, 13*(2), 335–345.

Yosso, Tara J. (2005). Whose Culture Has Capital? A Critical Race Theory Discussion of Community Cultural Wealth. *Race Ethnicity and Education, 8*(1), 69–91.

IMMIGRATION AND LATINA/O INCORPORATION

CHAPTER 2

New Latino Destinations

Manuel A. Vásquez
Chad E. Seales
Marie Friedmann Marquardt

INTRODUCTION

On April 10, 2006, Latino immigrants and their allies took to the streets in more than 100 cities throughout the United States to advocate for comprehensive immigration reform. In Albertville, Alabama (population 20,000), more than 5,000 demonstrators marched, some carrying signs that read "Sweet Home Alabama." In Jackson, Mississippi, approximately 500 participants joined together in singing a Spanish translation of "We Shall Overcome," a song closely linked with the African American Civil Rights Movement (Hardin, 2006). Three Nebraska cities—South Sioux City, Lincoln, and Omaha—saw a combined 20,000 participants (Gonzalez & Stickney, 2006). Approximately 3,000 demonstrators gathered in Siler City, North Carolina (population 8,079) bearing signs that read, "We love Siler City" and "I pay taxes." In Atlanta, Georgia, more than 50,000 protestors took to the streets, significantly surpassing the number of participants in such traditional immigrant gateway cities as San Diego, Los Angeles, and Miami (Skiba & Forester, 2006). As news reports documented rallies from Charleston, South Carolina to Indianapolis, Indiana; from Jackson, Mississippi to Garden City, Kansas, they highlighted the complex physical, cultural, and economic contours of a new map of Latino presence in the United States. Although the policy impact of this mobilization remains to be seen, one thing is perfectly clear: The cartographies of settlement for Latino and Latina immigrants have shifted in recent decades, and as Latinos filled the streets in protest, they mapped these shifts onto the landscapes of cities and towns throughout the United States.

Who were these Latino demonstrators? How is it that they have come to reside in municipalities, states, and regions that, as recently as 20 years ago, had negligible Latino populations? What is the impact of their presence on socioeconomic, political, and cultural life in new destinations? In this chapter, we survey the small but growing literature on Latinos in new destinations and analyze the available data to sketch preliminary answers to these questions and to identify some key emergent issues and themes. The chapter begins by describing the geography of new destinations. We highlight the dynamics of Latino settlement on the regional, state, county, and municipal levels. We then explore some of the characteristics of Latino populations in new destinations, focusing significant attention on national origin but also attending to immigration status, age, and gender. After examining the geography and demography of new destinations, we offer an analysis of three interrelated causes for Latino dispersion: changes in immigration policy from the federal to the municipal level, restructuring of the U.S. economy in relation to global economic change, and the formation of immigrant social and economic networks.

Rapid Latino population increases in new destinations often bring into stark relief issues of interracial and interethnic relations, concerns about immigrant incorporation, and questions about the role of civic and religious organizations, all of which are critical to our understanding of the role Latinos are playing in the construction of an increasingly multiethnic post-1965 America. In the final section of this chapter, we explore the case of Siler City, North Carolina to offer a glimpse into how these issues are engaged at the local level. This case not only offers insight into the complex dynamics of new receiving destinations but also points toward some of the most significant emergent themes to be addressed as we move forward with the study of new Latino destinations.

THE GEOGRAPHY OF NEW DESTINATIONS

In the last two decades, the composition and settlement patterns of immigration from Latin America have experienced significant shifts. Historically, Latinos in the United States have concentrated in large metropolitan areas in the Southwest and Northeast. According to the 1990 U.S. census, 16.8% of all Latinos lived in the Northeast, whereas 45.2% resided in the West and 30.3% in the South. Within these regions, Latino immigrants have usually settled in six states with long histories of immigration: California, Texas, New York, Florida, Illinois, and New Jersey. Collectively, in 1990, these states contained 78% of the U.S. Latino population. Within those states, Latino immigrants have tended to settle in gateway cities such as Los Angeles, Houston, Dallas, New York City, Miami, and Chicago. Regional and metropolitan clustering has also dovetailed with national origin, giving rise to the heuristic rule of thumb that Mexicans live mostly in the Southwest and the snowbelt around Chicago, whereas Puerto Ricans concentrate in the Northeast and Cubans in Florida and New Jersey.

From roughly the mid-1980s on, however, Latinos have increasingly dispersed, moving to new destinations in the South, Midwest, and, to some extent, in the West, ranging from small rural towns like Siler City, North Carolina and Dalton, Georgia to large cities such as Atlanta, Omaha, and Reno. Changes in the cartography of settlement are accompanied by a diversification in the national origin, such that there are now significant numbers of Guatemalans in North Carolina, Salvadorans in Northern Virginia and Phoenix, Puerto Ricans and Colombians in Central Florida, Brazilians in Boston and Atlanta, Venezuelans in Nebraska, and Mexicans in New York City, just to give some striking examples (Duany & Matos-Rodríguez, 2006; Fink, 2003; Gouveia, 2005; Martes, 2000; Moran-Taylor & Menjívar, 2005; Smith, 2005). To understand more fully the complex dynamics of Latino spatial deconcentration, it is helpful to explore this process at the regional, state, and county levels.

Regional Level

Although between 1990 and 2000 the Latino population grew in all regions of the country, the Midwest registered the highest rate of growth (81%), followed by the South (71.2%). By 2000, 8.9% of Latino families in the country resided in the Midwest, up from 7.7% in 1990. Moreover, during the same decade, the South's share of Latino households grew from 30.3% to 32.8%. This is because the Latino population in the South doubled from 1990 to 2000, going from 2.4 million to 4.9 million. In fact, during this decade, Latinos accounted for close to 23% of the 11 million persons added to the population in the South (Saenz et al., 2003). Conversely, the Northeast's share of the overall national Latino population went down from 16.8% to 14.9%, whereas in the West, it declined from 45.2% to 43.5% (Guzman & McConnell, 2002).

State Level

The shift toward new destinations at the state level is even more remarkable. As Table 1 indicates, 9 of the 10 states with the fastest growing Latino population are in the South and Midwest. Hypergrowth rates of over 300% in states such as North Carolina, Arkansas, and Georgia contrast sharply with those of traditional settlement states, which maintain a large immigrant base but have exhibited much lower rates of growth. For example, the Latino population in California grew only by 43%, whereas in New York, it gained only 30%, well below the national growth rate of 58%. Of the six traditional settlement states, only Illinois registered a Latino growth rate above the national average (at 69%). Table 1 also shows that the percentage growth for Latinos is substantially higher across the board than for the general population, even in states such as Nevada, which is the fastest growing in the union. Indeed, in absolute numbers, Nevada received the largest influx of Latinos

TABLE 1. Population Changes for the 10 States with the Highest Rates of Latino Growth, 1990–2000

State	Total population		Change 1990 to 2000		Hispanic population		Change 1990 to 2000	
	1990	2000	Numeric	Percentage	1990	2000	Numeric	Percentage
North Carolina	6,628,637	8,049,313	1,420,676	21.4	76,726	378,963	202,237	394
Arkansas	2,350,725	2,673,400	322,675	13.7	19,876	86,866	66,990	337
Georgia	6,478,216	8,186,453	1,708,327	26.4	108,922	435,227	226,105	300
Tennessee	4,877,185	5,689,283	812,098	16.7	32,741	123,838	91,097	278
Nevada	1,201,833	1,998,257	796,424	66.3	124,419	393,970	269,551	217
South Carolina	3,486,703	4,012,012	525,309	15.1	30,551	95,076	64,525	211
Alabama	4,040,587	4,447,100	406,513	10.1	24,629	75,830	51,201	208
Kentucky	3,685,296	4,041,769	356,473	9.7	21,984	59,939	37,955	173
Minnesota	4,375,099	4,919,479	544,380	12.4	53,884	143,382	89,498	166
Nebraska	1,578,385	1,711,263	132,878	8.4	36,969	94,425	57,456	155
Illinois	11,430602	12,419,293	988,691	8.6	904,446	1,530,262		69
United States	**248,709,873**	**281,421,906**	**32,712,033**	**13.2**	**22,354,059**	**35,305,818**	**12,951,759**	**58**

Source: U.S. Census Bureau, 1990 and 2000 Census Sample Data.

TABLE 2. **Percentage of Latino Population by State 1990–2000**

State	1990 Percentage of Hispanics	2000 Percentage of Hispanics
Nevada	10.3	19.7
Nebraska	2.3	5.5
Georgia	1.7	5.3
North Carolina	1.2	4.7
Arkansas	0.9	3.2
Minnesota	1.2	2.9
South Carolina	0.9	2.4
Tennessee	0.7	2.2
Alabama	0.6	1.7
Kentucky	0.6	1.5
United States	**9.0**	**12.5**

Source: U.S. Census Bureau, 1990 and 2000 Census Sample Data.

during the 1990's, followed by Georgia and North Carolina. Table 2 shows the impact of the influx of Latino immigrants on the demographics of the new destination states.

County and Municipal Levels

While in 2000 over 90% of Hispanics lived in metro areas (Kandel & Cromartie, 2004), there has been a shift toward suburbanization, accompanied by hypergrowth in particular rural areas. Indeed, in the 1990s, the Latino population in nonmetropolitan areas grew by 67% compared to only 57% in metropolitan areas (Saenz & Torres, 2003). As a result of this growth, roughly 3.1 million Latinos live in nonmetro counties, representing over 25% of the 1990–2000 overall nonmetro population growth (Lichter & Johnson, 2006). It is important to note that, for all its speed, the growth of rural Latinos has been fairly concentrated. One-third of rural Latinos reside in only 109 nonmetropolitan counties, less that 5% of all the 2,289 nonmetropolitan counties (Kandel & Parrado, 2005). Thus, it is more appropriate to speak of a selective rather than a generalized deconcentration of Latinos in the countryside. The nonmetropolitan/metropolitan residential gap and the clustered rural hypergrowth show regional variations, as illustrated by Table 3. During the 1990s, the Latino metropolitan population in the Southwest and West grew faster than its nonmetropolitan counterpart. The inverse took place in the South, Midwest, and Northeast.

TABLE 3. **Percentage of Change in Latino Population by Region and Metropolitan/Nonmetropolitan Residence, 1990–2000**

Region	Nonmetropolitan	Metropolitan
Midwest	112.8	77.0
Northeast	71.2	39.4
South	200.2	93.6
Southwest	35.3	50.3
West	81.7	130.3
United States	**67.1**	**57.9**

Source: Adapted from Saenz and Torres (2003).

Growth in nonmetropolitan areas in the South and Midwest has accompanied the restructuring of food processing industries, as well as changes in service construction and manufacturing sectors. For example, in Nebraska, cities with meatpacking plants have experienced the fastest Latino growth. This is certainly the case for two of the state's rural towns: Lexington, where between 1990 and 2000 the Latino population grew by 1,457%, and Schuyler, with a 1,377% increase among Latinos and a 25% decline in the Euro-American population (Gouveia & Powell, 2005).

In North Carolina, the nongateway state experiencing the fastest Latino growth, the counties that have registered the highest increases are just east of the Southern Appalachian Mountains, in the so-called Piedmont Triad, which includes Alamance, Davidson, Forsyth, and Gilford counties. These counties contain some of the largest and most dynamic cities in the state, such as Winston-Salem, Greensboro, and High Point, affording Latinos plentiful jobs in an economy that still relies heavily on agriculture, poultry processing, and meatpacking but is increasingly expanding its manufacturing, construction, and service sectors. Between 1990 and 2000, the Latino population increased by 1,124% in Alamance County, 905% in Davidson, 898% in Forsyth, and 533% in Guilford (Bailey, 2005). Other areas that have registered significant growth include the Research Triangle (Durham, Raleigh, and Chapel Hill), as well as the counties around Charlotte. In Chatham County, the proportion of Latinos did not grow as fast as in the Piedmont Triad. However, Hispanics make up 11.4% of the population, one of the highest concentrations in the state. Siler City, which we will discuss later, is located in Chatham County.

In Georgia, Latinos have had a strong presence in Hall County, particularly in Gainesville, which has been described as the "poultry capital of the world" since the 1970s (Guthey, 2001). Between 1990 and 2000, the Latino population in Hall County grew by 657%, and by 2004, Hispanics comprised 24.1% of Gainesville's population. However, the fastest rates of Latino growth in Georgia in the past decade took place in the Northwest corner of the state, in counties with an expanding manufacturing sector anchored on the production of carpeting and flooring materials. For example, Murray County, home of World Carpets Inc. and Aladdin Manufacturing Corps, saw a 1,375% increase in the Hispanic population between 1990 and 2000. Neighboring Gordon County, with a similar industrial base, experienced a 1,534% growth in the Latino population during the same decade (Kochhar, Suro, & Tafoya, 2005). Also, although in Whitfield County the Latino population grew by only 600% by 2000, Hispanics accounted for 40% of the overall population of Dalton, the county's largest city (Hernández-León & Zúñiga, 2005).

The final trend in Georgia parallels construction booms throughout Atlanta's suburbs and exurbs. For instance, in Cobb, Cherokee, and Gwinnett counties, the Latino population has grown by 399%, 627%, and 657%, respectively. This suburbanization is part of a larger trend in Mexican migration. Between 1995 and 2000, 51% of Mexicans immigrants who arrived in nongateway states settled in suburbs, in contrast to only 23% of those who came between 1985 and 1990 (Durand, Massey, & Capoferro, 2005).

In Florida, although Latinos continue to be heavily concentrated in Miami-Dade and Broward Counties, there has been a gradual drift northward, especially toward the Interstate 4 corridor in the center of the state, which connects Tampa, Orlando, and Daytona Beach. For instance, Otomís from the municipality of Ixmilquipan in the state of Hidalgo, Mexico have moved in large numbers to Clearwater, a city close to Tampa. They are now estimated to constitute 15% (about 20,000 persons) of the city's population (Schmidt & Crummett, 2004). Moreover, a growing number of Guatemalans, mainly Jacaltecs and Kanjobals, who have had a long-standing presence in Florida's tomato fields in places like Immokalee and Indiantown (Burns, 1993), are settling at the periphery of rapidly expanding planned and gated communities in cities such as Jupiter, Naples, and Fort Myers (Steigenga & Palma, 2003).

Simultaneously, increasing numbers of Latinos have moved to Orlando to work in the tourist and service industry. During the 1990s, Florida replaced New Jersey as the state with the second largest concentration of Puerto Ricans on the U.S. mainland. This is because Florida's share of mainland Puerto Ricans went from 2% in 1960 to 14% in 2000. Most Puerto Ricans settled in Orlando and surrounding areas. By 2003, 206,000 Puerto Ricans lived in Central Florida, as compared to 155,000 in the counties of Miami-Dade and Broward (Duany & Matos-Rodríguez, 2006).

Finally, New Orleans bears special mention. In the 1990s, the city emerged as a new destination for Latinos, particularly for Hondurans, whose connections with the United Fruit Company had brought them to the "Crescent City" in the 1960s. According to the 2000 census, there were roughly 64,000 persons of Hispanic origin in the greater metropolitan area of New Orleans, 24% of whom were Honduran. However, the post-Katrina cleanup and reconstruction efforts have attracted as many as 20,000 Mexicans and Central Americans, who have come directly to the city or have traveled from other areas of the South (Quiñones, 2006). It is too early to assess the characteristics and potential impact of this population.

CHARACTERISTICS OF LATINOS IN NEW DESTINATIONS

Who are the Latinos settling in new destinations? A snapshot of the state of Georgia begins to highlight several of the most important contours of these diverse populations. The 2004 American Community Survey revealed that 4.6% of the total population of Georgia was of Mexican origin and 2.2% was "Other Hispanic." Of the more than 390,000 Mexicans in Georgia, 34.3% are U.S. citizens by birth, 3% are naturalized U.S. citizens, and 62.7% are not citizens (Kochut & Humphreys, 2006). Of noncitizens, a very high proportion, yet to be accurately counted, is undocumented. In Georgia, 95.7% of children under the age of 5 who have Mexican parents were born in the United States, and almost 70% of U.S.-born Mexicans living in Georgia are under 15 years old (Kochut & Humphreys, 2006).

The first characteristic evident in the case of Georgia is that immigrants dominate the Latino population of new destinations to a much greater extent than in traditional settlement areas. In 2000, 57% of all Latinos in six new settlement states of the South (Alabama, Arkansas, Georgia, North Carolina, South Carolina, and Tennessee) were foreign born. By contrast, only 41% of the Latino population nationwide was born outside of the United States (Kochhar, Suro, & Tafoya, 2005). In the 36 new settlement counties of the region exhibiting the most significant population growth between 1990 and 2000, immigrants comprised two-thirds (66%) of the Latino population.

The Georgia data also highlights a second characteristic: Immigrant and native-born Latinos in new destinations are young. The trend holds across the six new settlement states of the U.S. South, where foreign-born Latinos have a median age of 27, compared with 33 nationally. The median age of native-born Latinos in these states was 15 in 2001, reflecting the fact that Latino immigrants in this region, as throughout the United States, have high rates of fertility (Kochhar, Suro, and Tafoya, 2005). The Latino population of children age 4 and younger increased by 382% between 1990 and 2000, and the number of Latinos added to the population in this age range was significantly larger than the number of whites (110,000 vs. 43,000).

Fertility rates link closely to the third notable characteristic of the Latino population in new destinations: this population's changing gender composition. Among foreign-born Latinos in the six new settlement states, there were 173 men for every 100 women in 2001 (Kochhar, Suro, & Tafoya, 2005). Yet, several ethnographic studies of new settlement areas have pointed toward a trend that the numbers do not yet reflect. The pattern of the single male sojourner appears to be decreasing in prevalence while migration for family reunification and family unit migration are on the rise (Griffith, 2005; Rich & Miranda, 2005; Zúñiga & Hernández-León, 2005a). This is related, in part, to the increasing difficulty of back-and-forth migration for undocumented workers, which paradoxically works as an inducement to the settlement of entire families in new destinations. As Zúñiga and Hernández-León (2001, 2005a) and Griffith (2005) highlight, the feminization of the Latino population and the phenomenon of family unit migration have a broader impact on local communities than temporary male migrations. Not only workplaces but also schools, churches, hospitals, and other cultural and social institutions are shaped by the presence of Latino immigrant families.

Much research remains to be done on gendered shifts in the dynamics of migration to new destinations, but one area in which the impact of these shifts has been documented and examined is public school systems. In the six new settlement states of the South, the Latino school age population grew by 322% between 1990 and 2000. Because Latinos were starting from a very small base, their share of the school population in 2000 was only 4% (Kochhar, Suro, & Tafoya, 2005). This broad statistic masks the fact, related to patterns of selective deconcentration discussed earlier, that the impact of Latino immigration is disproportionately felt in particular districts and schools. For example, 4% of students in the city schools of Dalton, Georgia were Latino in 1989, but by 2000, more than 51% of students were Latino, and one-third of Dalton elementary schools had reached 70% Latino by 1998 (Zúñiga & Hernández-León, 2001, 2005a).

The fourth significant characteristic of these Latino populations is the high proportion of undocumented immigrants, 81% of whom, nationwide, come from Latin America. Although 62% of the undocumented population lives in the big six immigrant states, since the mid-1990s, the most accelerated growth of this population has taken place outside of those states. During the period between 2002 and 2004, an estimated 39% of the total undocumented immigrant population, calculated at 10 million, resided in states other than California, Texas, New York, Florida, Illinois, and New Jersey, up from only 12% in 1990 (Passel, 2005). In fact, Arizona, Georgia, and North Carolina, where the unauthorized immigrant populations fall in the range of 250,000–350,000 for each state, might have surpassed New Jersey as a primary destination.

Finally, most of the Latino immigrants settling in nongateway states are Mexican. Between 1990 and 2000, the Mexican immigrant population increased more than 1,800% in North Carolina, Tennessee, and Alabama; more than 1,000% in Arkansas and Minnesota; over 800% in Georgia; and between 500% and 700% in Utah, Iowa, Indiana, and Nebraska (Zúñiga & Hernández-León, 2005b). Simultaneously, the percentage of Mexican immigrants residing in California has declined from 57.8% to 47.8%, whereas in Texas, it has gone down from 22.1% to 19.0%. Also, whereas 63% of the Mexicans who arrived in the United States between 1985 and 1990 went to California, only 35% of those who came between 1995 and 2000 went to the Golden State. In contrast, the proportion of Mexicans settling in new destination states grew from 13% to 35% (Durand, Massey, & Capoferro, 2005).

One of the most striking examples of shifts in the geography of Mexican immigration is the rapid growth of the Mexican-origin population in New York City. In 1980, there were between 35,000 and 40,000 Mexicans in the city. By 1990 that figure had grown to 100,000, swelling to between 250,000 and 275,000 in 2000. Some estimates place the number of Mexicans in the greater New York area at half a million (Smith, 2001). A large majority of these Mexicans migrants are Poblanos and Mixtecos, but there are increasing numbers from the nontraditional sending states of Tlaxcala, Tabasco, and Morelos, as well as from Mexico City (Smith, 2005). As a result of this growth, Mexicans now constitute 13% of New York City's Latino population, the third largest Hispanic group, just behind Puerto Ricans and Dominicans.

The case of New York demonstrates that Mexican immigrants are not a homogeneous group, because many Mexicans heading to new destinations do not come from traditional sending states, such as Hidalgo and Michoacan, but from indigenous communities in Chiapas and Oaxaca. More than ever, Mixtecos, Zapotecas, Tzotziles, and Mames are part of the new geography of Latino migration (Fox, 2006). These groups bring specific histories and cultural, linguistic, religious, and social resources that shape their relations with other immigrants, as well as with native populations.

Despite the preponderant role that Mexican immigrants, in all their diversity, are playing in the dispersion of Latinos throughout the United States, other national groups are also contributing to this process. For example, in the 1990–2000 decade, the percentage of other Latinos living in the Northeast decreased from 30% to 25%. During the same period, the proportion of other Latinos in the South went up from 17.6% to 18.5% and in the Southwest, it went from 43.2% to 47.0% (Saenz, 2004). In particular, the growing presence of other Latinos in some southern states is striking. By 2000, Latinos from countries other than Mexico, Puerto Rico, and Cuba accounted for 62.5% of all Hispanics in Virginia, 55.1% in Louisiana, 34% in Mississippi, and 31% in Kentucky (Mohl, 2003). Similar processes are occurring in the Midwest. For instance, 24% of all Latinos in Nebraska come from Central and South America (Gouveia, Carranza, & Cogua, 2005). Obviously, this is a topic on which more research is needed.

CAUSES OF THE EMERGING GEOGRAPHY

The reasons for the dispersion of Latinos are diverse, complex, and interconnected, although they can be grouped in three categories. The first set of causes involves policymaking at the federal, state, and municipal levels. Foremost among these causes are the unintended consequences of the passage of the Immigration Reform and Control Act (IRCA) in 1986 (Massey, Durand, & Malone, 2002). In effect, IRCA legalized roughly 3 million undocumented Latino immigrants, allowing them the mobility needed to search for better jobs and affordable housing throughout the country. At the same time, in the post-IRCA period there was an increased militarization of the border, as demonstrated by Operation Gatekeeper in San Diego–Tijuana in 1994. By driving up the cost and risk of crossing the border, the drastic escalation of enforcement also provided incentives for Latinos to extend their stay or even to settle permanently in the United States. Rather than engaging in an ongoing transnational commute, which had been a yearly routine (particularly among many Mexicans in the pre-IRCA years), it made more sense for immigrants to bring their families in once and for all.

The strengthening of the Mexico–California border, combined with increasing municipal political controls on migration, had the effect of diverting the flow of immigration east. As California state government and specific municipalities actively sought to restrict unwanted migration through the passage of ordinances related to housing quality, drivers licenses, minimum wage and health care, their policy had the combined effect of "deflecting immigration" (Light, 2006) toward new destinations. As a result, such states as Arizona and New Mexico have emerged at the frontline of immigration reform debates in recent years. These states were also experiencing a housing boom during this time. In the midst of this boom, many Latinos found jobs as day laborers in construction, landscaping, and services, as was the case with growing numbers of Mexicans and Central Americans in Phoenix and surrounding areas (Moran-Taylor & Menjívar, 2005).

The second cluster of factors behind the new geographies of Latino migration relates to changes in the economy at the state, regional, national, and global levels. During the early 1990s,

California's economy suffered due to cutbacks in defense-related industries at the end of the Cold War. This recession not only dried up the job supply for both natives and immigrants but also dovetailed with growing anti-immigrant feelings that came to a head with the passage of Proposition 187, denying public social services to undocumented immigrants and requiring local and state officials to report them to the Immigration and Naturalization Service (INS). The result was a sociopolitical and economic climate that "pushed" Latino immigrants to seek opportunities elsewhere. Because close to 55% of the 2.3 million Mexicans legalized through IRCA lived in California, the state's labor markets were flooded with legalized immigrants. Thus, it is not surprising that many of them moved to alternative destinations in the West, South, and Midwest. Under these conditions, California's share of Mexican immigrants declined from 57.8% in 1990 to 48% in 2000. During the same decade, the proportion of Mexican immigrants in Colorado went up from 8.5% to 10.7%, in Nevada from 8.3% to 9.7%, and in Arizona from 3.4% to 5.3% (Durand, Massey, & Capoferro, 2005).

Also in the 1990s, several regions of the country and sectors of the economy experienced substantial growth and labor shortages. In rural areas in the Midwest and South, for instance, the agro-food sector underwent a massive restructuring. Responding to an exploding demand for meat, producers not only consolidated through corporate mergers but also moved their operations to nonmetropolitan areas in order to be close to raw materials, receive special land deals and tax breaks, and have access to a nonunionized labor force. Relocation was accompanied by changes in the assembly line that rendered it faster and more labor-intensive. Given the high turnover and dangerous work conditions, particularly on the so-called kill floor, where carcasses are carved and sectioned into predetermined portions, the new processing plants created an inexhaustible demand for disposable workers, which Latinos have filled (Stull, Broadway, & Griffith, 1995). Despite the hazardous conditions, meatpacking jobs are relatively well paid in comparison to work harvesting crops. This, plus access to inexpensive housing and the possibility of raising their children away from the violence, crime, and deficient schools that characterize big cities, proved attractive to Latinos. Agro-food conglomerates understood these circumstances and undertook aggressive recruitment in the countries of origin (Krissman, 2000). As a result, in 1980 only 8.5% of the meat processing workforce was Hispanic but, by 2000, this number had grown to 28.5%; and 82% of Hispanics working in this industry are foreign-born (Kandel & Parrado, 2005).

Regional changes in the South go beyond the restructuring of the agro-food sector. The region has become increasingly globalized, with a growing number of transnational corporations, such as CNN, Coca-Cola, Home Depot, Daimler-Benz, Toyota, Wal-Mart, and Fed-Ex locating their headquarters or production plants there. These corporations operate through a post-Fordist regime of production that attracts more than just highly skilled and high-income professional and managerial class. Post-Fordism also depends on a vast low-skilled force, hired under various types of temporary and precarious arrangement, among other things, to take care of the housing, consumption, and lifestyle requirements of the professional class (Sassen, 1998). Although there has been some migration of highly skilled industrial workers from Latin America, the great majority of Latinos have been integrated into this flexible unskilled labor pool, working in construction, dry walling and roofing companies, landscaping firms, hotels, restaurants, and manufacturing plants, not only in cities such as Atlanta and Raleigh but also in Birmingham, Huntsville, Memphis, and Little Rock.

The service sector has its own peculiarities in states like Florida, where the hospitality industry is a major economic force. Particularly after 9-11, when domestic tourism saw a substantial increase, hotels, casinos, entertainment parks, retirement communities, and restaurants experienced a labor shortage. Fleeing from Miami's saturated job market, Latino immigrants have helped to ease the pressure. This explains the emergence of new Latino communities beyond Miami-Dade County.

Changes in immigration policy and in the structure of the U.S. economy have coincided with the economic crises and civil wars of the 1980s and the disorderly transitions to democracy of the 1990s in Latin America. These crises and transitions have not only conditioned increased migration from Mexico but also new flows from Central and South America. As we move into the new millennium, the implementation of NAFTA, CAFTA, and other initiatives within a neoliberal framework has produced considerable dislocation. In particular, the elimination of trade barriers in Latin America, in tandem with the continuation of farm subsidies in the United States, has put enormous pressure on small producers and subsistence agriculture, contributing to international migration from places like Oaxaca, Chiapas, and eastern Guatemala.

The final piece in the puzzle has to do with the role that immigrant networks play in the emergence and growth of new destinations. Corporations have relied heavily on formal and informal immigrant networks to secure a steady supply of workers. Agro-food industries, in particular, have engaged in a host of recruiting practices beyond the H2A and H2B visa programs, encouraging workers to refer their families and friends, advertising job openings in hometowns heavily represented in particular plants, and using labor contractors operating transnationally to avoid legal responsibility (Johnson-Webb, 2002; Taylor & Stein, 1999). This has generated an entire legal and illegal procurement, transportation, and support industry with its own financial logics, which is often run by immigrants themselves. Diverse actors are part of this industry, ranging from smugglers, *raiteros*, couriers, and restaurant owners and shopkeepers, who not only bring Latin American products to the rural communities but often run lending, check-changing, and remittance businesses (Hernández-León, 2006).[1]

Although immigrant networks are often co-opted by the state and business elites, they are not reducible to a purely for-profit, or even economic, logic. They are embedded in broader transnational social fields that constitute the fabric of daily life and provide immigrants multiple sociocultural resources, including narratives and symbols to make sense of their journey, memories to recreate the homeland abroad, and practices to carve out new spaces of belonging. As we will see in the case of Siler City, these resources help immigrants confront the challenges of life in new gateways.

Thus, the new geography of Latino immigration stems from the complex interplay of factors, including immigration policies, economic restructuring at the state, regional, national, and global levels, informal and officially sanctioned recruitment strategies, and the immigrants' sociocultural resources. The rapid influx of Latinos to places with little or no history of recent migration raises a host of issues about interracial relations, incorporation, and the role of religious and civic organizations in the process of settlement (Johnson et al., 1999). We turn to these issues in a more local focus in the following two sections.

THE IMPACT OF LATINO MIGRATION ON NEW DESTINATIONS

As Latinos have settled in new destinations, they inevitably have shaped the life of local communities. Although comprehensive comparative studies that include rural, suburban, and urban cases do not yet exist, several case studies of small manufacturing cities in the Southeast and Midwest offer evidence of the new Latino presence contributing to economic revitalization (Engstrom, 2001; Grey & Woodrick, 2005; Griffith, 2005; Mohl, 2003; Rich & Miranda, 2005; Zúñiga & Hernández-León, 2005a). This revitalization can be understood as twofold. First, as discussed earlier, Latino immigrant workers are filling labor market shortages and contributing significantly to the profitability of rural industries. Some case studies document the impact of surging profitability accompanied by flat wages and the impact that this phenomenon has had on interethnic relations (Mohl, 2003; Rich & Miranda, 2005). As industrial leaders proclaim the salvific effect of the Latino work ethic on their communities, working-class whites and African Americans perceive job competition and wage pressures. Groups opposed to immigration, such as the Federation for American Immigration Reform (FAIR), the Minutemen, and Voices of Citizens Together/American Patrol (VCT), have tapped into these perceptions, often intensifying them through association with national security fears—that U.S. sovereignty is being violated by invading hordes of "law breakers." This manufactured linkage has made it possible to advance draconian anti-immigrant legislation at the local and state levels.[2]

In terms of scholarship, the debate about the impact of immigration on the labor market is far from settled. On the one hand, there is evidence that Latino employment is positively correlated with employment rates for native-born. Kochhar (2006), for instance, shows that the growth in Latino employment in 2005 has concentrated in the construction industry (40% of the jobs generated) and in booming areas of the country like the South and the West. Therefore, the rise in employment for Latinos is part of a widespread economic expansion that has also created jobs for native-born workers. It remains to be seen if this dynamic will be sustained as the real estate market and the construction industry cools down. On the other hand, Borjas (2004) argued that immigration has a strong negative impact on the earnings of natives without a high school diploma, who represent roughly 10% of the labor force. Between 1980 and 2000, immigrants, by increasing the labor supply, have reduced the wages of less qualified native workers by 7.4%. According to Borjas, this impact is magnified for African Americans and native-born Hispanics.

Given the contradictory evidence, the safest conclusion we can draw at this juncture is that Latino migration has differential effects on the job market, with no discernable national pattern. Immigrants might displace and/or replace native-born workers depending on factors such as the sector of the economy, the local employment conditions, the level of skill, and the nature of immigrant networks involved. Data from new Latino destinations has yet to be systematically incorporated into the debate.

Beyond the dynamics of the job market, Latino immigrants play a second revitalizing role in small cities, reviving declining downtown business districts by establishing shops and restaurants as part of growing local ethnic economies. During the massive "a day without Latinos" protests in March 2006, there were indications that Latinos have become important to the commercial life of many communities. In Milwaukee, for example, about 90 Latino-owned businesses closed in solidarity with the marchers for all or part of the day, effectively shutting down the city's south side (MSNBC, 2006). Scenes like this were repeated throughout the country in April and May. Although we are beginning to have a sense of the contribution of Latino immigrants to the overall economy, more research has to be undertaken to study the differential impact they have on the economy and quality of life of local communities.[3]

Latino immigrants also fill residential and school districts that have experienced decline (Engstrom, 2001; Grey & Woodrick, 2005; Griffith, 2005; Zúñiga & Hernández-León, 2001). As discussed earlier, the presence of complete families in new destinations significantly shapes religious, educational, and health care institutions while also introducing new racial and ethnic dynamics.[4] One of the most consistently noted cultural phenomena in new destinations of the South is the subversion of a long-standing biracial order (Rich & Miranda, 2005 Studsill & Nieto-Studsill, 2001; Zúñiga & Hernández-León, 2005a). This and many other economic, cultural, social, and political effects of immigration on new destinations still require significant scholarly attention. To give a glimpse of these dynamics at work we now turn to a case study.

THE DYNAMICS OF SETTLING IN A NEW DESTINATION: A CASE STUDY

New Latino migration to Siler City, North Carolina, a manufacturing town located on Highway 64 between Raleigh and Greensboro, is one example of the process of selective deconcentration discussed earlier. With only an estimated total population of 8,079 residents, Siler City is the largest town in rural Chatham County. Following the arrival of the railroad in 1884, Siler City became the county's primary distribution hub for agricultural and industrial goods, including poultry and textiles. Incorporated in 1887, it was populated by Euro-American and African American Protestants who moved from surrounding farms to fill factory jobs in the early 20th century. This settlement pattern, combined with the industrialization of the town, has left indelible marks on the local religious and cultural landscape. Until the arrival of Latino migrants in the early 1990s, Siler City had been a racially segregated and religiously Protestant place.

Poultry plants and textile mills have remained the backbone of Siler City's economy, employing African American and Euro-American workers for much of the long 20th century. In the late 1980s, however, when manufacturers sought less expensive labor, recruiting directly from Mexico and Central America, the local demographics changed drastically. In 1990, the Siler City population of 4,955 was 68% White, 27% African American, and 3% Hispanic. However, by 2000, the Hispanic population increased to nearly 40% of the town's total population.

Like many new destinations, Siler City lacked the necessary resources and infrastructure to accommodate the massive influx of Spanish-speaking migrants in the mid-1990s. Housing was scarce, public schools were overwhelmed, and adequate health care was not widely available. As in other rural communities experiencing a rapid influx of immigrants, Latinos rejuvenated the town's declining business district, becoming visible in the city's main public spaces through their stores, restaurants, and storefront churches. This visibility, however, came at the cost of increasing resentment from natives. Tensions arose as Latinos disrupted segregated residential patterns, first moving into the historically African American neighborhood of Lincoln Heights and then into other low-income predominantly White sections of the city (Cravey, 1997; Stocking, 1997a). The impact of Latinos on the local school system was equally dramatic. By 2003, over 60% of kindergarteners were Latino (Bailey, 2005). With no English as a Second Language (ESOL) programs and certified bilingual and Latino educators, Siler City's public school system struggled to retain Latino students and communicate with their parents. At the same time, a number of middle-class white parents, including a former school official, withdrew their children and enrolled them in private institutions (Stocking, 1997b).

Tensions came to a head in 2000, when, at the invitation of a small group of residents, former Klansman and Louisiana state legislator David Duke visited Siler City and gave a speech against the town's Spanish-speaking population. Even though Siler City officials denounced Duke, many Latinos assumed that local officials sponsored the rally because it took place on the steps of Town Hall (Glasscock, 2000). Duke's speech led to a further deterioration in the relations between Latinos and city hall, which had been rocky since the publication of a brochure in Spanish that asked the newcomers not to "keep goats in the yard, beat your wife, or watch T.V. after 10 PM" (Stocking, 1996).

Given the hostility and scarcity of institutional resources and infrastructure, religious organizations have played a critical social role for new migrants in Siler City. In fact, religious networks play a key, albeit hitherto not sufficiently studied, role in new destinations, particularly in the early stages of community formation (Marquardt, 2005; Menjívar, 2006;Odem, 2004). Although congregations might not have the necessary resources to act as full-fledged social service agencies, they often provide material, legal, and moral support, as well as mutual-aid networks used to operate transnationally (Vásquez & Marquardt, 2003). In some instances, religious lay leaders might create hometown associations as one aspect of their congregational work—for example, collecting funds to rebuild the church in their village of origin or to send bodies for burial in the homeland (Finke, 2003). These associations might eventually become civic organizations independent of church structures. Because religious networks entail a high level of intimacy, trust, and affect, they can be very effective in the construction of collective identities. By sponsoring activities like festivals, soccer leagues, and family picnics, they also serve as familiar, comfortable spaces in which simply to gather for entertainment and solace in the face of difficult work schedules and a hostile new environment. In some cases, churches offer space and resources for organizing toward civic engagement (Marquardt, 2005). The heavily Latino congregation of St. Julia Catholic church, for example, hosts an annual celebration of Our Lady of Guadalupe, patroness of Mexico and the Americas. In 2005, congregants constructed a large shrine to the Virgin in the colors of the Mexican flag, and some attached a Guatemalan flag to its side. On the evening of the festivities, over 600 Latinos filled the crowded sanctuary to honor Her with words, songs, flowers, and candles.

In Siler City, congregations are, by far, the most pervasive organizational form of civic engagement. As of August 2006, there were 43 congregations within a 3-mile radius of Siler City, compared to just two community and social service agencies. Religious institutions are not, of course, always civically engaged, nor are they free from contradictions and tensions. For instance, although some preexisting Euro-American churches in Siler City provide resources for Latino religious activities, most often in the form of a meeting space, new migrants are seldom integrated into preexisting congregations. Here, the language barrier has been a significant factor in the formation of separate rather than multiethnic congregations. Because many of the Latino Protestant ministers in Siler City are bilingual, they frequently play a mediating role between their congregants and the English-speaking community. They are also able to develop rapport within the community through ministerial networks and alliances, and some are readily familiar with U.S. law and institutional processes, because they often come from Puerto Rico or states such as Texas or California. This linguistic and cultural competence effectively makes religious leaders in new destinations power brokers, with mixed results. They might help immigrants to secure resources from host communities but they also mighty reproduce patron–client asymmetries common in the societies of origin.

Despite these contradictions, churches have the potential for building interethnic bridges. For example, when David Duke arrived to Siler City in 2000, white supremacists targeted the Latino congregants at St. Julia, rearranging the letters on the church marquee to spell "White Power" (O'Neill, 2000). In response to Duke, another group of Siler City residents gathered 2 months later, during Holy Week, to show their support for their Latino neighbors. Representatives from local congregations, including historically African American and Euro-American Protestant churches, joined members of St. Julia as part of the Jubilee Pilgrimage for Peace and Justice. A similar interethnic coalition came together for a local rally on April 10, 2006, which was organized by the advocacy group Hispanic Liaison as part of nationwide demonstrations. Although there were few African Americans present among the 3,000 demonstrators, the legacy of Martin Luther King Jr. was invoked by a variety of speakers, including a white woman who sang Woody Guthrie's "This Land is Your Land."

LINKING THE MICRO TO THE MACRO: THE AGENDA FOR THE FUTURE

The case of Siler City offers a glimpse of local dynamics behind the rise of new destinations, dynamics of interethnic tension and solidarity that emerge in the shared spheres of work, school, health, religion, housing, and everyday life. The growing ethnographic literature that has focused on the local impact of the new cartography of Latino settlement must be deepened to gather the perceptions, attitudes, and experiences of immigrants and native populations, particularly of African Americans and poor, rural Euro-Americans. This new research should explore comparatively the practices, institutions, and contexts that shape the ways in which Latino newcomers relate to host groups. Under what conditions do these two groups ignore, accommodate, collaborate, or express overt hostility toward each other (Hernández-León & Zúñiga, 2005)? Answers to this question will help scholars revise theories of immigrant incorporation and evaluate the impact of Latino migration on the bipolar racial formation still dominant in new gateways in the South (Waters & Jiménez, 2005).

To rise above the particularities of case studies, contextual analysis needs to engage studies of long-term trends and changes in the demographics and economics of Latino migration. Linking levels of analysis will make it possible to assess the specificity of new destinations: how they reproduce and break with patterns in traditional gateways. As Jones-Correa (2005) puts it, "We need more comparisons across groups, across places, across institutional levels, and across time periods" (p. 88).

Finally, the study of new Latino destinations has to take into account the evolving politics of immigration at the local, state, and national level. Whether it is a question of municipal zoning laws that limit the number of tenants per housing unit or state initiatives such as S.B. 529 in Georgia or proposals at the federal level like H.R. 4437, both of which criminalize undocumented workers, immigration policy is bound to have an impact on the way immigrants are received and integrated in new destinations.

The rise of a new geography of Latino settlement is a developing story. The 2005 American Community Survey confirms the rapid growth of Latino populations in the Midwest and South, but it also shows that this growth is now extending further into New England (New Hampshire), the upper Midwest (South Dakota), and the West (Montana). In short, much research remains to be done.

NOTES

1. The legality, level of institutionalization, and morphology of recruitment networks varies according to the industry, the context of reception, and length of settlement. In the Atlanta suburbs, for example, the rapid influx of immigrants who came after the 1996 Olympics to work in construction, landscaping, and housecleaning has been facilitated primarily by networks based on kinship, friendship, *paisanaje*, and church affiliation, rather than on deliberate recruiting by corporations, as was the case in Dalton (Hernández-León & Zúñiga, 2005). Many of these immigrants work as freelancers or have their own small businesses.

2. Ordinances directly targeting immigrants have emerged in places as diverse as Avon Park, Florida, Hazleton, Pennsylvania, Arcadia, Wisconsin, Farmingville, New York, and Riverside, New Jersey (Fried, 2006).

3. Raul Hinojosa ("Embracing Illegals," 2005) argued that undocumented Latino immigrants generate every year a net added value of about $800 billion through consumption.

4. For a wide-ranging discussion of the educational challenges Latinos face in new destinations, see Bohon, McPherson, & Atiles (2005) and Gouveia & Powell (2005). On the impact of Latino immigrants on health care, Erwin (2003) found that despite the challenges of a poor rural infrastructure—the high numbers of immigrants suffering

job-related health problems and without insurance—Latinos tend to have greater use of physician and hospital services in rural communities than in urban settings. This might reflect rural medical practices, which "were more likely to afford patients the ability to pay over time, make partial payments, and barter for services than would be likely in urban practice" (Erwin, 2003:65).

REFERENCES

Bailey, R. (2005). New Immigrant Communities in the North Carolina Piedmont Triad: Integration Issues and Challenges. In E. Gozdziak & S. F. Martin (Eds.), *Beyond the Gateway: Immigrants in a Changing America* (pp. 57–85). Lanham, MD: Lexington Books.

Bohon, S., Macpherson, H., & Atiles, J. (2005). Educational Barriers for new Latinos in Georgia. *Journal of Latinos and Education, 4*(1), 43–58.

Borjas, G. (2004). Increasing the Supply of Labor Through Immigration: Measuring the Impact on Native-born Workers. *Backgrounder.* Center for Immigration Studies: Washington, DC. Retrieved November 28, 2006, from http://www.cis.org/articles/2004/back504.pdf,

Brain, R., & Miranda, M. (2005). The Sociopolitical Dynamics of Mexican Immigration in Lexington, Kentucky, 1997 to 2002: An Ambivalent Community Responds. In V. Zúñiga & R. Hernández-León (Eds.), *New Destinations: Mexican Immigration in the United States* (pp. 187–219). New York: Russell Sage Foundation.

Burns, A. (1993). *Maya in Exile: Guatemalans in Florida.* Philadelphia: Temple University Press.

Cravey, A. (1997). Latino Labor and Poultry Production in Rural North Carolina. *Southeastern Geographer, 37*(2), 295–300.

Duany, J., & Matos-Rodríguez, F. (2006). *Puerto Ricans in Orlando and Central Florida.* New York: Centro de Estudios Puertorriqueños, Hunters College (CUNY).

Durand, J., Massey, D. S., & Capoferro, C. (2005). The new geography of Mexican migration. In V. Zúñiga & R. Hernández-León (Eds.), *New Destinations: Mexican Immigration in the United States* (pp. 1–20). New York: Russell Sage Foundation.

Engstrom, J. D. (2001). Industry and Immigration in Dalton, Georgia. In A.D. Murphy, C. Blanchard, & J. Hill (Eds.), *Latino Workers in the Contemporary South* (pp. 44–55). Athens: University of Georgia Press.

Erwin, D. O. (2003). An Ethnographic Description of Latino Immigration in Rural Arkansas: Intergroup Relations and Utilization of Health Care Services. *Southern Rural Sociology, 19*(1), 46–72.

Fink, L. (2003). *The Maya of Morganton: Work and Community in the Nuevo New South.* Chapel Hill: University of North Carolina Press.

Fox, J. (2006). Reframing Mexican Migration as a Multi-ethnic Process. *Latino Studies, 4*(1–2), 39–61.

Fried, D. (2006, September 2). Local Illegal Immigration Laws Draw a Diverse Group of Cities. *NC Times.* Retrieved November 29, 2006, from http://www.nctimes.com/articles/2006/09/03/news/top_stories/21_40_499_2_06.txt.

Glascock, N. (2000, February 20). Rally Divides Siler City. *News and Observer,* p. B1.

Gonzalez, C., & Stickney, V. (2006, April 11). Immigration Rally Cry: 'Today we are making History.' *Omaha World-Herald,* pp. A1.

Gouveia, L. (2005, February 2). *Divergent Origins, Converging Destinies? Venezuelans, Colombians, and Mexicans in the Heartland.* Paper presented at the Russell Sage Conference on Immigration to the United States: New Sources and Destinations, New York.

Gouveia, L., Carranza, M. A., & Cogua, J. (2005). The Great Plains Migration: Mexicanos and Latinos in Nebraska. In V. Zúñiga & R. Hernández-León (Eds.), *New Destinations: Mexican Immigration in the United States* (pp. 23–49). New York: Russell Sage Foundation.

Gouveia, L., & Powell, M. A. (with E. Carmargo). (2005). *Educational Achievement and the Successful Integration of Latinos in Nebraska: A Statistical Profile to Inform Policies and Programs.* Omaha: Office of Latino/Latin American Studies at the University of Nebraska at Omaha.

Griffith, D. (2005), Rural Industry and Mexican Immigration and Settlement in North Carolina. In V. Zúñiga & R. Hernández-León (Eds.), *New Destinations: Mexican Immigration in the United States* (pp. 50–75). New York: Russell Sage Foundation.

Grey, M. A., & Woodrick, A. (2005). 'Latinos Have Revitalized Our Community.' Mexican migration and Anglo responses in Marshalltown, Iowa. In V. Zúñiga & R. Hernández-León (Eds.), *New Destinations: Mexican Immigration in the United States* (pp. 133–154). New York: Russell Sage Foundation.

Guthey, G. (2001). Mexican Places in Southern Spaces: Globalization, Work, and Daily Life in and Around the North Georgia Poultry Industry. In A. D. Murphy, C. Blanchard, & J. A. Hill (Eds.), *Latino Workers in the Contemporary South* (pp. 57–67). Athens: University of Georgia Press.

Guzman, B., & McConnell, E. D. (2002). The Hispanic population: 1990–2000 Growth and Change. *Population Research and Policy Review, 21*, 109–128.

Hardin, J. (2006, April 11). It's Time for Us to Talk, Be Loud. *News & Record*, p. A1.

Hernández-León, R. (2005). *The migration Industry in the Mexico–U.S. Migratory System*. Online working paper, Center for Population Research, UCLA. Paper CCPR 049 05. Retrieved November 28, 2006, from http://repositories.cdlib.org/cgi/viewcontent.cgi?article=1127&context=ccpr.

Hernández-León, R., & Zúñiga, V. (2005). Appalachia Meets Aztlán: Mexican Migration and Intergroup Relations in Dalton, Georgia. In V. Zúñiga & R. Hernández-León (Eds.), *New Destinations: Mexican Immigration in the United States* (pp. 244–273). New York: Russell Sage.

Hinojosa, Raul. (2005, July 18). Embracing Illegals: Companies Are Getting Hooked on the Buying Power of 11 Million Undocumented Immigrants. *Business Week*. Retrieved November 28, 2006, from http://www.businessweek.com/magazine/content/05_29/b3943001_mz001.htm.

Johnson, J. H., Johnson-Webb, K. D., & Farrell, W. C. (1999). Newly Emerging Hispanic Communities in the U.S.: A Spatial Analysis of Settlement Patterns, In-Migration Fields, and Social Receptivity. In F. Bean & S. Bell-Rose (Eds.), *Immigration and Opportunity: Race, Ethnicity, and Employment in the United States* (pp. 263–310). New York: Russell Sage Foundation.

Johnson-Webb, K. D. (2002). Employer Recruitment and Hispanic Labor Migration: North Carolina Urban Areas at the End of the Millennium. *Professional geographer, 54*(3), 406–421.

Jones-Correa, M. (2005). Bringing Outsiders in: Questions of Immigrant Incorporation. In R. Hero & C. Wolbrecht (Eds.). *The Politics of Democratic Inclusion* (pp. 75–101). Philadelphia: Temple University Press.

Kandel, W., & Cromartie, J. (2004). *New Patterns of Hispanic Settlement in Rural America*. Washington, DC: United States Department of Agriculture.

Kandel, W., & Parrado, E. A. (2005). Restructuring of the US Meat Processing Industry and New Hispanic Migrant Destinations. *Population and Development Review, 31*(3), 447–471.

Kochhar, R. (2006). *Latino Labor Report, 2006: Strong Gains in Employment*. Washington, DC: The Pew Hispanic Center.

Kochhar, R., Suro, R., & Tafoya, S. (2005). *The New Latino South: The Context and Consequences of Rapid Population Growth*. Washington, DC: Pew Hispanic Center.

Kochut, B. D., & Humphreys, J. (2006). *Going North: Mexicans in Georgia*. Atlanta: Selig Center for Economic Growth, University of Georgia.

Krissman, F. (2000). Immigrant Labor Recruitment: U.S. Agribusiness and Undocumented Migration from Mexico. In N. Foner, R. Rumbaut, & S. Gold (Eds.), *Immigration Research for a New Century* (pp. 277–300). New York: Russell Sage Foundation.

Lichter, D. T., & Johnson, K. M. (2006). Emerging Rural Settlement Patterns and the Geographic Redistribution of America's New Immigrants. *Rural Sociology, 71*(1), 109–131.

Light, I. (2006). *Deflecting Immigration: Networks, Markets, and Regulation in Los Angeles*. New York: Russell Sage Foundation.

Marquardt, M. (2005). Structural and Cultural Hybrids: Religious Congregational Life and Public Participation of Mexicans in the New South. In K. Leonard, A. Stepick, M. Vásquez, & J. Holdaway (Eds.), *Immigrant Faiths: Transforming Religious Life in America* (pp.189–218). Walnut Creek, CA: Alta Mira.

Martes, A. C. (2000). *Brasileiros nos Estados Unidos: Um Estudo Sobre Imigrantes em Massachussetts*. Rio de Janeiro: Paz e Terra.

Massey, D. S., Durand, J., & Malone, N.J. (2002). *Beyond Smoke and Mirrors: Mexican Immigration in an Era of Economic Integration*. New York: Russell Sage Foundation.

Menjívar, C. (2006). Introduction. Public Religion and Immigration Across National Contexts. *American behavioral scientist, 41*(11), 1447–1454.

Mohl, R. A. (2003). Globalization, Latinization, and the Nuevo New South. *Journal of American Ethnic History, 22*(4), 31–66.

Moran-Taylor, M., & Menjívar, C. (2005). Unpacking Longing to Return: Guatemalans and Salvadorans in Phoenix, Arizona. *International Migration Review, 43*(4), 91–121.

MSNBC (2006, March 23). Day Without Latinos' Protest Roils Wisconsin: Thousands in Milwaukee, Racine Oppose Targeting Undocumented Workers [Television broadcast.]. City: MSNBC. Retrieved November 28, 2006, from http://www.msnbc.msn.com/id/11981744/.

Odem, M. (2004, Fall). Our Lady of Guadalupe in the New South: Latino Immigrants and the Politics of Integration in the Catholic Church. *Journal of American Ethnic History, 23*, 29–60.

O'Neill, P. (2000, May 3). Jubilee: Siler City Residents Reclaim Their Town from David Duke. *Independent*. Retrieved November 28, 2006, from http://www.indyweek.com/gyrobase/Content?oid=oid%3A14289.

Passel, J. S. (2005). *Unauthorized Immigrants: Numbers and Characteristics*. Washington, DC: Pew Hispanic Center.

Quiñones, S. (2006, April 4). Latinos Find Gold Rush in New Orleans. *Los Angeles Times*. Retrieved November 28, 2006, from http://www.latimes.com/news/nationworld/nation/la-na-labor4apr04,0,5618062.story?coll=la-home-headlines.

Saenz, R. (2004). *Latinos and the Changing Face of America*. New York: Russell Sage Foundation.

Saenz, R., & Torres, C. C. (2003). Latinos in rural America. In D. L. Brown & L. E. Swanson (Eds.), *Challenges for rural America in the Twenty-First Century* (pp. 57–70). University Park: The Pennsylvania State University Press.

Saenz, R., Donato, K., Gouveia, L., & Torres, C. (2003). Latinos in the South: A Glimpse of Ongoing Trends and Research. *Southern Rural Sociology, 19*(1), 1–19.

Sassen, S. (1998). *Globalization and Its Discontents*. New York: The New Press.

Schmidt, E., & Crummett, M. (2004). Heritage Recreated: Hidalguenses in the U.S. and Mexico. In J. Fox & G. Rivera-Salgado (Eds.), *Indigenous Mexican Migrants in the United States* (pp. 417–48). La Jolla: Center for Comparative Immigration, University of California, San Diego.

Skiba, K., & Forester, S. (2006, April 11), Throngs Rally for Immigrants: Across Nation, Wave of Newcomers Is Called Future of America. *Milwaukee Journal Sentinel*, p. 1.

Smith, R. C. (2001). Mexicans: Social, Educational, Economic and Political Problems and Prospects in New York. In N. Foner (Ed.), *New Immigrants in New York* (pp. 275–300). New York: Columbia University Press.

Smith, R. C. (2005). *Mexican New York: Transnational Worlds of New Immigrants*. Berkeley: University of California Press.

Stocking, B. (1996, June 30). Siler City Leaders Deny Brochure for Latino Newcomers Is Racist. *News and Observer*, p. B1.

Stocking, B. (1997a, May 4). Side by Side: Worlds Apart. *News and Observer*, p. A1.

Stocking, B. (1997b, September 3). Language Gap Strains Schools. *News and Observer*, p. A1.

Steigenga, T., & Palma, I. (2003, March 27–29). *Religion, Transnationalism, and Public Action Among the Maya of Jupiter, Florida: Recreated Images of Home and Collective Identity*. Paper presented at the Latin American Studies Association XXIV International Congress, Dallas, TX.

Studstill, J. D., & Nieto-Studstill, L. (2001). Hospitality and Hostility: Latin Immigrants in Southern Georgia. In A.D. Murphy, C. Blanchard, & J. Hill (Eds.), *Latino Workers in the Contemporary South* (pp. 44–55). Athens: University of Georgia Press.

Stull, D. D., Broadway, M. J., & Griffith, D. (Eds.). (1995). *Any Way You Cut It: Meat Processing and Small-Town America*. Lawrence: University of Kansas Press.

Taylor, M., & Stein, S. (1999, July 4). Network Help Recruit Immigrants for U.S. Job Market. *The Fort Worth Star-Telegram*, p. A30.

Vásquez, M., & Marquardt, M. F. (2003). *Globalizing the Sacred: Religion Across the Americas*. New Brunswick, NJ: Rutgers University Press.

Waters, M., & Jiménez, T. (2005). Assessing Immigrant Assimilation: New Empirical and Theoretical Challenges. *Annual Review of Sociology, 31*, 16.1–16.21.

Zúñiga, V., & Hernández-León, R. (2001). A New Destination for an Old Migration: Origins, Trajectories, and Labor Market Incorporation of Latinos in Dalton, Georgia. In A.D. Murphy, C. Blanchard, & J. Hill (Eds.), *Latino Workers in the Contemporary South* (pp. 44–55). Athens: University of Georgia Press.

Zúñiga, V., & Hernández-León, R. (2005a). Appalachia Meets Aztlán: Mexican Immigration and Intergroup Relations in Dalton, Georgia. In V. Zúñiga & R. Hernández-León (Eds.), *New Destinations: Mexican Immigration in the United States*. New York: Russell Sage Foundation.

Zúñiga, V., & Hernández-León, R. (Eds.). (2005b). *New Destinations: Mexican Immigration in the United States*. New York: Russell Sage Foundation.

CHAPTER 3

Latino Incorporation in the United States in Local and Transnational Contexts

ROBERT COURTNEY SMITH

INTRODUCTION

Latino incorporation into the United States reflects this country's political involvements abroad and its political economy at home, set within an evolving global system and varying levels of transnational life. The timing of a particular group's incorporation into the United States, and the peculiarities of the locality in which it settles, also affect its context of reception and its trajectory. This chapter will look at how various groups have become incorporated into the United States over time, focusing on variations in their contexts of reception, including the following: their labor market and geographical concentration; the political context of their initial out-migration from their home countries and their immigration into the United States, including their legal status; their continued links with their home states and societies; and the transnational life that emerges from these.

The process of Latino incorporation into the United States is set within a larger system I call the Inter-American Migration System (Smith, 2003a, 2003b). The Inter-American Migration System theory sees migration as resulting from economic and other pressures stemming from globalization; from politics, including the pressures stemming from U.S. immigration policies and foreign policies, and sending state policies that tend to directly or indirectly produce migration; and from the self-perpetuating nature of migration, including a transnational social field that engages home country politics, to varying extents, with U.S. politics. In some cases, such as Cubans, the overwhelmingly political nature of the causes of their migration and their context of reception has been most important and has given them a political and social importance beyond their numbers and a relatively prosperous incorporation. In other cases, such as Central Americans, the political causes of their migration and their subsequent context of reception have led to the opposite effect: a diminution of their political and social power relative to their numbers and a relatively impoverished incorporation. In other cases, such as the Dominicans, their initial out-migration began largely for political reasons, but as American politics changed, the country lost its foreign policy importance, and the primary cause of migration incorporation has become economic. Moreover, over time, the transnational world that Dominicans have forged between their two islands has been determined much more by their primary settlement in New York than by larger U.S. policy.

For each group, we discuss their social, economic, and political incorporation, with attention given as well to racial dynamics of incorporation. A discussion of the transnational life of each group is presented while identifying particularly interesting developments for each group, such as the effect of their legal status or changes in it on their likely incorporation.[1] We highlight how the home country's position in the global system or its relationship to the United States is likely to affect incorporation in the long term. The focus of this chapter will be on the incorporation of the first generation of immigrant Latino groups, but will, wherever possible, examine data on the second or subsequent generations. One final introductory note is in order. Relatively less time will be spent discussing the "big three" groups—Mexicans in the southwest, Puerto Ricans in the northeast and Cubans—who usually dominate historical discussions of Latino immigration. These three have been capably dealt with by many authors (Acuña, 1996; Montejano, 1987; Portes & Rumbaut, 1994; Rodriguez, 1990; Sanchez-Karrol, 1994). Consequently, more time will be spent discussing the experiences of other newer groups that receive relatively less attention: Dominicans, Salvadorans, Colombians, Ecuadorians, Peruvians, and Mexicans migrating to the east coast.

Mexican, Cubans, and Puerto Ricans: The Big Three

Mexicans, Cubans, and Puerto Ricans are the most frequently discussed Latino immigrant groups, and they present interesting comparisons. Mexicans can be understood as primarily a low-wage labor migration, whose members have been subject, at various times, to intense racial discrimination and whose futures are still uncertain today. Cubans are characterized as a politically, economically, and socially advantaged group that, on the whole, has had greater socioeconomic success than most and that today has political power well in excess of its numbers (Portes & Rumbaut, 1994). Puerto Ricans are between a rock and hard place. As U.S. citizens, they do not encounter the issue of undocumented status that many immigrant groups do, but they also had particularly unfortunate luck in terms of the timing and location of their immigration, and racialized antagonism and stigma from American society.

Mexicans

Mexicans are, by far, the largest group, accounting for about 60% of the total Latino population in the United States (U.S. Census, 2000). The Mexican population in the United States stems back from the war between Mexico and the United States in 1848 when, as Garcia y Griego (1981), who hails from New Mexico, says "The border crossed us" when Mexico was forced to cede much of its northern territory to the United States. The incorporation of Mexicans into U.S. society and politics over the subsequent 160 years has been checkered, but not without resistance and optimism, and not uniform throughout the United States (Acuña, 1996; Estrada et al., 1988). Mexican elites intermarried with American elites in Texas (Montejano, 1987), but the overwhelming pattern in the United States was one of low-wage incorporation into the United States (Acuña, 1996; Portes & Rumbaut, 2001). This was true both for the majority of native-born Mexicans in the United States and immigrants. The growth of Mexican immigration to the United States was fostered in part by U.S. government policy. Driven by wartime labor shortages, the United States concluded an agreement with the Mexican government known as the Bracero Program, which brought nearly 5 million Mexicans to the United States to work between 1942 and 1964, when it was ended due in large part to protests over the bad working conditions of the braceros (Calavita, 1992; Garcia y Griego, 1981). The Bracero Program laid out immigration pathways that continued after the program ended, and many of the more than 20 million Mexican-descendant people in the United States can trace their roots to it.

Mexicans have experienced complex and sometimes contradictory incorporation into the United States. Although the descendants of Mexican immigrants do better educationally than their parents, the returns to those additional years of education are not as rich as for their parents, in large part because they are entering a different labor market (Myers & Cranford, 1998). In today's information economy, higher levels of education, usually a bachelor's degree, are needed for entry-level jobs. Nationally, Mexican Americans drop out at a rate of 35–40%, according to the U.S. Department of Education, and the nonenrollment rate and dropout rate for recent immigrants is higher, about 50%, especially in new destinations (Smith, 2002). In an interesting pattern also seen among other groups, including Whites, Mexican girls are much more likely to go to college and graduate than their male counterparts (Myers & Cranford, 1998). Reasons for this difference are not completely clear, but include growth in sectors of the labor market where women are preferred, combined with employer preferences where racial and gender stereotypes work against Latino men. For example, one study showed that employers prefer minority women in jobs where services require soft skills for dealing with people (Moss & Tilly, 1996).

Politically, Mexicans have fared better than they have economically, but there is still a great deal of bitter history with which to reckon. In some parts of the southwest, especially Texas, Mexicans were subjected to the same kinds of Jim Crow laws and practices as Blacks, and the disregard for their civil rights was just as brutal. A less well-known case than *Brown v. Board of Education*, the *Mendez v. Westminster* (1946) case was a landmark because it ruled that separate "Mexican" schools were unconstitutional and denied Mexican students equal protection under the law. Much of this momentum came from the return of Latino GIs from the Second World War and their fight against racism in Europe. Having risked their lives and lost friends and family for the United States, their patience for being treated as second-class citizens had worn a bit thin. Among other things, this stance spurred on the League of United Latin American Citizens (LULAC) to pursue the case. Other organizations such as the Mexican American Legal Defense and Education Fund and the National Council of La Raza later became important players.

In the last 20 years, Mexican Americans in the United States have witnessed a paradox in politics. Although they have failed to see an increase in their social and economic fortunes commensurate with their numbers, they have become increasingly powerful in politics, and their future as the country's largest minority promises even greater influence (de la Garza, 1997, 1982; DeSipio, 1998; Garcia, 1988). Their importance has been amplified by their concentration in key electoral states, such as California, New York, Texas, and Florida, which either have many electoral votes or are key contests. Although Mexican Americans have historically voted Democratic, the Republican Party is attempting to make inroads into that constituency by emphasizing the confluence between the Republicans' more conservative agenda and the social conservatism and religiosity among many Latinos.

Cubans

Cubans' positive incorporation trajectory has its roots in the Cold War. Fleeing Castro's Cuba, Cubans coming to the United States in the early 1960s were given, in effect, the "royal treatment": immediate refugee status, which made them legally eligible to work, gain access to social insurance programs, small business loans, and similar programs, and a generally positive image in the public mind—think Ricky Ricardo on prime-time television in the 1950s–1960s. Initial Cuban refugees also had higher levels of social and human capital that facilitated their adjustment and advancement in American society. Later Cuban inflows were also political creatures, but this time as a foreign policy move by Castro to send to the United States the Marielitos. Often portrayed in the media as criminals, the Marielitos have done less well than prior migrants in U.S. society, partly because of their own human capital characteristics and partly because their "blacker" phenotype has made them more likely to suffer effects of racial discrimination in the United States (Portes & Stepick, 1993).

Cubans have acquired a disproportionate share of political power relative to their numbers and compared to other Latino groups. This power is due to the confluence of several factors. Cubans are concentrated in, among other places, Florida, many of whose cities have become political strongholds for Cuban politicians, from local officials to state officeholders. Their political incorporation has been aided by their having an open route to US. citizenship directly from refugee status and by the fact that they now have more than 40 years since the first big influx, so that their U.S. born children are now grown adults. Their relative prosperity has also facilitated political mobility. Moreover, Florida is a key electoral state in presidential races, and the Cubans—whose leadership has been fiercely anti-Castro, politically conservative—have become a key political constituency for a Republican party that has attempted, with increasing success, to seek the votes of the emerging Latino constituency in the United States.

Puerto Ricans

Puerto Ricans are primarily concentrated in the U.S. northeast, although they are also present throughout the US mainland. They have had the significant advantage of being U.S. citizens from birth, but they have had a number of disadvantages as well. First, their phenotypes often have features that White and often non-White Americans see as "black," making them more subject than most immigrants to the cumulative and negative consequences of racial discrimination in the United States (Massey, 1990; Rodriguez, 1996). Puerto Ricans also lost out because of the timing and location of their migration. They came to the U.S. mainland and the northeast during the 1940s–1970s in large numbers and into industries that were dying—garment making, manufacturing, agriculture—or that were paid poorly—such as services (Morales & Bonilla, 1993; Rodriguez, 1990; Smith, Cordero-Guzmán & Grosfoguel, 2001).

Although there is a growing middle class and Puerto Ricans in suburbs outside major cities do better than those inside, Puerto Ricans as a whole have faced difficult structural circumstances. Cordero-Guzmán (1997) analyzed how structurally negative positions translate into constrained choices and poor outcomes for Puerto Rican youth. On the other hand, recent work by Aranda (2006) shows that middle-class Puerto Ricans have had different relationships with racialization than their poorer counterparts and have made choices about where to live based in part on their perceptions of local opportunities and where they will be able to negotiate local racial and ethnic hierarchies.

Puerto Ricans might be the original population to inhabit a kind of postmodern, hybrid cultural space. The island's status as a commonwealth of the United States has facilitated migration because there is no citizenship obstacle to Puerto Ricans coming to the United States. It has also fostered a biculturality both in New York and elsewhere on the mainland and on the island (Flores & Yudice, 1997). This hybridity has been a source of cultural vibrancy and innovation, although it has also clashed with dominant language policies, such as those emphasizing the transition to English only as the goal of second language classes (Zentella, 1997). Puerto Rican transnational migrants also often feel the liminality of being betwixt and between the United States and Puerto Rico (Perez, 2004).

Puerto Ricans, as a group and like other groups, have encountered fewer obstacles in political, artistic, and intellectual arenas than in socioeconomic ones, and their achievements have had significant impacts in New York and the region, as well as across the United States. These achievements include a caucus in the New York State Assembly and many officeholders in the northeastern states. Puerto Ricans have had a huge positive impact at the City University of New York (CUNY) and other institutions of higher education. Their mobilization in favor of open admissions and to demand departments of Puerto Rican studies in the early 1970s led to the formation of such departments at many CUNY institutions and others, including the State University of New York (SUNY) and to the creation of the Centro de Estudios Puertorriqueños at Hunter College, widely recognized as a leader in research, teaching, and community service. This commitment to combine scholarship and community organizing in community development lives on in the work of Haslip-Viera, Falcon, and Matos Rodríguez (2005) and Flores (2005). Flores observed that class differences between Puerto Rican workers and American employers exacerbate difficulties and underline the need to improve working conditions for Puerto Ricans. The 1974 ASPIRA consent decree in New York State, the result of a lawsuit brought by the Puerto Rican Legal Defense and Education Fund (PRLDEF), set a national precedent in the right to bilingual education—even if the educational philosophy is less the balanced biculturalism sought in that lawsuit, and more transitional education. Similarly, PRLDEF's work in *Torres v. Sachs* pushed Congress to extend the Voting Rights Act to language minorities in 1975, setting the stage for subsequent litigation and extension of minority voting rights across the country. Most recently, PRLDEF fought for the educational rights of undocumented immigrants in New York, when it sued CUNY in 2002 (Cruz, 2005; Falcon, 2005).

Puerto Rico's status as a commonwealth makes it difficult to characterize political and other activity between the mainland and the island. There has long been an independence movement that has had strong influence in departments of Puerto Rican studies in New York and that has, at various times, been active in U.S. politics (Duany, 2002). In addition, the Puerto Rican government has, at times, had a very vigorous set of diasporic institutions attending to the needs of their migrants in the United States. These included a labor migration program between agricultural regions on the east coast and Puerto Rico (CUNY, 2006).

Newer Latino Immigrants

DOMINICANS   Dominican incorporation into the United States has a complex history and trajectory. Dominican migration initially began largely as a political migration. After the death of Trujillo in 1961, many of those who benefited from his regime left. Later, democratically elected president Juan Bosch was ousted by a military junta backed by conservative elements in civil society. The 1965 civil war and the U.S. invasion led it to use its immigration policy as foreign policy. The United States opened its doors to dissidents and tried to help the military regime "export" political dissent and prevent "another Cuba," a policy in which the American ambassador to the Dominican Republic was directly involved (Hernandez, 2002; Mitchell, 1992). The political nature of Dominican migration persisted. Duany (2005) documents a spike in admissions to Puerto Rico from the Dominican Republic each time Balaguer was reelected President during his 1966–1978 regime (p. 247). Political events over the next 40 years have made the Dominican Republic less politically important to the United States as a whole. As the Dominican Republic's democracy became more consolidated and the Cold War ended, the country largely fell off the political radar of the United States.

Over the last 30 years, Dominican migration and incorporation into the US has assumed a fascinating form (Torres-Saillant & Hernandez, 1998). The Dominican population is primarily concentrated in New York, but also with significant concentration in Boston and Florida and in suburbs surrounding major cities. It has become, increasingly, an economically driven wage migration, with the initially middle-class and elite migrants giving way to peasant migrants and then urban dwellers with lower income and education levels. In the United States, Dominicans have concentrated in the light manufacturing and low-income service economies. The Dominican population in New York consists of more women than men and has lower levels of undocumented status than in other large populations, such as Mexicans, especially among women. Fuentes (2005) reported that Dominican women often prefer to live on their own because they have access to better employment than many Dominican men, and they see marriage as a burden.

Dominican incorporation into the United States shows complex racial dynamics (Duany, 1998; Torres-Saillant, 2000; Torres-Saillant & Hernandez, 1998). Dominicans migrating into the United States bring with them a racialized notion of the Dominican Republic as a White or European nation. Motivated in part by such concerns, the Dominican Republic continues to deny citizenship to Haitians born in the Republic, on the basis of the argument that their parents, who might have been in the country for decades, are "in transit." They also bring a more varied, nuanced sense of racial identity that does not fit in with a Black-and-White racial binary in the United States. The racialized notion of the Dominican Republic as a White country has sometimes led Dominican parents to urge their children to "mejorar la raza" (better the race) by marrying lighter-skinned spouses. The latter leads them to confusion when they confront anti-Black racial discrimination in New York. Dominicans experience the full measure of racial disadvantage usually reserved for Blacks in the United States, including concentration in the worst schools, geographic segregation, high levels of unemployment, and other problems. Dominicans are also helping to remake the racial and ethnic order in New York and other parts of the United States. Generally, in the life world of Latinos and their children in New York, a Black/White binary does not actually hold sway the way most theories suppose. Rather, a pan-minority, often cosmopolitan racial and ethnic reality holds sway, as discussed with respect to Mexicans in a later subsection.

Dominicans have also one of the most interesting political stories of recent immigrant incorporation. "Los Dominicanyork" have simultaneously incorporated into the politics of

New York and of the Dominican Republic (Graham, 2001; Guarnizo, 1997; Torres-Saillant & Hernandez, 1998). The 1991 New York City redistricting led to the redrawing of a "Dominican" electoral district in upper Manhattan and the subsequent election of the first Dominican to the New York City Council, Guillermo Linares. At the same time, they had more power in the Dominican Republic because of the rewriting of the constitution. These developments were presupposed by a very high transnationalization of political party life between the Dominican Republic and New York (Levitt, 2001). However, these twin developments—the creation of a Dominican district in New York and the enfranchisement of the Dominicanyork—served to further catalyze transnational life between the two islands. The result has been a quotidian political transnationalism more pronounced than most others. Dominican political parties have headquarters in New York City and actively campaign during elections. Moreover, Dominicans have become part of New York's political life to an increasing degree. When Hillary Rodham Clinton ran for the U.S. senate the first time, she took a trip to the Dominican Republic to campaign. Similarly, Leonel Fernandez, elected president of the Dominican Republic in 1996, went to New York City public schools; he also holds a U.S. green card. When he ran for president, his mother in the Dominican Republic did a radio spot for him urging Dominicans in New York to vote for him. His victory was based partly in his being identified as the migrant candidate.

SALVADORANS   Salvadoran migration to the United States is more directly, relative to other migration streams, attributable to U.S. foreign policy (see Aguayo & Weiss Fagen, 1988; Hamilton & Chincilla, 1991). During the civil wars of the 1980s, the United States often supported right-wing regimes in Central America against their leftist guerilla opponents. This support included direct training in the United States in counterinsurgency techniques and supervision in Latin America. Salvadoran migration, which had been negligible before the implementation of these techniques, grew exponentially during the 2–3-year period following their implementation. By 1985, between 20% and 35% of the total population was uprooted, including some 500,000 internally displaced and the remainder outside of the country. It is estimated that between 5% and 6% of the Salvadoran population was living in the United States in 1985 (Diaz-Briquets, 1989). By 2000, there were at least 500,000 Salvadorans living in the United States, most of whom had come during the 1980–1992 civil war (Alison & Gammage, 2004; Menjivar, 2000).

The massive scale of the migration cannot be accounted for simply by the understandable desire to avoid being caught in the fighting between insurgents and government troops; rather, it was a flight from systematic terror, attributable to the implementation of a counterinsurgency strategy "aimed at definitively breaking up the logistic base, social support, and the possible sympathy of the civilian population" (Torres-Rivas, 1985:15). It is this strategy that led to notorious massacres at El Mozote and dozens of other villages in El Salvador. The intersection of U.S. policy and out-migration came in the change in strategy by the Salvadoran government, which began a policy attempting to deprive the opposition of its base of support among the local populations. In addition, both the government and the guerillas forced people to join them or face death, including children as young as 12 years old. The result was a dramatic and sudden increase in migration.

The evolution of Salvadoran relationships with the Salvadoran and U.S. states is fascinating. Salvadorans initially came to the United States as undocumented refugees, aided by the Sanctuary movement of the 1980s. Despite well-documented country conditions that should have been the basis for legitimate claims for asylum or refugee status, the U.S. government did not want, in the words of one Salvadoran refugee, "to accept us as refugees because it would be admitting that the military aid it sends to El Salvador does not help, rather destroys and creates refugees" (Garcia, 2006:84; Repak, 1995). Similarly, the approval rating for their refugee and asylum applications were the mirror images of those from Russia or Cuba: Whereas those fleeing Communist countries were granted refuge at rates over the 90th percentile, those fleeing from civil wars, where the United States had a close relationship with the home regime, had approval ratings in the low single digits (Anker, 1990). It was more an expression of a cold war logic than anything else that drove these differing rates. However, after the end of the civil war with the Chapultepec Accords in 1992 and the later restoration of formal democratic institutions in El Salvador, the government began to vigorously seek to aid its migrants in the United States because of the tremendous boost they gave to the economy. Hence, the Salvadoran state moved to help its citizens in the United States fill out asylum applications. These were claims that argued that if these immigrants returned to their country of origin, they would face a well-founded fear of persecution! The United States gave Salvadorans temporary protected status—the right to stay until conditions in their home country improved. The rationale for this move was, in part, to avoid the negative economic consequences that forcing the return of Salvadoran migrants in the United States would have had in El Salvador (Coutin, 2000).

Salvadorans were also aided by a strong Sanctuary movement in the United Statesthat was morally opposed to U.S. interventions in Central America, and felt the United States had a moral obligation to accept its refugees, who were in the United States at least indirectly because of U.S. actions (Coutin, 1993). Hence, Salvadorans have had an evolving legal status in the United States and a curiously changing relationship with the Salvadoran state. The U.S. state has alternatively tried to deport, protect, and ignore them, whereas the Salvadoran state has alternatively tried to persecute them at home and protect them while abroad and to utilize their remittances. As it now stands, most Salvadorans still live in a legal limbo in which they must wait to see if the U.S. government renews their temporary protected status, introducing tremendous uncertainty into their lives and the lives of their U.S.-citizen children.

In the United States, Salvadorans have socioeconomic profiles of incorporation similar to Mexicans, with relatively low levels of education and income but increasing levels in both areas for most youth of the second generation. Salvadorans are concentrated geographically in several urban areas: Los Angeles, Washington, DC, northern Virginia, Houston, Long Island, and the New York metropolitan region.

Salvadorans show interesting paradoxes with respect to transnational life. Some scholars have noted how little transnational life there was among most Salvadorans, and they trace this to the ongoing violence in the country, the lack of security and rule of law even after the restoration of formal democracy, the tragic state of the economy, and high rates of undocumented status (Hagan, 1994; Menjivar, 2000). More than a decade after the end of formal hostilities, there are still significant problems in El Salvador regarding police conduct, gangs, and persistent hunger. El Salvador's rural economy, based largely on coffee exports, is in decline, and its new export-led economic development strategy as part of the Caribbean Basin Trade Partnership Act (and since 2004, the U.S.–Central America Free Trade Agreement, CAFTA) has failed to generate enough employment or income for the country's population. Gammage (2005) convincingly argues that the Salvadoran state's development strategy is to export people and recruit remittances, a practice that is encouraged by major multinational institutions.

This economic vulnerability has helped promote transnational life of various kinds. First, the Salvadoran economy received some 2.5 billion dollars in remittances in 2004, amounting to 17% of the Gross Domestic Product (GDP) by itself; considering multiplier effects, remittances are, by far, the largest source of income for families of migrants and perhaps the largest in the country, which can be used to promote development (Landhold, 2001). In 2001, El Salvador made the U.S. dollar a legal currency, all but replacing the colon.

Second, Salvadorans have actively organized since their earliest time in the United States. For example, El Rescate (The Rescue) was founded in 1981 to defend Central Americans' rights in the United States and to promote peace in El Salvador. El Rescate adopted explicitly transnational goals when 23 member municipios formed the COMUNIDADES (Comunidades Unificados en Ayuda Directa a El Salvador; Communities Unified in Direct Support of El Salvador) in 1993. In 2003, El Rescate organized its first International Convention of Salvadorans in the World, an event explicitly diasporic in its outlook. The most recent convention, in November 2006, has among its goals the following: the promotion of Salvadoran women's leadership in diaspora-Salvadoran relations; economic development; and the right of migrants to vote from abroad. Gammage (2005) also documented how the Salvadoran government created a bureaucratic department with the expressed goal of aiding hometown associations with links in the United States and El Salvador, such as applying for grants in El Salvador. Taken together, these steps indicate a working diaspora with important institutionalization.

Third, Salvadoran gangs, or maras, have established themselves throughout El Salvador, Honduras, and Guatemala and in various places in the United States (Chincilla & Hamilton, 1999; Moser & Winton, 2002; Santacruz Giralt, 2001). The intense police action in the United States and El Salvador and the U.S. policy of deporting them have facilitated the transnationalization of gangs as their members have been deported from the United States; they have organized new or strengthened existing chapters of their gangs in El Salvador. In El Salvador, gang members face disappearances and assassination by vigilantes and the police themselves. Deported gang members face an intense stigma upon return to Salvadoran society and are often unable to find work and housing. Deported gang members, with the help of local activists, clergy, and international organizations, have started Homies Unidos, to try to help these youth readjust in El Salvador.

COLOMBIANS, ECUADORIANS, AND PERUVIANS   There are now significant numbers of Colombians, Ecuadorians, and Peruvians in the United States and their numbers are concentrated in the great New York region, including the city's suburbs and New Jersey. A recent study by Mollenkopf et al. (2005) treated these three groups as one, calling them CEPs, and compares them with native Whites, Blacks, and Puerto Ricans and other immigrants, such as the Chinese, Russians, and West Indians. Although Colombians, Ecuadorians, and Peruvians do encounter many of the same kinds of problems that other immigrants encounter, including undocumented status for some (Guarnizo, Portes, & Haller, 2003), low wages, and sometimes ethnic discrimination, the CEPs as a group seem to be faring better than the children of native-born Blacks or Puerto Ricans, or of Dominicans and West Indians. Part of the explanation for this lies in the fact that Colombians, Ecuadorians, and Peruvians are more likely to have at least one parent with a college degree than most other immigrants, including Dominicans, Puerto Ricans, West Indians, native-born Blacks, and Chinese. Moreover, they are more likely to pursue familial strategies of upward mobility more like the Chinese, such as living at home with both parents well into their twenties, which saves money for education and offers other benefits. Some 29% of CEPs live with both parents, compared to 16% of Dominicans, 12% of Puerto Ricans, and 47% of Chinese (Mollenkopf et al., 2005:480). Another factor that might contribute to their faring better than other groups is that CEPs are all less likely to have Black phenotypes, relative to Puerto Ricans and Dominicans, and many more of them are likely to appear phenotypically White, especially Colombians. Peruvians, and Ecuadorians typically appear more "Andean," the sociological importance of which might be to clearly mark them as not Black. The larger point about these three groups of CEPs is that Latino incorporation into U.S. labor markets, social structures, and ethnic and racial hierarchies is likely to become increasingly varied over the coming decades.

Transnational life among Colombians and Ecuadorians differs interestingly (less is written about Peruvian transnational life; see Julca, 2001). Among Ecuadorians are significant numbers of indigenous Otavalans, who have excelled at a kind of small-scale, transnational entrepreneurship. Cutting out the middle man, they produce sweaters and similar goods, traveling in Europe and the United States to sell them (Kyle, 1999; Pribilsky, 2004). The Ecuadorian state has created a Program for Ecuadorians Abroad, modeled on the Mexican program. Since 2002, it has published *Migrantes*, aimed at informing migrants of pertinent news. However, there is much less institutionalization of this political life, with much less capacity on the part of the Ecuadorian state and among its organizations in the United States, with a much shorter history of such organizing, than among Mexicans. The First International Forum of Ecuadorian Organizations, held in 2005 in Spain, for example, criticized the lack of movement toward giving Ecuadorians abroad the right to vote in elections at home (Ecuatorianos en el Exterior, 2006). Finally, indigenous people in Ecuador have used transnational links to fight different kinds of oppression, from oil companies to their home state government.

Colombians show particularly interesting political dynamics. The Colombian state has done much more than most to institutionalize its relationship with its diaspora. Indeed, it rewrote parts of its constitution (as part of a larger rewriting of it) to enable it to treat Colombians abroad as part of its political community, and it made provision for Colombians abroad to elect a senator from the diaspora, meaning, in practice, the senator from New York City (Sanchez, 1997). Sanchez reported that part of the plan was for the Colombian state to enlist Colombians in the United States as lobbyists and image makers to change the perception of Colombia as a country that produces drugs and terror. Colombians in the United States have also had the right to vote in the presidential elections in Colombia for over a decade, but the turnout in such elections is usually quite modest. Guarnizo and his colleagues (1999, 2003) argued that this is because distrust resulting from systemic violence has so permeated Colombian political culture that it has been exported to the United States as well. Hence, despite the Colombian state's attempts to institutionalize political activity in its diaspora, it has had limited success.

Mexicans and Other New Latinos in the Eastern United States

Mexicans migrating to the east coast can be thought of as a new migration with perhaps a different incorporation trajectory than their longer-term counterparts in the southwest. As documented by Hernandez Leon and Zuñiga (2005; see also Cortina & Gendreau, 2003; Galvez, 2004; Smith, 2001, 2006), Mexican migration to the east coast of the United States has increased tremendously over the past 15 years. For example, the Latino population in Georgia and North Carolina, most of which is Mexican but also includes Guatemalans and other Central Americans, increased several times over during the 1990s. In North Carolina, the Census data show the population increased from under 78,000 Latinos in 1990 to nearly 380,000 in 2000, with over 300,000 undocumented immigrants in 2002. Georgia had over 390,000 Latinos in 2000, with some 200,000–250,000 undocumented (Passell, 2005). These Latinos are coming into different social and political contexts than those in the southwest, and differ from each other as well. They face different local political economies, racial and ethnic hierarchies, and educational and social contexts. Those moving into older northeastern cities, such as Philadelphia, or Hartford and New Haven, Connecticut, or New Brunswick or Camden, New Jersey, Newburgh, New York, or, to some extent, New York City or Boston, enter a seemingly paradoxical situation. These new immigrants encounter great demand for their labor, and employers in these cities seek to recruit new workers through their current workers. Hence, these immigrants enter what appears to be a promising labor market. However, they are entering and contracting economic niches in older central cities.

Olvera and Rae (2007) document how Latinos in New Haven, Connecticut have rapidly come to occupy most of the entry-level service jobs in that city's small businesses. However, the industrial and commercial bases that sustained earlier groups of immigrants, such as the Italians of the early 20th century, are gone. Hence, it is feared that these immigrants might be getting set up for their ethnic niches to turn into racial traps (Kasinitz & Vickerman, 2001), as the children of these immigrants want better jobs and living standards, but are being raised in structural contexts inhibiting the mobility required to support such lifestyles.

In places like New York and Boston, the situation is quite a bit different. There is more of an internal labor market and more chance for people with less education to move up. Take the restaurant industry as one example in which there is significant internal diversity in the size of firms and what they pay–ranging from small restaurants run by the owners, to large private clubs with a larger internal labor market and many well-paying jobs. An immigrant with little education can start as a busboy and end up as a waiter making $70,000 per year. This is not meant to sound Pollyannaish or to suggest that opportunity awaits all, given that the exploitation of workers in such places is a critical issue. However, it is noteworthy that there is nontrivial upward mobility within the families of immigrants with little education, through the opportunities to convert sweat to equity based on higher salaries.

The key issue for Mexicans in New York and the northeast is how high a percentage of the population is undocumented. Indeed, a study by McNees, Suilc, and Smith (2003) showed that, in a convenience sample of over 500 Mexicans in public places in New York City, some 91% who had been in the United States 10 years, 86% who had been here up to 15 years, and 39% of those who had been here more than 15 years were undocumented. Most will have little or no chance to adjust their status in the future. Part of this impact is mitigated by New York State and New York City policies. For example, there is a program known as Child Health Plus that provides health insurance to all poor children who have no other means of support, including undocumented ones. As a result, most undocumented Mexican children are covered by health insurance and have regular access to a doctor. Such a generous policy is in striking contrast to that in other states, where undocumented people are denied feasible access to medical and educational services. However, the federal government's stance on these issues makes life difficult, even in immigrant-friendly states such as New York. Indeed, there are many young immigrants who came to New York as children and have graduated from high school and college and must they remain in the same labor market they have always been in–working low-wage, dead-end jobs–despite the fact that they have supported themselves over time and graduated. This is fundamentally unjust and inconsistent with American values of fairness and with the "American Dream." However, there might be an alternative to this problem–the Dream Act–which would give such students the right to legalize their status after graduating from high school. Although these youth and others would still face serious inequalities in American society, this would at least allow them to take advantage of the same institutions and opportunities open to most youth in the country. Congress would invest well in America's future to pass it.

In the southeast, the situation is a bit different. Again, new Latino immigrants are being incorporated into older or contracting industries, like agriculture, but also into ones that are growing or are still robust, like poultry processing. The key thing will be to what extent these jobs allow these immigrants to enter the middle class and enable their children to move up the economic ladder. There is an irony here in that the southeast might be much better than the northeast in terms of offering immigrants opportunities for economic mobility. For example, it is possible to buy a house fairly inexpensively in the Carolinas or Georgia, whereas purchasing a house in many cities in the northeast is impossible, particularly for low-income immigrants; owning a house is still key to intergenerational wealth transfer for most families in the United States.

These new immigrants also face at least two different racial and ethnic worlds. First, there is the cosmopolitan, polyglot world of New York. Although New York has its share of racial problems, it is not a city that is conceived in black and white, as many American cities are. Latinos and Asians have complicated the picture (Haslip-Viera, 1996). In my current research, we find that there are many Mexican young men moving into decent jobs in the service and retail sectors in New York, in contradiction to what the literature predicts will happen—that they will not want to do such work because they see it as demeaning, and that employers will not want to hire them because they fear them (Kasinitz & Rosenberg, 1993; Moss & Tilly, 1996). Instead, they are benefiting from what Victoria Malkin keenly called the "Beneton effect," invoking the bus ads that that company promoted some years ago featuring ambiguously ethnic models in their clothes. The bottom line is that these youth are getting opportunities that their gender and ethnicity would, according to theory, prevent them from getting or taking advantage of.

In other regions in the east, new Latino immigrants are settling in areas not only with Black/White racial binaries but also with a whole set of social relations and rituals arising around them (Hernandez Leon & Zuñiga, 2005). In such areas, it is still not clear whether Mexicans and other Latinos will be treated more like Blacks or Whites or how their position in the racial hierarchy will be changed. This is complicated even more because in many of these places, the last immigrants came in from Europe over 100 years ago and so they are not used to dealing with outsiders. Moreover, the speed of the settlement and magnitude of the growth of the Latino population has engendered strong reactions from some locals. Some Blacks and Whites fear labor market competition, whereas others resent the increased costs of educating these new local populations.

CONCLUSION

This chapter has focused mainly on new Latino immigrant groups: Dominicans, Salvadorans, Colombians, Peruvians, and Ecuadorians, and Mexican migrants to the east coast of the United States. However, we also examined, albeit briefly, the experiences of the "big three": Mexicans (in the Southwest), Puerto Ricans, and Cubans. We examined how these groups have incorporated themselves into U.S. social, economic, and racial hierarchies, how U.S. policies and foreign policy have shaped both out-migration and incorporation into the United States, and how transnational life is experienced among these different groups. It finds both significant cause for concern and optimism in how America is welcoming these new immigrants and their children.

Suggestions for Future Research

Research on the incorporation of Latinos into the United States and their transnational links will grow in the coming decades. As Latinos continue to increase as a percentage of the population, and given their location in key electoral states, they will no doubt gain greater attention in politics and public policy. However, this greater political attention does not ensure that Latinos will be invited or permitted to join American society as full members. One job of scholars studying Latinos will be to make sure that we have the analysis needed to help in the fight for their equal inclusion in American society. Another task will be to analyze how Latinos are helping remake American society and have done so in the past. The following is a nonexhaustive discussion of issues that should be researched.

First, there are emerging research issues on Latino immigrants and their children, and later generations, in new geographical areas. One significant issue will be how Latinos are changing racial and ethnic hierarchies in the areas into which they settle. In the American south and in many suburbs throughout the United States, Latinos are complicating what were in the past literally Black and White hierarchies. This has raised several issues. The first is what happens politically when Latinos come to represent a significant part of the population in an area in which there is little experience dealing with diversity or where all the social and political pacts for dealing with it are between African Americans and Whites? Will Latinos form coalitions with African Americans, or with Whites, or will race and ethnicity not be the main lines along which politics is organized? To what extent will local electoral and other political systems be adapted, voluntarily or by force of federal law, to accommodate Latinos, either as newcomers or as old timers whose population has grown significantly? How will Latinos relate to more established political groups, including both Whites and African Americans, as they begin to gain more political power?

A second area for this kind of research will be in how changes in everyday life will be affected by Latinos' growing numbers and the accompanying changes in racial and ethnic hierarchies and patterns of interaction. How, for example, have long established patterns of daily, racial interaction in the Deep South changed in places where Latinos have emerged as significant populations? How do African Americans, Whites, and Latinos understand each other in these places?

Another key area for future research will be relations between established, long-time Latinos and Latino newcomers and their children. Emerging research (Duarte, 2007) showed that many Latinos in the third and later generations feel that they are treated as being shamefully "less Mexican" (or Latino) by immigrants, because they might not be fluent in Spanish. On the other side, Anglos and African Americans express surprise that they speak English fluently and ask them to explain aspects of the immigrant experience that are far removed from their own lives. These dynamics merit further study.

Education is a key factor in the incorporation of Latinos into the United States, and the United States has failed to take appropriate measures to ensure that Latinos have equal educational opportunities. Part of the issue has been the mid-20th-century assimilationist bias in educational language policy in the United States. This can be seen through the evolution of language policy over the three decades since the right to instruction in Spanish (or other native language) was won in part through the ASPIRA consent decree in 1974. The intent of those pursuing this right was to make Spanish an equal language to English, more on the model of a dual-language program, where instruction is in both languages and both are equally valued. Such an approach makes even more sense now, with the more globalized world in which we live. Yet, the emphasis over more than 30 years of language policy has been toward shorter and shorter transition times, with the goal being not to maintain the second language but to eliminate it by converting the student entirely to English. This kind of approach has made America what one observer called "the graveyard of languages" and has made it a nation of monolingual English speakers in a world where multilingualism is the norm in developed countries. Given the documented positive effects to multilingualism, a key research area should be to analyze the political work needed to implement and sustain such policies. Even in the liberal New York City public school district in which my children have been enrolled, dual-language programs are constantly underfunded and in need of defense.

Another area for further research and policy action will be on the ways in which Latinos that have been in the United States for decades, or longer, have fared in the educational system and how to improve their access to opportunity. Part of the problem has been a larger disinvestment in urban areas, driven in part by racial prejudice that has starved the educational system and its supporting social infrastructure. Another part of the problem is that the school system can adopt policies that disproportionately affect Latinos and others, as in the emphasis on high-stakes testing. Driven by the need to raise scores on high-stakes tests as embodied in the No Child Left Behind law, many schools engage in what Valenzuela (1999) called "subtractive schooling," engaging in practices that make the students feel they do not belong, and even counseling many Latino and immigrant students out of regular schools and into Graduate Equivalency Diploma programs, where their scores will not be counted as part of the district. Such policies amount to an attack on these students and must stop; they should be replaced with increased support for programs that enable all students to achieve their potential.

Future research is also needed on the relationship between diasporic activity and incorporation into the United States. There is a common belief that involvement in one's home country retards incorporation, but I believe the relationship is more complex than that and involves the issues of how subsequent generations fare in U.S. society and the relationship of the home state with the United States and with its first-generation emigrants. Empirically, it seems that those more involved in diasporic action are also more involved in addressing issues in the United States. This makes sense, because community leaders will address problems wherever their community is. The long-term sustainability of this relationship, into the second, third, and subsequent generations, will depend on various factors, including how much effort the sending state puts into it and the extent to which postimmigrant generations have lived in the home country.

Policy Recommendations

In concluding, I want to make a few recommendations and/or reflections about public policy and the alternative futures of Latinos in the United States, and particularly in the northeast. First, Latinos, both immigrants and the native born, will continue to move to the suburbs, out of major cities, and face both a new set of issues and the same old issues in new contexts. For example, Westchester County, New York entered into a Consent Decree in 2005 to provide Spanish language assistance in voting, including a ballot in Spanish, an issue which had long been settled in New York City and in much of the rest of the country (*U.S.A. v. Westchester County Board of Elections*, 7-19-05). Advocacy organizations will need to be alert to political exclusion in such "new frontiers." Similarly, suburban school districts are now serving increasing numbers of Latino and language minority students, and these schools will need to develop ways to address the needs of these groups.

Second, the country must invest more in its urban centers and especially in urban education. Public universities have been raising their tuition at increasing rates across the United States, making it harder for low-income students to attend. Some public universities seem to be trading higher test scores, which favor the more affluent, over greater access. Public universities offer subsidized education with the idea that they will serve as engines of mobility for newcomers and the poor. If they keep increasing the economic and other barriers to entry, they might achieve higher test scores, but they will exclude the very people they are meant to serve. Moreover, urban school systems often get shortchanged financially compared to those in more affluent suburbs. This is the basis of the 13-year (so far) lawsuit by the Campaign for Fiscal Equity seeking equal funding for New York City public school children. Imagine what could be accomplished if we instituted a Students' Bill of Rights, guaranteeing students a high-quality, free or low-cost education through college.

Finally, I would highlight a key long-term issue, and one of the most important in my own work: the incorporation of undocumented children of immigrants. Each year, up to 65,000 undocumented children graduate from U.S. high schools (National Council of La Raza, 2006), and very few of them go on to college. Those who do finish college, graduate back into undocumented status in the labor market. It reflects very poorly on the United States that it continues to penalize these youth who play by the rules; who beat the very high odds to graduate from high school, and some even from college; and who do so without any government financial aid available to students who are U.S. citizens. In my view, the single most important step forward that the United States could take would be to pass the Dream Act, which would provide these students with access to legal residency in the United States through their high school graduation. This would move us in the right direction toward a fairer policy for these youth; It would contribute to advancing the U.S. larger interest in having more productive and active citizens who are permitted to invest themselves in the country's future.

NOTE

1. This framework draws on the context of the reception approach to analyzing incorporation of immigrants (see Portes & Bach, 1985), but it also incorporates transnational and larger systemic factors into the analysis, as per Zolberg and Smith (1996) and Smith (2003a, 2003b).

REFERENCES

Acuña, Rodolfo. (1996). *Anything But Mexican: Chicanos in Contemporary Los Angeles*. New York: Verso.

Aguayo, Sergio, & Weiss Fagen, Patricia. (1988). *Central Americans in Mexico and the United States: Unilateral, Bilateral, and Regional Perspectives*. Washington, DC: Center for Immigration Policy and Refugee Assistance, Georgetown University.

Alison, Paul, & Gammage, Sarah. (2004). *Home Town Associations and Development: The Case of El Salvador*. New Brunswick, NJ: Women's Studies Department, Rutgers University.

Anker, Deborah. (1990). US Immigration and Asylum Policy: A Brief Historical Perspective. In Lydio Tomasi (Ed.), *In Defense of the Alien*. Staten Island, NY: Center for Migration Studies.

Aranda, Elizabeth. (2006). *Emotional Bridges to Puerto Rico*. Lanham, MD: Rowman and Littlefield.

Cavalita, Kitty. (1992). *Inside the State: The Bracero Program and the INS*. New York: Routledge.

Chinchilla, Norma, & Hamilton, Nora. (1999). Changing Networks and Alliances in a Transnational Context: Salvadoran and Guatemalan Immigrants in Southern California. *Social Justice, 26*(3), 4–27.

Cordero Guzman, Hector. (1997). The Structure of Inequality and the Status of Puerto Rican Youth in the US. In Antonia Darder, Rodolfo Torres, & Henry Gutierrez (Eds.), *Latinos and Education* (pp. 80–94). New York: Routledge.

Cortina, Regina, & Gendreau, Monica. (2003). *Immigrants and Schooling: Mexicans in New York*. Staten Island, NY: Center for Migration Studies.

Coutin, Susan Bibler. (1993). *The Culture of Protest: Religious Activism and the US Sanctuary Movement*. Boulder, CO: Westview Press.

Coutin, Susan Bibler. (2000). *Legalizing Moves: Salvadoran Immigrants Struggle for US Residency*. Ann Arbor, MI: University of Michigan Press.

Cruz, Jose E. (2005). The Changing Socioeconomic and Political Fortunes of Puerto Ricans in New York City, 1960–1990. In G. Haslip Viera, A. Falcon, & F. Matos Rodriguez (Eds.), *Boricuas in Gotham: Puerto Ricans in the Making of Modern New York City* (pp. 37–84). Princeton, NJ: Markus Weiner Publishers.

CUNY. (2006). Centro de Estudios Puertorriqueños. Retrieved September 12, 2006, from http://www.centropr.org.

de la Garza, Rodolfo O. (1997). Foreign Policy Comes Home: The Domestic Consequences of the Program for Mexican Communities Abroad. In Rodolfo de la Garza & Jesus Velasco (Eds.), *Beyond the Border: Mexico's New Foreign Policy* (pp. 69–88). Lanham, MD: Rowan and Littlefield.

de la Garza, Rodolfo O. (1982). Chicano-Mexican relations: A Framework for Research. *Social Science Quarterly, 63*(1), 115–130.

DeSipio, Louis. (1998). *Making Americans/Remaking America: Immigrants and Immigration in the Contemporary United States.* Boulder, CO: Westview.

Diaz-Briquets, Sergio. (1989). *The Central American Demographic Situation: Trends and American Population and US Immigration Policy* (pp. 33–54). Austin: University of Texas at Austin Center for Mexican American Studies.

Duany, Jorge. (1998). Reconstructing Racial Identity: Ethnicity, Color and Class among Dominicans in the United States and Puerto Rico. *Latin American Perspectives, 25*(3), 147–172.

Duany, Jorge. (2002). *The Puerto Rican Nation on the Move: Identities on the Island and in the United States.* Chapel Hill: University of North Carolina Press.

Duany, Jorge. (2005). Dominican Migration to Puerto Rico: A Transnacional Perspective. *Centro Journal, 17*(1), 243–269.

Duarte, Cynthia. (2007). *Between Shame and Authenticity: Negotiating Ethnic Identity Among Third and Later Generation Mexican Americans.* Doctoral dissertation. New York: Department of Sociology, Columbia University.

Ecuatorianos en el Exterior. Retrieved August 26, 2006; from www.victimasdelaprensa.com.

Estrada, Leobardo, Garcia, F. Chris, Macias, Reynaldo, & Maldonado, Lionel. (1988). Chicanos in the United States: A History of Exploitation and Resistance. In F. Chris Garcia (Ed.), *Latinos and the Political System* (pp. 28–64). Notre Dame, IN: University of Notre Dame Press.

Falcon, Angelo. (2005). From Civil Rights to the "Decade of the Hispanic": Boricuas in Gotham, 1960–1990. In G. Haslip-Viera, A. Falcon, & F. Matos Rodriguez (Eds.), *Boricuas in Gotham: Puerto Ricans in the Making of Modern New York City* (pp. 85–106). Princeton, NJ: Markus Reiner Publishers.

Flores, Juan (Ed.). (2005). *Puerto Rican Arrival in New York: Narratives of the Migration, 1920–1950.* Princeton, NJ: Markus Wiener Publishers.

Flores, Juan, & Yudice, George. (1997). Living Borders/Buscando America: Languages of Latino Self-Formation. In Antonia Darder, Rodolfo D. Torres, & Henry Gutiérrez (Eds.), *Latinos and Education* (pp. 174–200). New York: Routledge.

Fuentes, Norma. (2005). *Mexican and Dominican Women in Racialized and Ethnicized Labor and Housing Markets.* Doctoral dissertation. New York: Columbia University.

Galvez, Alyshia. (2004). *In the Name of Guadalupe: Religion, Politics and Citizenship among Mexicans in New York City.* Doctoral dissertation. New York: New York University.

Gammage, Sarah. (2005). Exporting People and Recruiting Remittances. Retrieved September 8, 2006, from www.noapparentmovie.org/papers/gammage.

Garcia, F. Chris (Ed.). (1988). *Latinos and the Political System.* Notre Dame, IN: University of Notre Dame Press.

Garcia, Maria Cristina. (2006). *Seeking Refuge: Central American Migration to Mexico, the United States and Canada.* Berkeley: University of California Press.

Garcia y Griego, Manuel. (1981). *The Importation of Mexican Contract Laborers to the US, 1941–1964.* La Jolla, CA: Center for US–Mexico Studies.

Graham, Pamela. (2001). Political Incorporation and Re-incorporation: Simultaneity in the Dominican Migrant Experience. In Hector Cordero-Guzman, Robert Smith, & Ramon Grosfoguel (Eds.), *Migration, Transnationalization and Race in a Changing New York* (pp. 87–108). Philadelphia: Temple University Press.

Guarnizo, Luis. (1997). Los Dominicanyorks: The Making of a Binational Society. In Mary Romero, Pierrette Hondagneu-Sotelo, & Vilma Ortiz (Eds.), *Challenging Fronteras* (pp. 161–174). New York: Routledge.

Guarnizo, Luis A., & Elizabeth Roach. (1999). Mistrust, Fragmented Solidarity and Transnational Migration: Colombians in New York City and Los Angeles. *Ethnic and Racial Studies, 22*(2), 367–397.

Guarnizo, Luis Eduardo, Portes, Alejandro, & Haller, William. (2003). Assimilation and Transnationalism: Determinants of Transnational Political Action among Contemporary Migrants. *American Journal of Sociology, 108*, 1211–1248.

Hagan, Jacqueline. (1994). *Deciding to Be Legal.* Philadelphia: Temple University Press.

Hamilton, Nora, & Chincilla, Norma Stoltz. (1991). Central American Migration: A Framework for Analysis. *Latin American Research Review, 26*(1), 75–111.

Haslip-Viera, Gabriel. (1996). The Evolution of the Latino Community in New York City: Early Nineteenth century to the Present. In G. Haslip-Viera & S. Baver (Eds.), *Latinos in New York: Communities in Transition* (pp. 3–29). Notre Dame, IN: University of Notre Dame Press.

Haslip-Viera, Gabriel, Falcón, Ángelo, & Matos Rodríguez, Félix (Eds.). (2005). *Boricuas in Gotham: Puerto Ricans in the Making of Modern New York City.* Princeton, NJ: Markus Wiener Publishers.

Hernandez, Ramona. (2002). *The Mobility of Workers under Advanced Capitalism: Dominican Migration to the United States.* New York: Columbia University Press.

Hernandez Leon, Ruben, & Zuñiga, Victor (Eds.). (2005). *New Destinations for Mexican Migration*. New York: Russell Sage Foundation.

Julca, Alex. (2001). Peruvian Networks for Migration in New York City's Labor Market, 1970–1996. In Hector Cordero-Guzman, Robert Smith, & Ramon Grosfoguel (Eds.), *Migration, Transnationalization, & Race in a Changing New York* (pp. 239–257). Philadelphia: Temple University Press.

Kasinitz, Philip, & Rosenberg, Jan. (1993). Missing the Connection: Social Isolation and Employment on the Brooklyn Waterfront. *Social Problems*, 43(2), 180–196.

Kasinitz, Philip, & Vickerman, Milton. (2001). Ethnic Niches and Racial Traps: Jamaicans in the New York Regional Economy. In Hector Cordero-Guzman, Robert Smith, & Ramon Grosfoguel (Eds.), *Migration, Transnationalization, & Race in a Changing New York* (pp.191–211). Philadelphia: Temple University Press.

Kyle, David. (1999). The Otavalan Trade Diaspora: Social Capital and Transnational Entrepreneurship. *Ethnic and Racial Studies*, 22(2), 422–447.

Landholt, Patricia. (2001). Salvadoran Economic Transnationalism: Embedded Strategies for Household Maintenance, Immigrant Incorporation, and Entrepreneurial Expansion. *Global Networks: A Journal of Transnational Affairs*, 1(3), 217.

Levitt, Peggy. (2001). *Transnational Villagers*. Berkeley: University of California Press.

Massey, Douglas S. (1990). American Apartheid: Segregation and the Making of the Underclass. *American Journal of Sociology*, 96(2), 329–357.

McNees, M., Suilc, N., Flores A., & Smith, R. (2003). *Immigrant Health in New York*. Final Report to the United Hospitals Corporation. New York: Lutheran Medical Center

Menjivar, Cecilia. (2000). *Fragmented Ties: Salvadoran Immigrant Networks in America*. Berkeley: University of California Press.

Mitchell, Christopher. (1992). US Foreign Policy and Dominican Migration to the United States. In Christopher Mitchell (Ed.), *Western Hemisphere and United States Foreign Policy* (pp. 89–123). University Park: Pennsylvania State University Press.

Mollenkopf, John, Waters, Mary, Holdaway, Jennifer, & Kasinitz, Philip. (2005). The Ever Winding Path: Ethnic and Racial Diversity in the Transition to Adulthood. In R. Setterson, F. Furstenberg, & Rumbaut, R. (Eds.), *On the Frontier of Adulthood: Theory Research and Public Policy* (pp. 454–497). Chicago: University of Chicago Press.

Montejano, David. (1987). *Anglos and Mexicans in the Making of Texas*. Austin: University of Texas Press.

Morales, Rebecca, & Bonilla, Frank (Eds.). (1993). *Latinos in a Changing US Economy*. Newberry Park, CA: Sage.

Moser, Caroline, & Winton, Ailsa. (2002). *Violence in the Central American Region: Towards an Integrated Framework for Violence Reduction*. London: Overseas Development Institute.

Moss, P., & Tilly, C. (1996). "Softz" Skills and Race: An Investigation of Black Men's Employment Problems. *Work and Occupations*, 23(3), 252–276.

Myers, Dowell, & Cranford, Cynthia. (1998). Temporal Differentiation in the Occupational Mobility of Immigrant and Native Born Latinas. *American Sociological Review*, 63, 68–93.

National Council of La Raza. (2006). Dream Act: Overview. Retrieved September 6, 2006, from http://nclr.org/content/policy/detail/1331/.

Olvera, Jacqueline, & Rae, Douglas. (forthcoming, 2007). Mexican Immigration After Urbanism: The New Haven Case. In Hilary Silver (Ed.), *New Immigrants in Urban New England*. Unpublished manuscript.

Passell, Jeffrey. (2005). *Estimates of the Size and Characteristics of the Undocumented Population*. Pew Hispanic Center Report. Washington, DC: Pew Hispanic Center.

Perez, Gina. (2004). *The Near Northwest Side Story: Migration, Displacement, and Puerto Rican Families*. Berkeley: University of California Press.

Portes, Alejandro, & Bach, Robert. (1985). *Latin Journey*. Berkeley: University of California Press.

Portes, Alejandro, & Rumbaut, Ruben. (1994). *Immigrant America*. Berkeley: University of California Press.

Portes, Alejandro, & Rumbaut, Ruben. (2001). *Legacies*. Berkeley: University of California Press.

Portes, Alejandro, & Stepick, A. (1993). *City on the Edge: La Presidencia de la República Geografía de la Marginalización en México Coordinación*. Mexico, D.F.: General del Plan Nacional de Zonas Deprimidas y Grupos Marginados.

Pribilsky, Jason. (2004). 'Aprendemos A Convivir': Conjugal Relations, Co-parenting, and Family Life Among Ecuadorian Transnational Migrants in New York and the Ecuadorian Andes. *Global Networks*, 4(3), 313–334.

Repak, Terry. (1995). *Waiting on Washington: Central American Workers in the Nation's Capital*. Philadelphia: Temple University Press.

Rodriguez, Clara. (1990). *Puerto Ricans: Born in the USA*. Boston: Unwin Hyman.

Rodriguez, Clara. (1996). Racial Themes in the Literature: Puerto Ricans and Other Latinos. In Gabriel Haslip-Viera and Sherrie L. Baver (Eds.), *Latinos in New York: Communities in Transition* (pp. 104–125). Notre Dame, IN: University of Notre Dame Press.

Sanchez, Arturo Ignacio. (1997). Transnational Political Agency and Identity Formation Among Colombian Immigrants. Paper presented at Conference "Transnational Communities and the Political Economy of New York City in the 1990s." New York: New School for Social Research.

Sanchez-Karrol, Virginia. (1994). In Their Own Right: A History of Puerto Ricans in the USA. In Alfredo Jimenez (Ed.), *Handbook of Hispanic Cultures in the United States* (pp. 281–301). Houston, TX: History, Arte Público Press.

Santacruz Giralt, Maria. (2001). *Barrio Adentro: La Solidaridad Violento de las pandillas*. San Salvador: Universidad Centroamericana.

Smith, Robert C. (1996). Mexicans in New York City: Membership and Incorporation of New Immigrant Group. In G. Haslip-Viera & S. Baver (Eds.), *Latinos in New York: Communities in Transition*. Notre Dame, IN: University of Notre Dame Press.

Smith, Robert C. (2001). Mexicans: Social, Educational, Economic, and Political Problems and Prospects. In Nancy Foner (Ed.), *New Immigrants in New York* (pp. 275–300). New York: Columbia University Press.

Smith, Robert C. (2002). Gender, Ethnicity, and Race in School and Work Outcomes of Second Generation Mexican Americans. In Marcelo Suarez-Orozco & Mariela Paez (Eds.), *Latinos Remaking America*. Berkeley: University of California Press.

Smith, Robert C. (2003a). Migrant Membership as an Instituted Process: Migration, the State, and the Extra-Territorial Conduct of Mexican Politics. *International Migration Review*, 37(2), 297–343.

Smith, Robert C. (2003b). Diasporic Memberships in Historical Perspective: Comparative Insights from the Mexican and Italian Cases. In Josh DeWind, Steven Vertovec, & Peggy Levitt (Eds.), *International Migration Review* [Special Issue], 37(3), 724–759.

Smith, Robert C. (2006). *Mexican New York: Transnational Lives of New Immigrants*. Berkeley: University of California Press.

Smith, Robert C., Cordero-Guzmán, Héctor, & Grosfoguel, Ramón. (2001). Introduction. In Héctor Cordero-Guzmán, Robert C. Smith, & Ramón Grosfoguel. (Eds.), *Migration, Transnationalization, and Race in a Changing New York* (pp. 1–32). Philadelphia: Temple University Press.

Torres-Rivas, Eldelberto. (1985). *Report on the Condition of Central American Refugees and Migrants Hemispheric Migration Project*. Washington, DC: Center for Immigration Policy and Refugee Assistance, Georgetown University.

Torres-Saillant, Silvio. (2000). The Tribulations of Blackness: Stages in Dominican Racial Identity. *Callalo*, 23(3), 1086–1111.

Torres-Saillant, Silvio, & Hernandez, Ramona. (1998). *The Dominican Americans*. New York: Greenwood Publishing Group.

US Census Bureau. (2000). Demographic Profile Highlights. Retrieved September 8, 2006, from http://www.census.gov.

Valenzuela, Angela. (1999). Subtractive Schooling: U.S. Mexican Youth and the Politics of Caring (pp. 3–5). Albany: State University of New York Press.

Zentella, Ana Celia. (1997). Returned Migration, Language and Identity: Puerto Rican Bilinguals in Dos Mundos/Two Worlds. In Antonia Darder, Rodolfo Torres, & Henry Gutierrez (Eds.), *Latinos and Education* (pp. 302–318). New York: Routledge.

Zolberg, Aristide, & Smith, Robert. (1996). *Migration Systems in Comparative Perspective: An Analysis of the Inter-American Migration System with Comparative Reference to the Mediterranean-European System*. Report to US Department of State, Bureau of Population, Refugees, and Migration. Washington DC. US Department of State.

THE SOCIAL DEMOGRAPHY OF LATINAS/OS

CHAPTER 4

Demographic Patterns: Age Structure, Fertility, Mortality, and Population Growth

JORGE DEL PINAL

INTRODUCTION

One of the most important recent demographic events in the United States is the emergence of the Latino population as the largest minority population. The rapid growth of the Hispanic population in the last three or four decades has in effect rejuvenated the aging U.S. population by adding children and working-age adults, at the same time making it more ethnically diverse. Saenz (2005) noted that the size of the Latino population doubled between 1980 and 2000, but more importantly, Latinos also accounted for 40% of the country's population growth. That rapid growth has continued since 2000, accounting for almost half the increase of the U.S. population (U.S. Census Bureau, 2006). In this chapter we will seek to answer the following questions: Why is the Latino population growing rapidly? What are some of the demographic causes of that growth? What are the factors that might affect future growth? In order to answer these questions, we need to examine the basic demographic components affecting the growth of the Hispanic population: fertility, mortality, and international migration. Past changes in these components affected the current age structure and will affect future population growth. Another crucial factor in the future growth of Hispanics, as we will see, is the degree to which Latinos marry non-Latinos and the degree to which children of mixed-origin marriages choose to identify with their Hispanic origin.

Previous research has shown that Latinos,[1] as a population, are young and socioeconomically diverse and growing very rapidly in the United States. More importantly, the rate of growth and

57

the youth of the Hispanic population are vital factors in rejuvenating an aging U.S. population. Although their presence predates the founding of the United States, Hispanics were not an officially recognized population group until 1976 as a result of Congressional action (Public Law 94–311) and government regulation (OMB Statistical Directive No. 15; see del Pinal, 1996). In creating the new Hispanic category, significant differences in national origin, migration history, legal status, and socioeconomic status were hidden (Bean & Tienda, 1987; del Pinal & Singer, 1997; Frank & Heuveline, 2005; Rumbaut, 2005; Saenz, 2005; Tienda & Mitchell, 2006).

Demography is the scientific study of human populations. Among the factors studied by demographers are those that determine changes in a population's size, composition, and distribution. The geographic distribution of the Hispanic population in the United States is primarily determined by the historical patterns of immigration and immigrants' ties to the gateway cities in the West, South, Midwest, and Northeast through which immigrant Latinos arrived in the United States.

In recent years, Latinos, particularly the foreign-born, have responded to emerging economic opportunities in states that were not the traditional gateway states. Between 1995 and 2000, more Latinos left the West and Northeast to go to other parts of the United States than moved to the West or Northeast from elsewhere in the United States. The South and Midwest recorded net immigration of Latinos (Schachter, 2003). Thus, new Latino communities have emerged in new settlement areas of the South and Midwest (Saenz, 2005).

The presence of Hispanics predates the founding and expansion of the United States as a country. There might have been around 500,000 Latinos in the United States in 1900 (Saenz, 2005:352). However, it is the massive immigration from Latin America and the Caribbean in the last three and a half decades that has played the major role in the demography of the Latino population in the United States. In 2005, about 68% of Hispanics were either immigrants (40%) or children of immigrants (28%). Nevertheless, about 60% of Latinos were born in the United States or its possessions and are therefore U.S. citizens by birth. Another 10% were foreign-born and have since become naturalized U.S. citizens. In sum, 7 of every 10 Hispanics are currently U.S. citizens, either by birth or by naturalization.[2]

AGE STRUCTURE

The age structure of a population is affected by past changes in the demographic components (fertility, mortality, and net international migration), but the strongest influence is usually fertility—the number of births in a population. When fertility is high for an extended period of time, the proportion of younger age groups tends to be much larger than that of older age groups. Aside from catastrophic events like natural disasters, pandemic disease outbreaks, famine, civil strife, and war that lead to abnormally high mortality, international migration in or out of a country can also affect the age structure of a population. International migrants are sometimes displaced by political instability and violence or other catastrophic events in their home countries. Others are motivated to move for economic reasons. Economic motivation tends to be selective of young and healthy adults and proportionately more males. Migrants tend to be those who are much more able to cope with the challenges and stresses associated with moving and who have fewer primary attachments than those who do not move. Sometimes, both displacement and economic circumstances impel people to move, and Latinos immigrants have been motivated by these factors (Durand, Telles, & Flashman, 2006).

TABLE 1. Median Age and Selected Age Groups: United States, 2004

	Median age	Under 18	18 to 44	45 to 64	65 and older
Total U.S. Population	36.2	25.5	38.0	24.5	12.0
White alone, not Hispanic	40.1	22.3	35.8	27.3	14.5
Hispanic	26.9	34.3	45.3	15.2	5.1
Mexican	25.3	36.6	46.0	13.4	4.1
Puerto Rican	28.3	33.7	42.1	18.2	6.0
Cuban	40.6	21.2	36.3	24.2	18.3
Dominican	29.2	33.4	42.3	18.4	5.9
Central American	29.4	27.8	53.7	15.4	3.1
Guatemalan	28.2	27.5	57.6	13.0	1.9
Honduran	28.0	31.5	52.2	13.5	2.7
Salvadoran	29.3	28.0	54.6	14.8	2.6
South American	33.1	25.3	48.8	20.2	5.7
Colombian	33.5	25.9	47.1	21.2	5.8
Ecuadorian	31.4	26.9	49.9	16.8	6.5
Peruvian	35.1	23.4	49.3	21.5	5.6
All Other Hispanic	26.4	36.9	38.2	17.9	6.9

Source: U.S. Census Bureau, compiled from individual Selected Population Profiles, American Community Survey, 2004.

The Latino population of the United States is said to be a young population, particularly when compared to the White population.[3] What that means in simple terms is that the proportion of young people exceeds the proportion of older people. There are several ways to show that this is the case. As can be seen in Table 1, each Latino group shown has a lower median age than the White population (40.1 years), with the exception of the Cuban-origin population (40.6 years). This indicator shows that most Latino population subgroups are composed of younger people than Whites.

Table 1 also shows the proportion of each population divided into four large age groups. The first is under age 18 (children); the second is ages 18 to 44 years (early working ages); the third is ages 45 to 64 years (older working ages); and the fourth is over age 65 (older adults). Again, with the exception of Cubans (21.2%), most Hispanic groups have a higher proportion of children than do Whites (22.3%). Almost 37% of Mexicans are children. Conversely, with the exception of Cubans (18.3%), Latinos have proportionately fewer older adults (ages 65 and over) than do Whites (14.5%). Only 4.1% of Mexicans and 3.1% of Central Americans are older adults. Central Americans (53.7%) and South Americans (48.8%) show very high proportions in the younger working ages compared to Whites (35.8%), reflecting recent migration, which tends to be mostly composed of working-age adults.

Figures 1–7 show the 5-year age-sex composition (structure) for each of the major Latino groups based on data from Census 2000. Each bar represents the proportion of the total population represented by each 5-year age-sex group. The left-hand bars represent the males and the right-hand bars represent the females. Each bar can have up to four segments representing the native-born and foreign-born segments of each age-sex group. The native-born proportion is shown as the innermost part of each bar. Succeeding segments indicate the proportion of foreign-born by period of arrival to the United States. The outermost segment

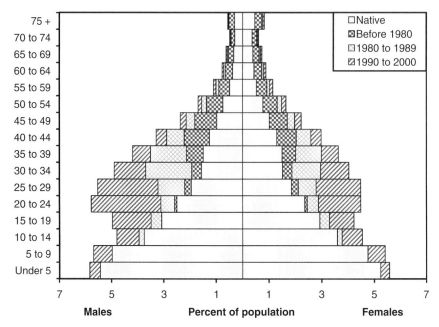

FIGURE 1. Age-Sex Composition of Mexican-Origin Population by Nativity and Year of Entry: 2000. From U.S. Census Bureau, 2000 Census Sample Data.

indicates the proportion of immigrants who arrived since 1990. If applicable, the second segment from the outside indicates the proportion of immigrants who arrived from 1980 to 1989, and the third indicates the proportion that arrived before 1980. As we will see, immigration has impacted the age-sex structure of some Latino groups much more than others, and these differences are related to differences in the migratory history of each group (Durand, Telles, & Flashman, 2006).

Mexican-Origin Population

Looking first at the age-sex-nativity composition of the Mexican-origin population (Figure 1), we note a wide base on the pyramid-shaped distribution indicating high fertility but also showing a small proportion of immigrants in the younger ages. Recall that the innermost segment of the bars represents the native-born proportions, whereas the outermost segments represent the proportion of immigrants by period of arrival. The very wide inner segments of the bars indicate a large native-born segment in the younger years.

Note that as you look up the pyramid, and particularly in the early working ages (20–34 years), the bars flare, indicating the much greater role played by immigration in determining the age structure. Also note that the bars on the left-hand side flare a bit more than those on the right, indicating that Mexican migration tends to be male dominated. Between ages 20 and 29, recent immigration (after 1990) accounts for a larger proportion of the age groups, whereas between 30 and 39 years, the immigrants who came in the 1980s are a much larger proportion.

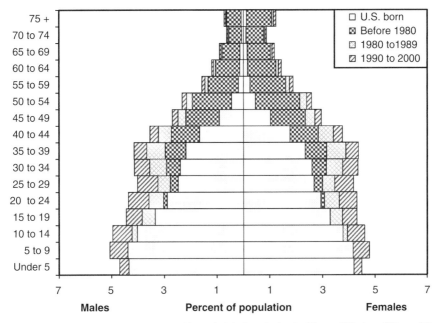

FIGURE 2. Age-Sex Composition of Puerto Rican-Origin Population by Place of Birth and Year of Entry to the United States: 2000. From U.S. Census Bureau, 2000 Census Sample Data.

Puerto Rican-Origin Population

Turning to the Puerto Rican-origin population in the United States, Figure 2 shows the age-sex distribution. Island-born Puerto Ricans are U.S. citizens and can come and go as any other U.S. citizen. Still, net migration from the island to the mainland has increased the size of the Puerto Rican-origin population on the mainland over a period of years. The innermost bar segments show the proportion born in the United States, whereas the outermost segments show those born outside of the United States, including Puerto Rico, and their period of arrival on the mainland. The pyramid base is much narrower than was the case for the Mexican-origin population. This suggests that fertility has declined somewhat among Puerto Ricans. The Puerto Rican pyramid also shows wider bars at older ages, indicating an older population. Larger migrant segments at older ages also indicate that migration occurred earlier and is more heavily composed of migrants that came before 1980 than was the case for Mexicans.

Cuban-Origin Population

In contrast to Mexicans and Puerto Ricans, the Cuban-origin population's age-sex-nativity composition does not resemble a pyramid at all (Figure 3). It has a very narrow base, suggesting very low fertility, and extremely wide bars at ages above 25 years, indicating a much older population. In addition, the older bars are heavily composed of immigrants, particularly those who

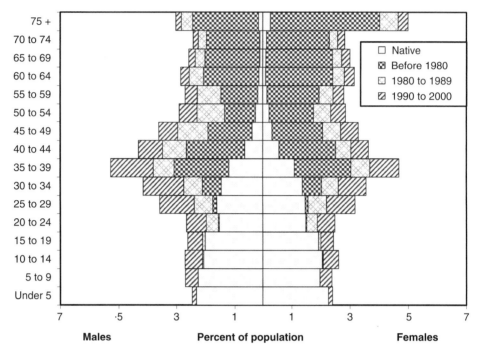

FIGURE 3. Age-Sex Composition of Cuban-Origin Population by Nativity and Year of Entry: 2000. From U.S. Census Bureau, 2000 Census Sample Data.

arrived before 1980. It is also interesting to note that unlike Mexicans and Puerto Ricans, the Cuban age-sex structure shows significant segments from each period of entry. This is consistent with refugee-type flows rather than the economic-induced migration, which tends to select for working-aged migrants.

Dominican-Origin Population

In contrast to the Cuban-origin population's age-sex distribution, the Dominican age-sex structure resembles a jug, with proportionately more people in the working and younger ages (Figure 4). Even more so than the Cuban case, the Dominican age structure is heavily influenced by immigration in all three periods, suggesting a continuing pattern of heavy immigration. Unlike Cubans, Dominicans have a substantial proportion of younger (under 25 years), native-born people, suggesting much higher fertility. Unlike other Latino groups, Dominican women appear to dominate the migration flows, as can be seen by the bulging right side of the pyramid, particularly between ages 30 and 44 years.

Central American-Origin Population

Even more so than the Dominicans, the age structure of Central Americans is dominated by very recent immigration (Figure 5). Rather than a pyramid shape, the Central American age structure looks like a bird with its wings extended, showing high proportions of immigrants in

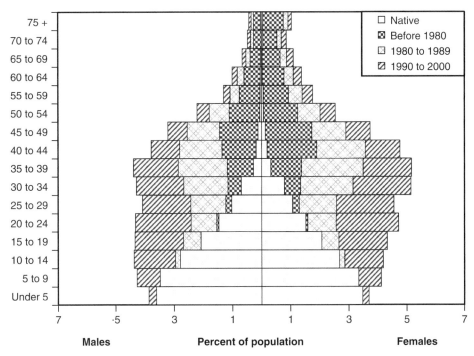

FIGURE 4. Age-Sex Composition of Dominican-Origin Population by Nativity and Year of Entry: 2000.
From U.S. Census Bureau, 2000 Census Sample Data.

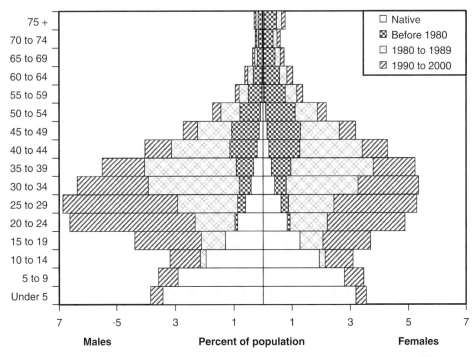

FIGURE 5. Age-Sex Composition of Central American-Origin Population by Nativity and Year of Entry: 2000.
From U.S. Census Bureau, 2000 Census Sample Data.

the 20–39 age range. Because the left-hand side extends out more than the right, males have dominated that migration stream. Similar to Dominicans, the Central American population has substantial proportions of younger (under 25 years), native-born people, also suggesting high fertility. It is important to note that the Central American category includes six national origins whose populations have different migration histories. They also differ in their socio-economic status. It is not possible to show individual age-sex pyramids for each national origin group, but Table 1 shows differences in the age structure among the largest of these national origin groups.

South American-Origin Population

Like Central Americans, the age structure of the South American population is dominated by recent immigration, and it also has a bird shape, albeit with less extended wings (Figure 6). Unlike Central Americans, South American migration appears to be less selective of males and more gender balanced. Similar to Central Americans, the South American population has a good-sized pyramid of younger (under 25 years), native-born people, but with a proportionately narrower base, suggesting somewhat lower fertility. Again, it is important to note that the South American category includes nine national origins with different migration histories and significant differences in their socioeconomic status. Table 1 shows some of the age structure differences among the largest of these national origin groups.

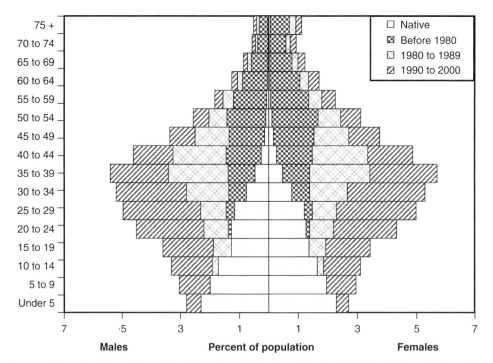

FIGURE 6. Age-Sex Composition of South American-Origin Population by Nativity and Year of Entry: 2000.
From U.S. Census Bureau, 2000 Census Sample Data.

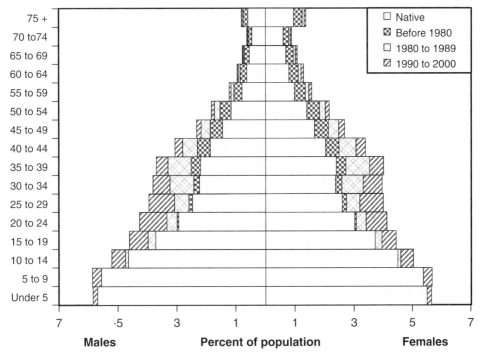

FIGURE 7. Age-Sex Composition of Other Hispanic-Origin Population by Nativity and Year of Entry: 2000.
From U.S. Census Bureau, 2000 Census Sample Data.

Other Hispanic-Origin Populations

Unlike Mexicans, Cubans, Dominicans, Central Americans, and South Americans, the age structure of the Other Hispanic population is much less dominated by immigration (Figure 7). It has a very large pyramid base consisting mostly of native-born people, which is consistent with high fertility. What is more puzzling is the relatively high proportion of immigrants in the younger working-age group (20–34 years). Most people think of this group as the more highly integrated, if not totally acculturated of Hispanic groups. Its members do not identify with any of the specific Latino groups. There is some evidence, however, that the changes to the Hispanic origin item in Census 2000 (such as dropping "origin" and specific examples from the question) might have resulted in some respondents providing pan-ethnic, rather than a specific group response (Cresce & Ramirez, 2003). This would have resulted in the inclusion of people who should have been in specific groups, such as Dominican and Salvadoran, rather than in a pan-ethnic group such as "Hispanic" or "Latino." Because many of these people were born outside of the United States, their presence tends to exaggerate the role that immigration might have played on the age structure of the "Other Hispanics" group.

FERTILITY

Another important aspect of the demography of Hispanics in the United States is a relatively high rate of childbearing or fertility. A higher birth rate combined with an early entry into, and late exit from, childbearing, plus a relatively young age structure produces a large number of births.

TABLE 2. Crude Birth Rates, General Fertility Rates, and Total Fertility Rates by Hispanic Origin of Mother and by Race for Mothers of Non-Hispanic Origin: United States, 1990 and 2000

	Crude birth rate			General fertility rate			Total fertility rate		
	1990	2000	Change	1990	2000	Change	1990	2000	Change
Total population	16.7	14.4	−13.8%	70.9	65.9	−7.1%	2,081	2,056	−1.2%
Hispanic total	26.7	23.1	−13.5%	107.7	95.9	−11.0%	2,960	2,730	−7.8%
Mexican	28.7	25.0	−12.9%	118.9	105.1	−11.6%	3,214	2,907	−9.6%
Puerto Rican	21.6	18.1	−16.2%	82.9	73.5	−11.3%	2,301	2,179	−5.3%
Cuban	10.9	9.7	−11.0%	52.6	49.3	−6.3%	1,460	1,528	4.7%
Other Hispanic	27.5	21.8	−20.7%	102.7	85.1	−17.1%	2,877	2,564	−10.9%
White, non-Hispanic	14.4	12.2	−15.3%	62.8	58.5	−6.8%	1,851	1,866	0.8%
Black, non-Hispanic	23.0	17.3	−24.8%	89.0	71.4	−19.8%	2,548	2,179	−14.5%

Source: Adapted from Sutton and Mathews (2006:Table 1, p. 2).

Latinos in the United States were just over 14% of the population in 2000 but had about 23% of the births between July 1, 2004 and July 1, 2005 (U.S. Census Bureau, 2006).

Table 2 shows three different measures of fertility: crude birth rates, general fertility rates, and total fertility rates. The crude birth rate represents the number of live births per 1,000 population, whereas the general fertility rate is the number of live births per 1,000 women aged 14 to 44 years. The total fertility rates (TFRs) are the sums of birth rates for 5-year age groups multiplied by 5. The TFR is a measure of fertility that takes into account the age distribution of the population and is interpreted as the number of children 1,000 women would have through their reproductive years if the age-specific rates observed stayed constant during that time.

By most measures shown in Table 2, Latino fertility has declined somewhat between 1990 and 2000. The exception is a slight increase in the TFR for Cubans, which increased almost 5%. White fertility also increased slightly by 1%. It is also clear that with the exception of Cubans, the Latino fertility was higher than that of Blacks and Whites. In 2000, the Mexican TFR was about 56% higher than the White rate, whereas the Cuban rate was 18% lower. The TFR of Puerto Ricans and Blacks was 17% higher than that of Whites in 2000. To put these differences in perspective, Mexican women average about one more child than White women based on the age-specific rates observed in 2000.

It is interesting to note that the TFR in Mexico was about 7,200 (about 7.2 children per woman) in the early 1960s but has since declined to about 2,400 (about 2.4 children per woman) compared to about 2.9 children among Mexican-origin women in the United States (Tuiran, Partida, et al., 2005). Frank and Heuveline (2005) found higher levels of overall fertility among Mexican-origin women in the United States than among Mexican women in Mexico. In large part, the highly successful family-planning program in Mexico is responsible for the fertility crossover, but there were also changes in the fertility behavior of the U.S. Mexican-origin population, such as increases in the fertility of recent immigrants and of younger native-born Mexican-origin women.

Whereas the fertility of Latinos in the United States is higher than that of other groups, it is not dramatically higher. Still, higher birth rates combined with a very large Latino population in the reproductive years produce a substantial number of births. Latinos had about 23% (935,000) of over 4.1 million births in the United States between 2004 and 2005 (U.S. Census Bureau, 2006).

MORTALITY

In what has been termed an "epidemiological paradox," Latinos appear to have lower mortality than might be expected by their socioeconomic status and lack of health insurance (Escarce, Morales, & Rumbaut, 2006; also see Acevedo-Garcia and Bates in this volume). Some recent studies of the issue suggest that Latinos do experience relatively low mortality, perhaps even lower than that of Whites. For example, Palloni and Arias (2004) found that foreign-born, but not native, Latinos experienced a mortality advantage compared with non-Hispanic Whites after controlling for demographic characteristics and socioeconomic status. Elo et al. (2004) also found a Latino mortality advantage over Whites among those age 65 and over. Among the factors that have been suggested that provide a mortality advantage to Hispanics are better health behaviors, greater social support through extended family and kinship networks, selection of healthy people through immigration, and the emigration of less healthy people to their country of origin (see Escarce, Morales, & Rumbaut, 2004, and Acevedo-Garcia and Bates in this volume for additional discussion). However, Elo et al. (2004) suggested that limitations in the data used to calculate mortality (vital statistics and census data) raises questions about the accuracy of mortality estimates for Latinos. Among the data problems they found are age misreporting and the lack of comparability between the Hispanic-origin information collected in vital statistics and that collected in census data. Death certificate information is often filled by a physician, health worker, or coroner based on observation, whereas census information is usually self-reported by respondents. Observation tends to be much less accurate than self-identification.

Whether or not Latinos experience a mortality advantage over Whites, we do know that Hispanics account for relatively few of the deaths each year in the United States. Latinos had less than 5% of the deaths from 2004 to 2005 even though they constituted a bit over 14% of the population (U.S. Census Bureau, 2006). The principal reason for the low number of deaths is a very young Latino population age structure; mortality rates tend to be lower among the young compared to the older population.

POPULATION GROWTH

The basic demographic story of the Latino population is one of exceptionally rapid population growth, particularly in the last three and a half decades. One estimate suggests there were about 500,000 Hispanics in the United States in 1900 (Saenz, 2005:352), but the regular collection of statistics on Latinos did not begin until 1970. The 1970 Census puts the Hispanic population at 9.1 million by the most accepted of several data collection methods used in that census (del Pinal, 1996). Bean and Tienda (1987:42–54, 59) put the Latino population at 10.5 million after adjusting for an estimated undercount. The 1980 Census recorded 14.6 million Hispanics using the self-identification method with the Spanish Origin question, whereas the 1990 Census showed an increase of 53% in the number of Latinos, whose population now reached 22.4 million. Incredibly, Census 2000 recorded another 58% increase for a total of 34.5 million Hispanics in the United States. This does not take into account the Latino population of Puerto Rico in 2000, which was in excess of 3.8 million, virtually all of whom are Hispanics.

Demographically speaking, a population changes over specified periods of time through the addition of births and immigrants (in-migrants) and the subtraction of deaths and emigrants (out-migrants). The natural increase of a population is defined as the births minus deaths, and the net international migration is the balance of immigrants minus emigrants. According to the latest Census Bureau estimates, the Hispanic population of the United States (excluding Puerto Rico) was 42.7 million as of July 1, 2005, casting aside any remaining doubts that Latinos are the largest minority population in the United States and one of the fastest growing population segments (U.S. Census Bureau, 2006).

Although Latinos were only 14.1% of the total population in 2004, they contributed 49% of the total population growth from 2004 to 2005. During that time, the Hispanic population grew by 3.3% or just over 1.3 million persons; about 60% of that growth was due to natural increase (births minus deaths) and 40% to net international migration. Latinos also had about 23% of all births and 5% of all deaths in the United States. As discussed previously, Hispanics have a disproportionately high number of births and a low number of deaths, which is primarily a result of a much younger population age structure. As a result, more Latinos were added through births and fewer were subtracted through deaths. Finally, Hispanics were almost 51% of immigrants, so the growth in the Hispanic population accounted for about half of the total U.S. population growth during this period (U.S. Census Bureau, 2006).

This suggests that Latino births and immigrants are major contributors to the nation's overall population growth. Because Hispanic immigrants have some of the births, it can be difficult to estimate the true contribution of immigration. In order to answer the question of which contributes more to population growth, it is necessary to estimate how many births foreign-born Latinos contributed. One set of estimates suggests that only about 17% of the Hispanic population growth during the 1980s was a result of births to natives, 27% was due to births of foreign-born Latinos, and 56% was due to actual immigration. During the 1990s, births to natives contributed about 24% of the growth, whereas births to the foreign-born contributed 28% and immigration contributed 48% (Durand, Telles, & Flashman, 2006:68). From this, it is clear that immigration (including births to immigrants) has played the dominant role in the growth of the Latino population since the 1980s, but it is also clear that births to natives is growing in importance.

Other factors can cause changes in the size and composition of a population. Changes in territory, such as when parts of Mexico became a part of the United States, created a larger Latino population in the United States. Changes in the definition of the Latino population produce different estimates of its size. Also, improved data collection methodologies have reduced the undercount and increased coverage of the Hispanic population (del Pinal, 1996; Rumbaut, 2006). Finally, a greater willingness to identify as Latino can increase the population count. Although most of these factors affected the size and growth of the Hispanic population of the United States, it is the identification with the Latino population that will be as important for the future growth of the Latino population as immigration.

In the process of assimilation into American society, some immigrant groups tend to lose some or all the markers of ethnic identity and have intermarried with the mainstream population, effectively merging into America's "melting pot." Many of the early Latino immigrants had similar experiences, but in the last decade and a half, marketing researchers have noted the rise of what they call "born-again Hispanics," who have rediscovered their buried past. According to Landale, Oropesa, and Bradatan (2006), the level of out-marriage or exogamy varies by Latino group and generation. Mexican-origin married women are most likely to be married to a Mexican-origin man or to another Latino (87%). The comparable figures were 83%for Cuban women, 79% for Central and South Americans, 74% for Puerto Ricans, and 67% for Other Hispanic women (adapted from Landale, Oropesa, & Bradatan, 2006:Table 5.6, pp. 160–161). The percentage of Latino women marrying outside their group also increases with future generations, with the highest out-marriage rate among native-born women of native-born parents. Because Latinos have a fairly high rate of out-marriage or exogamy, the future rate of Latino population growth will depend on the proportion of children of mixed-Hispanic and non-Hispanic heritage who choose to identify as Latinos.

Several researchers note that future size of an ethnic group is not just a function of fertility, mortality, and international migration but also depends on the extent of intermarriage with other groups and the degree of ethnic identification (attribution) of children with multiple ancestry (Edmonston, Lee, & Passel, (2002); Landale, Oropeso, & Bradatan, 2006; Saenz, 2005). If few of these children identify with the ethnic group (low ethnic attribution), the growth of the ethnic population will be less than if most or all do (high ethnic attribution). In projections using different levels of ethnic attribution, Edmonston, Lee, & Passel (2002:247) showed that the Hispanic population in 2050 could vary from 69.1 million, with very low Hispanic attribution, to 126.5 million, with very high Hispanic attribution. Recent projections from two sources that do not take into account the multiple-origin populations suggest that the Latino population might reach 101 to 103 million by 2050 (Durand, Telles, & Flashman, 2006:93; U.S. Census Bureau, 2004).

SUMMARY

The Hispanic population is among the fastest growing population segments in the United States. There is every expectation that rapid growth will continue, but the pace of that increase will depend on the level of immigration and the degree to which children of mixed-ethnic marriages identify with their Latino roots. The Latino population has a young population age structure, in part because of a large number of past births and, in part, because of significant international in-migration, which tends to consist of young adults. Mortality rates among Hispanics are probably as low as, or maybe lower, than those of the general population. In addition, the younger age structure means that the Latino population loses proportionately fewer members each year. Higher birth rates combined with the younger age structure also means that the Hispanic population adds proportionately more members each year. Finally, immigration also plays a large role in adding new Latinos to the population. The Census Bureau estimates that the Latino population added to its numbers with almost 935,000 births and 534,000 immigrants from July 1, 2004 to July 1, 2005, but also lost almost 119,000 through deaths.

This suggests that about 64% of the annual additions to the Hispanic population are from births whereas immigration adds about 36%. However, this ignores the fact that immigrant parents contribute a large portion of the births, as discussed previously. The role of immigration is also quite evident in the age structure of all Hispanic groups shown, with the possible exception of Other Hispanics. It is worth repeating that, currently, about 68% of Latinos are either immigrants (40%) or children of immigrants (28%). Still, about 60% of Latinos were born U.S. citizens. Another 10% are naturalized U.S. citizens. Whereas 7 out of every 10 Hispanics are U.S. citizens, by birth or naturalization, it is very clear that immigration has and will probably continue to have a large role in the demography of Latinos in the United States. Although immigration is receiving much attention currently, another factor to consider affecting future population growth is intermarriage and the degree to which children of these marriages identify with the Latino population.

The degree of identification with the Hispanic population, now and in the future, will dramatically affect its size and composition. Even so, the Latino population is expected to grow regardless of the level of immigration and the degree of identification, because of its youth and higher fertility. Only the pace of the growth will be dramatically affected by continued immigration and high levels of identification, as shown by Edmonston, Lee, & Passel (2002).

FUTURE RESEARCH

As we have seen in this chapter, the Latino population is a young, rapidly growing, and a vital component of the U.S. population growth that is destined to become an ever larger fraction of this population. Consequently, future research needs to include ongoing studies focusing on international movements from Latin America to the United States and the fertility patterns of Latinos, as these are the strongest factors affecting their growth. Fortunately, annual data are collected by the U.S Census Bureau and the National Center for Health Statistics on these topics, respectively, making future research in these areas very practical. On the other hand, the mortality of Latinos is much more difficult to study because of data deficiencies; nevertheless, more research needs to be focused on this important topic. Finally, there is a dearth of research on the extent to which Latinos of mixed heritage choose to identify as Latinos and how that changes over the life cycle. As we have seen, this factor will play a decisive role in the future growth of Latino population in the United States.

NOTES

1. The terms "Hispanic" and "Latino" are used interchangeably in the text.
2. Based on the author's tabulation of the 2005 Annual Social and Economic Supplement (ASEC) of the Current Population Survey.
3. The terms "White" and "Black" as used in the text refers to the "White alone, not Hispanic" and "Black alone, not Hispanic" populations, respectively, which consists of persons who indicated they were not Hispanic and were of one race—White or Black.

REFERENCES

Bean, F. D., & Tienda, M. (1987). *The Hispanic Population of the United States*. New York: Russell Sage.

Cresce, R. C., & Ramirez, R. R. (2003). *Analysis of General Hispanic Responses in Census 2000*. U.S. Census Bureau, Population Division Working Paper No. 72. Washington, DC: Census Bureau. Retrieved October 12, 2006, from http://www.census.gov/population/www/documentation/twps0072/twps0072.pdf.

del Pinal, J. (1996). Treatment of and Counting of Latinos in the Census. In R. Chabrán & R. Chabrán (Eds.), *The Latino Encyclopedia* (pp. 272–278). New York: Marshall Cavendish.

del Pinal, J., & Singer, A. (1997). Generations of Diversity: Latinos in the United States. *Population Bulletin 52*(3). Washington DC: Population Reference Bureau.

Durand, J., Telles, E., & Flashman, J. (2006). The Demographic Foundations of the Latino Population. In M. Tienda & F. Mitchell (Eds.), *Hispanics and the Future of America* (pp. 66–99). Washington, DC: The National Academies.

Edmonston, B., Lee, M. S., & Passel, J. S. (2002). Recent Trends in Intermarriage and Immigration and Their Effects on the Future Racial Composition of the U.S. Population. In J. Perlmann & M. C. Waters (Eds.), *The New Race Question, How the Census Counts Multiracial Individuals* (pp. 227–255). New York: Russell Sage Foundation.

Escarce, J. J., Morales, L. S., & Rumbaut, R. G. (2006). The Health Status and Health Behaviors of Hispanics. In M. Tienda & F. Mitchell (Eds.), *Hispanics and the Future of America* (pp. 362–409). Washington, DC: The National Academies.

Elo, I. T., Turra, C. M., Kestenbaum, B., & Ferguson, B. R. (2004). Mortality Among Elderly Hispanics in the United States: Past Evidence and New Results. *Demography, 41*, 109–128.

Frank, R., & Heuveline, P. (2005). A crossover in Mexican and Mexican-American fertility rates: Evidence and explanations for an emerging paradox. *Demographic Research, 12*, 77–104. Retrieved October 13, 2006, from http://www.demographic-research.org/volumes/vol12/4/.

Landale, N.S., Oropesa, R.S., & Bradatan, C. (2006). Hispanic Families in the United States: Family Structure and Process in an Era of Family Change. In M. Tienda & F. Mitchell (Eds.), *Hispanics and the Future of America* (pp. 138–178). Washington, DC: The National Academies.

Palloni, A., & Arias, E. (2004). Paradox Lost: Explaining the Hispanic Adult Mortality Advantage. *Demography, 41*, 385–415.

Rumbaut, R. G. (2006). The Making of a People. In M. Tienda & F. Mitchell (Eds.), *Hispanics and the Future of America* (pp. 16–65). Washington, DC: The National Academies.

Saenz, R. (2005). Latinos and the Changing Face of America. In R. Farley & J. Haaga (Eds.), *The American People Census 2000* (pp. 352–379). New York: Russell Sage.

Schachter, J. P. (2003). *Migration by Race and Hispanic Origin: 1995 to 2000*. Census 2000 Special Reports CENSR-13. Washington, DC: Government Printing Office.

Sutton, P. D., & Mathews, T. J. (2006). Birth and Fertility Rates for States by Hispanic origin subgroups: United States, 1990 and 2000. *Vital Health Statistics (21)*57. Washington, DC: National Center for Health Statistics. Retrieved October 15, 2006, from http://www.cdc.gov/nchs/data/series/sr_21/sr21_057.pdf.

Tienda, M., & Mitchell, F. (Eds.) (2006). *Hispanics and the Future of America*. Washington, DC: The National Academies.

Tuiran, R., Partida, R., Mojarro, O., & Zúñiga, E. (2005). *Fertility in Mexico: Trends and Forecast*. New York: United Nations Population Division. Retrieved November 23, 2006, from http://pdfdl.oceighty.net/pdf2html.php?url=http://www.un.org/esa/population/publications/completingfertility/RevisedTUIRAN-PARTIDApaper.PDF.

U.S. Census Bureau. (2004). *U.S. Interim Projections by Age, Sex, Race, and Hispanic Origin*. Washington, DC: Government Printing Office. Retrieved October 12, 2006, from http://www.census.gov/ipc/www/usinterimproj/natprojtab01a.pdf.

U.S. Census Bureau. (2006). *Nation's Population One-Third Minority* (CB06–72). Washington, DC: Government Printing Office. Retrieved October 12, 2006, from http://www.census.gov/Press-Release/www/releases/archives/population/006808.html.

CHAPTER 5

Through Children's Eyes: Families and Households of Latino Children in the United States

JENNIFER E. GLICK

JENNIFER VAN HOOK

INTRODUCTION

The children of Latinos today are a diverse group along several dimensions. They differ in generational composition. Some are children of recent immigrants, whereas others are born in the United States from families with several generations of U.S. citizens. They differ in ethnic origins. Some originate from Mexico, but they also come from countries in Central America, South America, and the Caribbean. They identify as different races. These children might or might not accept a pan-ethnic identity as their own.

This great diversity in origins is also associated with differential outcomes in the United States. Concerns about the well-being of Latino children stem from their lower socioeconomic position relative to other pan-ethnic groups and the lower educational attainment evidenced by second-generation children, particularly those of Mexican origin (Bean & Stevens, 2003). This has led to a debate over generational progress and whether some Latino groups are likely to become permanently disadvantaged in the United States (Portes & Zhou, 1993).

Although the concern about children's well-being stems from the lower socioeconomic background of Latino families in general, other characteristics might mitigate negative effects of low socioeconomic status on children. This is because the disadvantaged structural position of some Latinos is not associated with the same family behavior patterns associated with other disadvantaged groups in the United States (Perlmann, 2005). For example, age at marriage tends to be lower among Mexican- and Central/South American-origin adults than non-Latino Whites, a pattern that is consistent with the cultural stereotype emphasizing marriage and religious conservatism. Low divorce rates, high marriage rates, and greater extended family coresidence are also commonly cited as traditional "familistic" patterns that might be protective for Latino children (Feliciano, Bean, & Leach, 2005). Even among second-generation youths in the United States, family formation patterns are more similar to non-Latino Whites than other minorities with similar economic profiles (Glick et al., 2006; Wildsmith & Raley, 2006).

However, even within Latinos, considerable diversity remains. Lower marriage rates persist among those of Puerto Rican origin for example. Puerto Ricans have some of the highest rates of nonmarital fertility and cohabitation than any other racial or ethnic group in the United States (Landale & Fennelly, 1992). Those of Cuban origin, on the other hand, evidence a higher average age at marriage and lower nonmarital fertility (Landale, Oropesa, & Bradatan, 2006) than among other groups. Socioeconomic disparities and structural barriers faced in the United States might indeed play a role in this diversity (Portes & Rumbaut, 2001).

Some differences in family patterns are, in part, attributable to the recent immigration of many from Central and South America. Family structures and practices might be brought from the country of origin and might change as immigrants adapt to the family formation and living arrangement norms in the United States. Yet there is great variation in the family behavior patterns of Latinos in the United States and it is difficult to conclude that these differences are solely based on cultural preferences from the origin community.

This chapter examines the considerable diversity in the family and household structures experienced by Latino children in the United States and the association of these structures with children's outcomes. The role of family and household composition on children from different Latino groups has not been extensively documented in national studies because so few surveys contain sufficient samples of Latinos as one pan-ethnic group, let alone allow for an in-depth analysis across ethnic groups or generation statuses. Here we document these variations across as many groups as possible. We examine the living arrangements of Latino children, highlighting the diversity of patterns among various Latino subgroups and differences from native Whites and Blacks. We specifically examine whether children live with one, both, or neither parent and whether children live with other adult relatives or nonrelatives. We consider not only the ethnic or national group of origin but also the possibility that family structures vary by generation status. Then we examine the effects of various living arrangements and their stability on children's academic achievement. We pay particular attention to the extent to which differences in performance across generation status and ethnic origins are attributable to socioeconomic status, family structure and stability, and the social environment provided in the child's home. The analyses shed light on the extent to which children's family structure helps offset the possible negative effects of low socioeconomic status on academic achievement, a key indicator of children's well-being.

"FAMILISM" AS A PROTECTIVE FACTOR FOR CHILDREN

Latinos as a group have been perhaps the most stereotyped by their orientation toward family, perceived as "familistic," placing a high value on marriage and childbearing and committed to sharing support among extended kin (Valenzuela & Dornbusch, 1994). This stereotype receives support when the higher marriage and fertility rates among various Latino groups are compared to lower marriage and fertility rates among non-Latino Whites and Blacks (Landale, Oropesa, & Bradatan, 2006). The prevalence of extended kin sharing households is also viewed as evidence that Latinos in the United States are more "familistic" than other groups. Immigrants, in particular, might favor coresidence with extended kin as the ideal family form. Latinos in general are more likely to live in extended family households at much higher rates than non-Latino Whites or Blacks (Burr & Mutchler, 1992; Van Hook & Glick, 2007).

In the past, scholars suggested this orientation toward family would lead to detrimental outcomes for children in the United States, but there is reason to expect they could be associated with positive outcomes for children that mitigate the disadvantages associated with low economic status or mobility (Valenzuela & Dornbusch, 1994). For example, family disruptions in the form of divorce, cohabitation, and remarriage are associated with negative outcomes for children in general (Casper & Bianchi, 2002; McLanahan, 1997). Certainly, lower rates of divorce and cohabitation (for some Latino groups) could result in positive outcomes for Latino children (for some subgroups) when compared to other children from similar socioeconomic backgrounds.

Additionally, living with extended kin, particularly grandparents, can be associated with positive outcomes for children both by increasing the earnings of parents freed from child-care costs and by increasing the number of adults available for supervision and support (Perez, 1994). Although the research on the effects of living with extended relatives is not as well developed as the literature on parental marital status, extended-family coresidence might well be associated with greater attention and interaction with loving, consistent caregivers.

Family and household size and complexity could be associated with greater focus on children's activities. Just as there are ethnic and generational differences in family formation patterns and living arrangements, it is likely that families also differ in the social environment for children, and families might behave in ways that promote academic success for their children (Fuligni, 1997). Engaging children in academically oriented activities might enhance subsequent educational outcomes (Sy & Schulenberg, 2005). Extended households could provide children greater opportunities for involvement in activities that enhance their academic achievement because more adults are available than in nonextended households.

"FAMILISM" MIGHT NOT BE ENOUGH

Although it is clear that Latino children are more likely to live with extended family members than children from other backgrounds in the United States, such structures might be formed to meet the needs of adults rather than children and thus would not necessarily enhance children's development and well-being. Here there might be larger differences in household/family structure by immigration status than across Latino groups. Children are impacted by migration when they are left in the country of origin in the care of other relatives while one or both parents migrate (Hondagneu-Sotelo & Avila, 1997; Menjivar, 2000). However, migration can also disrupt family patterns in the United States. Children of immigrants might live in families in a state of flux and change as their parents adjust to the economic opportunities and constraints facing new arrivals while other family members might be housed temporarily (Chavez, 1990; Feliciano, Bean, & Leach 2005; Van Hook & Glick, 2006). These households are likely to be more unstable than other households as new arrivals come in and others move out. It is possible that such instability is associated with disruptions in schooling and inconsistent caregivers. The picture is further complicated if households contain family members from multiple nativity statuses, including U.S.-born citizens, longer-resident immigrants, and recent arrivals. Mixed-nativity households add to the complexity in children's lives. For example, U.S.-born children are eligible for social services to which their foreign-born family members do not have access.

Additionally, children themselves might be the newest arrivals as they migrate to join parents who have left the country of origin before their children. Also, children migrate as labor migrants in their own right. This is more common among Central Americans than other groups (Menjivar, 2006). These children are likely to live without any parents in the household temporarily or long term. Thus, the complex living arrangements associated with immigration might also be associated with greater instability for children's lives and poorer subsequent outcomes. Because immigrants' family behaviors are directly impacted by the challenges of the migration process and further complicated by unauthorized migration status (Menjivar, 2006), the effects of family structure on children might be different for children of immigrants than children of natives even within the same ethnic group.

Certainly we cannot understand the outcomes for Latino children in the United States without considering the diversity of their origins and nativity statuses. Thus, our first task is to document the diversity of living arrangements of children across multiple Latino groups and by generation status using a large nationally representative data source—the Current Population Survey (CPS). We expect that Latino children will be more likely to live with married parents and with extended relatives, but also more likely to live in households that do not include their parents, especially among children in the first and second generations. We further posit that greater family and household stability might be evidenced among those in the higher-order generations, as children of immigrants experience their own immediate family's settlement in the United States and quite possibly the addition of other family members.

Our second task is to explore the possible associations of Latino children's living arrangements with academic achievement. If Latino children's family structure ameliorates the negative effects of poverty among Latino families, we would expect to see significant positive effects of living with married parents and extended-kin coresidence on achievement. In addition, we would expect the effects of Latino ethnicity (relative to native Whites) to increase (become more positive) when socioeconomic status alone is controlled, but then to decrease once family structure and socio-economic status are both controlled (i.e., we expect to see a suppression effect). This outcome is expected to be stronger for groups with both relatively high poverty and intact family structures.

DATA AND MEASURES

We used the pooled 2000, 2001, 2002, 2003, 2004, and 2005 March CPS to document the living arrangements of Latino children aged 0–17 years. The strength of the CPS data lies in its sample size. The pooled CPS sample contains 54,574 Latino children, among whom 9,036 are foreign-born (first generation), 36,906 are U.S.-born children of foreign-born parents (second generation), and 8,632 are U.S.-born children of U.S. natives (third and higher generation). The large sample permits the analysis of numerically small Latino subgroups, including first, second, and third or higher generations of Mexican-, Cuban-, and Puerto Rican-origin children (numbering 35,538, 1,469, and 4,930, respectively). It is impossible to determine the specific national ancestry of the third and higher generation of other Latino groups (these groups are not identified by the "Hispanic ethnicity" variable available in the CPS). However, we are able to identify the first and second generation according to their country of birth and parents' country of birth. In this way, we are able to compare the family/household structures of first- and second-generation Salvadorans ($N = 2,303$), Guatemalans ($N = 1,030$), Hondurans ($N = 692$),

Nicaraguans ($N = 412$), Dominicans ($N = 1,956$), Columbians ($N = 985$), Ecuadorians ($N = 627$), and Peruvians ($N = 1,962$).

Although we can use the CPS to document the family and household composition of children in all of these groups, we cannot directly observe the association between these arrangements and children's outcomes using the CPS. We therefore turn to a smaller dataset with a longitudinal design, the Early Childhood Longitudinal Study—Kindergarten Cohort (ECLS-K), to explore the extent to which family and household structure, stability, and involvement with children are associated with academic outcomes for one cohort of young children. We examine family and household structure in the kindergarten year as well as changes in family and household structure by the third-grade year. We then use regression analyses to examine the associations of these structures and changes with subsequent academic achievement in the third grade. We cannot separate all groups with the same detail as with CPS, but we can compare third- and higher-generation children whose parents identify them as "Hispanic" to those who are identified as non-Hispanic White or non-Hispanic Black. We also include a comparison to children with foreign-born parents. Children are included if at least one parent originated in Mexico, Central America (includes Belize, Costa Rica, El Salvador, Guatemala, Honduras, and Nicaragua), South America (includes Argentina, Chile, Uruguay, Bolivia, Peru, Ecuador, Colombia, Venezuela, Guyana, Brazil, and Panama), Cuba or other Caribbean countries (includes Aruba, Bahamas, Bermuda, Dominica, Haiti, Jamaica, Puerto Rico, Trinidad and Tobago, Virgin Islands, and Dominican Republic who also identified as "Hispanic").

DIVERSITY BY NATIONAL ORIGINS AND GENERATION STATUS

Latino children are much more likely to be impacted by recent immigration within their own families than White or Black children. Children of immigrants, whether they migrated themselves (1.5 generation) or are the U.S.-born children of immigrants (second generation), all share the unique position of being socialized in the United States by foreign-born parents. The generation status of children in the United States today is shown in Table 1. The vast majority of non-Latino White and Black children are in the third or higher generation; that is, they are removed from the migration experience by at least two generations and many are five or more generations removed from their families' origin countries. On the other hand, children of Latino origin are much more likely to be the U.S.-born children of immigrants, or the second generation. The majority of all Mexican-, Cuban-, and Puerto Rican-origin children aged 0–17 are the children of immigrants or are immigrants themselves. The numbers are even higher for children of other national origins.

FAMILY STRUCTURES EXPERIENCED BY CHILDREN

National origin and generational status of Latino children are associated with different family structures. Table 2 demonstrates this, focusing on the largest groups discernable in the CPSs by generation status. Over half of all Mexican-, Cuban-, Salvadoran-, Honduran-, Columbian-, Ecuadorian-, and Peruvian-origin children of all generations reside with two married parents. A sizable minority live with two cohabiting partners. Such cohabitation is most commonly experienced by Central American- and South American-origin children, including Salvadoran-, Nicaraguan-, and Ecuadorian-origin children. Although we cannot go beyond the descriptive

TABLE 1. Race/ethnic and Generational Composition of U.S. Children

	Number[a]	%	% 1st Gen	% 2nd Gen	% 3rd+
Non-Latino White	45,683,768	62.7	1.3	5.5	93.2
Non-Latino Black	11,006,741	15.1	2.1	7.3	90.6
Other Non-Latino	4,721,595	6.5	14.0	46.1	39.9
Latino	11,425,360	15.7	16.1	67.4	16.4
Mexican	7,761,925	10.7	15.3	66.4	18.2
Puerto Rican	886,760	1.2	15.2	60.5	24.3
Cuban	309,515	0.4	16.6	74.8	8.6
Other Latino	2,467,160	3.4	18.9	72.1	9.0
Salvadoran	460,700	0.6	13.1	86.9	
Guatemalan	186,237	0.3	19.7	80.3	
Honduran	140,301	0.2	19.9	80.1	
Nicaraguan	85,480	0.1	22.2	77.8	
Dominican	371,182	0.5	18.6	81.4	
Colombian	189,562	0.3	29.1	70.9	
Ecuadorian	124,459	0.2	20.6	79.4	
Peruvian	422,206	0.6	27.7	72.3	
TOTAL	72,837,465	100.0	4.6	18.1	77.3

[a]Average population 2000–2005.
Source: March CPS 2000–2005.
Sample: Children ages 0–17.
Note: "Other Latino" subgroups include only 1st and 2nd generation children.

patterns here, we note the meaning of cohabitation might differ for these groups just as it does outside the United States (Landale & Fennelly, 1992).

When married and cohabiting parents are combined, children from the remaining national-origin groups are also likely to live with two parents or parental figures in the case of married or cohabiting stepparents. However, for several groups, living with a single mother is also quite common. Dominican- and Puerto Rican-origin children are the most likely to live with a single mother, but these families are certainly prevalent among all of the groups we examine here.

One key component so much of the research on Latinos has addressed is the extent to which their generational progression is less positive than might have been the case for others (Alba & Nee, 2003), and family structure, to the extent that it is associated with positive or negative outcomes, might be an important indicator for this. Table 2 demonstrates that a simple story of generational progression does not hold for all Latinos. For example, first- and second-generation Mexican children are less likely to live with a single mother than their third- and higher-generation counterparts, a pattern consistent with a story of negative adaptation if one considers that single-mother families are generally associated with less favorable outcomes than two married parent families. However, this story is much less clear in the case of Cuban-origin children for whom single-mother families are more prevalent in the second generation than third or higher.

Table 2 also offers some insight into the likelihood of living with neither parent. There might be several reasons why children do not reside with either parent, including parental death, migration, or the removal of children from the parental home by social service agencies. One might imagine that first- and second-generation children are more likely than third- and higher-generation children to experience separation from their parents due to migration as parents seek employment or work in live-in situations. For most of the Latino groups, first-generation children are the

TABLE 2. Parental Status by Generational Status among Latino Children, 2000–2005

	Mexican	Puerto Rican	Cuban	Salvadoran	Guatemalan	Honduran	Nicaraguan	Dominican	Colombian	Ecuadorian	Peruvian
Married Parents											
1st Generation	68.2	36.2	58.9	56.2	46.6	53.9	45.9	42.7	58.8	59.5	65.0
2nd Generation	66.3	42.5	51.5	60.5	58.7	54.5	59.0	36.7	62.2	64.8	63.4
3rd+ Generation	51.6	40.2	68.2	–	–	–	–	–	–	–	–
Cohabiting Parents											
1st Generation	7.7	11.7	14.5	14.3	8.4	6.3	15.3	9.3	20.1	12.5	14.6
2nd Generation	10.0	10.5	18.5	13.5	11.3	9.9	15.9	12.2	12.7	16.4	13.1
3rd+ Generation	8.4	10.5	14.6	–	–	–	–	–	–	–	–
Mother Only											
1st Generation	12.3	43.4	19.6	17.8	19.0	15.6	26.4	36.5	11.8	15.2	12.3
2nd Generation	17.8	38.9	22.1	18.9	21.5	26.7	18.8	43.4	20.0	11.1	17.9
3rd+ Generation	28.7	39.4	11.8	–	–	–	–	–	–	–	–
Father Only											
1st Generation	2.6	1.3	4.8	2.4	2.1	5.9	5.7	5.0	1.9	5.1	2.0
2nd Generation	2.3	2.6	2.7	3.7	5.1	2.5	2.7	2.1	2.1	3.9	3.6
3rd+ Generation	4.2	2.1	2.0	–	–	–	–	–	–	–	–
No Resident Parent											
1st Generation	9.2	7.4	2.3	9.4	23.9	18.3	6.7	6.4	7.5	7.7	6.2
2nd Generation	3.6	5.6	5.1	3.3	3.4	6.4	3.6	5.6	2.9	3.8	2.0
3rd+ Generation	7.1	7.8	3.4	–	–	–	–	–	–	–	–

Source and Sample: See Table 1.

most likely to live without a parent in their household. The high proportions of Guatemalan and Honduran first- generation children residing without a parent might reflect a greater likelihood of children migrating to join parents among Central Americans (Menjivar, 2006). It might also reflect a number of adolescents who are labor migrants in their own right who do not have parents to join in the United States. Over half of the Guatemalan, Nicaraguan, and Colombian children living without parents are teenagers. When only foreign-born children are considered, we find that approximately two-thirds of all children living without parents present are teenagers (with the notable exception of Cuban foreign-born youth).

The cross-sectional descriptive picture we have presented so far illustrates the diversity of family structures among Latino children. We can also address the extent to which young children experience changes in their family's structure by utilizing longitudinal data on a smaller sample of children. Although the ECLS-K cohort does not provide as many groups to compare as is possible with the CPS data, we observe similar patterns in family structure by ethnic origins in the kindergarten year as we did in CPS with a sample of children from birth to age 17. Table 3 reveals that all of the young children of Latino origins, regardless of generation status, are more likely to live with two married parents than non-Latino Black children, and their living arrangements are quite close to the pattern observed for non-Latino White children.

The greatest frequency of living with cohabiting parents occurs among children of Puerto Rican-born parents, but there are also fairly high levels of cohabitation among other children of immigrants, including those of Mexican origin. By third grade, the majority of children are still residing with two married parents. There is a decrease for most groups in cohabiting families. These families might have dissolved or moved into formal marriages. The proportion of children living with a single mother also decreases for several groups. Most notably, we observe fewer Puerto Rican-origin third- and higher-generation children in these families by third grade. A similar decrease is observed among Puerto Rican children of immigrants. We observe only small changes in the proportions of children residing with neither parent, suggesting few children are reunited with their parents or experience the separation from their parents in these few years.

Children Living in Extended Family Households

Extended-family households are formed for many reasons, including the addressing the needs of aging parents, pooling income in hard times, and providing enough caregivers to young children. Thus, there are many reasons why other relatives might reside in children's households. Because extended-family households containing relatives at different points of the life course might meet different needs and are prevalent to a very different extent among different groups, we consider the extent to which children live with a variety of relatives. Table 4 demonstrates that having adult siblings in the same home is more common among first-generation children of all groups with the exception of Cubans. For immigrant families, adult children might represent important contributors to the economic stability of the household. Sharing a household with a grandparent, on the other hand, varies more across groups and by generation status. In part, this could reflect greater kin availability among children in the third and higher generation whose grandparents are, by definition, more likely to be proximate (i.e., possibly born in the same country as the grandchild). However, although an increasing prevalence of grandparents in the household occurs across generations for Mexican- and Puerto Rican-origin children, the same is not necessarily the case for all groups. Cuban-origin children in the third and higher generation are the least likely to share a household with a grandparent.

Jennifer E. Glick and Jennifer Van Hook

TABLE 3. Living Arrangements of One Cohort of Young Children Over Time

	Married parents		Cohabiting parents		Mother only		Father only		No resident parent		Grandparent in household	
	Year 1	Year 4	Year 1	Year 4	Year 1	Year 4	Year 1	Year 4	Year 1	Year 4	Year 1	Year 4
Non-Latino, Third and higher generation												
Whites	81.3	81.4	3.3	2.9	12.8	12.5	1.5	1.9	1.0	1.0	9.2	8.4
Blacks	41.3	47.6	5.8	3.3	45.0	41.4	1.2	1.2	6.7	6.5	17.5	16.3
Latino, Third and higher generation:												
Mexican origin	69.6	73.1	5.3	2.2	22.3	21.1	1.0	2.4	1.8	1.2	14.9	11.6
Puerto Rican origin	63.4	72.9	3.0	3.8	27.8	18.8	3.3	3.6	0.7	0.7	17.5	15.0
Other Latino	63.2	76.5	6.3	6.4	26.0	12.9	0.9	0.9	3.5	3.3	14.1	9.8
Latino Children of Immigrants												
Mexican origin	78.1	85.1	7.8	2.0	13.3	11.7	0.3	0.4	0.5	0.9	8.1	6.7
Puerto Rican origin	66.5	78.9	9.2	4.7	24.3	15.2	–	–	–	–	3.4	6.6
Carribean origin	62.6	72.4	3.5	2.4	28.7	24.4	–	–	–	–	6.5	6.9
Central American	73.4	72.4	5.6	3.4	19.7	18.6	–	–	–	–	8.2	9.4
South American	81.1	88.5	1.8	0.7	17.1	9.0	–	–	–	–	10.5	15.7

Source: Early Childhood Longitudinal Study-Kindergarten Cohort
Note: Sample weighted and adjusted for design effects; unweighted sample size presented

TABLE 4. Extended Family Living Arrangements of Latino Children by Generational Status, 2000–2005

	Mexican	Puerto Rican	Cuban	Salvadoran	Guatemalan	Honduran	Nicaraguan	Dominican	Colombian	Ecuadorian	Peruvian
Older Sibling[a]											
1st Generation	14.6	13.2	7.8	14.9	14.1	16.8	20.6	17.4	10.9	15.9	14.3
2nd Generation	11.2	11.2	11.1	9.0	12.3	5.3	6.4	14.0	13.1	10.7	12.4
3rd+ Generation	8.9	8.4	4.0	–	–	–	–	–	–	–	–
Grandparent[b]											
1st Generation	4.4	4.6	10.9	6.0	2.5	7.1	7.0	7.8	5.4	16.2	6.7
2nd Generation	8.2	9.4	13.3	9.0	8.0	8.1	8.5	13.0	12.2	8.1	8.7
3rd+ Generation	15.9	11.3	8.8	–	–	–	–	–	–	–	–
Other Relative[c]											
1st Generation	20.8	7.7	11.9	24.4	17.6	20.6	8.6	10.8	5.3	20.9	11.2
2nd Generation	12.5	6.7	4.9	14.6	14.3	11.2	8.9	8.3	3.1	16.2	4.4
3rd+ Generation	6.3	6.6	5.4	–	–	–	–	–	–	–	–
Non-relative[d]											
1st Generation	6.1	7.1	4.2	7.9	13.9	8.4	8.1	9.5	6.4	6.1	3.1
2nd Generation	3.9	3.8	2.7	6.1	6.5	7.2	6.2	5.3	3.8	4.4	3.0
3rd+ Generation	5.2	5.5	5.1	–	–	–	–	–	–	–	–

Source and Sample: See Table 1.

[a]Child lives with sibling age 18+, but no other related adults besides parents.

[b]Child lives with a grandparent. Child *may* live with other relatives or parents as well.

[c]Child lives with an extended relative other than a grandparent. Child *may* live with siblings or parents as well.

[d]Child lives with a non-relative age 18+, but no related adults besides parents.

A similar pattern of living with grandparents is also found in the longitudinal ECLS-K data. The last column of Table 3 demonstrates that more third- and higher-generation Mexican, Puerto Rican, and other Latino children live with grandparents than their counterparts who are children of immigrants. This is again likely associated with the greater availability of grandparents for children who are the grandchildren of immigrants to the United States. There is also some change in the prevalence of grandparents in the homes of these young children over time. This could be associated with grandparent's aging but could also be associated with decreased needs for childcare provided by grandparents as children age and progress through school.

Grandparents might become more common in households across generations, but other relatives and nonrelatives become less common household members for children in the third and higher generations. As we see when we return to Table 4, other relatives are more common for some first- and second-generation groups than others. More than 20% of first-generation children of Mexican, Salvadoran, Honduran, and Ecuadorian origin share a home with a relative outside of their immediate or vertically extended families (i.e., relatives other than an adult sibling, parent, or grandparent). Some in these groups are also likely to face added uncertainty from undocumented status (Menjivar, 2006). It seems likely that for these families, coresidence provides an important resource in precarious economic or legal situations.

FAMILY STRUCTURE AND CHILDREN'S OUTCOMES

Certainly one reason scholars have been concerned with family structure is the likelihood that these living arrangements are associated with differential outcomes and childhood well-being. If "familism" is indeed protective for children, then the negative impact of low economic status might be offset by the benefits afforded by living with two-parent families or having access to additional coresident kin. On the other hand, if these households are less stable than others, the benefits of additional kin will be offset and we might conclude that the attributes associated with "familism" are neutral for children, at most.

Here we offer a basic comparison of academic progress of young Latino children by looking at standardized reading test scores from the spring of 2002. Early reading success is necessary for subsequent educational attainment. The analyses examine the relative impacts of parental education, household income, and family and household composition and stability on children's trajectories over time. The analyses also include measures of the resources families provide to enhance their children's academic opportunities. These activities include being enrolled in sports or arts classes outside of the school in their kindergarten year. In addition to formal enrollment in classes, we include two variables for outings taken with any member of the family and the focal child in the previous month. The first variable represents outings to the library and the second represents other outings, including trips to zoos, museums, aquariums, concerts, plays, or sporting events. These measures are particularly useful for our purposes because they include involvement by anyone in the household. In this way, we are able to consider the direct involvement of extended-family members with the child. There is considerable variation in the types of activity and the level of activity children are exposed to in kindergarten. For example, Latino children are all more likely to be enrolled in a non-English language class outside of school than are non-Latino Whites or Blacks. Yet, children of immigrants are less likely to be enrolled in other activities outside of school. There is somewhat less variation in the likelihood children are taken to the library and we note that there is considerable similarity by generation status across Latino groups. Children of immigrants are less likely to be taken on other outings than their

Latino counterparts in the third and higher generation, possibly reflecting the ability to pay for such activities.

To address the extent to which family structure, household structure, household stability and activities all contribute to children's reading success, Table 5 presents the regression results predicting children's third-grade Item Response Theory scaled reading scores while also controlling

TABLE 5. Regression of Children's Reading Test Scores in Third Grade

	Model 1	Model 2	Model 3	Model 4
Race/ethnicity/generation status (vs. non-Latino Whites, third+ generation)				
Non-Latino Blacks, 3rd+ generation	−0.41***	−0.32***	−0.31***	−0.30***
Mexican origin, 3rd+ generation	−0.25***	−0.17**	−0.16**	−0.16**
Other Latino, 3rd+ generation	−0.12**	−0.07	−0.07	−0.07
Mexican origin, 1st or 2nd generation	−0.28***	−0.12*	−0.13*	−0.10*
Carribean origin[c], 1st or 2nd generation	−0.30***	−0.26*	−0.26*	−0.23*
Central American, 1st or 2nd generation	−0.11	0.01	0.00	0.03
South American, 1st or 2nd generation	0.00	0.02	0.02	0.04
Male		−0.07***	−0.07***	−0.07***
Child's Age (in months)		0.00	0.00	0.00
Parent Age (in years)		0.01*	0.01*	0.00
Family Income (log)		0.03***	0.03***	0.02**
Parent Education (vs. more than college)				
Less than High school		−0.44***	−0.43***	−0.40***
High school graduate		−0.25***	−0.25***	−0.23***
Some College		−0.13***	−0.13***	−0.13***
Four year degree		0.00	0.00	−0.02
Family Structure (vs. Both Parents)				
Parent & Partner			−0.02	−0.02
Single Parent			−0.03	−0.01
Neither Parent			−0.09	−0.06
Household Structure				
Grandparent in Household			0.03	0.01
Other relative in Household			0.00	0.00
Changes in Family/Household Structure				
Lost Parent from Household			−0.08*	−0.08*
Parent added to Household			0.03	0.03
Lost Grandparent from Household			−0.06	−0.06
Grandparent added to Household			−0.06	−0.06
Non-school involvement (Kindergarten year)				
Sports or Arts classes/activities[a]				0.05*
Non-English language instruction				0.00
Went to library in last month[b]				0.06**
Other outings in last month				0.05**
Reading Test Score in 2000	0.69***	0.65***	0.65***	0.64***
Intercept	0.09	0.13	0.14	0.09
R square	0.56	0.58	0.58	0.58

Source: Early Childhood Longitudinal Study- Kindergarten Cohort

Note: Sample weighted and adjusted for design effects; unweighted sample size presented

[a]Child was enrolled in an organized sport, took dance, music or arts classes

[b]Family/household member took child to one of these in previous month: museum, zoo, aquarium, play or concert, game.

[c]Includes Puerto Rican origin

for their previous test scores from first grade. In other words, the results demonstrate the extent to which children's scores are associated with various characteristics net of their underlying abilities as measured by the previous test. The results show that reading scores vary greatly by ethnicity and generation status even when we take previous performance into account. Children of immigrants, however, do not have the lowest scores. Mexican- and Caribbean-origin Latino children have lower scores than non-Latino Whites, but their scores are also significantly higher than non-Latino Blacks (results not shown). Family income and parents' education are important predictors of initial school performance. Model 2 reveals that differences are further reduced when family income and parents' education are added to the model. Note that this is still controlling for previous test scores. This strongly suggests that the structural position of the child's family is of continued importance in academic achievement over time and explains some of the difference across ethnic and generation status groups.

Model 3 adds family structure and instability to our analyses. Although living in a stepparent family or family with neither parent present is associated with lower test scores initially (results not shown), little of the difference in reading scores over time is explained by family structure. Nor are the effects of ethnicity or generation status suppressed when family structure is added, which is what we would expect if family mitigates other disadvantages. However, family dissolution (i.e., losing a parent or guardian between kindergarten and third grade) is associated with a negative academic trajectory.

In addition, family activities are important predictors of improvement in reading scores even when we control for family income that might make these activities less affordable for some families. We observe a modest reduction in the coefficients for first- and second-generation children that is not observed for non-Hispanic Black third- and higher-generation children when moving from model 3 to model 4 in support of our expectations. Interactions of ethnicity and generation status with these activities are not significant, suggesting that all children benefit similarly from such extracurricular activities and outings. Further interactions of family and household structure and race/ethnic group also fail to achieve statistical significance. Thus, we do not conclude that there are group differences in the effects of family instability on children. Rather, we suggest that the benefits of family involvement, as evidenced by the positive effect of extracurricular activities and outings, are offset by types of instability, as evidenced by the negative effect of losing a parent or guardian from the household, and that these factors affect outcomes similarly across groups.

CONCLUSIONS

Latino children in the United States are a diverse group representing multiple ethnic origins as well as the legacy of past and recent migration. Because family structure and stability are important assets for children's well-being, we present a detailed look at family structure among Latinos in the United States from the perspective of these children. We find that many children of Latino origin are more likely to live with two parents than non-Latino Black or non-Latino Whites, as suggested by the "familistic" stereotype sometimes applied with one broad brush to all Latinos. However, considerable variation across ethnic groups and generation status suggests that such images are limited. We also note that the extended-family households among Latino children contain a wide variety of different types of kin and our analyses of one cohort of young children suggests that these households are not the stable living arrangements depicted by the same "familistic" stereotype. Rather, we suggest that the benefits of two-parent homes with extended kin who provide resources or care are offset by the instability of such households. This instability is more likely in the households of immigrant youth across Latino groups. With federal efforts aimed at "promoting" marriage among low-income groups, we suggest marriage alone is not a guaranteed path to family stability. Rather, our results suggest that instability in children's homes is present in the face of structural constraints even for groups where marriage is prevalent.

When considering the diversity of family structures among these children, we note particularly the greater likelihood of living with nonrelatives and without parents present among Central American first-generation youth. These children are likely to be in the least stable living arrangements. Losing their parent or guardian is likely to be associated with negative outcomes and more precarious status overall. Current debates over immigration have not addressed the needs of these vulnerable migrants who might remain outside the scope of school or social service outreach.

There is one significant impact of migration on Latino children that we were not able to address here. Many children are left behind in origin countries when parents migrate to the United States. These families face considerable challenges as they work to maintain close ties and struggle with their roles as parents (Hondagneu-Sotelo & Avila, 1997). Such "transnational" families also once again highlight the importance of grandparents. Grandparents play important roles as caregivers when parents migrate, creating "skipped-generation" households in origin countries. Further research from the perspective of these households would extend our understanding of the extent to which grandparents play key roles in children's development within the context of international migration.

Latino families cannot be described under a single "familistic" rubric. Some groups are more typified by married two-parent families. For other groups, single-parent families are more common. Further, living arrangements across groups are complex, as reflected by the greater prevalence of coresident adult children or grandparents in some groups or the prevalence of children living without either parent in the case of others; many households, particularly those containing recent immigrants, experience turnover and instability. We suggest that these characteristics offer offsetting strengths and vulnerabilities for children. For children from groups with the most recent migration histories and precarious economic or legal status in the United States, the challenges might be large indeed.

There are several areas in need of further investigation as researchers address the considerable diversity within the large Latino pan-ethnicity. Although many excellent smaller detailed studies exist, we must rely on large national-level datasets to provide the answers to questions of comparability across diverse groups. We are limited by the few, but growing, data sources that address both family and household complexity *and* detailed ethnic and generation status information. It is not enough to paint all Latino families with one broad brush, but few data sources would permit a detailed comparison.

Beyond data limitations, the research we present here raises intriguing questions about the dynamics of living arrangements for Latino children and their own experiences with the migration process. We need a better understanding of how family members' migration impacts children's opportunities and well-being. Perhaps, children are helped by the arrival of grandparents or, perhaps, children are disrupted by the turnover in their households as new arrivals seek assistance. More longitudinal analyses of children's progress and family dynamics that include children from diverse origins can help address these questions.

ACKNOWLEDGMENT

This research is supported by grants from the National Institute of Child Health and Human Development (RO3 HD044006 and R03 HD44700-01A1).

REFERENCES

Alba, R., & Nee, V. (2003). *Remaking the American Mainstream: Assimilation and Contemporary Immigration.* Cambridge: Harvard University Press.

Bean, F., & Stevens, G. (2003). *America's Newcomers and the Dynamics of Diversity.* New York: Russell Sage Foundation

Burr, J. A., & Mutchler, J. (1992). The Living Arrangements of Unmarried Elderly Hispanic Females. *Demography, 29,* 93–112.

Casper, Lynne M., & Bianchi, Suzanne M. (2002). *Continuity & Change in the American Family.* Thousand Oaks, CA: Sage Publications.

Chavez, L. R. (1990). Coresidence and Resistance: Strategies for Survival Among Undocumented Mexicans and Central Americans in the U.S. *Urban Anthropology, 19,* 31–61.

Feliciano, C., Bean, F. D., & Leach, M. (2006). The Emphasis on Family Among Latinos: Cultural Myth or Social Capital Asset? In Harry Pachon, Rodolfo de la Garza, & Louis DeSipio (Eds.), *Latinos: Past Influence, Future Power.* Philadelphia: Temple University Press.

Fuligni, A. (1997). The Academic Achievement of Adolescents from Immigrant Families: The Roles of Family Background, Attitudes and Behavior. *Child Development, 68*(2), 351–363.

Glick, J. E., Ruf, S.D., Goldscheider, F., & White, M. J. (2006). Education and Early Family Formation: Patterns by Race, Ethnicity and Generation Status. *Social Forces, 84,* 1391–1415.

Hondagneu-Sotelo, P., & Avila, E. (1997). I'm Here, But I'm There: The Meanings of Latina Transnational Motherhood. *Gender and Society, 11,* 548–571.

Landale, N. S., & Fennelly, K. (1992). Informal Unions Among Mainland Puerto Ricans: Cohabitation or an Alternative to Legal Marriage? *Journal of Marriage and the Family, 54,* 269–280.

Landale, N. S., Oropesa, R. S., & Bradatan, C. (2006). Hispanic Families in the United States: Family Structure and Process in an Era of Family Change. In Marta Tienda & Faith Mitchell (Eds.), *Hispanics and the Future of America.* Washington, DC: The National Academies Press.

McLanahan, Sara S. (1997). Parent Absence or Poverty: Which Matters More?. In Greg J. Duncan & Jeanne Brooks-Gunn (Eds.), *Consequences of Growing Up Poor* (pp. 35–48). New York: Russell Sage Foundation.

Menjivar, C. (2000). *Fragmented Ties: Salvadoran Immigrant Networks in America.* Berkeley: University of California Press.

Menjivar, C. (2006). Liminal Legality: Salvadoran and Guatemalan Immigrants' Lives in the United States. *American Journal of Sociology, 111,* 999–1037.

Perez, L. (1994). The Household Structure of Second-Generation Children: An Exploratory Study of Extended Family Arrangements. *International Migration Review, 28*(4): 736–747.

Perlmann, J. (2005). *Italians Then, Mexicans Now: Immigrant Origins and Second Generation Progress, 1890 to 2000.* New York: Russell Sage Foundation.

Portes, A., & Zhou, M. (1993). The New Second Generation: Segmented Assimilation and Its Variants. *The Annals of the American Academy of Political and Social Science, 530,* 74–96.

Portes, A., & Rumbaut, R. G. (2001). *Legacies: The Story of the Immigrant Second Generation.* Berkeley: University of California Press.

Sy, S. R., & Schulenberg, J. E. (2005). Parent Beliefs and Children's Achievement Trajectories During the Transition to School in Asian American and European American Families. *International Journal of Behavioral Development, 29,* 505–515.

Valenzuela, A., & Dornbusch, S. M. (1994). Familism and Social Capital in the Academic Achievement of Mexican Origin and Anglo Adolescents. *Social Science Quarterly, 75,* 18–36.

Van Hook, J., & Glick, J. E. (2006). Mexican Migration to the United States and Extended Family Living Arrangements. Annual Meeting of the Population Association of America, Los Angeles, CA.

Van Hook, J., & Glick, J. E. (2007). Immigration and Living Arrangements: Moving Beyond the "Instrumental Needs Versus Acculturation" Dichotomy. *Demography, 44*(2), 225–249.

Wildsmith, E., & Raley, R. K. (2006). Race-Ethnic Differences in Nonmarital Fertility: A Focus on Mexican American Women. *Journal of Marriage and Family, 68,* 491–508.

CHAPTER 6

U.S. Latinos/as and the "American Dream": Diverse Populations and Unique Challenges in Housing

Eileen Diaz McConnell

INTRODUCTION

Housing has numerous impacts on the daily lives of individuals and families. For example, the cost of shelter influences what can be spent on other items such as education, transportation, or entertainment. Inferior-quality housing can lead to accidents and poor health. Housing conditions such as overcrowding influence whether household members have privacy and space to engage in various activities such as homework. Critical housing issues include the affordability of housing, the extent to which families are "cost-burdened" due to the high cost of housing, housing quality, the value and equity of owned-housing, and the stability of households, among others.[1] These matters have important consequences for children, families, communities, and the nation as a whole. Further, common practices such as redlining, a widespread banking policy after World War II through the 1970s that excluded racial and ethnic minorities from obtaining mortgage loans, real estate agents steering minorities to particular neighbourhoods, and other housing practices have had differential impacts on Americans by race and ethnicity (Squires, 1992) and have been particularly devastating for minorities, including Latinos (Diaz, 2005). Given this context, it is especially important to evaluate how housing outcomes continue to differ across racial and ethnic lines.

Housing issues matter for the substantial Latino population in the United States, their physical and mental health, and their ability to save and to accumulate wealth. Latinos are a significant and fast-growing component of the housing market, because of international migration, fertility rates, and their relative youth. Indeed, between 1995 and 2005, Latino-headed households increased at a faster rate than non-Latino households, accounting for more than 27% of the total increase in U.S. households (JCHS, 2006). In the decade after 1995, Latino households grew by at least 50% in nearly every state in the country, accounting for *all* of the household growth in central cities, 26% in suburban households, and offset non-Latino declines in rural households (Ready, 2006).

Latinos have economic impacts in housing. They spent $61 billion on shelter in 2000, about 20% of their total spending, their second highest expenditure after transportation (Humphreys, 2002). Latino buying power in housing is very concentrated, given that many Latino groups reside in just a few cities, especially Los Angeles (Mexicans, Guatemalans, Salvadorans, and Costa Ricans) and New York City (Puerto Ricans, Dominicans, and Colombians) (Lewis Mumford Center, 2002). The overall buying power of Latinos is increasing faster than any other group, more than tripling between 1990 and 2000 (Humphreys, 2002), and they represent an increasingly attractive market for mortgage lenders and the financial market overall (Gallagher, 2005; Grow et al., 2005). Reports indicate that even unauthorized Latino immigrants potentially could take out $44 billion in home mortgages if given the opportunity (Paral & Associates, 2004). Banks, credit unions, and mortgage companies have tapped into this market by translating applications into Spanish, changing criteria for assessing credit, accepting alternative documents to driver's licenses and social security numbers, and marketing specifically to Latinos (Gallagher, 2005; Grow et al., 2005).

This chapter has two primary objectives. This first is to summarize the experiences of Latinos in housing, including the characteristics of their residences and neighborhoods, the costs of shelter, differences in rental versus owned-housing, homeownership rates, and the value and equity of Latino-owned homes. Where data are available, I identify variation within Latinos by country and by nativity and contextualize these patterns via comparisons with non-Hispanic Whites, Blacks, and Asians. Moreover, the chapter includes information about both the housing situation nationally and in cities with large Latino populations, including Chicago, Los Angeles, New York City, and Miami. Thus, the chapter highlights the extensive heterogeneity of Latinos in housing by nativity, group, and U.S. location.

The second objective is to describe the state of current housing research vis-à-vis Latinos. Despite the importance of housing for the social and economic well-being of this rapidly growing population, housing scholarship focusing on Latinos is at a relatively nascent stage, compared with research about non-Hispanic Whites and African Americans. The earliest Latino-focused work generally explored the history and development of Latinos in Southwestern cities or the experiences of Latino households and Latino neighborhoods known as *barrios* (e.g., Acuña, 1972; Barrera, 1979; reviewed in Diaz, 2005). Contemporary housing scholarship increasingly includes Latinos rather than examining only White-Black gaps in housing outcomes. I provide a brief overview of this literature, with a particular focus on the most developed of this research – homeownership and housing equity.[2] The chapter concludes with new housing challenges and directions for future research.

Readers will note that housing information about this population is typically presented for all Latinos or for one or more of the three largest Latino groups (Mexicans, Puerto Ricans, and/or Cubans). Even research reports describing the state of housing in America generally (JCHS, 2006) or particularly about Latinos (McConnell, 2005; Ready, 2006; Vargas-Ramos, 2005) take this approach. This is partly due to the small sample sizes of Latinos in many national surveys, preventing analyses that are disaggregated by group. Additionally, important data sources, such as the American Housing Survey, do not collect information about detailed Latino groups, noting instead the *nativity* of Latinos (born in the United States, Puerto Rico, or elsewhere). For these reasons, it is difficult to uncover information about housing outcomes for different Latino groups, especially the smaller ones. Clearly, this reality makes it difficult to provide a truly comprehensive portrait of Latino experiences in housing. In spite of these limitations, the chapter provides a snapshot of the diversity and challenges facing Latinas/os in housing.

CHARACTERISTICS OF LATINO HOUSEHOLDS AND NEIGHBORHOODS

Latinos have unique household characteristics, which have important consequences for their experiences in housing. For instance, Latino household heads are younger than other groups. In 2003, the mean age of Latino household heads was 42 years old, significantly younger than the mean age of 46 years old for Blacks and 50 years old for Whites (McConnell, 2005). Latino households also are significantly larger than other types of household: 3.3 persons, compared with 2.5 and 2.4 for Black and White households, respectively, in 2003 (McConnell, 2005).

The majority of Latino households in 2000, about 80%, were comprised of families, individuals related by bloodlines or marriage; nearly 54% of all Latino households are married-couple families, as opposed to male- or female-headed households (Guzmán & McConnell, 2002). Latinos who live in extended families tend to do so because of their stage in the life course or to facilitate sharing of caretaking responsibilities for children and older individuals (Blank & Torrecilha, 1998). Living arrangements vary by national origin. For example, Mexican and Cuban immigrants are more likely to reside in extended living arrangements than those from Puerto Rico (Blank & Torrecilha, 1998).

Latinos are an overwhelmingly urban population, with nearly 94% of Latino households located in urban areas in 2000, compared with 75% of White households and 90% of Black households (U.S. Census Bureau, n.d.).[3] Approximately 47% of all Latino household heads live in the central cities of metropolitan areas, compared with 52% of Blacks and 23% of Whites (McConnell, 2005). Cuban households are the most urban (98%), followed by Puerto Rican households (97%), those of Mexican descent (92%), and other Latinos (94%) (U.S. Census Bureau, n.d.). These patterns are significant for Latinos, as characteristics such as age and residence in urban areas, within central cities, and/or suburbs are important factors in housing tenure (Coulson, 1999; Flippen, 2001) and housing equity (Flippen, 2004; Krivo & Kaufman, 2004).

The spatial locations of Latinos and the types of neighborhood in which they reside also are unique, with implications for their quality of life (Lewis Mumford Center, 2002). Trends in recent decades show that Latinos are generally more residentially segregated than non-Hispanic Whites but less segregated than African Americans. Latino neighborhoods are dynamic; between 1990 and 2000, more Latinos were added to neighborhoods with small proportions of other Latinos than to neighborhoods that were majority Latino (Suro & Tafoya, 2004). In 2000, the majority of Latinos, about 57%, resided in neighborhoods where Latinos comprised more than 7% of the population (Suro & Tafoya, 2004). The other 43% of Latinos resided in neighborhoods where the majority of the population is Latino. Living in a majority- or minority-Latino neighborhood varies by nativity, language(s) spoken, income, and other factors (Suro & Tafoya, 2004). For example, more than 75% of monolingual English-speaking Latinos lived in minority-Latino neighborhoods, whereas monolingual Spanish-speaking Latinos reside in both minority- and majority-Latino neighborhoods (Suro & Tafoya, 2004).

Like African Americans, Latinos live in neighborhoods characterized by lower average neighborhood median household incomes and higher rates of poverty compared with Whites and Asians, and the quality of their neighborhoods declined between 1990 and 2000 (Lewis Mumford Center, 2002). This association holds even for higher-income Latinos: Latinos in Los Angeles, Miami, New York City, and Washington D.C. dwell in neighborhoods with lower levels of human capital (lower percent of highly educated, professional, and employed neighbors) and higher levels of ethnic isolation, compared with non-Hispanic Whites (Lewis Mumford Center, 2002).

CONDITIONS AND COSTS OF HOUSING

Housing challenges for Latinos extend to other aspects of shelter, such as crowding. Research consistently shows that Latinos are much more likely to live in crowded households than other groups, typically defined as more than one person per room in the unit. Indeed, 26% of Latino households in 2003 lived in crowded conditions, compared with 8% of African American households and 4% of White households (McConnell, 2005). Foreign-born Latinos tend to be even more crowded (35%) than U.S.-born Latinos (15%) and those born in Puerto Rico or other U.S. territories (24%) (McConnell, 2005). The proportion of Latinos living in overcrowded households varies dramatically by metropolitan area. For instance, in 2003, about 4% of Latino households were considered to be crowded in Miami, 12% in Phoenix, 28% in Chicago, and 41% in Los Angeles (McConnell, 2005; Vargas-Ramos, 2005). Such patterns underscore similarities and differences across housing experiences for Latinos.

Housing quality is another challenge. Nearly 10% of all households with Latino heads in 2003 lived in dwellings that were moderately or severely inadequate, perhaps lacking a complete kitchen, plumbing, or electricity, rodent activity, and other issues (McConnell, 2005). Although residing in these conditions is less prevalent for Latinos than for African Americans (12%), it is more than double the rate for Whites (4%) (McConnell, 2005). Moreover, compared with other racial and ethnic groups, Latinos are much more likely to live in older homes, structures with external structural deterioration, with unsafe water to drink, and to feel uncomfortably cold during the winter (Vargas-Ramos, 2005). Clearly, such housing environments pose significant problems for the physical and mental health of Latino families and communities.

Despite the inferior conditions of housing for Latinos, this population pays a high price for shelter. Latinos spent ~33% of their pretax income on housing expenditures in 2003, far higher than the 26% spent by non-Latinos (Bureau of Labor Statistics, 2005). This is partly due to the concentration of Latinos in high-cost areas.[4] Latinos overwhelmingly reside in urban areas, and, overall, urban residents spend a larger percentage of total average expenditures on housing than rural residents (34% and 27%, respectively, in 2003) (Bureau of Labor Statistics, 2005). Latinos are also concentrated in the most expensive metropolitan areas in the United States. For instance, they comprise ~29% of all households in Los Angeles, 14% in New York City, and 11% in Chicago (U.S. Census Bureau, n.d.).[5] Housing costs in these cities account for a higher percent of total annual average household expenditures in places such as New York City (38%) compared with national expenditures (33%) (Bureau of Labor Statistics, 2005).

Dealing with high housing costs is a challenge for Latinos. In New York City in 1990, Puerto Rican and Dominican renters spent ~41% and 43% of their household income on housing costs, twice the cost burden of African Americans in the city (Elmelech, 2004). In 1999, only 29% of Latino households could afford a median-priced home in California compared with 49% of Whites and 55% of Asians (Lopez-Aqueres, Skaga, & Kugler, 2003). Nationally in 2003, nearly

17% of all Latino households were severely cost-burdened due to housing, compared with less than 11% of White households, but as equally likely as Black households (McConnell, 2005).

Housing cost burdens can vary significantly by area and by group. For example, the proportion of Latino owners spending more than 50% of their income on housing is about 38% in San Jose, 17% in San Diego, and 22% in Los Angeles, far higher than for their African American counterparts (Lopez-Aqueres, Skaga, & Kugler, 2003). Housing affordability is problematic in the East, as well. Indeed, fully 35% of Puerto Rican households in New York City spend more than 50% of their income on housing costs. Foreign-born Latino households in New York City are also severely cost-burdened (28%), much higher than other racial and ethnic groups (McConnell, 2005). The rental market overall tends to be expensive and relevant for Latino immigrants, especially since 85% of immigrant Latinos reside in rental housing (Center for Puerto Rican Studies–CUNY, 2003).

Another challenge for Latinos is the availability of housing. In many places, there is too little housing to meet current or future demand. In 2001, the rental vacancy rate in California was more than 4% and the owner-occupied vacancy rate was 1%—far below the benchmark of 5% that indicates a housing shortage (Lopez-Aqueres, Skaga, & Kugler, 2003). Other locales have even lower availability of housing. Indeed, New York City has declared a "housing emergency" since 1966; in 2002, less than 3% of rental units were vacant, with even lower availability in rent-stabilized and low-rent units in the city (Center for Puerto Rican Studies–CUNY, 2003). Again, housing issues in states like California and New York are particularly relevant to Latinos, who are concentrated in those states.

HOUSING TENURE

Renting

Current statistics show that about half of all Latinos in the United States own and the other half rent. The number of Latino renter-occupied households increased by 25% between 1995 and 2005 (Ready, 2006). Although renting is common for Latinos, many are extremely interested in homeownership, even in high-cost areas. In one recent survey of Mexican-heritage families renting in Los Angeles, Houston, and Atlanta 85% of Mexican renters surveyed in Los Angeles reported wanting to become homeowners, with the majority of those either actively in the process of purchasing a home or planning to do so within the next 5 years (Lee, Tornatzky, & Torres 2004).

There are substantial differences between Latino household heads who own their homes and those who rent. Latino household heads who rent are about 37 years old, 10 years younger than Latino household heads who own their own homes. They are also more likely to be foreign born, to be recently arrived immigrants, and to earn nearly half of what their home-owning peers do ($32,122 vs. $63,636) (McConnell, 2005). Given the lower income of Latino renters, their monthly housing costs are significantly higher. Indeed, Latino renters spend about 38% of their monthly income on housing, whereas Latino homeowners spend 27% (McConnell, 2005).

Despite this cost burden, Latinos are much less likely to receive rent subsidies than their non-Latino peers (Vargas-Ramos, 2005) and are the largest proportion of those on waiting lists for public housing or housing vouchers in cities such as New York (Center for Puerto Rican Studies–CUNY, 2003). Moreover, Latino households who rent are significantly larger and are more likely to live in crowded conditions (McConnell, 2005).

Owning

Homeownership is an important component of the "American Dream," a commonly used measure of national progress and achievement in the United States. Extensive research demonstrates the positive benefits associated with owning one's home for individuals, families, and communities, as it is an important avenue for the creation of wealth (Alba & Logan, 1992). In fact, it is the "cornerstone" of household wealth in America (Di, 2005). Owning a home in a neighborhood with high levels of owner-occupied homes has a positive relationship with housing values and the social distribution of wealth. Housing tenure is strongly associated with individual and household well-being (Flippen, 2001). Homeownership also has societal impacts, as neighborhoods with higher proportions of homeowners are more likely to have well-kept properties, lower crime rates and more community participation in local organizations than neighborhoods with lower tenure rates (e.g., Dietz, 2002).

Homeownership is currently at the highest rate in U.S. history: ~69% in the last quarter of 2005 (Callis & Cavanaugh, 2006). Reflecting other forms of stratification in society, there are significant racial and ethnic disparities in housing tenure. For instance, in the fourth quarter of 2005, non-Hispanic Whites have homeownership rates of 76% (Callis & Cavanaugh, 2006). In recent years, Latinos and African Americans have the lowest rates of homeownership of all racial and ethnic groups in the United States: 50% and 48%, respectively (Callis & Cavanaugh, 2006). This can change from year to year; in 2003, the Latino homeownership rate was 47%, lower than African Americans (U.S. Census Bureau, n.d.).

There is extensive heterogeneity within the homeownership patterns of the Latino population by national origin, nativity, and region in the United States. In 2000, homeownership rates were ~20% for Dominicans, 34% for Puerto Ricans, 48% for Mexicans, and 57% for Cubans (U.S. Census Bureau, n.d.). Homeownership rates also differ by nativity. For example, 2003 American Housing Survey data shows that 54% of U.S.-born Latinos in 2003 were homeowners, compared with 31% of Puerto Ricans and 42% of foreign-born Latinos (McConnell, 2005).

Similar to overall gains in U.S. homeownership rates, Latino households also have made significant progress in housing tenure. Latino homeowners increased from 3% of all owner-occupied households in 1990 to 6% in 2000. Naturalized Latin American immigrants increased their homeownership rates from 56% in 1994 to 62% in 2002; noncitizen Latin American immigrants increased their homeownership from about 30% in 1994 to more than 32% in 2002 (Callis, 2003). In the 10 years after 1995, Latinos experienced an overall 81% growth in owner-occupied housing compared with a 19% increase for non-Hispanic households (Ready, 2006). Latino achievement of homeownership is related to various factors, such as the 34% drop in mortgage interest rates between 1991 and 2000 and the growth of the Latino middle class (Lopez-Aqueres et al., 2003).

Latinos are taking out mortgages in record numbers, increasing from about 157,000 mortgage loans in 1993 to more than 528,000 ten years later, a 236% increase over the decade (FFIEC, 2004). This increase was the highest of any racial and ethnic group in the United States. Government-backed home-purchase loans to Latinos increased nearly 68% between 1993 and 2003 (FFIEC, 2004). Overall, in 2003, ~12% of all mortgage loans went to Latino applicants, 8% went to Black applicants, and 70% went to White applicants (FFIEC, 2004). Despite such gains, Latinos continue to have denial rates for home-purchase loans that are substantially higher than for their non-Hispanic White peers. More than 17% of all Latino applicants for both conventional and government-backed mortgages in the United States were denied for home mortgage loans in 2003, compared with 11% for Whites (McConnell, 2005).

Analyses of Homeownership

The majority of housing scholarship that includes Latinos has been devoted to housing tenure and, not surprisingly, shows that this population experiences a level of disadvantage that is similar to African Americans (Alba & Logan, 1992; Krivo, 1986). About half of the studies focusing on the determinants of homeownership disaggregates Latinos by national origin, such as Mexicans, Puerto Ricans, Cubans, and Dominicans (e.g., Alba & Logan, 1992; Borjas, 2002; Elmelech, 2004; Krivo, 1995; McConnell & Marcelli, 2007; Rosenbaum & Friedman, 2004); the other half includes variables for nativity, citizenship, and/or year of arrival to the United States and do not disaggregate Latinos (e.g., Coulson, 1999; Flippen, 2001; Friedman & Rosenbaum, 2004; Painter, Gabriel, & Myers, 2001).[6]

In general, housing scholarship demonstrates strong positive relationships between homeownership and human capital variables such as income, education, English proficiency, nativity, time in the United States if foreign born, life-course factors such as marital status and the presence of children, and contextual variables such as cost of housing, urban versus suburban, and region (e.g., Alba & Logan, 1992; Borjas, 2002; Coulson, 1999; Flippen, 2001; Krivo, 1995; McConnell & Marcelli, 2007; Toussaint-Comeau & Rhine, 2004). For example, U.S.- and foreign-born Latinos with higher incomes have higher levels of homeownership, whether their heritage is Mexican, Puerto Rican, Cuban, or "Other Hispanic" (e.g., Alba & Logan, 1992; Flippen, 2001; Krivo, 1995; Rosenbaum & Friedman, 2004).

Similarly, stage in the life cycle is also relevant to Latino homeownership. Older individuals, those who are married, and those with children have higher odds of housing tenure. Such results apply to all Hispanics (e.g., Krivo, 1995), Hispanic immigrants (e.g., Clark, 2003; Flippen, 2001), Mexican immigrants specifically (McConnell & Marcelli, 2007), and recent Hispanic movers (Blank & Torrecilha, 1998). Homeownership clearly is linked with key transitions in families and households over the life course and with individual and family characteristics.

In considering housing tenure for immigrants, researchers associate homeownership with assimilation. As immigrants participate in the process of assimilation (e.g., obtain a better job, increase their pay and social capital) and decide to remain in the country (Alba & Logan, 1992), they are more likely to become homeowners. Studies consistently document the positive link of U.S. nativity with Latino homeownership (e.g., Clark, 2003; Coulson, 1999; Lee, Tornatzky, & Torres, 2004; Ready, 2006). This is not surprising, because to qualify for a mortgage, applicants generally need a sizable down payment, a social security number, proof of wages for the previous year, previous tax returns, of current stable employment, homeowner's insurance, and must meet other requirements. Time in the United States is another measure of assimilation, and immigrants with longer residence in the country have higher rates of homeownership (e.g., Borjas, 2002; Callis, 2003; Clark, 2003; Elmelech, 2004).

In the current social, economic, and political context surrounding immigration, especially Mexican migration, documentation to live and work in the United States can be vitally important for housing tenure. Recent data collected by the U.S. Census Bureau indicates that naturalized Mexican immigrants have homeownership rates of 69%, compared with 34% of noncitizen Mexican immigrants (Callis, 2003). Legal status has important implications for homeownership, even if Latino immigrants are "assimilated" in other ways. Indeed, it is deemed to be one of the most important factors for immigrant homeownership (Clark, 2003; Coulson, 1999; Toussaint-Comeau & Rhine, 2004). Barriers to homeownership for unauthorized immigrants often includes not having financial transaction accounts, lacking credit, or not having acceptable identification to open accounts or take out a mortgage. Consequently, numerous studies show that, even after accounting for factors such as income, English skills, years since migration, and characteristics of the location, U.S. citizenship is positively associated with owning a home for Latino immigrants (Clark, 2003; Coulson, 1999; Toussaint-Comeau & Rhine, 2004).[7]

The housing literature to date indicates that factors such as neighborhood composition and housing costs also are associated with homeownership. One study found that Latinos are less likely to be homeowners in neighborhoods with higher proportions of coethnic residents, perhaps because of low levels of resources in the form of high proportions of poor and non-English-speaking households (Toussaint-Comeau & Rhine, 2004). However, other analyses indicate that higher levels of Latino U.S.- and/or foreign-born residents in a neighborhood can serve as resources for Latino immigrants and, consequently, promote higher rates of homeownership. This positive relationship holds for Latinos of Mexican and/or Cuban descent (Alba & Logan, 1992; Borjas, 2002), but a higher coethnic context is linked with lower homeownership for Puerto Ricans and "Other Hispanics" (Alba & Logan, 1992; Krivo, 1995). Perhaps the tendency of Latinos to rely on coethnics to recommend trustworthy agents and lenders (Lee, Tornatzky, & Torres, 2004) can be helpful in many locales, but not in high-cost areas such as New York City, where Puerto Ricans are likely to reside with coethnics.

Indeed, the unique geographic concentration of Latinos in high-cost areas is particularly important for their homeownership. Research shows that as the value of housing increases, the likelihood of ownership for Mexicans, Puerto Ricans, Cubans, and other Hispanics decreases (Krivo, 1995), which partially explains why Latino homeownership rates are higher in affordable areas such as the South and the Midwest, compared to the Northeast and West (Flippen, 2001). Unfortunately, housing prices are rising nationwide; the average home price increased from $139,000 to nearly $209,000 between December 2000 and December 2005 (Ready, 2006). Rising home prices are eroding housing affordability in large housing markets such as Phoenix, Washington D.C, and Los Angeles (JCHS, 2006). Clearly, this is an issue that is relevant for both Latinos and non-Latinos.

Homeownership studies show that after controlling for many influential variables, immigrants from the Dominican Republic, Mexico, and Cuba, Puerto Ricans and Dominican Americans are still less likely to be homeowners than U.S.-born Latinos or non-Hispanic Whites (Borjas, 2002; Elmelech, 2004). Other research shows important variations by generation status for Latinos (Rosenbaum & Friedman, 2004) or that Mexicans, Puerto Ricans, and Cubans would have substantially higher housing if they had the mean socioeconomic status of African Americans (Alba & Logan, 1992). Such intriguing findings point to the need for additional research on Latino homeownership by national origin, nativity, and citizenship.

Analyses of Housing Values and Equity

There are significant racial and ethnic inequalities in numerous aspects of owned-housing, including value and equity. The financial value of homeownership is important to low-income and minority households because it "helps temper the racial inequality in the wealth distribution" (Di, 2005:293). For most American homeowners, the value of their home is a significant source of their net wealth. However, for Latinos and African Americans, it comprises nearly two-thirds of their total wealth, a much higher proportion than for non-Hispanic Whites (Kochhar, 2004). In addition to having fewer sources of wealth, Latinos generally have far lower levels of wealth overall. Latino households in 2002 held a median net worth of ~$8,000, less than 10% of the median wealth of White households ($89,000) (Kochhar, 2004). Part of the Latino-White wealth gap is due to the much lower homeownership rates of Latinos compared with their non-Hispanic White counterparts. Indeed, the comparison of wealth for Latino renters versus owners is startling. In 2001, Latino renters had a median net worth of $2,650, whereas Latino owners had a median net worth of $70,560, a ratio of 1:27 (Di, 2005).

Lower levels of overall wealth for Latinos also stems from the relatively low median values of Latino-owned housing, ~$106,000 for Latinos in 2000. In contrast, the median value of single-family detached homes was $123,000 for non-Hispanic Whites and nearly $200,000 for Asians (U.S. Census Bureau, n.d.). African American-owned homes were worth less, ~$81,000. The worth of Latino-owned homes would be even lower if they did not live in the West, a region with high housing values (Flippen, 2001). Housing values for homes owned by Latinos vary by metropolitan statistical area. For example, Latino-owned homes in 2000 were worth about $154,000 in Washington, D.C.; $128,000 in Miami; $159,000 in Los Angeles; and $178,000 in New York City (U.S. Census Bureau, n.d.). Similar to national patterns, Latino-owned homes in each of those cities were worth less than those owned by non-Hispanic Whites or Asians. In Washington, D.C. and Miami, Latino-owned homes were worth more than those owned by African Americans but worth less in Los Angeles and New York City (U.S. Census Bureau, n.d.).

There is significant diversity in the real estate equity among Latinos. For example, all Latinos held ~$36,000 in real estate wealth in 1992 constant-dollars, varying from ~$31,000 for Puerto Ricans, $42,000 for U.S.-born Mexican Americans, and $57,000 for U.S.-born "Other Hispanics" (Cobb-Clark & Hildebrand, 2006a). Foreign-born Latinos have lower home equity than U.S.-born Latinos; and among immigrants, those who lack citizenship or are recent arrivals have lower equity (Krivo & Kaufman, 2004). For example, Cuban immigrants have real estate equity of ~$57,000; Central and South American immigrants possess about $40,000; Mexican immigrants have ~$24,000 and the U.S.-born population (of any race) has about $69,000 (Cobb-Clark & Hildebrand, 2006a, 2006b). Mexican, Central American, and South American immigrant groups have lower real estate equity than European and Asian immigrant households, even after accounting for income, timing of immigration, and citizenship status (Cobb-Clark & Hildebrand, 2006b).

On average, Latino homeowners have lower home equity than non-Hispanic Whites, partially due to the population's relative youth, lower household incomes, and education (Flippen, 2004; Krivo & Kauffman, 2004).[8] Yet, analyses show that even after controlling for important factors such as age, marital status, education, and locational characteristics, Latinos still have lower home equity than non-Hispanic Whites (Flippen, 2001). Explanations for the White-Hispanic equity gap include lower returns to high income and education for Latinos than Whites and lower prevalence in employment that provides benefits or stability (Flippen, 2001). Also difficult for Latino homeowners is that, despite increasing access to homeownership, their homes are not experiencing the same level of appreciation over time as homes owned by Whites (Flippen, 2004). This situation is similar to the lower home equities and appreciations of African Americans, due in part to the racial and ethnic compositions of their neighborhoods (Flippen, 2004).

Another area of concern is access and cost of homeowner's insurance to protect the value of their homes. Latinos and other minorities tend to pay higher premiums per $1,000 of the value of their home and, consequently, are less able to afford comprehensive homeowner's insurance coverage compared with Whites (Van Kerkhove, 2005). Paired-test studies examining the practices of major insurers document that Latino and other minority applicants are unfairly treated, referred to other insurers, and receive higher quotes for the same levels of insurance as Whites (Squires, 1997). This form of discrimination undoubtedly affects the security of Latino housing wealth in the event of natural or man-made disasters, and the lower equity and appreciation of Latino-owned dwellings significantly decreases the ability of both groups to accumulate housing wealth and to transfer wealth to future generations.

NEW CHALLENGES IN HOUSING

Numerous changes have occurred in the mortgage market, which have implications for future levels of Latino homeownership. Perhaps the most important change in housing overall is the increasing unaffordability of housing. Indeed, between 2000 and 2005, median home prices rose 23% for new single-family homes, 28% for existing single-family homes, and 43% for existing condominiums and co-ops (JCHS, 2006). Increasing costs impact renters, owners, native- and foreign-born alike, with particularly dire consequences for low-income and immigrant families (Lipman, 2005).

A related issue is the rapid and dramatic growth of the subprime mortgage market (Williams, Nesiba, & McConnell, 2005), rising from 5% of the conventional mortgage market in 1994 to fully 20% by 2005 (Fishbein & Woodall, 2006; JCHS, 2006). Since 2001, the volume of subprime loans increased from $210 billion to $625 billion in 2005 (JCHS, 2006). Subprime loans are higher risk loans for those who earn relatively low incomes, have poor credit scores, and/or have high debt-to-income ratios. The share of home-purchase loans in metropolitan areas made by subprime lenders, or those who lend to individuals with poorer credit, in low-income, predominantly minority communities has shot up dramatically (Fishbein & Woodall, 2006). The number of subprime mortgages increased more than eightfold for Latino homebuyers between 1995 and 2001 nationwide (ACORN, 2002), likely due to "steering" to subprime loans, especially if they do not meet automated underwriting guidelines for qualifying for prime loans because of their financial behavior or do not live in areas with commercial banks offering prime loans (Chandrasekhar, 2004). By 2005, nearly 38% of Latino mortgages were subprime, compared with about 22% of White borrowers (Fishbein & Woodall, 2006).

The expansion of the subprime mortgage market might have provided more access to home loans for more Latinos and other groups; however, the higher interest rates and fees associated with such loans can significantly increase the cost of owning a home and reduce wealth accumulation (Williams, Nesbia, & McConnell, 2005). Moreover, some subprime loans practices qualify as "predatory lending" because of unethical and usurious practices (Chandrasekhar, 2004). By 2005, nearly 41% of all conventional loans made to Latinos were high-cost, nearly double the proportion for Whites and more than triple the proportion for Asians but lower than the rate of African American homebuyers taking out conventional loans (55%) (National Community Reinvestment Coalition, 2006). Latino homeowners in some locales are even more likely to have such loans: 30% of Latino homeowners in 2004 in San Antonio, Texas and Hartford, Connecticut; 24% in Chicago, and 20% in Miami have subprime loans (Ready, 2006). These numbers are of concern because subprime loans are seven times more likely than prime loans to be delinquent or in foreclosure (JCHS, 2006), putting Latino homeownership and housing equity in serious jeopardy.

There is increasing evidence that the housing market has softened, with high housing inventories and rising interest rates (Llana, 2006). This is especially problematic for the millions of homeowners who have borrowed against their homes, with the expectation that their homes would appreciate in value. Moreover, many recent homebuyers took out interest-only mortgages or mortgages at introductory teaser rates that reset after 2 or 3 years (Tedeschi, 2006). Approximately $1 trillion dollars in outstanding mortgages, out of a total of $9 trillion dollars, will reset in 2007 (Derus, 2006). Many of these homeowners will not be able to afford the "true" cost of the mortgage. Indeed, a recent estimate of national trends suggests that approximately "19 percent of the 7.7 million adjustable rate mortgages (ARMs) taken out in 2004 and 2005 are at risk of defaulting" (Tedeschi, 2006). Default notices, the first step in the foreclosure process, were up more than 100% in California and California counties such as Ventura, San Diego, and Orange in the third quarter of 2006, compared to the same period in 2005 (Steitfield & Zimmerman, 2006). If such dire predictions become reality, this will have devastating consequences for Latinos and others, felt at both the local and national levels.

DIRECTIONS FOR FUTURE RESEARCH

As outlined in this chapter, Latinos face housing challenges along multiple lines, with implications for Latino families and communities and, indeed, for the nation as a whole. Much more research is needed to fully document how Latinos fare in housing. Future research should be directed toward the following:

1. Examine the housing situations and outcomes for "other" Latino groups. This gap in the literature is partially due to limitations in housing datasets and/or small sample sizes. Scholars need better and more data on Latinos, which includes providing more detailed information about Latinos in important sources such as the American Housing Survey. When the data are available, researchers should, whenever possible, disaggregate Latino samples by national origin, nativity, and legal status.

2. Explore additional geographic areas in housing studies. Clearly, recent Latino demographic growth across the country and the heterogeneity in housing across locales indicate the need for housing studies in more locales across the country. The housing landscape is rapidly changing in "new" areas experiencing high Latino population growth, such as North Carolina, Nevada, Georgia, and in rural areas. Investigating housing outcomes in such locales will provide a more comprehensive portrait of the experiences of Latinos in housing.

3. Investigate how the important changes occurring in the mortgage market, such as increased marketing to Latinos, the rapid increase in the subprime mortgage market, home equity loans, and growing foreclosure rates, will impact current and future homeownership, housing foreclosures, and home equity/appreciation.

4. Identify possible sources of housing discrimination, such as treatment by landlords, financial institutions, and lending personnel; and conduct qualitative and quantitative studies that can detect steering by real estate agents and mortgage brokers.

5. As housing scholarship about Latinos develops further, the research must be disseminated to policy makers. Targeted housing policies should address the specific housing needs and challenges of different racial and ethnic groups in different areas of the United States and outline the "best practices" for increasing homeownership and home equity. A "one-size-fits-all" approach to improving housing conditions and increasing household wealth is not likely to be as successful as attending to the unique situations of Americans, whomever and wherever they might be.

ACKNOWLEDGMENTS

The author appreciates the financial support of the University of Illinois at Urbana-Champaign and Arizona State University during the writing of this chapter. The author is grateful to Havidán Rodríguez and two anonymous reviewers for their comments on an earlier draft of the chapter and to Keri Niehans for her editorial assistance. All errors are solely the responsibility of the author.

NOTES

1. Many housing issues that are relevant for Latinos are beyond the scope of this chapter such as the following: the history of redlining and other racist practices; the dismantling of the low-income housing opportunities and the experiences of Latinos in public and affordable housing; explanations for the location decisions of Latinos; the causes and consequences of living in *colonias*, unincorporated settlements with no or few basic services; and the connections between homeownership in Latin America and the United States.
2. This chapter briefly summarizes research about other housing outcomes for Latinos: living arrangements (Blank, 1998; Blank & Torrecilha, 1998), housing quality (Friedman & Rosenbaum 2004), and housing costs and crowding (e.g., Elmelech 2004; Krivo 1995).
3. References in the text to the U.S. Census Bureau were dynamically generated using American Factfinder. See the References section for more details.
4. Diaz (2005) outlines additional explanations for the crushing costs of housing for Latinos.
5. Data on the total size of the Latino population shows that Latinos are an even larger proportion of the total population in each metropolitan area than the household figures show.
6. One study incorporates the two strands: Papademetriou and Ray (2004) examine the determinants of homeownership for Mexican and Central American immigrants combined, compared with other immigrant groups.
7. One study (McConnell and Marcelli, 2007) does not find a statistically significant association between legal status and homeownership for Mexican immigrants. That project examined Mexican immigrant homeownership only in Los Angeles County, and various factors, including the unique context of Los Angeles and recent changes in the mortgage market, could explain their results.
8. Flippen (2001) and Krivo and Kaufman (2004) do not disaggregate the Latino population but do include variables that differentiate between Latinos, such as region, income, nativity, and citizenship.

REFERENCES

Acuña, R. F. (1972). *Occupied America*. San Francisco: Canfield Press.

Alba, R. D., & Logan, J. R. (1992). Assimilation and stratification in the homeownership patterns of racial and ethnic groups. *International Migration Review, 26*, 1314–1341.

ACORN (Association of Community Organizations for Reform Now). (2002, November). *Separate and Unequal: Predatory Lending in America*. ACORN Predatory Lending Report. Washington, DC: ACORN.

Barrera, M. (1979). *Race and Class in the Southwest*. Notre Dame: University of Notre Dame Press.

Blank, S. (1998). Health and Home: The Living Arrangements of Mexican Immigrants and U.S.-Born Mexican Americans. *Sociological Forum, 13*, 35–59.

Blank, S., & Torrecilha, R. (1998). Understanding the living arrangement of Latino immigrants: A Life Course Approach. *International Migration Review, 32*, 3–19.

Borjas, G. (2002). Homeownership in the immigrant population. *Journal of Urban Economics, 52*(3), 448–476.

Bureau of Labor Statistics. (2005). Current Metropolitan Statistical Areas Tables. Tables 7, 8, 21, 22, 24: Selected Metropolitan Statistical Areas: Average Annual Expenditures and Characteristics, Consumer Expenditure Survey, 2002–2003. Table 2200: Hispanic or Latino origin of reference person: Average annual expenditures and characteristics, Consumer Expenditure Survey, 2003.

Callis, R. R. (2003, September). *Moving to America—Moving to Homeownership: 1994–2002* U.S. Census Bureau, Current Housing Reports, H121/03-1. Washington, DC: U.S. Government Printing Office.

Callis, R. R., & Cavanaugh, L. B. (2006, January). *Census Bureau Reports on Residential Vacancies and Homeownership*. Washington, DC: U.S. Department of Commerce.

Center for Puerto Rican Studies–CUNY. (2003). Housing Emergency and Overcrowding: Latinos in New York City. *Centro Policy Brief, 1*(1), 1–8.

Chandrasekhar, C. A. (2004). Can New Americans Achieve the American Dream? Promoting Homeownership in Immigrant Communities. *Harvard Civil Rights Civil Liberties Law Review, 39*, 169–216.

Clark, W. A. V. (2003). *Immigrants and the American Dream: Remaking the Middle Class*. New York: Guilford Press.

Cobb-Clark, D. A., & Hildebrand, V. (2006a, January). *The Portfolio Choices of Hispanic Couples*. Discussion Paper No. 1948. Bonn: Institute for the Study of Labor (IZA).

Cobb-Clark, D. A., & Hildebrand, V. (2006b). The Wealth and Asset Holdings of U.S.-Born and Foreign-Born Households: Evidence from SIPP data. *Review of Income and Wealth, 52*(1), 17–42.

Coulson, N. E. (1999). Why Are Hispanic and Asian-American Homeownership Rates So Low? Immigration and Other Factors. *Journal of Urban Economics, 45*, 209–227.

Derus, M. (2006, October 24). 4 times as many home foreclosures predicted; Heavy debt, housing. *Milwaukee Journal Sentinel*.

Di, Z. X. (2005). Does Housing Wealth Contribute to or Temper the Widening Wealth Gap in America? *Housing Policy Debate, 16*(2), 281–296.

Diaz, D. R. (2005). *Barrio Urbanism: Chicanos, Planning, and American Cities*. New York: Routledge.

Dietz, R. (2002). The Estimation of Neighborhood Effects in the Social Sciences: An Interdisciplinary Review. *Social Science Research, 31*, 539–575.

Elmelech, Y. (2004). Housing Inequality in New York City: Racial and Ethnic Disparities in Homeownership and Shelter-Cost Burden. *Housing, Theory, and Society, 21*(4), 163–175.

FFIEC (Federal Financial Institutions Examination Council). (2004). *Federal Financial Institutions Examination Council Reports-Nationwide Summary Statistics for 2003 HMDA Data*. Aggregate Report Search by Metropolitan Statistical Areas, (Tables 4-1, 4-2). FFIEC. Arlington: VA.

Fishbein, A. J., & Woodall, P. (2006). Subprime Locations: Patterns of Geographic Disparity in Subprime Lending. Washington, DC: Consumer Federation of America. September 5.

Flippen, C. A. (2001). Racial and Ethnic Inequality in Homeownership and Housing Equity. *The Sociological Quarterly, 42*(2), 121–149.

Flippen, C. A. (2004). Unequal Returns to Housing Investments? A Study of Real Housing Appreciation Among Black, White, and Hispanic Households. *Social Forces, 82*(4), 1523–1551.

Friedman, S., & Rosenbaum, E. (2004). Nativity Status and Racial/Ethnic Differences in Access to Quality Housing: Does Homeownership Bring Greater Parity? *Housing Policy Debate, 15*(4), 865–901.

Gallagher, M. (2005). Alternative IDS, ITIN Mortgages and Emerging Latino Markets. *Protfitwise News and Views*, Newsletter of the Federal Reserve Bank of Chicago. March, 2–7.

Grow, B., Carter A., Crockett, R.O., & Smith, G. (2005, July 18). Embracing Illegals. *Business Week*, No. 3943:56–62.

Guzmán, B., & McConnell, E. D. (2002). The Hispanic population: 1990–2000 growth and change. *Population Research and Policy Review, 21*(1–2), 109–128.

Humphreys, J. M. (2002). The Multicultural Economy: Minority Buying Power in the New Century. *Georgia Business and Economic Conditions, 62*(2), 1–27.

JCHS (Joint Center for Housing Studies, Harvard University). (2006). *The State of the Nation's Housing 2006*. Cambridge, MA: Harvard University.

Kochhar, R. (2004, October). *The Wealth of Hispanic Households: 1996 to 2002,* Pew Hispanic Center Report. Washington, DC: Pew Hispanic Center.

Krivo, L. J. (1986). Homeownership Differences Between Hispanics and Anglos in the United States. *Social Problems, 33*, 319–334.

Krivo, L. J. (1995). Immigrant Characteristics and Hispanic-Anglo Housing Inequality. *Demography, 32*(4), 599–615.

Krivo, L. J., & Kauffman, R. L. (2004). Housing and Wealth Inequality: Racial-Ethnic Differences in Home Equity in the United States. *Demography, 41*(3), 585–605.

Lee, J., Tornatzky, L., & Torres, C. (2004). *El Sueño de Su Casa: The Homeownership Potential of Mexican-Heritage Families*. Claremont, CA: Tomás Rivera Policy Institute CA.

Lewis Mumford Center for Comparative Urban and Regional Research. (2002). *Separate and Unequal: Racial and Ethnic Neighborhoods in the 21ˢᵗ Century and Sortable Lists of Population Data for Hispanic National-Origin Groups*. Albany, NY: University of Albany–SUNY.

Lipman, B. (2005, April). The Housing Landscape for America's Working Families, 2005. *New Century Housing*. Washington, DC: Center for Housing Policy, 5(1).

Llana, S. M. (2006, March 21). Homeowners Stretched Perilously. *Christian Science Monitor*.

Lopez-Aqueres, W., Skaga, J., & Kugler, T. (2003). *Housing California's Latino Population in the 21ˢᵗ Century: The Challenge Ahead* (Research Report 1050). Claremont, CA: Tomás Rivera Policy Institute.

McConnell, E. D. (2005, June 1). *No Place Like Home: The State of Hispanic housing in Chicago, Los Angeles, and New York City, 2003* (Research Report). Notre Dame, IN: University of Notre Dame.

McConnell, E. D., & Marcelli, E. A. (2007). Buying into the American Dream? Mexican Immigrants, Legal Status, and Homeownership in Los Angeles County. *Social Science Quarterly, 88*(1), 199–221.

National Community Reinvestment Coalition. (2006, May). *The 2005 Fair Lending Disparities: Stubborn and Persistent II*. National Community Reinvestment Coalition Report. Washington, DC: National Community Reinvestment Coalition.

Painter, G. D., Gabriel, S., & Myers, D. (2001). Race, Immigrant Status, and Housing Tenure Choice. *Journal of Urban Economics, 49*, 150–167.

Papademetriou, D., & Ray, B. (2004). From Homeland to a Home: Immigrants and Homeownership in Urban America. *Fannie Mae Papers. 3*(1), 1–16.

Paral, R., & Associates. (2004). *The Potential for New Latino Homeownership Among Undocumented Latino Immigrants.* Report prepared for the National Association of Hispanic Real Estate Professionals. Washington, DC: National Association of Hispanic Real Estate Professionals.

Ready, T. J. (2006, June). *Hispanic housing in the United States 2006*. Research Report. Notre Dame, IN: University of Notre Dame, Institute for Latino Studies and Esperanza USA).

Rosenbaum, E., & Friedman, S. (2004). Generational Patterns in Home Ownership and Housing Quality Among Racial/Ethnic Groups in New York City, 1999. *International Migration Review, 38*(4), 1492–1533.

Squires, G. D. (1992). *From Redlining to Reinvestment*. Philadelphia: Temple University Press.

Squires, G. D. (Ed.). (1997). *Insurance Redlining: Disinvestment, Reinvestment, and the Evolving Role of Financial Institutions*. Washington, DC: The Urban Institute Press.

Steitfield, D., & Zimmerman, M. (2006). More Homeowners Going into Default. *Los Angeles Times*. October 19, 2006.

Suro, R., & Tafoya, S. (2004, December 27). *Dispersal and Concentration: Patterns of Latino Residential Settlemen*. Pew Hispanic Center Report. Washington, DC: Pew Hispanic Center.

Tedeschi, B. (2006). It Seemed Like a Good Bet at the Time. *New York Times*. September 24, 2006.

Toussaint-Comeau, M., & Rhine, S. L.W. (2004). Tenure Choice with Location Selection: The Case of Hispanic Neighborhoods in Chicago. *Contemporary Economic Policy, 22*(1), 95–110.

U.S. Census Bureau. (n.d.) *2000 Census of Population and Housing, Summary File 1 (SF1), Summary File 2 (SF2), Summary File 3 (SF3)* (generated by Eileen Diaz McConnell using American Factfinder). Retrieved July 14, 2006, from http://factfinder.census.gov/home/saff/main.html?_lang=en.

Van Kerkhove, B. (2005). *The Homeowners Insurance Gap: How Race and Neighborhood Composition Explain Cost and Access Disparities in Rochester and Monroe County, NY*. Report for Public Interest Law Office of Rochester.

Vargas-Ramos, C. (2005, Spring). *The State of Housing for Hispanics in the United States* (Policy Brief, 2(1)). New York: Center for Puerto Rican Studies, Hunter College (CUNY).

Williams, R. A., Nesiba R., & McConnell, E. D. (2005). The Changing Face of Mortgage Lending. *Social Problems, 52*(2), 181–208.

CHAPTER 7

Latino Health Paradoxes: Empirical Evidence, Explanations, Future Research, and Implications

Dolores Acevedo-Garcia

Lisa M. Bates

INTRODUCTION

In the last decades, the growth of the U.S. Latino population and the adaptation of Latino immigrants have increasingly been the subject of scholarly and policy attention. Some see the growth of the Latino population as a positive force that will redefine U.S. society and might strengthen diversity and democracy (Suarez-Orozco & Paez, 2002). On the other hand, some argue that Hispanic immigration constitutes a threat to the Anglo-Protestant values and practices that form the core of American culture (Huntington, 2004). In health research, the topic of Latino health paradoxes (defined below) is also becoming the subject of increased debate. For some, the health advantage that Latinos appear to have might be rooted in their "cultural orientation" and strong social networks. For others, the so-called paradoxes are the result of selection processes that bring to the United States Latino immigrants that are healthier than their nonimmigrant conationals. Hence, this school argues, "paradoxes" are, after all, not paradoxical.

This chapter describes the empirical evidence on Latino health paradoxes and discusses possible explanations for and implications of such paradoxes. We argue that research on Latino health should be embedded in a complex understanding of the context of Latino immigration, including the Latin American sending countries and the process of immigrant adaptation. Thus, studying Latino health should involve an interdisciplinary dialogue between sociologists of immigrant adaptation and public health researchers.

Large-scale Latino immigration is relatively recent and is rapidly evolving (e.g., the emergence of secondary destinations in addition to the traditional metro area gateways, the growth of non-Mexican Latin American immigration, and the resurgence of highly contentious immigration politics and policy debates). Because of this fluidity, understanding Latino immigration and Latino health often seems elusive. Therefore, the objective of this chapter is not to provide answers but to suggest research approaches that might enrich our inquiry into Latino health. Other chapters in this volume discuss in-depth important dimensions of the Latino experience in the United States, such as the demographics of the U.S. Latino population and immigrant adaptation. Here we discuss how these factors might influence Latino health and highlight some issues that are critical for understanding observed patterns of health in this population.

THE DEMOGRAPHICS AND SOCIOECONOMIC STATUS OF THE *U.S.* LATINO POPULATION

Latinos are the largest U.S. racial/ethnic minority group: 12.5% (35.3 million) of the U.S. population in 2000 and 24.4% (102.6 million) by 2050 (U.S. Census Bureau, 2004). The foreign-born from Latin America represent 52.2% of the total U.S. foreign-born population (32.5 million; 11.5% of the total U.S. population) (Schmidley, 2003; U.S. Census Bureau, 2003b). Mexicans comprise 66.9% of the U.S. Latino population (25.1 million) and 8.9% of the total U.S. population. Given the size of the Mexican-origin population, discussions of Latino immigration and health often focus on this Latino subgroup. In other cases, Latinos are not disaggregated by national origin, which might conceal important variation across Latino subgroups.

During 1970–2000, the first generation (i.e., foreign-born Latinos) contributed 45% of the growth of the Latino population, whereas the second generation (i.e., U.S.-born Latinos of immigrant parents) contributed 25%. In contrast, in 2000–2020, the second generation will contribute 47% of the growth of the Latino population, whereas the first generation will contribute only 28%. The second generation will surpass the first generation in size by 2020 (Suro & Passel, 2003). Given that foreign-born Latinos appear to have a health advantage over U.S.-born Latinos, the increase in the second generation might have implications for the health status of Latinos.

Overall, Latinos experience low socioeconomic status (SES) (Ramirez & De la Cruz, 2003). In 2002, among those aged 25+ years, 27% of Latinos had not completed ninth grade, whereas only 4% of non-Hispanic Whites had such low educational attainment. The Mexican-origin population is more likely to be of low SES than other Latino subgroups.

LATINO HEALTH PARADOXES

Some patterns in Latino health have received attention because they appear to contradict our expectations based on the well-documented social gradient in health [i.e., individuals of a higher SES have better health than those of a lower SES (Berkman & Kawachi, 2000) and the pervasive patterns of poor health among African Americans vis-à-vis Whites (Williams, 2001)]. However, the question of Latino health paradoxes is far from settled due to ambiguity in the definition(s) of paradox, limited comparable empirical evidence, limited testing of possible explanations for it, and limited discussion of its policy and intervention applications (Franzini, Ribble, & Keddie, 2001; Palloni & Arias, 2004 Palloni & Morenoff, 2001; Jasso et al., 2004).

TOWARD A WORKING DEFINITION OF LATINO HEALTH PARADOXES

The term *health* or *epidemiologic paradox* typically refers to a pattern of morbidity and/or mortality for a particular group (e.g., Latinos, immigrants) that is at odds with what would be expected given its socioeconomic profile. However, definitions and reference groups are often not explicit and might vary from study to study. For example, epidemiologic paradoxes are sometimes defined in relation to the *average* SES of a population group (e.g., it is paradoxical that Latinos have low rates of low birth weight given that, on average, they have a low SES). In other cases, the term *paradox* is used to denote a *residual protective effect* of Latino (or foreign-born) status that cannot be accounted for by measured demographic, socioeconomic, behavioral, and/or medical risk factors.

Because the notion of a health paradox presumes a socioeconomic gradient in health, an important first step should entail examining whether the association between SES and health is different among Latinos than among other racial/ethnic groups. Ideally, understanding Latino health paradoxes requires addressing the combined effects of race/ethnicity, immigrant status (i.e., nativity), and SES on health outcomes.

A significant issue in the study of health paradoxes is the choice of an appropriate reference group. Some studies have compared immigrants with the majority (i.e., U.S.-born non-Hispanic White) population, whereas others have compared immigrants to their U.S.-born racial/ethnic counterparts (e.g., foreign-born Mexicans to U.S.-born Mexicans) or to other U.S.-born racial/ethnic minorities (e.g., African Americans). Social science and health research on immigrant adaptation suggests that all these comparisons might be important, because Latino immigrants follow multiple adaptation pathways, including *assimilation* into the majority culture and preservation of an ethnic identity and assimilation into a U.S.-born ethnic minority group (Portes & Rumbaut, 2001a). Additionally, intergenerational comparisons within a given national-origin group allow us to test whether there is intergenerational advancement in health (or other) outcomes (Smith, 2003).

As described below, research has documented that Latino immigrants often exhibit a health advantage over non-Latinos and their U.S.-born counterparts. The protective effect of immigrant status though is not exclusive to Latinos. For some outcomes, immigrants of other racial/ethnic groups have also been shown to exhibit better health than their U.S.-born counterparts. A central research question is the extent to which Latino health paradoxes are related to Latino ethnicity versus immigration. Given that Latino health paradoxes are often attributed to cultural and/or social factors presumed to be specific to Latinos, the comparison with other immigrant groups might help clarify the role of such factors vis-à-vis immigrant health selectivity.

EMPIRICAL EVIDENCE ON LATINO HEALTH PARADOXES

Due to limited comparability across studies and the variety of health outcomes examined, it is difficult to characterize the empirical evidence on Latino health paradoxes. The fact that a U.S.-born comparison group is not used consistently across studies alone makes it difficult to draw conclusions about the extent and nature of these "paradoxes." Several review articles (Franzini, Ribble, & Keddie, 2001; Hayes-Bautista, 2002; Jasso et al., 2004; Palloni & Arias, 2004 Palloni & Morenoff, 2001) indicate that there is evidence that some Latino health outcomes exhibit paradoxical patterns. Instead of offering another review of the literature, this chapter presents some examples of mortality and health outcomes for which a Latino health advantage has been documented. We focus on highlighting the questions that should inform future research on Latino health.

Adult Mortality

Based on the National Longitudinal Mortality Study (1979–1989), Singh and Siahpush (2001) found that all-cause mortality was significantly lower among immigrants than among the U.S.-born (18% lower for men and 13% lower for women), after adjusting for age, race/ethnicity, marital status, urban/rural residence, education, occupation, and family income. Black and Latino immigrant men (47% and 22% lower, respectively) and women (45% and 37% lower, respectively) exhibited a stronger reduction in mortality risk vis-à-vis their U.S.-born counterparts than immigrant White men (17% lower) and women (11% lower). Compared with U.S.-born whites of equivalent socioeconomic and demographic background, foreign-born Blacks, Latinos, Asians/Pacific Islanders (APIs), and Whites had respectively 48%, 45%, 43%, and 16% lower mortality risks. U.S.-born APIs and U.S.-born Hispanics also had lower mortality risk than comparable U.S.-born whites (32%, and 26%, respectively), whereas U.S.-born Blacks had an 8% higher mortality risk (Singh & Siahpush, 2002).

Research by Singh and Siahpush (2001) highlighted the need to study Latino health using as a comparison the experience of other racial/ethnic groups. The mortality data discussed earlier suggest that both Latino immigrants and U.S.-born Latinos have a health advantage over U.S.-born whites of comparable SES. However, the health advantage of Latino immigrants over Whites appears greater than that of U.S.-born Latinos.

Infant Health

Several studies have documented that infants born to Latino immigrant women tend to have better birth outcomes [i.e., lower rates of low birth weight (birth weight <2,500 g; LBW) and infant mortality (death during the first year of life)], than infants of U.S.-born women (Acevedo-Garcia, Soobader, & Berkman, 2005). In the 2004 Pediatric Nutrition Surveillance System, the crude prevalence of LBW was highest among Black infants (13.1%) and lowest among Latinos (7.6%), with White (8.8%) and API (8.3%) infants falling in the middle.

Using data from the 1998 Vital Statistics, Acevedo-Garcia and colleagues (Acevedo-Garcia, Soobader, & Berkman, 2005) showed that although immigrant status was not protective against LBW among Whites and it increased the risk among Asians by 24%, it reduced the risk by about 25% among Blacks and by about 19% among Latinos, after adjusting for maternal age, prenatal care, health behaviors and medical risk factors during pregnancy, and education. By educational attainment, for Whites, Blacks, and Latinos, the protective effect of foreign-born status was stronger among women with low education (i.e., 0–11 years) than among women with more education. The association between maternal education and LBW was less pronounced among foreign-born White, Black, and Hispanic women than among their U.S.-born counterparts. Although there was a clear negative education gradient (i.e., LBW rates decreased as education level increased) among U.S.-born women in these three racial/ethnic groups, the gradient was less pronounced among foreign-born Whites and Blacks and nearly flat among foreign-born Hispanics. This research illustrates again that the health advantage of immigrants vis-à-vis the U.S.-born is not confined to Latinos. Here, as in the above mortality example, the immigrant health advantage was strongest among Blacks. Also, instead of merely controlling for SES, this research examined whether the effect of SES on health is different among immigrants than among the US-born. It appears that a low SES increases the risk of LBW among U.S.-born Latinos but not Latino immigrants.

Additionally, the research on infant health outcomes has shown that there are variations across Latino subgroups. Immigrant status is associated with a reduced risk of LBW among Mexicans by about 20% but does not seem to be protective against LBW among other Latino subgroups (i.e., Puerto Ricans, Cubans, and Central/South Americans) (Acevedo-Garcia, Soobader, & Berkman, in press).

Health Behaviors

Some studies suggest that Latinos and immigrants have more positive health behaviors, particularly related to substance use, than their non-Latino and U.S.-born counterparts. For example, compared to non-Latino whites, Latinos are less likely to consume cigarettes or alcohol, independent of SES (Abraido-Lanza, Chao, & Florez, 2005). Foreign nativity has also been found to be protective for illicit drug use among Mexican Americans, particularly women (Vega et al., 1998). Data from the 1995–1996 Tobacco Use Supplement of the Current Population Survey indicated that for all racial/ethnic groups, smoking rates were lower among first-generation immigrants (foreign born) and also among the second generation (those born in the United States of foreign-born parents) than among the third generation (those born in the United States of U.S.-born parents) (Acevedo-Garcia, Pan, et al., 2005).

The protective effect of being second generation or of being foreign born varied across racial/ethnic groups. For Whites, Asians, and Latinos being second generation or being foreign born were similarly protective against smoking. In contrast, for Blacks, although being foreign born was highly protective, being second generation was not. The protective effect of foreign-born status was highest for Blacks [odds ratio (OR) = 0.32] and lowest for Whites (OR = 0.77), whereas Asians (OR = 0.45) and Latinos (OR = 0.42) fell in the middle.

Mental Health

Research also suggests that Latino ethnicity and foreign nativity might be protective against psychiatric disorders. In broad racial/ethnic comparisons, "Hispanics" as well as non-Hispanic Blacks were at lower risk for disorders such as depression, generalized anxiety disorder, and social phobia compared to non-Hispanic Whites (Breslau et al., 2006). In national estimates, foreign-born Mexicans were at lower risk for substance use and mood and anxiety disorders compared to their U.S.-born counterparts, and U.S.-born Mexican Americans were, in turn, at lower risk than U.S.-born non-Hispanic Whites (Grant et al., 2004). Once again, however, it is not clear that this relative advantage extends to all Latinos (Ortega et al., 2000) or, conversely, that it is unique to Mexican Americans; foreign nativity has also been shown to be protective for non-Hispanic Whites (Grant et al., 2004).

Challenges to Latino Health

Although the focus of this chapter is on Latino health paradoxes, it is essential to recognize that there are health conditions for which Latinos do not exhibit a health advantage [e.g. diabetes, obesity, human immunodeficiency virus/autoimmunodeficiency syndrome (HIV/AIDS)]. In some cases (e.g., overweight/obesity) although Latino immigrants show lower rates than U.S.-born

Latinos, the rates among both groups are high from a clinical perspective as well as compared to other racial/ethnic groups. National estimates show the prevalence of obesity (among Mexican Americans) to be comparable to that of non-Hispanic Whites in 2001–2002 (31.0% and 30.2%, respectively) but considerably higher in 2003–2004 (36.8% compared to 31.0%, respectively) (Ogden et al., 2006). In 2002–2003, the prevalence of obesity among Latinos overall was 29.1%, compared to 9.4% among Asian Americans (Bates et al., 2008). These data also reveal dramatic increases in obesity among Latinos with each generation in the United States, ranging from 25.4% among the foreign-born to 35.7% in the third generation (U.S. born with two U.S.-born parents) (Bates et al., 2008). A similar pattern is suggested by analyses showing that obesity appears to increase among immigrants with years in the United States (Antecol & Bedard, 2006; Goel, McCarthy, Phillips, & Wee, 2004).

There are also health conditions for which some Latino subgroups show a disadvantage while other Latino subgroups show an advantage. For instance, although Puerto Ricans are the U.S. racial/ethnic group with the highest adult asthma rate (17% vs. a national average of 8.9%), Mexicans have the lowest rate (3.9%) (Rose, Mannino, & Leaderer, 2006). Whereas Puerto Rican children have the highest prevalence of lifetime asthma (26%), compared with Black children (16%) and White children (13%), Mexican children have the lowest prevalence (10%) (Lara et al., 2006).

Similarly, the attention toward Latino health paradoxes should not make us overlook the considerable barriers facing the Latino population: the highest health uninsurance rates (Brown & Yu, 2002); large numbers of individuals with undocumented immigrant status; and limited access to social benefits for immigrants who entered the United States after the 1996 Welfare Reform Act (Fix & Passel, 2002). For example, among individuals under 65 years, Mexicans have the lowest rate of health insurance (less than 60%), compared to both of the other Latino subgroups, such as Cubans (75%) and Puerto Ricans (85%), and to non-Hispanic Whites (87%) (National Center for Health Statistics, Centers for Disease Control and Prevention and Services, 2002). Also, certain Latino subpopulations, such as migrant farm workers (Villarejo, 2003) and residents of *colonias* along the Mexico-U.S. border (Weinberg et al., 2004) are at high risk for dangerous occupational and environmental exposures, such as musculoskeletal disorders, infectious diseases, and injuries.

PROPOSED EXPLANATIONS FOR LATINO HEALTH PARADOXES

There are least three types of explanation for Latino health paradoxes. First, some studies maintain that paradoxes are due to *cultural and/or social protective factors* (Hayes-Bautista, 2002), such as social support, familism, religion, and norms related to diet and substance use. This hypothesis is often presented in association with an acculturation hypothesis—that is, that there is an erosion of such protective factors with time spent in the United States (within one generation) and across generations, which results in a deterioration of health outcomes. Some studies have shown that the initial health advantage that Latino immigrants have over their U.S.-born counterparts declines with length of residence and/or in subsequent generations. However, acculturation is often poorly defined and is operationalized through demographic and/or English-language-use proxy indicators (Hunt, Schneider, & Corner, 2004). Some health research also tends to romanticize the experience of being a Latino immigrant, by speculating about (but rarely measuring) the role that social networks and families might play in protecting health while ignoring that socioeconomic hardship and tenuous immigration status might severely compromise the effectiveness of these social supports (Menjivar, 2000).

Second, several authors contend that health paradoxes arise from a process of *healthy immigrant selection*. According to this view, some patterns in Latino health indeed run against our expectations based on social epidemiologic regularities observed in other populations, but they should not be interpreted as paradoxical because they reflect this selection effect (Palloni & Morenoff, 2001). A parallel selection process might also yield an "unhealthy remigration effect." There is evidence that the likelihood of staying in the destination country or reemigrating occurs selectively (Lindstrom, 1996) in ways that might similarly correspond to health status.

Third, some researchers suggest that paradoxical patterns might be due to data artifacts, including undercount of Latino deaths, inconsistent definitions of Latino identity (e.g., self-identification vs. Latino surnames), and underreporting of health problems (Franzini, Ribble, & Keddie, 2001; Jasso et al., 2004; Palloni & Morenoff, 2001). Additionally, some nonhealth studies of Mexican intergenerational performance suggest that inappropriate cross-sectional comparisons might create an erroneous impression of deterioration in health outcomes across generations (Jasso et al., 2004).

LIMITATIONS OF RESEARCH ON LATINO HEALTH

For the most part, the possible explanations for Latino health paradoxes have not been empirically tested, due to the interplay of conceptual and data limitations. Palloni and Morenoff (2001) argued that testing of these hypotheses might be precluded by a tendency to prematurely dismiss selection and data artifacts as possible mechanisms. Our reading of the relevant literature indicates that studies that advance selection as a possible explanation also dismiss complementary and/or alternative explanations, such as social and cultural factors. A tendency in some studies is to exclude the possibility that several mechanisms might be operating simultaneously and/or to acknowledge that with the data at hand, the ability to test for competing explanations is limited.

Other conceptual issues seem to prevent a more comprehensive examination of Latino health paradoxes. The notion of "acculturation" has been used in health research with a limited attention to its conceptualization. Often, immigrant health outcomes are examined with a focus on demographic variables or English use as markers for acculturation, without considering the broader concept of immigrant adaptation (i.e., social integration) as postulated, for example, in the segmented assimilation theory (Portes & Rumbaut, 2001a). Encouragingly, though, health studies have begun to address socioeconomic factors, contextual factors, and discrimination in the host society along with acculturation (Arcia et al., 2001). For instance, Finch, Kolody, & Vega (2000) showed that perceived discrimination and acculturative stress had independent effects on depression among Mexican-origin adults in California.

Another conceptual limitation, strongly influenced by lack of relevant data, is the limited attention paid to the country of origin background and influence. Some studies have begun to examine Latino health in relation to the immigrants' country of origin. Using health data for Mexico and the United States, Soldo, Wong, and Palloni (2002) examined the health of Mexican immigrants in the United States vis-à-vis their nonimmigrant counterparts in Mexico and those immigrants to the United States who did return to Mexico. Increasingly, health researchers realize that a meaningful examination of immigrant health will require health data on the origin and destination countries.

TESTING POSSIBLE EXPLANATIONS FOR LATINO HEALTH PARADOXES

Although it appears that for various health outcomes, Latino and/or foreign-born Latino status confer a protective effect, new research designs are needed to test possible explanations. For instance, on average, immigrants might have better health than those in their country of origin who do not migrate and than those immigrants who return to their country of origin. Ideally, in order to explore the issue of selection, we would like to compare health outcomes among the foreign-born from a given country of origin with their U.S.-born ethnic counterparts, as well as with comparable individuals in their country of origin, including both those who have never migrated and return migrants. If we are interested in testing the effect of immigrant adaptation on health outcomes, we need longitudinal study designs that allow the long-term follow-up of immigrant trajectories since arrival in the United States. The New Immigrant Survey (Jasso et al., 2000) will allow such analyses for several documented immigrant cohorts.

To date, research has suggested intriguing patterns in Latino health, but the findings are open to different interpretations. In our research, we have found that education gradients in LBW are considerably attenuated among immigrant women (Latino and non-Latino) compared to their U.S.-born counterparts (Acevedo-Garcia, Soobader et al., 2005; Acevedo-Garcia et al., in press). This pattern leaves room for several explanations. If immigrant women are selected for being healthier or having better health behaviors across education levels, such health selection might override the education gradient. If, as suggested by Jasso et al. (2004), there is a minimum health level that would make migration worthwhile, selection might limit the dispersion in health outcomes among immigrants, thus flattening SES gradients. Alternatively, if present across SES levels, protective cultural factors might attenuate SES gradients.

Some studies have integrated data from multiple sources with the development of migration models of health selectivity (Jasso et al., 2004) or simulation exercises (Palloni & Morenoff, 2001). These studies strongly suggest that paradoxical patterns in Latino health could result from migrant health selection. Some data presented to support this view are suggestive but not conclusive. Jasso et al. (2004) have shown that foreign-born Latinos (and Asians) in the United States have higher life expectancy than their U.S.-born counterparts and than those in their sending regions. Although compelling, these data do not prove that the health advantage among the foreign-born is driven entirely or even primarily by immigrant selection.

Disentangling the potential effects on health of selection processes, immigration, and long-term adaptation in the receiving country is at best only approximated by existing study designs. Currently available data do not allow definitive determination of the causal role of any of these factors; theory would suggest that all three play a role to some degree and that the relative influence of each might vary by immigrant subgroup. For example, the selection hypothesis suggests that, other factors being equal, health selection would be stronger among immigrant groups that have to overcome greater obstacles (e.g., longer distances) to migrate to the United States. The evidence of health paradoxes among Mexicans might not be consistent with this logic. Until the mid-1980s, border controls along the Mexico-U.S. border were relatively loose, and Mexican immigration was dominated by a largely male-initiated, *circular* migration flow (seeking work in the United States during a specific season) (Massey, Durand, & Malone, 2002). Despite the relative smoothness that characterized Mexican migration to the United States prior to 1986, there is empirical evidence of health paradoxes among Mexicans. In fact, the articulation of the Latino health paradox has been based largely on the Mexican case.

DIRECTIONS FOR FUTURE RESEARCH

Research on Latino health paradoxes might benefit from better explicit definitions of what is meant by health paradox, including the variables involved (e.g., race/ethnicity, immigrant status, SES), the group of interest, and the reference group (Palloni & Morenoff, 2001). Research questions should involve both the verification of Latino health paradoxes and their possible explanations. Ideally, studies should simultaneously and rigorously address the three types of explanation discussed earlier and allow for the possibility that more than one explanation might account for the observed patterns. Exploring possible explanations for Latino health paradoxes should involve explicit definitions (and sound operationalization) of concepts such as "acculturation," "protective cultural factors," and "social support." Qualitative study designs might allow a better conceptualization and measurement of protective factors at the individual level, as well as various contextual levels (e.g., family, neighborhood). For example, although it is often assumed that social networks are supportive, under economic hardship and unfavorable contexts of reception, immigrant social networks might offer limited support (Menjivar, 2000). Therefore, examining the role of social factors in Latino health paradoxes might require measuring the structure of social networks, the content of their exchanges in different contexts, and specifically how these exchanges benefit (or hinder) health.

EXPLICIT RESEARCH DESIGNS TO STUDY LATINO IMMIGRANTS AND THEIR ADAPTATION

Health researchers should be more proactive, incorporating theories and research designs that have been fruitful in the study of Latino immigrant adaptation. Only recently, new health surveys have begun to incorporate such information. The National Latino and Asian American Study (NLAAS) is a nationally representative study of psychiatric morbidity and mental health service use among Latino and Asian American adults that samples eight ethnic subgroups (Puerto Ricans, Cubans, Mexicans, other Latinos, Chinese, Filipinos, Vietnamese, and other Asians). The survey was administered in five languages and provides extensive data on immigration parameters (e.g., generation status, length of time in the United States, citizenship), acculturation processes, SES, and important aspects of immigrants' experience of the social context (e.g., social capital and support, and perceptions of discrimination and neighborhood safety) (Alegria et al., 2004). Similarly, studies of immigrant adaptation such as the New Immigrant Survey (Jasso et al., 2000), a longitudinal study of several documented immigrant cohorts, have begun to include extensive questions on health status, health behaviors, and access to health care before and after immigration to the United States.

As noted earlier, previous research has highlighted heterogeneity in health outcomes among Hispanics/Latinos showing, for example, a higher burden of asthma, LBW, and self-reported physical limitations among Puerto Ricans on the U.S. mainland (Hajat, Lucas, & Kington, 2000; Mendoza et al., 1991 Rose, Mannino, & Leaderer, 2006) and higher levels of obesity among U.S.-born Mexican Americans (Bates et al., 2008). However, nationally representative prevalence data accounting for the full heterogeneity of Latinos are rare, and sample size limitations almost always preclude analyses of subgroup differences in health determinants. Study designs should ideally allow comparisons across various national-origin groups and among immigrants with different durations in the United States, their U.S.-born ethnic counterparts (including the second generation), their nonmigrant counterparts in the country of origin, and return migrants. Due to the large size of the Mexican-origin population, any distinct pattern among Mexicans is likely to dominate patterns among Latinos overall. Differences across Latino subgroups might reflect differences in country of origin background factors, migration experiences, as well as incorporation into U.S. society. Puerto Ricans constitute an important subgroup both because they often have unfavorable health outcomes compared to other Latino groups and because they can serve as a reference group to test the selection hypothesis. As U.S. citizens, Puerto Ricans face relatively lower obstacles to migration to the mainland and therefore might be less health selected—or selected differently—than other Latino subgroups.

There is also need for studies that address the issue of immigration broadly and allow us to compare Latino health paradoxes for different outcomes to the health profiles and trajectories of other immigrant groups and to examine what individual and contextual factors account for any differences. The NLAAS (Alegria et al., 2004) and the New Immigrant Survey (Jasso et al., 2000) constitute important steps in this direction.

The lack of longitudinal data on immigrant health is a significant limitation. Important developments in sociological research on immigrant adaptation have relied on longitudinal surveys that collect information from immigrant parents and their children on various domains of life such as family relations, employment, and school performance (Portes & Rumbaut, 2001b; Suarez-Orozco & Suarez-Orozco, 2001). In addition to longitudinal studies, using sound analytic methods to make proper intergenerational comparisons might lead to reassessing whether health and other outcomes deteriorate across generations (Alba et al, 2006; Jasso et al., 2004). Studying intergenerational health patterns in light of differences in the context of immigration might help us assess the role of selection. For example, Mexicans who migrated to the United States after stricter border controls were implemented in 1986 (Massey, Durand, & Malone, 2002) might be more health-selected than those who migrated earlier.

IMPLICATIONS OF LATINO HEALTH PARADOXES
IN THE CONTEXT OF DEMOGRAPHIC CHANGE

Why should we pay attention to Latino health paradoxes? Given the growing demographic significance of the Latino population, the apparent resilience of Latinos in relation to some health outcomes might imply that the health of the overall U.S. population is considerably better than it would have been if Latinos did not have paradoxical health outcomes. Consider, for example, the relatively low rates of LBW among Latino women with less than a high school education (Acevedo-Garcia, Soobader et al., 2005). Given that 43% of U.S. Hispanic women have less than high school education (U.S. Census Bureau, 2003b), what would be the implications if Latino women with limited education had the high rates of LBW of U.S.-born White women or African American women with the same educational attainment?

Because it appears that the first generation has a better health profile than Latinos born in the United States, the rapid growth in the second generation might imply that the health profile of the total U.S. Latino population might worsen over time, assuming no persistence of health paradoxes from the first into the second generation. Neither the selection nor acculturation hypotheses explicitly negate the possibility of preserving the foreign-born health advantage into the second generation and beyond. The presumed bases for health selection are not well specified in the literature, but both genes and behaviors consistent with good health can potentially be passed on to subsequent generations. However, empirical evidence to date, although limited, is not consistent with this scenario. Further research should clarify whether this apparent deterioration in health across generations is real and inevitable or whether in fact through immigration policies and programs that facilitate successful immigrant adaptation (e.g., by strengthening immigrant families; Portes & Rumbaut, 2001a), the health advantages of the foreign born could be sustained.

REFERENCES

Abraido-Lanza, A. F., Chao, M. T., & Florez, K. R. (2005). Do Healthy Behaviors Decline with Greater Acculturation? Implications for the Latino Mortality Paradox. *Social Science and Medicine, 61*(6), 1243–1255.

Acevedo-Garcia, D., Pan, J., Jun, H. J., Osypuk, T. L., & Emmons, K. M. (2005). The Effect of Immigrant Generation on Smoking. *Social Science and Medicine, 61*(6), 1223–1242.

Acevedo-Garcia, D., Soobader, M. J., & Berkman, L. F. (2005). The Differential Effect of Foreign-Born Status on Low-Birthweight by Race/Ethnicity and Education. *Pediatrics, 115*, e20–e30.

Acevedo-Garcia, D., Soobader, M. J., & Berkman, L. F. (in press). Low Birthweight Among US Hispanic/Latino Subgroups: The Effect of Maternal Foreign-Born Status and Education. *Social Science and Medicine*.

Alba, R. D., Abdel-Hady, D., Islam, T., & Marotz, K. (2006). Downward Assimilation and Mexican-Americans: An Examination of Intergenerational Advance and Stagnation in Educational Attainment. In Alba, R. and Waters, M. (Eds.), *Proceedings from the Second Generation Conference*.

Alegria, M., Takeuchi, D., Canino, G., Duan, N., Shrout, P., Meng, X., Vega. W., Zane, N., Vila, D., Woo, M., Vera, M., Guarnaccia, P., Aguilar-Gaxiola, S., Sue, S., Escobar, J., Lin, K., & Gong, F. (2004). Considering Context, Place and Culture: the National Latino and Asian American Study. *International Journal of Methods in Psychiatric Research, 13*(4), 208–220.

Antecol, H., & Bedard, K. (2006). Unhealthy Assimilation: Why Do Immigrants Converge to American Health Status Levels? *Demography, 43*(2), 337–360.

Arcia, E., Skinner, M., Bailey, D., & Correa, V. (2001). Models of Acculturation and Health Behaviors Among Latino Immigrants to the US. *Social Science and Medicine, 53*(1), 41–53.

Bates, L., Acevedo-Garcia, D., Alegria, M., & Krieger, N. (forthcoming Jan, 2008). Immigration and Generational Trends in Body Mass Index and Obesity in the United States: Results of the National Latino and Asian-American Survey (NLAAS), 2002–2003. *American Journal of Public Health*.

Berkman, L., & Kawachi, I. (Eds.). (2000). *Social Epidemiology*. New York: Oxford University Press.

Breslau, J., Aquilar-Gaxiola, S., Kendler, K., Su, M., Williams, D., & Kessler, R. (2006). Specifying Race-Ethnic Differences in Risks for Psychiatric Disorder in a USA National Sample. *Psychological Medicine 36*(1), 57–68.

Brown, E. R., & Yu, H. (2002). Latinos'' Access To Employment-Based Health Insurance. In M. M. Suarez-Orozco & M. Paez (Eds.), *Latinos Remaking America* (pp. 215–235). Berkeley: University of California Press; David Rockefeller Center for Latin American Studies.

Finch, B., Kolody, B., & Vega, W. (2000). Perceived Discrimination and Depression Among Mexican-Origin Adults in California. *Journal of Health and Social Behavior, 41*(3), 295–313.

Fix, M., & Passel, J. (2002). Assessing Welfare Reform's Immigrant Provisions. In A. Weil & K. Finegold (Eds.), *Welfare Reform: The Next Act* (pp. 179–202). Washington, DC: The Urban Institute.

Franzini, L., Ribble, J. C., & Keddie, A. M. (2001). Understanding the Hispanic Paradox. *Ethnicity and Disease, 11*(3), 496–518.

Goel, M. S., McCarthy, E., Phillips, R., & Wee, C. (2004). Obesity Among US Immigrant Subgroups by Duration of Residence. *Journal of the American Medical Association, 292*(23), 2860–2867.

Grant, B., Stinson, F., Hasin, D., Dawson, D., Chou, S., & Anderson, K. (2004). Immigration and Lifetime Prevalence of DSM-IV Psychiatric Disorders Among Mexican Americans and Non-Hispanic Whites in the United States: Results from the National Epidemiologic Survey on Alcohol and Related Conditions. *Archives of General Psychiatry, 61*(12), 1226–1233.

Hajat, A., Lucas, J. B., & Kington, R. (2000). Health Outcomes Among Hispanic Subgroups: Data from the National Health Interview Survey, 1002-95. *Advance Data, 310*, 1–14.

Hayes-Bautista, D. E. (2002). The Latino Health Research Agenda for the Twenty-first Century. In M. M. Suarez-Orozco & M. Paez (Eds.), *Latinos Remaking America* (pp. 215–235). Berkeley: University of California Press; David Rockefeller Center for Latin American Studies.

Hunt, L. M., Schneider, S., & Corner, B. (2004). Should "Acculturation" Be a Variable in Health Research? A Critical Review of Research on US Hispanics. *Social Science and Medicine, 59*(2004), 973–986.

Huntington, S. P. (2004). *Who Are We? The Challenges to America's National Identity*. New York: Simon and Schuster.

Jasso, G., Massey, D. S., Rosenzweig, M. R., & Smith, J. P. (2000). The New Immigrant Survey Pilot (NIS-P): Overview and New Findings about US Legal Immigrants at Admission. *Demography, 37*(1), 127–138.

Jasso, G., Massey, D. S., Rosenzweig, M. R., & Smith, J. P. (2004). Immigrant Health Selectivity and Acculturation. In N. B. Anderson, R. A. Bulatao, & B. Cohen, In Panel on Race Ethnicity and Health in Later Life and National Research Council (Eds.), *Critical Perspectives on Racial and Ethnic Differences in Health in Late Life* (pp. 227–266). Washington, DC: The National Academies Press.

Lara, M., Akinbami, L., Flores, G., & Morgenstern, H. (2006). Heterogeneity of Childhood Asthma Among Hispanic Children: Puerto Rican Children Bear a disproportionate Burden. *Pediatrics, 117*(1), 43–53.

Lindstrom, D. P. (1996). Economic Opportunity in Mexico and Return Migration from the United States. *Demography, 33*(3), 367–374.

Massey, D. S., Durand, J., & Malone, N. J. (2002). *Beyond Smoke and Mirrors: Mexican Immigration in an Era of Economic Integration*. New York: Russell Sage Foundation.

Mendoza, F. S., Ventura, S. J., Valdez, R. B., Castillo, R. O., Saldivar, L. E., Baisden, K., & Martorell, R. (1991). Selected Measures of Health Status for Mexican-American, Mainland Puerto Rican, and Cuban-American Children. *Journal of the American Medical Association, 265*(2), 227–232.

Menjivar, C. (2000). *Fragmented Ties: Salvadoran Immigrant Networks in America*. Berkeley: University of California Press.

National Center for Health Statistics, Centers for Disease Control and Prevention, Department of Health and Human Services. (2002). A Demographic and Health Snapshot of the U.S. Hispanic/Latino Population. 2002 National Hispanic Health Leadership Summit, National Center for Health Statistics, Centers for Disease Control and Prevention, 2006. Retrieved July 17, 2006, from http://www.cdc.gov/NCHS/data/ hpdata2010/chcsummit.pdf.

Ogden, C., Carroll, M., Curtin, L., McDowell, M., Tabak, C., & Flegal, K. (2006). Prevalence of Overweight and Obesity in the United States, 1999–2004. *Journal of the American Medical Association, 295*(13), 1549–1555.

Ortega, A. N., Rosenheck, R., Alegria, M., & Desai, R. A. (2000). Acculturation and the Lifetime Risk of Psychiatric and substance Use Disorders Among Hispanics. *Journal of Nervous and Mental Disease, 188*(11), 728–735.

Palloni, A., & Arias, E. (2004). Paradox Lost: Explaining the Hispanic Adult Mortality Advantage. *Demography, 41*(3), 385–415.

Palloni, A., & Morenoff, J. D. (2001). Interpreting the Paradoxical in the Hispanic Paradox: Demographic and Epidemiologic Approaches. *Annals of the New York Academy of Sciences, 954*, 140–174.

Portes, A., & Rumbaut, R. G. (2001a). *Legacies: The Story of the Immigrant Second Generation*. Los Angeles: University of California Press, Russell Sage Foundation.

Portes, A., & Rumbaut, R. G. (2001b). *The New Americans*. Los Angeles: University of California Press, Russell Sage Foundation.

Ramirez, R. R., & De la Cruz, G. P. (2003). *The Hispanic Population in the United States: March 2002* (U.S. Census Bureau No. 8). Washington, DC: Government Printing Office.

Rose, D., Mannino, D., & Leaderer, B. (2006). Asthma Prevalence Among US Adults, 1998–2000: Role of Puerto Rican Ethnicity and Behavioral and Geographic Factors. *American Journal of Public Health, 96*(5), 880–888.

Rumbaut, R. G. (1999). Assimilation and Its Discontents: Ironies and Paradoxes. In C. Hirschman, J. Dewind, & P. Kasinitz, (Eds.), *The Handbook of International Migration: The American Experience* (pp. 172–195). New York: Russell Sage Foundation.

Schmidley, A. D. (2003). *The Foreign-Born Population in the United States: March 2002* (U.S. Census Bureau No. 70). Washington, DC: Government Printing Office. Retrieved July 17, 2006, from http://www.census.gov/prod/ 2003pubs/p20-539.pdf.

Singh, G. K., & Siahpush, M. (2001). All-Cause and cause-Specific Mortality of Immigrants and Native Born in the United States. *American Journal of Public Health, 91*(3), 392–399.

Singh, G. K., & Siahpush, M. (2002). Ethnic-Immigrant Differentials In Health Behaviors, Morbidity, and Cause-Specific Mortality in the United States: An Analysis of Two National Data Bases. *Human Biology, 74*(1), 83–109.

Smith, J. P. (2003). Assimilation Across the Latino Generations. *AEA Papers and Proceedings, 93*(May), 315–319.

Soldo, B., Wong, R., & Palloni, A. (2002). Migrant Health Selection: Evidence from Mexico and the US. Annual Meetings of the Population Association of America, Atlanta, GA, May 9–11.

Suarez-Orozco, C., & Suarez-Orozco, M. M. (2001). *Children of Immigration*. Cambridge, MA: Harvard University Press.

Suarez-Orozco, M. M., & Paez, M. (Eds.). (2002). *Latinos Remaking America*. Berkeley, CA: University of California Press, David Rockefeller Center for Latin American Studies.

Suro, R., & Passel, J. S. (2003). *The Rise of the Second Generation: Changing Patterns in Hispanic Population Growth*. Washington, DC: Pew Hispanic Center.

U.S. Census Bureau. (2003b). Table 7.2. Educational Attainment of the Population Age 25 years and over by Sex and Hispanic Origin Type: March 2002, U.S. Census Bureau, Population Division, Ethnic & Hispanic Statistics Branch, 2005. Available at: http://www.census.gov/population/socdemo/hispanic/pp1–165/tab07–2.pdf.

U.S. Census Bureau. (2004). Table 1a. Projected Population of the United States, by Race and Hispanic Origin: 2000 to 2050, U.S. Interim Projections by Age, Sex, Race, and Hispanic Origin, Washington, DC: US Census Bureau. Retrieved July 17, 2006, from http://www.census.gov/ipc/www/usinterimproj/natprojtab01a.pdf.

Vega, W.A., Alderete, E., Kolody, B., & Aguilar-Gaxiola, S. (1998). Illicit drug use among Mexicans and Mexican Americans in California: The Effects of Gender and Acculturation. *Addiction, 93*(12), 1839–1850.

Villarejo, D. (2003). The Health of U.S. Hired Farm Workers. *Annual Review of Public Health, 24*, 175–193.

Weinberg, M., Hopkins, J., Farrington, L., Gresham, L., Ginsberg, M., & Bell, B. (2004). Hepatitis A in Hispanic Children Who Live Along the United States-Mexico Border: The Role of International Travel and Food-Borne Exposures. *Pediatrics, 114*(1), e68–e73.

Williams, D. R. (2001). Racial Variations in Adult Health Status: Patterns, Paradoxes, and Prospects. In N. J. Smelser, W. J. Wilson, F. Mitchell, & National Research Council (Eds.), *America Becoming: Racial Trends and Their Consequences* (pp. 371–410). Washington, DC: National Academy Press.

CHAPTER 8

Latino Crime and Delinquency in the United States

Ramiro Martinez, Jr.

INTRODUCTION

There are considerable race and ethnic disparities in violence across the nation. Public health data illustrate that Latinos were three times *more* likely than non-Latino Whites to be a victim of homicide but almost three times *less* likely than Blacks to be killed (Keppel, Pearcy, & Wagenar, 2002). More recent national crime victimization surveys indicate that Latinos and Blacks were victims of robbery at similarly high rates, but Latinos were victims of aggravated assault at a level comparable to that of Whites and Blacks (Catalano, 2006). These differences remind us that social science research on racial/ethnic variations in crime must incorporate Latinos and consider variations within Latino groups in order to fully understand group differences in criminal and delinquent behavior.

Indeed, research on Latinos and violent crime has been lagging behind that of Black or White violent crime even in the face of long-held beliefs and stereotypes about crime-prone Latinos by some politicians and the mass media (for details, see Martinez, 2002, 2006). A recent search of citations in *Social Science Full Text* produced 80 journal articles on Latinos/Hispanics and crime. In contrast, there were almost 700 journal articles on African Americans/Blacks and crime over the 1990–2006 period. The lack of criminological research on the Latino population limits our understanding of the sources and extent of racial and ethnic disparities in violent crime and serious delinquency research (Morenoff, 2005; Peterson & Krivo, 2005).

In this chapter, the key findings on Latinos and criminal or serious delinquent behavior in the United States are reviewed. The chapter begins by outlining the shape of ethnic disparities in violent crime and serious delinquent behavior; that is, Latino criminal activity relative to Whites,

Blacks, and "Other" race and within Latino groups from two major self-report surveys of victimization and offending. This is done to draw from some of the most extensive national sources of crime and delinquency while directing attention to Latinos in general and Latino groups specifically. This is followed by a discussion of the quantitative analyses that has focused on Latino or ethnic group comparisons because most of the work on ethnicity and violent crime directs attention to the impact of economic disadvantage or deprivation in Latino areas rather than individual level studies (Peterson & Krivo, 2005). Although qualitative and ethnographic studies are important to consider, they remain limited in number relative to quantitative studies on Latinos and crime (see Dohan, 2003, and Kil & Menjívar, 2006, for exceptions). The final section considers some initial results from an ongoing analysis of nonlethal violence reported to the police in two cities—Houston and Miami—and highlights findings on ethnic disparities in delinquent behavior among youths in Chicago neighborhoods. I close by highlighting the importance of policy and addressing issues for future research as well.

NATIONAL VICTIMIZATION SURVEY

The primary source of survey-based crime data in the United States is the National Crime Victimization Survey (NCVS), a nationally representative study of person and household victimization administered by the U.S. Census Bureau. Unlike the Uniform Crime Reports (UCR), which is regarded as the primary source of official crime data in the United States,[1] the NCVS records the race (White, Black, or Other) and "Hispanic" origin of the victim (Hispanic or non-Hispanic). The incorporation of ethnicity in the NCVS that permits estimates of both racial and ethnic differences[2] in crime or criminal victimization probably makes this survey the leading source of Hispanic/Latino crime across the United States.

Table 1 summarizes violent crime rates based on the 2005 NCVS. Other researchers have noted that racial and ethnic disparities are usually not as heightened in the NCVS as they are in official police crime or arrest statistics, and that is probably the case for most types of criminal victimization, but attention here is directed to violence because the literature on Latinos and property or minor crimes is almost nonexistent (Morenoff, 2005). African Americans, or Blacks, are more likely than Whites to be victims of crime and, this difference is greater for violent crimes than it is for property crimes. Similar to the UCR police data, racial differences in the

TABLE 1. NCVS Rates of Violent Crime by Race and Ethnicity, 2005

	Victim race			Victim ethnicity	
	White	Black	Other	Hispanic	Non-Hispanic
All violent	20.1	27.0	13.9	25.0	20.6
Rape/sexual assault	0.6	1.8	0.5	1.1	0.7
Robbery	2.2	4.6	3.0	4.0	2.4
All assaults	17.2	20.6	10.4	19.9	17.5
Aggravated assault	3.8	7.6	2.5	5.9	4.1
Simple assault	13.4	13.0	7.9	14.0	13.4

Note: Victim rates for violent crimes are per 1,000 persons age 12 years or older.
Source: National Crime Victimization Survey, 2005 (Catalano, 2006).

NCVS victimization rates are greatest for robbery, followed by aggravated assault. The Black robbery victim rate (7.2 black robberies per 1,000 black persons) is much higher than the White robbery victim rate (2.7 white robberies per 1,000 white persons) and the Hispanic/Latino robbery rate (5.0 Hispanic robberies per 1,000 Hispanics) is in between both groups. Put another way, Latinos[3] are 1.7 times more likely to be victims of robbery than non-Hispanics, and the Black robbery victim rate is in line with that of Hispanics (4.6 to 4.0). Victimization differences between Latinos and other racial/ethnic group members for other types of violent crime are usually minor, but Latinos are 1.6 times more likely to be victims of aggravated assault than Whites.

Information regarding gender disparities in Latino crime is scarce and violent crime research on Latinas is in even more short supply, but the NCVS has demonstrated that some gender differences in violence exist. There are obvious disparities between Latino male and female victimization, but that difference varies by type of violence and even the relationship between victim and offender. For example, Latino male youths encounter significantly higher risks of stranger violence than Latina youths (Lauritsen, 2003). This finding is not surprising, given traditionally high levels of violence among young males in violent crime studies. In contrast, levels of nonstranger violence were similar among Latino and Latina youths; this is an interesting finding probably linked to protective factors at home or some other influence not included in the survey (Lauritsen, 2003). This area requires more research and should attract more attention in the future.

The NCVS has also collected race and ethnicity information since, at least, 1993, allowing the examination of changes over time in violent crime victimization. The overall violent victimization rate among Latinos has declined dramatically, in fact by almost 55%, between 1993 and 2005 (see Catalano, 2006). This decline, however, was consistent across all racial and ethnic groups: Whites declined by 58%, Blacks by 59.9%, other race respondents by 65.1%t, and non-Hispanics by 58.4%. Thus, Latinos appear equally likely to have experienced similar declines in violent crime victimization as other racial/ethnic group members. This finding is important because it counters beliefs by immigrant opponents in the popular media who contend that immigrants have "contributed" to crime rates in their local areas. It goes without saying that these are incorrect assumptions, and ideas regarding high crime rates among Latino immigrants by extension are fatally flawed. Latinos, legality aside, as a whole have long had the same levels of violent crime as Whites and Blacks, and violent crime victimization has declined among all groups even in an era of intense immigration (Martinez, 2002, 2006).

NATIONAL SELF-REPORT SURVEYS

There are a few national studies that gather self-report of delinquency, risk, and health-related behaviors. These include Monitoring the Future, an annual national survey of secondary school students conducted by the University of Michigan's Institute for Social Research or the Center for Disease Control's Youth Risk Behavior Surveillance System, which is a biannual school-based survey of representative samples of high school students (Morenoff, 2005). However, most of these studies have traditionally focused on Black or White delinquency, avoiding Latinos, or have a limited set of questions on delinquency and risk-taking behavior such as illegal substance use.

Another national survey of self-reported delinquent behavior and exposure to violence is the National Longitudinal Study of Adolescent Health (Add Health), a study that initially explored the causes of health-related behaviors in a nationally representative sample of adolescents in grades 7 through 12 in the United States in the 1994–1995 school year. The Add Health survey seeks to examine the impact of various types of social context (families, friends, peers, schools, neighborhoods, and communities) on adolescents' health and risk behaviors. Data at the individual, family, school, and community levels were collected in two waves between 1994 and 1996, and later, in 2001 and 2002, respondents were reinterviewed in a third wave to investigate the influence that adolescence has on young adulthood. Unlike most of the other national surveys, the Add Health asks the respondents to provide detailed information on Latino background— Mexican, Chicano, Cuban, Puerto Rican, Central American, and Other Latino (heavily South American)—which provides a unique opportunity to examine the range of groups that comprise the Latino population.

The self-report of delinquent behavior[4] within the Latino population is summarized in Table 2. A couple of points are worth noting. First, attention is directed in Table 2 to variations *within* Latino groups, thus Blacks and Whites are not included as reference categories. Second, the 12-month counts of self-reported delinquency are recoded so "Yes" equals at least one or more times the following happened in the past 12 months or "No," which means it did not happen. The recoding allowed us to create proportions (or percentages when multiplied by 100), which facilitates the presentation and compresses the findings into a readable format. For most of the self-reported behaviors, Latino group variations are relatively minor, but in the cases where differences exist, there are some interesting findings that should be examined in more detail in the future. Respondents who identify themselves as Chicano or Puerto Rican are usually more likely than Mexican, Cuban, Central American, or Other Latinos to have seen a shooting or stabbing, had a knife or gun pulled out on them, or involved in a physical fight. In two of those self-reported behaviors, the percentages were highest among Chicano respondents, and in the other, Chicano and Puerto Rican youths had equal proportions (27%) exposed to viewing a shooting or stabbing.

In two other items, Chicano respondents had much higher proportions of violent activity than all other Latino groups. For example, almost one-third of Chicano respondents reported being jumped or assaulted, a level twice that of Mexicans, Puerto Ricans, Other Latinos, and Central Americans and almost three times that of Cubans. Although relatively low, about 14% of

TABLE 2. Latino Background Differences in Exposure to Physical Violence. (During the Past 12 Months, How Often Did the Following Things Happen?)

	Mexican	Chicano	Cuban	Puerto Rican	Central American	Other Latino
Saw shooting/stabbing of person	0.21	0.27	0.16	0.27	0.16	0.17
Had knife/gun pulled on you	0.19	0.30	0.11	0.20	0.15	0.13
Someone shot you	0.02	0.04	0.02	0.03	0.02	0.01
Someone stabbed you	0.06	0.07	0.05	0.08	0.04	0.09
Got into a physical fight	0.35	0.52	0.27	0.42	0.32	0.35
Was jumped	0.17	0.33	0.12	0.17	0.15	0.16
Pulled a knife/gun on someone	0.06	0.14	0.05	0.08	0.05	0.04
Shot stabbed someone	0.03	0.07	0.02	0.04	0.03	0.02

Note: Delinquency items in percent. Descriptive statistics provided by Dr. Stephen Demuth.
Source: Add health data.

surveyed Chicano youths reported having pulled a knife/gun on someone, which was a level at least twice that of Other Latino respondents. For most of the remaining behaviors, all six groups are almost equally exposed to low levels (less than 10%) of being shot, stabbed, or actually shooting or stabbing someone. Still, at even such a low level, some Latino group variations emerged. Other Latinos (i.e., South Americans) were more likely to be stabbed than Puerto Ricans and Chicanos. Also, Chicanos were more likely to have been shot and much more likely to have shot or stabbed someone else.

As a whole, the comparison of racial/ethnic differences across various national data sources illustrates that the primary difference in violent crime victimization among Blacks, Whites, and Latinos appears sizable in the case of robbery and modest on other types of violent crime. When focusing on Latino youths, withinLatino-group disparities are greater for some types of violent activity, at least for Chicanos, and to a lesser extent for Puerto Ricans, when compared to Cubans, Mexicans, Central Americans, and Other Latinos. Perhaps the most important outcome of this section is that although reliable Latino crime data are rare, existing sources confirm that including Latinos and distinct Latino groups is important in the study of racial and ethnic disparities in crime. Regardless of the findings or the surveys, it is clear that researchers can no longer focus on racial dichotomies of Black or White when considering racial/ethnic disparities in crime.

CITY/COMMUNITY-LEVEL STUDIES

Much of the recent research on race/ethnicity and crime has been conducted at the aggregate level with official crime data (See Morenoff, 2005; Peterson & Krivo, 2005; Sampson & Bean, 2006). This literature does not ponder individual variations in propensity to engage in criminal offending but, instead, considers variations in violent crime victimization or offending across places such as metropolitan areas or cities (Morenoff, 2005). Ecological research on crime and violence also draws attention to the relationship between race/ethnicity and place, whether at the city, metropolitan, or community level, and proposes that racial disparities are linked to the varying social contexts in which population groups exist. A consistent finding in this literature is that violent crime rates, both offending and victimization, are higher in places with greater proportions of Blacks or African Americans, and this finding persists over time (Morenoff, 2005; Sampson & Bean, 2006). Most of these studies use homicide or violent crime rates or counts of racial/ethnic-specific violence as the dependent variable because homicides are routinely detected and reported to the police, but even these studies typically focus on Black or White crime differences (see Martinez, 1996, 2000, and Phillips, 2002, for exceptions).

These aggregate-level studies have been valuable because they demonstrate the need to consider racial disparities in crime and, in some cases, to encourage scholars to push conceptions of race and crime to include Latino composition in crime studies (Peterson & Krivo, 2005). Unfortunately, this literature has, until very recently, rarely considered the level of Latino crime or compared Latinos to other ethnic minority groups largely due to official crime data limitations.[5] This omission, in part, has led some researchers to revisit the long tradition of research on communities and crime, a tradition in criminology that dates back to the founding of American criminology[6] (Sampson & Bean, 2006).

Most of the handful of early ethnicity and crime studies focused on European immigrants in Chicago. A notable exception to this pattern is *Mexican Labor in the United States, Volume II* (Taylor, 1932/1970), which is perhaps the earliest quantitative study on Mexican immigration to the United States. In this study, Taylor described the labor market, educational, criminal justice, and fertility experiences of Mexican-origin persons in Chicago. By explicitly linking arrest statistics (felonies and misdemeanors) to local population sizes, he was able to compare White and Mexican criminal activities. Although Mexicans were arrested at a percentage two to three times their population size, most of the arrests were not related to violence but were for property- and alcohol-related offenses, a finding that Taylor linked to the high number of single males in the population. Regarding violence, Taylor (1932/1970) noted that "The offenses of Mexicans are concentrated much more than average in these two groups of charges, probably mainly because of the very abnormal age and sex composition of the Mexican population in Chicago" (p. 147). This is important to highlight because patterns of criminal involvement were shaped by social factors, including neighborhood poverty and the age and sex distributions of the immigrant population, not the inherent criminality of immigrant Latinos.

Few pioneering scholars, however, acknowledged the presence of Latino or non-European immigrants. This was probably due to the passage of restrictionist national-origin quota laws in the 1920s and assimilation campaigns that gradually rendered the study of the immigrant European experience obsolete and forced scholars to focus on race or "Black versus White" crime. The emphasis on Blacks and Whites is now changing. For at least 10 years, scholars have been examining violent crime counts across census tracts within a city with varying levels of racial and ethnic composition.[7] Some compare and contrast the characteristics of Black, White, and Latino homicides in Chicago, Houston, Los Angeles, and Miami (Martinez, 2003; Riedel, 2003; Titterington & Damphousse, 2003) or control for social and economic determinants of crime thought to shape racial/ethnic disparities across neighborhoods (Lee, Martinez, & Rosenfeld, 2001; Morenoff & Sampson, 1997). None have found evidence that more immigration means more homicides in a given area (Martinez, 2002, 2006).

This body of work is important because there is a strong relationship among economic disadvantage, affluence, and violent crime, and this connection has received a great deal of attention given the racial/ethnic differences in the strength of the association between crime and socioeconomic context at the community level. To a large extent, this notion is rooted in the claim by Sampson and Wilson (1995) that the "sources of violent crime appear to be remarkably invariant across race and rooted instead in the structural differences across communities, cities, and states in economic and family organization" (p. 41), which helps explain the racial/ethnic differences in violence. Thus, as Sampson and Bean (2006:8) noted, the premise is that community-level patterns of racial inequality give rise to the social isolation and ecological concentration of the truly disadvantaged, which, in turn, leads to structural barriers and cultural adaptations that undermine social organization and, in turn, shape crime. Therefore, "race" is not a cause of violence but, rather, a marker deriving from a set of social contexts reflecting racial disparity in U.S. society. This thesis has become known as the "racial invariance" in the fundamental causes of violent crime. Still, the racial invariance thesis has rarely been applied to ethnicity and crime and this issue is discussed in the next section (Sampson & Bean, 2006). Although other conceptual or theoretical overviews on Latino crime and delinquency exist (see Morenoff, 2005), attention is directed to macro-level approaches because this is where the bulk of Latino violence research is located (Peterson & Krivo, 2005).

LATINOS AND IMMIGRATION

Sampson and Wilson (1995) were concerned about explaining crime differences between Blacks and Whites when applying their "racial invariance" thesis and did not focus on ethnicity and crime. This seemed logical at the time because most of the race and violence research stemmed from observations about the deep-rooted social and economic divisions between

Blacks and Whites in urban America, especially in areas where the loss of manufacturing jobs devastated the local economy. However, historical peaks of immigration have transformed the ethnic composition across the nation, and Latinos have emerged as the largest ethnic minority group in the United States (Sampson & Bean, 2006). Latinos now comprise about 14% of the population and most migrated from Spanish-speaking Latin American countries. Some scholars have started to address the compelling issue of what does or does not influence Latino violence and have begun to push research on violent crime beyond Blacks and Whites, particularly toward analyses of Latinos.

In general, researchers have evaluated whether the structural conditions relevant for Black and White violence also apply to Latinos (Peterson & Krivo, 2005). Martinez and colleagues have been at the vanguard of recent ecological analyses of Latino violence and provided results worth noting because they laid the groundwork for future research by suggesting the predictors of Latino violence or homicide are unique (Peterson & Krivo, 2005). Using homicide or violent crime data gathered directly from police departments and linked to census tracts that are widely used as proxies for communities, Martinez and colleagues in a series of articles analyzed Latino-specific homicide either alone or in comparison with models for native-born Blacks and Whites, and sometimes immigrant Haitians, Jamaicans, or Latino subpopulations (e.g., Mariel Cubans) (Lee, Martinez, & Rosenfeld, 2001; Martinez, 1996, 2003). They noted that Latinos usually follow the familiar pattern, as among Blacks and Whites, in terms of the all-encompassing effect of concentrated disadvantage even though some predictors of Latino homicide are, to some extent, distinct. Thus, the basic linkages among disadvantage and homicide hold for African Americans, Haitians, and Latinos in the city of Miami, and similar findings hold in other places for Blacks and Latinos, such as in the cities of San Diego and El Paso. For the most part, these studies support the racial/ethnic invariance hypothesis forwarded by Sampson and Wilson (1995), leading Martinez (2003) to conclude that "the basic links among deprivation, disorganization, and homicide are similar for all three ethnic groups [African Americans, Haitians, and Latinos]. Therefore it seems that the racial invariance thesis holds in the case of Latinos and might be extended to ethnic invariance in terms of community-level causes of violence, especially disadvantage" (p. 40).

One issue influencing Latinos much more so than Whites or Blacks is the impact of immigration on crime, in general, and Latino violence, specifically.[8] For example, some scholars have written about the "Latino Paradox" where Latinos, especially immigrants, do much better on certain indicators including violence than Blacks, and in some cases Whites, given relatively high levels of disadvantage (Sampson & Bean, 2006). Thus, Latinos have high levels of poverty but lower levels of homicide or violence than expected, given the power of economic disadvantage (or deprivation). The impact of recent immigration[9] and the role of immigrant concentration is one that appears to construct a different story with respect to violence than the concentration of African Americans in the race and crime literature (Sampson & Bean, 2006).

Martinez and colleagues have also been at the forefront of researchers debunking the popular notion that higher levels of immigration lead to increased violence and challenge the belief that more immigrants means more homicide (Peterson & Krivo, 2005; Sampson & Bean, 2006). In fact, it generally has no effect on violence contrary to expectations dating back to the turn of the last century that an influx of immigrants disrupts communities, creates neighborhood instability, and contributes to violent crime[10] (see Bursik, 2006). If immigration increases violent crime, it should do so among Latinos and in Latino communities because movement from abroad is heavily concentrated in Spanish-speaking Caribbean and Latin American countries. Instead, the studies in this section support the finding that extreme disadvantage matters more for violence across racial, ethnic and even immigrant groups than the presumed deleterious impact of immigration on violence forwarded by immigrant opponents (Martinez, 2006). Immigration policy makers should heed research that more immigrant Latinos usually means less violent crime. Still, future researchers should pay closer attention to potential variations across and within groups of various immigrant and ethnic variations, especially among Latino groups (see also Mears, 2001).

CURRENT PROJECTS ON CRIME IN IMMIGRATION COMMUNITIES

At least two important studies have extended these lines of inquiry. Recently, Stowell (2005) completed a comprehensive dissertation designed to build on the nascent body of research on immigration and crime. He used more specific measures of immigration containing information about both nativity and country of origin and included measures of official crime reported to the cities of Miami and Houston police departments: aggravated assault and armed robbery. This allows for a test of the degree to which the impact of immigration on violence varies across nonlethal violence at the census tract level in two immigrant destination places.

In Table 3, the descriptive statistics are included for both cities. The disparities in reported violent crime are evident and the average levels in Miami are more than twice as high as the corresponding levels in Houston. Although rates of violent crime are more prevalent in Miami, the relative proportion of robbery and aggravated assaults is similar in both cities. In Miami and Houston, aggravated assaults accounted for a larger share of the observed levels of violence, with robberies comprising less than half of the total.

Nearly 40% of the average neighborhood in Miami is composed of individuals born outside of the United States. On average, one-quarter of the neighborhood population in Miami were born in Cuba. The remaining three largest immigrant groups (Nicaraguans, Hondurans, and Haitians) represent much smaller shares of the total neighborhood populations. Approximately 12% of the average neighborhood in Houston is composed of individuals born in Mexico. Compared to Miami, the next three largest immigrant groups (Vietnamese, Salvadoran, and Chinese) represent less than 2% of the population in Houston. It is also clear that the average poverty rate in Miami neighborhoods is higher than in Houston (31.4% compared to 17.3%) and that

TABLE 3. Two City Descriptive Statistics of Crime and Latino Population

	Miami		Houston
Dependent variables			
Violent crime rate	108.03		41.04
Robbery	46.89		17.03
Aggravated assault	61.15		24.00
Immigration measures			
% Cuban	25.00	% Mexican	11.86
% Nicaraguan	6.25	% Chinese	0.63
% Honduran	4.15	% Vietnamese	1.20
% Haitian	5.42	% Salvadoran	1.70
Neighborhood measures			
% Poverty	31.37		17.13
Ethnic/RACIAL HETEROGENEITY	0.28		0.46

Source: Stowell (2005).

neighborhoods in Miami tend to be less racially/ethnically heterogeneous. The disparities in levels of unemployment also point to the relatively higher levels of economic disadvantage in Miami (12.3% compared to 7.8%). Although the average is slightly higher in Houston, neighborhoods in both cities have similar shares of young males (5.4% and 4.6%).

Based on the descriptive information, it is evident that average levels of neighborhood violence are higher in Miami than in Houston, a pattern that holds for each of the three dependent variables. More generally, these results illustrate the differences in the social structural contexts between these cities. In Miami neighborhoods, not only are immigrants a larger share of the overall neighborhood populations, but they also tend to be more economically distressed. Nevertheless, the Stowell regression results (not shown here) are consistent with prior research on immigration. With the inclusion of ethnic-specific measures of immigration, the findings yielded a combination of negative and null effects of the presence of foreign-born ethnic groups on violent crime. In other words, more immigrants in Houston or Miami neighborhoods means either less violent crime or no impact on violent crime, contrary to the popular impression that immigrant communities are crime-prone (Stowell, 2005; see also Martinez, 2002, 2006).

In an influential publication based on the Project on Human Development in Chicago Neighborhoods, a study designed to examine individual and neighborhood immigration status, along with ethnicity, in range of developmental outcomes including juvenile crime, Sampson and colleagues investigated delinquency among Chicago's Mexican-origin population (Sampson, Morenoff, & Raudenbush, 2005). They reported that the lower rate of violence among the Mexican-origin groups, relative to Whites and Blacks, was explained by a combination of having married parents, living in an area with a high concentration of immigrants, and being an immigrant individual. Moreover, they found that first-generation immigrants have lower violence rates than second-generation immigrants, who, in turn, have lower rates of violence than third-generation Americans.

Thus, despite having lower levels of socioeconomic status than any racial/ethnic group in the Chicago study, the Mexican-origin population has the lowest levels of involvement in delinquent activity across a wide range of outcomes. Within the Mexican population, criminal activity increases across generations, even though there is a corresponding increase in socioeconomic status, suggesting that exposure to U.S. society or an "Americanization" effect is probably criminogenic or that recent Mexican immigrants differ from others in some other unmeasured attribute (see Morenoff, 2005). Yet again, immigrants, in general, and Mexican-origin population, specifically, are less violent, even more so when they live in heavily immigrant neighborhoods (Martinez, 2002, 2006).

MULTILEVEL STUDIES

The integration of macro-level structural factors into multilevel models of racial and ethnic differences in violence represents a growing research trend in criminology (Peterson & Krivo, 2005). Beyond the examples mentioned earlier by Sampson and colleagues in Chicago, others have also determined whether individual differences in violence, disaggregated by race and ethnicity, are explained by a host of individual and context factors (Lauritsen, 2003). Lauritsen (2003) discovered that concentrated disadvantage and individual factors explained most of the higher risks of nonlethal violent victimization among Blacks and Latinos relative to Whites. This study was noteworthy because census tract- or area-identified data were linked to individual NCVS data, permitting analysis of Black, White, and Latino male and female victimization risk.

Others have also reported that the effect of neighborhood-level disadvantage is similar among all racial and ethnic groups. While examining serious violence among Asian, Black,

Latino, White, and Native American youths, McNulty and Bellair (2003a, 2003b), in two different datasets, (Add Health and the National Educational Longitudinal Study or NELS) reported that individual and neighborhood disadvantage usually explained variations for violence across all groups. The exception was for Native Americans in the NELS data. McNulty and Bellair (2003a, 2003b) also discovered that the gaps between Blacks and White were influenced by variations in neighborhood disadvantage, but the Latino-to-White gap was more strongly influenced by individual level sources.

CONCLUSION

Overall, this chapter yields at least one clear conclusion: Studies of racial and ethnic disparities in violent crime must broaden their focus beyond Blacks and Whites to include Latinos and Latino groups whenever possible. The growth of Latinos across broad sectors of U.S. society requires a renewed focus on multiple racial/ethnic/immigrant groups when comparing levels of violence across a variety of communities and regions, some of which, until recently, rarely encountered Latinos (Martinez, 2002). The incorporation of Latinos will help scholars of violent crime and serious delinquency produce a broader understanding of the race/ethnic and violent crime linkages and expand our focus to include the diverse ecological contexts in which Blacks, Whites, and Latinos reside (Peterson & Krivo, 2005).

There are a number of important questions that should be addressed in the future. More data collection is necessary to answer important questions on Latino violence. For example, how does economic disadvantage operate to produce violence within and across Latino groups in similar communities? This issue has been directed to apparently comparable conditions related to Blacks and Latinos (Martinez, 2002). These groups have similar levels of disadvantage, but many Latino communities have higher levels of labor market attachment, even though typically it might mean employment in menial jobs, than found in many African American areas. This, of course, has a parallel in many Latino communities and more data should be collected on the country of origin as well to help us better understand complex neighborhood dynamics. As immigrant Latinos move into older Latino areas, should we expect more or less crime in places like Miami, where Cubans are replaced by Columbians or Nicaraguans? Or does Latino violence rise in cities like Los Angeles and Houston, where a dominant Mexican-origin population (native and foreign-born alike) resides when Salvadorans and other Latino group members move in? Perhaps it decreases over time, as suggested by some researchers. It is also possible that, as disadvantaged as conditions in U.S. barrios might be, immigrant Latinos might use their sending countries, with even worse economic and political conditions, as reference points when assessing their position relative to others, thus canceling out possible inequality effects.

There is also a need to conduct more qualitative and ethnographic research to provide important insights on emerging populations and broaden the portrait of Latino violence. At least two require attention. First, there are a number of ways that thorough and detailed qualitative case studies of Latino communities could be compared and contrasted to each other, to Black or Whites areas, and expanded to rural or suburban settings while considering immigrant status. For example, qualitative studies comparing the sources of violence in rural areas with new immigrant populations to those with little or no Latino influx would help expand research on Latino crime and delinquency. Studies examining the implications of Latino movement into formerly White suburban communities, if crime follows or not, would also help broaden our understanding of economic deprivation, affluence, and, of course, ethnicity and violence.

Second, it is also important to note that violence is shaped by gender, and the case of Latinas has been ignored in the social science literature. Research should explore a variety of issues: Little is known about the extent or sources of Latina victimization or offending; if Latina violence is shaped by interpersonal relations at home, work, school, or in the streets; and if immigrant status matters when Latinas report crime. These suggestions could be extended to include the comparison of Latinas to females of other racial/ethnic groups and in various neighborhood settings ranging from extremely poor to ethnically mixed middle communities and in heavily immigrant communities or primarily native-born ones to shed more light on Latina crime research. Future studies, moving beyond quantitative studies, should help us understand why Latinos are less crime-prone than expected in various settings and fill in the gap in the Latina violence literature.

This chapter also serves as a reminder about the importance of sound immigration policy based on research, not political rhetoric. The growing ethnic diversity across the nation is renewing a focus on the assumed influence of immigration on criminal activity, which, according to long-held wisdom, means that Latinos have high rates of violence or that immigrants are crime-prone predators (for recent examples, see Martinez, 2006). These are long-held beliefs promoted by some self-styled populist commentators in the mass media or are stereotypes perpetuated by conservative politicians, rooted in anecdotes or impressions. These groups have ignored the broad reductions in violence simultaneous with increased Latino immigration over the last decade, the protective mechanism of concentrated immigration, and other aspects of the unique Latino experience articulated in this chapter and others in this volume. It is no longer reasonable to assume that immigration and immigrant Latinos have a deleterious impact on violent crime in contemporary U.S. society or that singling out Latinos with legislation to deter the movement of undocumented workers into communities will decrease crime, as some advocate in the current rabid anti-immigration climate. In fact, the opposite might occur as Latinos are targeted for selective enforcement of immigration laws and removed from communities, reducing neighborhood stability and setting the stage for more crime now and perhaps later among the children of immigrants stigmatized by mean-spirited legislation.

Finally, scholars should move beyond the contemporary time frame and examine changes over time in violent crime among racial and ethnic group members during an era of intense isolation and segregation. Going back in time will enable researchers to compare periods of high crime to low crime and permit the comparison in racially and ethnically diverse or homogenous communities. Given the growth of Latinos and the corresponding increase in ethnic diversity across the country, it is important to not only ask more questions about Latino violence and delinquency but also to answer them with more serious cutting-edge research studies on violence crossing theoretical and methodological approaches, academic disciplines, and data sources. This chapter highlights many studies focusing on Latinos that serve as starting points for future research, but much more work remains to help assess the powerful protective role of immigration in Latino communities and provide more meaningful context to explanations of ethnicity and crime.

NOTES

1. The UCR is a nationwide collection of police reports from most law enforcement agencies across the country. The UCR data includes information on victim and offender or arrestee race (i.e., White, Black, American Indian/Alaskan, or Asian/Pacific Islander), but it does not consistently contain information on offender ethnicity. The exclusion of ethnic identifiers in official data has probably been the primary contribution to the dearth of research on crime among Latinos.
2. The NCVS also asks victims about the characteristics of the offenders by whom they were victimized and includes a question about the victims' perception of the offender race (White or Black). Unfortunately a "Hispanic" category is not included as a choice and it is difficult to assess the extent of offending among Latinos.

3. In order to maintain consistency in the chapter, I use "Latino" to reflect activity among the total Latino population without referring to males and females.
4. I thank Dr. Stephen Demuth, Faculty Associate in the Center for Family and Demographic Research at Bowling Green State University, for his generous assistance in accessing these data.
5. For more on the methodological problems associated with "place-based disparities in crime," see Morenoff (2005:152).
6. See Bursik (2006) for more on European immigrants and crime.
7. This is not to suggest that some studies did not include Latino composition or examine Latino violence, especially in cities such as Houston, Texas. For a succinct review of this literature, see Titterington and Damphousse (2003).
8. This potentially transcends race because the movement of Black immigrants into some communities has impacted notions of race and crime in many places, especially those with large Haitian and African communities (Nielsen & Martinez, 2006).
9. Some studies have also focused on the impact of immigration on Latino violence. Peterson and Krivo (2005:345) noted that immigration has been considered a source of violent crime by pioneering and contemporary scholars because (a) an influx of immigration into a community contributes to social disorganization by obstructing communication and cooperation among residents, (b) immigrants might turn to crime more than the native-born as a way of adjusting to blocked opportunities (i.e., strain), and (c) immigrants reside in areas where oppositional culture is evident (see Martinez & Lee, 2000, and Mears, 2001, for more detailed discussions of these arguments).
10. Research examining immigration and violence for cities in the southwestern United States (Hagan & Palloni, 1998) and metropolitan areas (Butcher & Piehl, 1998) also finds negligible influences of immigration on crime. Moreover, family and community characteristics at the census tract level were attached to NCVS data in a special release to examine factors shaping violent victimization (see Lauritsen, 2003). No relationship was found between percent foreign-born or percent Latino on the incidence of violent victimization (again, see Lauritsen, 2003).

REFERENCES

Bursik, Robert J., Jr. (2006). Rethinking the Chicago School of Criminology in a New Era of Immigration. In Ramiro Martinez, Jr. & Abel Valenzuela (Eds.), *Immigration and Crime: Race, Ethnicity, and Violence* (pp. 20–35). New York: New York University Press.

Butcher, Kristin F., & Piehl, Anne M. (1998). Cross-city Evidence on the Relationship Between Immigration and Crime. *Journal of Policy Analysis and Management, 17*, 457–493.

Catalano, Shannon M. (2006, September). *National Crime Victimization Survey: Criminal Victimization, 2005.*, Bureau of Justice Statistics Bulletin: NCJ 214644. Washington, DC: U.S. Government Printing Office.

Dohan, Daniel. (2003). *The Price of Poverty: Money, Work, and Culture in the Mexican American Barrio.* Berkeley: University of California Press.

Hagan, John, & Palloni, Alberto. (1998). Immigration and Crime in the United States. In J. P. Smith & B. Edmonston (Eds.), *The Immigration Debate* (pp. 367–387). Washington, DC: National Academy Press.

Keppel, Kenneth G., Pearcy, Jeffrey N., & Diane K. Wagener. (2002, January). Trends in racial and ethnic-specific rates for the health status indicators: United States, 1990–98. *Healthy People Statistical Notes, No 23.* Hyattsville, Maryland: National Center for Health Statistics.

Kil, Sang Hea, & Menjívar, Cecilia. (2006). The "War on the Border": Criminalizing Immigrants and Militarizing the U.S.-Mexico Border. In Ramiro Martinez, Jr. & Abel Valenzuela (Eds.), *Immigration and Crime: Race, Ethnicity, and Violence* (pp. 20–35). New York: New York University Press.

Lauritsen, Janet L. (2003, November). How Families and Communities Influence Youth Victimization: Individual and Contextual Factors in the NCVS. *Office of Juvenile Justice and Delinquency Prevention Juvenile Justice Bulletin.* Washington, DC: U.S. Department of Justice, Office of Justice Programs, Office of Juvenile Justice and Delinquency Prevention. NCJ 201629.

Lee, Matthew T., Martinez, Ramiro, Jr., & Rosenfeld, Richard. (2001). Does Immigration Increase Homicide? Negative evidence from Three Border Cities. *The Sociological Quarterly, 42*, 559–580.

Martinez, Ramiro, Jr. (1996). Latinos and Lethal Violence: The Impact of Poverty and Inequality. *Social Problems, 43*, 131–146.

Martinez, Ramiro, Jr. (2000). Immigration and Urban Violence: The Link Between Immigrant Latinos and Types of Homicide. *Social Science Quarterly, 81*, 363–374.

Martinez, Ramiro, Jr. (2002). *Latino Homicide: Immigration, Violence and Community.* New York: Routledge.

Martinez, Ramiro, Jr. (2003). Moving Beyond Black and White Violence: African American, Haitian, and Latino Homicides in Miami. In Darnell F. Hawkins (Ed.), *Violent Crime: Assessing Race and Ethnic Differences* (pp. 22–43). New York: Cambridge University Press.

Martinez, Ramiro, Jr. (2006). Coming to America: The Impact of the New Immigration on Crime. In Ramiro Martinez, Jr. & Abel Valenzuela (Eds.), *Immigration, Ethnicity, and Crime* (pp. 1–21). New York: New York University Press.

McNulty, Thomas, & Bellair, Paul. (2003a). Explaining Racial and Ethnic Differences in Adolescent Violence: Structural Disadvantage, Family Well-being and Social Capital. *Justice Quarterly, 20*, 201–231.

McNulty, Thomas, & Bellair, Paul. (2003b). Explaining Racial and Ethnic Differences in Serious Adolescent Violent Behavior. *Criminology, 41*, 709–729.

Mears, Daniel P. (2001). The Immigration-Crime Nexus: Toward an Analytic Framework for Assessing and Guiding Theory, Research, and Policy. *Sociological Perspectives, 44*, 1–19.

Morenoff, Jeffrey D. (2005). Racial and Ethnic Disparities in Crime and Delinquency in the United States. In Marta Tienda & Michael Rutter (Eds.), *Ethnicity and Causal Mechanisms* (pp. 139–173). New York: Cambridge University Press.

Morenoff, Jeffery D., & Sampson, Robert. (1997). Violent Crime and the Spatial Dynamics of Neighborhood Transition: Chicago, 1970–1990. *Social Forces, 76*, 31–64.

Nielsen, Amie, & Martinez, Ramiro, Jr. (2006). Multiple Disadvantages and Crime among Black Immigrants: Exploring Haitian Violence in Miami's Communities. In Ramiro Martinez, Jr. & Abel Valenzuela (Eds.), *Immigration and Crime: Race, Ethnicity and Violence* (pp. 212–234). New York: New York University Press.

Peterson, Ruth D., & Krivo, Lauren J. (2005). Macrostructural Analyses of Race, Ethnicity, and Violent Crime: Recent Lessons and New Directions for Research. *Annual Review of Sociology, 31*, 331–356.

Phillips, Julie A. (2002). White, Black and Latino Homicide Rates: Why the Difference? *Social Problems, 49*, 349–373.

Reidel, Marc. (2003). Homicide in Los Angeles County: A Study of Latino Victimization. In Darnell F. Hawkins (Ed.), *Violent Crime: Assessing Race and Ethnic Differences* (pp. 44–66). New York: Cambridge University Press.

Sampson, Robert, & Wilson, William J. (1995). Toward a Theory of Race, Crime, and Urban Inequality. In John Hagan & Ruth Peterson (Eds.), *Crime and Inequality* (pp. 37–56). Stanford, CA: Stanford University Press.

Sampson, Robert J., & Bean, Lydia. (2006). Cultural Mechanisms and Killings Fields: A Revised Theory of Community-Level Racial Inequality. In Ruth D. Peterson, Lauren J. Krivo, & John Hagan (Eds.), *The Many Colors of Crime* (pp. 8–38). New York: New York University Press.

Sampson, Robert J., Morenoff, Jeffrey D., & Raudenbush, Stephen. (2005). Social Anatomy of Racial and Ethnic Disparities in Violence. *American Journal of Public Health, 95*, 224–232.

Stowell, Jacob I. (2005). Does Immigration Beget Crime? Understanding the Direct and Indirect Impacts of Immigration on Violence. Unpublished doctoral dissertation. Albany: University at Albany, State University of New York.

Taylor, Paul S. (1970). Economic Correlates of Racial and Ethnic Disparity in Homicide: Houston, 1945–1994. *Mexican Labor in the United States, Volume II*. New York: Arno Press/New York Times. (Original work published 1932)

Titterington, Victoria E., & Damphousse, Kelly R. (2003). In Darnell F. Hawkins (Ed.), *Violent Crime: Assessing Race and Ethnic Differences* (pp. 67–88). New York: Cambridge University Press.

SCHOOLING, WORK, AND INCOME AMONG LATINAS/OS

CHAPTER 9

The Educational Experiences of Latinos in the United States

WILLIAM VÉLEZ

INTRODUCTION

The educational conditions of Latinos in the United States in the first decade of the 21st century can be described only with a sense of alarm, given the dismal statistics we can use to capture attainment levels. For example, in 2003 only about half (48.7%) of the Mexican- and the Dominican-origin (51.7%) population (25 years and older) had completed at least a high school education (Falcon, 2004). This compares with just over three-fifths (63.3%) of Puerto Ricans and 68.7% of Cubans completing a high school education, which means that all of the major Latino subgroups were lagging behind the majority White-population high school completion rate of 84% by a wide margin.

The historical context under which the Latino educational situation has developed in the United States is very complex and can be summarized under relations of subjugation, colonization, and the specific institutional mechanisms used in different locations to segregate and track Latino students. Latinos have struggled for more than a century to preserve their "raices" (cultural roots) in the face of a public educational system embarked on an "Americanization" mission, obsessed with erasing the Spanish language and any historical connections to Latin America (Garcia, 2001). The schooling of Latinos is frequently discussed under the umbrella of "immigrant" adaptation and bilingual education, even though the majority of U.S. Latinos were born in the continental United States (Bean, Lee, Batalova, & Leach, 2004) and their first language is English. However, emphasis on comparing the native-born with immigrants reflects a desire to see the second and third generation outpace the educational and occupational gains of their parents and grandparents, with specific attention to returns on educational credentials.

For example, Bean et al. (2004) reported that full-time workers of Mexican origin were earning about 30% less than U.S.-born White males, irrespective of education level. However, when the comparison is made to U.S.-born Mexican workers, the differences shrink considerably, although White workers with at least some college education still make 21% more than comparable Mexican workers, suggesting the presence of discriminatory labor markets.

This chapter is organized as follows: In the next section I outline some of the major historical events that have shaped the educational experiences of Latinos in this country. The following section covers some of the most relevant factors or variables behind the educational attainment of Latinos at both the secondary and postsecondary level. The final section contains recommendations for future research in light of more recent developments (e.g., the No Child Left Behind Act) at the state and federal levels.

HISTORICAL BACKGROUND

Mexican Americans

In the 19th century, the recently independent nation of Mexico lost close to half of its territory to the United States. As a result, many Mexicans in the southwest found themselves in a subordinate position within a vastly expanding United States, which had promised equal protection under the law, including private property and language rights in the Treaty of Guadalupe Hidalgo signed with Mexico in 1848. As Anglos consolidated their political and economic power throughout the region, they extended their dominance in the cultural domain by restricting the use of Spanish. In Texas, for example, the state legislature passed a new school law in 1870 mandating English as the language of instruction in all schools. Coupled with widespread poverty and poor public school facilities, the new law made schooling unavailable for most Mexican children in the state (Velez, 1994).

More wealthy *Tejanos* had access to religious institutions and private Mexican schools, like the Incarnate Word of Brownsville, established in 1853 by four nuns, that enrolled females between 5 and 18 years of age (San Miguel, 1987). For poor *Tejano* parents, however, public schools were the only alternative. In a pattern that would be repeated for many decades, these schools were usually segregated, overcrowded, and lacked adequately trained staff and school equipment.

In the early 20th century, the decline of the cattle industry coupled with the development of commercial agriculture led to a system of exploitative wages and extreme segregation practices in Texas and other southwestern states. The Mexican Revolution that started in 1910 and the loss of communal lands that affected millions of peasants in that country led to a substantial increase in Mexican immigration to the United States between the years 1900 and 1930. Rampant use of child labor and the denial of schooling by many boards of education to migrant children meant that the majority of Mexican migrant children never went beyond the primary grades in Texas (Warburton, Wood, & Crane, 1943). Curricular reforms began in the 1920s aimed at providing Mexican children in Texas with vocational education (San Miguel, 1987). Agriculture classes, industrial training, and home economics instruction were widely offered to these children by 1929. Thus, schools were used to train Mexican Americans to be domestics and farm hands and to occupy the lower rungs of the manufacturing sector.

In response to these discriminatory conditions, the League of United Latin American Citizens (LULAC) was founded in 1929. The organization's constitution declared that one of its aims was "to assume complete responsibility for the education of our children as to their rights and duties and the language and customs of this country; the latter insofar as they may be good customs" (cited in Montejano, 1987). Over the years, LULAC has won many important legal victories to secure political and educational rights for Latinos. Perhaps the most well-known legal victory resulted from LULAC coming to the aid of several MexicanAmericans that were challenging the practice of school segregation in California. The suit, known as *Mendez v. Westminster School District*, charged that a number of school districts in Orange County were denying Mexican and Latino children their constitutional rights by forcing them to attend separate "Mexican" schools. On February 18, 1946, the court ruled against the district, and under appeal, the decision was upheld 14 months later, on April 14, 1947. This was a very important victory from a legal standpoint, because the court reinterpreted the Plessy "separate but equal" doctrine. The presiding judge, Paul J. McCormick, made a distinction between physical equality (facilities) and social equality. The existence of separate facilities was unconstitutional because it fostered social inequality. Moreover, McCormick found no evidence that showed segregation aided in the development of English proficiency. Thus, he ruled that the segregation of Mexican children lacked legal and educational justifications (González, 1990).

Another organization that fought for educational equity is the Mexican American Legal Defense and Education Fund (MALDEF). One of the primary concerns of MALDEF was eliminating segregated schools for Mexican Americans. MALDEF went to court to challenge the federal government's practice, through the Office for Civil Rights, of treating Mexican Americans as White, thus allowing some school districts to appear to have "integrated" schools by pairing Blacks with Mexican Americans while leaving the all-Anglo schools intact. In order to change this, MALDEF sought court decisions declaring Mexican Americans an identifiable ethnic minority group that had been subjected to a system of pervasive official discrimination. The crucial decision was rendered by the U.S. Supreme Court in 1973 in *Keyes v. School District Number One, Denver, Colorado*, declaring Mexican Americans an identifiable minority for desegregation purposes.

More recent attempts to deny education to immigrant children have also reached the U.S. Supreme Court. In *Plyler v. Doe*, 1982, the Supreme Court rejected an attempt by one school district in Texas to exclude Mexican immigrant students from public school altogether. The Supreme Court found such exclusion unconstitutional. In 1994, California voters approved Proposition 187, which attempted to cut off social services, including public education, to undocumented immigrant families and children. In March 1998, a federal district judge found Proposition 187 unconstitutional. The reasoning behind the Supreme Court's decision on this issue revolves around the equal protection clause, which was intended to cover any person physically within a state's borders regardless of the legality of his/her presence. As Garcia (2001) stated, "denying children an education would make them illiterate and would prevent them from advancing on their individual merit and becoming useful members of U.S. society."

Integration by itself could not guarantee equal educational opportunity for all Mexican American children, because many of them were monolingual Spanish speakers and could not be integrated into the regular classroom. It was necessary to address the special needs of these children by implementing a new curriculum, one that was designed to deal with linguistic minorities. The crucial legal decision that paved the way for demanding bilingual programs was the 1974 Supreme Court ruling in the *Lau v. Nichols* case. The court ruled that bilingual education was to be provided to facilitate equal access to the instructional program of students who were English learners.

Bilingual education has proved to be an arena for persistent debate and controversy both among Latinos and non-Latinos. Although most research supports the educational benefits of bilingual programs for Spanish-speaking children (Garcia, 1999), political pressure against it has developed in some areas of the country. In 1998, for example, California voters passed Proposition 227, an initiative outlawing most forms of bilingual education, with about 40% of Latinos supporting the initiative. It made bilingual education available only through parental requests and prescribed a 1-year course called "Structured English Immersion." However, without assistance using their native language, it is very improbable that immigrant children can acquire English effectively. Moreover, evidence on the effects of Proposition 227 shows widespread failure in its ability to allow these immigrants to become proficient in English. In the academic year 2002–2003, 5 years after the implementation of Proposition 227 in California, only 42% (of the total population in 1998) of English language learners had become proficient in English (Crawford, 2003).

Puerto Ricans

Puerto Ricans became politically linked to the United States as a result of the Treaty of Paris, which ended the Spanish American War in 1898, with Spain ceding Cuba, Puerto Rico, and the Pacific territories of the Philippines and Guam to the United States. Puerto Ricans have been U.S. citizens since 1917, when Congress passed the Jones-Shafroth Act. Since 1952, the political status of Puerto Rico is that of a commonwealth, and although retaining some local autonomy, Puerto Rican affairs have been closely controlled by U.S. business interests and federal agencies.

Most of the initial U.S. colonial policies were based on prejudiced and patronizing views of the Puerto Rican people, aimed at Americanizing the Island (Acosta-Belén & Santiago, 2006). The school system was forced to adopt English as the language of instruction, and the Island's schools were used to inculcate U.S. values and promote the learning of English (Negrón de Montilla, 1971).

As part of their forced acculturation mission, U.S. administrators of Puerto Rico sent 60 Puerto Rican students to the Carlisle Indian Industrial School in Pennsylvania between 1898 and 1905. The school had been founded in 1879 with the goal of erasing the cultural identity of American Indian children and acculturating them into U.S. western society (Navarro-Rivera, 2006). The Puerto Rican students and their families had been deceived into thinking that they would receive a professional education at Carlisle, and most were disappointed with its Americanizing and vocationally oriented curriculum. As a result, many students returned to Puerto Rico on the orders of their parents, and at least five Puerto Rican students ran away from the school (Navarro-Rivera, 2006).

Puerto Ricans first migrated to the United States in the second half of the 19th century as a result of political persecution from the colonial Spanish authorities. The majority of these political migrants settled in New York, as did many of the Puerto Ricans migrating to the United States in the first three decades of the 20th century. By 1940, there were about 70,000 Puerto Ricans living in the United States, having formed communities in East Harlem, the Brooklyn Navy Yard Area, the South Bronx, and the Lower East Side in New York. Economic and political transformations in Puerto Rico aimed at industrializing the Island's economy were accompanied by a government-sponsored plan to facilitate the migration of Puerto Rican surplus workers in what is called the "great migration" during the 1946–1964 period (Alicea, 1994). Although Puerto Ricans are now geographically dispersed throughout the United States, they remained heavily concentrated in the New York area until the 1970s.

The initial reaction of school officials in New York City to the increasing enrollments of Puerto Rican students in the postwar period was a forced immersion approach. Under community pressure, the New York City Board of Education decided to undertake a study in 1954. The study, known as the "Puerto Rican Study," lasted 3 years, and in its final report, it recommended proper screening, placement, and periodic assessment of non-English-speaking children (Santiago-Santiago, 1986). These recommendations were ignored; they were never implemented at the system level, leaving it at the discretion of the local schools to follow them.

The abysmal failure of the city's schools to educate and graduate its Puerto Rican students was reflected in their large dropout rates, estimated at between 80% and 85% throughout the 1960s (Vélez, 1994). By 1969, Puerto Ricans constituted 22% of the student population but filled less than 1% of all teacher and guidance positions. Parental demands and community activism led to the creation of three experimental school districts in New York City by the late 1960s: Independent School 201, Two Bridges, and Ocean-Hill Brownsville. These districts had large representations of Puerto Rican students, and one of the first bilingual programs established without state or federal support was set up as a mini-school in Ocean-Hill Brownsville in 1968 (Fuentes, 1980).

When it became clear that the Board of Education had taken inadequate measures to meet the needs of Puerto Rican children, as yet another study (Jenkins, 1971) had conclusively demonstrated, Aspira of New York, a nonprofit educational agency, decided to litigate. In 1972, the Puerto Rican Legal Defense Fund filed a suit on behalf of Aspira of New York (*Aspira v. Board of Education of the City of New York*). The suit persuasively argued that Puerto Rican children had been denied their right to equal educational opportunity by the board as a function of their ethnicity and language. It also petitioned to implement a bilingual educational program. This suit resulted in the Aspira Consent Decree, signed by both parties on August 29, 1974 (Santiago-Santiago, 1978).

Bilingual education and the decentralization of New York City's schools was not an effective remedy for the high dropout rates affecting Puerto Rican students in that city. First, many language-minority children were still being denied bilingual education after 10 years under the consent decree (Educational Priorities Panel, 1985). Also, second- and third-generation Puerto Rican students were more negatively influenced by educational practices like tracking and the combined effects of low educational expectations and inadequate facilities (National Commission of Secondary Education of Hispanics, 1984).

Because they hold citizenship status and because they frequently engage in circulatory migration patterns, Puerto Ricans are a unique case requiring targeted attention from educators and policy makers. Grosfoguel, Negrón-Muntaner, and Georas (1997), in their explanation of this legacy of colonialism and how it impacts Puerto Ricans' situation in the United States, classified them as an "increasingly deterritorialized ethno-nation" (p. 19). Walsh (2002) suggested that the resistance of many White school administrators to acknowledge cultural differences and the assumption of a colonial attitude toward Puerto Rican students and their parents are at the root of the poor education received by this community in the nation's schools.

Cubans

The origins of the Cuban presence in the United States dates back to the first half of the 19th century when about 1,000 Cubans moved to cities such as New Orleans, Philadelphia, and New York. Expanding commercial ties between Cuba and the United States attracted professionals and merchants and a growing dissatisfaction with Spain's colonial system brought political exiles into the United States at various points during that century. Cuban-owned cigar factories were established in Florida to avoid the import tariffs on cigars and fueled the out-migration of cigar workers from Havana and western Cuba. The domination of Cuban economic and political affairs by the United States in the first half of the 20th century also led to steady migratory steams in the 1940s and 1950s as Cubans fled political violence and a deteriorating economic situation; most of them came to New York and Miami (Poyo & Díaz-Miranda, 1994).

However, it is the two migration waves known as the "Golden Exiles" and the "Marielitos" that set the stage for the social, political, and economic assimilation of Cubans in South Florida in the last four decades of the 20th century. About 270,000 Cubans escaped the socialist government of Fidel Castro between 1959 and 1962; their composition was mostly representative of the socio-economic elite and the middle classes, and they received generous economic support from the United States. In contrast, the so-called "Marielitos," who came in 1980 (about 124,000), were primarily male and of working-class background and were racially diverse, but, most importantly, they were portrayed in the media as dangerous criminals and "social deviants" (Garcia, 1996).

In their quest for establishing a strong ethnic community in South Florida, Cubans built an ethnic enclave that at first emphasized an exile identity enveloped by Cuban nationalism obsessed with overthrowing Castro's government. A key ingredient for creating the enclave was to nurture *Cubanidad* (Cubanness), and one of the most important vehicles to accomplish this was the founding of dozens of small private schools in Miami and Hialeah that became known as *las escuelitas Cubanas* (the little Cuban schools). Taking advantage of the expulsion of the Jesuit priests that were running Havana's best private schools, Cuban exiles reopened schools (closed by Castro) such as LaSalle and Loyola (Garcia, 1996). The most renowned of these private schools was Belén Jesuit, founded in Cuba in 1854. In 1961, the Belen Jesuit School started operations in downtown Miami; and in 1981, the now called Belen Jesuit Preparatory School moved to an impressing facility in the southwest Miami suburbs. What sets these private schools apart, in addition to their academic rigor, is a strong emphasis on developing bilingual skills in Spanish and English.

In trying to model the school performance of native-born children of foreign parents, Portes and Rumbaut (2001) concluded that the pre-Mariel Cuban children had better grades and test scores than the Mariel and post-Mariel children. They also found a causal relationship between attending private bilingual schools and becoming a fluent bilingual. Females and students living in more affluent homes were also more likely to become fluent bilinguals. Thus, the earlier success of the Golden Exiles allowed them to create the right conditions (e.g., bilingual schools) for a privileged group of children to succeed educationally, but this advantage was not passed on to Cuban children whose parents came in more recent periods.

Due to their more privileged background and more positive government reception, Cubans have one of the highest levels of educational attainment among Latino subgroups. In 2000, for example, approximately one of every five (21%) adult Cubans had a college degree, much higher than the college attainment levels of Puerto Ricans and Mexicans (12.5% and 7.5%, respectively; see Acosta-Belén & Santiago, 2006).

Central Americans

As a result of civil war and government repression in their countries of origin, Central Americans began arriving in large numbers in the United States during the 1970s and 1980s. In the Los Angeles region, for example, the number of foreign-born Salvadorans went from 4,800 in 1970 to 241,509 in 1990 (Sabagh & Bozorgomehr, 1996). The Los Angeles neighborhoods of Pico Union and Westlake have the largest concentrations of Central Americans, where you can find churches, businesses, and community-based organizations catering to the needs of this population. Arriving with limited English skills, of mostly peasant and working-class background, and with high rates of undocumented status (especially Salvadorans and Guatemalans), these young immigrants have very low levels of educational attainment. Only 3% of Salvadorans and 4% of Guatemalans (ages 25–64) in the Los Angeles region had a college degree in 1990, compared to 12% of other Central Americans and 24 % of the rest of the population (Lopez, Popkin, & Telles, 1996).

An ethnographic study of Central American immigrant adolescents conducted by Suarez-Orozco (1989) revealed a strong belief in the value of schooling for achieving economic mobility as well as a strong desire to graduate from high school and pursue college studies. In their study of second-generation eighth- and ninth-grade students (in South Florida), Portes and Zhou (2005) found that about four of every five Nicaraguan students aspired to a college education or higher.

Through the efforts of Central American activists in Los Angeles, a number of refugee service organizations were developed in the 1980s, and some of these, like the Central American Refugee Center, have developed programs to help students in the local schools. For example, following the 1992 riots in Los Angeles, CARECEN launched the Nueva Generación program, which provided tutoring and computer training as well as internships for high school students (Hamilton & Chinchilla, 2001). In 1997, CARECEN joined the Los Angeles Bridge program, a coalition of local community organizations, and was able to provide bilingual tutoring in math and other subjects, art workshops, and training in computer skills for students in the Berendo Middle School located in the Westlake district (Hamilton & Chinchilla, 2001).

The educational outlook for Central American students is heavily dependent on the quality and the policies of the Los Angeles Unified School system. However, the Los Angeles Board of Education changed the graduation requirements in 2003, requiring students to pass a year of algebra and a year of geometry or an equivalent class to earn a high school diploma. There is increasing evidence that Central American students are having great difficulties in passing their algebra classes, and as a result, their dropout rates are very high (Helfand, 2006).

Dominicans

Political and economic ties between the Dominican Republic and the United States go back to the 19th century, including military interventions and massive investments in the country by American business interests (Grasmuck & Pessar, 1991). Mass migration to the United States began in the early 1960s, and by 1998, there were an estimated 412,000 foreign-born Dominicans residing in New York City (Foner, 2000). The disappearance of manufacturing jobs and fierce competition for jobs from other immigrant groups in New York City has led to high unemployment and poverty rates among Dominicans (Pessar & Graham, 2001). Dominicans have the lowest educational levels of the major Latino subgroups (Falcon, 2004).

Increasing geographical concentrations in Washington Heights and other parts of northern Manhattan and parts of the South Bronx meant living in neighborhoods characterized by overcrowded housing and schools, as well as exposure to drug-related violence and poorly maintained parks and physical facilities. However, as a consequence of their relative high segregation, Dominicans have been able to mobilize along ethnic lines to achieve local representation and empowerment. In 1991, Guillermo Linares was the first Dominican elected to the New York City Council (Pessar, 1995), and in 1996, Dominican-born Adriano Espaillat was elected to the New York State Assembly as the representative from District 72 in northern Manhattan (Pessar & Graham, 2001).

By the early 1980s, Dominicans made up the majority of students in New York's Community School District 6 (in the Washington Heights neighborhood), at that time home to the city's most overcrowded schools. It was then that the Community Association of Progressive Dominicans confronted the school board and superintendent to demand bilingual education and other services for recently arrived immigrant families. The concerted efforts of community organizations, a parents' network throughout the district, and an aggressive voter registration drive led to greater Dominican representation on neighborhood school boards (and a majority in District 6). As a result, bilingual programs were started, new schools were constructed in the district, and, in 1994, a Dominican was appointed principal of a community high school where three-quarters of the student body was of Dominican origin (Pessar, 1995). Examples of schools serving immigrant students include the Gregorio Luperon High School for Science & Mathematics and the Twenty-First Century Academy (P.S. 210; K–6), both of which have partnerships with Dominican community organizations.

Dominican students are the largest Latino subgroup in New York City's public school at a time when Latinos have the highest dropout rate of the major ethnic/racial groups in the city's schools (see New York City Department of Education, 2005). However, signs of hope for those born in the United States are present in the study done by Hernandez and Rivera-Batiz (2003), who found that second-generation Dominicans had higher college attainment levels than other Latino groups in the country. They found that, in the year 2000, 22% of U.S.-born Dominicans (25 years of age or older) had completed a college education, compared to only 13% and 12% respectively of their Mexican and Puerto Rican counterparts. Hernandez and Rivera-Batiz (2003) also reported that Dominican students in New York City have high school retention rates that are substantially higher than for the overall Latino population.

EXPLAINING EDUCATIONAL ATTAINMENT

One of the most common indicators used to illustrate the struggles faced by Latinos in educational institutions is the dropout rate. For example, the status dropout rate (the percentage of an age group that is not enrolled in school and has not earned a high school credential) for Latinos 16–24 years old in 2001 was 27%, or about four times larger than the status dropout rate of similar Whites, which stood at 7.3% (NCES, 2003). More disturbing, in retrospect, comparisons of dropout rates over time also illustrate that the educational gap between Latinos and other ethnic and racial groups has not closed very much in more than two decades. Between 1972 and 2001, the status dropout rates for White and Black young adults declined significantly (41% and 49%, respectively) while the decline in the Latino rate was more modest (21%).

Some, but not all, of the high Latino dropout rates can be explained by greater dropout rates among Latino immigrants, many of whom have never enrolled in U.S. schools. However, even among Latino young adults born in the United States, the status dropout rate in 2001 was 15.4%, slightly more than twice the rate for White students and about 40% higher than the status dropout rate for Black students (NCES, 2003).

In reviewing the literature on school-leaving among Latinos, Vélez and Saenz (2001) suggested that the best approach to understanding the dropout activity of these students is the ecological model, which makes linkages between individuals, the groups in which they participate, and the environment in which they live. They identified three clusters—individual, family, and structural—useful in organizing or making sense of the growing research findings around high school attrition. Before beginning the discussion of the three clusters of factors affecting Latino dropout rates, it is important to point out that many of the empirical observations based on Latino youth are consistent with results based on their peers from other racial and ethnic groups.

Individual Factors Explaining the Educational Attainment of Latinos[1]

Alienation from educational goals and school officials and/or peer pressure (see Valenzuela, 1999) leads some students to engage in what has been called "confrontational practices" or behaviors that oppose or violate specific rules of school. Velez (1989) concluded that Puerto Rican and Chicano high school students who cut classes were more likely to drop out of school. Disruptive behaviors frequently lead to school sanctions such as suspensions, which have been found to be associated with leaving high school before graduation (Velez, 1989). Ironically, schools are frequently slow to catch on to oppositional behaviors such as cutting classes, suggesting that the staff is either indifferent or uncaring (see Flores-González, 2002).

Although oppositional behaviors often have negative consequences for students, there are instances when students act out of a critical interpretation of schools as an oppressive institution. In such cases, one can argue for the presence of what some scholars call "resistance" of a transformative form (Yosso, 2005), which involves conscious efforts to challenge and overcome practices and attitudes harmful to students of color.

Ogbu (1987) asserted that involuntary minorities are especially likely to develop an oppositional culture due to the rejection that they experience from mainstream society. Involuntary minorities consist of those groups whose initial incorporation into the United States occurred through military conquest, slavery, or other aggressive means. Involuntary minorities include Chicanos, Puerto Ricans, African Americans, and Native Americans. In contrast, voluntary minorities initially came to this country through their free will and, as a result, experience less conflictive relations with the mainstream society. Hence, members of these groups are more likely to embrace the cultural values of the host society because they are less likely to experience rejection from the mainstream society. For example, recent data on intermarriage rates suggesting that Chinese Americans have high out-marriage rates (mostly to Whites) was used by Bonilla-Silva (2006) to buttress his argument that some Asian American groups have achieved what he calls "honorary white" status.

Students with involuntary minority backgrounds develop identities in opposition to school culture when they believe in the existence of job ceilings that make the acquisition of educational credentials irrelevant for socioeconomic mobility. For them, hard work in school does not necessarily lead to economic success in the future because society has been structured so that class or ethnicity circumscribes one's opportunities (Fine, 1991). Among Latinos, Mexicans and Puerto Ricans are characterized as having experienced "castelike" conditions of socioeconomic incorporation, whereas Cubans experienced a warmer government reception and developed ethnic enclaves in Florida that gave them an edge in the local economy (Bohon, Johnson, & Gorman, 2006).

Another important argument made by oppositional theory is that involuntary minorities tend to experience difficulty in maintaining a racial/ethnic identity and academic success simultaneously because academic success is perceived by them as a characteristically "White" (or middle class) behavior (Fordham & Ogbu, 1986). Success in school comes at the expense of their own culture (and the friendship of coethnic peers) as they embrace "White" culture (McLaren, 1994). However, in studying academic achievement among Latino students, some researchers have concluded that success in school does not necessarily come at the expense of ethnic identity (Antrop-Gonzalez, Velez, & Garrett, 2005; Flores-González, 2002). For example, a study in a predominantly Latino high school in Chicago concluded that high achievers did not associate school success with "whiteness" and that although some were initially harassed by their peers, they went on to occupy their own social space in school and were not pressured to underachieve (Flores-González, 1999). In another study of Puerto Rican high achievers (Antrop-Gonzalez, Velez, & Garrett, 2005), the authors observed that "they were very clear about their Puerto Rican identity, always stating to their friends that they were 'Boricua' or 'puertor-riqueño' and proud about it" (p. 86). So it appears that many successful Latino students engage in "accommodation without assimilation" (Gibson, 1988) by navigating between different cultural worlds, such as the home, community, and schools, while keeping the cultural framework acquired at home (and in their countries of origin for immigrant students).

Ogbu's (1987) model of voluntary/involuntary minorities can also be criticized for generalizing assumptions about specific ethnic groups and ignoring the internal variability frequently present in these groups. Olneck (2003) noted, for example, that sometimes immigrant students from voluntary minority backgrounds (e.g., some Asian groups) do better in school than their U.S.-born counterparts. This means that the often-cited advantages in school performance that members of voluntary minorities enjoy can disappear. He also suggested that resistance to schooling at times can be inspired by "cultural revitalization movements that redefine ethnic identities in ways conducive to educational achievement."

Academic Expectations and Performance

Student orientations toward the future and parental expectations for college are often cited in the literature as being related to school persistence. Students who plan to attend college tend to finish high school at higher rates than those who do not plan to go on to college (Velez, 1989). In their study of native-born children of immigrant parents, Portes and Rumbaut (2001) found that Mexican-origin students had the lowest levels of educational expectations of all the Latino subgroups, whereas Cuban students who attended bilingual private schools in Miami had the highest level of educational expectations

Bohon, Johnson, & Gorman (2006) found that Cuban adolescents have stronger college aspirations and expectations than non-Latino Whites, whereas Mexican and Puerto Rican youth have significantly weaker college aspirations and expectations than non-Latino White youth. Controlling for family socioeconomic status, test scores, and other demographic factors eliminates the Mexican disadvantage in college aspirations and expectations vis-à-vis Whites, whereas for Puerto Ricans, the addition of these variables eliminates differences from non-Latino Whites in college expectations, but not aspirations. Additionally, the stronger Cuban college aspirations and expectations remained after adjusting for socioeconomic status and other factors.

Planning for college has significant effects for the probability of completing college among Latinos. The authors of a recent study of Latino college attainment concluded that Latino students planning for some college (vs. none) increased the probability of completion by 48%, and those who planned for a bachelor's degree increased the probability by 53% (Swail et al., 2005).

Parents exert a strong and decisive influence on the formation of educational expectations among Latino students (Cabrera & La Nasa, 2001). Portes and Rumbaut (2001) found that about three out of every four parents of Cuban and Nicaraguan descent expected their children to graduate from college. Using logistic regression analysis, Swail et al. (2005) found that although Latino parental expectations for their children to attend some college or to get a bachelor's degree (ves. none) was not related to finishing college, parental expectation of advanced degrees increased the probability of completing a 4-year degree by 46%.

Academic performance as measured by school grades appears to be negatively associated with the risk of dropping out among Latino students (Driscoll, 1999; Velez, 1989). Put simply, students with higher grades are less likely to become high school dropouts compared to those with poorer scholarly performance. Gatekeepers such as school counselors and teachers frequently use grades as the main criterion to grant entry to college-oriented classes and/or privileged academic programs with small class sizes and strong teacher-student relationships (Conchas, 2006). Good grades can be a boost to the academic self-concept of high-achieving Latino students and makes future learning easier or less costly than for their less successful counterparts.

Generational Status and Acculturation

Immigrant students face a broad array of educational needs and problems. In addition to the need for learning English, these children and youths face problems like high residential mobility, poverty, the emotional stress associated with adjusting to a new social and physical environment, and inadequate social support to compensate for broken community ties in their native countries and loss of support necessary for psychological well-being (Ream, 2005; Valdés, 2001). Previous studies have found consistently higher dropout rates for foreign-born Latino youths and students with limited English proficiency (see Velez, 1989; Warren, 1996).

However, some research has observed that recent immigrants actually do better in school than U.S.-born Latinos (Conchas, 2006; Suarez-Orozco & Suarez-Orozco, 1995). Driscoll (1999), in her research distinguishing among first-, second-, and third-generation Latino youth when modeling dropout behavior, found no generational differences in the odds of dropping out of high school early (by the sophomore year). However, among students who made it through the first 2 years of high school, she found that both first- and second-generation students were less likely to become dropouts than third-generation students, net of class, school performance, aspirations, and family structure.

These contradictory results suggest that immigrant status is associated with a variety of factors and situations, some of which promote dropping out (e.g., lower family income and less educated parents) and others that encourage school retention and completion. For example, Conchas (2006) suggested that Latino immigrant students have a more positive view of the opportunity structure and are willing to work harder than their U.S.-born counterparts.

Portes and his colleagues (Portes & Rumbaut, 2001; Portes & Zhou, 1993) noted that the particular track that immigrants take depends on their access to resources within their families and communities. The road to educational success is dependent on a socially supportive environment that promotes selective acculturation and fluent bilingualism. An example of this would be the pre-1980 Cuban exile community in southern Florida, who constructed a solid and institutionally diversified ethnic economy that included a system of bilingual private schools (Portes & Rumbaut, 2001). Under the segmented assimilation model proposed by Portes and his colleagues, attention is paid to the interaction among the economic and human capital of different groups, the context of exit from their countries of origin, and the context of reception (including racial stratification, spatial segregation, and government policies) in determining how immigrant groups adjust to life in the United States.

One important asset for immigrant youth in pursuing advanced levels of education is their legal status. Significant numbers of Mexicans, Salvadorans, and Guatemalans are undocumented youth and, as such, face legal and economic barriers to higher education (Abrego, 2006). Even if they graduate from high school with good academic records, undocumented students often fail to qualify for in-state tuition and federal and local financial aid for college.

Immigrants' Educational Selectivity

The selective migration argument is sometimes used to explain earnings and health disparities among immigrants' children (Borjas, 1987; Landale, Oropesa, & Gorman, 2000). By calculating the sending countries' average levels of educational attainment as well as the average educational attainment of immigrants for a particular cohort or time period, Feliciano (2005) tested the predictive power of the selective migration model to explain college attainment among the second generation of 32 national-origin groups. Her findings suggest that as educational selectivity among Mexican immigrants declined over time (1960–1990 period), there has been a similar decline in the percent college educated among immigrant children. Controlling for group educational selectivity (as well as parents' socioeconomic status) eliminates the lower college expectations among Latinos and cancels the advantage of belonging to an Asian ethnic group. These findings challenge cultural explanations that are used to account for ethnic group differences in educational success and suggest that class reproduction appears to be taking place from the generation of immigrants to their children.

Spanish Language Use

Spanish language use is commonly targeted as an extremely important factor to explain the educational failure of Latino youth. However, research on high school students suggests that speaking Spanish at home, per se, does not lead to lowered academic performance (Yeung, Marsh, & Suliman, 2000). In their study of second-generation children, Portes and Rumbaut (2001) reported a negative effect of losing the parental language on school achievement, measured as scores in standardized tests and grade point average.

Family-Related Factors

The family is often seen in the literature as responsible to a significant extent for the success or failure of students in the educational system (see Stanton-Salazar, 2001). Given that Latinos have often been viewed as a group characterized by high levels of familism, the family-related factors need to be considered when examining the educational outcomes of Latino students.

FAMILY STRUCTURE The literature provides consistent evidence regarding the relationship between family structure and school completion. In particular, widespread research has concluded that students with two parents at home are more likely to continue their schooling than are those with only one parent at home (Velez, 1989). Although two-thirds of Latino families are married-couple families (Perez, 2001), high rates of female-headed households are prevalent in some Latino subgroups, in particular among Puerto Ricans (Acosta-Belén & Santiago, 2006).

A study comparing Latino subgroups suggests that the positive effects of having two parents (in decreasing dropout behavior) are greater for Puerto Rican and Cuban students than for Chicanos (Velez, 1989).

FAMILY SOCIOECONOMIC BACKGROUND   The literature is also very clear on the impact of family socioeconomic status (SES) on the probability of school completion, with low SES being one of the most frequently mentioned causes of dropping out (Hauser, Simmons, & Pager, 2000). Economic constraints can force some students to drop out because they or their families need their earnings immediately (Romo & Falbo, 1996; Rumberger & Thomas, 2000).

The family's economic position can also have an impact on the neighborhood of residence, with consequences for the quality of life and the quality of the schools that Latino students attend. Living in a neighborhood characterized by concentrated poverty is associated with inadequate housing, high crime rates, high unemployment rates, and higher exposure to health hazards, all of which have direct or indirect effects on the educational chances of children (Sampson, Morenoff, & Gannon-Rowley, 2002).

The geographic concentration of poor minorities as a factor in educational outcomes of minority youth is especially important in the case of Latinos. Recent research by the Harvard Civil Rights Project has shown increasing levels of school segregation among minorities, particularly in the case of Latinos (Orfield & Lee, 2006). The average Latino student attends a school that is 28% White, whereas the average White student attends a school that is 78 % White.

The effects of housing and school segregation during early childhood have long-term educational consequences for Latino students. Comparing Latinos who grew up in segregated neighborhoods to those growing up in predominantly majority settings, Massey and Fischer (2006) found that the latter group completed more advanced placement courses in high school. They also concluded that Black and Latino students growing up in integrated surroundings earned higher grades during their first three terms of college than their counterparts who came of age in segregated settings.

As a result of an unstable economic situation, many Latino families tend to move frequently within the United States. Ream (2005) argued that student mobility limits the acquisition of social capital because it prevents close-knit and trusting peer interactions. This makes it more difficult for students to feel "connected" to their schools and teachers. Thus, changing schools because of family moves is often found to increase a student's probability of dropping out (Velez, 1989) and is also associated with lower test scores in 12th grade among Mexican-origin youth (Ream, 2005). Family socioeconomic background also impacts postsecondary educational outcomes among Latinos. Swail et al. (2005) concluded that middle-income Latinos had a 17 % higher probability of earning a BA compared to low-income Latinos.

SOCIAL CAPITAL   Discussions related to the effect of SES on educational outcomes often involve paying attention to cultural capital, frequently characterized as a cluster of dispositions and "tastes" (Bourdieu, 1977). The cultural knowledge of the upper and middle classes are highly valued, so those who are not born into these families must access this knowledge through formal schooling. Assuming a critical race theory perspective, Yosso (2005) criticized the cultural capital paradigm for assuming a deficit view of communities of color and proposed an alternative concept called "community cultural wealth" (see below).

The family also impacts the social capital available to the student (i.e., the degree and quality of middle-class forms of social support present in a young person's interpersonal network) (see Coleman, 1988). This is usually conceptualized to affect students from two perspectives. In the first, high levels of parental social capital are associated with the ability of adults to control the student's behavior by way of shared norms and expectations that can readily be enforced. Teachman, Paasch, and Carver (1997) called this process "connectivity." They found that parents who interact with their children and their children's schools have children who are more likely to remain in school. The second conceptualization of social capital focuses on the presence or lack of opportunities for generalized exchange between adults and youths. To succeed in school, students must acquire a set of skills known as "funds of knowledge." These funds of knowledge allow the student to decode the school's institutional culture. By knowing and displaying institutionally sanctioned discourses and by their ability to solve school-related problems, students are identified as insiders; that is, they receive the school's approval or sponsorship (Stanton-Salazar, 2001).

An overemphasis on middle-class forms of social and cultural capital assumes that students come to school without the normative cultural knowledge and skills and that their parents neither value nor support their child's education. Basing her theoretical constructs on research findings on Latinos and other communities of color, Yosso (2005) argued for the presence of "community cultural wealth" useful as survival strategies under oppressive conditions by conceptualizing six forms of capital: (a) aspirational capital—ability to maintain hopes and dreams for the future, allowing children to "dream of possibilities beyond their present circumstances" (p. 78); (b) linguistic capital—language and communication styles attained in more than one language; (c) familial capital—cultural knowledge nurtured and transmitted through kinship ties, where one learns "the importance of maintaining a health connection to our community and its resources" (p. 79); (d) social capital—networks of people and community resources that provide both instrumental and emotional support to navigate through society's institutions; (e) navigational capital—the ability or skills to maneuver through social institutions like schools that create stressful and hostile situations that place students "at-risk" of failing; and (f) resistant capital—"those knowledges and skills fostered through oppositional behavior that challenges inequality" (p. 80) and that have the potential to transform oppressive structures of domination.

STRUCTURAL-LEVEL FACTORS

The literature on Latino dropouts, as is the case with the general dropout literature, focuses primarily on individual- and family-level factors in efforts to develop an understanding of the forces explaining students' dropout behavior (Velez & Saenz, 2001). Implicitly, this analytical approach emphasizes deficiencies of students and their families in accounting for the failure of students in the educational system. As such, schools and communities are let off the hook when it comes to explaining why certain students do not succeed in the educational system (Hispanic Dropout Project, 1998).

School Practices

In their quest for maintaining order and for pursuing educational excellence, educational systems develop a variety of school practices and policies. For example, tracking or curricular placement is one institutional practice that has immediate and long-term effects for high school students, affecting not only their chances of finishing school but also their chances of attending college and attaining a college degree (Kao & Thompson, 2003; Velez, 1985, 1989). Students enrolled in the college preparatory track are exposed to more rigorous material, receive more attention from teachers and school staff, and complete more advanced placement classes than those who are enrolled in other curricular tracks (Oakes, 1985). However, Latinos are less likely to take the courses associated with school retention and college preparation, as evidenced by their low completion of advanced science and mathematics courses in high school (Kao & Thompson, 2003; Swail et al., 2005). Taking pre-calculus and calculus has been found to be significantly associated with the probability of completing a 4r-year degree among Latinos (Swail et al., 2005).

The practice of grade retention or holding back students because of language difficulties, learning disorders, poor attendance, or academic failure has also been found to have negative effects on high school graduation (Farkas, 2003). Students who have been delayed in their schooling as a result of grade retention tend to experience higher rates of withdrawal from school (Jerald, 2006). Latino students have very high incidences of grade retention (National Association of School Psychologists, 2003).

Community Economic and Demographic Context

A study of Latino college students in a Midwestern university concluded that those residing in a predominately Latino neighborhood were less likely to persist in college (Velez, 2002). This finding, if generalizable to students in the rest of the nation, augurs lower completion rates for Latino college students, given increasing rates of residential segregation in the nation's largest metropolitan areas between Whites and Latinos (Velez & Martin, 2003).

PUBLIC POLICY IMPLICATIONS

In terms of its impact on access to education, federal action on immigration reform is one of the most important issues of the 21st century. A streamlined path to legal residency and citizenship would enhance the social, economic, and political assimilation of the millions of undocumented Latinos living in the United States, allowing them and their children to secure rights to an advanced education, including financial aid. In the meantime, some states (e.g., California) have taken the lead in providing some remedy for the legal vulnerability of undocumented youth by passing legislation that qualifies many of them for a waiver of out-of-state tuition (Abrego, 2006). However, these measures do not go far enough, which is why it is very important that the U.S. Congress pass the Development, Relief, and Education for Alien Minors Act, which would grant many youth access to legal residency and federal financial aid.

It is also very important to encourage Latino students to prepare for college as early as possible. Thus, federal programs like GEAR UP and Upward Bound should continue to be funded, as they help low-income students, starting in middle school, to learn more about post secondary education and the curricular choices they have to make to achieve their occupational plans. However, there are also excellent nonfederal programs that have proven successful in engaging Latino students early, such as AVID in San Diego, El Puente in New York City, and Aspira of America, that can be replicated in other places.

At the curricular level, state and local school leaders should develop policies to encourage the selection of Algebra I at the eighth grade in order to open up further academic options for students in high school (Swail et al., 2005). It is also crucial that public schools provide remedial English programs for Latino students and well-run bilingual programs for English learners.

At the college level, it is imperative to develop financial aid policies that provide sufficient support and enable Latino students to maintain continuous enrollment while bringing about engagement with faculty and staff. Student success needs to be enhanced through collaborative action by faculty and staff who adopt the persistence and graduation of their students of color as their "mission" and who treat their students as members of a family (AASCU, 2005). Access to residence halls that provide coordinated student services and opportunities for undergraduate Latino students to work closely with faculty members on research projects are other campus policies that have been used in many college campuses to promote student success among Latinos (AASCU, 2005).

DIRECTIONS FOR FUTURE RESEARCH

After surveying the methodological and sampling shortcomings of previous federally funded educational surveys, Velez and Saenz (2001) called for a large-scale nationally representative longitudinal survey that would focus on the educational outcomes of Latino students. Such a study would collect data from students, teachers, administrators, peers, and parents. It also would provide information about the neighborhoods and communities where students live and precise information about the nativity and immigration status of students to determine the length of stay of students and their parents in the United States. Such a longitudinal study needs to include an adequate sample of undocumented Latino/a youths, a sizable and growing population that is facing exclusionary immigration policies and legal barriers that block their access to educational mobility.

The passage of what can be considered anti-immigrant legislation in a number of states requires the continued and future attention of researchers. For example, implementation of Proposition 227 in California made enrollment in bilingual programs problematic for many Latino students. It also failed to deliver on its promise that limited-English-proficient students would become proficient in English within 1 year (Crawford, 2003). Additional studies that document the impact of Proposition 227 and similar measures in other states and that assess the efficacy of bilingual programs (e.g., see Greene, 1998) to enhance academic subject mastery and English acquisition are needed.

Similarly, the passage of the No Child Left Behind Act (NCLB) and its mandatory testing of all children, even those who are English learners, poses a real threat to the self-esteem and academic progress of many Latino students. These tests have to be administered in English with only minor special accommodations for some of the limited-English-proficient children, even though research shows that it takes between 5 and 7 years to gain mastery of academic English. Under this new "audit" culture, public schools (but not private) are subjected to strong accountability measures, teachers are forced to "teach to the test," and a student's worth is reduced to her or his test scores (Apple, 2006). Evidence on the effects of graduation tests in Texas show rising grade retention and high school dropout rates for Latino students (Valenzuela, 2005). New studies are need to determine the adequacy and impact of NCLB as applied to immigrant Latino students in our nation's school systems.

Finally, the school reform trends of the early 21st century include efforts to impose a "market logic" on public schools where students and their parents can behave as consumers presented with a wide array of services (Apple, 2006). This has resulted in the development of school vouchers, tax credits, and publicly funded "choice" schools in a number of states. More research is needed to ascertain the impact of these school reforms on Latino students.

NOTE

1. This section is partially drawn from themes found in an article authored by William Velez and Rogelio Saenz (2001) titled "Toward a Comprehensive Model of the School Leaving Process Among Latinos." *School Psychology Quarterly, 16*(4), 445–467.

REFERENCES

AASCU (American Association of State Colleges and Universities). (2005). Student Success in State Colleges and Universities: A Matter of Culture and Leadership. Washington, DC: American Association of State Colleges and Universities.

Abrego, Leisy J. (2006). "I Can't Go to College Because I Don't Have Papers": Incorporation Patterns of Latino Undocumented Youth. *Latino Studies, 4*, 212–231.

Acosta-Belén, Edna, & Santiago, Carlos E. (2006). *Puerto Ricans in the United States: A Contemporary Portrait*. Boulder, CO: Lynne Rienner Publishers.

Alicea, Marisa. (1994). The Latino Immigration Experience: The Case of Mexicanos, Puertorriqueños, and Cubanos. In Felix Padilla (Ed.), *Handbook of Hispanic Cultures in the United States* (pp. 35–56). Houston, TX: Arte Publico Press.

Antrop-González, R., Vélez, W., & Garrett, T. (2005). Dónde Están los Estudiantes Puertorriqueños Exitosos [Where Are the Successful Puerto Rican Students]? Success Factors of High Achieving Puerto Rican High School Students. *Journal of Latinos and Education, 4*(2), 77–94.

Apple, Michael W. (2006). *Educating the "Right" Way: Markets, Standards, God, and Inequality*. New York: Routledge.

Bean, Frank, Lee, Jennifer, Batalova, Jeanne, & Leach, Mark. (2004). *Immigration and Fading Color Lines in America*. Washington, DC: Population Reference Bureau.

Bohon, Stephanie A., Johnson, Monica Kirkpatrick, & Gorman, Bridget K. (2006). College Aspirations and Expectations Among Latino Adolescents in the United States. *Social Problems, 53*, 207–225.

Bonilla-Silva, Eduardo. (2006). We Are All Americans! The Latin Americanization of Racial Stratification in the U.S.A. In Elizabeth Higginbotham & Margaret L. Andersen (Eds.), *Race and Ethnicity in Society: The Changing Landscape* (pp. 419–425). Belmont, CA: Thomson Wadsworth.

Borjas, George J. (1987). Self-Selection and the Earnings of Immigrants. *The American Economic Review, 77*, 531–553.

Bourdieu, Pierre. (1977). *Reproduction in Education, Society, and Culture*. London: Sage Publications.

Cabrera, Alberto F., & La Nasa, S. M. (2001). On the Path to College: Three Critical Tasks Facing America's Disadvantaged. *Research in Higher Education, 42*, 119–149.

Coleman, James S. (1988). Social Capital in the Creation of Human Capital. *American Journal of Sociology, 94*, S95–S120.

Conchas, Gilberto Q. (2006). *The Color of Success: Race and High Achieving Urban Youth*. New York: Teachers College Press.

Crawford, James. (2003). *A Few Things Ron unz would prefer you didn't know about…English Learners in California*. Retrieved November 1, 2006, from www.humnet.ucla.edu/humnet/linguistics/people/grads/macswan/unz.htm.

Driscoll, Anne K. (1999). Risk of high school dropout among immigrant and native Hispanic youth. *International Migration Review, 33*(4), 857–875.

Educational Priorities Panel. (1985). *Ten Years of Neglect: The Education of Children of Limited English Proficiency in New York Public Schools*. New York: Interface.

Falcon, Angelo. (2004). *Atlas of Stateside Puerto Ricans*. San Juan: Puerto Rico Federal Affairs Administration.

Farkas, George. (2003). Racial Disparities and Discrimination in Education: What Do We Know, How Do We Know It, and What Do We need To Know? *Teachers College Record, 105*, 1119–1146.

Feliciano, Cynthia. (2005). Does Selective Migration Matter? Explaining Ethnic Disparities in Educational Attainment among Immigrants' Children. *International Migration Review, 39*, 841–871.

Fine, Michelle. (1991). *Framing Dropouts: Notes on the Politics of an Urban Public High School*. Albany: State University of New York Press.

Flores-González, Nilda. (1999). Puerto Rican High Achievers: An Example of Ethnic and Academic Identity Compatibility. *Anthropology and Education Quarterly, 30*, 343–362.

Flores-González, Nilda. (2002). *School Kids/Street Kids: Identity Development in Latino Students*. New York: Teachers College Press.

Foner, Nancy. (2000). *From Ellis Island to JFK: New York's Two Waves of Immigration*. New Haven: Yale University Press.

Fordham, S., & Ogbu, J. U. (1986). Black Students' School Success: Coping with the Burden of Acting White. *The Urban Review, 18*, 176–206.

Fuentes, Luis. (1980). The Struggle for Local Political Control. In C. E. Rodriguez, V. S. Korrol, & J. O. Alers (Eds.), *The Puerto Rican Struggle: Essays on Survival in the U.S.* (pp. 111–120). New York: Puerto Rican Migration Research Consortium.

Garcia, Cristina. (1996). *Havana USA: Cuban Exiles and Cuban Americans in South Florida, 1959–1994*. Berkeley: University of California Press.

Garcia, Eugene E. (1999). *Understanding and Meeting the Challenge of Student Cultural Diversity* (10th ed.). New York: Houghton Mifflin.

Garcia, Eugene E. (2001). *Hispanic Education in the United States*. Lanham, MD: Rowman & Littlefield.

Gibson, Margaret A. (1988). *Accommodation Without Assimilation*. Ithaca, NY: Cornell University Press.

Gonzalez. G. (1990). *Chicano Education in the Segregation Era: 1915–1945*. Philadelphia: The Balch Institute.

Grasmuck, Sherri, & Pessar, Patricia R. (1991). *Between Two Islands: Dominican International Migration*. Berkeley: University of California Press.

Greene, Jay P. (1998). *A Meta-Analysis of the Effectiveness of Bilingual Education*. Los Angeles: The Tomas Rivera Policy Institute.

Grosfoguel, R., Negrón-Muntaner, F., & Georas, C. (1997). Beyond Nationalist and Colonialist Discourses: The Jaiba Politics of the Puerto Rican Ethno-nation. In F. Negrón-Muntaner & R. Grosfoguel (Eds.), *Puerto Rican Jam: Essays on Culture and Politics* (pp. 1–38). Minneapolis: University of Minnesota Press.

Hamilton, Nora, & Chinchilla, Norma S. (2001). *Seeking Community in a global city: Guatemalans and Salvadorans in Los Angeles*. Philadelphia: Temple University Press.

Hauser, Robert M., Simmons, Solon J., & Pager, Devah I. (2000). *High School Dropout, Race-Ethnicity, and Social Background from the 1970s to the 1990s*. New York: Russell Sage Foundation.

Helfand, Duke. (2006, January). A Formula for Failure in L.A. Schools. *Los Angeles Times*. Retrieved December 22, 2006, from http://www.latimes.com/news/education/la-me-dropout30jan30,0,3211437.story.

Hernandez, Ramona, & Rivera-Batiz, Francisco. (2003). *Dominicans in the United States: A Socioeconomic Profile, 2000*. New York: The CUNY Dominican Studies Institute.

Hispanic Deopout Project. (1998). *No More Excuses: The Final Report of the Hispanic Dropout Project*. Madison, WI: University of Wisconsin-Madison.

Jenkins, Mary. (1971). *Bilingual Education in New York City*. New York: New York City Board of Education, Office of Recruitment and Training of Spanish-Speaking Teachers.

Jerald, Craig D. (2006). *Identifying Potential Dropouts: Key Lessons for Building an Early Warning Data System*. New York: Achieve, Inc., American Diploma Project Network.

Kao, Grace, & Thompson, Jennifer S. (2003). Racial and Ethnic Stratification in Educational Achievement and Attainment. *Annual Review of Sociology, 29*, 417–442.

Landale, Nancy S., Oropesa, R. S., & Gorman, B. K. (2000). Migration and Infant Death: Assimilation or Selective Migration among Puerto Ricans? *American Sociological Review, 65*, 888–909.

Lopez, David E., Popkin, Eric, & Telles, Edward. (1996). Central Americans: At the Bottom, Struggling to Get Ahead. In R. Waldinger & M. Bozorgmehr (Eds.), *Ethnic Los Angeles* (pp. 279–304). New York: Russell Sage Foundation.

Massey, Douglas S., & Fischer, Mary J. (2006). The Effect of Childhood Segregation on Minority Academic Performance at Selective Colleges. *Ethnic and Racial Studies, 29*, 1–26.

McLaren, Peter L. (1994). *Life in Schools*. New York: Longman.

Montejano, David. (1987). *Anglos and Mexicans in the Making of Texas, 1836–1986*. Austin: University of Texas Press.

National Association of School Psychologists. (2003). *Position Statement on Student Grade Retention and Social Promotion*. Bethesda, MD: National Association of School Psychologists.

National Commission on Secondary Education for Hispanics. (1984). *"Make Something Happen": Hispanics And Urban School Reform*. Washington, DC: Hispanic Policy Development Project.

Navarro-Rivera, Pablo. (2006). Acculturation Under Duress: The Puerto Rican Experience at the Carlisle Indian Industrial School 1898–1918. *CENTRO Journal, 18*, 223–257.

NCES (National Center for Education Statistics). (2003). *The Condition of Education, 2003*. Washington, DC: U.S. Government Printing Office.

Negrón de Montilla, Aida. (1971). *Americanization in Puerto Rico and the Public School System*. Rio Piedras, Puerto Rico: Editorial Universitaria.

New York City Department of Education. (2005). *The Class of 2005 Four-Year Longitudinal Report and 2004–2005 Event Dropout Rates*. New York: Department of Education, Division of Assessment and Accountability.

Oakes, Jeannie. (1985). *Keeping Track: How Schools Structure Inequality*. New Haven, CT: Yale University Press.

Ogbu, John U. (1987). Variability in Minority School Performance: A Problem in Search of an Explanation. *Anthropology and Education Quarterly, 18*, 312–334.

Olneck, Michael E. (2003). Immigrants and Education in the United States. In James A. Banks & Cherry A. McGee Banks (Eds.), *Handbook of Research on Multicultural Education* (pp. 381–403). San Francisco: Jossey-Bass.

Orfield, Gary, & Lee, Chungmei. (2006). *Racial Transformation and the Changing Nature of Segregation*. Cambridge, MA: The Civil Rights Project at Harvard University.

Perez, Sonia M. (2001). *Beyond the Census: Hispanics and an American Agenda*. Washington, DC: National Council of La Raza.

Pessar, Patricia. (1995). *A Visa for a Dream: Dominicans in the United States*. Boston: Allyn and Bacon.

Pessar, Patricia R., & Graham, Pamela M. (2001). *Dominicans: Transnational Identities and Local Politics*. In Nancy Foner (Ed.), *New Immigrants in New York* (pp. 251–274). New York: Columbia University Press.

Portes, Alejandro, & Rumbaut, Ruben G. (2001). *Legacies: The Story of The Immigrant Second Generation*. Berkeley: University of California Press.

Portes, Alejandro, & Zhou, Min. (1993). The New Second Generation: Segmented Assimilation and Its Variants. *Annals of the American Academy of Political and Social Sciences, 530*, 74–96.

Portes, Alejandro, & Zhou, Min. (2005). The New Second Generation: Segmented Assimilation and Its Variants. In M. Suarez-Orozco, C. Suarez-Orozco, & D. Baolian Quin (Eds.), *The New Immigration: An Interdisciplinary Reader* (pp. 85–104). New York: Routledge.

Poyo, Gerald E., & Diaz-Miranda, Mariano. (1994). Cubans in the United States. In Felix Padilla (Ed.), *Handbook of Hispanic Cultures in the United States: History* (pp. 302–320). Houston, TX: Arte Publico Press.

Ream, Robert K. (2005). Toward Understanding How Social Capital Mediates the Impact of Mobility on Mexican American Achievement. *Social Forces, 84*, 201–224.

Romo, Harriett D., & Falbo, Toni (1996). *Latino High School Graduation: Defying the Odds*. Austin: University of Texas Press.

Rumberger, Russell W., & Thomas, Scott L. (2000). The Distribution of Dropout and Turnover Rates Among Urban and Suburban High Schools. *Sociology of Education, 73*, 39–67.

Sabagh, Georges, & Bozorgmehr, Mehdi. (1996). Population Change: Immigration and Ethnic Transformation. In R. Waldinger & M. Bozorgmehr (Eds.), *Ethnic Los Angeles* (pp. 79–108). New York: Russell Sage Foundation.

Sampson, Robert J., Morenoff, Jeffrey D., & Gannon-Rowley, Thomas. (2002). Assessing Neighbourhood Effects: Social Processes and New Directions in Research. *Annual Review of Sociology, 28*, 443–478.

San Miguel, Guadalupe, Jr. (1987). *"Let All of Them Take Heed," Mexican Americans and the Campaign for Educational Equality in Texas, 1910–1981*. Austin: University of Texas Press.

Santiago-Santiago, Isaura. (1978). *A Community's Struggle for Equal Educational Opportunity: Aspira v. Board of Education* (Monograph No. 2, Office of Minority Education). Princeton, NJ: Educational Testing Service.

Santiago-Santiago, Isaura. (1986). *Aspira v. Board of Education* Revisited. *American Journal of Education, 95*, 149–199.

Stanton-Salazar, Ricardo D. (2001). *Manufacturing Hope and Despair: The School and Kin Support Networks of U.S.-Mexican Youth*. New York: Teachers College Press.

Suarez-Orozco, Marcelo M. (1989). *Central American Refugees and U.S. High Schools*. Stanford, CA: Stanford University Press.

Suarez-Orozco, M., & Suarez-Orozco, C. (1995). *Transformations: Immigration, Family Life, and Achievement Motivation Among Latino Adolescents*. Stanford, CA: Stanford University Press.

Swail, Walter Scott, Cabrera, Alberto F., Lee, Chul, & Williams, Adriane. (2005). *Latino Students & the Educational Pipeline, Part III: Pathways to the Bachelor's Degree for Latino Students*. Stafford, VA: Educational Policy Institute.

Teachman, J. D., Paasch, K., & Carver, K. (1997). Social Capital and the Generation of human Capital. *Social Forces, 75*, 1343–1359.

Vélez, William. (1985). Finishing College: The Effects of College Type. *Sociology of Education*, 58, 191–200.

Valdés, Guadalupe. (2001). *Learning and Not Learning English*. New York: Teachers College Press.

Valenzuela, Angela. (1999). *Subtractive Schooling: U.S.-Mexican Youth and the Politics of Caring*. Albany: State University of New York Press.

Valenzuela, Angela. (2005). Accountability and the Privatization Agenda. In A. Valenzuela (Ed.), *Leaving Children Behind: How "Texas-style" Accountability Fails Latino Youth* (pp. 263–294). Albany: State University of New York Press.

Vélez, William. (1989). High School Attrition Among Hispanic and Non-Hispanic White Youths. *Sociology of Education*, *62*, 119–133.

Vélez, William. (1994). Educational Experiences of Hispanics in the United States: Historical Notes. In Felix Padilla (Ed.), *Handbook of Hispanic Cultures in the United States: Sociology* (pp. 151–159). Houston, TX: Arte Publico Press.

Vélez, William. (2002). The Impact of Ethnic Consciousness and Neighborhood Characteristics on College Retention Amongst Latino Students. *Practicing Anthropology*, *24*(3), 24–28.

Vélez, William, & Martin, Michael E. (2003). Latino Segregation Patterns in Metro Areas: Historical Trends and Causes. Paper presented at the Color Lines Conference, Cambridge, MA, August 29–September 1, 2003.

Vélez, William, & Saenz, Rogelio. (2001). Towards a Comprehensive Model of the School Leaving Process Among Latinos. *School Psychology Quarterly*, *16*(4), 445–467.

Walsh, Catherine E. (2000). The Struggle of 'Imagined' Communities in School: Identification, Survival, and Belonging for Puerto Ricans. In Sonia Nieto (Ed.), *Puerto Rican Students in U.S. Schools* (pp. 97–114). Mahwah, NJ: Lawrence Erlbaum Associates.

Warburton, Amber A., Wood, Helen, & Crane, Marian M. (1943). *The Work and Welfare of Children of Agricultural Workers in Hidalgo County, Texas*. (U.S. Department of Labor, Children's Bureau Publication No. 298). Washington, DC: Government Printing Office.

Warren, John Robert. (1996). Educational Inequality among White and Mexican-Origin Adolescents in the American Southwest: 1990. *Sociology of Education*, *69*(2), 142–158.

Yeung, Alexander Seeshing, Marsh, Herbert W., & Suliman, Rosemary. (2000). Can Two Tongues Live in Harmony: Analysis of the National Educational Longitudinal Study of 1988 (NELS88) Longitudinal Data on the Maintenance of Home Language. *American Educational Research Journal*, *37*(4), 1001–1026.

Yosso, Tara J. (2005). Whose Culture Has Capital? A Critical Race Theory Discussion of Community Cultural Wealth. *Race Ethnicity and Education*, *8*, 69–91.

CHAPTER 10

Latinos in the United States Labor Market

Lisa Catanzarite
Lindsey Trimble

INTRODUCTION

Latinos constitute a large and growing share of the United States' labor force. Hence, they are—and will increasingly be—critical to the productivity of the U.S. economy. Yet, Latinos experience a number of significant labor market disadvantages, including high unemployment rates, low wages, overrepresentation in low-level occupations, and limited mobility.

Discussions of Latinos in the labor force are necessarily complicated by the diversity of the Latino population in terms of skill levels, ethnic origin, class background, immigration, and geographic concentrations. For example, the above-noted disadvantages vary for workers of different nativity, skill levels, and ethnic groups: Native-born workers do better than immigrants, those with more education fare better than those with less, and Cubans and South Americans are generally better off than Central Americans, Mexicans, and Puerto Ricans (and, these factors are interrelated). Although the Latino population is quite heterogeneous, most Latino workers are foreign-born, the preponderance of both natives and immigrants is poorly educated, and the vast majority hails from the less privileged ethnic groups. Thus, the aforementioned problems are widespread. In addition, undocumented workers (who make up a large share of recent immigrants) derive from the most disadvantaged groups and face employment restrictions imposed by the 1986 Immigration Reform and Control Act (IRCA), which further exacerbate their labor market difficulties.

This chapter provides an overview of Latinos' position in the workforce. We profile Latino workers with up-to-date statistics on various aspects of incorporation, giving attention to critical dimensions of diversity among Latinos. Interspersed with the presentation of these data, we review recent literature on the research areas we identified as dominant in the current scholarship on Latino workers: labor force participation, unemployment, spatial and skills mismatch, occupations, ethnic economies, social networks, and immigrant complementarity versus competition.[1]

Studies of Latino workers have been guided by several theoretical frames that focus on the following: individual deficits in education, language, and labor force experience (human capital); discrimination; and structural factors (including spatial and skills mismatch resulting from industrial restructuring, employment in ethnic enclaves, occupational segregation, and social networks). We cannot adjudicate between these here, but, instead, review research that reflects the dominant, current discussions of Latino incorporation and disadvantage.

LABOR FORCE SHARE

Latinos constitute a sizable share of the current U.S. workforce, and their numbers are expected to rise disproportionately in coming years. Figure 1 outlines the composition of the 2005 labor force in terms of race/ethnicity and nativity.[2] Latino workers, who number 19.8 million and comprise 13.3% of the workforce, have now passed Blacks as the largest minority racial/ethnic group.[3] Seven percent of all workers were foreign-born Latinos, and 6% were native-born Latinos. Foreign-born Latinos outnumbered their native-born counterparts by a small margin and made up 54% of the Latino workforce.[4] Note also that Latinos comprised almost half (47%) of foreign-born workers.[5]

In the coming years, the Latino presence is expected to expand substantially. According to Census Bureau projections, Latinos will account for almost half (45%) of population growth between 2000 and 2020 (author calculations, Table 1b, U.S. Census Bureau, 2004). As the Latino population increases, so too will its share in the labor force. Latinos are projected to contribute disproportionately to workforce growth in upcoming decades (Fullerton & Toosi, 2001; Suro

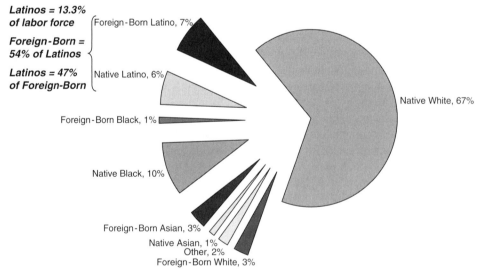

Source: Table 1, "Foreign-Born Workers: Labor Force Characteristics in 2005." April 14, 2006. U.S. Department of Labor, BLS.
a. White, Black, Asian, and Other are Non-Latino in this figure.

FIGURE 1. Labor Force by Race[a]/Ethnicity and Nativity, 2005.

& Passell, 2003). Whereas immigration is expected to account for a large fraction of the increase, more important will be the rising numbers of native-born Latinos, particularly second generation (Suro & Passell, 2003).

ETHNIC MAKEUP OF THE LATINO WORKFORCE

The Latino workforce is heterogeneous with respect to ancestry. Figure 2 details the ethnic origins of Latino workers in 2000.[6] Those who self-identified as Mexican-origin made up the majority (58%), numbering 8.6 million. The next largest group was "other Hispanic," at 14% (2.1 million); these workers identified as Latino but did not name the country of origin.[7] Puerto Ricans comprised 9% of Latino workers, followed by Cubans (4%), Salvadorans (2.5%), Dominicans (2.3%), and Colombians (1.8%). Other Central and Latin American countries combined account for 7.7% of Latino workers (and none of the remaining countries comprised more than 1.5%).

The different Latino ancestry groups have divergent histories, class backgrounds, skill sets, and modes of incorporation into the U.S. labor force. Those of Mexican origin are a heterogeneous group that includes individuals with long-term roots in the Southwest (predating the annexation of territory following the Mexican–American War), descendants of more recent generations of immigrants, and—the largest group—immigrants themselves. The Mexican-origin workforce was historically overrepresented in agriculture, but it is now a predominantly urban population, still regionally concentrated in the Southwest, but with growing populations in the Midwest, and, more recently, the South. Central Americans are disproportionately foreign-born and constitute the newest immigrant group. Immigrants from Mexico and Central America have low average educational levels, and a large share of recent arrivals is undocumented (Passell, 2005). Although Puerto Ricans are U.S. citizens, both island- and mainland-born are relatively disadvantaged

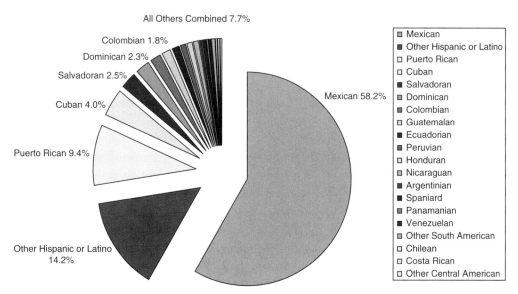

Source: Author calculations from 2000 Census Demographic Profile Highlights Fact Sheets, U.S. Census Bureau, American Factfinder.
a. Census figures for "Hispanics/Latinos" include ancestry from Spain and exclude non-Spanish speaking Latin American countries.

FIGURE 2. Ethnic Breakdown of Latino Labor Force[a], 2000.

in terms of socioeconomic background and have low average educational attainment. They are concentrated in the urban Northeast and were historically overrepresented in less-skilled manufacturing. The presence of Cubans in the United States traces primarily to the postrevolution migration of middle- and upper-class Cubans to Miami, where they established and continue to maintain a strong ethnic enclave. Whereas more recent immigrants are from less advantaged backgrounds, Cubans remain the most privileged of the large Latino groups.[8]

LATINO LABOR FORCE PARTICIPATION, UNEMPLOYMENT, AND PART-TIME WORK

What share of Latinos is in the workforce and how does Latino labor force participation (LFP) compare with that of other groups? Figure 3 provides 2005 LFP rates by sex and for youth (ages 16–19) for Latinos overall, the three largest Latino ethnic groups, and for Whites, Blacks, and Asians.

Eighty percent of Latino men were in the labor force, and Latino men are more likely to work than any other group. The opposite is true for Latina women, whose LFP rate of 55% is below rates for White, Black, and Asian women. Among Latino groups, Mexican men have considerably higher LFP rates than Puerto Ricans or Cubans (82% vs. 68% and 70%, respectively).

Research on Latino LFP has focused largely on participation and—to a lesser degree—work effort (hours and weeks worked) for *women*. Like the general literature on women's LFP, studies of Latinas have investigated the influences of human capital (sometimes via expected wage), family context (children, marital status, coresident adults, other family income), and local labor market demand for female labor. Research generally suggests that (1) Latina women's relatively low LFP rates are related to low human capital, large families, and high marriage rates and (2) ethnic differences in LFP among Latinas persist even when comparing otherwise similar women

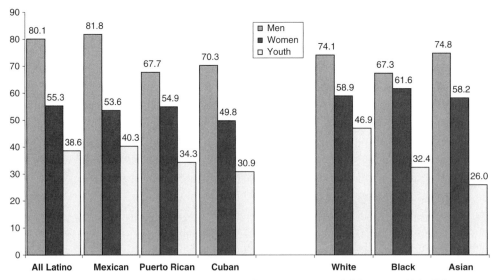

Source: Author calculations from Tables 5 and 6, Employment and Earnings. January 2006. U. S. Department of Labor BLS.
a. Whites, Blacks, and Asians include Latinos in this figure.
b. Youth are ages 16-19.

FIGURE 3. Percent in Labor Force by Latino Ethnicity, Race,[a] Sex, and Age,[b] 2005.

(e.g., Kahn & Whittington, 1996). Qualitative research has helped explicate work decisions, highlighting the salience of women's contributions to the household budget and cultural norms regarding work (e.g., husband's influence, family work history) (Segura, 1991).

Studies have illuminated influences on work behavior for particular groups of Latinas (e.g., Greenlees & Saenz, 1999, on Mexican immigrant wives) or identified differences relative to Blacks or Whites. For example, Latina women's LFP is less strongly related to education than is true for Blacks or Whites (Kahn & Whittington, 1996); coresident adults facilitate work effort (hours and weeks) for single mothers among Puerto Ricans and Blacks, but not Whites (Figueroa & Meléndez, 1993); local labor market conditions might have differential effects on Puerto Ricans (Figueroa & Meléndez, 1992) or on Latinas in general (Kahn & Whittington, 1996) than on Blacks or Whites.

How do Latinos fare in terms of unemployment, and what share works part-time? Individuals are classified as unemployed if they were actively seeking work in the 4 weeks prior to the survey. Part-time refers to employment less than 35 hours per week, both voluntary and involuntary. Figure 4 provides unemployment rates overall and for youth, along with part-time rates.

Figure 4 shows Latino unemployment rates lower than those of Blacks and higher than those of Whites and Asians. (Unemployment rates for Latinos overall and for Mexicans are 5% of men and 7% of women; for Puerto Ricans, 7% of men and 8% of women; versus 11% of men and 10% of women for Blacks; and 4% of both men and women for Whites and Asians.[9]) Some research shows that unemployment spells are longer for Latinos and Blacks than for Whites (Hsueh & Tienda, 1996), whereas other work suggests unemployment duration comparable to that of Whites (Thomas-Breitfeld, 2003). (Note that unemployment for Latina women is higher than for Latino men, in contrast to the patterns for other groups.) Youth unemployment rates are far higher but follow the same pattern: 18% for Latinos (22% for Puerto Ricans), in between Blacks (33%) and Whites and Asians (14% and 12%, respectively). Further, data not shown here demonstrate that native Latinos have higher unemployment rates than immigrants (7.2% vs. 5.0%, from Table 1, U.S. Department of Labor BLS, 2006a), and less educated workers have higher unemployment rates than the more educated (Table 7, U.S. Department of Labor BLS, 2006b).

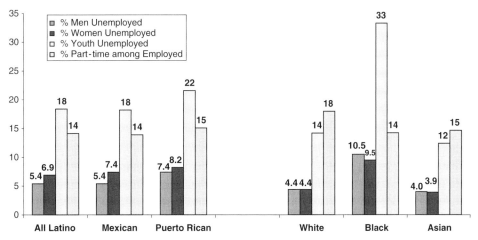

Source: Author calculations from Tables 5 and 6, Employment and Earnings. January 2006. U. S. Department of Labor BLS.
a. Youth are ages 16-19.
b. Whites, Blacks, and Asians include Latinos in this figure.

FIGURE 4. **Unemployment by Sex, Youth Unemployment,[a] and Part-Time Emlpoyment by Latino Ethnicity and Race,[b] 2005.**

Part-time employment is slightly less common for Latinos than for Whites, but it is comparable to levels for Blacks and Asians. These data are not broken out by gender, but a larger share of the White labor force is female than is true for Latinos (47% of White workers and 39% of Latinos[10]). We can infer that part-time employment is more likely to be voluntary for Whites than for Latinos, both because of the gender composition of the workforce and the lower likelihood of discrimination and resulting underemployment for Whites than for minorities in general. Consistent with this inference, De Anda (2005) demonstrated a higher incidence of involuntary part-time employment for Mexican-origin than White women (De Anda, 2005) and men (De Anda, 1998).

A small set of studies has investigated work instability for both women and men. Even when comparing individuals similar in other respects (e.g., education, age), (1) instability is worse for Latinos and Blacks than for Whites (Hsueh & Tienda, 1996) and (2) employment hardship (defined as joblessness, involuntary part-time work, and working poverty) is worse for Mexican-origin women than for Whites (De Anda, 2005).

Latino unemployment and underemployment, particularly for youth, are likely to become more problematic in the future, given the low education levels of both native and immigrant Latinos (discussed later) and the expected increase in the share of the labor force comprised of U.S.-born Latinos (Suro & Passell, 2003). This is an area that merits further research. Additionally, we will need more research on LFP and underemployment of Latina women, as the secular increase in women's LFP and the decline in men's real wages continue. Moreover, studies of employment for poor Latina heads of household will be critical in the context of the time limits and mandatory work requirements imposed by the 1996 welfare reform.

Latinos' relatively low levels of education and experience contribute to higher unemployment rates. Other factors are hiring discrimination against Latino workers (e.g., Kenney & Wissoker, 1994) and the negative effect of economic restructuring and the decline in manufacturing employment on Latinos (e.g., Morales, 2000; Toussaint-Comeau, Smith, & Comeau, 2005; Ortiz, 1991). With respect to the impact of economic restructuring, it is possible that labor market mismatches contribute to Latinos' disadvantage, and we now turn to research on this question.

SKILLS AND SPATIAL MISMATCH

Are Latino unemployment and underemployment due to skills or spatial mismatch? Skills mismatch is posited when workers' skills do not match those sought by employers. Spatial mismatch occurs when workers are geographically ill-matched to local job opportunities, because of the joint processes of residential segregation and job decentralization. The arguments are essentially that jobs requiring low skills have moved out of inner-city areas where less-skilled minorities concentrate. Limited research has examined the spatial and skills mismatch hypothesis for Latino workers, and existing studies show mixed results. McLafferty and Preston (1996) found no spatial mismatch when examining commuting times of Latina women in New York. Aponte's (1996) analysis of skills and spatial mismatch among Puerto Rican and Mexican immigrant men in Chicago showed mismatch effects for Puerto Ricans but not Mexicans: Mexican men had consistently high levels of employment, even with little education (skills) and access to transportation (spatial). Pastor and Marcelli (2000) found spatial mismatch effects for native and established immigrant Latinos but not for new immigrants. Additionally, Stoll (1998) showed that job decentralization negatively affected young Latino men's rates of unemployment. Analyses of Boston, Detroit, Los Angeles, and Atlanta support the existence of spatial mismatch for Blacks and Latinos combined, especially high school dropouts (Holzer & Danziger, 2001; also see Stoll, Holzer, & Ihlanfeldt, 2000). Thus, the jury is still out on the degree to which Latinos suffer from spatial or skills mismatch. Further research is needed and should attend to ethnic, nativity, gender, age, and regional differences. As the composition of the Latino labor force shifts toward native Latinos, the mismatch explanations might become more salient.

LATINO EDUCATIONAL DISADVANTAGE

Latino workers exhibit educational attainment levels substantially lower than those for the labor force as a whole. Figure 5 provides information on the educational composition of the Latino labor force, by nativity, relative to the non-Latino workforce.

The Latino educational distribution is distinctly bottom heavy. For the total workforce (immigrant and native combined), more than one in three Latino workers (35%) had not completed high school in 2005; the comparable figure for non-Latinos was only 6%. At the higher degree end of the educational spectrum (bachelor's and higher), Latinos also show a pronounced deficit: Only 14% of Latino workers held higher degrees (bachelor's or higher) versus 35% of the non-Latino workforce.

The educational disadvantage for native-born Latinos is less pronounced than for immigrants, but it is still striking. Native Latinos are almost three times as likely as non-Latinos to have less than a high school education (17% vs. 6%), and they are far less likely to obtain higher degrees: 18% of Latinos versus 34% of non-Latinos completed a bachelor's degree or above.

Immigrant Latinos show extreme educational disparities: Almost half (49%) of Latino immigrants completed less than 12 years of education and only 11% achieved Bachelor's or higher degrees. This represents a distinct disadvantage relative to native-born Latinos. However,

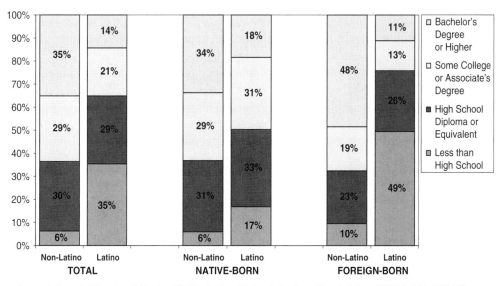

Source: Author calculations from Tables 1 and 3, "Foreign-Born Workers: Labor Force Characteristics in 2005." April 14, 2006. U.S. Department of Labor, BLS, and Table 7, Employment and Earnings , January 2006. U.S. Department of Labor, BLS.

FIGURE 5. Educational Attainment of Labor Force (Ages 25+), Non-Latino and Latino by Nativity, 2005.

the divergence is even more pronounced when immigrant Latinos are compared with their non-Latino counterparts. The above figures are inverted: 10% had less than high school and almost half (48%) obtained bachelor's or higher degrees. Thus, whereas Latino immigrants are relatively poorly educated, other immigrants are generally well educated, not just relative to Latinos but also to native-born non-Latinos.

In the economy as a whole, less-educated workers face declining prospects relative to the better educated (e.g., Blackburn, Bloom, & Freeman, 1990; Juhn, Murphy, & Brooks, 1993). Related to these declines are secular decreases in (better paid) manufacturing occupations and increases in (lower paid) service employment.[11] These shifts are particularly important for Latinos, who generally fall at the low end of the educational distribution. The following section provides detail on occupational prospects for Latino workers.

LATINOS' OCCUPATIONS, SEGREGATION, AND MOBILITY

Given their relatively low average educational attainment, it is not surprising that Latinos are concentrated in occupations where educational requirements are also low. Figure 6 bears this out, showing the share of Latinos versus the total workforce, by sex, in each of 10 major occupation groups (MOGs). The MOG categories are not ordered by skill, but they do divide white and blue-collar occupations, as well as the pink collar (female-dominated) MOG of office and administrative support (clerical). These divisions roughly correspond to formal schooling requirements. However, the bars are not stacked in terms of earnings. For example, pay is sometimes higher in construction than in clerical, sales, and some professional occupations.

Very small shares of Latinos are in managerial and executive occupations (6.8% of Latinos, 7.8% of Latina women) relative to the total workforce (15.5% of men, 13.2% of women). Similarly, professional occupations employ a relatively small share of Latino men (7.0% vs. 16.6% of total male workforce) and women (14.4% vs. 24.6% of total female workforce). Note that women in professional occupations are heavily concentrated in a limited set of female-dominated

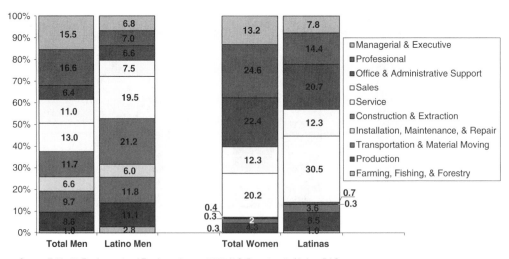

Source: Table 10, Employment and Earnings , January 2006. U.S. Department of Labor, B LS

FIGURE 6. Major Occupation Group by Sex, Total Labor Force and Latinos, 2005.

"semiprofessions" in education, health care, and social services; women, in general, and Latinas, in particular, are underrepresented in the better paying and more prestigious professional occupations (Table 11, U.S. Department of Labor, BLS, 2006a).

At the other extreme of the distribution, much larger shares of Latino men and women are service workers than is true overall (19.5% of Latino men vs. 13.0% of all men; 30.5% of Latinas vs. 20.2% of all women). Similarly, although production (manufacturing) employs a small share of all workers (8.6% of men, 4.3% of women), this MOG accounts for a relatively larger share of Latinos (11.1% men, 8.5% women). Given their concentrations in service and manufacturing, Latinos have been especially vulnerable to structural economic changes in recent years (e.g., Toussaint-Comeau et al., 2005).

The MOG data also reflect substantial gender segregation. The most common MOG for Latino men is construction/extraction (21.2% of Latino men; 11.7% of men overall). Latinas, by contrast, are most commonly in service (30.5%, as noted earlier), and—like other women—are well represented in clerical (20.7% vs. 22.4% of all women).

We now turn to the distribution of workers in *detailed* occupational categories. (The Census breaks out about 500 detailed categories; e.g., lawyers, elementary school teachers, cashiers, drywallers). Latinos have become hypersegregated in particular occupations. Table 1 lists occupations with pronounced overrepresentations of Latinos.

Latinos represented 13.1% of the total employed labor force in 2005, yet comprised more than 20% of workers in each of the occupations in Table 1. In several construction, manufacturing, and service occupations, Latinos constituted a vastly disproportionate share of workers. For example, Latinos were 54% of cement masons, 47% of drywallers, 42% of hand packagers, 35% of maids, 29% of cooks, and 21% of electrical\electronics assemblers. Further, in geographic areas where Latinos concentrate, the composition of local occupations is even more skewed than these national data suggest.

Latinos are highly segregated from other ethnic groups, and—for women and men—segregation is more pronounced for Central Americans, Mexicans, and Dominicans than for Cubans, Puerto Ricans, and South Americans (Cotter, Hermsen, & Vanneman, 2004). Segregation has been rising for Latinos overall and Latino immigrants nationally (Kochhar, 2005), Mexican immigrants (Ortiz, 1996), and newcomer Latinos in Los Angeles' *brown-collar* occupations (fields with an overrepresentation of immigrant Latinos) (Catanzarite, 2000). Segregation apparently contributes to Latinos' wage disadvantage above and beyond the impact of English proficiency and schooling (Catanzarite, 2000; Catanzarite & Aguilera, 2002). Longitudinal analyses demonstrate both that newcomer Latinos are hired into already low-paid occupations (i.e., they find employment in less desirable occupations) and, importantly, wages *erode* over time—for both immigrants and natives—in precisely the occupations where newcomer Latinos concentrate (i.e., the occupations worsen after new immigrants enter) (Catanzarite, 2002). Pay dynamics underscore the vulnerability of brown-collar occupations. Segregation and its attendant wage pressures constitute important structural barriers to Latino advancement.

Although most research on immigrant assimilation focuses on earnings, several recent studies attend to the question of occupational mobility. Myers and Cranford (1998) find limited opportunities for immigrant Latinas to move out of low-level occupations, and better possibilities for native Latinas. Kossoudji and Cobb-Clark's research on undocumented Latinas (2000) and Latino men (1996, 2000) demonstrates considerable occupational movement, but it is characterized not by mobility into better occupations but by occupational "churning" in and out of a small set of migrant-heavy occupations; their research on men legalized under IRCA indicates that legalization does significantly improve access to better occupations

TABLE 1. Occupations with Overrepresentations[a] of Latinos, 2005

Occupation	% Latino
Cement masons, concrete finishers, and terrazzo workers	54
Drywall installers, ceiling tile installers, and tapers	47
Roofers	42
Butchers and other meat, poultry, and fish processing workers	42
Packers and packagers, hand	42[b]
Construction laborers	41
Graders and sorters, agricultural products	41[b]
Carpet, floor, and tile installers and finishers	40
Helpers, construction trades	39
Helpers—production workers	38
Packaging and filling machine operators and tenders	38[c]
Grounds maintenance workers	37
Pressers, textile, garment, and related materials	36[b]
Dishwashers	35
Maids and housekeeping cleaners	35[b]
Painters, construction and maintenance	35
Brickmasons, blockmasons, and stonemasons	34
Sewing machine operators	34[b]
Cleaners of vehicles and equipment	34
Dining room and cafeteria attendants and bartender helpers	30[c]
Laundry and dry-cleaning workers	29[b]
Cooks	29[c]
Cutting workers	29
Pest control workers	28
Janitors and building cleaners	27[c]
Upholsterers	27
Miscellaneous media and communication workers	27[c]
Parking lot attendants	26
Painting workers	26
Bakers	25[c]
Food preparation workers	24[b]
Carpenters	24
Tailors, dressmakers, and sewers	24[b]
Crushing, grinding, polishing, mixing, and blending workers	24
Industrial truck and tractor operators	24
Baggage porters, bellhops, and concierges	22
Food batchmakers	22[c]
Electrical, electronics, and electromechanical assemblers	21[b]
Shipping, receiving, and traffic clerks	21[c]
Molders and molding machine setters, operators, and tenders, metal and plastic	20
First-line supervisors/managers of housekeeping and janitorial workers	20[c]
Welding, soldering, and brazing workers	20
Total Employed, 16 years and over	13.1

[a]Overrepresentation is defined as 1.5 times the labor force share.
[b]Occupation is heavily female (over 60%).
[c]Occupation is gender integrated (30–60% female).
Source: Table 11, U.S. Department of Labor BLS (2006a).

(2000). Findings have been mixed on the degree to which English proficiency, education, and labor force experience promote access to better occupations (Kochhar, 2005; Kossoudji & Cobb-Clark, 1996, 2000, 2002).

A number of studies have investigated immigrant Latinos' experiences in particular low-skill occupations. Two prime examples are day laborers and domestic servants.[12] Valenzuela (e.g., Valenzuela, Kawachi, & Marr, 2002; Valenzuela, 2003) has developed a body of work on day laborers who seek temporary work at street-side hiring sites. Immigrant Latino men are the primary labor force for this burgeoning employment form in U.S. cities. Work is generally heavy manual labor in construction and landscaping. Valenzuela's work documentes the extent of day labor, the hiring process, working conditions, and problems for workers. Domestic service has become a stronghold of immigrant Latinas in the current period. Hondagneu-Sotelo's (2001) and Romero's (2002) studies explore employment relations and working conditions, providing nuanced understandings of the operation of class, race/ethnicity, and gender in private household cleaning and childcare jobs.

Clearly, occupations are critical to wage attainment and worker mobility. Further research on occupational locations, segregation, and mobility opportunities for both native and immigrant Latinos will aid in understanding the relative importance of structural versus individual factors that contribute to Latino disadvantage.

LATINOS IN THE PUBLIC SECTOR, PRIVATE SECTOR, AND SELF-EMPLOYMENT

How do Latinos fare in terms of public and private sector employment and self-employment? Figure 7 provides data for the total workforce, all Latinos, and the three largest Latino groups.

Latinos are more prevalent in the private sector than is true for the workforce as a whole (84% vs. 79% of workers), with Mexicans most likely to be in the private sector, followed by

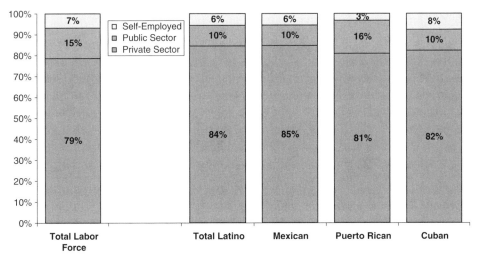

Source: Author Calculations from Tables 13 and 15, Employment and Earnings January 2006, U.S. Department of Labor BLS.
a. Nonagricultural Paid Labor Force

FIGURE 7. Private, Public, and Self-Employment,[a] Total Labor Force, Latinos, and Largest Latino Groups, 2005.

Cubans, then Puerto Ricans. On the flip side, self-employment is less common for Latinos as a whole (6%) than for the overall workforce (7%), with the important exception of Cubans, whose self-employment rate is relatively high, at 8%. The broad figures provided here indicate that ethnic economies and entrepreneurship are likely to be more important sources of employment for Cubans than for other Latinos (see Valdez's chapter in this volume). We discuss the issue of ethnic economies in the next section.

Public sector employment is currently less common for Latinos (10%) than for the total labor force (15%). However, Puerto Ricans constitute an important exception, with 16% in government employment. Published data on native-born Latinos separated from immigrants are not available, and there is little scholarship on public sector employment for Latinos (but see McClain, 1993; Sisneros, 1993). However, we suspect that the government is a significant employer for native Latinos and will increase in importance as the Latino population grows and attains higher levels of education. The public sector has been an important source of opportunity and mobility for Black workers in the past half-century, particularly for better educated Blacks, who have encountered less discrimination in the public than private sector (Carrington, McCue, & Pierce, 1996; Hout, 1984; Long, 1975; Pomer, 1986).[13] Public sector employment for Latinos warrants further research.

THE ETHNIC ECONOMY: BENEFICIAL FOR WORKERS?

The ethnic economy refers to immigrant-owned businesses that employ coethnic workers, and ethnic enclaves are geographic areas with concentrations of such firms. Wilson and Portes (1980) argued that enclave employment is superior to the secondary labor market, where immigrants are otherwise likely to be confined, and that ethnic enclaves are comparable to the primary labor market in terms of career ladders and earnings returns to human capital. The ethnic economy purportedly facilitates immigrants' mobility, as entrepreneurs mentor employees, providing training and skills that can later be applied to workers' own entrepreneurial ventures (Bailey & Waldinger, 1991; Portes & Jensen, 1989).

Evidence has been mixed on the effect of the ethnic economy for immigrant workers. Research on Cubans in Miami supports the argument (Portes & Jensen, 1989). Bohon's (2000) research suggests that destination cities that already have a strong Latino enclave environment provide more successful labor market outcomes to Latino immigrants, particularly Cubans, Colombians, and other South Americans. However, this did not hold true in Los Angeles, which is home to the nation's largest Latino population.

A number of studies show no benefit of employment in the ethnic economy. Sanders and Nee (1987) demonstrated no pay advantage for Cuban and Chinese employees in the ethnic economy. Hum's (2000) analysis of Mexicans and Central Americans in Los Angeles employed in the ethnic economy suggested that workers were apt to experience labor market conditions similar to those of the secondary labor market (i.e., menial, poor paying jobs with limited fringe benefits and opportunities for skill acquisition).[14]

Research on Dominicans and Colombians in New York shows no advantage of the ethnic economy over the secondary sector for women (Gilbertson, 1995) or men (Gilbertson & Gurak, 1993). Based on analyses of multiple metropolitan areas and ethnic groups, Logan, Alba, and McNulty (1994) concluded that—with the exception of the Cuban economy in Miami, which is large and highly diversified—most minority entrepreneurship is concentrated in low-wage, poorly capitalized sectors.

The divergent findings by ethnicity raise doubts as to whether ethnic economies generally provide benefits to workers in terms of pay, working conditions, or entrepreneurship avenues, or if they constitute another exploitative ghetto for particular groups of immigrant workers. Future research should attend to differences by country of origin, time of arrival, gender, and local labor market conditions to further understanding of the impact of ethnic economies on immigrant labor market outcomes.

SOCIAL NETWORKS: EMBEDDED ECONOMIC OPPORTUNITY OR ENTRENCHED EXPLOITATION?

Social scientists have long been interested in the effects of social networks on labor market experiences, beginning with Granovetter's (1973) pioneering work on the strength of weak ties. Research demonstrates that individuals who utilize network ties to secure employment reap benefits such as increased wages, longer job tenure (Simon & Warner, 1992), and mobility (Podolny & Baron, 1997).

Studies of Latinos (which overwhelmingly focus on immigrants) demonstrate that networks influence a number of outcomes. Social networks shorten the job search for Mexican immigrants (Aguilera & Massey, 2003) and increase Latino LFP (Aguilera, 2002); self-employment (Sanders & Nee, 1996), wages for Salvadoran immigrants (Greenwell, Valdez, & DaVanzo, 1997), Puerto Rican women (Aguilera, 2005), and Mexican immigrants (Aguilera & Massey, 2003); and job tenure for Mexican immigrants (Aguilera, 2003). Most of these outcomes appear positive.

Portes (1998) drew attention to negative aspects of social networks: ties that bind certain people together simultaneously exclude others. Social networks also constrain individual freedoms through conformity demands and can inhibit business efficiency (Portes & Landolt, 1996). Based on her study of Mexican and Central American janitors in Los Angeles, Cranford (2005) argued that network ties were exploitative for workers and facilitated employers' control during job restructuring.

This work suggests that use of networks by immigrant Latinos and their employers might exacerbate the isolation of these workers in job ghettos. Falcón and Meléndez (2001) showed that Latinos are more likely than any other racial/ethnic group to utilize social networks to find employment and are more likely than other groups to use strong ties (family and close friends; i.e., individuals who are socially similar). This might be a disadvantage because greater diversity of network members provides more unique job information (Granovetter, 1995). Latino networks could be providing redundant job information that serves to confine workers to less desirable jobs and thereby reproduces economic disadvantage (Portes & Landolt, 1996).

Further research should attend to potentially deleterious consequences of networks (e.g., the extent to which social networks might reinforce occupational segregation or provide greater benefits to employers than to workers). Other fruitful avenues include differences in outcomes when workers activate weak versus strong ties; and network usage and its consequences for *native* Latinos.

IMMIGRANT EFFECTS ON OTHER WORKERS?

This chapter would be incomplete without a discussion of the potential impact of Latino immigrants on other workers. The question of whether newcomers compete with or complement other workers is complex, politically charged, and continues to lack a definitive answer. Most studies examine aggregate differences in wages or unemployment between metropolitan areas with and without high immigration levels and provide mixed and limited evidence (e.g., Johnson, 1998; Kposowa, 1995; Reimers, 1998; Smith & Edmonston, 1997). In national analyses, Borjas (2003, 2004) found negative effects of immigration on wages for less-skilled workers.

One argument hones in on jobs and occupations and suggests that less-skilled immigrants (including Latinos) take the most undesirable jobs at the bottom rungs of the occupational ladder—jobs that native workers generally do not want (Catanzarite, 2000, Piore, 1979). To the degree that some native workers do want these jobs, immigrants might displace them. Competition can be indirect: Few native workers might apply for these positions, in part because employers signal their hiring intentions. Employer interviews reveal extensive use of referral hiring (Waldinger & Lichter, 2003) and strong preferences for immigrant Latinos in low-level jobs (Moss & Tilly, 2001; Waldinger & Lichter, 2003).

Research suggests that other workers' wages are suppressed when they do find employment in occupations where immigrants concentrate (Catanzarite, 1998, 2003, 2004, 2006; Howell & Mueller, 2000). Catanzarite's research shows that wages deteriorate over time for both immigrants and natives in brown-collar occupations (2002); pay penalties are substantial for incumbents, especially earlier-immigrant Latinos, followed by native Blacks and native Latinos (2003, 2006).[15] Latino workers are least segregated from new immigrant coethnics; thus, they are more likely to experience within-occupation wage effects than are other workers.

At the same time, immigrants might push some workers up the occupational hierarchy into better jobs (Piore, 1979; Waldinger & Lichter, 2003). Benefits are likely to accrue to better educated workers who can take advantage of new opportunities (e.g., in the public sector).

Further, it is important to recognize that, in the aggregate, immigration creates new jobs (Smith & Edmonston, 1997). Thus, immigrants are not competing with natives for a fixed set of opportunities. The consequences of immigration are nuanced. Immigrants are likely to act as complements in some occupations and as substitutes in others (e.g., Rosenfeld & Tienda, 1999). They appear to benefit the owners of capital but to disadvantage less-skilled workers (Borjas, 1999). Certainly, the vulnerable status of less-skilled immigrants, particularly the undocumented, contributes to their exploitability and exacerbates consequences for other workers. This suggests that increased worker protections are likely to benefit both immigrants and natives at the low end of the labor market.[16]

Much of the research in this area focuses on the impact of immigration on less-skilled workers, minorities, and, particularly, African Americans (e.g., Hamermesh & Bean, 1998; Shulman, 2004), many studies do not differentiate Latino immigrants from other immigrants, and most studies are concerned with consequences for native workers. We need further research on the extent to which newcomer Latinos provide benefits or constrain opportunities for other Latinos, including earlier cohorts of immigrants.

CONCLUSION

In general, the disadvantaged labor market position of Latinos—both natives and immigrants—is the combined result of human capital deficits (e.g., low education, work experience), employer discrimination, and structural disadvantages (e.g., occupational segregation, spatial and skills mismatch, economic restructuring, and the accompanying expansion of dead-end, low-paid service jobs). We will continue to need studies that disentangle the relative influences of these factors. Because of the ongoing changes in Latino demographics, longitudinal research must give careful attention to the relative impacts of supply-side and demand-side influences. In general, we will need research on the relative importance of education and English proficiency, immigration status, employer discrimination, local labor market structure, occupational dynamics, and social networks in determining labor market outcomes. Findings will be crucial to formulating a policy agenda that effectively addresses barriers for Latino workers.

Latinos make up a disproportionate share of the working poor, and research on these workers will be critical in the coming years. The welfare and immigration reforms of the late 1990s will put more pressure on Latinos' wages in several ways. On the one hand, wages will be more important to Latino economic well-being with the cutbacks in public assistance programs in general and for immigrants in particular. On the other hand, the increase in LFP of former welfare recipients is likely to adversely influence other workers at the low-wage end of the labor market (Bartik, 2000; Burtless, 2000). Further, the new emphasis in poverty policy on expansions to the Earned Income Tax Credit (EITC), although beneficial to the working poor who file taxes, will not give any relief to those who do not, including the substantial population of undocumented immigrants among Latinos. More broadly beneficial to Latinos would be raising the federal minimum wage and indexing it to inflation. New initiatives that provide relief in the areas of health insurance and retirement benefits will also be crucial, as Latinos have the lowest rates of these employer-provided benefits (Herz, Meisenheimer, & Weinstein, 2000; National Council of La Raza, 2002, per Thomas-Breitfeld, 2003).

Finally, we note that the existing labor market literature focuses disproportionately on Latino immigrants, and research on native Latinos has generally taken a back seat. Future research should give greater attention to a variety of labor market processes and outcomes for native-born Latinos. This will be progressively more important as native-born workers increase their labor force share in the coming years.

NOTES

1. We do not take up the issues of wage inequality, unions, or entrepreneurship, as these are the subjects of separate chapters in this volume.
2. All charts and tables are for the civilian labor force, ages 16 and up in 2005, unless otherwise noted.
3. In 2000, Latinos constituted 10.9% of the labor force and Blacks were 11.8% (author calculations from Geographic Profile of Employment and Unemployment. U.S. Department of Labor BLS, 2002).
4. Whereas immigrants outnumber natives among male Latino workers, the opposite is true for Latina women. This is related to immigrant Latino men's higher LFP rates than native Latino men and the reverse for Latina women: (85% vs. 75% of immigrant vs. native Latino men, and 53% vs. 61% for immigrant vs. native Latinas in 2000, from Mosisa, 2002, Table 3). The fact that immigrant Latinas are less likely to work than native Latinas is largely due to higher fertility and marriage rates and lower educational attainment for immigrant than native women (Mosisa, 2002, Table 3).
5. Asians made up 22% of foreign-born workers. Most Asian workers were foreign-born (77%).
6. The Census includes individuals of Spanish ancestry with Hispanics and omits Latin Americans from non-Spanish-speaking countries. We follow the Census definition for consistency with other published tables. Note that Spaniards accounted for less than 1% of the total Latino/Hispanic labor force in 2000. We use the term "Latino" to refer to Latinos and Hispanics.
7. We expect that this "other Hispanic group" is comprised disproportionately of the native-born (because this group would be less likely to identify country or countries of ancestry and includes those who identify as residents of Aztlán) and Mexican-origin (because this group accounts for the lion's share of Latinos).
8. This discussion draws on Meléndez, Rodriguez, & Figueroa (1991), Bean & Tienda (1987), and Browne and Askew (2006), which provide further detail on differences between groups.
9. Cubans are omitted because the base of 16- to 19-years-old is smaller than the BLS cutoff for published data. Unemployment rates for Cuban men and women are 3.1% and 3.7%, respectively, and the share of part-time workers is 9%. Thus, Cubans fare better than other Latinos and Whites on these measures.

10. Author calculations, Tables 12 and 13, U.S. Department of Labor BLS 2006a.
11. With respect to manufacturing occupations, note that Latinos, particularly Mexican and Central American immigrants, constitute a preferred labor force for low-level, poorly paid nondurable goods manufacturing (e.g., Bonacich, 1993; Ortiz, 2001).
12. Also, see research on janitors (Zlolniski, 2006; Waldinger, Erickson, Milkman, Mitchell, Valenzuela, et al., 1996), street vendors (Zlolniski, 2006), and entry-level occupations in select industries (Waldinger, 1996; Waldinger & Lichter, 2003).
13. Public sector employment continues to be substantial for Blacks: in 2005, one in five Black workers (19.6%) was in this sector (author calculations, Table 12, U.S. Department of Labor BLS, 2006b).
14. Note that this study used supervisor's (not owner's) race/ethnicity; hence, the findings might say more about predominantly Latino workplaces (i.e., segregation) than about ethnic enclaves.
15. That earlier immigrants are most affected within occupations is consistent with other studies of immigration effects more generally (Altonji & Card, 1992; Grossman, 1982; Smith & Edmonston, 1997).
16. In this vein, Catanzarite (2004) shows smaller brown-collar wage penalties in heavily unionized occupations.

REFERENCES

Aponte, Robert. (1996). Urban Employment and the Mismatch Dilemma: Accounting for the Immigration Exception. *Social Problems, 43*, 268–283.

Aguilera, Michael B. (2002). The Impact of Social Capital on Labor Force Participation: Evidence from the 2000 Social Capital Benchmark Survey. *Social Science Quarterly, 83*, 853–874.

Aguilera, Michael B. (2003). The Impact of the Worker: How Social Capital and Human Capital Influence the Job Tenure of Formerly Undocumented Mexican Immigrants. *Sociological Inquiry, 73*, 52–83.

Aguilera, Michael B. (2005). The Impact of Social Capital on the Earnings of Puerto Rican Migrants. *The Sociological Quarterly, 46*, 569–592.

Aguilera, Michael B., & Massey, Douglas S. (2003). Social Capital and the Wages of Mexican Migrants: New Hypotheses and Tests. *Social Forces, 82*, 671–701.

Bailey, Thomas, & Waldinger Roger. (1991). Primary, Secondary, and Enclave Labor Markets: A Training Systems Approach. *American Sociological Review, 56*, 432–445.

Bartik, Timothy J. (2000). Displacement and Wage Effects of Welfare Reform. In Rebecca Blank & David Card (Eds.), *Finding Jobs: Work and Welfare Reform* (pp. 72–122). New York: Russell Sage Foundation.

Bean, Frank D. & Tienda, Marta. (1987). *The Hispanic Population of the United States*. New York: Russell Sage Foundation.

Blackburn, McKinley L., Bloom, David E., & Freeman, Richard B. (1990). The Declining Economic Position of Less Skilled American Men. In Gary Burtless (Ed.) *A Future of Lousy Jobs? The Changing Structure of U.S. Wages* (pp. 31–76). Washington, DC: Brookings Institute.

Bohon, Stephanie. (2001). *Latinos in Ethnic Enclaves*. New York: Garland.

Bonacich, Edna. (1993). Asian and Latino Immigrants in the Los Angeles Garment Industry: An Exploration of the Relationship between Capitalism and Racial Oppression. In Ivan Light & Parminder Bhachu (Eds.), *Immigration and Entrepreneurship: Culture, Capital and Ethnic Networks* (pp. 51–74). New Brunswick, NJ: Transaction Books.

Borjas, George J. (1999). *Heaven's Door: Immigration Policy and the American Economy*. Princeton, NJ: Princeton University Press.

Borjas, George J. (2003). The Labor Demand Curve *Is* Downward Sloping: Re-Examining the Impact of Immigration on the Labor Market. *The Quarterly Journal of Economics, 118*(4): 1335–1374.

Borjas, George J. (2004). Increasing the Supply of Labor Through Immigration: Measuring the Impact on Native-Born Workers. *Backgrounder* (pp. 1–12). Washington, DC: Center for Immigration Studies.

Browne, Irene & Askew, Rachel. (2006). Latinas at Work: Issues of Gender, Ethnicity and Class. In Marge Karsten (Ed.), *Gender, Ethnicity and Race in the Workplace* (pp. 223–251). Westport, CT: Praeger Press.

Burtless, Gary. (2000). Can the Labor Market Absorb Three Million Welfare Recipients? In Kelleen Kaye & Demetra Smith Nightingale (Eds.) *The Low-Wage Labor Market: Challenges and Opportunities for Economic Self-Sufficiency* (pp. 65–84). Washington, DC: U.S. Department of Health and Human Services.

Carrington, William J., McCue, Kristin, & Pierce, Brooks. (1996). Black/White Wage Convergence: The Role of Public Sector Wages and Employment. *Industrial and Labor Relations Review, 49*, 456–471.

Catanzarite, Lisa. (1998). Immigrant Latino Representation and Earnings Penalties in Occupations. *Research in Social Stratification and Mobility, 16*, 147–179.

Catanzarite, Lisa. (2000). Brown-Collar Jobs: Occupational Segregation and the Earnings of Recent-Immigrant Latinos. *Sociological Perspectives, 43*(1), 45–75.

Catanzarite, Lisa. (2002). The Dynamics of Segregation and Earnings in *Brown-Collar* Occupations. *Work and Occupations, 29*(3), 300–345.

Catanzarite, Lisa. (2003). Occupational Context and Wage Competition of New Immigrant Latinos with Minorities and Whites. *Review of Black Political Economy, 31*(1–2), 77–94.

Catanzarite, Lisa. (2004). Immigration, Union Density, and Brown-Collar Wage Penalties. *State of California Labor, 4*, 107–130.

Catanzarite, Lisa. (2006). *Wage Penalties and Discounted Returns to Education in Brown-Collar Occupations.* Unpublished manuscript, Washington State University.

Catanzarite, Lisa, & Aguilera, Michael B. (2002). Working with Co-Ethnics: Earnings Penalties for Latino Immigrants at Latino Jobsites. *Social Problems, 49*(1), 101–127.

Cotter, David A., Hermsen, Joan M., & Vanneman, Reeve. (2004). *Gender Inequality at Work.* New York: Russell Sage Foundation.

Cranford, Cynthia J. (2005). Networks of Exploitation: Immigrant Labor and the Restructuring of the Los Angeles Janitorial Industry. *Social Problems, 52*, 379–397.

De Anda, Robert M. (1998). Employment Instability and Earnings of Mexican-Origin Men. *Hispanic Journal of Behavioral Sciences, 20*, 363–374.

De Anda, Robert M. (2005). Employment Hardship Among Mexican-Origin Women. *Hispanic Journal of Behavioral Sciences, 27*, 43–59.

Falcón, Luis M., & Meléndez, Edwin. (2001). Racial and Ethnic Differences in Job Searching in Urban Centers. In Alice O'Connor, Chris Tilly, & Lawrence Bobo (Eds.), *Urban Inequality: Evidence from Four Cities* (pp. 341–371). New York: Russell Sage Foundation.

Figueroa, Barry, & Meléndez, Edwin. (1992). The Effects of Local Labor Market Conditions on Labor Force Participation of Puerto Rican, White, and Black Women. *Hispanic Journal of Behavioral Sciences, 14*, 76–90.

Figueroa, Barry, & Meléndez, Edwin. (1993). The Importance of Family Members in Determining the Labor Supply of Puerto Rican, Black, and White Single Mothers. *Social Science Quarterly, 74*, 867–883.

Fullerton, Howard N., Jr., & Toossi, Mitra. (2001). Labor Force Projections to 2010: Steady Growth and Changing Composition. *Monthly Labor Review, 124*, 21–38.

Gilbertson, Greta A. (1995). Women's Labor and Enclave Employment: The Case of Dominican and Colombian Women in New York City. *The International Migration Review, 29*, 657–665.

Gilbertson, Greta A., & Gurak, Douglass T. (1993). Broadening the Enclave Debate: The Labor Market Experiences of Dominican and Colombian Men in New York City. *Sociological Forum, 8*, 205–220.

Granovetter, Mark. (1973). The Strength of Weak Ties. *American Journal of Sociology, 78*, 1360–1380.

Granovetter, Mark. (1995). *Getting a Job: A Study of Contacts and Careers.* Chicago: University of Chicago Press.

Greenlees, Clyde S., & Saenz, Rogelio. (1999). Determinants of Employment of Recently Arrived Mexican Immigrant Wives. *International Migration Review, 33*, 354–377.

Greenwell, Lisa, Valdez, R. Burciaga, & DaVanzo, Julie. (1997). Social Ties, Wages, and Gender in a Study of Salvadorian and Pilipino Immigrants in Los Angeles. *Social Science Quarterly, 78*, 559–577.

Hamermesh, Daniel S., & Bean, Frank D. (1998). *The Economic Implications of Immigration for African Americans.* New York: Russell Sage Foundation.

Herz, Diane E., Meisenheimer, Joseph R., II, & Weinstein, Harriet G. (2000). Health and Retirement Benefits: Data from Two BLS Surveys. *Monthly Labor Review.* Washington, DC: U.S. Department of Labor, Bureau of Labor Statistics.

Holzer, Harry J., & Danzinger, Sheldon. (2001). Are Jobs Available for Disadvantaged Workers in Urban Areas? In Alice O'Connor, Chris Tilly, & Lawrence Bobo (Eds.), *Urban Inequality: Evidence from Four Cities* (pp. 496–538). New York: Russell Sage Foundation.

Hondagneu-Sotelo, Pierrette. (2001). *Doméstica: Immigrant Workers Cleaning and Caring in the Shadows of Affluence.* Berkeley: University of California, Press.

Hout, Michael. (1984). Occupational Mobility of Black Men: 1962–1973. *American Sociological Review, 49*, 308–322.

Howell, David R., & Mueller, Elizabeth J. (2000). Immigration and Native-Born Male Earnings: A Jobs-Level Analysis of the New York City Metropolitan Area Labour Market, 1980–90. *Journal of Ethnic and Migration Studies, 26*(3), 469–493.

Hsueh, Sheri, & Tienda, Marta. (1996). Gender, Ethnicity and Labor Force Instability. *Social Science Research, 25*, 73–94.

Hum, Terry. (2000). A Protected Niche? Immigrant Ethnic Economies and Labor Market Segmentation. In Lawrence D. Bobo, Melvin L. Oliver, James H. Johnson, & Able Valenzuela, Jr. (Eds.), *Prismatic Metropolis: Inequality in Los Angeles* (pp. 279–314). New York: Russell Sage Foundation.

Johnson, George E. (1998). The Impact of Immigration on Income Distribution Among Minorities. In Daniel S. Hamermesh & Frank D. Bean (Eds.), *Help or Hindrance? The Economic Implications of Immigration for African Americans* (pp. 17–50). New York: Russell Sage Foundation.

Juhn, Chinhui, Murphy, Kevin M., & Brooks, Pierce. (1993). Wage Inequality and the Rise in Returns to Skill. *Journal of Political Economy, 101*(3), 410–442.

Kahn, Joan R., & Whittington, Leslie A. (1996). The Labor Supply of Latinas in the USA: Comparing Labor Force Participation, Wages, and Hours Worked with Anglo and Black Women. *Population Research and Policy Review, 15*, 45–77.

Kenney, Genevieve M., & Wissoker, Douglas A. (1994). An Analysis of the Correlates of Discrimination Facing Young, Hispanic Job Seekers. *American Economic Review, 88*, 674–683.

Kochhar, Rakesh. (2005). *Latino Labor Report, 2004: More Jobs for New Immigrants, But at Lower Wages*. Washington, DC: Pew Hispanic Center.

Kossoudji, Sherrie A., & Cobb-Clark, Deborah A. (1996). Finding Good Opportunities Within Unauthorized Markets: U.S. Occupational Mobility for Male Latino Workers. *International Migration Review, 30*, 901–924.

Kossoudji, Sherrie A., & Cobb-Clark, Deborah A. (2000). IRCA's Impact on the Occupational Concentration and Mobility of Newly-Legalized Mexican Men. *Journal of Population Economics, 13*, 81–98.

Kossoudji, Sherrie A., & Cobb-Clark, Deborah A. (2002). Coming out of the Shadows: Learning About Legal Status and Wages form the Legalized Population. *Journal of Labor Economics, 20*, 598–628.

Kposowa, Augustine J. (1995). The Impact of Immigration on Unemployment and Earnings Among Racial Minorities in the United States. *Ethnic and Racial Studies, 18*(3), 605–628.

Logan, John R., Alba, Richard D., & McNulty, Thomas L. (1994). Ethnic Economies in Metropolitan Regions; Miami and Beyond. *Social Forces, 72*, 691–724.

Long, James E. (1975). Public-Private Sectoral Differences in Employment Discrimination. *Southern Economic Journal, 42*(1), 89–96.

McClain, Paula D. (1993). The Changing Dynamics of Urban Politics: Black and Hispanic Municipal Employment—Is There Competition? *The Journal of Politics, 55*(2), 399–414.

McLafferty, Sara, & Preston, Valerie. (1996). Spatial Mismatch and Employment in a Decade of Restructuring. *Professional Geographer, 48*, 420–431.

Meléndez, Edwin, Rodriguez, Clara E. & Figueroa, Barry J. (1991). *Hispanic in the Labor Force*. New York: Plenum Press.

Morales, Rebecca. (2000). What a Latino Worker Finds in the U.S. Labor Market. In Sonia M. Pérez (Ed.), *Moving Up the Economic Ladder: Latino Workers and the Nation's Future Prosperity*. Washington, DC: National Council of La Raza.

Mosisa, Abraham T. (2002). The Role of Foreign-Born Workers in the U.S. Economy. *Monthly Labor Review, 125*, 3–14.

Moss, Phillip I., & Tilly, Chris. (2001). *Stories Employers Tell: Race, Skill and Hiring in America*. New York: Russell Sage Foundation.

Myers, Dowell, & Cranford, Cynthia J. (1998). Temporal Differentiation in the Occupational Mobility of Immigrant and Native-Born Latina Workers. *American Sociological Review, 63*, 68–93.

National Council of La Raza. (2002, September 30). *Statement of Raul Yzaguirre, NCLR President, on New Census Data Showing High Levels of Uninsurance Among Latinos* (Press Release). Washington, DC: U.S. Government Printing Office.

Ortiz, Vilma. (1991). Latinos and Industrial Change in New York and Los Angeles. In Edwin Meléndez, Clara E. Rodriguez, & Barry J. Figueroa (Eds.) *Hispanics in the Labor Force* (pp. 119–132). New York: Plenum Press.

Ortiz, Vilma. (1996). The Mexican-Origin Population: Permanent Working Class or Emerging Middle Class? In Roger Waldinger & Mehdi Bozorgmehr (Eds.), *Ethnic Los Angeles* (pp. 247–277). New York: Russell Sage Foundation.

Passell, Jeffrey. (2005). *Unauthorized Migrants: Numbers and Characteristics*. Washington, DC: Pew Hispanic Center.

Pastor, Manuel, & Marcelli, Enrico A. (2000). *Social, Spatial, and Skill Mismatch in Los Angeles*. La Jolla, CA: Center for Comparative Immigration Studies.

Piore, Michael J. (1979). *Birds of Passage: Migrant Labor and Industrial Societies*. New York: Cambridge University Press.

Podolny, Joel M., & Baron, James N. (1997). Resources and Relationships: Social Networks and Mobility in the Workplace. *American Sociological Review, 62*, 673–693.

Pomer, Marshall I. (1986). Labor Market Structure, Intragenerational Mobility, and Discrimination: Black Male Advancement Out of Low-Paying Occupations, 1962–1973. *American Sociological Review, 51*, 650–659.

Portes, Alejandro. (1998). Social Capital: Its Origins and Applications in Modern Sociology. *Annual Review of Sociology, 24*, 1–24.

Portes, Alejandro, & Jensen, Leif. (1989). The Enclave and the Entrants: Patterns of Ethnic Enterprise in Miami Before and After Mariel. *American Sociological Review, 54*, 929–949.

Portes, Alejandro, & Landolt, Patricia. (1996, May-June). The Downside of Social Capital. *The American Prospect, 26*, 18–22.

Reimers, Cordelia W. (1998). Unskilled Immigration and Changes in the Wage Distributions of Black, Mexican American and Non-Hispanic White Male Dropouts. In Daniel S. Hamermesh & Frank D. Bean (Eds.), *Help or Hindrance? The Economic Implications of Immigration for African Americans* (pp. 107–148). New York: Russell Sage Foundation.

Romero, Mary. (2002). *Maid in the USA* (10th anniversary edition). New York: Routledge.

Rosenfeld, Michael J., & Tienda, Marta. (1999). Mexican Immigration, Occupational Niches, and Labor-Market Competition: Evidence from Los Angeles, Chicago, and Atlanta, 1970 to 1990. In Frank D. Bean & Stephanie Bell-Rose (Eds.), *Immigration and Opportunity: Race, Ethnicity, and Employment in the United States* (pp. 64–105). New York: Russell Sage Foundation.

Sanders, Jimi M., & Nee, Victor. (1987). Limits of Ethnic Solidarity in the Enclave Economy. *American Sociological Review, 52*, 745–773.

Sanders, Jimy M., & Nee, Victor. (1996). Immigrant Self-Employment: The Family as Social Capital and the Value of Human Capital. *American Sociological Review, 61*, 231–249.

Segura, Denise A. (1991). Ambivalence or Continuity? Motherhood and Employment Among Chicanas and Mexican Immigrant Women Workers. *Aztlan: A Journal of Chicano Studies, 20*, 119–150.

Shulman, Steven. (2004). *The Impact of Immigration on African Americans.* New Brunswick, NJ: Transaction Books.

Simon, Curtis, & Warner, John. (1992). Matchmaker, Matchmaker: The Effect of Old Boy Networks on Job Match Quality, Earnings and Tenure. *Journal of Labor Economics, 10*, 306–330.

Sisneros, Antonio. (1993). Hispanics in the Public Service in the Late Twentieth Century. *Public Administration Review, 53*, 1–7.

Smith, James P., & Edmonston, Barry (Eds.). (1997). *The New Americans: Economic, Demographic, and Fiscal Effects of Immigration.* Washington, DC: National Academy Press.

Stoll, Michael A. (1998). When Jobs Move, Do Black and Latino Men Lose? The Effect of Growth in Job Decentralization on Young Men's Jobless Incidence and Duration. *Urban Studies, 35*, 2221–2239.

Stoll, Michael A., Holzer, Harry J., & Ihlanfeldt, Keith R. (2000). Within Cities and Suburbs: Racial Residential Concentration and the Spatial Distribution of Employment Opportunities Across Submetropolitan Areas. *Journal of Policy Analysis and Management, 19*, 207–232.

Suro, Robert, & Passell, Jeffrey. (2003). *The Rise of the Second Generation: Changing Patterns in Hispanic Population Growth.* Washington, DC: Pew Hispanic Center.

Thomas-Breitfeld, Sean. (2003). *The Latino Workforce.* Washington, DC: National Council of La Raza.

Toussaint-Comeau, Maude, Smith, Thomas, & Comeau Jr., Ludovic. (2005). *Occupational Attainment and Mobility of Hispanics in a Changing Economy.* Washington, DC: Pew Hispanic Center.

U.S. Department of Labor, BLS (Bureau of Labor Statistics). (2002). *Geographic Profile of Employment and Unemployment 2000.* Bulletin 2550. Washington, DC: U.S. Government Printing Office. (June).

U.S. Department of Labor, BLS, (Bureau of Labor Statistics). (2006a). *Employment and Earnings.* Washington, DC: U.S. Government Printing Office.

U.S. Department of Labor, BLS (Bureau of Labor Statistics). (2006b). *Foreign-Born Workers: Labor Force Characteristics in 2005.* Washington, DC: U.S. Government Printing Office.

Valenzuela, Abel, Jr. (2003). Day Labor Work. *Annual Review of Sociology, 29*, 307–333.

Valenzuela, Abel, Jr., Kawachi, Janette A., & Marr, Matthew D. (2002). Seeking Work Daily: Supply, Demand, and Spatial Dimensions of Day Labor in Two Global Cities. *International Journal of Comparative Sociology, 43*, 192–219.

Waldinger, Roger. (1996). *Still the Promised City? African-Americans and New Immigrants in Post-Industrial New York.* Cambridge: Harvard University Press.

Waldinger, Roger, & Lichter, Michael. (2003). *How the Other Half Works: Immigration and the Social Organization of Labor.* Berkeley: University of California Press.

Waldinger, Roger, Erickson, Chris, Milkman, Ruth, Mitchell, Daniel, Valenzuela, Abel & Wong, Kent. (1996, April). Helots No More: A Case Study of the Justice for Janitors Campaign in Los Angeles. Los Angeles: UCLA Ralph and Goldy Lewis Center for Regional Policy Studies, Working Paper Series. Paper 15.

Wilson, Kenneth L., & Portes, Alejandro (1980). Immigrant Enclaves: An Analysis of the Labor Market Experiences of Cubans in Miami. *American Journal of Sociology, 86*, 235–313.

Zlolniski, Christian. (2006). *Janitors, Street Vendors, and Activists: The Lives of Mexican Immigrants in Silicon Valley.* Berkeley: University of California Press.

CHAPTER 11

Latino/a Entrepreneurship in the United States: A Strategy of Survival and Economic Mobility

Zulema Valdez

INTRODUCTION

The Latino/a population in the United States has more than doubled between 1980 and 2000. Recent Census figures indicate that this population has increased from 22.4 million in 1990 to 35.3 million in 2000 (a 58% increase) (Saenz, 2004). Not surprisingly, the rise in the Latino/a population has contributed to an unprecedented growth in Latino/a business ownership. In 2002, Latino/as owned a reported 1.6 million nonfarm businesses and employed 1.5 million persons. From 1997 to 2000, Latino/a business ownership increased by 31% (compared to only 6% for non-Latino/a businesses). Over this same period, revenues for Latino/a businesses totaled *$220 billion dollars* (U.S. Census Bureau, 2006).

Although Latino/a business owners maintain a considerable presence in the U.S. economy, it is noteworthy that their economic progress has not kept pace with that of non-Latino/as. To illustrate, sales and receipts for Latino/a businesses increased by 19% from 1997 to 2000; however, those of non-Latino businesses rose even higher (22%). Moreover, although Latino/as currently reflect 12.5% of the total U.S. population, the Latino/a business community makes up only 7% of business firms nationwide and garners just 1% of firm sales and receipts. Additionally, fewer than 2,000 Latino/a firms employ 100 workers or more.

Importantly, then, the growth of Latino/a business in the United States requires a consideration of the causes and consequences of Latino/a business ownership within the larger context of the U.S. economy, including the potential for economic progress (or decline).

Moreover, it is important to consider differences across distinct national-origin groups, as the pan-ethnic Latino/a or Hispanic identity masks intergroup differences in business ownership. The quintessential Cuban ethnic entrepreneurs thriving in "Little Havana" (the Cuban ethnic enclave in Miami), the undocumented Mexican day laborers and *domésticas* in Los Angeles who work on their own account, and the Central American transnational entrepreneurs who conduct business on both sides of the border all reflect a diversity of experiences that constitute Latino/a self-employment.

In this chapter, I provide a theoretical and empirical overview of the entrepreneurial experience of Latino/as in the United States. In the first section, I discuss the traditional approach to ethnic enterprise. Next, I provide an exploratory investigation of self-employment among diverse Latino/a-origin groups. Because many of these Latino/a groups are recent migrants to the United States and/or their populations are small, this analysis serves as a preliminary "first look" at self-employment across distinct Latin American national-origin groups. Finally, although ethnic entrepreneurship among the Latino/a population overall remains understudied (with the exception of Cuban immigrants and their descendants), I present research that has explored the entrepreneurial and self-employment practices of the more traditional and larger Latino/a population in the United States.

A NOTE ON ENTREPRENEURSHIP VERSUS SELF-EMPLOYMENT

Social scientists define entrepreneurship differently. The definition may include innovators or managers, the "pure" self-employed (those who are self-employed with no employees), or business owners who hire workers and work in part, for themselves (Schumpeter, 1934, 1951/1989; Hakim, 1988, p. 430; Waldinger, Aldrich, Ward, & Associates, 1990, p. 17). With respect to actual occupations, then, this definition comprises the following: marginal, low-skilled, and part-time self-employment, such as day laborers and *domésticas*; full-time, mid-range occupations, such as owner/managers of garment factories, restaurants, or auto repair shops; and highly skilled, technological occupations or those requiring specialized knowledge, such as translators or real estate brokers.

Ethnic entrepreneurship constitutes business ownership among immigrants, ethnic group members, or both. Research on ethnic entrepreneurship generally uses the terms *entrepreneur/ entrepreneurship* for all forms of self-employment activity; however, it is important to note that the vast majority of "entrepreneurs" (approximately 80%) are self-employed small business owners who hire one or no employees or who rely solely on unpaid family labor (Hakim, 1988; Rath, 2002: Sanders & Nee, 1996). This is especially true for ethnic minorities (Sanders & Nee, 1996). Therefore, I use the terms *ethnic entrepreneurs/ethnic entrepreneurship*, in keeping with the literature, but also use the terms *self-employed workers/self-employment* when discussing understudied groups with low self-employment participation rates. By underscoring "ethnic entrepreneurship" as "self-employment," an attempt is made to reflect more accurately the actual working conditions of this self-employed majority.

THEORIZING ETHNIC ENTREPRENEURSHIP

The traditional approach to ethnic entrepreneurship presents a supply-side argument that focuses on the characteristics and attributes of the ethnic group itself. This approach posits that resource mobilization based on ethnic group membership facilitates ethnic entrepreneurship (Light, 1972;

Light & Bonacich, 1988; Portes & Bach, 1985; Portes & Rumbaut, 1990; Waldinger et al., 1990). The "interaction" (Waldinger et al., 1990) and "modes of incorporation" (Portes & Rumbaut, 1990) models extend this approach to include the demand side of entrepreneurship (i.e., the opportunity structure of the host society). This model maintains that ethnic entrepreneurship is explained by the interaction of the particularistic features of an ethnic group with the opportunity structure of the larger economy and society.

Light and Bonacich (1988) forwarded a supply-side approach and suggested that specific class and ethnic resources associated with an ethnic group promote entrepreneurship. Class resources consist of private property, wealth, and "bourgeois values, attitudes, and knowledge" that are associated with the aggregate social class of an entrepreneurial ethnic group (Light & Bonacich, 1988, pp. 18–19). Ethnic resources are defined as the intergenerational transfer of information, attitudes, leadership potential, and solidarity among coethnics (Light & Bonacich, 1988, pp. 18–19). In sum, class and ethnic resources combine the following; individual-level, human capital such as skills, education, and experience; tangible material goods related to class background, such as property and wealth; and social capital, a more "intangible" resource that is rooted in ethnic group membership and that fosters group solidarity, trust, and reciprocal obligations (Coleman, 1988, p. s98; Portes & Sensenbrenner, 1993, p. 1322). Ultimately, class and ethnic resources supply the essential ingredients that facilitate ethnic entrepreneurship.

For example, research indicates that ethnic group membership provides a basis for mutual aid between coethnics. In particular, some Cuban entrepreneurs in Miami acquired their start-up capital from informal "character loans"—loans granted to co-ethnics based solely on their family reputation in Cuba (Portes & Stepick, 1993). Similarly, ethnic banking institutions sometimes grant loans more readily to coethnics (Light & Bonacich, 1988; Portes & Zhou, 1992; Sanders & Nee, 1996, p. 232). Additionally, Korean, Japanese, and Chinese rotating credit associations are well-documented, ethnic group-specific lending institutions that foster their capital accumulation (Light, 1972; Light & Bonacich, 1988). Participation in mutual aid associations requires specific ethnic group and social class features: One must be a member of the ethnic group and one must have a reputable social class standing or sufficient market capital. In this way, the combination of ethnic and class resources promote ethnic entrepreneurship (Light & Bonacich; Portes & Rumbaut, 2001; Waldinger et al., 1990). Although class and ethnic resources explain the supply side of ethnic entrepreneurship, newer research extends this approach to consider the demand side (i.e., the interaction of the specific features of a given group with the larger economy and society for a more comprehensive picture).

Waldinger and colleagues (1990) suggested that three sets of characteristics explain ethnic entrepreneurship. Premigration characteristics are similar to class and ethnic resources and include the education and skills, work experience, and entrepreneurial attitudes that immigrants possess before they migrate (Waldinger et al., 1990, p. 41). Circumstances of migration relate to factors that stem from the larger socioeconomic context. For example, disadvantaged minorities in the United States, such as Mexican immigrants, might engage in enterprise as a survival strategy (Light & Roach, 1986) or to avoid blocked mobility—the discriminatory practice of employers to limit advancement and promotion of ethnic minority workers (Borjas, 1990; Piore, 1979). In contrast, more "advantaged" minorities, such as Cuban immigrants, might participate in entrepreneurship as a strategy of economic mobility, helped along by start-up capital provided by U.S. government-backed refugee loans and other social welfare benefits (Portes & Bach, 1985). Circumstances of migration also include the settlement process: whether a group settles temporarily or permanently. In particular, research shows that a pattern of permanent settlement and family migration characterizes those groups that are more likely to engage in ethnic entrepreneurship. In contrast, those groups that are more likely to come to the United States as individual migrants or sojourners, such as Mexican and Puerto Rican immigrants, are less likely to own businesses (Massey et al., 1987; Piore, 1979; Sanders & Nee, 1996). Finally, postmigration characteristics refer primarily to the occupational position of the immigrant group upon entry to the receiving country. Strategic occupational positions—those that provide business opportunities—emerge from a combination of prior skills, "random factors," and "cumulative social advantage" (Waldinger et al., 1990, p. 45). Waldinger and colleagues (1990) argued that membership in a group with characteristics that "favor business success … gain access to needed business skills …," whereas those immigrants who are not members of business-oriented groups are "more likely to work for natives" (pp. 45–46). In support of this contention, Light, Bernard, and Kim (1999) argued that Mexican and Central American "working-class migrations" generate few entrepreneurs.

Overall, Waldinger and his associates (1990) argued that pre-migration characteristics, circumstances of migration, and postmigration characteristics explain ethnic entrepreneurship (pp. 155–156). They concluded that although the combination of these factors might be different across groups, the strategies employed are similar. Likewise, Portes and Rumbaut (1990) argued that specific ethnic group characteristics combine with the larger context of the host society, such as a positive or negative societal reception context, specific government immigration policies, and a favorable or unfavorable social climate. They argued that ethnic group differences in entrepreneurship rest on such "modes of incorporation" (Portes & Rumbaut, 1990, pp. 83–93).

Finally, this ethnic entrepreneurship paradigm characterizes those ethnic groups with negligible rates of entrepreneurship as disadvantaged. For these groups, individual and group deficiencies, such as limited education and work experience, a weak or weakened coethnic social structure, and few structural opportunities in the larger economy and society, are presumed to impede enterprise (Borjas & Bronars, 1990; Fratoe, 1988; Lee, 2002, pp. 42–47; Light, 1972; Logan, Alba, & McNulty, 1994, pp. 693–694; Portes & Bach, 1985, p. 245; Wilson, 1980, p. 121 1987, p. xi). As Portes and Rumbaut (2001) argued, the limited economic progress of Mexican-origin population is, in part, due to "weak communities that have emerged under their precarious conditions of arrival and settlement" (p. 278). Moreover, Portes and Bach (1985) contrasted Cubans' entrepreneurial participation and economic success with an absence of Mexican entrepreneurship and concluded that a lack of community support relegates the Mexican-origin population to low-wage work in the U.S. labor market and subsequent economic stagnation (Portes & Bach, 1985, p. 245).

Although rates of entrepreneurship among disadvantaged groups are low, the few who attempt such enterprises face greater hardships than those with economically supportive social networks. For example, disadvantaged ethnic entrepreneurs are more vulnerable to "consumer discrimination, whereby white consumers dislike purchasing goods and services from blacks and other minorities" (Borjas & Bronars, 1989, p. 582). Additionally, because entrepreneurial activity is constrained to begin with, such enterprises provide few "multiplier effects for the community" (Wilson & Martin, 1982, p. 150). Hence, whereas business ownership is widespread among some Latino/a national origin groups, such as Cubans, it is negligible for other groups, such as Mexicans (Portes & Bach, 1985).

In sum, the ethnic entrepreneurship paradigm asserts that the specific characteristics associated with a given group interact with the opportunity structure of the larger economy and society to explain ethnic entrepreneurship. Moreover, this approach suggests that in the absence of such factors, entrepreneurial activity is suppressed. Finally, these approaches argue that understanding differences in ethnic entrepreneurship is essential because entrepreneurial activity is associated with economic success (Nee & Sanders, 1985; Logan et al., 1994; Portes & Zhou, 1992; Sanders & Nee, 1987, 1996; Waldinger, 1986; Waldinger et al., 1990).

ETHNIC ENTREPRENEURSHIP AND ECONOMIC PROGRESS

Previous research demonstrated that ethnic entrepreneurs are better off than their coethnic worker counterparts (Portes & Rumbaut, 1990; Portes & Stepick, 1993; Waldinger et al., 1990). For instance, Portes and Bach (1985) argued that entrepreneurial activity partially explains the economic progress of Cubans in the United States. However, mixed findings among more recent waves of Mariel Cubans challenge the notion that ethnic entrepreneurship results in economic progress (Portes & Jensen, 1989, pp. 945–946). Additionally, Valdez (2006) found that the self-employment earnings of Mexicans who reside in the Southwest are lower than those of their wage-worker counterparts, regardless of skill. Such findings call into question the presumed upward mobility trajectory associated with ethnic entrepreneurship.

Additionally, researchers observe that some ethnic groups favor entrepreneurship as a survival strategy or "economic lifeboat"—that is, as a last ditch alternative to unemployment, rather than one of upward mobility (Light & Roach, 1996, p. 193). As Hakim (1988) stated, "it cannot be assumed that the self-employed are invariably entrepreneurs who are building businesses that will eventually employ more people than themselves" (p. 430). On the contrary, research has shown that self-employed workers are likely to work on their own account, with few, if any, paid employees. Such findings challenge assumptions that ethnic entrepreneurship promotes economic success. In the case of the Latino/a population, whose socioeconomic outcomes reflect "… signs of group progress matched by signs of decline and stagnation" (Camarillo & Bonilla, 2001, p. 104), self-employment might also serve as a strategy of economic survival. In the following section, I explore the self-employment outcomes of a number of distinct Latino/a national-origin groups. Specifically, I examine self-employment participation rates, earnings, and industry concentration.

SELF-EMPLOYMENT IN THE LATINO/A POPULATION

Table 1 displays the percentage of the working population that is self-employed across select Caribbean, Central and South American groups, and Mexicans. Among U.S.-born men, Cubans report the highest self-employment rate (7.3%), followed by Peruvians (5.8%) and Argentines (5.8%). Similarly, foreign-born Argentine (11.9%), Cuban (9.9%), and Peruvian (6.5%) men are more likely to be self-employed than the other foreign-born groups; additionally, these groups exceed the self-employment rate of their U.S.-born counterparts. Notably, these groups' self-employment rates are considerably higher than that of the U.S.-born working male population as a whole (5.1%) (U.S. Census Bureau, 2006). In contrast, U.S.-born Ecuadorian and Dominican men report substantially lower rates of self-employment (2.0% and 2.4%, respectively), and foreign-born Honduran (3.8%) and Puerto Rican (3.7%) men fall behind all other foreign-born groups.

Among women, U.S.-born Hondurans (4.9%) and Nicaraguans (4.1%) are more likely to be self-employed than the other U.S.-born Latina groups. Moreover, foreign-born Columbian (6.7%) and Peruvian (5.2%) women, like their foreign-born male counterparts, report the highest self-employment rate among foreign-born Latina groups. Moreover, these U.S.- and foreign-born groups exceed the self-employment rate among women in the general population (2.2%) (U.S. Census Bureau, 2006). In contrast, self-employment among U.S.-born Guatemalan and Peruvian women is negligible, as is the self-employment rate of foreign-born Cuban women (0.04%).

Table 2 shows the earnings of wage workers and self-employed workers across different Latino/a origin groups, by nativity and gender. These data show that among men, the earnings of the self-employed are higher than those of wage workers, regardless of Latino national-origin or nativity. Additionally, the earnings of U.S.-born self-employed men are generally higher than

TABLE 1. Percent Self-Employed Workers Among Latino/as in the U.S. Labor Force, ages 25–64

	Men		Women	
	U.S.-born	Foreign-born	U.S.-born	Foreign-born
Caribbean				
Cuban	7.26	9.88	3.31	0.04
Dominican	2.42	5.15	2.12	3.98
Puerto Rican	3.30	3.70	2.00	2.11
Central American				
Guatemalan	2.50	4.79	0.64	4.86
Honduran	3.92	3.77	4.90	5.11
Nicaraguan	4.73	4.86	4.05	4.48
Salvadoran	3.89	4.23	1.67	4.68
South American				
Argentinian	5.56	11.93	3.85	5.00
Colombian	4.52	6.40	2.01	6.65
Ecuadorian	1.95	6.37	1.95	3.89
Peruvian	5.80	6.48	0.003	5.21
North American				
Mexican	4.56	5.28	2.47	2.59

Source: US Census Bureau (Census 2000, 5% IPUMS).

TABLE 2. Mean Annual Earnings Among Latino/a Wage and Self-Employed Workers in the United States, ages 25–64

	Men				Women			
	US-born		Foreign-born		US-born		Foreign-born	
	Wage work	Self-employed	Wage work	Self-employed	Wage work	Self-employed	Wage work	Self-employed
Caribbean								
Cuban	48,236	64,730	40,708	56,258	33,171	43,817	27,009	34,642
Dominican	34,423	81,750	29,034	41,747	28,446	46,100	21,148	38,860
Puerto Rican	38,540	55,742	35,329	49,026	28,371	33,933	25,352	27,959
Central American								
Guatemalan	48,628	87,000	23,406	28,185	26,769	10,000	17,800	14,734
Honduran	48,079	144,600	24,293	34,595	25,926	12,838	16,342	11,913
Nicaraguan	52,029	85,800	29,941	39,620	31,067	17,100	19,121	15,965
Salvadoran	54,870	193,333	25,083	31,404	24,610	5,900	16,539	17,386
South American								
Argentinian	53,993	64,177	55,936	71,522	40,745	129,589	30,915	43,581
Columbian	38,930	39,583	37,941	48,175	31,447	22,400	22,140	19,364
Ecuadorian	43,451	86,560	30,942	37,125	31,668	31,255	21,508	22,429
Peruvian	43,502	71,546	36,450	46,383	34,140	34,514	22,517	21,153
North American								
Mexican	34,878	47,112	24,270	33,667	24,327	28,031	16,242	18,630

Source: US Census Bureau (Census 2000, 5% IPUMS).

their foreign-born counterparts (with the exception of self-employed foreign-born Argentines and Colombians, who earn more than the U.S.-born). These earnings data clearly show that self-employed Latino men are better off than Latinos who work for wages in the U.S. labor market.

The earnings data are not as favorable or clear-cut for self-employed Latina women. First, Latina women earn less than their male counterparts, regardless of worker status (wage worker or self-employed) or nativity. Second, self-employed Latina women do not always exceed the earnings of their wage-earning counterparts. Although self-employed Caribbean and Mexican women earn more than wage workers, self-employed Central American (with one exception), Argentine, foreign-born Ecuadorian, and U.S.-born Peruvian women earn less. Finally, although most U.S.-born Latina women earn more than the foreign-born, foreign-born Guatemalan and Salvadoran women earn more than their U.S.-born counterparts. Findings suggest that self-employment might provide a strategy of economic mobility for men and most women; however, for Central American women, self-employment might provide a strategy of survival. Findings further suggest that women experience a less favorable context of reception than men, likely due to occupational segregation in the gendered labor market.

Finally, Table 3 displays the distribution of the self-employed Latino/a-origin groups by industry. Findings reveal that most groups concentrate in similar industries, regardless of national origin. Specifically, the construction, professional services (i.e., translator, real estate), and other services (i.e., auto repair) industries represent the top three industries for 9 of the 12 Latino/a groups presented here. Furthermore, Argentine, Colombian, and Dominican groups report two of these three industries in their top three. Although these groups might possess different premigration characteristics or experience different circumstances of migration, the overwhelming concentration of Latino/a national-origin groups in specific and limited industries suggests that these groups share a similar context of reception. As Latino/as, these groups likely face similar structural opportunities (and constraints) in the U.S. labor market that shape their entrepreneurial endeavors.

Taken together, these findings highlight similarities and differences in the self-employment experiences of Latino/a national-origin groups. Although the entrepreneurial Cubans and "non-entrepreneurial" Mexicans dominate the ethnic entrepreneurship literature, these exploratory findings reveal intragroup and intergroup variation in self-employment, by nativity and gender. Notably, these findings reveal that understudied groups show even greater disparities than those groups that are represented in the literature. To illustrate, I observe that foreign-born Argentine men surpass Cubans in entrepreneurship, and Puerto Rican and Central American men fall behind Mexican men (Table 1). Additionally, there is evidence of industrial concentration among the Latino/a population; in particular, findings reveal that self-employed Latino/as overwhelmingly concentrate in the construction, professional services, and other services industries. Findings suggest the presence of pan-ethnic "occupational niches" (Waldinger, 1986) among the self-employed Latino/a-origin population (Table 2).

Finally, with respect to earnings, findings show that Latino men earn more than women, regardless of worker status (i.e., self-employed or wage worker). Additionally, U.S.-born Latinos earn more than foreign-born Latinos, and self-employed workers earn more than wage workers. Although Caribbean and Mexican women follow similar trends, the earnings data for Central American and South American women is mixed. Overall, findings suggest that self-employment might be a strategy of survival (Light & Roach, 1996) for Central American and some South American women and a strategy of upward mobility for Latin American men and Caribbean and Mexican women. These preliminary findings highlight the need for more research in this area. In the next section, I present four cases of Latino/a enterprise that illustrate the diversity of entrepreneurial experiences among Latino/as in the United States.

TABLE 3. Industry Concentration among Latino/a Self-Employed Workers in the US, 25–64 (percent)

Industry	Mexican	Puerto Rican	Cuban	Guatemalan	Honduran	Nicaraguan	Salvadoran	Argentinian	Columbian	Ecuadoran	Peruvian	Dominican
Agriculture	3.5	1.0	1.6	0.8	0.6	0.5	0.0	0.6	0.1	0.0	0.8	0.9
Mining	0.2	0.0	0.0	0.0	0.0	0.0	0.0	0.3	0.0	0.0	0.0	0.0
Construction	20.2	15.7	16.7	18.7	22.2	17.0	13.4	12.5	10.0	13.9	13.1	10.6
Manufacturing	4.3	3.0	4.8	2.4	3.7	2.1	1.7	6.3	4.3	4.8	4.1	3.5
Wholesale	2.7	3.9	5.1	1.6	1.2	3.2	1.5	6.9	3.9	5.2	2.6	3.1
Retail	10.0	9.9	10.2	6.4	5.6	6.9	6.4	10.9	9.2	10.9	7.5	15.9
Transportation	4.4	4.2	6.3	4.4	3.7	5.3	5.9	4.6	7.0	10.4	7.5	9.3
Information & communications	0.0	1.2	1.6	0.8	0.6	1.1	0.5	1.0	1.4	0.4	3.0	0.4
Finance	4.3	5.5	7.5	2.8	2.5	7.5	1.7	6.6	6.2	5.2	7.5	4.9
Professional services	17.1	16.8	19.8	13.9	13.0	16.0	17.8	16.8	16.9	17.8	15.4	11.1
Education; health; social services	9.1	15.5	10.7	7.2	6.8	11.2	9.9	14.9	13.5	6.5	12.4	21.7
Entertainment; food service	6.0	7.0	5.1	5.2	3.1	3.7	6.2	7.6	5.2	5.7	5.2	3.1
Other services (i.e., auto)	17.4	16.5	10.7	35.9	37.0	25.5	34.9	10.9	22.4	19.1	21.0	15.5
Unweighted N	10,311	1,310	2,449	251	162	188	404	303	728	230	267	226

Note: Non-self-employment industries excluded (utilities, public administration, and armed services). Analysis of variance (ANOVA) results indicate that Latino groups differ significantly by industry concentration: F-value = 18.

Source: US Census Bureau (Census 2000, 5% IPUMS).

THE ETHNIC ENCLAVE ECONOMY: THE CASE OF THE CUBAN ENTREPRENEURS

The Souto family coffee business was established in Cuba during the late 1800s. Following Castro's regime change, it closed its doors in 1959. The Souto family, José "Pepe" Souto (whose dad, Angel, founded the business) and his wife Haydeé fled to Miami, where they started it anew. "Our father encouraged us to come to the business, but he never insisted," José Enrique recalls. However, as the Cuban population in Miami grew, so did their sales, and the brothers left their steady jobs to join their parents. Today, the Souto coffee business ranks among the top 100 fastest growing Latino/a businesses (Hispanic Online, 2006).

Like the Souto family, many middle- and upper-class Cuban migrants fled the Castro regime in the early 1960s to the late 1970s. Cuban immigrants' settlement in the United States was made easier with U.S. government support in the form of financial aid, health care, education loans, scholarships, and business loans (Portes & Stepick, 1993). Additionally, ethnic solidarity within the coethnic Cuban community elicited trust and reciprocal obligations that further facilitated Cuban immigrants' settlement and enterprise (Portes & Bach, 1985; Sanders & Nee, 1996; Wilson & Martin, 1982; Wilson & Portes, 1980).

Wilson and Portes (1980) first defined the ethnic enclave as a spatially concentrated ethnic business sector of coethnic employers, employees, and businesses that provides goods and services to coethnics and eventually others (Portes & Jensen, 1992, p. 419; Portes & Stepick, 1993, p. 127; Wilson & Portes, 1980, p. 304). In Miami, residential segregation coupled with few white-owned businesses in areas of Cuban immigrant and ethnic settlement created a greater supply and demand for Cuban-specific specialty goods and services. Such factors ushered in the development of the Cuban enclave economy.

The Cuban ethnic enclave in Miami provides Cuban entrepreneurs with an available source of coethnic, low-wage or unpaid family labor. Cuban business owners often hire family or coethnic members, thereby "mobilizing direct connections to the ethnic community from which they emigrated" (Waldinger et al., 1990, p. 38). Family members experience the "reciprocal obligation" to work in the family business, often without pay (Wilson & Portes, 1980, p. 315). Beyond family or immediate kin, the geographically concentrated Cuban community itself provides a source of low-wage labor.

In the 1980s, a new wave of disadvantaged Cuban immigrants settled in the United States, known as "Marielitos" (in reference to the Mariel boatlifts). Unlike previous professional, middle- and upper-class Cuban refugees, the Marielitos constituted a group characterized by the Cuban government as "undesirable" and "disaffected" (Portes & Stepick, 1985, p. 495). Nevertheless, the Marielitos have benefited from the strong ethnic enclave economy that was established by the previous generation. Facilitated by coethnic networks, this most recent and disadvantaged group has been able to integrate into the Cuban enclave economy and has achieved some measure of socioeconomic progress, relative to other disadvantaged Latino/a groups.

THE ETHNIC ECONOMY: AN ALTERNATIVE TO THE ETHNIC ENCLAVE ECONOMY

In contrast to the ethnic enclave economy, which requires a geographically-district, ethnic community, the ethnic economy perspective provides a more general concept of ethnic entrepreneurship. Importantly, the ethnic economy does not require ethnic concentration in business location, residence, or industry; nor does it specify the necessity of a coethnic customer base, coethnic hiring practices, or the buying and/or selling of ethnic-specific goods and services. As such, the ethnic economy hypothesis allows for multiple entrepreneurial scenarios and can be applied widely without the need to "squeeze an ethnic economy into an ethnic enclave economy definition" (Light, Sabagh, & Kim, 1994, p. 78). In the ethnic economy, ethnic entrepreneurs are often well suited for a particular occupation and have the capacity to access specific goods or skills; "... it is presumed that they enjoy a favorable competitive position in some niche of the economy" (Logan et al., 1994, p. 694). Central American restaurateurs in the Southwest, Puerto Rican bodega owners in New York, and Latino/a auto mechanics and subcontractors in the construction or garment industries, who might or might not cater to a diverse Latino/a customer base, are all engaged in the ethnic economy.

THE TRANSNATIONAL ECONOMY: THE SALVADORAN VIAJEROS AND OTHER TRANSNATIONAL ENTREPRENEURS

Transnationalism refers to "the continuing relations between immigrants and their places of origin ... and the impact that such activities [have] in communities at both ends of the migration stream" (Portes, Guarnizo, & Haller, 2002, p. 279). Recent research on Salvadoran immigrants found that transnational enterprises are common, and range from *viajeros*, couriers who transfer goods between borders for small and large firms, to *return migrant microenterprises*, businesses established in El Salvador by return migrants from the United States, and that rely on U.S. contacts (Landolt, Autler, & Baires, 1999; Portes et al., 2002). Dominicans are also engaged in transnational enterprises. In particular, Dominican remittance agencies and specialty goods stores in the United States and the importation of U.S. businesses to the Dominican Republic (such as laundromats or video stores) are some examples of Dominican transnational enterprises at work. The study of transnational entrepreneurs is relatively new and, as such, has largely focused on Central Americans and other recent immigrant groups to the United States; however, it is likely that other Latino/a (and non-Latino/a) immigrant groups engage in transnational enterprise as well. As Portes et al. (2002) recently concluded in their study of transnational entrepreneurs, "... transnational entrepreneurs represent a large proportion, often the majority, of the self-employed persons in immigrant communities" (p. 293).

THE INFORMAL OR UNDERGROUND ECONOMY: DAY LABORERS AND *DOMÉSTICAS*

Day laborers constitute a temporary low-wage workforce of immigrant men who work on their own account and are usually of Mexican descent (although a growing number identify as Central American) (Valenzuela, 2001). Day laborers are a familiar presence across the nation. A recent report by the Center for the Study of Urban Poverty indicated that 42% of day laborers concentrate in the West, 23% of day laborers concentrate in the East, 18% concentrate in the Southwest, 12% concentrate in the South, and 4% concentrate in the Midwest (Valenzuela, Theodore, Melendez, & Gonzalez, 2006, p. 2).

Day labor is considered an informal economic activity because the work is generally unstable and insecure with little or no government oversight or regulation. Day laborers might seek work in a variety of informal ways, which include standing on street corners or near home improvement stores or moving/storage companies. Sites that are more formal include government or community-based day labor work centers.

Domésticas are Latina immigrants (the majority of whom are of Mexican, Guatemalan, or Salvadoran descent) who work as house cleaners/keepers, live-in/out maids, and nannies (Hondagneu-Sotelo, 2001). Although *domésticas* might work for a firm, many work on their own account and are paid "under the table" (neither they nor their clients pay taxes on their income). Although some day laborers and *domésticas* might *choose* this type of work over standard work (i.e., formal employment, regular hours) for increased autonomy or a more flexible schedule, nonstandard work practices are first and foremost a strategy of survival (Valenzuela, 2001, p. 335). The preliminary analysis of self-employment earnings among Central American women presented earlier in this chapter support this claim, because self-employed Central American women earn less than their wage-worker counterparts. Self-employed day laborers and *domésticas* earn more than those who are not employed (e.g. unemployed or jobless). Additionally, the Latino/a self-employed may earn more than wage workers in the low-skilled labor market, who may be more likely to face blocked mobility due to racial and ethnic discrimination, limited skills, education, and work experience. As such, day laborers and *domésticas* employ strategies similar to "survivalist entrepreneurs" (Valenzuela, 2001, p. 349). Additionally, and akin to ethnic entrepreneurship more generally, day laborers and *domésticas* often rely on coethnic networks and information channels for job opportunities.

CONCLUSION

In the 1970s, the emergence of global capitalism forced an economic restructuring of the U.S. economy. Economic restructuring resulted in the decline of good-paying "blue collar" jobs in durable manufacturing and a rise in low-skilled low-wage non-durable-goods manufacturing (small electronics, garment manufacturing), and service jobs. Such changes have hit the Latino/a population particularly hard. The negative effect of economic restructuring on the wages and job opportunities of foreign-born and U.S.-born Latino/as persists to this day (Moore & Pinderhughes, 1993; Morales & Bonilla, 1993; Ortiz, 1996). In addition, and during this same period, immigration policy reforms, such as the Hart-Cellar Act of 1965, the Immigration Reform and Control Act of 1986, and the Immigration Act of 1990, have dramatically increased Latino/a migration to the United States. Alongside legal immigration, undocumented Mexican and Central American migrants continue to cross the border in record numbers.

Overall, economic restructuring coupled with the growth of the Latino/a population has increased labor market competition, racial and ethnic discrimination, and wage inequality in the U.S. labor market (Davila, Pagan, & Grau, 1998; Phillips & Massey, 1999; Valdez, 2006). In this context, ethnic enterprise provides a necessary and alternative means to Latino/a economic incorporation.

The ethnic entrepreneurship paradigm maintains that class and ethnic resources interact with the opportunity structure of the larger economy to explain ethnic entrepreneurship. For highly skilled and "advantaged" Latino/a groups, those with class and ethnic resources and a positive context of reception, business ownership likely provides an opportunity for economic progress. For disadvantaged groups, however, self-employment might offer, at best, an alternative to low-skilled low-wage work at the bottom of the economic ladder, where opportunities for advancement are rare.

Although some research has demonstrated that low-skilled self-employed workers do not benefit economically from microenterprise assistance programs (Sanders, 2002; Servon & Bates, 1998), research has not examined whether disadvantaged ethnic minorities engaged in microenterprise might achieve modest economic gains. Research on Latino/a survivalist entrepreneurs, then, will supply policy makers with information to understand the benefits of microenterprise assistance programs that promote self-sufficiency through informal self-employment.

Such limited and targeted programs might enable low-skilled disadvantaged Latino/as to escape from poverty by providing an opportunity for self-employment as an alternative to unemployment or underemployment.

In sum, this chapter attempts to provide a theoretical and empirical overview of Latino/a entrepreneurship in the United States. Primarily, this chapter reveals intergroup and intra group differences in ethnic entrepreneurship among Latino/a national-origin groups. This diversity of entrepreneurial experiences is often hidden or masked, as researchers limit their investigations to traditional groups, such as Cubans or Mexicans, conduct analyses on pan-ethnic "Latinos" or "Hispanics" only, and/or neglect to consider the gendered aspects of entrepreneurship. This chapter highlights the need for continued research in the area of Latino/a enterprise that goes beyond existing theoretical frameworks and encourages the investigation of self-employment as a strategy of survival among disadvantaged Latino/a groups.

REFERENCES

Borjas, George J. (1990). *Friends or Strangers: The Impact of Immigrants on the American Economy*. New York: Basic Books.

Borjas, George J., & Bronars, Stephen G. (1989). Consumer Discrimination and Self-Employment. *The Journal of Political Economy, 97*, 581–605.

Camarillo, Albert M., & Bonilla, Frank. (2001). Hispanics in a Multicultural Society: A New American Dilemma? In Neil J. Smelser, William Julius Wilson, & Faith Mitchell (Eds), *America Becoming: Racial Trends and Their Consequences, Volume 1* (pp. 103–134). Washington, DC: National Academy Press.

Coleman, James S. (1988). Social Capital in the Creation of Human Capital. *American Journal of Sociology, 94*, S95–S120.

Davila, Alberto, Pagan, Jose A., & Grau, Montserrat Viladrich. (1998). The Impact of IRCA on the Job Opportunities and Earnings of Mexican-American and Hispanic-American Workers. *International Migration Review, 32*(1), 79–95.

Fratoe, Frank. (1988). Social Capital and Small Business Owners. *The Review of Black Political Economy, 16*, 33–50.

Hakim, Catherine. (1988). Self-Employment in Britain: Recent Trends and Current Issues. *Work, Employment and Society, 2*, 421–450.

Hispanic Online. (2006). 2001 Hispanic Entrepreneur 100. Retrieved November 15, 2006, from http://www.hispaniconline.com.

Hondagneu-Sotelo, Pierrette. (2001). *Doméstica: Immigrant Workers Cleaning and Caring in the Shadows of Affluence*. Berkeley: University of California Press.

Landolt, Patricia, Autler, Lilian, & Baires, Sonia. (1999). From 'Hermano Lejano' to "Hermano Mayor': The Dialectics of Salvadoran Transnationalism. *Ethnic and Racial Studies, 2*, 290–315.

Lee, Jennifer. (2002). *Civility in the City: Blacks, Jews, and Koreans in Urban America*. Cambridge, Massachusetts, and London, England: Harvard University Press.

Light, Ivan, Bernard, Richard B., & Kim, Rebecca. (1999). Immigrant Incorporation in the Garment Industry of Los Angeles. *International Migration Review, 33*, 5–25.

Light, Ivan, & Bonacich, Edna. (1988). *Immigrant Entrepreneurs: Koreans in Los Angeles*. Los Angeles: University of California Press.

Light, Ivan, & Roach, Elizabeth. (1996). Self-Employment: Mobility Ladder or Economic Lifeboat? In Roger Waldinger & Mehdi Bozorgmehr (Eds.), *Ethnic Los Angeles* (pp.193–214). New York: Russell Sage Foundation.

Light, Ivan, Sabagh, Georges, Bozorgmehr, Mehdi, & Der-Martirosian, Claudia. (1994). Beyond the Ethnic Enclave Economy. *Social Problems, 41*, 65–80.

Light, Ivan Hubert. (1972). *Ethnic Enterprise in America: Business and Welfare among Chinese, Japanese and Blacks*. Berkeley: University of California Press.

Logan, John R., Alba, Richard D., & McNulty, Thomas. (1994). Ethnic Economies in Metropolitan Regions: Miami and Beyond. *Social Forces, 72*(3), 691–724.

Massey, Douglas S. (1987). Understanding Mexican Migration to the United States. *American Journal of Sociology, 92*, 1372–1403.

Moore, Joan, & Pinderhughes, Raquel (Eds). (1993). *In the Barrios: Latinos and the Underclass Debate*. New York: Russel Sage Foundation.

Morales, Rebecca, & Bonilla, Frank (Eds). (1993). *Latinos in a Changing US Economy*. Newbury Park: Sage Publications.

Nee, Victor and Sanders, Jimmy. (1985). The Road to Parity: Determinants of the Socioeconomic Achievement of Asian Americans. *Ethnic and Racial Studies*, *8*, 75–93.

Ortiz, Vilma. (1996). The Mexican-Origin Population: Permanent Working Class or Emerging Middle Class? In Roger Waldinger & Mehdi Bozorgmehr (Eds.), *Ethnic Los Angeles* (pp. 247–278). New York: Russell Sage Foundation.

Phillips, Julie A., & Massey, Douglas S. (1999). The New Labor Market: Immigrants and Wages after IRCA. *Demography*, *36*(2), 233–246.

Piore, Michael J. (1979). *Birds of Passage: Migrant Labor and Industrial Societies.* Cambridge: Cambridge University Press.

Portes, Alejandro, & Bach, Robert. (1985). *Latin Journey: Cuban and Mexican Immigrants in the United States.* Berkeley: University of California Press.

Portes, Alejandro, Guarnizo, Luis Eduardo, & Haller, William J. (2002). Transnational Entrepreneurs: An Alternative Form of Immigrant Economic Adaptation. *American Sociological Review*, *67*, 278–298.

Portes, Alejandro, & Jensen, Leif. (1989). The Enclave and the Entrants: Patterns of Ethnic Enterprise in Miami Before and After Mariel. *American Sociological Review*, *54*, 929–949.

Portes, Alejandro, & Jensen, Leif. (1992). Disproving the Enclave Hypothesis. *American Sociological Review*, *57*, 418–420.

Portes, Alejandro, & Rumbaut, Ruben G. (1990). *Immigrant America: A Portrait.* Berkeley: University of California Press.

Portes, Alejandro, & Rumbaut, Ruben G. (2001). *Legacies: The Story of the Immigrant Second Generation.* Berkeley: University of California Press.

Portes, Alejandro, & Sensenbrenner, Julia. (1993). Embeddedness and Immigration: Notes on the Social Determinants of Economic Action. *American Journal of Sociology*, *93*, 1320–1350.

Portes, Alejandro, & Stepick, Alex. (1985). Unwelcome Immigrants: The Labor Market Experiences of 1980 (Mariel) Cuban and Haitian Refugees in South Florida. *American Sociological Review, 50*, 492–514.

Portes, Alejandro, & Stepick, Alex. (1993). *City on the Edge: The Transformation of Miami.* Berkeley: University of California Press.

Portes, Alejandro, & Zhou, Min. (1992). Gaining the Upper Hand: Economic Mobility Among Domestic Minorities. *Ethnic and Racial Studies*, *15*, 491–522.

Rath, Jan. (2002). *Unraveling the Rag Trade: Immigrant Entrepreneurship in Seven World Cities.* Oxford: Berg Press.

Saenz, Rogelio. (2004). *Latinos and the Changing Face of America.* New York: Russell Sage Foundation.

Sanders, Cynthia K. (2002). The Impact of Microenterprise Assistance Programs: A Comparative Study of Program Participants, Nonparticipants, and Other Low-Wage Workers. *Social Service Review, 76*, 321–340.

Sanders, Jimmy M., & Nee, Victor. (1987). Limits of Ethnic Solidarity in the Enclave Economy. *American Sociological Review, 52*, 745–773.

Sanders, Jimmy, & Nee, Victor. (1996). Social Capital, Human Capital, and Immigrant Self-Employment: The Family as Social Capital and the Value of Human Capital. *American Sociological Review*, *61*, 231–249.

Servon, Lisa J., & Bates, Timothy. (1998). Microenterprise as an exit route from poverty: recommendations for programs and policy makers. *Journal of Urban Affairs, 20*, 419–432.

Schumpeter, Joseph A. (1934). *The Theory of Economic Development.* Cambridge: Harvard University Press.

Schumpeter, Joseph A. (1989). *Essays on Entrepreneurs, Innovations, Business Cycles, and the Evolution of Capitalism.* New Brunswick, NJ: Transaction Publishers. (Original work published 1951)

Swedberg, R., & Granovetter, M. (1992). *The Sociology of Economic Life.* Boulder, CO: Westview Press.

U.S. Census Bureau. (2006). Hispanic-Owned Firms: 2002. *Economic Census, Survey of Business Owners.* Washington, DC: U.S. Department of Commerce, Economics and Statistics Administration, U.S. Government Printing Office.

Valdez, Zulema. (2006). Segmented Assimilation Among Mexicans in the Southwest. *The Sociological Quarterly*, *47*(3), 397–424.

Valenzuela, Abel, Jr. (2001). Day Labourers as Entrepreneurs? *Journal of Ethnic and Migration Studies*, *27*, 335–352.

Valenzuela, Abel, Jr., Theodore, Nik, Melendez, Edwin, & Gonzalez, Ana Luz. (2006). *On the Corner: Day Labor in the United States.* Report, Center for the Study of Urban Poverty, Working Papers.

Waldinger, Roger. (1986). Immigrant Enterprise: A Critique and Reformulation. *Theory and Society*, *15*, 249–285.

Waldinger, Roger, Aldrich, Howard, Robin Ward, % Associates. (1990). *Ethnic Entrepreneurs: Immigrant Business in Industrial Societies.* Newbury Park, CA: Sage Publications.

Wilson, Kenneth, & Martin, W. A. (1982). Ethnic Enclaves. A Comparison of Cuban and Black Economies in Miami. *American Journal of Sociology*, *88*, 135–160.

Wilson, Kenneth L., & Portes, Alejandro. (1980). Immigrant Enclaves: An Analysis of the Labor Market Experiences of Cubans in Miami. *American Journal of Sociology*, *86*(2), 295–316.

Wilson, William J. (1980). *The Declining Significance of Race: Blacks and changing American Institutions.* Chicago: University of Chicago Press.

Wilson, William J. (1987). *The Truly Disadvantaged.* Chicago: University of Chicago Press.

CHAPTER 12

Income, Earnings, and Poverty: A Portrait of Inequality Among Latinos/as in the United States

ALBERTO DÁVILA

MARIE T. MORA

ALMA D. HALES

INTRODUCTION AND BACKGROUND

Poverty rates are higher and income levels are lower on the average for Latinos than for non-Hispanic Whites.[1] In the year 2000, more than 1 out of every 5 Latinos lived below the poverty line in the United States in contrast to 1 out of 13 non-Hispanic Whites. Also, the median household income of non-Hispanic Whites was over one third greater than that of Hispanics in 2000. Figures 1 and 2 provide these poverty and household income statistics from 1975 to 2004 for these two demographic groups.

A cursory comparison of Figures 1 and 2 predictably shows that the poverty and income numbers mirror each other. The sources of the income gap between Latinos and non-Hispanic Whites arguably provide one means to understand the poverty differentials between these two groups. Indeed, a host of studies indicates that the high poverty rates and low income levels of Latinos can be largely explained by their relatively low levels of human capital, including education, work experience, and English-language proficiency [for a recent example, see Duncan, Hotz, and Trejo (2006)]. Stemming from such studies, the general policy prescription implies that an increase in the human capital wealth of Hispanics should enhance their socioeconomic status.

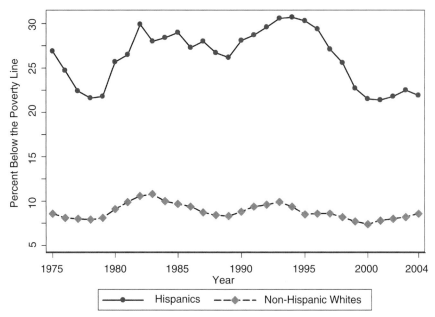

FIGURE 1. Percentage of Hispanic and Non-Hispanic White Populations Living Below the Poverty Line
in the United States: 1975–2004. *Note*. This figure is based on the U.S. Census Bureau estimates
reported in Table B-1 by DeNavas-Walt, Proctor, & Lee (2005).

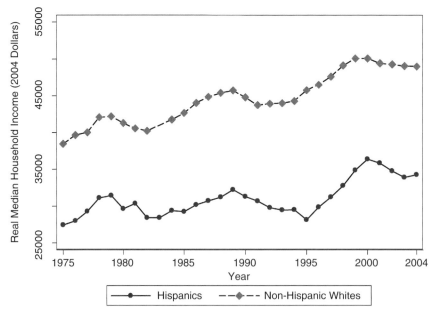

FIGURE 2. Real Median Income (in 2004 Dollars) for Households Headed by Hispanics and Non-Hispanic
Whites in the United States: 1975–2004. *Note*. This figure is based on the U.S. Census Bureau estimates
reported in Table A-1 by DeNavas-Walt et al. (2005).

However, there appears to be more to this policy story, particularly when one considers that the vast majority of recent reports on the earnings and poverty status of Latinos rely on data from the year 2000. Consider that, according to the trends reported in Figures 1 and 2, Latinos made progress relative to non-Hispanic Whites with respect to income growth and poverty reduction between the mid-1990s and 2000. However, such progress tapered off thereafter, with Latinos experiencing a slightly larger decline in real median household income than non-Hispanic Whites between 2000 and 2003. The salient observation of this point highlights the temporal dynamics of these differentials and the importance of continued empirical analysis of the labor market outcomes of Hispanic populations in the United States.

To be sure, analyzing the socioeconomic status of Latinos using the most recent available data relates to policy. Consider that the size of Latino populations in the United States has increased dramatically in recent years, as illustrated by the rise in their population share of nearly two percentage points—from 12.6% to 14.4%—between 2000 and 2005 (see the U.S. Census Bureau, 2006). Their rising presence has led to a variety of policy debates on Hispanic-oriented issues. For example, the current immigration (and national security) discourse stems partly from the growing presence of Latinos in this country. Also, the recent (re)surgence of the "English-only" debate, including H.R. 997 (the English Language Unity Act—legislation with 161 cosponsors as of July 2006 and pending in the U.S. House of Representatives) and the growing public support, even among Latinos, that immigrants should learn the English language (Pew Hispanic Center, 2006), seem to be spun from the perceived increasing prevalence of the use of the Spanish language in a variety of settings.

Insight into how these recent demographic changes have affected the socioeconomic status of Latinos can be garnered using a relative supply/relative demand framework. An implication of the growing Latino population is that, under the same relative labor-demand conditions, the earnings disparity between Latinos and non-Hispanic Whites should have widened after 2000.

However, there are reasons to suspect that the relative demand for Latino workers did not stay the same after 2000, although the direction of this change is ambiguous. If the rising demand for skilled workers that occurred during the 1980s and 1990s (e.g., Juhn, Murphy, & Pierce, 1993; Welch, 1999, 2000) continued in the early 2000s, the wages of Latino workers conceivably fell vis-à-vis non-Hispanic Whites since 2000, as Latinos have lower skill levels on average. Compounding this potential earnings decline is the possibility that growing xenophobia and national security concerns in the aftermath of the terrorist events of September 11 reduced the demand for Hispanic immigrant labor (Orrenius & Zavodny, 2006). However, countervailing events could have put upward pressure on the relative demand for Latino workers after 2000. First, as noted by Mora and Dávila (2006b, 2006c), the demand for Hispanic-related products, including entertainment, clothing, and food, has increased in recent years. Because the demand for labor comes from product demand, this evidence implies that the relative demand for Latino workers has been rising, given their comparative advantage (e.g., their inherent knowledge of the culture) over non-Hispanic Whites in producing such goods and services. Second, Latino men have been disproportionately shifting into construction jobs and Latinas into services, compared to non-Hispanic Whites (Kochhar, 2005). Construction and services represent two of only four occupational categories projected to have above-average employment growth between 2002 and 2012 (Hecker, 2004), such that the relative demand for Latino workers might be rising in particular industries.

Without empirical insight, it is unclear how these potential changes in relative labor demand and supply have affected the socioeconomic status of Hispanics since 2000. This framework provides a benchmark to empirically analyze the labor market earnings of Latinos after 2000, as we will explore in the remainder of this chapter.

In all, this chapter seeks to address two related questions. First, after accounting for human capital levels, what happened to the Latino/non-Hispanic White earnings disparity after the year 2000? Second, and following from the first question, to the extent that this earnings disparity changed, did it similarly affect (1) immigrants and natives as well as (2) low- versus high-income Hispanics?

THE CHARACTERISTICS OF LATINO WORKERS IN 2000 AND 2004

We analyze recent labor market earnings of Latinos using data collected by the U.S. Census Bureau and provided by Ruggles, Sobek, Alexander, Fitch, Goeken, et al. (2004) in the Integrated Public Use Microdata Series (IPUMS). Specifically, we employ the 1/100 Public Use Microdata Sample (PUMS) from the 2000 decennial census as well as the 1/239 sample from the 2004 American Community Survey (ACS)—the most recent large-scale dataset available at the time this chapter was written. To maintain the national representation of the samples, all of our analyses will utilize the IPUMS-provided statistical weights.

Our sample of interest includes U.S.- and foreign-born Latinos and U.S.-born monolingual-English non-Hispanic Whites between the ages of 25 and 64 who report wage and salary income. The use of this non-Hispanic White sample is standard in the literature, under the assumption that it represents the most assimilated population in the United States. To obtain a sample committed to labor market activities, we only include individuals who worked at least 32 weeks in the previous year and were not enrolled in school at the time of the survey. Moreover, all of the analyses separate men and women, given that gender affects a variety of labor market outcomes.

Table 1 provides selected mean characteristics of Latino and U.S.-born non-Hispanic White workers in 2000 and 2004.[2] Similar to Figure 2, Latinos earned less on average than non-Hispanic Whites in both years, regardless of measuring wage and salary income annually or on an hourly basis (estimated by annual wage and salary income divided by usual weekly work hours times weeks worked).

Table 1 also reports the growth rate of hourly earnings between 2000 and 2004. Note that the wages of Hispanic men and women increased by the same proportion (10.7%) between 2000 and 2004, such that the gender-related earnings gap for this group did not change. However, the wages of non-Hispanic Whites grew by a larger percentage than for Latinos (13.5% for men and 15.5% for women), causing the Hispanic/non-Hispanic-White wage differential to widen during this relatively short time period.

This relative deterioration of the wages of Latinos vis-à-vis non-Hispanic Whites after 2000 could be related to a continuation of the increasing returns to skill mentioned earlier. As Table 1 shows, the average education of non-Hispanic Whites exceeded that of Latinos by nearly 3 years for men (14 vs. 11 years) and 2 years for women (14 vs. 12 years). Although this schooling gap narrowed slightly between 2000 and 2004, an increase in the returns to education during this time might have overshadowed the growth in the average schooling levels of Latino workers. The potential labor market experience (defined here using the *age–education–5* convention) of non-Hispanic Whites also exceeded the average experience levels of Latinos, particularly in 2004.

Table 1 further indicates an increase in the presence of immigrants among Latino workers in the United States, particularly among men. This observation is consistent with the rise in immigration from Latin America in the early 2000s. It also relates to the higher proportion of the limited-English-proficient (LEP, defined here as individuals who do not speak the English language "well") in 2004 than in 2000 among Latinos.

TABLE 1. Mean Characteristics of Latino and U.S.-Born Monolingual-English Non-Hispanic White Workers in 2000 and 2004

Characteristic	Men		Women	
	2000	2004	2000	2004
Latino workers				
Annual wage	30,980	34,602	24,003	27,375
& salary income	(29,290)	(28,829)	(22,510)	(22,562)
Natural log of	2.464	2.571	2.334	2.441
hourly earnings	(0.640)	(0.670)	(0.619)	(0.667)
Earnings growth	10.7%		10.7%	
Education	10.697	11.214	11.564	12.158
	(4.077)	(3.796)	(3.718)	(3.432)
Experience	22.726	22.518	22.912	22.931
	(10.477)	(10.483)	(10.630)	(10.585)
LEP	0.276	0.309	0.211	0.236
Foreign-born	0.609	0.623	0.487	0.493
Years in U.S. if foreign-born	16.176	16.217	18.335	18.532
	(10.013)	(10.573)	(10.750)	(11.416)
N (unweighted)	52,754	19,221	35,026	13,968
N (weighted)	5,615,531	7,297,092	3,718,912	4,562,737
U.S.-born monolingual-English non-Hispanic White workers				
Annual wage & salary income	51,652	58,201	30,873	36,516
	(50,158)	(47.489)	(27,580)	(30,853)
Natural log of hourly earnings	2.867	3.002	2.567	2.722
	(0.681)	(0.722)	(0.612)	(0.656)
Earnings growth	13.5%		15.5%	
Education	13.752	14.045	13.812	14.105
	(2.468)	(2.405)	(2.291)	(2.265)
Experience	23.736	24.329	23.976	24.838
	(10.202)	(10.334)	(10.397)	(10.579)
N (unweighted)	356,112	157,211	299,107	138,948
N (weighted)	35,409,184	34,430,566	29,355,955	29,305,434

Notes: The parentheses contain the standard deviations of the continuous variables. The reported time immigrants have spent in the United States is only estimated for the foreign-born. These figures reflect the appropriate sampling weights to preserve the national representation of the IPUMS samples, which are from the 2000 1% PUMS and the 2004 ACS. See the text for sample selection.

Table 2 presents the average characteristics of Latinos when partitioning this population between those born in the United States (including its territories) and those born abroad. Consistent with conventional wisdom, Latino immigrants earn less on average than their U.S.-born counterparts. Moreover, Table 2 indicates that the immigrant/native wage differential rose between 2000 and 2004, especially for women, where the hourly earnings of U.S.-born Latinas grew by more than twice the rate experienced by foreign-born Latinas (14.8% vs. 7.1%).

When comparing Tables 1 and 2, the wage gap between U.S.-born Latinos and non-Hispanic White men remained fairly constant between 2000 and 2004. For U.S.-born Latinas, although losing ground to non-Hispanic White women, the male/female wage gap narrowed in these 4 years. This finding suggests that the earnings trends for Latinas vis-à-vis Latinos and female non-Hispanic

TABLE 2. Mean Characteristics of U.S.- and Foreign-Born Latino Workers in the United States: 2000 and 2004

Characteristic	U.S.-born latinos		Foreign-born latinos		U.S.-born latinas		Foreign-born latinas	
	2000	2004	2000	2004	2000	2004	2000	2004
Annual wage &	35,952	42,349	27,794	29,910	26,790	31,999	21,070	22,715
salary income	(29,310)	(33,142)	(28,830)	(24,718)	(22,458)	(25,095)	(22,191)	(18,552)
Natural log of	2.614	2.750	2.368	2.463	2.448	2.596	2.213	2.284
hourly earnings	(0.621)	(0.749)	(0.633)	(0.592)	(0.595)	(0.659)	(0.621)	(0.637)
Earnings growth	13.6%		9.5%		14.8%		7.1%	
Education	12.431	12.814	9.586	10.245	12.838	13.285	10.408	11.021
	(2.792)	(2.735)	(4.373)	(4.015)	(2.491)	(2.423)	(4.338)	(3.893)
Experience	21.493	21.266	23.516	23.277	21.339	21.409	24.568	24.463
	(10.356)	(10.426)	(10.479)	(10.445)	(10.231)	(10.360)	(10.788)	(10.589)
LEP	0.038	0.044	0.428	0.469	0.031	0.029	0.400	0.444
N (weighted)	2,193,382	2,752,693	3,422,149	4,544,399	1,906,996	2,290,242	1,811,916	2,272,495
N (unweighted)	20,488	8,116	32,266	11,105	18,033	7,519	16,993	6,449

Notes: The parentheses contain the standard deviations of the continuous variables. These figures reflect the appropriate sampling weights to preserve the national representation of the IPUMS samples, which are from the 2000 1% PUMS and the 2004 ACS. See the text for sample selection.

Whites observed in earlier data (e.g., Browne, 1999; Mora & Dávila, 2006b) continued for U.S. natives in the early 2000s.

Education differences likely explain part of the relatively low wage growth accrued by foreign-born Latinos between 2000 and 2004. The immigrant/non-Hispanic White education differential was nearly 4 years for men (10 years for Latino immigrants vs. 14 years for non-Hispanic White men) and 3 years for women (11 years for Latina immigrants vs. 14 years for non-Hispanic White women). Foreign-born Latinos also had less labor market experience on average than non-Hispanic Whites and had a higher share of the LEP in 2004 than in 2000. In an era of increasing returns to skill, these relative low levels of human capital presumably widened the earnings disparity between Latino immigrants and U.S. natives.

EMPIRICAL METHODOLOGY AND RESULTS

Thus far, we have attributed changes in the relative earnings of Latinos between 2000 and 2004 to increasing returns to skill. We now turn to a more in-depth analysis by estimating the following earnings function:

$$\ln(\text{Wage}) = Latino \, \beta + XB + e, \tag{1}$$

where ln(Wage) denotes the natural logarithm of hourly earnings. *Latino* represents a vector that includes (1) a binary variable equal to 1 for U.S.-born Latinos (and equal to zero otherwise), (2) a binary variable equal to 1 for Latino immigrants (and equal to zero for workers born in the United States), and (3) a continuous variable for the number of years immigrants have resided in the United States (which equals zero for U.S. natives). β is the vector of coefficients for the variables in *Latino*—the coefficients of interest to this study. Vector X contains other observable socioeconomic characteristics related to earnings (including education, experience,

experience-squared, being LEP, being married, geographic region, and a constant term), and B serves as the coefficient vector for X. Finally, e is the Normally distributed error term.

Table 3 presents the results from estimating Eq. (1) for 2000 and 2004 for men and women. To determine if the coefficients significantly changed, we also estimate an extended version of Eq. (1) that pools individuals from both years and interacts a binary variable equal to 1 for those in 2004 (zero otherwise) with all of the right-hand-side variables. t-Tests on these 2004 interaction terms provide the levels of the statistical significance for the changes in coefficients from 2000 to 2004.

United States-born Latinos in both years earned significantly less—about 9% less—on average than non-Hispanic Whites,[3] *ceteris paribus*. The average wages of U.S.-born Latinas were also less than those accrued by female non-Hispanic Whites when controlling for other characteristics, but the difference is considerably smaller (with U.S.-native Latinas earning about 2.4% less than non-Hispanic White women in 2004). This finding is consistent with other studies using data from previous years, in that observable characteristics explain a large portion of observed female Hispanic/non-Hispanic White wage differentials (e.g., Antecol & Bedard, 2002). Note also that the Latino earnings "penalty" did not significantly change for U.S.-born Hispanics between 2000 and 2004 for either men or women.

TABLE 3. Earnings Regression Results for Latinos and Non-Hispanic Whites (Dependent Variable = Natural Logarithm of Hourly Earnings)

Characteristic	Men			Women		
	2000	2004	Significantly different?	2000	2004	Significantly different?
U.S.-born Latino	−0.092[a]	− 0.091[a]	No	−0.009[c]	− 0.024[b]	No
	(0.005)	(0.013)		(0.005)	(0.010)	
Foreign-born Latino	−0.268[a]	−0.335[a]	Yes[a]	− 0.187[a]	−0.280[a]	Yes[b]
	(0.009)	(0.016)		(0.013)	(0.026)	
Immigrants' years in U.S.	0.008[a]	0.009[a]	No	0.008[a]	0.008[a]	No
	(0.0004)	(0.001)		(0.001)	(0.001)	
LEP	−0.012	0.005	No	0.047[a]	0.003	Yes[c]
	(0.008)	(0.013)		(0.011)	(0.021)	
Education	0.086[a]	0.094[a]	Yes[a]	0.101[a]	0.107[a]	Yes[a]
	(0.0005)	(0.001)		(0.001)	(0.001)	
Experience	0.029[a]	0.031[a]	Yes[b]	0.016[a]	0.018[a]	Yes[c]
	(0.0005)	(0.001)		(0.0005)	(0.001)	
Experience^2/100	−0.041[a]	−0.048[a]	Yes[a]	− 0.024[a]	−0.028[a]	Yes[b]
	(0.001)	(0.002)		(0.001)	(0.002)	
Married	0.194[a]	0.187[a]	No	−0.006[a]	0.016[a]	Yes[a]
	(0.002)	(0.005)		(0.002)	(0.004)	
Constant	1.146[a]	1.158[a]	No	0.989[a]	1.000[a]	No
	(0.009)	(0.017)		(0.010)	(0.019)	
R^2	.201	.213		.184	.191	

Note: The parentheses contain robust standard errors. These regressions employ the appropriate sampling weights to preserve the national representation of the samples. Other binary variables in the regressions include the geographic region: New England, Middle and South Atlantic, North Central, South Central, Mountain, and Pacific (base). These IPUMS samples are from the 2000 1% PUMS and the 2004 ACS. The unweighted (weighted) sizes of the samples are 408,866 (41,024,715) men and 334,133 (33,074,867) women in 2000, and 176,432 (41,727,658) men and 152,196 (33,868,171) women in 2004. See the text for the sample selection as well as for the discussion of the estimation of the statistical significance of the change in the coefficients between 2000 and 2004.
[a, b, c] Statistically significant at the 1%, 5%, or 10% level, respectively.

However, Table 3 shows that Latino *immigrants* lost significant ground to U.S.-born Latinos and non-Hispanic Whites in the early 2000s with respect to labor market earnings when controlling for human capital. Indeed, Latino immigrants without U.S. tenure earned 27% less on average than otherwise similar U.S.-born men in 2000; by 2004, the magnitude of this earnings penalty significantly increased to over 33%. Foreign-born Latinas experienced an even greater deterioration in their relative earnings during this time, with their wage penalty vis-à-vis U.S.-born women rising from almost 19% in 2000 to 28% 4 years later. Although U.S. tenure offset part of these immigrant earnings penalties, the returns to such tenure (0.8% per year of U.S. residence) did not significantly change during this time period.[4]

Table 3 further indicates that the returns to education and experience increased between 2000 and 2004 for both men and women. For example, each year of schooling enhanced the earnings of men by 8.6% in 2000 and 9.4% in 2004. It therefore appears that, similar to the 1980s and 1990s (e.g., Welch, 1999, 2000), increasing returns to skill continued in U.S. labor markets in the early 2000s. Moreover, these results indicate that observed differences in human capital, and changes in their returns, do not fully account for the observed earnings penalty or relatively low average wage growth of foreign-born Latinos between 2000 and 2004.

Table 3 also shows that limited English-language proficiency per se did not dampen the average earnings of Latino workers in 2000 or 2004. This finding is consistent with Mora and Dávila (2006a, 2006c), who report that the well-known LEP earnings penalty observed in the 1980s and 1990s (e.g., McManus, Gould, & Welch, 1983) dwindled for Hispanic men by 2000.[5] These results imply that policies aimed at improving the socioeconomic status of Latinos might be more effective if they focused on enhancing the levels of traditional forms of human capital, such as education.

In all, the results in Table 3 indicate that *something* happened to reduce the relative earnings of foreign-born Latinos in the United States between 2000 and 2004. Such a reduction is consistent with a declining relative demand for, and/or increasing supply of, Latino immigrants during this time period. If a decline in their relative labor demand explains this finding, it would indicate that the growing xenophobic sentiments in the United States in the early 2000s more than offset the potential labor demand effects caused by the rising demand for Latino-related products described earlier.

Of course, it might be possible that this relative earnings decline simply reflects a decrease in the unobservable skills of recent arrivals; that is, perhaps immigrants who migrated after 2000 had lower unobservable skill levels, thus reducing the average quality (hence the earnings) of foreign-born Latino workers by 2004. This possibility does not appear to be the case, however. When reestimating Eq. (1) while excluding immigrants who arrived to the United States after 2000 (results not shown to conserve space), we continue to observe a significant decline in the relative wages of Latino immigrants between 2000 and 2004. Excluding the post-2000 arrivals from the 2004 sample, the estimation of the earnings function yields the coefficients (standard errors) of −0.317 (0.017) for Latino immigrants and −0.270 (0.029) for Latina immigrants; both of these coefficients are significantly larger in magnitude than the respective 2000 coefficients. It follows that a decreasing quality of recent immigrants from Latin America was not the driving force behind the growing wage disparities between foreign-born Latinos and other workers in the early 2000s.

The Earnings of Specific Latino Ethnic Groups

Another question that arises from this analysis is whether the loss in relative earnings among Latino immigrants between 2000 and 2004 only occurred for a particular Hispanic-ethnic group. Other studies, including some of the chapters in this volume, have illustrated that specific Latino populations do not always experience the same labor market conditions (see, also Bansak, 2005; Dávila, Pagán, & Grau, 1998; Mora & Dávila, 2006b). We therefore reestimate Eq. (1) while partitioning Latinos into the seven largest distinct Latino ethnic groups in our sample: Mexican Americans, Puerto Ricans, Cubans, Guatemalans, Salvadorans, Dominicans, and Colombians. We combine the remaining Latino populations into a composite group of "Other" Latinos.

Table 4 reports the coefficients for the U.S.- and foreign-born members of these Latino populations in 2000 and 2004; the remaining results (similar to those observed in Table 3) can be obtained from the authors. As with Table 3, in this exercise we estimate an additional version of Eq. (1) pooling both years while including a *2004* binary variable (1 for those in 2004, zero otherwise) interacted with all of the right-hand-side variables. *t*-Tests on these interaction terms reveal whether the coefficients significantly changed between 2000 and 2004.

Table 4 shows that many of the specific U.S.-born Latino groups earned statistically similar wages to their non-Hispanic White counterparts in both years. For example, among men, only three groups of U.S.-born Latinos (Mexican Americans, Puerto Ricans, and Other Latinos) earned less on average than non-Hispanic Whites (8–11% less—similar to the penalty observed in Table 3 for U.S.-born Latinos as a group). Among U.S.-born Latinas, only a few of the ethnic coefficients are statistically significant, and many exhibit *positive* signs. It therefore appears that combining all U.S.-born Hispanic populations into one composite category masks important earnings differences that exist among specific Latino groups. These results further suggest that differences in human capital represent a major source of the earnings penalties accrued by many U.S.-native Latino workers.

Moreover, with the exception of U.S.-born Salvadoran women, none of the U.S.-born Latino populations, male or female, lost significant ground relative to non-Hispanic Whites between 2000 and 2004. *F*-Tests on the group of Latino categories (see the footnote to Table 4) provide further support for this observation. As such, the general pattern observed in Table 3 that U.S.-born Latinos did not gain or lose ground in the early 2000s holds for almost all of the specific Latino groups. The dramatic decline in the relative earnings of U.S.-born Salvadoran women in the early 2000s is, on the surface, an intriguing finding. However, a closer perusal of our data indicates that the sample of female U.S.-born Salvadorans is quite small ($N = 33$ in 2000, and 17 in 2004), raising questions about the reliability of this finding.

Focusing on foreign-born Latinos, although varying in magnitude, all but one of the coefficients for the different populations are negative and statistically significant (the exception being foreign-born Puerto Rican women in 2004). These results affirm a host of studies using data from previous years, which finds that Latino immigrants, regardless of their country of origin, earn less on average than non-Hispanic Whites even when controlling for human capital and U.S. tenure. Foreign-born Salvadoran men and women accrued the smallest earnings penalty out of the eight Latino populations in 2000, whereas male Dominican immigrants and Cuban-born women accrued the largest penalty that year relative to U.S.-born workers of the same gender.

Of particular interest, the coefficients on all of the Latino immigrant ethnic groups increased in magnitude between 2000 and 2004 (with the exception, again, being foreign-born Puerto Rican women), and in many cases, the changes are statistically significant. *F*-Tests (provided in the footnote to Table 4) also indicate that, as a group, the relative earnings of the eight Latino immigrant populations significantly changed between 2000 and 2004. It follows that, similar to the above discussion that combined Latino immigrants into one population, something adversely affected their average labor market earnings relative to U.S. natives between 2000 and 2004.

In all, Table 4 provides evidence that the use of a "generic" Latino label imprecisely reflects the actual labor market outcomes of specific ethnic populations, indicating the importance of

TABLE 4. Earnings Regression Results for Specific Latino Groups (Dependent Variable = Natural Logarithm of Hourly Earnings)

Characteristic	Men 2000	Men 2004	Significantly different?	Women 2000	Women 2004	Significantly different?
U.S.-born Mexican American	-0.094[a]	-0.087[a]	No	0.002	-0.011	No
	(0.006)	(0.018)		(0.006)	(0.011)	
U.S.-born Puerto Rican	-0.105[a]	-0.112[a]	No	-0.016	-0.060[b]	No
	(0.010)	(0.025)		(0.010)	(0.026)	
U.S.-born Cuban	0.004	-0.001	No	0.078[b]	0.078[c]	No
	(0.041)	(0.049)		(0.031)	(0.043)	
U.S.-born Guatemalan	-0.057	0.010	No	0.088	0.045	No
	(0.079)	(0.124)		(0.084)	(0.111)	
U.S.-born Salvadoran	-0.052	-0.135	No	-0.008	-0.327[b]	Yes[c]
	(0.088)	(0.143)		(0.086)	(0.163)	
U.S.-born Colombian	-0.042	0.030	No	0.094	0.086	No
	(0.089)	(0.071)		(0.066)	(0.065)	
U.S.-born Dominican	-0.091	0.008	No	0.006	-0.083	No
	(0.063)	(0.089)		(0.062)	(0.077)	
U.S.-born Other Latino	-0.083[a]	-0.094[a]	No	-0.033[a]	-0.023	No
	(0.010)	(0.029)		(0.010)	(0.023)	
Foreign-born Mexican American	-0.244[a]	-0.301[a]	Yes[a]	-0.161[a]	-0.230[a]	Yes[b]
	(0.010)	(0.017)		(0.014)	(0.026)	
Foreign-born Puerto Rican	-0.347[a]	-0.438[a]	No	-0.188[a]	0.003	Yes[c]
	(0.073)	(0.097)		(0.072)	(0.087)	
Foreign-born Cuban	-0.385[a]	-0.414[a]	No	-0.293[a]	-0.382[a]	Yes[c]
	(0.019)	(0.030)		(0.022)	(0.042)	
Foreign-born Guatemalan	-0.256[a]	-0.281[a]	No	-0.174[a]	-0.225[a]	No
	(0.026)	(0.046)		(0.036)	(0.055)	
Foreign-born Salvadoran	-0.213[a]	-0.256[a]	No	-0.118[a]	-0.235[a]	Yes[c]
	(0.019)	(0.031)		(0.028)	(0.057)	
Foreign-born Colombian	-0.350[a]	-0.494[a]	Yes[a]	-0.244[a]	-0.380[a]	Yes[a]
	(0.027)	(0.040)		(0.028)	(0.041)	
Foreign-born Dominican	-0.409[a]	-0.535[a]	Yes[b]	-0.285[a]	-0.366[a]	Yes[c]
	(0.023)	(0.056)		(0.027)	(0.040)	
Foreign-born Other Latino	-0.297[a]	-0.401[a]	Yes[a]	-0.207[a]	-0.321[a]	Yes[a]
	(0.012)	(0.022)		(0.016)	(0.039)	
R^2	.201	.214		.184	.191	

Note: The parentheses contain robust standard errors. These regressions employ the appropriate sampling weights to preserve the national representation of the samples. Foreign-born Puerto Ricans include individuals reporting Puerto Rican ethnicity but were born outside of the U.S. mainland, Puerto Rico, and other U.S. territories. Other variables in the regressions include education, experience, experience-squared, U.S.-tenure, limited-English-proficiency, being married, binary variables for geographic region, and a constant term. These IPUMS samples are from the 2000 1% PUMS and the 2004 ACS. The unweighted (weighted) sizes of the samples are 408,866 (41,024,715) men and 334,133 (33,074,867) women in 2000 and 176,432 (41,727,658) men and 152,916 (33,868,171) women in 2004. See the text for the sample selection as well as for the discussion of the estimation of the statistical significance of the change in the coefficients between 2000 and 2004. F-Tests reveal that between 2000 and 2004, the coefficients on the eight Latino populations did not significantly change for U.S.-born Latinos as a group (where $F = 0.25$ for men and 0.94 for women), but they did for foreign-born Latinos as a group (where $F = 3.34$ for men and 2.3 for women).
[a, b, c] Statistically significant at the 1%, 5%, or 10% level, respectively.

analyzing different Latino populations rather than focusing on one pan-Latino group. However, particularly among the foreign-born, studies using the latter approach have value with respect to capturing overall labor market trends affecting many Latino groups in the United States.

Earnings Results by Occupations

Another issue worth exploring relates to the occupational profiles of Latino immigrants. Recall from earlier that construction and service occupations are projected to have some of the fastest employment growth between 2002 and 2012. These sectors have also witnessed a rapid increase in their workforce representation of Latinos (construction for men and services for women). Did foreign-born Latinos in these high-growth sectors experience a relative wage decline between 2000 and 2004?

For insight, we estimate Eq. (1) for Latino and non-Hispanic White men in construction and then for Latina and non-Hispanic White women in service occupations. The results from this exercise (available from the authors) indicate that foreign-born Latino construction workers (and Latina service workers), despite accruing statistically significant earnings penalties in 2000, did *not* experience significant wage declines on average between 2000 and 2004. Indeed, holding U.S. tenure constant, foreign-born Latinos earned 27.5% less than non-Hispanic white construction workers in 2000 and 26.9% less in 2004—penalties statistically indistinguishable between the 2 years. Similarly, the earnings penalty (about 11%) accrued by Latina immigrants among service workers did not significantly change between 2000 and 2004. Also, the influence of U.S. tenure on earnings statistically remained the same in both years.

When estimating Eq. (1) for men outside of construction and for women outside of services (results available from the authors), however, the same pattern emerges as in Table 3: The wage disparity between foreign-born Latinos and non-Hispanic Whites in non-construction (and for women, in non-service) professions significantly widened between 2000 and 2004. In fact, these estimated earnings disparities are similar in magnitude to those in Table 3 (with the foreign-born Latino coefficients in 2000 and 2004 equal to respectively −0.287 and −0.361 for men outside of construction and respectively −0.173 and −0.274 for women in nonservice occupations).

These ancillary findings suggest that the relative demand for Latino immigrants did not change "across the board." In some occupational segments, this relative demand seems to have increased enough to offset their rising relative labor supply. Despite the overall increasing returns to skill observed in the U.S. labor market after 2000, foreign-born Latinos in construction (men) or services (women) did not lose further ground to their non-Hispanic White counterparts with respect to earnings.

Earnings Quantiles

We next consider whether Latino immigrants at the lower end of the wage distribution experienced the same loss in relative earnings as those at the high end between 2000 and 2004. The results from focusing on construction and service workers indicate that the growing wage disparities between foreign-born Latinos and non-Hispanic Whites were not evenly dispersed among the Latino immigrant workforce. We therefore use conditional quantile regression as discussed by Koenker and Hallock (2001) to estimate a series of earnings functions [based on Eq. (1)] for nine distinct wage deciles in 2000 and 2004.[6] Estimates of the coefficients for foreign-born

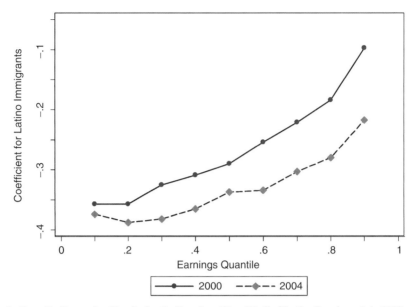

FIGURE 3. Quantile Regression Results for the Earnings "Penalties" of Latino Immigrants in 2000 and 2004.
Note. **These figures provide the estimated coefficients on the Latino immigrant variable using quantile regression analysis; the base group of comparison is non-Hispanic White men. Other variables in the regressions include U.S.-born Latinos, immigrants' years in the United States, being married, being LEP, education, experience, experience-squared, and binary variables for geographic region. These IPUMS samples are from the 2000 1% PUMS and the 2004 ACS. The unweighted (weighted) sizes of the samples are 408,866 (41,024,715) in 2000 and 176,432 (41,727,658) in 2004. See the text for the sample selection.**

Latinos by earnings quantile are presented in Figures 3 and 4, where the horizontal axes display the quantile and the vertical axes display the coefficients on the Latino immigrant binary variable. (The authors will provide other results from these regressions upon request.) As the sample sizes of some of the specific Latino populations in each earnings decile are quite small, we conduct this analysis combining Latinos into one population. However, as datasets with larger samples of Hispanic ethnic groups become available, future studies should investigate differences across these populations with respect to their locations in earnings distributions.

At least three points should be made with respect to Figures 3 and 4. First, foreign-born Latinos faced larger earnings penalties in the lower wage quantiles than in the higher ones, particularly in 2000. For example, holding U.S- tenure constant, in 2000 foreign-born Latino men earned about 36% less than U.S.-born men, and Latina immigrants earned 24% less than U.S.-born women at the bottom tenth of the conditional wage distribution. However, at the ninth decile, male Latinos earned about 10% less than other men, and Latinas earned about 7% less than other women. This observation corresponds to the fact that the relative labor supply of Latinos is largest in low-wage jobs.

Second, consistent with the increase in the relative labor supply of Latino workers after 2000, the downward shift in the coefficient curves show that foreign-born Latinos at all wage deciles experienced a decline in their relative earnings between 2000 and 2004. This finding parallels the above results, in that Latino immigrants lost ground to U.S. natives with respect to earnings, emphasizing the importance of analyzing Hispanic labor markets beyond the year 2000.

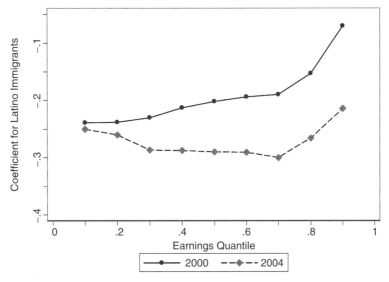

FIGURE 4. Quantile Regression Results for the Earnings "Penalties" of Latina Immigrants in 2000 and 2004. *Note.* These figures provide the estimated coefficients on the Latina immigrant variable using quantile regression analysis; the base group of comparison is non-Hispanic White women. Other variables in the regressions include U.S.-born Latinas, immigrants' years in the United States, being married, being LEP, education, experience, experience-squared, and binary variables for geographic region. These IPUMS samples are from the 2000 1% PUMS and the 2004 ACS. The unweighted (weighted) sizes of the samples are 334,133 (33,074,867) in 2000 and 152,196 (33,868,171) in 2004. See the text for the sample selection.

Third, this decline was not parallel; indeed, Latino immigrants lost more ground at the higher end of the wage distribution than at the lower end. To illustrate, the earnings of foreign-born Latinos (Latinas) negligibly fell by less than two (one) percentage points vis-à-vis U.S. natives at the first wage decile between 2000 and 2004, but they decreased by 12–14 percentage points at the ninth decile.

This latter observation is of particular interest to this study and reinforces the occupational results discussed earlier. Both relative demand and supply forces appear to have influenced the earnings of foreign-born Latino workers after 2000. However, these quantile regression results suggest that the relative labor demand for foreign-born Latinos increased more in low-wage jobs than in high-wage ones.

CONCLUDING COMMENTS

This chapter's primary aims were to investigate the recent earnings experience of Latinos in the United States and to determine if this experience varied according to immigration status and along the income distribution. Our empirical results show that while U.S.-native Latinos maintained their labor-market standing relative to non-Hispanic Whites between 2000 and 2004, Latino immigrants, particularly at the high end of the income distribution, lost ground relative to this group. We interpret these results using a relative demand-and-supply framework.

Future research should continue to investigate the relative earnings of Latino populations by further exploring the links among labor market earnings, total personal income, and poverty.

Indeed, despite being highly correlated, earnings are not the same metric as income. A quick perusal of 2000 and 2004 data indicates that the ratio of wage and salary income to total personal income for individuals between the ages of 25 and 64 years varies across Latino populations. To illustrate, we estimate this ratio to be 80.4% for U.S.-born Latinos in the 2004 ACS but 89.7% for Latino immigrants. Although additional work on this issue is clearly warranted, on the surface it appears that earned income represents a higher share of the wealth portfolio of Latino immigrants than U.S. natives. It follows that changes in the labor market outcomes of Latino populations would not evenly impact their overall socioeconomic outcomes (such as poverty).

In all, our findings in this chapter point to the importance of continued analyses of the socioeconomic status of Latinos in the United States. With the wide range of policy issues being currently debated—from immigration reform to national language policies—that might have long-term impacts on U.S. labor markets, it behooves policy makers to go beyond labor market evidence based on decennial census data for Latino populations. Extant research provides keen insights into how Latino labor markets work, but the dynamic nature of this ethnic group's earnings experience, as evidenced in this chapter for some Latino subpopulations, arguably requires updated research on this topic.

Indeed, as national datasets with larger specific Latino populations become available, future research should explore the underlying mechanisms driving the labor market outcomes and socioeconomic profiles of the different Latino groups in the United States. Issues that would be particularly fitting to meet this aim include patterns in net migration flows between specific Latin American countries and the United States, as well as the geographic distributions, human capital characteristics, and wealth and asset-accumulation patterns of Latino populations in the United States.

NOTES

1. In this chapter, we use the term "Latino" interchangeably with "Hispanic." We realize that, technically, "Latino" is a male term, but to facilitate the discussion, the reader should consider this term as gender neutral.
2. We report two sample sizes in Table 1: unweighted (the size of our IPUMS sample) and weighted (the estimated population size reflected by the sample). The decrease in the weighted size of the non-Hispanic White population between 2000 and 2004 reflects their declining employment levels and labor force participation (see the Bureau of Labor Statistics at www.bls.gov).
3. For ease of interpretation, we discuss the estimated coefficients on the binary variables as the actual effects of these variables on earnings. The reader should be aware that, given the semi logarithmic construction of Eq. (1), more precise effects can be obtained using the method discussed by Kennedy (1981).
4. Recall that our sample includes individuals who worked at least 32 weeks in the previous year. When further restricting the sample to those working full time (i.e., 35 or more hours per week), the results observed in Table 3 continue to hold. To illustrate, the coefficients (standard errors) on U.S.-born Latinos did not statistically change between the two years: −0.098 (0.005) and −0.094 (0.013) for Latino men and −0.026 (0.005) and −0.038 (0.010) for women, in 2000 and 2004. The coefficients (standard errors) for foreign-born Latinos significantly were significantly larger in magnitude in 2004 [−0.335 (0.016) for men and −0.296 (0.026) for women] than in 2000 [−0.284 (0.009) for men, and −0.231 (0.013) for women].
5. Despite being outside of the scope of this chapter, an issue in Table 3 worth noting is the change in the signs on the "married" variable for women. Standard in the literature, a negative relationship between marital status and the labor market earnings of women is assumed to reflect the time-allocation pressures that married women experience. In 2004, however, Table 3 suggests that married women earned slightly more (1.6% more) than their unmarried peers, ceteris paribus. Welch (1999) suggested in passing that an increase in the "marriage premium" is consistent with greater wage dispersion, as such dispersion relates to the timing of marriage and the incidence of divorce. Future research should address whether temporal changes in wage-dispersion differentials between Latinos and non-Hispanic Whites have spillover effects with respect to their marriage market outcomes and female labor force participation.
6. Clearly, 10 wage deciles exist, but when using quantile regression for the wage deciles, workers in the top decile have no comparison group by definition.

REFERENCES

Antecol, H., & Bedard, K. (2002). The Relative Earnings of Young Mexican, Black, and White Women. *Industrial and Labor Relations Review, 56*, 122–135.

Bansak, C. (2005). The Differential Wage Impact of the Immigration Reform and Control Act on Latino Ethnic Subgroups. *Social Science Quarterly, 86*, 1279–1297.

Browne, I. (1999). Latinas and African American Women in the US Labor Market. In I. Browne (Ed.), *Latinas and African Americans at Work: Race, Gender, and Economic inequality* (pp. 1–31). New York: Russell Sage Foundation.

Dávila, A., Pagán, J., & Grau, M. (1998). The Impact of IRCA on the Job Opportunities and Earnings of Mexican American and Hispanic American Workers. *International Migration Review, 32*(1), 80–95.

DeNavas-Walt, C., Proctor, B. D., & Lee, C. H. (2005). *Income, Poverty, and Health Insurance Coverage in the United States: 2004* (U.S. Census Bureau, Current Population Reports, P60-229). Washington, DC: U.S. Government Printing Office.

Duncan, B., Hotz, V. J., & Trejo, S. (2006). Hispanics in the U.S. Labor Market. In M. Tienda & F. Mitchell (Eds.), *Hispanics and the Future of America* (pp. 228–290). Washington, DC: National Academy Press.

Hecker, D. E. (2004, February). Occupational Employment Projections to 2012. *Monthly Labor Review, 127*, 80–105.

Juhn, C., Murphy, K. M., & Pierce, B. (1993). Wage Inequality and the Rise in the Returns to Skill. *Journal of Political Economy, 101*(3), 410–442.

Kennedy, P. (1981). Estimations with Correctly Interpreted Dummy Variables in Semilogarithmic Equations. *American Economic Review, 71*(4), 801.

Kochhar, R. (2005, December). *The Occupational Status and Mobility of Hispanics* (Pew Hispanic Center Report). Washington, DC: Pew Hispanic Center.

Koenker, R., & Hallock, K. F. (2001). Quantile Regression. *Journal of Economic Perspectives, 15*(4), 143–156.

McManus, W. S., Gould, W., & Welch, F. (1983). Earnings of Hispanic Men: The Role of English Language Proficiency. *Journal of Labor Economics, 1*(2), 101–130.

Mora, M. T., & Dávila, A. (2006a). A Note on the Changes in the Relative Wages of LEP Hispanic Men Between 1980 and 2000. *Industrial Relations, 45*(2), 169–172.

Mora, M. T., & Dávila, A. (2006b). Hispanic Ethnicity, Gender, and the Change in the LEP-Earnings Penalty in the U.S. During the 1990s. *Social Science Quarterly, 87*(5), 1295–1318.

Mora, M. T., & Dávila, A. (2006c). *The Decline in the Limited-English-Proficient Earnings Penalty for Hispanic Men in the U.S.: 1980–2000* (Working paper 03/2006). Unpublished manuscript, Department of Economics and Finance, The University of Texas—Pan American.

Orrenius, P., & Zavodny, M. (2006, January). *Did 9/11 Worsen the Job Prospects of Hispanic Immigrants?* Unpublished manuscript, Federal Reserve Bank of Dallas.

Pew Hispanic Center. (2006, June). *Hispanic Attitudes Toward Learning English* (Fact Sheet). Washington. DC: Pew Hispanic Center. Retrieved November 14, 2006, from www.pewhispanic.org

Ruggles, S., Sobek, M., Alexander, T., Fitch, C. A., Goeken, R., Hall, P. K., et al. (2004). *Integrated Public Use Microdata Series: Version 3.0* [machine readable database]. Minneapolis: Minnesota Population Center. Retrieved July 17, 2006, from http://www.ipums.org

U.S. Census Bureau. (2006). *Annual Estimates of the Population by Sex, Race, and Hispanic or Latino Origin: April 1, 2000 to July 1, 2005* (Report NC-EST2005-03; Population Division). Washington, DC: Author. Retrieved July 18,2006, from http://www.census.gov/popest/national/asrh/

Welch, F. (1999). In Defense of Inequality. *American Economic Review, 89*(2), 1–17.

Welch, F. (2000). Growth in Women's Relative Wages and in Inequality Among Men: One Phenomenon or Two? *American Economic Review, 90*(2), 444–449.

LATINA/O CULTURE

CHAPTER 13

Mapping the Dynamic Terrain of U.S. Latina/o Media Research

ISABEL MOLINA GUZMÁN

INTRODUCTION: MAPPING A DYNAMIC TERRAIN

The contemporary Latina/o media landscape is a diverse, complex, and constantly shifting terrain. Three key factors have played a role in redefining Latina/o media and the scholarship that surrounds it: (1) the demographic shifts within the U.S. Latina/o population; (2) the global visibility of Latina/o performers and cultural forms; and (3) the profitability of dual-market transnational media. Consequently, once predominantly homogenous urban media markets such as Los Angeles, Miami, and New York are now increasingly defined by the heterogeneity of their Latino populations. Latina/o musicians such as Marc Anthony and Shakira move easily, albeit problematically, across national, racial, and ethnic borders. Emerging hybrid media genres such as Reggaeton and television programs such as "Ugly Betty" are popular across diverse linguistic, ethnic, racial, and gender categories. Additionally, the successful marketing of Latinas/os as a commodity audience is drawing unprecedented attention from both general-market and Spanish-language media.

Media scholarship about Latina/o audiences and texts that capture the contradictions and tensions embedded in these contemporary shifts is emerging (Del Rio, 2006; Valdivia 2004a). However, a majority of the established Latina/o media scholarship remains grounded in traditional social scientific approaches focused around the three largest Latina/o groups: Cubans, Mexicans, and Puerto Ricans (Rodriguez, 1997). Additionally, because of the dominant development of Latina/o media in the Southwest, much of the research focuses specifically on Mexican and Chicana/o media in California and Texas.

Thus, it is only recently that Latina/o media researchers have focused on other populations, such as Colombians and Venezuelans, and regions, such as the Midwest. For instance, the work of Acosta-Alzuro (2003, 2005) focusing on the cultural production and reception of Venezuelan *telenovelas* and Mayer (2004) studying the racialized relationship of recent Argentinian immigrants to dominant definitions of pan-Latinidad are examples of ethnographic work stepping outside of the dominant boundaries. Additionally, scholarship by Valdivia (2000, 2002) and Cepeda (2003) on U.S. media representations of Chileans, Colombians, and Guatemalans are repositioning the borders of Latinidad within research about mainstream popular culture.

The chapter begins with a brief overview of the U.S. Latina/o media and contemporary changes within that landscape. Next, it briefly outlines traditional academic approaches to studying U.S. Latina/o media and discusses the contributions of contemporary Latina/o critical media studies to understanding the industry's dynamic shifts. Finally, the chapter concludes by discussing theoretical strategies for future research.

DEFINING LATINA/O MEDIA AND AUDIENCES

In a multicultural society that believes that diverse ethnic and racial groups should coexist equally, "the right to communicate" is one of the basic tenets necessary for political recognition within the public sphere: "With the increasing social complexity and mobility that characterizes late-twentieth century societies the mass media have been perceived as having an increasingly central role in facilitating dialogue among citizens" (Husband, 2000, p. 201). Not only do the ethnic media provide a space for political dialogue, but they also perform a central cultural function in defining the parameters of citizenship itself (Riggins, 1992). Cultural, political, and economic access to the public sphere is central for constructing citizenship and imagining community. Not surprisingly, Latina/o communities in the United States have a long established tradition of producing media. However, as with other media, the social and historical forces surrounding the development of Latina/o media, marketing, and advertising are thus varied and complex. The antecedents of Latina/o media rest with three primary historical developments: (1) the ongoing complex relationship between Mexico and the United States in the Southwest; (2) the Cuban revolution of 1959 that resulted in the mass exodus of Cuban media professionals to Miami and New York; and (3) "Operation Bootstrap," which encouraged and rewarded the labor migration of mostly women from Puerto Rico to manufacturing and garment industries in New York and the Midwest during the 1950s.

Latina/o Media in the Southwest

The oldest location for Latina/o print and radio media in the South and Southwest regions. Latina/o newspapers and radio stations in California, New Orleans, and Texas targeted at Mexican and Spanish citizens have existed since the 19th and early 20th century (Gutiérrez, 1977; Rodríguez, 1999). The 1848 Treaty of Guadalupe Hidalgo further motivated the development of Spanish-language newspapers and radio in Southern California and Texas, as Mexican citizens turned U.S. residents used the media to build community in the newly acquired and racially hostile territories (Rodríguez, 1999). A second historical event, the Mexican Revolution of 1910, led to the development of prorevolutionary and antirevolutionary newspapers in the region. Media outlets produced during these two periods were primarily dependent on local and regional advertisers and specifically aimed at local, regional, and transnational Mexican and U.S. Mexican communities. Not surprisingly, 6 of the top 10 Latina/o media markets today are still in California and the Southwest: Los Angeles (3), San Antonio (4), Dallas (5), Houston (8), San Francisco (9), and Phoenix (10) (Advertising Age, 2005, p. 43). San Antonio is also home to the oldest Latina/o media market in the United States, launching the first full-time Spanish-language radio station in the country in 1922 (Rodríguez, 1999). Some of the most prominent Latina/o newspapers also arose during the postrevolution era: Los Angeles' *La Opinión* (1926) and San Antonio's *La Prensa* (1926).

Latina/o Media in the East and Midwest

The rest of the top Latina/o media markets are located in the Midwest and East coast: New York (1), Miami (2), Detroit (6), and Chicago (7) (Advertising Age, 2005, p. 43). Unlike the history of Latina/o media in the Southwest, which was predominantly influenced by the U.S. war with Mexico (1846–1848) and the Mexican Revolution of 1910, the development of Latina/o media elsewhere has been driven by other external political and economic forces. Although the development of Latina/o media in the Midwest is the most recent, established Puerto Rican and Mexican community media outlets have existed in the Midwest since the Great Western Cattle Trail of the 1800s and Puerto Rico's more recent "Operation Bootstrap" (1950s to 1960s).

However, Latina/o media growth in the East and Midwest was primarily fueled by a second wave of development during the 1960s, resulting from the immigration of exiled Cuban media professionals to the United States (Dávila, 2001; Rodríguez, 1999). Unlike the regional media in the Southwest, Cuban media professionals sought to work with national media outlets throughout the United States and Latin America. Rather than specializing in a particular region or local ethnic group, such as U.S. Mexicans in Los Angeles or Puerto Ricans in New York, U.S. Cuban media outlets specialized in selling specific ethnic Latina/o audiences to national advertisers and programmers. Thus, U.S. Cuban media firms were the first to actively market Latinas/os as a commodity audience for U.S. products through the Spanish-language media (Dávila, 2001).

Not surprisingly, it was during the 1960s that Latina/o media giant Univisión (1961) was founded by Mexican nationals in San Antonio, Texas (Rodríguez, 1999). Univisión pioneered the art of developing ethnically ambiguous programming in Mexico and Latin America and broadcasting it to Latina/o communities in the United States. Univisión is currently the fifth largest network behind ABC, CBS, NBC, and FOX, and in the Los Angeles, New York, and Miami markets, it often wins the prime-time evening ratings. Univisión is the largest owner of Spanish-language television and radio stations in the United States. Telemundo, established in 1985 and owned by NBC, is its closest competitor. Both networks are currently headquartered in Miami, making Miami the transnational Latina/o media capitol of the world (Sinclair, 2003). Some critics have complained that the centrality of Miami and its U.S. Cuban community is affecting the Mexican-dominant content of the networks, and there is discussion that Univisión is planning to move its headquarters to Mexico City in order to be closer to the development of its most profitable programming, the *telenovelas*. Televisa, headquartered in Mexico City, is the largest multinational corporation producing and distributing *telenovelas* throughout the globe (Sinclair, 1990).

One of the primary forces driving changes within the Latina/o media industry is the increasing demographic diversification of the U.S. Latina/o community. Although the Latina/o population in the Southwest has historically been predominantly Mexican and U.S. Mexican, the demographics of these communities are quickly changing, forcing the local media to respond. For example, in the city of Los Angeles, although Mexicans make up 36.6% of the population, Latinas/os from El Salvador (3.1%) and Guatemala (2.2%) are quickly growing in numbers and represent Los Angeles' second and third largest Latina/o population, respectively (U.S. Census, 2005a). As the Latina/o population in Los Angeles increases and diversifies so does its media content. Thus, Los Angeles is home to six major Spanish-language stations with news bureaus in Tijuana, Mexico and San Salvador, El Salvador. Los Angeles currently holds the highest concentration of Latina/o viewers and is the most profitable Latina/o market in television and radio.

Similar changes have occurred in the media landscapes of the East Coast. For example, in the Miami-Dade County, where Cubans are the largest Latina/o group (31.6%), Nicaraguans (4.1%), Colombians (3.9%), and Puerto Ricans (3.5%), the second, third, and fourth largest Latina/o groups, respectively, are quickly changing the county's audience makeup (U.S. Census, 2005b). Latinas/os from Mexico, the Caribbean, and Central and South America make up the largest ethnic/racial group in the county (61.1%) and consistently contribute to Univisión's number one ranking in the Nielsen ratings. Likewise, Latino radio in New York City often ranks first in audience numbers in an urban market where Puerto Ricans (9.9%) are being matched by the growth of Dominicans (6.7%) and Mexicans (3.1%) (U.S. Census, 2005c). When all Latina/o groups are combined, the ratings for Spanish-language television and radio often outpace those of its general-market competitors. Changes in the content and success of the Latina/o media in the three largest media markets (Los Angeles, Miami, New York) in the United States is representative of the diversity of Latina/o populations.

FROM ESTABLISHED TO DYNAMIC: THE CONTEMPORARY FIELD OF LATINA/O MEDIA STUDIES

Traditional approaches to the study of Latina/o media have focused on two areas: advertising and journalism. Research on Latinas/os and advertising explores the uses and effectiveness of Spanish-language media. Much of this scholarship has been funded by the Latina/o advertising and marketing industry, which is particularly interested in documenting the effectiveness of Spanish-language media in reaching specific Latina/o audiences, particularly Cuban, Mexican, and Puerto Rican. Most of the work conducted on advertising and media use highlights the media preferences of Mexican immigrants and U.S. Mexican consumers (Korzenny, Neundorf, Burgoon, Burgoon, & Greenberg, 1983; Roslow & Nicholls, 1996; Ueltschy & Krampf, 1997).

Nevertheless, the research in this area is not definitive, especially because issues of language and acculturation are complex and difficult to measure, particularly as second- and third-generation Latinas/os take on increasingly hybrid identity positions consuming both English- and Spanish-language media (Johnson, 2000). In a 2004 survey, the Pew Hispanic Center reported that almost 50% of the Latina/o population uses both English and Spanish-language media for information and entertainment (Suro, 2004). Language and media preferences shift from Spanish to English for U.S.-born Latinas/os, but nearly a quarter of third-generation U.S. Latinas/os reported using media in both languages (Suro, 2004, p. 43). Thus, one of the flaws of advertising research on media use is that it rarely takes a comparative approach for analyzing differences and similarities across gender, generation, and nationality, all three of which are becoming increasingly important as the U.S. Latina/o population changes.

Journalism research is the second traditional area of Latina/o media scholarship. Researchers in this area center on the history and political efficacy of Spanish-language journalism and issues of positive versus negative representations in the English-language news media. The majority of historical scholarship on Latina/o journalism emphasizes the development of Spanish-language newspapers as tools for "political and social activism; the promotion of civic duties; the defense of the population against the abuse of authorities and other organized groups" (Leal, 1989, p. 159). Again, the dominant focus of this research deals with the development of the

U.S. Mexican press in the Southwest (Di Stefano, 1985; Kanellós, 1994; Meléndez, 1997). For instance, the work of Gutiérrez (1977) and Leal (1989) examines the shift from 19th-century bilingual and Spanish-language newspapers in the South and Southwest that served primarily as forms of propaganda for upper-class Spaniards, Mexicans, and the local Anglo elite, to the politicization of Spanish-language newspapers financed and published by Mexican citizens in response to the U.S. conquest of the Southwest and California. The scholarship suggests that these more political newspapers often protested discrimination and violence against Mexicans and Mexican descendents, and newspapers such as San Antonio's *La Prensa* or Los Angeles's *La Opinión* still demonstrate this type of political content (Di Stefano, 1985; Medeiros, 1980; Rodríguez, 1999).

Although the majority of scholarly work regarding the Latina/o news media focuses on California and the Southwest, other scholars have documented how the imperialistic United States relationship with Puerto Rico spurred the migratory flow of Puerto Ricans from the island to the mainland, where they met with racial and linguistic discrimination for the first time. Scholars suggest that it was this experience with racialization that led to the subsequent development of Latino newspapers in the Northeast, with a particular political orientation targeted at Puerto Ricans living in the United States (Downing, 1992). Likewise, research on Miami illustrates how the political strength of U.S. Cuban exiles shaped the proliferation and political content of the local Spanish-language and English-language news media (Molina Guzmán, 2005, 2006a; García, 1996; Soruco, 1996).

Finally, journalism scholars have worked in two other areas: the efficacy of Spanish-language news to disseminate information and the positive/negative representation of Latinas/o in the English-language news media (Subervi, 1986, 2003). Both research traditions are heavily grounded in quantitative social science approaches. Research dealing with the quality of information or ability to disseminate information through the Latina/o news media points to a problematic finding. Although Latina/o news outlets are better able to reach Spanish-dominant audiences, the quality of information it disseminates is less accurate and helpful than information provided through the general-market news media. For example, research on the reporting of health news demonstrates that whereas first-generation Latina/o immigrants depend on the Spanish-language media for information gathering, they often receive inadequate or inaccurate health information about important health issues such as the increase of diabetes in the Latino community (Subervi, 2004; Vargas & dePyssler, 1999).

Likewise, most of the research on general-market news representations of Latinas/os point to troubling trends. The Annual "Network Brown Out Report" conducted by the National Association of Hispanic Journalists shows that general-market news outlets continue to underreport news about Latinas/os (Méndez-Méndez & Alverio, 2001, 2002, 2003, Montalvo & Torres, 2006; Subervi, 2003, 2004). From 2000 to 2006, the major networks devoted less than 1% of their news coverage to Latinas/os. When Latinas/os are reported about in the network news, the focus is often on crime, personalities, immigration, and sports (Montalvo & Torres, 2006). Furthermore, research by Molina Guzmán (2005) and Vargas (2000) also shows that when Latinas/os are the focus of general-market news coverage, they are often constructed in racialized and gendered ways that marginalize the community. For instance, with regard to network reporting of the Elián González custody case, which is the most reported Latina/o news in the history of network news, the U.S. Cuban community was often depicted as extremely religious and hyperemotional, both attributes associated with femininity. Additionally, U.S. Cubans were often represented as hot-headed, violent, and irrational, racially marked characteristics (Molina Guzmán, 2005).

Critical Roots of Latina/o Media Studies

The release of the 1980 U.S. Census documenting the rapid increase of the Latina/o community created a watershed moment for Latina/o media production and scholarship (Goodson & Shaver, 1994; Kramer, 2002). Latina/o media, advertising, and marketing agencies have extended their reach in both English- and Spanish-language media by moving away from ethnic-specific Latina/o marketing/programming to pan-ethnic Latina/o marketing/programming (Dávila, 2001; Santiago & Valdés, 2002; Garza, 1994). Prior to 1980, media strategies that emphasized the cultural differences among Cubans, Puerto Ricans, and Mexicans prevailed within the industry. Contemporary Latina/o media, advertising, and marketing campaigns have shifted away from ethnic-specific audience constructions toward a pan-ethnic and unified image of Latina/o consumers, emphasizing the similarities, rather than differences, among the more than 50 Latina/o groups that currently live in the United States. Latina/o marketing and advertising agencies have turned the focus away from nationality-specific programming targeted at particular groups or regions toward the notion of Latinas/os as one unified pan-ethnic market that share common cultural values and norms. At the center of this strategy is the use of English and nonaccented Spanish, Anglo-appearing models with stereotypical black hair and dark eyes, and generic appeals to Latino values, traditions, family, and other community structures. The result is a problematic trend toward economic, racial, and ethnic homogenization, where Latinas/os are increasingly represented as white and Latinidad in the general-market and Spanish-language media is expressed only through stereotypic notions of food, music, sexuality, and gender.

Shifts in the industry's orientation from ethnic-specificity to pan-ethnicity demand new lines of academic inquiry (Valdivia 2004a). Contemporary critical Latina/o media research has worked to open emerging areas of research and capture this dynamic terrain filled with tensions and contradictions. One of the primary tensions surrounds the definition of Latina/o media. Several scholars define Latina/o media as that which is produced by Latina/o media professionals for Latina/o audiences. Given this definition, Latina/o access to institutions and institutional resources plays an important political role. Thus, Noriega's field-defining work documented the political activism of Chicana/o activists during the 1960s, 1970s, and 1980s targeting the general-market television and film media (Noriega, 1992, 2000; Noriega & López, 1996). Noriega demonstrates how Chicana/o political organizations, such as the National Council of La Raza, helped to open the industry doors for some Latina/o media professionals but did little to change the quantity or quality of representations about Mexicans and other Latinas/os in television and film. Similar political work by the National Associations of Hispanic Journalist (NAHJ) has had mixed results. NAHJ surveys show that the numbers of Latina/o journalists in general-market news outlets hovers at less than 5% (Montalvo & Torres, 2006).

However, as Noriega (2000) noted, one of the primary consequences of Latina/o media activism has been an increase in independent film and television production. Emerging scholarship in this area documents how Chicana/o and Latina/o film producers are creating hybrid genres of cinematic texts that often explore the fluidity of the symbolic and geopolitical U.S.-Mexico/U.S.-Puerto Rican borders and transnational border citizens—citizens who occupy multiple spaces and positions of identity (Fregoso, 1993, 2003; Ramírez-Berg, 2002; Valdivia, 2000). As a consequence, defining Latina/o media texts is increasingly problematic as both audiences and production are situated transnationally. Often times, such as in the case of *Real Women Have Curves* (2002) or *Frida* (2002), the movies, although produced by Latinas, are performed in English for an international market. In other cases, such as in the work of director Lourdes Portillo, the work is produced in Spanish but for an international and transnational U.S./Mexican/Chicana/o audience (Fregoso & Portillo, 2001).

New Directions in Latina/o Media Studies

One of the central goals of critical Latina/o communication scholarship is exploring the hybrid nature of contemporary media production and reception in order to analyze how these texts speak to the always changing and increasingly unstable positions of Latinidad, Latina/o and Latin American audiences (Acosta-Alzuru, 2003, 2005; Mayer, 2003; Rojas, 2004). Within critical Latina/o communication studies, hybridity is defined as part of the process of cultural formations produced from the unstable dynamic mixing of ideologically established systems of classifications. As a theoretical concept, it draws into question notions of purity, authenticity, and the historical stability of categories in the era of globalization (Garcia Canclini, 1995; Levine, 2001; Shome & Hedge, 2002; Valdivia, 2004b). Consequently, critical Latina/o communication scholarship problematizes notions of authenticity, homogeneity, and ethnic essentialism.

For instance, critical scholarship on Latina/o produced television such as Univisión and Telemundo programming foreground the transnational and conglomerated nature of its production base. Both networks depend on Mexico for the production of its most popular programming, the *telenovelas* (Sinclair, 1990). Although the networks are headquartered in Miami, most of the creative and production labor is outsourced to Latin America. Ironically, little of their programming content is produced in the United States for the specific consumption of U.S. Latina/o audiences (Sinclair, 2003). Thus, Latina/o audiences in the United States are often watching content produced in Mexico for Mexican audiences or produced in Mexico for pan-Latina/o audiences. In addition, media conglomeration within places such as Puerto Rico is creating a situation in which locally produced content is decreasing and multinational pan-ethnic programming is increasing (Rivero, 2005). Further problematizing definitions of Latina/o media content are forays by general-market outlets into Latina/o themed network programming. The ABC network has led the way with two popular shows: "The George López Show" (2000–2007), based on the life of comedian George López, and "Ugly Betty," based on the globally popular Colombian telenovela "Yo soy Betty, La Fea" (1999).

Within the area of critical Latina/o media studies, some of the most interesting work is being conducted on television. Scholarship on television has focused both on transnational U.S. Latina/o audiences and audiences located in the Caribbean and Latin America, particularly Venezuela, Mexico, and Puerto Rico (Acosta-Alzuru, 2003, 2005; Rivero, 2005; Rojas, 2004). Work in this area generally centers on understanding the relationship among media texts, audiences, and the construction of national and ethnic identities. Moreover, it foregrounds how television programs speak to audience negotiations over national identity as they intersect with issues of class, gender, and race. For scholars studying transnational Latina/o audiences living in the United States, the process of racialization is often highlighted, especially with regard to how racialization makes issues of cultural representation and identity particularly problematic (Molina Guzmán, 2006b; Rojas, 2004); that is, for second- and third-generation Latinas/os, the consumption of Spanish-language Latina/o programming is sometimes marked as a source of difference, whereas for more recent Latinas/os, it is used as a transnational symbolic link to their home countries. U.S. Latina audiences specifically perceive the hypersexualized, hyperfeminized representations of women in Spanish-language programming as contributing to their stigmatization in the United States (Rojas, 2004).

Moving to a different mode of communication, the transnational fluidity of texts and audience reception is central to critical Latina/o media scholarship dealing with popular music. For instance, the scholarship surrounding Tejano music and Puerto Rican reggaeton is grounded in an understanding of how multiple cultures come together to produce innovative hybrid texts that are then consumed by audiences across a multiplicity of national borders with sometimes competing interests and interpretations (Aparicio, 1998; Báez, 2006; Mayer, 2003; Rivera, 2003; Valdivia, 2001). For example, work on reggaetón documents its roots in the flow of people and cultures through its hybrid intersection in Jamaican dance hall, Dominican merengue, and Nuyorican salsa (Rivera, 2003). The cultural flow of reggaetón allows it to communicate differently to multiple audiences in disparate spaces. Thus, it signifies a classed-based identity on the island while communicating an ethnic/racial community identity in the United States.

Tejano, reggaetón, and salsa as hybrid cultural "Latina/o" forms also contribute to transnational community formations. For instance, the popularity of tejano music in the Southwest and northern Mexico and salsa in New York, Puerto Rico, Miami, and Los Angeles, among other places, help to create an imagined transnational community of listeners (Mayer, 2003). At the same time, contemporary scholarship demonstrates the ways music functions as a fluid ethnic signifier across Latina/o communities. For instance, salsa music crosses ethnic-specific borders, spawning the popularity of salsa nights in predominantly Mexican communities in the Midwest, Southwest, and California (Valdivia, 2001).

Finally, critical Latina/o communication studies analyze the tension between invisibility and the iconic hypervisibility surrounding particular Latinas/os, specifically women's bodies, within general-market U.S. popular culture (Molina Guzmán & Valdivia, 2004). As the U.S. Census continues to document the changing demographic position of Latinas/os, Latina/o bodies, music, and other cultural elements of Latinidad are increasingly used to sell a myriad of media programming, products, and services. Consequently, while Latinas/os remain invisible and marginalized within news narratives, film, and television, Latina/o bodies are harnessed in the service of global consumption. With regard to advertising, among the most visible Latina spokespeople are Penélope Cruz (Ralph Lauren), Salma Hayek (Lincoln Continental), Jennifer Lopéz (Pepsi), and Christina Aguillera (Versace). In addition, Jessica Alba, Salma Hayek, and Jennifer Lopéz have all been awarded coveted contracts as L'Oreal spokeswomen. Advertising campaigns from Bacardi Rum to Cuervo prominently feature Latina and Latino models dressed seductively in stereotypically bright colors with salsa background music. Among companies recently targeting Latinas/os are LEVI'S, Adidas, Target, Wal-Mart, and Blockbuster.

While increasing levels of media targeting Latinas/os and using elements of Latina/o culture to sell products denote a superficial change from the social periphery to the social center, it is also cementing the use of stereotyped racial representations and homogenizing ethnic images to sell products across a diversity of audiences. Critical Latina/o media scholarship on general-market media representations theorizes through the commodification of pan-Latinidad to problematize the discourses of authenticity, ethnic essentialism, and homogenization, predominantly but not exclusively circulated by the Latina/o marketing industry (Molina Guzmán, 2006b). Because of the contemporary dimensions of globalization and transnational immigration driven by gendered labor, the politics of representation surrounding women and women's bodies has been a primary focus for critical communication scholars examining Latinidad in U.S. general-market popular culture (Acosta-Alzuru, 2003; Aparicio, 2003a; Báez, 2006; Beltrán, 2002; Cepeda, 2003; Molina Guzmán, 2005, 2006b; Molina Guzmán & Valdivia, 2004; Rojas, 2004).

FUTURE RESEARCH IN CRITICAL LATINA/O MEDIA STUDIES

Latina/o media scholarship illustrates a field with depth across a variety of methodological approaches and empirical foci (Aparicio, 2003b). Interpretive projects in Latina/o media history and quantitative work on Latina/o media use and representations in the general-market media have established the foundational terrain for contemporary critical scholarship. However, contemporary critical scholarship in Latina/o media studies have turned away from quantification to a qualitative analysis of complicated cultural issues: What is Latina/o media in the context of globalization and multinational media corporations? How is Latinidad signified for ethnic-national communities historically characterized by the remnants of colonialism, imperialism, cultural syncretism, and racial fluidity? Why do cultural representations still matter? What are the social and political consequences of Latina/o cultural invisibility or hypervisibility?

Critical Latina/o media scholars are participating in a project that, in Poblete's words, provides "an analytical space where borders themselves can be investigated and with them all kinds of transnational, translingual, and transcultural phenomenon" (2003, p. xv). Of the most theoretically interesting borders to explore are those dealing with the cultural politics of identity—in particular, issues dealing with the intersection of Latinidad and gender, race, and class. Thus, like the field of Latina/o Studies at large, critical media scholarship ultimately seeks to (1) destabilize notions of nationality, citizenship, and the nation, (2) engage in a comparative ethnic and racial analysis that captures the increasing diversity and complexity of Latina/o life in the United States, and (3) position the United States as a site for postcolonial cultural analysis (Aparicio, 2003b; Valdivia, 2003). Given that it is more difficult today than ever before to neatly define the borders of a Latina/o media that is increasingly crossing over into the general market, being consumed by audiences in the United States, the Caribbean, and Latin America, and increasingly produced by multinational teams and corporations, I argue that an understanding of the contemporary dynamics of Latina/o media demands critical analysis.

REFERENCES

Acosta-Alzuru, C. (2003). Tackling the Issues: Meaning Making in a Telenovela. *Popular Communication, 1*(4), 193–215.

Acosta-Alzuru, C. (2005). Home Is Where My Heart Is: Reflections on Doing Research in My Native Country. *Popular Communication, 3*(3), 181–193.

Aparicio, F. R. (1998). *Listening to Salsa: Gender, Latin Popular Music, and Puerto Rican Cultures*. Hanover, NH: University Press of New England.

Aparicio, F. R. (2003a). Jennifer as Selena: Rethinking Latinidad in Media and Popular Culture. *Latino Studies, 1*(1), 90–105.

Aparicio, F. R. (2003b). Latino Studies. In J. Poblete (Ed.), *Critical Latin American and Latino Studies* (pp. 1–17). Minneapolis: University of Minnesota Press.

Báez, J. M. (2006). 'En Mi Imperio': Competing Discourses of Agency in Ivy Queen's Reggaetón. *CENTRO Journal, 18*(2), 62–81.

Beltrán, M. (2002). The Hollywood Latina Body as Site of Social Struggle: Media Constructions of Stardom and Jennifer Lopez's 'Cross-over Butt'. *Quarterly Review of Film and Video, 19*(1), 71–86.

Cepeda, M. E. (2003). Shakira as the Idealized, Transnational Citizen: A Case Study of *Colombianidad* in Transition. *Laitno Studies, 1*(2), 211–232.

Dávila, A. M. (2001). *Latinos, Inc.: The Marketing and Making of a People*. Berkeley: University of California Press.

Del Rio, E. (2006). The Latina/o Problematic: Categories and Questions in Media Communication Research. *Communication Yearbook, 30*(1), 387–429.

Di Stefano, O. (1985). 'Venimos a Luchar': Brief History of *La Prensa's* Founding. *Aztlán, 16*(1–2), 95–118.

Downing, J. (1992). Spanish-Language Media in the Greater New York Region During the 1980s. In S. H. Riggins (Ed.), *Ethnic Minority Media: An International Perspective* (pp. 256–275). Newbury Park, Calif.: Sage Publications.

Fregoso, R. L. (1993). *The Bronze Screen: Chicana and Chicano Film Culture*. Minneapolis: University of Minnesota Press.

Fregoso, R. L. (2003). *MeXicana Encounters: The Making of Social Identities on the Borderlands*. Berkeley: University of California Press.

Fregoso, R. L., & Portillo, L. (2001). *Lourdes Portillo: The Devil Never Sleeps and Other Films* (1st ed.). Austin, TX: University of Texas Press.

García Canclini, N. (1995). *Hybrid Cultures: Strategies for Entering and Leaving Modernity*. Minneapolis: University of Minnesota Press.

García, M. C. (1996). *Havana USA: Cuban Exiles and Cuban Americans in South Florida, 1959–1994*. Berkeley: University of California Press.

Garza, M. (1994). Growth Market: Mainstream Media Vie for Latino Readers. *Media Studies Journal, 8*(3), 18–21.

Goodson, S. R., & Shaver, M. A. (1994). Hispanic Marketing: National Advertiser Spending Patterns and Media Choices. *Journalism Quarterly, 71*(1), 191–198.

Gutiérrez, F. (1977). Spanish Language Media in America: Background, Resources, History. *Journalism History, 4*(2), 34–41, 65–67.

Husband, C. (2000). Media and the Public Sphere in Multi-Ethnic Societies. In S. Cottle (Ed.), *Ethnic Minorities and the Media: Changing Cultural Boundaries* (pp. 199–214). Buckingham: Open University Press.

Johnson, M. A. (2000). How Ethnic Are U.S. Ethnic Media: The Case of Latina Magazines. *Mass Communication and Society, 3*(2–3), 229–248.

Kanellos, N. (1994). *The Hispanic Almanac: From Columbus to Corporate America*. Detroit: Invisible Ink.

Korzenny, F., Neuendorf, K., Burgoon, M., Burgoon, J. K., & Greenberg, B. S. (1983). Cultural Identification as a Predictor of Content Preferences of Hispanics. *Journalism Quarterly, 60*(4), 677–685, 770.

Kramer, L. (2002, January 7). Ethnic Ad-Vances; Hispanic Agencies Are Industry's Hot Spots. *Crain's New York Business*, p. 3.

Leal, L. (1989). The Spanish Language Press: Function and Use. *The Americas Review, 17*(3/4), 157–162.

Levine, E. (2001). Constructing a Market, Constructing an Ethnicity: U.S. Spanish-Language Media and the Formation of a Syncretic Latino/a Identity. *Studies in Latin American Popular Culture, 20*, 33–50.

Mayer, V. (2003). *Producing Dreams, Consuming Youth: Mexican Americans and Mass Media*. New Brunswick, N.J.: Rutgers University Press.

Mayer, V. (2004). Please Pass the Pan: Retheorizing the Map of Panlatinidad in Communication Research. *The Communication Review, 7*(2), 113–124.

Medeiros, F. (1980). *La Opinión*, a Mexican Exile Newspaper: A Content Analysis of Its First Years, 1926–1929. *Aztlán, 11*(1), 65–87.

Meléndez, A. G. (1997). *So All Is Not Lost: The Poetics of Print in Nuevomexicano Communities, 1834–1958* (1st ed.). Albuquerque: University of New Mexico Press.

Méndez-Méndez, S., & Alverio, D. (2001). *Network Brownout 2001: The Portrayal of Latinos in Network Television News, 2000*. Washington, D.C.: National Association of Hispanic Journalists.

Méndez-Méndez, S., & Alverio, D. (2002). *Network Brownout 2002: The Portrayal of Latinos in Network Television News, 2001*. Washington, D.C.: National Association of Hispanic Journalists.

Méndez-Méndez, S., & Alverio, D. (2003). *Network Brownout 2003: The Portrayal of Latinos in Network Television News, 2002*. Washington, D.C.: National Association of Hispanic Journalists.

Molina Guzmán, I. (2005). Gendering Latinidad through the Elián News Discourse About Cuban Women. *Latino Studies, 3*(2), 179–204.

Molina Guzmán, I. (2006a). Competing Discourses of Community: Ideological Tensions between Local General-Market and Latino News Media. *Journalism: Theory, Practice and Criticism, 7*(3), 281–298.

Molina Guzmán, I. (2006b). Mediating Frida: Negotiating Discourses of Latina/o Authenticity in Global Media Representations of Ethnic Identity. *Critical Studies in Media Communication, 23*(3), 232–251.

Molina Guzmán, I., & Valdivia, A. (2004). Brain, Brow or Bootie: Iconic Latinas in Contemporary Popular Culture. *The Communication Review, 7*(2), 205–221.

Montalvo, D., & Torres, J. (2006). *Network Brownout Report 2006: The Portrayal of Latinos & Latino Issues in Network Television News, 2005*. Washington, D.C.: National Association of Hispanic Journalists.

Noriega, C. A. (2000). *Shot in America: Television, the State, and the Rise of Chicano Cinema*. Minneapolis: University of Minnesota Press.

Noriega, C. A. (Ed.). (1992). *Chicanos and Film: Essays on Chicano Representation and Resistance*. New York: Garland Publishing.

Noriega, C. A., & López, A. M. (Eds.). (1996). *The Ethnic Eye: Latino Media Arts*. Minneapolis, Minn.: University of Minnesota Press.

Poblete, J. (Ed.). (2003). *Critical Latin American and Latino Studies*. Minneapolis: University of Minnesota Press.

Ramírez Berg, C. (2002). *Latino Images in Film: Stereotypes, Subversion, Resistance*. Austin, TX: University of Texas Press.

Riggins, S. H. (Ed.). (1992). *Ethnic Minority Media: An International Perspective*. Newbury Park, Calif.: Sage Publications.

Rivera, R. Z. (2003). *New York Ricans from the Hip Hop Zone* (1st ed.). New York: Palgrave Macmillan.

Rivero, Y. M. (2005). *Tuning out Blackness: Race and Nation in the History of Puerto Rican Television*. Durham: Duke University Press.

Rodríguez, A. (1999). *Making Latino News: Race, Language, Class*. Thousand Oaks: Sage Publications.

Rodriguez, C. E. (1997). *Latin Looks: Images of Latinas and Latinos in the U.S. Media*. Boulder, Colo.: Westview Press.

Rojas, V. (2004). The Gender of Latinidad: Latinas Speak About Hispanic Television. *The Communication Review, 7*(2), 125–153.

Roslow, P., & Nicholls, J. A. F. (1996). Targeting the Hispanic Market: Comparative Persuasion of TV Commercials in Spanish and English. *Journal of Advertising Research, 36*(3), 67–77.

Santiago, C., & Valdes, I. (2002). *Missed Opportunities: Vast Corporate Underspending in the U.S. Hispanic Market*. (2002). McLean, VA: Association of Hispanic Advertising Agencies.

Shome, R., & Hegde, R. S. (2002). Postcolonial Approaches to Communication: Charting the Terrain, Engaging the Intersections. *Communication Theory, 12*(3), 249–270.

Sinclair, J. (1990). Televisa: Mexico's Multinational. *CENTRO Journal, 2*(8), 92–97.

Sinclair, J. (2003). 'The Hollywood of Latin America': Miami as Regional Center in Television Trade. *Television and New Media, 4*(3), 211–229.

Soruco, G. R. (1996). *Cubans and the Mass Media in South Florida*. Gainesville: University Press of Florida.

Subervi-Vélez, F. A. (1986). The Mass Media and Ethnic Assimilation and Pluralism: A Review and Research Proposal with Special Focus on Hispanics. *Communication Research, 13*(1), 71–96.

Subervi-Vélez, F. A. (2003). The Mass Media and Latinos: Policy and Research Agendas for the Next Century. *Aztlán, 24*(2), 131–147.

Subervi-Vélez, F. A. (2004). Spanish-Language Television Coverage of Health News. *Howard Journal of Communications, 10*(3), 207–228.

Subervi, F., Torres, J., & Montalvo, D. (2005). *Network Brownout Report 2005: The Portrayal of Latinos & Latino Issues on Network Television News, 2004 with a Retrospect to 1995*. Austin, Texas and Washington, D.C.: National Association of Hispanic Journalists.

Suro, R. (2004). *Changing Channels and Crisscrossing Cultures: A Survey of Latinos on the News Media*. Washington, D.C.: Pew Hispanic Center.

Ueltschy, L. C., & Krampf, R. F. (1997). The Influence of Acculturation on Advertising Effectiveness to the Hispanic Market. *Journal of Applied Business Research, 13*(2), 87–101.

U.S. Census Bureau. (2005a). *Hispanic or Latino Population by Specific Origin*. (Los Angeles City, California. American Community Survey). Retrieved January 27, 2006, from http:/factfinder.census.gov/servlet/DTTable?_bm=y&geo_id=16000 USO6440008-ds_na

U.S. Census Bureau. (2005b) *Hispanic or Latino Population by Specific Origin*. (Miami City, Florida. American Community Survey). Retrieved January 27, 2006, from http:/factfinder.census.gov/servlet/DTTable?_bm=y&geo_id=16000 US2450000&-ds_na

U.S. Census Bureau. (2005c). *Hispanic or Latino Population by Specific Origin*. (New York City. American Community Survey). Retrieved January 27, 2006, from http:/factfinder.census.gov/servlet/DTTable?_bm=y&geo_id=16000 US3651000&-ds_na

Valdivia, A. N. (2000). *A Latina in the Land of Hollywood and Other Essays on Media Culture*. Tucson: University of Arizona Press.

Valdivia, A. N. (2001). Community Building through Dance and Music: Salsa in the Midwest. In M. M. Flores & C. von Son (Eds.), *Double Crossings: Entrecruzamientos* (pp. 153–176). New Jersey: Ediciones Nuevo Espacio.

Valdivia, A. N. (2002). What Is Over? Ruminations from One Who Has Already Lived through Another September 11. *Cultural Studies <=> Critical Methodologies, 2*(3), 354–358.

Valdivia, A. N. (2004a). Latina/o Communication and Media Studies Today: An Introduction. *The Communication Review, 7*(2), 107–112.

Valdivia, A. N. (2004b). Latinas as Radical Hybrid: Transnationally Gendered Traces in Mainstream Media, *Global Media Journal*, 3(4). Online journal available at http://lass.calumet.purdue.edu/cca/gmj/sp04/gmj-sp04-valdivia.htm

Vargas, L. (2000). Genderizing Latino News: An Analysis of a Local Newspaper's Coverage of Latino Current Affairs. *Critical Studies in Media Communication, 17*(3), 261–293.

Vargas, L. C., & dePyssler, B. J. (1999). U.S. Latino Newspapers as Health Communication Resources: A Content Analysis. *Howard Journal of Communications, 10*(3), 189–205.

CHAPTER 14

As the Latino/a World Turns: The Literary and Cultural Production of Transnational Latinidades

Ana Patricia Rodríguez

INTRODUCTION

By the early 1990s, Latinos/as in the United States had attracted the attention of multinational corporations, transnational media, and the general public. Estimated, then, at 30 million people with buying power of over 100 billion dollars per year and projected to become the largest ethnic minority in the United States by 2025 (Flores & Yúdice, 1990), U.S. Latinos/as represented a growing body of consumers and markets, particularly in the untapped area of cultural and literary production. It was no coincidence, then, that in the months of May and June of 1993, the media conglomerate Univisión advertised Pepsi as the drink of Latinos/as, *Cosmopolitan* and *Harper's Bazaar* glossed on its cover pages the figure of Salvadoran American model Christy Turlington (June and September 1993), and *Fitness* magazine featured an exposé of MTV's Miami-based Daisy Fuentes (June 1993). With these public figures and products, Latinos/as formally entered the mass culture market (Dávila, 2001; García Canclini, 2001). Counting on the consumer value, purchasing power, and signifying potential of Latinos/as, major presses almost simultaneously began to publish and market a wide array of fiction and nonfiction works by U.S. Latino/a writers. Increasingly in the public eye, this expansive and diverse Latino/a literary and cultural production would transform the image of Latinos/as in the United States.

Focusing on what has been called and critiqued as the Latino/a cultural and literary "boom," this chapter explores the *transnationalization* of the Latino cultural imaginary and the production of more diverse *Latinidades* in the United States in the watershed decades of the 1980s and

1990s. Particular attention is paid to the intervention and impact of texts associated with the U.S. Latino/a cultural boom, whose condition of possibility was predicated and grounded in the context of increasing Latino immigration from Latin America and massive demographic shifts in the United States. These factors contributed not only to making Latinos/as one of the largest and most diverse ethnic populations in the United States but also to the cultural reconfiguration and expansion of Latino/a identities in the 20th and 21st centuries.

THE CRADLE OF LATINIDADES: THE LOST AND RELOCATED "DECADE OF THE HISPANIC"

Otherwise known as Latin America's "Lost Decade" and the "Decade of the Hispanic" in the United States, the 1980s through the 1990s was an era of military interventions, civil conflict, political upheavals, socioeconomic displacements, and mass movements of Latin American peoples to the United States and elsewhere. While people from Latin America were forced to flee their countries, the United States became increasingly more Latino, not only in numbers but also in cultural composition. During the 1980s and 1990s, Mexicans, Cubans, Dominicans, Salvadorans, Guatemalans, and other people from almost every Latin American country sought alternatives to rapidly deteriorating political and socioeconomic conditions in their homelands by immigrating to other locations. United States cities like Washington, DC, New York, Miami, San Francisco, and Los Angeles and regions such as the U.S. South and Midwest received critical masses of Latin American immigrants and newcomers. With the arrival of many Latino/a Americans, U.S. Latino/a cultural production would become more multifaceted and diffused in response to U.S. legislation, foreign policy, and domestic programs, which, in the 1980s and 1990s, dismally failed many Latinos/as.

As the "Decade of the Hispanic" finally waned with little fanfare in the United States and the "Lost Decade of Latin America" continued its decline in Central America, the so-called U.S. Latino/a literary and cultural boom was formally in session. Commenting on that watershed era, the feminist writer and cultural critic Cherríe Moraga (1995) affirmed that "[w]hat was once largely a Chicano/*mexicano* population in California is now *guatemalteco, salvadoreño, nicaragüense*" (p. 213), thus noting Latino/a demographic and discursive shifts not only in the U.S. Southwest but throughout the United States as well. In the midst of it all, a transnational Latino/a literary and cultural production appeared throughout the United States, one that represented recent arrivals and different issues and that was accompanied by translations of English titles into Spanish and vice versa. In many ways, U.S. Latino/a literature as of the 1990s mirrored contemporary immigration patterns, demographic shifts, transcultural processes, and the revitalization of Spanish in the United States.

Set against this historical backdrop, U.S. Latino/a cultural and literary production shifted from its historical domestic ethnocultural underpinnings, moving from its Chicano, Puerto Rican, and Cuban American foundations to more transnational orientations to include and represent the diversity of Latin American populations now intersecting in the United States. In regard to Chicano/Latino films produced during the "Decade of the Hispanic" under question here, the film critic Chon Noriega (1988/1990) examined the reception of four key films escaping the "cinema barrio" and entering "hybrid 'Hispanic Hollywood'" (p. 1). These path-breaking films were "La Bamba" (1987), "Born in East L.A." (1987), "The Milagro Beanfield War" (1988), and "Stand and Deliver" (1988). With these films, Noriega (1988/1990) noted the reconceptualization of "ethnic spaces, especially through the use of genre" (p. 11). It is telling that whereas most of these films represented Chicano/a culture and communities, "Born in East L.A." crossed the border into Tijuana, where the Chicano protagonist, once decentered, displaced, deported, and resignified as "Mexican," joined a diverse spectrum of would-be transnational immigrants in transit to the United States. The film also marked the appearance of a prototypical Salvadoran woman immigrant who would become the protagonist of her own Latino/a narratives and her Latinidades in later texts (Buss, 1991; Goldman, 1992; Limón, 1993; Viramontes, 1985).

Cultural and literary production, as seen here, participated in the reconfiguration of Latino/a identities, often playing out larger debates in various texts that asked the following questions: Who were the new Latino/a immigrants, and how would they transform and contribute to the re/formation of Latino ethnicity in the United States? How would U.S. Latino/a identities account for multiple histories, genealogies, cultures, and traditions? How would intersecting Latin American diasporas figure into the preexisting U.S. cultural and ethnic imaginary? What would a more pluralistic Latino cultural imaginary look like, sound like, feel like, and embody as a whole? Indeed, new terms would have to be invented to articulate and represent new Latino social constructs in the making; hence, the term *Latinidades* gained momentum among scholars and others.

EMBLEMATIC U.S. LATINO/A LITERARY *BOOMS*

As identified here, the first wave of Latino cultural and literary "boom" texts of the 1990s included Sandra Cisneros's *Woman Hollering Creek* (1991; *El arroyo de la Llorona y otros cuentos*, 1996), Cristina García's *Dreaming in Cuban* (1992; *Soñar en cubano*, 1993), Francisco Goldman's *The Long Night of White Chickens* (1992; *La larga noche de los pollos blancos*, 1994), Julia Alvarez's *How the García Girls Lost Their Accent* (1992; *De cómo las chicas García perdieron su acento*, 1994), Esmeralda Santiago's *When I Was Puerto Rican* (1994; *Cuando era puertorriqueña*, 1994), and Junot Díaz's *Drown* (1996; *Negocios*, 1997). These texts were emblematic of the crossings of Latino peoples, cultures, identities, histories, languages, traditions, nationalities, and ethnicities, among other things, during that period. Published in both English and Spanish and sometimes written in Spanglish and manifesting other forms for Latino linguistic and cultural code-switching, most of these texts became U.S. Latino/a bestsellers. The awarding of the Pulitzer Prize in 1990 to Oscar Hijuelos' *The Mambo Kings Play Songs of Love* (1989) not only represented Latino/a demographic shifts in process but also exemplified what came to be known as the "boom" in U.S. Latino/a culture and literature (Christie & González, 2006; Stavans, 1993a, p. 65).

As of the 1990s, major publishing houses also released numerous Latino/a anthologies, collections, and textbooks for the lucrative university market, including, to name only a few: *Iguana Dreams: New Latino/a Fiction* (HarperPerennial, 1992), *Growing Up Latino/a: Memoirs and Stories* (Houghton, 1993), *Short Fiction by Hispanic Writers of the United States* (Arte Público Press, 1993), *Barrios and Borderlands: Cultures of Latinos and Latinas in the United States* (Routledge, 1994), *Paper Dance: 55 Latino Poets* (Persea Books, 1995), *Daughters of the Fifth Sun: A Collection of Latina Fiction and Poetry* (Riverhead Books/G.P. Putnam's Sons, 1995), *Hispanic American Literature: A Brief Introduction and Anthology* (Addison Wesley Longman, 1995), *The Latino Reader: Five Centuries of an American Literary Tradition from Cabeza de Vaca to Oscar Hijuelos* (Houghton Mifflin, 1997), *New World Young Latino Writers: 23 Outstanding Stories from Exciting New Voices in the Hispanic Community* (Dell Publishing/Bantam Doubleday, 1997), *Touching the Fire: Fifteen Poets of Today's Latino Renaissance* (Anchor, 1998), *Hispanic American Literature: An Anthology* (NTC Publishing Group, 1998), *The Floating Borderlands: Twenty-five Years of U.S.*

Hispanic Literature (University of Washington Press, 1998), *Herencia: The Anthology of Hispanic Literature of the United States* (Oxford University Press, 2002), *The Prentice Hall Anthology of Latino Literature* (Prentice Hall, 2002), *Border-line Personalities: A New Generation of Latinas Dish on Sex, Sass, and Cultural Shifting* (HaperCollins/Rayo, 2004), and *Latino Boom: An Anthology of U.S. Latino Literature* (Pearson Longman, 2006). Anthologies of U.S. Latino/a literature published (and/or translated) thus far into Spanish include *Cuentos hispanos de los Estados Unidos* (Arte Público Press, 1998), *Cruzando Puentes: Antología de Literatura Latina* (Ventana Abierta, 2001), *Vistas y Voces Latinas* (Prentice Hall, 2002), and *En otra voz: Antología de la literatura hispana de los Estados Unidos* (Arte Público Press, 2002).

In quick succession, U.S. Latino/a books, anthologies, and press imprints not only introduced a growing number of well and less-known Chicano/a, Puerto/Neo Rican, Cuban American, Salvadoran American, and other authors writing under the expansive *U.S. Latino/a* umbrella but also contributed to the construction of an U.S. Latino/a cultural imaginary. Indeed, in *Latinos: A Biography of the People* (1992), Earl Shorris noted:

> Latinos/as now have a body of work, a literary mirror in which to see themselves, and the images in the mirror grow more interesting to the rest of society as they represent an increasingly large segment of the population. (p. 395)

Part-and-parcel of a marketing boom, the publication of works by writers like Alvarez, Castillo, Cisneros, García, Santiago, and others presented an unprecedented space for some Latinos/as to participate in the "overall effort of mapping contemporary, postmodern culture", as Marc Zimmerman claimed in the preface to his monograph titled *U.S. Latino Literature: An Essay and Annotated Bibliography* (1992, p. 3). An interrogation of this come-lately U.S. Latino/a literary and cultural boom would enable us to examine critically what Arlene Dávila (2001) called the making and marketing of Latinidades and Latino/a imaginaries.

Although some observers of this Latino literary and cultural explosion initially hailed it as a "revival" and "renaissance" of ethnic literature (González, 1998; Shorris, 1992, pp. 381–395; Stavans, 1993a), many academic scholars, however, have remained skeptical of the cultural "boom" phenomena and the marketing forces behind it (Dávila, 2001; Rostagno, 1997).[1] Since their first appearance, these texts have been part-and-parcel of the growing Latino/a culture market as well as new trends in the globalization of the publishing industry as noted by Robbins (2004).[2] Catching on to these trends, mainstream presses have been quick to experiment with Latino and Spanish language book imprints,[3] publishing to date not only works by recent U.S. Latino/a writers but also reprints by long-standing writers. Texts by reputable Chicano/a and U.S. Puerto Rican authors such as Rudolfo Anaya, Tato Laviera, Nicolasa Mohr, Tomás Rivera, Richard Rodriguez, Piri Thomas, José Antonio Villarreal, Victor E. Villaseñor, and other precursors to U.S. Latino/a literature of the 1990s and beyond have been reprinted, reread, and revitalized. Through archival projects such as "Recovering the U.S. Hispanic Literary Heritage" at the University of Houston, Latino/a texts embedded in older traditions, histories, and struggles like María Amparo Ruiz de Burton's post-1848 California historical romance *The Squatter and the Don* (1885) have been reprinted by Arte Público Press (1992) and Random House (2004). The U.S. Latino/a literary and cultural boom thus includes texts produced across various historical periods as well as those still on the horizon of the Latino/a cultural imaginary.

In an interview, the Cuban writer Alejo Carpentier (himself associated with the Latin American literary boom of the 1960s) once cautioned, however, against simply celebrating and accepting at face value so-called literary and cultural booms (Arias, 1977, p. 49), which might gain rapid diffusion and massive popularity all too quickly. As noted by Carpentier, such works by a handful of writers do not necessarily constitute an aesthetic or cultural "movement" with a central project and articulation (Arias, 1977, p. 47) but, rather, underscore a culture industry and market for which these texts are written. Carpentier's skepticism about the production and reception of the *big boom* of Latin American literature in the 1960s might be hereto put to task and redirected to examine the making and marketing of the post-1980s' U.S. Latino/a literary boom to consumers outside of endogenous Latino groups. What images of Latinos/as would sell and how (much) they would sell (for) continue to offer significant prospects and profits for the publishing world. In one telling example, a Houston Chronicle reviewer praised Sandra Cisneros's *Woman Hollering Creek* for "the chance to taste deeply of Hispanic culture while accompanied by a knowing and generous guide."[4] Drawing attention to the consumption of *authentic* Latino/a texts in the United States, the reviewer implicitly suggested that by reading U.S. Latino/a literature, readers could *taste deeply* and *knowingly* significant aspects of Latino/a culture. Moreover, by doing so, they would symbolically partake in multiculturalism, or what the Mexican-Chicano performance artist Guillermo Goméz-Peña has called *multicultism*.[5] In their own turn, Flores and Yúdice (1990) examined the role of mass media and the market of multiculturalism in the production of this Latino/a literary boom (p. 62), and Yúdice, Franco, & Flores (1992) suggested that U.S. Latino/a boom writers often function as cultural brokers. Indeed, for Yúdice, Franco, & Flores (1992), "[a]s culture becomes privatized, intellectuals and artists increasingly act as salespersons for free enterprise, hawking and making wares of 'otherness' familiar to transnational culture." They also noted that pluralist ideology tends to transform "difference" into a recognizable entity that is nonthreatening to the state and its market economy.

At the end of the 20th century, U.S. Latino/a "boom" literature was thus marketed as multicultural and/or ethnic literature (Stavans, 1993b). As such, this literature often contributed to the production and commodification of hegemonic images and discourses associated with Hispanic identities, especially those of exoticism, foreignness, and violence. Images of these appeared on book covers, reviews, and other paratextual forms in mainstream venues. The literary critic Gerard Genette (1997) identified as "paratexts" all those devices and conventions that "enable a text to become a book and to be offered as such to its readers and, more generally, to the public" (p. 1). Further, "peritexts" would include those devices such as book covers, forewords, illustrations, typeface, pocket-size and/or other formats, review inserts, and special series or imprints, which are generally used by publishing houses for the purpose of selling texts (Genette, 1997, pp. 16–36). The production, packaging, and marketing of 1990s Latino/a boom literature, I suggest here, gainfully employed many paratextual devices, producing particular emblems of Latinidad that blended exoticism, ethnicity, and culture into pan-Latino/a images, discourses, and products.

Indeed, anthologies and novels associated hereto with the U.S. Latino/a cultural boom wore the now all too familiar signs of commodified U.S. Latino-ness—jacket covers brown-washed with folkloric figures, picturesque motifs, or scenes of violence and disorder, as is the case for the texts about Central America/ns. These jacket covers caught the attention of would-be book buyers and reviewers, confirming that sex, violence, and magic sell well, especially in the representation, packaging, and marketing of Latinos/as in the United States. Many book reviews, which were printed on the covers or inserted into the pages of the books, attributed to U.S. Latinos/as an all-American immigrant experience and/or Latin American exotic magical realism, giving these texts their official stamp of "American" hybridity. Cristina García's *Dreaming in Cuban*, for example, was said to provide "a welcome addition to the growing literature of Latin American émigré experience deftly bridg[ing] two divergent cultures…At its lyrical best, García's writing owes a debt to the magical realism of Gabriel García Márquez and Isabel Allende"

(Hilma Wolitzer, "Chicago Tribune Book World"). Julia Alvarez's novel, *How the García Girls Lost Their Accent*, was "deft and magical...bring[ing] to attention many of the issues—serious and light—that immigrant families face" (Kirkus Reviews). Ana Castillo's (1993) *So Far from God* was read as a "surreal ode to the heartbreak and magic of life" (John Nichols).

Marked by distinct differences (exoticisms and familialisms), Latino/a texts thus have appealed to a general reading public and have generated large profits for mainstream publishing houses. Commenting on the penchant for the typecasting of Latino/a immigrant experiences as magical realist, the Nuyorican writer Victor Hernández Cruz (1986) rightly claimed that Latino/a literature is subject to a multicultural dictum that holds that the "unreal sells well as exotica" (p. 114). Further reflecting on the notion of a magical Latino/a American immigrant experience, Goldman (1999) in the *Book Word* section of *The Washington Post* wrote:

> Especially pernicious is the notion that magical realism is an authentically and uniquely Latino form of literary expression—magical realism as a kind of ethnic propaganda, a claim to specialness based on the idea that Latinos are magical, more sensual, childlike, folkloric, unthreatening, so pleasing to read about, if not to have to actually live next door to, or to share a school district with. (p. 16)

Goldman, Hernández Cruz, Aparicio, and Chavéz-Silverman (1997), and others do well to critique and deconstruct the prevailing images of exotic, magical, and mass commodified Latinidades in the 1990s. These images are no more aggrandized than in the overexposed hype around Jennifer López's well-endowed Latina-ness as represented in the media (Negrón-Muntaner, 2004).

Along the same lines, but in an entirely different context, novels and films about Central America and Central Americans in the United States in the 1990s were branded with hyperimages of violence and war, the eminent signs of Central America in U.S. cultural representations of the 1980s and 1990s. In many filmic and other visual texts of the period, Central America/ns figured as the war-trodden yet beautiful woman seeking refuge in the United States (Rodríguez, 2001), as can be seen in the films *El Norte* (Director G. Nava, 1983), *Salvador* (Director O. Stone, 1985), and *My Family/Mi Familia* (Director G. Nava, 1995). Likewise, novels, short stories, and poems about Central American refugees and immigrants also capitalized on the prolonged and extended war at home in El Salvador, Nicaragua, Guatemala, and the rest of Central America. A reviewer of Graciela Limón's *In Search of Bernabé*, a Chicana novel about the Salvadoran Civil War, wrote that the novel "presents with vivid detail and heartfelt sincerity the sorrow of a nation victimized by greed and power, the anguish of the survivors of slaughter and loss" (Berona, 1993, p. 153). Still, another reviewer identified Limón's novel as "a tragic family saga" of two warring factions (*Review of Graciela Limon's* In Search of Bernabé , 1993, p. 63). Finally, Guatemalan American Héctor Tobar's *The Tattooed Soldier*, a novel about the Guatemalan Civil War (1954–1996) and its diaspora, was reviewed as a "gripping tale of revenge set on the lower rung of L.A.'s social ladder." In the novel, two opposing sides of the civil war, represented by the student and the soldier, confront one another in the streets of Los Angeles (*Review of Héctor Tobar's* The Tattooed Soldier, 1998, pp. 48–50). Read as "the tragic story" of one nation divided into victims and victimizers, Tobar's novel, for the reviewer, represented the violence creeping into the United States from Central America.

In the 1990s, the U.S. Latino/a cultural and literary "boom" thus seemed both to propagate emblems and stereotypes of popular Latino/a ethnicity and, in many cases, to diversify the image of U.S. Latinos/as. Book reviews commented on the diverse experiences represented in these texts, whereas, as we have seen, book covers were filled with folkloric figures, picturesque suns and moons, tropical flora and fauna, and quaint houses and scenes of violence building below the surface. These paratexts and other marketing tools were key not only to the marketing of U.S. Latino/a texts but also for the discursive production of Latinidades in the

1980s and 1990s. Aparicio and Chávez-Silverman (1997) described these ambivalent and often conflicting signs of Latinidades as the *tropicalization* of Latino American peoples, cultures, and histories, and the imposition of "a particular space, geography, group, or nation with a set of traits, images, and values" through the circulation of official (and often unofficial) "texts, history, literature, and the media" (p. 8). Through these mechanisms of representation, Latinidades were shaped, reconstructed, and *tropicalized* by hegemonic discourses and debates on Latinos/as in the United States (Aparicio & Chávez-Silverman, 1997, p. 8). Debates on immigration and internal demographic shifts, international policy, and the expansion of free trade in the Americas (e.g., NAFTA), moreover, impinged on the production of hegemonic representations of Latinos/as in the media, films, and other texts (De la Mora, 2006).

U.S. LATINO/A HEMISPHERIC LITERATURES

In his introduction to *Short Fiction by Hispanic Writers of the United States*, Kanellos (1993) speculated that new Hispanic writing might be read as "an esthetic and epistemological experiment that is preparing the United States for the multicultural, hemispheric reality of the next century" (p. 10). Situated in the context and politics of transnationalism and globalization, U.S. Latino/a literature is thus a part of a long-standing *Americas* discourse that had gained wide currency by the end of the 20th century. Among the critics who had hereto theorized on *inter-Americas* paradigms and projects, Saldívar (1991) was instrumental in proposing what he identified as a *dialectics of our America*, a cross-cultural, transnational reading of intertextualities and intersectionalities linking North, Central, and South American and Caribbean texts. Invoking Martí's (1891) sign of *Nuestra América* as an organizing discursive principle, Saldívar designated an Inter-Americas topography of literature by Latin American, Chicano, African American, and Caribbean writers as well as initiated an archival hemispheric project later undertaken by Kirsten Silva Gruesz in *Ambassadors of Culture: The Transamerican Origins of Latino Writing* (2002). In her anthology, *Comparative American Identities: Race, Sex, and Nationality in the Modern Text* (1991), Hortense J. Spillers also compiled readings by U.S. and Canadian critics who disrupted the homogenizing category of *America* (read U.S.) and expanded the *borders* of *American* (U.S.) literature and studies.

Along these same lines, but focusing on Latin America, Gustavo Pérez-Firmat, in *Do the Americas have a Common Literature?* (1990), used the interrogative of the title of his book to cue readers to the *appositional* (not oppositional) strategies that underlie hemispheric intertextual readings. In other words, his book pondered how texts from different sites in the Americas might be read comparatively and in a parallel analogous fashion. Pérez-Firmat's initial work postulated a line of analysis of Cuban American literature further elaborated in *Life on the Hyphen: The Cuban-American Way* (1994). Though seemingly new and innovative at first glance, the hemispheric project to which Kanellos and others alluded and which prompted the production of a transnational U.S. Latino/a cultural critique could be traced back to the 19th century (trans)nation-building visions and programs of Simón Bolívar's Pan-Americanism (Bolivar, 1815) and José Martí's ideal of *Nuestra América* (1891). Thus the U.S. literary boom can be read as part of ongoing hemispheric projects, expanding the notion of an inter-Americas cultural imaginary.

Nonetheless, as late as 1986, when Kanellos published "U.S. Hispanic Literature in the Anglo-American Empire," U.S. Latino/a literature was far from reaching the status and circulation of a boom or inter-Americas cultural project. In that article based on a transcript of a speech he presented initially at a PEN conference, Kanellos exposed "[t]he publishing industry [as] an integral part of the capitalist State," which offered few opportunities for Latino/a writers to publish with "commercial houses" (1986, p. 104). Kanellos argued that the U.S. publishing industry was merely an instrument of the State that enforced a "caste system" (p. 105). By 1986, only a few novels by Latinos/as had been published by mainstream publishers, most notably among them, Piri Thomas's *Down These Mean Streets* (Knopf, 1978) and Nicholasa Mohr's *Nilda* (Harper & Row, 1973). Both of these Nuyorican novels were marketed as ethnic autobiographies or narratives of adolescent coming of age, acculturation, and reformation (Mohr, 1990, p. 84).

Calling for more equitable access to publishing opportunities for Latino/a writers and for more critical representations of Latinos/as, Kanellos (1986) critiqued the tendency of mainstream presses to publish mainly "ethnic autobiographies," which he argued "reinforce the myth of the State as a free democracy and an open market that responds to the ethic" (pp. 104–105). According to Kanellos (1986), the "ethnic autobiography" (p. 105) that gained wide acceptance was one in which the individual acculturated successfully and articulated a hegemonic national ethos (Rodriguez, 1982). Moreover, the "authentic" ethnic bestseller was marked by "sexual encounter, gang fights…the police and the community, drugs" (Mohr 1986, p. 108),[6] all of which reified negative or, at best, ambivalent images of Latinos/as held by the dominant society. Against these limited narrative horizons, Kanellos and others called for the production of more diverse Latino/a images, voices, and discourses and the representation of "a new world identity—mestizos, immigrants from the third world, former slaves, and wage slaves," as Kanellos put it (1986, p. 105). Arte Público Press, along with other small and independent presses, as well as large publishing houses, in the 1990s, were poised to publish this new Latino/a literature.

In the 1990s, U.S. Latino/a literature thus would gain expansive coverage and circulation, bringing to the fore "an hemispheric identity that has been five centuries in the making" (Kanellos, 1993, p. 10) to whose formation Latino/a writers and other cultural agents had long contributed. The work of Arte Público, Bilingual Press, Calaca Press, and other independent presses was instrumental in the production, publication, and promotion of early and contemporary Latino/a literature. Indeed, Kanellos underscored:

> [T]he important role that Hispanics—as well as other racial and cultural minorities play in redefining our nation's culture and the role our nation has to play in the newly reconceived and ever-evolving cultural makeup of the world. (1993, p. 10)

By situating Latino/a literary and cultural production in a history of struggle, Kanellos and other scholars of U.S. Latino/a history, culture, and literature challenged the overnight success story of the Latino/a boom and the seemingly unprecedented publication of Hijuelos's *The Mambo Kings Play Songs of Love* in 1989.

The "overnight success" myth constructed Latinos/as as the most recent arrivals to the literary scene, neither possessing historical precedence nor offering oppositional implications for the future. Indeed, Stavans claimed:

> In retrospect, 1990 may come to be seen as a signal date for this revival […] Suddenly, major trade publishing houses began to recognize the commercial value of Hispanics and rushed to sign new books. A plethora of novels and short-story collections materialized in a short period, and while some were disappointments, others, notably by Sandra Cisneros and Julia Alvarez and Cristina Garcia (women are among the leaders of this boom), were quite impressive. (1993a, p. 65)

In *Short Fiction by Hispanic Writers of the United States* (1993), Kanellos had thus predicted correctly that "[t]he day is not far off when a novel written in Spanish in New York can be published in Houston and distributed from Alaska to Tierra del Fuego" (p. 10).

By 1992, indeed, an increasing number of U.S. Latino/a writers were being published in English, Spanish, and interlingual languages for local, regional, national, transnational, and global consumption. At the same time, new discursive spaces were opened to representation of multiple Latinidades intersecting across the United States. As mentioned previously, Chicano/a, Puerto Rican, Cuban American, and Dominican American writers like Sandra Cisneros, Ana Castillo, Esmeralda Santiago, Cristina García, Julia Alvarez, Junot Díaz, and many others began to write from key sites of the Latino American diaspora such as Miami, New York, and other places. From San Francisco, Salvadoran émigré writers Martivón Galindo and Jorge Argueta, among others, wrote exile poetry and short stories, which were collected respectively in *Retazos* (Galindo, 1996; *Pieces*), *Las Frutas del Centro y Otros Sabores/Fruit from the Center and Other Flavors* (Argueta, 1997), and the San Francisco-based Latino cultural journals, *Voces* and *Cipactli* (La Raza Studes/San Francisco State University).

In Los Angeles, young Salvadoran Americans, who called themselves *Salvis*, paired up with their counterparts in San Francisco to produce *Izote Vos: A Collection of Salvadoran American Writing and Visual Arts* (Cowy, Serrano, Ramos, & Rocamora, 2000), and U.S. Central American performance artists such as Leticia Hernández-Linares, Maya Chinchilla, Karina Oliva Alvarado, Jessica Grande, and Mario Escobar collaborated in EpiCentro and other art collectives in California. This U.S.-born and/or raised generation of artists and writers, who Arias (2003) calls "Central American Americans," along with other post-1980s U.S. Latinos/as began to experiment with the forms, contents, and voices of historically based and emerging Latinidades, as well as to give shape to new cultural projects that will continue into the future and from different vantage points and locations.

In the context of Washington, DC, the home of diverse Latino communities, including a thriving Salvadoran community, Mayamérica Cortez wrote *Nostalgias y soledades* (1995) and Mario Bencastro produced several novels, including *Odyssey to the North* (1998) and *A Promise to Keep* (2004), all of which document Salvadoran transmigration to and from the United States and El Salvador. In 2001, the Chicano/Latino comedy troupe Culture Clash also came to Washington, DC, to conduct research on communities in the District of Columbia. In the fall of 2002, they performed at the Arena Stage their new production, titled *Anthems: Culture Clash in the District* (Culture Clash, 2003), a post-September 11 ode to the people, including Salvadorans, of Washington, DC Moreover, the Salvadoran American poet and performer Quique Avilés, a long-time Washington, DC resident, cofounded and coordinated several community art collectives: first *LatiNegro* and then *Sol & Soul*. In his poetry, performances, and cultural activism, articulated especially in *The Immigrant Museum* (2003), Avilés chronicled the immigrant and everyday lives of Salvadorans, Latinas/os, and others crossing paths in the greater Washington, DC Metropolitan Area. From other physical and subjective locations, U.S. Central Americans like Héctor Tobar (*The Tattooed Soldier*, 1998) and Francisco Goldman (*The Long Night of White Chickens*, 1992; *The Ordinary Seaman*, 1997) further explored Central American diasporic experiences in the United States. With Goldman, Tobar, Bencastro, Galindo, Cortez, Avilés, and other cultural producers mentioned herein, U.S. Latina/o literature is shown to dialogue critically with historical and contemporary issues and struggles.

THE RECOVERY OF CRITICAL U.S. LATINO/A BOOM NARRATIVES

In "Latino Sacrifice in the Discourse of Citizenship: Acting Against the 'Mainstream,' 1985–1988," Newman (1992), writing on films of that period, warned against "deemphas[ing] the history of struggle involved in bringing multicultural representations into circulation in the national culture" (p. 68), a critique that is moreover applicable to the U.S. Latino/a literary boom. She also noted the consistent "devalorization of Latinos/as as citizens" (p. 68) in the trans/national media and imaginary. Challenging the official propaganda of "The Decade of the Hispanic," long-standing and recently situated Latino/a literary and cultural producers, as we have seen, often exposed the social inequities affecting Latinos/as and other groups while ironically participating in the production of a critical double-voiced U.S. Latino/a cultural boom.

In her one-page story, titled "Bread," found in *Woman Hollering Creek and Other Stories*, Cisneros (1991) critiques the position of Latinos/as in U.S. society, especially when her Chicana protagonist, Italian American boyfriend in tow, recollects her old "city memories" of poverty, inadequate housing, and inaccessible healthcare (p. 84). She writes:

> Driving down the street with buildings that remind him, he says, of how charming this city is. And me remembering when I was little, a cousin's baby who died from swallowing rat poison in a building like these. (p. 84)

In Cisneros's stories, Latino/a protagonists embody the effects of historically produced social inequities in the United States. In lieu of institutional resources and economic means, Cisneros's characters make use of their own capacities and communities. Older siblings provide childcare ("Salvador Late or Early," 1991, pp. 10–11); children recycle hand-me-downs and second-hand goods ("Barbie–Q," 1991, pp. 14–16); young unwed mothers take that "crooked walk" and educate other young women by example ("One Holy Night," 1991, pp. 27–35); and men and women attempt to escape the loneliness of their gender alienation ("There was a Man, There was a Woman," 1991, pp. 133–134). In "Little Miracles, Kept Promises" (1991, pp. 116–129), the voice of one Chicana/o penitent sums up the needs of the community at large:

> Please send us clothes, furniture, shoes, dishes. We need anything that don't eat. Since the fire we have to start all over again and Lalo's disability check ain't much and don't go far. Zulema would like to finish school but I says she can just forget about it now. She's our oldest and her place is at home helping us out.... (117)

Cisneros's protagonists survive in *Woman Hollering Creek*, not by the aid of the State but through their own collective effort, resourcefulness, and empowering ability to "translate" oppression into the "special power" (p. 128) of cultural resilience. Cisneros's characters are never victims, but, rather, survivors of social inequities who stand up to the forces that would disempower them.

Along these lines, Pilar Puente—the disenchanted Cuban-born, U.S.-bred punk artist of Cristina García's *Dreaming in Cuban* (1992)—aptly poses the question that reverberates across many of the texts examined here: "We're living the American dream?" (p. 137). This statement turned into an interrogative articulates the linguistic sensibilities and critical consciousnesses taking shape in Pilar and new generations of Latinos/as in the United States. This form of linguistic and cultural code-switching and of articulating an interrogative, recognizable to the Spanish speaker by the rise in intonation at the end of the sentence (hence the question mark), situates Pilar at linguistic, cultural, and sociopolitical intersections. Like other protagonists of contemporary U.S. Latino/a cultural texts, Pilar is a transcultural subject embodying the intersections of language, culture, history, ethnicity, race, and gender. The youngest of three generations of women, which include her grandmother Celia, a devotee of the Cuban Revolution, and her mother Lourdes, an excessive capitalist who flees Cuba, Pilar negotiates two world orders: Communist Cuba and Capitalist USA. A novel about those who have broken with the Cuban Revolution of 1959 and immigrated to the United States, *Dreaming in Cuban*, like Cisneros's *Women Hollering Creek* and Alvarez's *How the García Girls Lost Their Accents*, is also about demythologizing history and examining the fissures where Latino/a subjects accommodate the local effects of State economies, policies, and ideologies in the 20th and 21st centuries.

Living between two ideological poles, Pilar Puente, as her name implies, is not only a "pillar" of street-smarts and defiance but a bridge between the painful vulnerabilities that the women in her family turn into strengths, depending on their sociopolitical contexts. Pilar demystifies the two ideologies represented by her grandmother and mother and comes to terms with the contradictions of her Latinidades. Upon momentarily visiting Cuba, she discovers that she must "return to New York," where she belongs, "not instead of here, but more than here…" (García, 1992, p. 236). Although Pilar reaches a temporary *seize fire* between her multiple identities (for the novel is really about her ethnicity as Cuban American), she also represents the possibility of constructing hybrid Latino/a cultural imaginaries, for, as she puts it, "there's only my imagination where our history should be" (García, 1992, p. 138). With the death and memoralizing of her grandmother, Pilar sets adrift her ties to Cuba, letting them blend and blur in reconstructions that show history, culture, and identity to be a product of narrative strategies, ideological (re)positionings, and emplotments of cultural forms (White, 1978). *Dreaming in Cuban*, hence, shows history to be a narrative construction and imaginary projection of desires for a mother, motherland, and a sense of belonging in diaspora.

With regard to Central America, Héctor Tobar's novel *The Tattooed Soldier* (1998) focuses on the relationship between homeland violence, displacement, and the relocation of millions of Central Americans to the United States. The novel, like García's *Dreaming in Cuban*, is about forging connections between Latino diasporas and their homelands. In *The Tattooed Soldier*, Tobar, however, traces the vertiginous movement of a Guatemalan refugee to the United States, as he is pursued by the memory of his family's massacre at the hands of an unknown *tattooed soldier*, who had been trained in methods of war at the U.S. School of the Americas. In the streets of Los Angeles, Antonio Bernal finally collides with his victimizer, Guillermo Longoria. Unbeknownst to one another, each man has fled Guatemala and now lives in the same city. In a symbolic reversal of histories and fates, or a moment of *poetic justice*, Bernal hunts down the man with the jaguar on his arm, taking matters into his own hands in the streets of Los Angeles during the uprisings of 1992.

In the midst of an ethnic war in Los Angeles, the clash between Bernal and Longoria recalls the wars in Central America in the 1980s, which displaced many people and forced them to flee their countries. Beyond a personal act of avenging his family's torture and killing in Guatemala, Bernal's run-in with his torturer on U.S. soil symbolizes the end of impunity for war crimes committed in Central America. It becomes quite apparent that this is no chance meeting. In confronting Longoria, Bernal challenges the war machine of the United States, which throughout the 1980s financed many of the regimes in Central America. At this moment of personal and historical reckoning, "Antonio spun in the flux between decades and countries, time and space distorted. He was in a park in Guatemala, a park in Los Angeles. The present, the past, somewhere in between" (Tobar, 1998, p. 79). The young immigrant Bernal, thus, is the carrier of the violent and violated history of Central America, which is unleashed in Los Angeles, amid the immigrant community who witnesses the clash of histories embodied by the jaguar man and the former university student. Bernal is part of a politicized youth forced into migrancy in the 1980s. It is this group, in particular, that contributes to the politicization of counterpart generations in Latino communities in the United States, interpellating them with revolutionary and solidarity discourses in the 1980s and 1990s.

Finally, in Julia Alvarez's *How the García Girls Lost Their Accent* (1992), the protagonist Yolanda García also travels to the United States with memories of untold violence and violations represented by the "black furred thing lurking in the corners of my life … wailing over some violation that lies at the center of my art" (p. 290). Like Pilar Puente of García's *Dreaming in Cuban* and Antonio Bernal of Tobar's *The Tattooed Soldier*, Yolanda in Alvarez's novel grapples with a history that eventually pulls her back to take care of unfinished family and national business in her native Dominican Republic. The reader learns that Yolanda's family belongs to the Dominican national bourgeoisie that profits from the dominant and oppressive social order. The "black furred thing" that immigrates with Yolanda to the United States signifies class and racial privilege built on socioeconomic and political violence, albeit much obfuscated and disavowed throughout much of Alvarez's text. Indeed, Latin American immigrants as of the 1990s come from all walks of life, bearing riches as well as great disadvantages and horrors.

As Alvarez, Cisneros, García, and Tobar show in their respective works, U.S. Latinos/as increasingly negotiate and reconstruct increasingly complex Latinidades that are situated in divergent histories, socioeconomic hierarchies, race and ethnic stratifications, gender and sexual violence, and geocultural displacements, among other things. Although Yolanda García longs to find a home in the Dominican Republic (Alvarez, 1992, p. 11) and Pilar Puente dreams of reconstructing Cuba in her imaginary way (García, 1992), Tobar's weary Guatemalan refugee finds neither safe haven nor peace in the United States. Many of Cisneros' Chicano/a characters also recognize that they, too, live in "that borrowed country" ("Tepeyac," 1991, p. 23), known to many as the United States. Thus, Cisneros, Garcia, Alvarez, Tobar, and other contemporary U.S. Latino/a authors write about transnational displacements and diasporas. They problematize what it means to relocate across territory and subjective spaces in the north and south of the Americas. Their texts not only link the United States to domestic and foreign transgressions but also represent local social inequities and global forces producing diasporic experiences. Whereas the U.S. Cuban embargo and blockade keeps Pilar from her grandmother, the 1965 U.S.-backed coup in the Dominican Republic forces the García family out of their country. In a similar vein, in María Helena Viramontes's short story "The Cariboo Cafe" (1985), the wars in Central America drive a woman mourning her murdered son out of her country (pp. 61–75); the same wars push the student Antonio Bernal into the belly of the monster in *The Tattooed Soldier*. In this transnational U.S. Latino/a literature, global issues are played out in the imaginary spaces of Latino/a protagonists, who carry the scars of larger injustices, displacements, and diasporas.

CONCLUSIONS

The production and publication of U.S. Latin/o texts representing long-standing and emerging Latinidades is thus situated in significant demographic and discursive shifts occurring not only in the U.S. multicultural and transnational publishing world but also in the politics of representation of Latinos/as, who participate significantly in "[i]nventing the Hispanic Psyche" (Stavans, 1993b). Actively engaged in the bringing about of new social formations and identities, U.S. Latino/a literature and cultural production participates in the production of more diverse and divergent images, discourses, voices, and texts across the hemisphere. Indeed, U.S. Latino/a literary and cultural production as of the 1990s serves as a site of contact and intersections, wherein peoples who had been separated by political borders translate, define, and imagine Latinidades across the hemisphere.

Through venues admittedly ambivalent, the corpus of U.S. Latino/a literary and cultural production examined here addresses the issues and needs of a growing constituency of transnational U.S. Latinos/as. The growing presence and popularity of this literature show U.S. Latinos/as to be a critical mass in the process of reimagining themselves in light of significant demographic and discursive shifts. This literature articulates and resonates with diverse Latinidades as well as the various historical and contemporary political, economic, and cultural issues of U.S. Latinos/as. As Aparicio (2004) notes, the writers identified with the U.S. Latino/a boom and thereafter "come from different social and class experiences and educational backgrounds, which in many cases differed from the marginal identities and self-taught formations of the authors, writers, and artists of the 1960s and 1970s" (p. 368). Indeed, U.S. Latino/a literature as of the 1980s opens up to the world at large, as the United States becomes more transnationalized by Latinos/as' transmigratory presence.

Among those gaining voice in the 1990s and thereafter are second-generation, English-dominant Latinos/as (Aparicio, 2004, p. 368) as well as recent immigrants from Latin America and Spain such as those whose stories are collected in *Los sueños de América* (González Viaña, 2001) and *Se habla español: Voces latinas en USA* (Paz Soldán & Fuguet, 2000), both of which are published in Spanish and by European transnational presses such as Alfaguara and Santillana. Edited by Paz Soldán and Fuguet (2000), *Se habla español* compiles a number of short stories focusing on "Latin American experiences in the U.S.," as imagined and written outside of the U.S. geographical territory, but within its expansive geocultural reach. Many of the writers whose works are included in *Se habla español* have never resided in or visited the United States, yet they identify with an imagined Latino diasporic condition spanning the globe. That such a book could purport to engage with and represent Latino/a cultural imaginaries and identities outside of historically traditional ethnic configurations and U.S. geographical locations signals the transnational diffusion of Latin American diasporas and the globalization of Latinidades across the world. Latinos/as can now be said to inhabit not only the United States but Latin America, Europe, and the entire world as well. And that is how the Latino world turns in the 21st century.

NOTES

1. Rostagno (1997) examined the marketing practices, translation politics, and role of large publishing corporations determining the publication of Latin American literature in the United States. She suggested that the 1960s' and 1970s' big *boom* of novels by Gabriel García Márquez and others staged the marketing of Latin America to U.S. readers.
2. Robbins (2004) examined the globalization of the publishing industry in Spain, offering insights into the commodification of certain Latin American texts and authors by mainstream presses like Random House. A subsidiary of the European publishing conglomerate Bertelsmann, Random House operates the Vintage Español division, which publishes for the Latino English and Spanish-speaking market. Vintage has published the works of Isabel Allende, Julia Alvarez, Ana Castillo, Sandra Cisneros, Laura Esquivel, Gabriel García Márquez, Pablo Neruda, and Esmeralda Santiago. In her study of the Spanish publishing market, Robbins suggested that although some authors and texts succeed in the transnational publishing industry, publishing opportunities for many Latin American and Latino/a writers, who might have once published with small and/or independent presses, are greatly diminished.
3. In 2001, HarperCollins inaugurated its Rayo Hispanic division—the first English/Spanish-language imprint in the United States, followed by Random House/Vintage Español, Penguin/Plume, and Ballantine/Un Mundo, and other divisions of major publishing houses. The Web site for HaperCollins Rayo imprint states, "Rayo publishes books that embody the diversity within the Latino community, in both English and Spanish-language editions, connecting culture with thought, and invigorating tradition with spirit." Latino/a authors listed at the Web site include Isabel Allende, Rudolfo Anaya, Carolina Garcia Aguilera, Yxta Maya Murray, Jorge Ramos, Esmeralda Santiago, Ilan Stavans, Victor Villasenor, and Alberto Fuguet, among others. Indistinguishably lumping together Latino/a writers from Latin America and the United States, Rayo, like Vintage Español, in effect, "transnationalizes" certain brands of Latino/a writers, texts, and Latinidades. See the HarperCollins Web site http://www.harpercollins.com/imprints. asp?imprint=Rayo. For a discussion on the "ethnic imprint debate," see also Herrera Mulligan (2004).
4. See *Woman Hollering Creek* for inset of reviews.
5. In an appearance at the University of California, Santa Cruz, in the spring of 1993, Guillermo Goméz Peña critiqued the appeal of and to multiculturalism in the hegemonic sphere, referring to it as "multicultist."
6. Mohr (1986) explained that her agent suggested that she write more "authentic" short stories filled with "sexual encounter, gang fights [...] the police and the community, drugs. Give us the kind of facts that would make this book a best seller" (p. 108).

REFERENCES

Alvarez, J. (1992). *How the García Girls Lost Their Accent*. New York: Plume.

Alvarez, J. (1994). *De cómo las chicas García perdieron su acento* (Jordi Gubert, Trans.). Barcelona: Ediciones B.

Aparicio, F. R. (2004). U.S. Latino Expressive Cultures. In D. G. Gutiérrez (Ed.), *The Columbia History of Latinos in the United States Since 1960* (pp. 355–390). New York: Columbia University Press.

Aparicio, F. R., & Chávez-Silverman, S. (Eds.). (1997). Introduction. In F. R. Aparicio & S. Chávez-Silverman (Eds.), *Tropicalizations: Transcultural Representations of Latinidad* (pp. 1–17). Hanover, MA: University Press of New England.

Argueta, J. (1997). *Las Frutas del Centro y Otros Sabores/Fruits From the Center and Other Flavors*. Berkeley, CA: Canterbury Press.

Arias, S. (Comp.) (1977). *Recopilación de textos sobre Alejo Carpentier*. La Habana: Casa de las Américas.

Arias, A. (2003). Central American Americans: Invisibility, Power, and Representation in the US Latino World. *Latino Studies, 1*(1), 168–187.

Avilés, Q. (2003). *The Immigrant Museum*. México, D.F.: PinStudio y Raíces de Papel.

Bencastro, M. (1998). *Odyssey to the North* (Susan Giersbach-Rascón, Trans.). Houston: Arte Público Press.

Bencastro, M. (2005). *A Promise to Keep* (Susan Giersbach-Rascón, Trans.). Houston: Arte Público Press.

Berona, D. A. (1993). Review of Graciela Limón's *In Search of Bernabé*. *Library Journal, 118*(3), 153.

Bolívar, S. (1815). Contestación de un americano meridional a un caballero de esta isla (Carta de Jamaica). In G. Soriano (Ed.) (1983), *Simón Bolívar: Escritos Políticos* (pp. 61–84). Madrid: Alianza Editorial.

Buss, Fan Leeper. (1991). *Journey of the Sparrow*. New York: Puffin Books/Penguin.

Castillo, A. (1993). *So Far From God: A Novel*. New York: W. W. Norton & Company.

Christie, J. S., & González, J. B. (Eds.). (2006). *Latino Boom: An Anthology of U.S. Latino Literature*. New York: Pearson/Longman.

Cisneros, S. (1991). *Woman Hollering Creek and Other Stories*. New York: Random House.

Cisneros, S. (1996). *El arroyo de la Llorona y otros cuentos* (Lilian Valenzuela, Trans.). New York: Vintage Español.

Cortez, Mayamérica. (1995). *Nostalgias y soledades*. San Salvador: Editorial Clásicos Roxsil.

Cowy Kim, K., Serrano, A., Ramos, L., & Rocamora, R. (Eds.). (2000). *Izote Vos: A Collection of Salvadoran American Writing and Visual Art*. San Francisco: Pacific News Service.

Culture Clash. (2003). Anthems: Culture Clash in the District. In *Culture Clash in Americca: Four Plays* (pp. 151–221). New York: Theatre Communications Group, Inc.

Dávila, A. (2001). *Latinos, Inc.: The Marketing and Making of a People*. Los Angeles: University of California Press.

De la Mora, Sergio. (2006). *Cinemachismo: Masculinities and Sexuality in Mexican Film*. Austin: University of Texas Press.

Díaz, J. (1996). *Drown*. New York: Riverhead Books.

Díaz, J. (1997). *Negocios* (Eduardo Lago, Trans.). New York: Vintage.

Flores, J., & Yúdice, G. (1990). Living Borders/Buscando America: Languages of Latino Self-formation. *Social Text, 8*(Fall), 57–85.

Galindo, M. (1996). *Retazos*. San Francisco: Editorial Solaris.

García, C. (1992). *Dreaming in Cuban: A Novel*. New York: Ballantine Books.

García, C. (1993). *Soñar en cubano* (Marisol Palés Castro, Trans.). New York: Ballantine Books.

García Canclini, N. (2001). *Consumers and Citizens: Globalization and Multicultural Conflicts* (George Yúdice, Trans.). Minneapolis: University of Minnesota Press.

Genette, G. (1997). *Paratexts: Thresholds of Interpretations*. Cambridge: Cambridge University Press.

Goldman, F. (1992). *The Long Night of White Chickens*. New York: The Atlantic Monthly Press.

Goldman, F. (1994). *La larga noche de los pollos blancos* (Jordi Beltrán, Trans.). Barcelona: Anagrama.

Goldman, F. (1997). *The Ordinary Seaman*. New York: Grove Press.

Goldman, F. (1999, February 28). State of the Art: Latino Writers. *The Washington Post*, p. 1, 8–10.

González, R. (Ed.). (1998). *Touching the Fire: Fifteen Poets of Today's Latino Renaissance*. New York: Anchor Books.

González Viaña, E. (Ed.). (2001). *Los sueños de América*. Miami: Santillana USA Publishing.

Hernández Cruz, V. (1986). Mountains in the North: Hispanic Writing in the U.S.A. *Americas Review, 14*(3–4), 114.

Herrera Mulligan, M. (2004). A Good Read: With a Pulitzer in Tow, Ethnic Publishing Imprints Are on the Rise. What Will That Mean for Books By and About People of Color? *Colorlines Magazine: Race, Action, Culture*. Retrieved December 10, 2006, from http://www.findarticles.com/p/articles /mi_m0KAY/is_3_7/ai_ n6178110/print

Kanellos, N. (1986). U.S. Hispanic Literature in the Anglo-American Empire. *Americas Review, 14*(3–4), 103–105.

Kanellos, N. (Ed.). (1993). Introduction. In N. Kanellos (Ed.), *Short Fiction by Hispanic Writers of the United States* (pp. 7–11). Houston: Arte Público Press.

Limón, G. (1993). *In Search of Bernabé*. Houston: Arte Públio Press.

Limón, G. (1997). *En busca de Barnabé* (Miguel Angel Aparicio, Trans.). Houston, TX: Arte Público Press.

Martí, José. (1891). Nuestra América/Our America. In D. Shnookal & M. Muñiz (Eds.) (1999), *José Martí Reader: Writings on the Americas*. New York: Ocean Press.

Mohr, N. (1986). On Being Authentic. *Americas Review, 14*(3-4), 106–109.

Mohr, N. (1990). The Journey Toward a Common Ground: Struggle and Identity of Hispanics in the U.S.A. *Americas Review, 18*(1), 81–85.

Moraga, C. (1995). Art in América con Acento. In L. Castillo-Speed (Ed.), *Latina: Women's Voices From the Borderlands* (pp. 211–220). New York: Touchstone Books.

Negrón-Muntaner, F. (2004). Jennifer's Butt: Valorizing the Puerto Rican Racialized Female Body. In *Puerto Ricans and the Latinization of American Culture* (pp. 228–246). New York: New York University Press.

Newman, K. (1992). Latino Sacrifice in the Discourse of Citizenship: Acting Against the "Mainstream," 1985–1988. In C. A. Noriega (Ed.), *Chicanos and Film: Representation and Resistance* (pp. 59–73.). Minneapolis: University of Minnesota Press.

Noriega, C. A. (1990). Chicano Cinema and the Horizon of Expectations: A Discursive Analysis of Film Reviews in the Mainstream, Alternative and Hispanic Press, 1987–1988. *Aztlán, 19*(2), 1–32. (Original work published 1988)

Paz Soldán, E., & Fuguet, A. (Eds.). (2000). *Se habla español: Voces latinas in USA*. Miami: Santillana USA Publishing/ Alfaguara.

Perez-Firmat, G. (Ed.). (1990). *Do the Americas Have a Common Literature?* Durham, NC: Duke University Press.

Perez-Firmat, G. (1994). *Life on the Hyphen: The Cuban American Way*. Austin: University of Texas Press.

Review of Graciela Limón's In Search of Bernabé. (1993). *Publishers Weekly, 240*(30), 63.

Review of Héctor Tobar's The Tattooed Soldier. (1998). *Publishers Weekly, 245*(15), 48–50.

Robbins, J. (2004). Neocolonialism, Neoliberalism, and National Identities: The Spanish Publishing Crisis and the Marketing of Central America. *Istmo 8* [online]. Retrieved December 10, 2006, from http://www.denison.edu/ collaborations/ istmo/n08/articulos/neocolonialism.html

Rodríguez, A. P. (2001). Refugees of the South: Central Americans in the U.S. Latino Imaginary. *American Literature, 73*(2), 387–412.

Rodriguez, R. (1982). *Hunger of Memory: The Education of Richard Rodriguez*. New York: Bantam Books.

Rostagno, I. (1997). *Searching for Recognition: The Promotion of Latin American Literature in the United States*. Westport, CT: Greenwood Press.

Saldívar, J. D. (1991). *The Dialects of Our America: Genealogy, Cultural Critique, and Literary History*. Durham, NC: Duke University Press.

Santiago, E. (1994). *When I Was Puerto Rican*. New York: Vintage.

Santiago, E. (1994). *Cuando era puertorriqueña*. New York: Vintage Español.

Spillers, H. J. (1991). *Comparative American Identities: Race, Sex, and Nationality in the Modern Text*. New York: Routledge.

Shorris, E. (1992). *Latinos: A Biography of the People*. New York: W. W. Norton & Co.

Silva Gruesz, K. (2002). *Ambassadors of Culture: The Transamerican Origins of Latino Writing*. Princeton, NJ: Princeton University Press.

Stavans, I. (1993a, January 18). Labyrinth of Plenitude. *The Nation*, 65–67.

Stavans, I. (1993b). Inventing the Hispanic Psyche. *MultiCultural Review, 1*(4), 20–38.

Tobar, H. (1998). *The Tattooed Soldier*. New York: Penguin.

Viramontes, H. M. (1985). The Cariboo Café. In *The Moths and Other Stories* (pp. 59–75). Houston, TX: Arte Público Press.

White, H. (1978). The Historical Text as Literary Artifact. In *The Tropics of Discourse: Essays in Cultural Criticism* (pp. 81–100). Baltimore: The Johns Hopkins University Press.

Yúdice, G., Franco, J., & Flores, J. (Eds.). (1992). *On Edge: The Crisis of Contemporary Latin American Culture*. Minneapolis: University of Minnesota Press.

Zimmerman, M. (1992). *U.S. Latino Literature: An Essay and Annotated Bibliography*. Chicago: MARCH/Abrazo Press.

CHAPTER 15

Religion and Religiosity

Miguel A. De La Torre

INTRODUCTION

Latinos/as are Catholics. They are also Protestants, Evangelicals, and Pentecostals. They bend their knees before Obatalá, Changó, and Oggún, *orishas* (African quasi-deities) from the religion known as *Santería*. Others proclaim a faith in one of the other major world religions (i.e., Judaism or Islam). In times of illness, some rely on the ancestral Amerindian religious traditions like *curanderismo*, whereas others found solace in the U.S.-based faiths of Mormonism or Jehovah Witnesses. Still, others are simply atheists. Hispanics are not a monolithic group, nor do they worship in a monolithic fashion. Contrary to popular stereotypes, all Latina/os are not Catholics. Although Hispanics are not monolithic, their faiths and beliefs, or lack thereof, do play an important role in understanding their overall identity. For this reason, a book such as this would be incomplete if it failed to examine the religiosity of the Hispanic community.

To seriously consider the religiosity of any group of people, in our case Latina/os, is to contradict Durkheim's sociological, Freud's psychological, or Marx's economic functionalism, each of which insisted that societal structures powerfully determine religious beliefs. As historian and philosopher of religion Mircea Eliade reminds us, the faith of a people, as the irreducible sacred, resists being reduced to an effervescence of the so-called underlying social reality. Instead, the reverse is claimed: Religion can shape society; it is not simply a dependent variable of other forces. Eliade asserted that society, psychology, or economics affects religion, but their influences are neither dominant nor determining (1963, p. xii). For this reason, this volume dedicates a chapter to the religiosity of Hispanics. Specifically, this chapter will explore the different faith traditions among Latinos/as and the impact they have on their community.

CHRISTIAN AFFILIATIONS

According to the most recent quantitative data about Hispanics' religious affiliations, as conducted by the Hispanic Churches in American Public Life (HCAPL), 93% of U.S. Latina/os identified with the Christian faith, 6% chose no particular religious preference, 1% declared practicing another world religion, and 0.37% claimed to be atheist or agnostic. For those who claimed Christianity, about 70% across all generations, identify themselves as Roman Catholic, whereas about 22% consider themselves Protestant. When compared to Protestants, Catholic Latinos/as are more likely to be immigrants (54%) and thus more likely to only speak Spanish (33%). When only Protestant denominations were considered, the first three traditions with the highest concentration of Latinos/as were Pentecostals. They were the Assembly of Christian Churches, the Pentecostal Church of God, and the Apostolic Assembly of Faith in Christ Jesus, which respectively ranked 3rd, 4th, and 10th among non-Catholic Christian traditions within the U.S. In general, these Protestant groups tended to be theologically and morally more conservative.

Hispanic Churches in American Life also discovered a growth of nondenominational religious affiliations. However, this does not necessarily mean a move toward secularism, for the vast majority who chose not to identify with a particular denomination did self-identify as a born-again Christian (75% or 37% of all Hispanics). This born-again movement has made significant inroads among Latina/os. Twenty-eight percent of all Latinos/as self-identified as born-again *and* Pentecostal, Charismatic, or spirit-filled. Twenty-one percent of all Hispanic mainline Protestants did likewise, as did 22% of all Latino/a Catholics.

One of the misconceptions that exists is that Hispanics are leaving Catholicism and becoming Protestants. In reality, those who are supposedly converting to Protestantism are in fact switching to Jehovah's Witness and Mormon traditions. This growth is not necessarily a new phenomenon, but rather has its roots in the 1920s. Today, Jehovah's Witness, with more than 800,000 Latina/o adherents and more than 2,200 Spanish-speaking congregations, is the largest non-Catholic Christian tradition among Hispanics, with the highest conversion rate among Hispanic immigrants of any other Latino/a non-Catholic tradition. Mormons rank eighth among Hispanic largest religious traditions (Espinosa, 2006, pp. 28–43).

Catholicism

One of the most enduring myths about Latino/a religiosity is that all Hispanics are Catholic. In reality, for every Hispanic who converts to Catholicism, four leave it. Recently, over 3 million Latina/os left the Catholic Church (Espinosa, 2006, p. 42). Since the territorial conquest of northern Mexico during the Mexican-American War, when the border crossed over Mexican Catholics, Hispanics found themselves in a hostile Eurocentric Protestant world that spared no expense in attempting to convert the natives. The religious component of Manifest Destiny tried to "save" the Latina/o Catholic "idolater." Race and religious supremacy, influenced by Euro-American hyperindividualism, stressed a personal piety that at times ignored the communal responsibilities crucial to the Mexican Catholic faith.

For Hispanic Catholics, an attempt is usually made to link popular movements (i.e., socio-political movements for human rights and dignity) with ecclesiastical authority. Commitment to social justice, as shaped by both papal encyclicals and the everyday struggles of Hispanics, becomes an expression of faith. Although the Catholic faith has advocated the importance of providing for the material needs of the poor, a shift from private charitable efforts to the civic sphere took shape. This development of a Hispanic perspective of Catholic thought viewed the hierarchical nature of the church with suspicion, for at times it imitated the race and class divisions existing within society (Stevens-Arroyo, 2006, pp. 169–175).

A Catholic movement influential among Hispanics has been *Cursillos de Cristiandad*. Originating in Franco's Spain, the movement was conservative and hierarchical, focusing on the sacraments. By the mid-1960s, this lay movement spread to every part of the United States where Hispanic Catholics resided. *Cursillos* are retreat-type events where participants renew their commitment to the faith. They are encouraged to make these commitments emotionally, providing Catholics with the "born-again" experiences that until now have been used by Protestants and Pentecostals against them in their proselyting ventures (Stevens-Arroyo, 2006, pp. 175–176).

Protestantism

"To be Hispanic and Protestant," according to David Maldonado, "means to exist in the margins of two realities, a Hispanic world in which being Protestant means being at the margins of a Catholic context, and a Protestant world in which being Hispanic means being at the margins of a non-Hispanic context" (1999, p. 16). The reason why many Protestants feel marginalized within the Latino/a context is due in part to how mainline Eurocentric Protestant denominations came in contact with the Latina/o world. The first phase of contact occurred in the early 1820s, culminating with Texas' declaration of independence from Mexico and the subsequent Mexican-American War. During this time, a gradual increase of Protestant evangelistic endeavors aimed at Mexican Catholics living in the newly conquered territories began to take place in earnest. Although reasons for conversion are scarce, it is reasonable to assume that among the motivating factors were the following: (1) opportunity for social mobility, (2) continuous grievances over both Roman Catholic doctrine and Spanish oppression, and (3) the perceived social and economic benefits of assimilating to the dominant culture. The second phase began in the aftermath of the 1898 Spanish-American War. The opening of new territories through conquest (Cuba and Puerto Rico) and economic exploitation (gunboat diplomacy) in Central America and the Caribbean provided Protestants with greater opportunities to evangelize.

Still, converting to Protestantism in the United States does not exclude the Hispanic convert from the prevalent racism and classism within the overall U.S. culture. The most significant challenges faced by Hispanic mainline Protestants are the following: (1) poverty (congregations tend to be poorer than Euro-American Protestant churches), (2) racial discrimination, which leads to resistant and limited resources from the national level of the denomination, and (3) limited access to higher education, which contributes to a more working-class congregation lead by non-seminary-trained clergy (Hernández, 2006, pp. 184–190).

Evangélica/os

Some evangélico/as will argue that the 70 % of Hispanics who identify with Roman Catholicism might be too high, especially when the phenomenon of "cultural Catholics" and "nominalism" are taken into consideration. They are suspicious of Latinos/as who are Catholic only in name, where ecclesial adhesion to the church might be more custom-based rather than the product of a deep religious conviction.

For the most part, the Latino/a evangélico/a mission for humanity is the proclamation of the entire gospel so that the world can be transformed. The good news they hope to share is the liberating message of Christ who died outside the gate, outside of church power and doctrines, and outside the realm of privilege. It is this rejected stone that is used by God that served as the foundation of a new creation. Thus, evangélico/as view the Hispanic church, in spite of its economic and political weakness, as empowered to usher in personal conversion and social transformation. Contrary to stereotypes that view evangélica/os as politically conservative, some would argue that the roots of evangélica/os have always promoted radical social change. Change within a sinful world is brought about through the repentance of sins (personal and public) and faith in Jesus Christ. Although hot-button issues like abortion, gay marriage, immigration, or family values might at times drive the political agenda for the evangélico/as, only a liberating gospel can transform and provide a public witness to the movement of God's hand among God's people (Traverzo Galarza, 2006, pp. 193–197).

Pentecostalism

Within the Protestant community, Pentecostals comprise 64%, which is distributed over 150 distinctive indigenous and autonomous denominations, councils, and independent movements within the United States, Mexico, and Puerto Rico. If we consider all of Latin America, we can add 1,991 Pentecostal denominations, traditions, and councils to the 150, of which 1,767 are completely independent of U.S. influence (Espinosa, 2006, pp. 37–38). The Latina/o Pentecostal tradition is grounded in an evangelical Christianity that stresses the gifts of the Spirit along with the baptism of the Spirit, which is signified by speaking in tongues (glossolalia). For the Hispanic who is made to feel inferior because he could not master the language of the dominant culture, speaking in tongues debunks the supremacy of English by making all believers equal in language before God.

An attempt is made to break free from *sola scriptura* (only scripture) by emphasizing the Spirit of God. Central to Hispanic Pentecostalism is the *testimonios*, the testimonies. These *testimonios* allow the person to (1) be a witness of the Holy Spirit's movement to the faith community, (2) allow the Spirit, as Comforter, to minister to the needs of the faith community, and (3) allow the faith community to enter the reality of the Holy Spirit's presence in the everyday, a presence that can be marked by physical or emotional healing, deliverance from a life-controlling problem, or miraculous deliverance from mundane obstacles.

When poverty prevents proper medical care, the laying of hands to secure a healing fills a need for the believer. However, healing encompasses more than simply physical ailments. It also encompasses deliverance from such "ailments" like drug or alcohol dependency. Healing services prove crucial in leading some Catholics to convert to Pentecostalism (Sánchez Walsh, 2006, pp. 199–205).

CHRISTIAN SOCIAL LOCATION

As we have seen, there is no monolithic Christian experience among Latinos/as. Nevertheless, among the divergences some commonalities exist, specifically the Hispanic incorporation of worship, family, and justice into their religiosity.

Centrality of Worship

Worship as *fiesta* allows Hispanic Christian communities to express their individual and corporate relationship with God. Although variety exists on how different Latinos/a congregations approach worship, many churches across Catholic/Protestant boundaries hold some common beliefs, as in the case of the sacred *fiesta* concept. *Fiesta* can be translated as "party," a time of joy, festivity, and celebration—a by-product of being in God's presence. Worship is not a scripted drama to be watched but, rather, a neighborhood party to which all are invited to participate. As Justo González reminds us, the difference between our worship and that of the dominant culture is that we think in terms of planning a party more than rehearsing a performance (1996, pp. 20–21). This sacred *fiesta* usually includes an informal time of greeting and assembly, enthusiastic singing, and freely expressed praise. Both sin and the One who forgives sins are confessed by the community of faith, the emphasis being on the communal. As can be expected, some from the dominant culture find this view of worship as *fiesta* inappropriate and even offensive. Still, Hispanic Christian religiosity, through the *fiesta* worship, has constructed its own alternative public space for such "God-talk" (De La Torre & Aponte, 2001, pp. 63–65).

Centrality of Familia

In a North American context in which individualism is on the increase, among U.S. Hispanics there exists a countervailing impulse in *comunidad*, community. Even within the diversity of national origins, race, language facilities, denominations, and class, the omnipresent prominence of the notion and experience of community is a unifying factor and a resource for ministry, engagement with the dominant Euro-American culture, and theology. This concept of *comunidad* is best expressed as *familia*, family, perhaps the most important social institution in Latino/a cultures. However, *familia* is more than the Euro-American understanding of the nuclear family; it encompasses a broadly extended network of relatives and fictive kinship. Even when there might not be literal blood relations, there often is a re-creation of family through the *compradrazgo* system. Among Latino/a Catholics and some Hispanic Protestants who practice infant baptism (or baby dedication), the sponsoring godparents (*padrino*, *madrina*) become "coparents" (*compadres*, *comadres*) and enter into lifelong relationships not only with the child but also with the family. Within Latino/a Christian circles, specifically Protestants, members of the congregation refer to each other as *hermano* (brother) and *hermana* (sister). In effect, the church becomes a *familia* of believers (De La Torre & Aponte, 2001, pp. 65–66).

The Importance of Justice

One of the central tenets of Hispanic theological thought is *praxis*, doing the deed of justice. For most Latinos/as Christians, to know God is to do justice. Along with the biblical mandate of unconditional love, justice is an important component of Christianity. However, for Hispanic Christians, justice might very well be the most important component. Justice based on love toward one's neighbor is a reflection of one's love for and by God. Unlike the Euro-American emphasis on individualism and its religious expression of personal piety, justice for the Latina/o is understood as an activity that can only be practiced in community, never in isolation—for the concrete reality of sin is always manifested in relation to others. Thus, justice can only manifest itself in relation to others. Rather than being a private expression of faith, justice is, by definition, a public action: a public manifestation of God's acting grace in the lives of Hispanics. Here then is the crux of the difference between the ways in which Euro-Americans and Latinas/os do theology (De La Torre & Aponte, 2001, pp. 67–68).

CHRISTIAN THEOLOGICAL PERSPECTIVES

If, indeed, theology is a second act, a reflection of the praxis (action) committed by the Latino/a faith community—a community quite different from the social location of Euro-Americans—it can then be expected to produce theological perspectives quite different from the dominant culture. The Christian theological perspectives of the Hispanic community are influenced by, and influences, both their culture and identity. A few theological examples will illustrate how differently from Euro-American Christianity Latinas/os understand their faith.

God

The importance of *familia* is manifested in how Hispanics understand God. God as *amor* (love) is part of the family, as expressed in the term of endearment, *Diosito* (my little God) or *Papa Dios* (Daddy God). God is seen more as a loving and affectionate friend than some impersonal king up in the heavens. Thus, God is spoken to in intimate terms that reveal a familial relationship. The ritual understanding of *Diosito* is most vividly expressed through worship songs known as *coritos* that give voice to the hope of a disenfranchised people and the God of their faith (Alanís, 2006, pp. 11–16).

Jesus

For many Hispanics, Jesus is a *mestizo*. *Mestizo* is a term that signifies the racial and cultural mixture of a people. The history of conquest within the Western Hemisphere created a race out of European, Native, and African stock. Unfortunately, White supremacy has relegated the nonpure Whites to subordinate and subjugate spaces, creating feelings of unworthiness and inadequacies. However, those whom the world dismisses as inferior, God chooses to reveal Godself. Virgilio Elizondo (1983) insisted that the *mestizo* reality Latinas/os find themselves in is a privileged place where God's revelation takes place. Jesus' Galilean identity was no accident. Like today's Hispanic, Jesus comes from where borders clash. Rather than coming from Jerusalem, the center of Jewish life, Jesus was born in Galilee, the margins of Jewish power, prestige, and privileges—an area viewed with suspicion by the pure-bred Jews of Jerusalem because of the area's racial mixing (Elizondo, 1983, p. 49).

The radicalness of the incarnation is not so much that the Creator of the universe became a frail human but, rather, that God chose to become poor, to take the form of a slave. As such, Jesus willingly assumed the role of the ultradisenfranchised. Like so many Hispanics today who live a life of deprivation, Jesus was born into, lived, and died in poverty—the ultimate act of solidarity with today's marginalized people (De La Torre, 2002, pp. 108–109).

Spirit

The charismatic revival experienced among many different religious traditions has produced among Hispanic believers a liberative theological response to their disenfranchisement. This response was explained by Eldin Villafañe (1993), who attempted to elucidate how Latina/os comprehend the working of the Spirit. Interpreting Galatians 5:25, Villafañe maintained that to live in the Spirit (a theological self-understanding) is to also walk in the Spirit (an ethical self-understanding). The historical project of the Spirit is to participate in God's Reign—a reign concerned with the establishment of justice by restraining evil and fostering conditions for an ethical moral order. Through the power of the Spirit, structures of sin and evil are challenged and confronted as disenfranchised Latino/a congregations receive charismatic empowerment and the spiritual resources to encounter social struggles (Villafañe , 1993, p. 195).

Trinity

Even though the dominant Euro-American culture emphasizes the Trinity as three separate entities, the average Christian still perceives a hierarchy, with Father being first, followed by the Son, and trailed by the Spirit. Yet, Father, Son, and Spirit do not exist in a hierarchy, rather, all three share equally in substance, power, and importance. For Hispanic churches to believe in the Trinity is not an attempt to explain this mystery intellectually but, rather, to follow the model set. The Triune God provides an economic pattern of sharing for those who claim belief in the doctrine of the Trinity, one that subverts any economic system requiring an undereducated and under-skilled reserve army of laborers so that the few can disproportionately hoard the majority of the wealth. Each person of the Trinity fully participates in divinity, sharing God's power and nature while maintaining their distinct functions—for God's nature is to share. This concept of sharing becomes the ideal model for how Latina/o congregations attempt to do church (De La Torre, 2004a, pp. 176–177).

Marianism

For Hispanics, specifically Catholics, the Virgin Mary plays a significant role within the faith community. Her manifestations as *Las Virgenes de Guadalupe* and *Cobre* impact and inform Hispanic religious thought by characterizing the hopes and aspiration of the faith community, regardless of national ethnicity. Several manifestations of Mary symbolize the birth of a new racial/ethnic identity, as she ceases to be a European White figure. Usually she appears as a bronzed woman of color, a color that symbolizes life, specifically as the color of the new Latin American race. She also provides dignity for the oppressed. Rather than first appearing to the religious leaders, she identified with the economic and racial outcasts by appearing to them in the color of oppression, thus severing the bond between inferiority and non-Whiteness. Not surprisingly, the earliest devotees of *la virgen* were Native Indians and slaves (De La Torre & Aponte, 2001, p. 92).

Sin

Unlike the dominant Euro-American culture, Latina/os also emphasize the importance of communal or corporate sin. Influenced by a hyperindividualism, the dominant culture seems to place a premium on personal piety. Additionally, although individual moral behavior is important, for the Hispanic community of faith so is the communal moral behavior. Sin is also understood to be inherent within social structures. Jesus' mission was not solely to save individuals from their sins but also, and just as importantly, to save the community from the sins of its social structures.

Oppression as Hispanic's ethnic discrimination transcends personal biases, for, in reality, it is the collective bias of society. These biases, in turn, are institutionalized by the dominant culture. Latinos/as facing discriminatory practices often realize that the source of this form of violence is not necessarily found in an individual within an organization, rather, the organization is constructed to protect the privileged space of the dominant culture at the expense of the disenfranchised. Hence, individual repentance is insufficient to change and/or challenge the status quo. Institutions also must repent by unmasking their normative procedures (De La Torre & Aponte, 2001, pp. 81–82).

Salvation

For many Hispanic Christians, it appears that Jesus links salvation with praxis (actions) of liberation. Such an understanding of salvation subverts the dominant Euro-American culture's reduction of the salvific act to the recitation of a proclamation of belief or a baptism ceremony. Influenced by Luther, Euro-Americans, specifically Protestants, insist that salvation can never be earned, but, rather, it is a gift from God. "We are saved by grace, not works, least anyone should boast." Although Latina/os agree that salvation begins as a love praxis from God, they insist that engaging in justice-based praxis is an outward expression of an inward conversion.

NON-CHRISTIAN AFFILIATIONS

Not all Latinas/os are Christians. Some belong to major world religions, others follow more indigenous traditions. Any study of Hispanic religiosity would be incomplete if it did not also explore these non-Christian expressions of faith.

Judaism and Latino/a Jews

With the expansion of the Roman Empires, Jewish communities existed in every corner of the empire, including the Iberian peninsula. There they flourished. Although periodically persecuted by both Christian and Muslim rulers, a large and culturally thriving Jewish community sustained itself. They were so successful that, to this day, half of the Jewish world is known as *Sephardi*, which means "Spanish." In spite of persecutions, many Iberian Jews served as advisors, linguists, and financiers in Muslim and Christian courts.

When Christian Iberia embarked on a campaign of *reconquista* (reconquest) of lands under Muslim control, Jews within those lands often faced the choice of conversion, expulsion, or death. Some changed their names to circumvent the royal decree that Jews could not immigrate to the new lands recently "discovered" by Columbus. Several of these *conversos* (converted Jews) fled to the outermost realms of New Spain, as far away as possible from the religious and political authorities. They settled in areas known today as California, Texas, New Mexico, and Arizona, where many of their descendants still live. For descendants of these exiles, Judaism has been an uninterrupted faith, and for many others, it has been a well-kept but persistent secret in family histories.

Family rites, traditions, customs, and stories containing suspiciously Jewish characteristics become clues for some Hispanics about their Jewish heritage. Once the family roots become known, some Hispanics have decided to lay aside the religion in which they were raised in favor of the religion of their ancestors. As they sought a new place within their community, these Latino/a converts found opposition from Jews who believe that they were not authentically Jewish, whereas some Christians charged them with abandoning their faith.

In addition to those reconnecting with their Jewish heritage, there are Latin American communities that have been openly Jewish, and their members have always struggled as a marginalized people. As some came to the United States and became part of Hispanic communities, they brought their faith and popular religiosity. For example, Cuba has been a major site for Jewish settlements composed of refugees escaping persecution. Spanish and Portuguese Jews arrived either with the conquering Spaniards as *conversos* and crypto-Jews (secret Jews) or in later migrations from the island of Curaçao, the center of Sephardic culture in the Caribbean. Later, in 1898, as a consequence of the United States' military presence on the islands of Puerto Rico and Cuba, there was a migration of American Jews. There were additional migrations of some European Jews to Latin America prior to World War II as they sought to escape the coming holocaust in Europe. Throughout Latin America, small Jewish communities were supplemented by later arrivals from Eastern Europe after World War II (De La Torre & Aponte, 2001, pp. 132–134).

Islam

In 711 C.E. a small army crossed the Straits of Gibraltar to spread via the sword the new faith of Mohammed throughout Europe. They were eventually stopped at the battle of Tours by Charles Martel in 732 C.E. Still, they took possession of the Iberian peninsula, except for a few extreme northern areas. From the very start of the Muslim presence in Iberia, a concerted Christian effort started to reclaim lost lands under the rubric of the *reconquista* (reconquest). This idea of holy war had a significant impact on the development of the Spanish kingdoms and the subsequent colonization of Latin America. The 700-year-old struggle to reclaim the land and vanquish the crescent by way of the cross merged nationalism with Catholicism. Holy war became an expression of faith.

The 700-year presence of Islam in Iberia left a profound and sometimes forgotten influence on Spanish culture. This imprint was transferred to the Americas with migration. Spanish literature, music, and thought are filled with African and Islamic themes. In fact, it is believed that a Moorish influence persists in Mexican-American *curanderismo*. Today, Hispanic Muslims include those, like Jews, responding to historical echoes, as well as those embracing the Islamic faith. In recent years, a small but growing number of Latinos/as converted to Islam (De La Torre & Aponte, 2001, p. 134).

Santería

During the 1950s, the character of Ricky Ricardo in the popular television sitcom "I Love Lucy" entertained us with his signature song "Babalu-Aye." What most television viewers failed to realize was that Ricky Ricardo was singing to one of the quasi-deities of the Afro-Cuban religion known as *Santería*. *Santería*, from the Spanish word "santo" (saint), literally means "the way of saints." This religion originated when the Yoruba people were brought from their homeland to colonial Cuba as slaves and forced to adopt Catholicism. They recognized existing parallels between their African religious beliefs and this new religion of their masters. Both religions consisted of a high god who conceived, created, and sustains all that exists. Additionally, both religions consisted of a host of intermediaries operating between this supreme God and believers. Catholics called these intermediaries saints, whereas Africans called them *orishas*.

Catholic saints became outward manifestation of traditional deities, a survival tactic from when the religion had to be hidden by masking African gods with Catholic "faces." So while the believer bent their knees to venerate St. Lazarus, in reality they were worshiping the African *orisha* known as *Babalu-Aye* who revealed himself to the white Catholic masters as St. Lazarus. Masters were believed to lack the spiritual knowledge to comprehend the true identity of their saints. These gods, manifested as Catholic saints, are recognized as the powerbrokers between the most high God (who remains too busy to directly interfere in human affairs) and humanity. These *orishas* personify the forces of nature and manifest themselves as amoral powers, which can have either positive or negative implications for humans. Like humans, they can be virtuous or exhibit vices as they express emotions, desires, needs, and wants. They do whatever pleases them, even to the detriment of humans.

Santería's components consist of an Iberian Christianity shaped by the Counter Reformation and Spanish "folk" Catholicism blended together with African *orisha* worship as practiced by the Yoruba of Nigeria and as modified by 19th-century Kardecan spiritualism, which originated in France and was later popularized in the Caribbean. *Santería* can best be understood as the product of a shared sacred space caused by the cultural clash of Christianity and African Yoruba beliefs, brought about by the introduction of slaves in the Americas (De La Torre, 2004b, pp. xi–xiv).

As the faith system of the marginalized, *Santería* has always been an underground religion in Cuba and the United States, due to its historical persecution. It was a slave religion that strengthened an oppressed people's will to survive. With the exodus of Cubans immediately following Castro's Revolution of 1959, *Santería* was brought to this country by new refugees. Today, it is recognized as a legitimate religion, for on June 11, 1992, the United States Supreme Court ruled that the practitioners of *Santería* had a constitutional right to sacrifice animals in connection with their rituals.

Santería is an amorphous and practical religion that promises power in dealing with life's hardships, power that is manifested in a variety of ways depending on the believer's situation. The focus is not on understanding the sacred forces like the *orishas*; rather, it is concerned with how these universal forces can be used for the betterment of humans. As a way of being and living, *Santería*, formed as a spiritual response to oppressive structures like slavery, developed into a symbol of protest. This way of life becomes a response against the societal forces bent on destroying the culture of the believers—a form of survival by way of cultural resistance. Since its inception, *Santería* has been an expression of a people's attitude toward finding harmony—harmony between one's life and one's environment, community, and the spiritual realm. For this reason, *Santería* can only be understood through the disharmony caused by the social and political climate of the believer. In a very real sense, *Santería* is created by the disenfranchised to resist their annihilation, a religious expression that protests their subjugation (De La Torre, 2004b, pp. 189–191).

Curanderismo

Curanderismo is a tradition that predates the Spanish conquest of Mexico that can be understood as a combination of Spanish and indigenous Meso-American popular religious outlooks and orientations to the physical world and spiritual realms. For many Mexicans, *curanderismo* attempts to find an expression to health practices and healing, hence the name that finds its roots in the Spanish verb *curar*, "to heal, cure." *Curanderismo* assumes that illnesses might have a natural or supernatural cause; therefore any given circumstance might require a natural or supernatural cure, or even a combination of both. Because the *curandero/a*, like the *santero/a* of *Santería*, is an herbalist, s/he understands the medicinal properties of plants, roots, leaves, and so forth. Cures for illness can be found by relying on the earth, by seeking harmony between the individual and both their physical and spiritual environments. Medicine can alleviate the symptoms, but it is unable to eliminate the cause of the person's disharmony. For this, a spiritual solution is required.

Illness, *mal de ojo* (the evil eye), and *susto* (loss of spirit and deep profound discouragement and hopelessness) are considered afflictions on material, spiritual, and mental levels and require spiritual as well as physical healing. The *curandero/as*, as specialized healers arising from the people, are recognized as having received a special gift or *el dón* for healing. They might prescribe an herbal remedy or conduct a religious ritual. Their knowledge is rooted in the ancient ways and includes remedies for a variety of sicknesses, physical complaints, and injuries. Because most followers of *curanderismo*, as well as *Santería*, historically came from marginalized communities that lacked any semblance of medical facilities, they turned to the supernatural for healing, seeking the assistance of the Catholic priest, the African healer, the *curandera/o*, or any combination thereof. *Curandero/as* filled the void of medical care by providing a means toward healing. However, as a Eurocentric form of health care developed, mainly in the large cities and some rural areas, the religion willingly moved toward a supporting role in the quest for the individual's cure from sickness and disease (De La Torre & Aponte, 2006, pp. 206–211).

Espiritismo

Founded by an engineer named Hippolyte Rivail, who wrote under the pseudonym Allan Kardec, *espiritismo* originated in France and spread to the Western Hemisphere in the mid-1800s. Known as Kardecism or Spiritism, it was considered by its adherents to be a scientific movement, not a religious movement. It was a combination of scientism, progressivist ideology, Christian morality, and mysticism. Rivail hoped to subject the spiritual world to human observation and then, from these observations, develop a positive science. As the movement spread, it took the form of small groups of mediums assisting their clients in communicating with the spirits of the dead. A group of believers would gather at someone's home, sit around a table, make specific invocations, fall into a trance, and allow a medium to become a bridge to the spirit world. They insisted that their practice was not ritualistic; rather, it was pure experimental science where the practitioner verified the experience by speaking with the dead through the medium who provided immediate solutions to what ailed them.

Among the first to be attracted to this movement were the middle and upper classes, but it quickly spread to other urban groups of less power and privilege, eventually reaching the rural countryside. Poorer segments of society turned to *espiritismo* for help and guidance with the struggle of daily life, specifically in areas of material need and health problems. In many cases, *espiritismo* absorbed into its practice elements of Spanish folk religion, specifically herbalism, African religious practices, and/or Amerindian healing practices (Brandon, 1997, pp. 85–87).

LATINA/O ETHNIC SUBGROUPS

Latinos/as comprise different cultures and nationalities. Although diverse religious expressions can be expected among different ethnic subgroups, a certain degree of blending also takes place. Some of these subgroups reside in the United States because of the conquest of their lands (Mexico and Puerto Rico). As Elizondo reminds us, Mexicans did not cross the border; rather, it was the border that crossed them (1988, pp. 44–45). The same can be said about Puerto Ricans. Others are here as a result of gunboat diplomacy (Central America and the Caribbean), following the resources extracted from their native lands due to unfair trade agreements and practices. Yet others find themselves in the United States due to the geopolitical struggles played out in their homelands (Chileans and Argentineans). For many Latina/os, they reside in the same country responsible for their expatriation, separated from the land that previously defined them. How then does the Hispanic's social location construct, impact, or influence his identity and religious understanding and practices?

People usually define their ethnicity, worldview, and spirituality by the land that witnessed their birth. For example, Puerto Ricans or Cubans refer to themselves as such, in part because they or their parents were born on those particular Caribbean islands. However, what happens when separated from the land that defines who the individual is? How do they understand themselves in a foreign and, at times, hostile land? How does this affect their religious views and rituals? (De La Torre & Aponte, 2001, pp. 44–46).

Mexicans

In spite of the ongoing rhetoric surrounding the 2006–2007 U.S. immigration debate aimed at Mexicans, their presence is a direct consequence of U.S. territorial expansion (the Mexican-American War of 1846–1848), making them foreigners in their own lands, mainly in the Southwest. Still others (Chicana/os) had occupied the land that would eventually be known as the United States for centuries prior to the European invasion. They were and are the consequences of Manifest Destiny.

The U.S. presence of Mexicans and their descendants has contributed to the Christian theological conversation. Three contributions are worth mentioning. The first is the notion of *mestizaje*. As previously mentioned, *mestizaje* refers to the biological mixture of different races. For Mexicans, more often than not, this means European (Spain) with indigenous nation groups. *Mestizaje* becomes a powerful mixing process in which physical, cultural, social, and religious identities merge to create a new identity, usually dominated by the characteristics of the conquerors. *Mestizaje* constitutes the new life—the new people conceived through the colonial conquest. Although this beginning produced death, pain, and confusion, a rich and unique identity and religious worldview developed.

The second contribution was discussed earlier; specifically overcoming the U.S.-imposed identity of inferiority through an understanding of Jesus as being a *mestizo*. Imposed inferiority is overcome by stressing the Mexican American unique identity and mission. The full potential of *mestizaje* can be reached by following the *mestizo* Jesus, the Jesus who arises from the culturally and linguistically mixed borderlands of Galilee. Like Jesus, the spiritual mission of Mexican Americans is to challenge the oppressive power structures that contribute to marginalization by proclaiming new life for those who suffer.

A third contribution is based on reflections of the "Virgin of Guadalupe," which is seen by some as providing a life-giving opportunity in reconciling the first violent clash that produced *mestizaje*, specifically the rape of indigenous women. Some Hispanic scholars will argue that the symbol of a *mestiza* Virgin of Guadalupe reclaims dignity for the offsprings caused by violence, moving them from degradation to pride, from rape to purity. A fourth contribution revolves around the concept of *nepatla*, the word that captures the reality of living in an in-between place, the disorientation of living in the borderlands. It is a space that requires questioning, tearing apart, and rebuilding, thus threatening a dominant culture that prefers to keep clear demarcations between them and their Others (Lozano, 2006, pp. 139–143).

Puerto Ricans

Like Mexicans, the presence of Puerto Ricans is a direct consequence of U.S. territorial expansion (Spanish American War, 1898) acquiring Puerto Rico as a colony—a colony it continues to hold. Granted U.S. citizenship, Puerto Ricans have migrated throughout the United States, specifically the Northeast, bringing with them their cultural and religious contributions. For example, the solidarity of Puerto Rican churches with the inhabitants of the island of Vieques in their struggle against the U.S. Navy found rich literary expression and theological reflection. Additionally, several books edited at the *Seminario Evangélico* in Puerto Rico, which focused on sermons delivered from Latina/o churches, have made a noteworthy contribution to the evangelical literature.

A significant portion of *Boricua* (i.e., Puerto Rican) religious thought appears to concentrate on the convergence of *evangélico* identity and intellectual curiosity. Although there exists no Puerto Rican (or any subgroup for that matter) religious essence, Puerto Rican identity has incorporated spiritual, existential, and intellectual aspects from the *evangélica* theological tradition, making the *evangélico* faith an important dimension of the Puerto Rican ethos (Rivera-Pagán, 2006, pp. 144–150).

Cubans

Unlike Mexicans and Puerto Ricans, who had the borders cross over them, Cubans arrived as political refugees. Their presence in this country is a direct result of U.S. foreign policies that deprived Cubans of sovereignty during the first half of the 20th century. Cubans had their independence from Spain abrogated due to the United States' multiple invasions of the island and its control of the Cuban economy, to the detriment of Cubans, due to forced trade agreements. After the Revolution of 1959, the majority of refugees who came to the United States were from the higher echelons of society. The vast majority were White, economically prosperous, and educated. It should therefore not be surprising that in spite of the ethnic discrimination faced and the economic struggles endured, the smallest of the three major Hispanic subgroups were able to create an economic enclave in Miami, Florida (and to a lesser extent in Union City, New Jersey) that propelled a disproportionately large number of Cubans (when compared to other Hispanics) into a middle- and upper-class lifestyle, entrepreneurship, and the academy (including religious studies).

Whereas other Hispanic subgroups might find comfort within the Democratic Party and political organizations that are more socially focused, many Cubans found a home in the Republican Party, mainly because of their pro-business stance and, during the Cold War era, their staunch anti-Communist stance. Probably more so than any other Hispanic group, Cubans might generally find themselves closer to the issues advocated by the Religious Right. Yet it is important to note that, generally speaking, Cubans who entered religious theological studies are usually more aligned with the political and religious worldviews of other Hispanic subgroups than with their own Cuban community.

Some of the contributions made by Cubans to the theological discourse revolved around issues of exilic existence. A Diaspora Theology has been developed throughout several books written by Cubans. Another issue is the introduction of the concept of *mulatez*. Like *mestizaje*, *mulatez* refers to the biological mixture of Spaniards and their African slaves. Several Cuban religious scholars have used the word in the same manner that Mexicans have used the word *mestizaje*. However, the term *mulatez* has proven to be more controversial. Although some Cubans use *mulatez* as a positive word to describe the Cuban identity, others question its racist connection to the word "mule." Can a term that Blacks and biracial Cubans find offensive be an acceptable word used for self-identity, especially when its imposition is mainly carried out by white Cubans?

Central and South Americans

As we have seen throughout this chapter, and throughout this book, the term "Hispanic" comprises a vastly diverse group representing a multiple of nations throughout the Americas, each with their own culture, worldviews, and religious practices. Unfortunately, when we attempt to examine the overall Latina/o community, we usually limit the discussion to the three largest U.S. Hispanic groups: Mexicans at 58.5% of the population, Puerto Ricans at 9.6%, and Cubans at 3.5%. Ignored is what is often referred to as "Other Hispanics." These "others," composed of any nationality other than Mexican, Puerto Rican, or Cuban, comprise 28.4% of the Hispanic population (Guzmán, 2001, p. 2).

The latter part of the 20th century witnessed an increase of Latin Americans (specifically non-Mexicans, non-Puerto Ricans, and non-Cubans) migrating to the United States. Many of these new immigrants are Central Americans, especially from Guatemala, El Salvador, and Nicaragua, settling in urban areas like New York City, Los Angeles, and Washington, DC. Among the Guatemalan immigrants are Mayans, many who maintained their indigenous cultural identity, speaking Spanish (if they know it) as a second language and participating in native religious rituals. Those from El Salvador and Nicaragua immigrated because of U.S. wars conducted in their country, either by supporting the oppressive regime (as in the case of El Salvador) or funding the rebel forces (as in the case of Nicaragua). The inability to contain military violence to just one nation would contribute to migration in the surrounding countries affected by the war. For example, the U.S.-sponsored Contras stationed on the Honduran side of the Nicaraguan border triggered a migration to the United States. Like the Guatemalans, many brought with them the native religious worldviews and rituals.

South American immigrants (especially during the 1970s and 1980s) included political refugees from bloody military regimes like Pinochet's Chile. The U.S.-backed right-wing dictatorships of South Americans led to Colombians, Ecuadorians, and Peruvians settling within the United States, with each nationality bringing its patron saints, its religious fraternities, and its own blending of indigenous traditions (De La Torre & Aponte, 2001, pp. 145–146).

Blending Among Subgroups

One can make the argument that because Mexicans constitute a *mestizaje* of Spanish and indigenous cultures, religious expressions like *curanderismo* will be found among this subgroup. Meanwhile, Cubans and Puerto Ricans, who come from a *mestizaje* rooted in a Caribbean context, where the mixture was Spanish and African, would more than likely participate in Afro-religious expressions like *Santería*. Although these assertions might hold some truth, caution is required in making such blanket generalizations. We need to pay attention to the question that Aponte asks: "What is Changó (the Caribbean orisha) doing in Oak Cliff, Texas (a heavily populated Mexican city)?" (2006, p. 46).

When Euro-Americans think of religious beliefs, they understand faithfulness to a religious tradition through the rejection of other faith traditions. You are either a Muslim or a Christian, you are either a Catholic or a Protestant, or you are either a Baptist or a Methodist. The idea of belonging to more than just one faith tradition would appear as if the individual was confused, if not naive. Yet, for some Hispanics, there exists an ability to participate in more than one faith tradition. There are good Catholics who attend mass in the morning and sacrifice a chicken to Changó at night. There are Southern Baptists (who abhor any graven images) who light a candle to *la Virgen de Cobre* every morning. Additionally, there are those who solely follow African-based religious traditions, like *Santería* or *curanderismo*, and borrow rituals and practices from each other.

CONCLUSION

Any discussion concerning Latina/o religiosity concludes with the recognition that they are indeed a multicultural, multiethnic, multiracial, and multireligious community. There is not, nor ever was there, a monolithic Hispanic religious expression. Yet, as we witnessed in this chapter, several commonalities do exist—commonalities that were created through similar marginalized experiences faced by a majority of Latinos/as living in the United States. From this Hispanic space, religiosity grows, develops, and matures. No doubt, Hispanic religiosity has much to offer the dominant Euro-American culture—religious insights that can contribute to and deepen the prevailing religious norms. Unfortunately, biases and cultural stereotypes of the dominant culture have prevented Euro-Americans from looking to their margins to see and hear what Hispanics can contribute to the discourse of faith and religion.

So what then can be expected about the future of Latino/a thought and religiosity? The field of Latina/o religious academic thought was birthed in 1969 with the publication of Gustavo Gutiérrez's classic text, *A Theology of Liberation*. His work laid the intellectual and spiritual foundation for the first generation of U.S. religious scholars. The Chicano, feminist, and Black civil rights movements and the new social-cultural history and postcolonial theory that arose in the late 1960s and 1970s also shaped the field. Many early Latino/a theologians created theologies that reflected these impulses and the struggle and spirituality of U.S. Hispanics. Equally important, they carved out a space in the academy for the critical study of this hitherto ignored community. Aside from work in anthropology, the first generation of Latino/a scholars focused almost exclusively on Catholic and, to a lesser extent, on Protestant Christianity. This was a natural development, as the vast majority (over 90%) of the community identified with the Christian religion. Furthermore, most of these scholars were trained at Christian seminaries and divinity schools.

We are now witnessing a new generation of Hispanic religious scholars pushing the boundaries of Latino/a religion and identity by moving beyond the liberationist framework and focusing on Christian Latina/o popular religiosity. Long-cherished notions are being critically interrogated while newer concepts, theories, and research outside of the traditional institutional religion are being explored. One of the reasons why the new generation of Hispanic scholars is moving beyond the field's traditional focus is because they realize that the emphasis on a common

Hispanic experience not only has the power to liberate but also to suppress, mask, and delegitimize the complex realities of hitherto marginalized voices within the very community it seeks to liberate (De La Torre, 2006, pp. 288–289).

REFERENCES

Alanís, Javier R. (2006). God. In Edwin David Aponte & Miguel A. De La Torre (Eds.), *Handbook of Latina/o Theologies* (pp. 11–16). St. Louis, MO: Chalice Press.

Aponte, Edwin David. (2006). Metaphysical Blending in Latino/a Botánicas in Dallas. In Miguel A. De La Torre & Gastón Espinosa (Eds.), *Rethinking Latino (a) Religion and Identity* (pp. 46–68). Cleveland, OH: Pilgrim Press.

Brandon, George. (1997). *Santería from Africa to the New World*. Bloomington: Indiana University Press.

De La Torre, Miguel A. (2002). *Reading the Bible from the Margins*. Maryknoll, NY: Orbis Books.

De La Torre, Miguel A. (2004a). *Doing Christian Ethics from the Margins*. Maryknoll, NY: Orbis Books.

De La Torre, Miguel A. (2004b). *Santería: The Beliefs and Rituals of a Growing Religion in America*. Grand Rapids, MI: William B. Eerdmans Publishing Company.

De La Torre, Miguel A. (2006). Religion and Power in the Study of Hispanic Religion. In Miguel A. De La Torre & Gastón Espinosa (Eds.), *Rethinking Latino (a) Religion and Identity* (pp. 286–297). Cleveland, OH: Pilgrim Press.

De La Torre, Miguel A., & Aponte, Edwin David. (2001). *Introducing Latino/a Theologies*. Maryknoll, NY: Orbis Books.

De La Torre, Miguel A., & Aponte, Edwin David. (2006). Alternative Traditions. In Edwin David Aponte & Miguel A. De La Torre (Eds.), *Handbook of Latina/o Theologies* (pp. 206–211). St. Louis, MO: Chalice Press.

Eliade, Mircea. (1963). *Patterns in Comparative Religion*. (Rosemary Sheed, Trans.). New York: Meridian Books.

Elizondo, Virgilio. (1983). *Galilean Journey: The Mexican-American Promise*. Maryknoll, NY: Orbis Books.

Elizondo, Virgilio. (1988). *The Future Is Mestizo: Life Where Cultures Meet*. New York: Crossroad.

Espinosa, Gastón. (2006). Methodological Reflections on Latino Social Science Research. In Miguel A. De La Torre & Gastón Espinosa (Eds.), *Rethinking Latino(a) Religion and Identity* (pp. 13–45). Cleveland, OH: Pilgrim Press.

González, Justo L. (1996). Hispanic Worship: An Introduction. In Justo L. González (Ed.), *!Alabadle! Hispanic Christian Worship*. Nashville, TN: Abingdon Press.

Guzmán, Betsy. (2001). *Hispanic Population: Census 2000 Brief*. Washington, DC: U.S. Census Bureau, U.S. Government Printing Office.

Hernández, Alberto. (2006). Historic Mainline Protestants. In Edwin David Aponte & Miguel A. De La Torre (Eds.), *Handbook of Latina/o Theologies* (pp. 184–190). St. Louis, MO: Chalice Press.

Lozano, Nora O. (2006). Mexicano/a Descent. In Edwin David Aponte & Miguel A. De La Torre (Eds.), *Handbook of Latina/o Theologies* (pp. 136–143). St. Louis, MO: Chalice Press.

Maldonado, David (Ed.). (1999). *Protestantes/Protestants: Hispanic Christianity Within Mainline Traditions*. Nashville, TN: Abington Press.

Rivera-Pagán, Luis N. (2006). Puertorriqueños/as. In Edwin David Aponte and Miguel A. De La Torre (Eds.), *Handbook of Latina/o Theologies* (pp. 144–151). St. Louis, MO: Chalice Press.

Sánchez Walsh, Arlene M. (2006). Pentecostals. In Edwin David Aponte & Miguel A. De La Torre (Eds.), *Handbook of Latina/o Theologies* (pp. 199-205). St. Louis, MO: Chalice Press.

Stevens-Arroyo, Anthony M. (2006). Latino/a Catholic Theology. In Edwin David Aponte & Miguel A. De La Torre (Eds.), *Handbook of Latina/o Theologies* (pp. 169–183). St. Louis, MO: Chalice Press.

Traverzo Galarza, David. (2006). Evangélicos/as. In Edwin David Aponte and Miguel A. De La Torre (Eds.), *Handbook of Latina/o Theologies* (pp. 191–198). St. Louis, MO: Chalice Press.

Villafañe, Eldin. (1993). *The Liberating Spirit: Toward an Hispanic American Pentecostal Social Ethic*. Grand Rapids, MI: William B. Eerdmans Publishing Company.

REDEFINING BORDERS:
THE LATINA/O POPULATION
IN THE UNITED STATES

CHAPTER 16

Latinos/os (in) on the Border

EMILY SKOP
BRIAN GRATTON
MYRON P. GUTMANN

In the early 21st century, no other area in the United States appears to have been as profoundly transformed by recent immigration from Latin America than the Southwest. This region, alongside the 2,000-mile stretch that separates the United States and Mexico, includes California, Arizona, New Mexico, Colorado, and Texas.[1] According to the latest estimates from the U.S. Census, the Southwest is currently home to more than half of all Latinos (nearly 56%). Because of intensive and extensive Latino geographic clustering, some have even gone so far as to label the region "Mex-America" and/or "New Aztlan." This categorization, in turn, encourages the broadly accepted notion that this ethnic concentration is both recent and the result of unprecedented and unparalleled growth.

In reality, the ancestors of Latinos were present in the Southwest territory of the United States even before it was a nation-state. Spanish exploration and settlement began in the 16th century, and during the 17th and 18th centuries, the Latino population continued to slowly grow, through both natural increase and net immigration, especially in New Mexico and Colorado. Then, after the Mexican-American war and U.S. jurisdiction, and especially in the late 19th and early 20th centuries, parts of California, Arizona, New Mexico, Colorado, and Texas saw tremendous change, as more Latino immigrants and their descendents (especially from Mexico) settled in the region. Thus, Latinos are both one of the oldest and one of the newest groups of U.S. immigrants; the Southwest, too, is one of the oldest and one of the newest regions of Latino settlement.

In this chapter, we describe the role of Latino immigration and settlement in the historical development of the Southwest border region. We confirm aspects of the broad narrative that already exists regarding Latinos in this region, but we also argue for a more dynamic view of the geography and demography of the Southwest.[2] The analysis links geographic data to demographic and economic conditions to assess the location and composition of the Mexican-origin population within the Southwest in the late 19th and early 20th centuries and it concludes with a brief discussion of the implications of these patterns in the early 21st century.[3] We focus specifically on Mexicans as a subset of the larger Latino population primarily because this group represents the vast majority of those living along the Southwest border during the period of study, although we do address how the composition of this region has changed in the present day with the immigration of other Latino subgroups.

In this analysis, we use the integrated public-use microdata samples of the U.S. Census (IPUMS), which we have designed to identify persons of Mexican-origin, using language, birthplace, and Spanish surname.[4] Designating State Economic Areas (SEAs) as our primary geographic unit, we reveal settlement patterns and major destination points from 1880 to 1950. We examine the 15 southwestern SEAs that capture more than 60% of the total population of the ethnic group across the period 1910–1950 (1880 is excluded for sampling reasons). We then compare the demographic experiences of persons residing in significant clusters of settlement along the Southwest border region during the first half of the 20th century. We find that the following:

- The Southwest has always been a Latino cultural region: until the early 20th century; however, the resident Mexican-origin population was small and confined to very particular communities within individual states along the border.
- By 1920, a rapid process of geographical expansion across the entire Southwest fortified and confirmed its status as a Latino cultural region: Nearly every SEA along the border had residents of Mexican origin and this development was largely a product of immigration from Mexico.
- This settlement process was highly urbanized: Cities were the site of expansion in the ethnic Mexican population in the Southwest.
- Urban areas became still more attractive across time, generally because they offered better job opportunities.
- Women immigrants played an important role in this new urban culture and were more likely to settle in cities.
- Female immigration led to declines in transitory household structure and the dominance of nuclear household patterns among persons of Mexican origin in all regions.

Throughout the analysis, we contend that place matters: The geographical context of arrival and settlement were key factors in differentiating Mexican American communities and the lives of those who lived within them in the early 20th century.

THE HISTORICAL GEOGRAPHY OF SETTLEMENT: THE ROLE OF POLITICAL, ECONOMIC, AND SOCIAL PROCESSES

The resident population of ethnic Mexicans in the United States in 1850 was rather small, amounting to about 80,000 persons (Gratton & Gutmann, 2006). In part, this was because indigenous groups in the area resisted efforts by, first, the Spanish and then, the Mexican government's efforts to broadly colonize the region with new settlers (Meinig, 1971). When the U.S. government eventually annexed the region, more difficulties ensued, especially in Arizona and New Mexico; even so, a natural increase encouraged the steady growth of the ethnic Mexican population from 1850 onward (Gutmann, Frisbie, & Blanchard, 1999). By 1880, around 290,000 persons of Mexican origin lived in the United States, nearly all in the Southwest and a majority of whom were native-born (Gutmann, McCaa, Gutiérrez-Montes, & Gratton, 2000).

Low levels of immigration to the United States from Mexico in the late 19th century was due in part because Mexican federal and state authorities saw emigration as threatening to the nationalist project and thus discouraged out-migration (Fitzgerald, 2006). As a result, fewer than 15,000 immigrants from Mexico arrived per year during this period (Gutmann et al., 2000). However, fundamental changes in the economic structure in the Southwest, accompanied by rapid modernization in Mexico, led to steep increases in immigration in the early 20th century. The expansion of mining enterprises, commercial agriculture, and the railroad networks needed to serve these enterprises occurred simultaneously under the Porfiarto regime in northern Mexico and in the southwestern United States, creating a unified economic system that, in turn, escalated labor demand. Both sides of the border saw a dramatic rise in their migrant populations, but because substantially higher wages were available in the United States, the northern side of the border saw the most growth (Arreola & Curtis, 1993). Indeed, immigration to the United States from Mexico rapidly became institutionalized, as both formal and informal mechanisms emerged to move labor across the border (Krissman, 2005; Peck, 2000). By 1910, annual immigration rates had reached an estimated 20,000 Mexicans per year (Gutmann et al., 2000).

The next two decades saw even more dramatic increases in Mexican immigration to the United States, largely as the result of political and economic circumstances. Although the Mexican Revolution had some effect on pushing workers north, even more critical was the disruption of European immigration streams by World War I, which was followed by a rising antagonism and xenophobia among U.S. citizens against Southern and Eastern Europeans in particular (Fernandez, Gonzalez, & Fernandez, 2003; Gutmann et al., 2000). When the National Origins Acts was passed in 1924, most immigration was prohibited, with the curious exception of Mexicans. In a story often told, the Congressmen representing the economic interests that had arisen in the Southwest exchanged their votes for general restriction so long as Mexican immigrants continued to be admitted. As the U.S. economy expanded, Mexican immigrants looked north for economic opportunities, at the same time that they became attractive to employers (and their recruitment agents) looking for an alternative (and easily exploited) source of immigrant labor (Krissman, 2005). In the Southwest, especially, jobs were available in commercial agriculture, mining, ranching, and railroads (Rosales, 1981). Labor contractors (*enganchistas*), too, responded by directing Mexican workers to particular employers in the region (Fitzgerald, 2006; Peck, 2000). Many of these migrants moved back and forth between the United States and Mexico as temporary laborers, but others became permanent settlers; as a result, given rapid growth in the Mexican origin population after 1920, when the population exceeded 1.2 million, it is likely that more than 1.5 million individuals of Mexican origin lived in the United States by 1930 (Gratton & Gutmann, 2006).

However, the Mexican immigration flow was again influenced by U.S. actors in the 1930s, as the ongoing economic depression, combined with growing animosity toward Mexican laborers and diminished demands from employers, created an abrupt halt to immigration. At the same time, return migration to Mexico began to occur. Many of those in the United States returned voluntarily, because the lack of job opportunities and a nativist backlash discouraged them from staying. Others (especially in California and Texas) were subject to forced repatriation to Mexico (Guerin-Gonzales, 1994; Hoffman, 1974). This strategy was used by the U.S. government as one way to ease the country's financial hardship. As a result, thousands of ethnic Mexicans were deported in the 1930s, including some Mexican American citizens born in the United States (Hoffman, 1974).

Once the U.S. economy began to recover during the Second World War, however, Mexican immigration began anew, as employers again searched for an inexpensive and flexible labor source to fill jobs at the bottom of the occupational hierarchy (Massey, 1999). The Bracero program was initiated in 1942 to allow Mexican nationals to take temporary agricultural work in the United States (Fitzgerald, 2006; Gamboa, 1990). Over the program's 22-year life, more than 4 million Mexican nationals were legally contracted for temporary work in the United States. In theory, the program was created to favor both the United States and Mexico, as a pool of unemployed laborers would facilitate the business of farming in the United States (because temporary guest workers were willing to take jobs at wages scorned by most Americans); at the same time, the emigrants would become a source of remittances. In reality, the Bracero program fed the circular migration patterns of Mexican migrants and created a "culture of migration" whereby, as Massey, Alarcon, Durand, and González (1987) argued, migration became difficult for state governments to regulate or control, because "the process of network formation lies largely outside their control and occurs no matter what policy regime is pursued" (p. 47).

Despite vacillating flows because of recruitment spikes and repatriation campaigns throughout the first half of the 20th century, a significant and increasing core population was now established: The number of persons of Mexican origin reached about 1.6 million in 1940 and 2.5 million in 1950. Importantly, by 1950, the ethnic Mexican population was now largely made up of persons born in the United States. Whereas in 1920, about half of the population was foreign-born, by 1950 only about 20% had been born in Mexico (Gratton & Gutmann, 2000, 2006). Significantly, the vast majority of ethnic Mexicans called the Southwest border region "home." This high concentration along the U.S.-Mexico border had important implications, especially in terms of altering the sociocultural, political, and economic landscapes of this region.

MAPPING THE DEVELOPMENT OF THE SOUTHWEST BORDER REGION, 1880–1950

Figures 1–4 illustrate the key role of the Southwest as a Latino culture region starting in the early 20th century. Using SEAs as the unit of analysis confirms the broad historical geography of this ethnic group (see Boswell & Jones, 1980; Durand, Massey, & Zenteno, 2001; Haverluk, 1997; Nostrand, 1975), but more clearly captures specific communities and the process of movement and settlement within states. To describe patterns of settlement, the number of ethnic Mexicans within an SEA was analyzed using a set of five population levels, beginning at 3,000 persons per SEA. These absolute measures identified communities better than relative measurement proportional to total population, especially when the numbers of migrants reached a certain magnitude. Both large and small population clusters suggest the establishment of permanent communities, to which subsequent migrants (both from abroad and domestically) have been pulled. What do these maps communicate about the role of individual communities in the Southwest border region in Mexican immigration and settlement? The early maps demonstrate that persons of Mexican origin had a significant presence in only a few select SEAs within the Southwest region of the United States. In 1880 (Figure 1), a small resident population (about 290,000), composed largely of native-born Mexican Americans, lived in a limited number of places close to the Mexican border, extending north only in New Mexico, Colorado, and California. This population was largely composed of *Hispanos*, a distinctive subgroup of Latinos whose cultural ancestry derives from the earliest Spanish colonial settlement of New Mexico and whose descendants continue to predominate in northern New Mexico and southern Colorado to this day. These individuals created what Nostrand (1993) described as a distinctive "Hispano homeland" with a unique history and

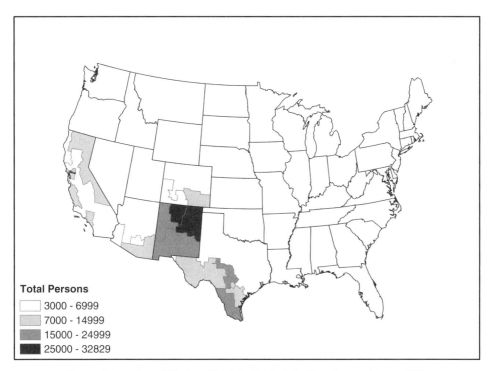

FIGURE 1. Number of Mexican-Origin Individuals by State Economic Area, 1880.

culture; interestingly, the subgroup's remnants still linger in this area, especially in the cultural landscapes of northern New Mexico (Smith, 2002).

By 1910 (Figure 2), expansion into new communities in the Southwest was noteworthy, a finding that has heretofore not been measured in the ethnic group's geographical history. Across this 30-year period, increasing portions of states within the Southwest became settled by persons of Mexican origin. For instance, whereas Northern California and San Francisco, rarely described previously as important magnets for migrants, had a significant Mexican ethnic presence very early in the ethnic group's settlement history, Southern California, a mecca of contemporary concentration, only became an important settlement area by 1910.

However, even in 1910, large areas of states like Texas were not home to ethnic Mexicans. Instead, south Texas and the lower Rio Grande Valley stood out as primary settlement areas. In this cultural province, as Arreola (2002) charted, Texans of Mexican ancestry established a unique subregion along the Texas-Mexico borderland that is unlike any other. Here, many factors made *Tejano* South Texas distinctive from other places along the border: the physical spaces of ranchos, plazas, barrios, and *colonias*; the cultural life of the small towns and the cities of San Antonio and Laredo; and the foods, public celebrations, and political attitudes that characterized the subregion.

It was only in 1920 (Figure 3) that the entire Southwest achieved its status as a distinctly Latino cultural region, when nearly all SEAs in California, Arizona, New Mexico, Colorado, and Texas reported at least 3,000 residents of Mexican origin. This broadening geographical shift again reveals the key role of labor demand and the deficiency of European immigrant sources in

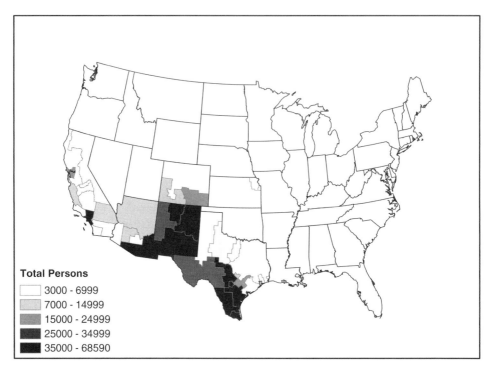

FIGURE 2.   Number of Mexican-Origin Individuals by State Economic Area, 1910.

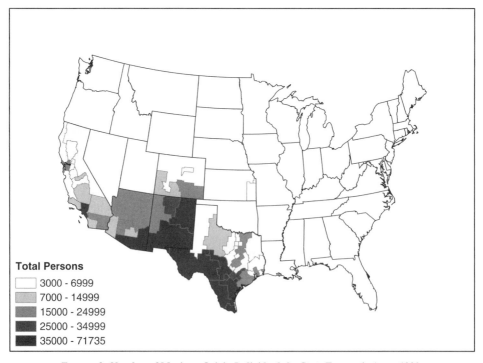

FIGURE 3. Number of Mexican-Origin Individuals by State Economic Area, 1920.

prompting the expansion of settlement. At the same time, the cumulative effect of migration and the social networks it created also began to prompt the expansion of settlement throughout the Southwest. The propensity for migrants to move along the same channels produced high levels of migration to certain destinations. As a result, greater cultural diversity began to appear within the broad Southwest region, as old *Hispano* settlements slowly made way for new communities composed largely of Mexican immigrants and their descendants.

Shifts in immigration law in the 1920s, which imposed national-origin quotas and reduced access of employers to European immigrant labor, accelerated flows from Mexico. This demand transformed the geography of the ethnic group in the Southwest, with new settlements visible throughout California, Arizona, New Mexico, Colorado, and Texas. Furthermore, labor shortages in the manufacturing sector drew Mexicans and Mexican Americans toward new areas of settlement. Indeed, growers' desire for inexpensive agricultural labor as well as manufacturers' need for inexpensive industrial workers eventually began to draw substantial numbers of Mexicans to northern Colorado, Nebraska, Kansas, Michigan, Illinois, and northwestern Ohio (Carlson, 1976; Oppenheimer, 1985; Rochen, Siles, & Gomez, 1996). The new levels of immigration created extensive social networks that then facilitated and encouraged still more migration northward from Mexico (Alvarez, 1966; Cornelius, 1992; Durand & Massey, 1992; Peck, 2000; Durand, Massey, & Charvet, 2001; Longmore & Hitt, 1943).

The unexpected hiatus of movement from Mexico to the United States and the increased deportations of laborers to Mexico from the United States in the 1930s meant that immigration was not a particularly important source of growth during this decade. Even so, population densities in certain areas of the Southwest increased, indicating the growing presence of Mexican Americans (and the role of natural increase in fueling growth) in this region. Additionally, with the initiation of the Bracero program in 1942, old migration routes were renewed and new ones established, once again revealing the way in which immigration can alter group demographics and settlement patterns.

By 1950, the rapid transformation and expansion of ethnic Mexican settlement outside the Southwest into other parts of the United States becomes apparent (Figure 4). The total number of SEAs in which persons of Mexican origin lived increased rapidly over time: In 1910, ethnic Mexicans were enumerated in 101 SEAs; in 1920, this number increased to 161; by 1950, there were 223 SEAs. Thus, by mid-century, ethnic Mexicans had sizable settlements in most SEAs in Colorado, a northward extension into portions of the upper Rocky Mountain States and the rather sudden appearance of ethnic Mexican workers in Midwestern industrial cities, including notable clusters in Chicago, Detroit, and other industrial Midwestern cities.

Despite the appearance of ethnic Mexicans in distant locales, the majority of ethnic Mexicans continued to concentrate in the Southwest, albeit in a diverse number of both smaller and larger communities. In fact, nearly 75% of ethnic Mexicans lived in the Southwest in 1910. By 1950, despite decreased immigration from Mexico and new out-migration to other parts of the United States, 62% of ethnic Mexicans continued to live in the Southwest. In every southwestern SEA, the ethnic group represented at least 5% of the total population, and in places like Southern and Central California, ethnic Mexicans represented between 11% and 35% of the total population. Meanwhile, the lower Rio Grande Valley in Texas had significant proportions of ethnic Mexicans; in some south Texas SEAs, the group was not only the majority but constituted upward of 70% of the total population living in the area. Thus, not only was the absolute population increasing through time, but the relative proportion of the Mexican-origin population compared to other ethnic groups in various SEAs increased as well. This remarkable concentration would have important implications not only for the immigrants and native-born residents living in the region at the time but also for their descendents and other newcomers who would arrive in the Southwest in the years to come.

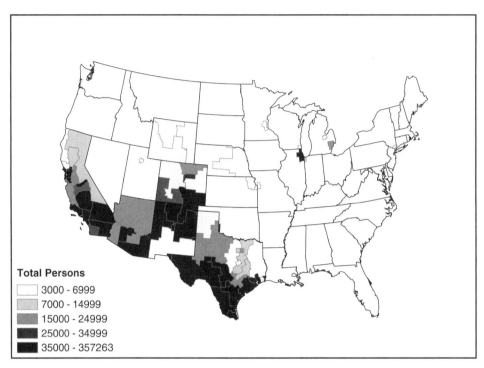

Total Persons
☐	3000 - 6999
☐	7000 - 14999
☐	15000 - 24999
☐	25000 - 34999
☐	35000 - 357263

FIGURE 4. Number of Mexican-Origin Individuals by State Economic Area, 1950.

DEMOGRAPHIC AND ECONOMIC DIVERSITY IN THE SOUTHWEST BORDER REGION, 1910–1950

The links between the historical geography and the demographic and economic characteristics of Mexican American communities in the Southwest are useful to explore; they reveal the remarkable diversity that exists within/between particular communities in the Southwest during the first half of the 20th century.[5] The most striking characteristics in these results are the differences between SEAs in certain demographic and economic traits. The percent foreign-born and the percent male, along with the divergent compositions of households (whether nuclear or augmented by nonrelatives, such as boarders and lodgers) and the occupational status for active workers, begin to capture the differentiating role of immigration in the process of settlement and geographic expansion. These individually measured, place-based characteristics also provide a novel picture of early Mexican-origin experience in the United States. Such distinctions imply the following: (1) The life of persons of Mexican origin was dissimilar from one area to another, especially *within* states and (2) across time, some areas went through significant changes, dictated largely by migratory forces. Much of this is a chronicle of the rise of an urban ethnic Mexican life, and much of the force behind this new life was immigrant and female.

Figure 5 illustrates the dramatic effects of immigration from Mexico in the various SEAs along the border during the first half of the 20th century. Most places in New Mexico (excepting the counties around Las Cruces nearer to the Mexican border) had very low percentages of Mexican immigrants. These figures reaffirm Nostrand's (1993) description of the distinctiveness of northern

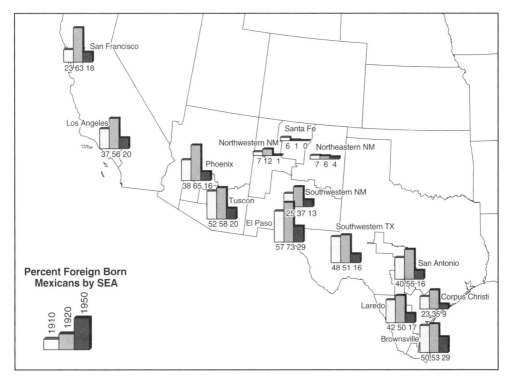

FIGURE 5. Percentage of Foreign-Born Mexicans by State Economic Area, 1910–1950.

New Mexico as the Hispano homeland, because the vast majority of Latino residents in these SEAs (95% or more) were native-born throughout the study period.

Whereas most of New Mexico had only a remote connection to Mexico (and, some claimed, a more direct one to Spain), other places in the Southwest were thoroughly and very recently Mexican. For instance, El Paso, Texas, directly on the border, had extremely high levels of immigration at all times. Foreign-born Mexicans exceeded 70% of the population in 1920, a remarkable percentage that illustrates the importance of this city as a gateway for migration from the south.

In 1910, when immigrants made up 38% of the entire Mexican-origin population of the Southwest, they were 42% of the Texas population and 49% in Arizona. California and Arizona SEAs tended to have large proportions of immigrants, revealing the capacity of cities like Los Angeles and Phoenix to attract newly arriving immigrants. Thus, the Southwest was sharply divided into two types of state: those that exhibited very little immigrant activity (i.e., New Mexico) and those that attracted large numbers of Mexican immigrants, like Arizona, Texas, and California.

By 1950, despite the emergence of the temporary Bracero guest worker program and increased migration from Mexico since 1942, the native-born represented nearly 80% of the ethnic Mexican population residing in the United States. The ethnic Mexican community, even in the new regions of the Southwest opened up by immigration in the early 20th century, was, by 1950, predominately native-born. In no area of settlement in the Southwest did the percentage of foreign-born exceed 30%, indicating the key role of a natural increase in weakening most immigration effects.

Still, in general, cities within the Southwest experienced more immigration from Mexico than rural areas. The economic advantages and opportunities to be found in cities were not lost on those individuals contemplating a long-distance move, and as a result, immigrants led the way in urban settlement, as was the case with nearly all immigrant groups in this era. In 1880, the proportion of foreign-born Mexicans living in urban places (defined as incorporated places with 2,500 or more residents) was small (14%) and lagged behind the national average of 24%. In 1910, as immigration from Mexico began to rise, 29% of the population lived in urban places and 10% lived in the central core of metropolitan areas. By this time, immigrants and their children were becoming increasingly likely to be residents of cities. In the first and second generation, nearly one-third lived in urban places, compared to only 22% of those in the third and higher generation. In 1920, when the nation first reported a majority of its population in urban places, the urbanizing influence of immigration was fully felt: Forty-five percent of Mexican immigrants lived in urban places.

By 1950, the urban/rural distribution of the Mexican-origin population was very similar to that of all persons in the United States, with the first indications that central cities, rather than the suburbs around them, would characterize ethnic Mexican urban life until at least the most recent period, when, as Frey (2006) demonstrated, the suburbs have become an increasingly important destination for all Latinos. In 1950, the majority of immigrants and their children lived in metropolitan areas and nearly a third resided in the central city. The main story, then, of the first half of the 20th century's process of expansion and settlement is urbanization, led by immigrants.

Some scholars have argued that the role of urban settlement has been exaggerated and that Mexican-origin men, in particular, remained tied to rural areas (Gamboa, 1990; González, 1994; Foley, 1998). Yet, there are few differences in urban/rural location by sex in any of the data we analyzed between 1910 and 1950; by 1950, the overall sex distribution was relatively balanced. Figure 6 illustrates the percentage of males of Mexican origin in each SEA. The highest male proportion for Phoenix, for instance, occurred in 1910 (when males represented 57% of the Mexican-origin population). In San Antonio, 53% of the population was male in 1920. Yet, by 1950, it was women who made up that percentage of the population. Similar patterns can be seen for Los Angeles, where the impact of female immigration was also clear. In 1920, when 56% of the population was in the first generation, women already made up more than 40% of the group. By 1950, male/female percentages reached near parity.

It would be logical to argue that labor demand would induce considerable migration by single native males, but our research indicates that the better explanation is that cities equally attracted female immigrants, keeping sex ratios close even during immigration. Just as our analysis confirms the preponderance of males in initial immigration streams, female immigration quickly followed. This is most clearly the case in Brownsville, Texas, where a disproportionate number of males resided in 1920. By 1950, however, the sex ratio had nearly equalized, indicating the important role of female migrants (and their U.S.-born daughters) in shifting community composition.

That female immigration closely followed male immigration from Mexico is clear. Male preponderance is relatively short-lived, repeating classic patterns found among most immigrant groups. The figures indicate that all communities had become considerably more balanced by 1920, with males at or slightly below 50% of the population. The typical pattern of single, male sojourner migration had been transformed into more permanent settlement as more women migrants crossed the border, a process prompted by the demands of the rapidly

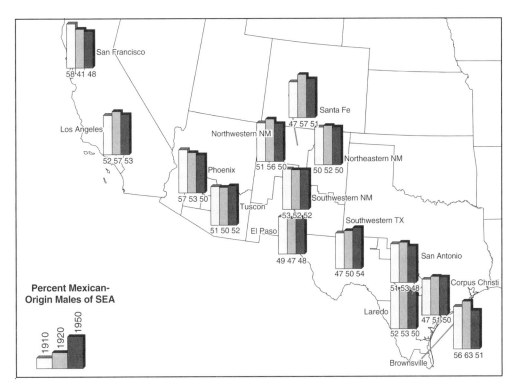

FIGURE 6. Percentage of Male Mexican-Origin Individuals by State Economic Area, 1910–1950.

industrializing economy of the Southwest and facilitated by U.S. immigration policy during the 1920s.

The transformation of household types early in the 20th-century history of the Mexican-origin population also reflects the arrival of female immigrants into the Southwest. In particular, the emergence of nuclear families rather than those households augmented by boarders or lodgers, a common housing choice of single males, signals the appearance of women in migration streams (Gratton, Gutmann, & Skop, 2004). Nuclear households typically develop when immigration becomes sex-balanced and becomes dominant when immigration wanes and more permanent settlement occurs. Figure 7 shows the proportion of persons living in nuclear households in the SEAs across the Southwest. Nuclear households always had a larger presence in the traditional, nonimmigrant region of northern New Mexico, extending into west Texas. Ethnic Mexicans were less likely to reside in nuclear households in California and Arizona, where immigration played a more dynamic role in the growth of the Mexican-origin population. In general, however, the nuclear family type increased over time and generally became more common throughout the Southwest by 1950, indicating not only the important influence of female immigration from Mexico but also the growing number of native-born ethnic Mexicans living in nuclear household living arrangements.

The impact of immigration on household formation is seen more clearly in Figure 8, which displays the percentage of persons living in augmented households (i.e., those households that include nonkin, such as boarders and lodgers). Rural SEAs in New Mexico show none of the boarding and lodging arrangements common to more urban immigrant communities. Yet, high

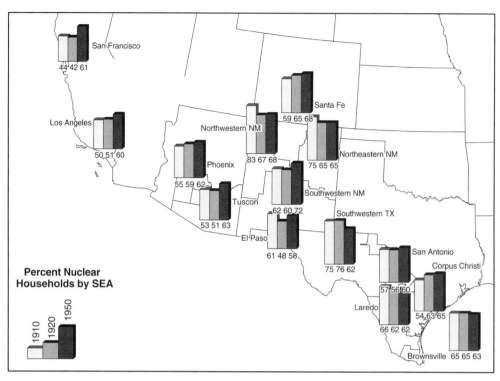

FIGURE 7. Percentage of Mexican-Origin Individuals Living in Nuclear Households by State Economic Area, 1910–1950.

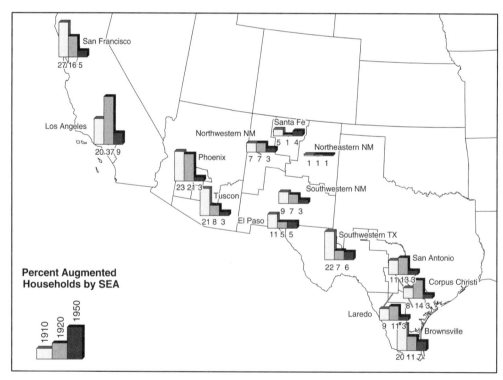

FIGURE 8. Percentage of Mexican-Origin Individuals Living in Augmented Households by State Economic Area, 1910–1950.

percentages of ethnic Mexicans residing in cities like Los Angeles, San Francisco, El Paso, Phoenix, and Brownsville lived in augmented households, especially in 1910 and 1920, when immigrants were most likely to gravitate toward these urban gateways. Indeed, heavy immigration revealed itself in the 1920 spikes seen in many of these places. Most Texas SEAs, on the other hand, lie between the extremes, reflecting their dual function as both areas of traditional settlement and entry zones for immigrants during that period. Still, the overall drift was clearly away from augmented households by 1950. This was in concert with the decline in augmented households for all ethnic groups in the United States during the 20th century (Gratton, Gutmann, & Skop, 2004).

To partially capture the economic implications of these patterns, Figure 9 illustrates the disparity in occupational levels among ethnic Mexicans living in different communities across individual states along the border. Occupational status is measured from 1910 to 1950 by using the "occscore" variable provided in the IPUMS dataset. "Occscore" is a constructed variable that assigns each occupation in all years a relative value for the median total income (in hundreds of 1950 dollars) of all persons with that particular occupation in 1950; that is, it provides a continuous measure of occupations according to the economic rewards enjoyed by people working in particular jobs in 1950 (see Ruggles, Sobek, Alexander, Fitch, Goeken, et al., 2004).

In all areas, occupational scores ranked toward the bottom end of the range, indicating the predominance of lower-skilled, lower-paying manufacturing, mechanical, mining, and service jobs among persons of Mexican origin. Across time, however, mean occupational scores rose for this population, and urban areas provided more economic opportunities than rural communities. For instance, northern and southwestern New Mexico had the lowest occupational ratings, joined by the poor agricultural regions in Texas's Rio Grande Valley. Conversely, cities in Arizona

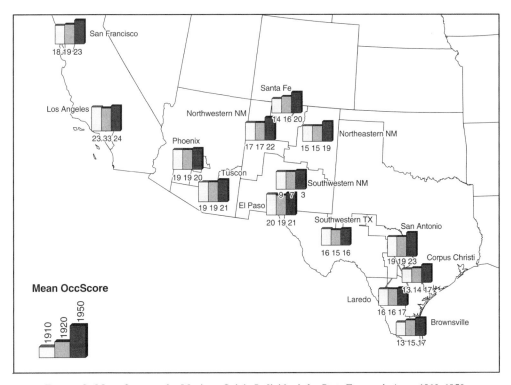

FIGURE 9. Mean Occscore for Mexican-Origin Individuals by State Economic Area, 1910–1950.

and California offered ethnic Mexicans better job prospects, as did El Paso and San Antonio in Texas. Thus, in 1920, the mean occupational score in urban SEAs averaged 20, whereas the mean occupational score in rural SEAs averaged 16. In other words, ethnic Mexicans working in urban SEAs earned, on average, 25% more than those working in rural SEAs. Even though improvement was evident in the rural areas that lagged behind originally by 1950, in general, cities in the Southwest offered more opportunities. These advantages were not lost on ethnic Mexicans and were particularly clear to immigrants, who led the way in making the ethnic group an urban rather than a rural people.

PLACE MATTERS: THE IMPLICATIONS OF SETTLEMENT IN THE SOUTHWEST BORDER REGION

Although many studies have shown that ethnic Mexicans remained largely confined to the five Southwestern states until very recently and that the Southwest is clearly one of the oldest regions of Latino settlement in the United States, the findings presented here suggest a more complex view of the historical geography of the Mexican-origin population, by including the significant role of immigration, and female immigration in particular, in shifting patterns of settlement, especially to urban destinations. So, in 1880, most regions within the vast Southwest had little in the way of an ethnic Mexican presence; the resident population after the Mexican-American War was both small and confined to limited areas. After 1900, and until about 1930, however, a dramatic process ensued whereby ethnic Mexicans became increasingly concentrated in the Southwest border region. During these three decades, parts of California, Arizona, New Mexico, and Texas saw tremendous change as more Latino immigrants and their descendents (especially from Mexico) settled in the region. By 1920, persons of Mexican origin lived in almost every SEA in California and were becoming an important minority group in southern and central Texas, among other places. With the rapid rise of second- and third-generation Mexican Americans, the filling in of the Southwest was largely complete by 1950. At this point, the Southwest was well established as a Latino culture region.

Even so, settlement did not expand traditional, rural community arrangements. Indeed, the rapid development of communities in urban centers in the Southwest, driven by immigrants, takes us away from the emphasis on the propensity of persons of Mexican origin to follow rural, agricultural pursuits. Instead, like most immigrant groups in the classic era, they pursued the better opportunities and socially distinct life of the city: By 1920, the ethnic Mexicans were not only as likely as other Americans to live in urban areas but, in concert with their fellow immigrants, still more likely to live in the urban core. No two sites are more evocative of this ascendancy of urban life than the demise of the traditional Hispano homeland of northern New Mexico and the rise of the dynamic city of Los Angeles. Whereas 9% of the Mexican-origin population in 1910 lived in northern New Mexico, only 2% of the total population lived there in 1950; in contrast, fewer than 6% of ethnic Mexicans lived in Los Angeles in 1910, but by 1950, 13% of the total population lived in that rapidly growing metropolis.

The shifting geography of ethnic Mexican settlement in the United States had important implications. The overriding consequence was that place mattered: In Southwest cities, regular contact with other groups was much more likely than in isolated rural regions, which, in turn, prompted greater opportunities, even in the face of segregation, discrimination in employment, and other prejudicial practices in everyday life (Moore & Pinderhughes, 1993). At the same time, large enough concentrations in urban centers permitted ethnic Mexicans, especially those in the first generation, to create facsimiles of life in the old country, the *México Lindo* of memory. Compared with other immigrant and migrant groups, persons of Mexican origin might not have formed a very large percentage of an urban SEA, but they were often great in number, as in Phoenix, where more than 50,000 ethnic Mexicans lived in 1950. Such numbers were sufficient to re-create, for a time, that image of a homeland so common and important to those who had to endure the difficult transition to a new life in a foreign land. In contrast to northern New Mexico or Colorado, where long-time settlements had created a distinctive Hispano culture, Los Angeles, San Francisco, Phoenix, and other cities had a decidedly Mexican stamp, one that undoubtedly altered the sociocultural, political, and economic landscapes of the Southwest for generations to come (Arreola, 2004).

Place also mattered for fortune. Our data illustrate much disparity in occupational levels among the ethnic Mexican communities in the Southwest. Clearly, better opportunities existed in cities like Los Angeles and Phoenix than in the New Mexico and Texas countryside. The traditional regions of settlement might have enjoyed familial stability, but they paid in terms of socioeconomic status, at least until 1950, when differences between urban and rural places leveled off. Across time, the wages of those living in urban places were often 25% higher than the wages earned by those living in rural places, especially in places like Los Angeles and San Francisco. Cities on the border, like Brownsville and El Paso, however, lagged well behind other urban centers and even behind some rural SEAs. These border towns attracted immigrants making their first step out of Mexico, but better wages in other areas of the country certainly beckoned many to venture further.

Women are an essential component of this urban history. Mexican immigration, like nearly all immigration in this period, was led by men and earlier censuses exhibited striking misbalances in sex ratios. In 1910, there were more than 150 males for every 100 females in the first generation. However, these ratios moved toward parity rapidly, falling to 135 in 1920 and 106 in 1940. The female immigrants who joined the male pioneers were very likely to move to cities, in part because they offered better -paying jobs (Ruiz, 1998). Urban SEAs, dominated by immigrants, had rather high male ratios at the onset of immigration; yet, these wide disparities collapsed with time, and more sex-balanced communities emerged.

Women also encouraged the rise of more stable living arrangements and family structure. The boarding and lodging choices characteristic of all immigrants—noticeable for ethnic Mexicans only in the regions to which immigrants moved—fell precipitously across the first half of the 20th century. In Los Angeles, nearly a quarter of the Mexican-origin population lived in augmented households in 1910, but only 9% by 1950. The proportion of nuclear households followed the reverse pattern in immigrant cities, becoming more common across time. Ironically, in the rural, traditional zones, there was a modest downward tendency in nuclear structure, likely a consequence of the out-migration of young males seeking better opportunities elsewhere.

In this dynamic historical geography of the southwestern United States, once-dominant communities fell behind newly emergent centers of settlement, and these changes resulted in important differences between rural and urban communities. The story owes more to the strategies employed by immigrants from Mexico than to the characteristics of native-born persons in the more established Hispano homelands. Settlement and growth occurred in places that captured the attention of immigrants, in general, and immigrant women, in particular. In Southwest cities particularly, a new Mexican American life was created, shaped by the hands of immigrants. It was these urban communities, firmly established by 1950, that greeted new waves of Mexican immigrants in the post-1965 era and, thus, reinforced the role of the Southwest in becoming what is today sometimes labeled "Mex-America" and/or the "New Aztlan."

CONCLUSION

We have argued that the geographic, demographic, and economic characteristics of ethnic Mexicans that emerged in the Southwest during the first half of the 20th century were the consequence of a variety of social, economic, and political processes. The results point especially to the key role of immigration policy and economic growth in contributing to the changing characteristics of the ethnic Mexican population living in the Southwest border region during this time period. As we have noted, this change was the product of an economic system that extended across the border, and that tied the United States and Mexico in an embrace of mines, farms, and railroads along the border. The higher demand for labor on the northern side and the higher wages that were offered, however, led to a powerful impetus for movement north, one sustained by both formal labor procurement and informal networks. This instrumental economic exchange was then furthered by political events. First, a world war interrupted the stream of European immigrants that had satisfied most American employers for 60 years. Second, common Americans' growing hostility toward Southern and Eastern European immigrants led to their exclusion. These forces created the context by which Mexican immigrants became the alternative source of labor for U.S. employers seeking an unskilled, flexible labor supply. The result was a U.S. immigration policy that facilitated higher levels of immigration from Mexico and that continued until the collapse of the American economy in 1929.

So, despite the fact that many areas in the Southwest had few or no residents of Mexican origin in the late 19th century, by 1930 geographic expansion had begun to emerge and ethnic Mexicans were now a significant minority group (and in some cases, a majority group) in a variety of places along the border. Even with the demise of immigration in the 1930s (and even the emergence of reverse flows), this area was firmly established as a Latino cultural region by 1950 and was largely composed of native-born, Mexican Americans. The stamp of ethnic Mexicans in the Southwest had by then become so clear that this region had become the standard by which the ethnic group was geographically imagined. The region housed a distinctive subculture, the long-time existence of Latino settlements, a rich Latino legacy, and even the presence of some Anglo-Americans who had been "Hispanicized" (Nostrand, 1970).

Importantly, this region has continued to govern Mexican settlement after 1950 and is especially important in the present day. Natural increase has played a significant role in the growth of the native-born Mexican American population, and immigration continuously reestablishes the Southwest as a Latino cultural region. Indeed, with the escalation of Mexican immigration after the 1965 Immigration Act, the concentration of Mexicans in the Southwest intensified in those areas where ethnic Mexicans had already established a foothold. Estimates suggest that more than 90% of Mexican immigrants from 1970 to 1990 moved to the Southwest, with the vast majority living in California (Durand, Massey, & Charvet, 2000). The clear trend in Mexican immigration and settlement, until very recently, has been one of growing concentration in the Southwest border region.

At the same time, because of dramatic shifts in U.S. immigration policy since 1965 (including the abolition of national quotas and the enactment of occupational and family preference measures), a burgeoning non-Mexican Latino population in the Southwest has also begun to increase significantly. Drawn by the growing importance of particular Southwest cities like Los Angeles, San Francisco, and Phoenix as large urban conglomerates that have become increasingly linked to the global economy, a rapidly diversifying Latino population now calls the Southwest "home" (Arreola, 2004; Menjivar, 2000; Skop & Menjivar, 2001). In contrast to earlier migratory movements from Mexico, however, new Latino immigration, especially from Central and South America, includes more refugees and people displaced by environmental and ethnic conflicts; at the same time, the racial and ethnic composition of these new flows is also more heterogeneous, as, for instance, indigenous Guatemalans (Mayans) and black Cubans begin to arrive in significant numbers. Importantly, new Latino immigrants bring different types of social and human capital that has begun to direct them in dissimilar paths of incorporation (see other chapters in this volume). Also, the growing feminization of migration from Latin America and the contribution of women in the settlement process influence how these immigrants have been received (Ehrenreich & Hochschild, 2004).

Thus, the Southwest has changed with regard to its composition of Latino groups. Yes, Mexican Americans continue to constitute the majority of Latinos in the region, but other Latino groups have arrived and continue to settle in this region. Indeed, there is a need for further research that both outlines the geography and demography of new Latino/a subgroups in the Southwest and that articulates how these patterns are transforming the way in which the cultural region is geographically imagined by residents and nonresidents alike.

Given the historical importance of the Southwest border region as the primary destination for both established and newer migrants, it might come as a surprise that new patterns of settlement among ethnic Mexicans have emerged in the United States since the 1990s. The number of alternative immigrant destinations in cities and regions where ethnic Mexicans have never had a presence has sharply risen in the past 15 years (Godziak & Martin, 2005; Jones, 2007; Suro & Singer, 2002). In part, this shifting geography is the result of the 1986 massive legalization campaign, which occurred against a backdrop of new employer sanctions, fluctuating economic conditions, and growing hostility against immigrants, especially in the Southwest border region (Durand, Massey, & Charvet, 2000). However, this recent geography is also emerging as a new class of second-tier metropolitan immigrant gateways emerge in the Southeast (Atlanta, Raleigh-Durham, and Charlotte), Southwest (Dallas/Fort Worth, Austin, and Las Vegas), upper Midwest (Minneapolis-St. Paul) and Northwest (Portland and Seattle), many of which have seen their immigrant population triple and quadruple in size as a result of recent immigration flows (Singer, Brettell, & Hardwick, 2007).

These unprecedented settlement patterns among ethnic Mexicans suggest that a new process has begun, linked to different economic and political circumstances and likely to lead to a shifting geographical map. As in the previous era, the new arrivals are largely immigrants, rather than those of native origin who migrate to new areas. Again, like the previous process, the stream is male-led but with relatively rapid movement toward sex parity. Importantly, drawn from still more distant parts of Mexico, these immigrants are participants in a much broader, global economic system that is not dependent on the specific ties between northern Mexico and the southwestern United States as in the early 20th century. Instead, formal and informal mechanisms have risen up to serve different employers, who are spread across the United States and who are often willing to take advantage of both documented and undocumented workers. At the same time, in the previous era, political circumstances (i.e. restrictive immigration policy) had a separate and determining effect. Also, it appears that politics might again have an important role to play in the vacillating flows of migration and new geographies of settlement from Mexico. A rising resentment against immigrants is once more becoming increasingly visible in the United States, and Mexican immigrants are at the very center of the controversy. Thus, as in the previous era, if restrictionists achieve victory, the new process of Mexican settlement that is unfolding in the early 21st century, might, in turn, be disrupted. What this means for the establishment of a broader, perhaps national geography of ethnic Mexicans remains to be seen, but it will surely have an impact, as previous policies did in the early 20th century.

ACKNOWLEDGMENTS

Support for the research was provided by a grant from the National Institute of Child Health and Human Development (HD37824-02) on "Assimilation Trajectories in Mexican American Families," Principal Investigator: Brian Gratton. The authors wish to acknowledge Paul A. Peters, a Ph.D. student in the Department of Sociology at the University of Texas at Austin, for helping to create maps for this research.

NOTES

1. This research focuses on four states that actually sit alongside the U.S.-Mexico border (California, Arizona, New Mexico, and Texas) along with one other nonborder state (Colorado, which is commonly treated as part of the Southwest).
2. A longer version of this essay appeared in Skop, Gratton, and Gutmann, The Professional Geographer, 58(1), 78–98, 2006. Permission was granted to the authors by Blackwell Publishing to use the material and on the understanding that nowhere in the original text do the publishers or authors acknowledge another source for the requested material.
3. Following Gutiérrez (1995), we use Mexican immigrants or Mexicans to describe persons born in Mexico and Mexican American for persons born in the United States or to refer to settings in this country, such as a Mexican American community or Mexican American history. To refer to the combined population, we use ethnic Mexican or Mexican origin.
4. A full description of the methods we used for identification can be found in Gratton and Gutmann (2000). Instructions on how to access the datasets and reconstruct them for analysis can be found at the Mexican American Trajectories Project Web site (www.icpsr.umich.edu/ATMAF/). For details on IPUMS, see Ruggles et al. (2004) and the Web site www.ipums.umn.edu.
5. Colorado is not included in this portion of the chapter because no SEAs in the state are among the 15 southwestern SEAs that capture more than 60% of the total population of the ethnic group across the period 1910–1950.

REFERENCES

Alvarez, J. H. (1966). A Demographic Profile of Mexican Immigration to the U.S., 1910–1950. *Journal of Inter-American Studies, 8*(6), 471–496.

Arreola, D. D. (2002). *Tejano South Texas: A Mexican American Cultural Province*. Austin: University of Texas Press.

Arreola, D. D, (Ed.). (2004). *Hispanic Spaces, Latino Places: Community and Cultural Diversity in Contemporary America*. Austin: University of Texas Press.

Arreola, D. D., & Curtis, J. (1993). *The Mexican Border Cities: Landscape Anatomy and Place Personality*. Tucson: The University of Arizona Press.

Boswell, T. D., & Jones, T. C. (1980). A Regionalization of Mexican Americans in the United States. *The Geographical Review, 70*(1), 88–98.

Carlson, A. W. (1976). Specialty Agriculture and Migrant Laborers in Northwestern Ohio. *Journal of Geography, 75*(3), 292–310.

Cornelius, W. A. (1992). From Sojourners to Settlers: The Changing Profile of Mexican Immigration to the U.S. In J. A. Bustamante, C. W. Reynolds, & R. Hinojosa-Ojeda (Eds.), *U.S.-Mexico Relations: Labor Market Interdependence* (pp. 155–195). Stanford, CA: Stanford University Press.

Durand, J., & Massey, D. S. (1992). Mexican Migration to the United States: A Critical Review. *Latin American Research Review, 27*(2), 3–42.

Durand, J., Massey, D. S., & Charvet, F. (2000). The Changing Geography of Mexican Immigration to the U.S.: 1910–1996. *Social Science Quarterly, 81*(1), 1–15.

Durand, J., Massey, D. S., & Zenteno, R. M. (2001). Mexican Immigration to the United States: Continuities and Changes. *Latin American Research Review, 36*(1), 107–127.

Ehrenreich, B., & Hochschild, A. R. (Eds.). (2004). *Global Woman: Nannies, Maids, and Sex Workers in the New Economy*. New York: Metropolitan Books.

Fernandez, R. E., Gonzalez, G. G., & Fernandez, R. A. (Eds.). (2003). *A Century of Chicano History: Empire, Nations and Migration*. New York: Routledge.

Fitzgerald, D. (2006). Inside the Sending State: The Politics of Mexican Emigration Control. *International Migration Review, 40*(2), 259–293.

Foley, N. (1998). *The White Scourge: Mexicans, Blacks, and Poor Whites in Texas Cotton Culture*. Berkeley: University of California Press.

Frey, W. H. (2006). *Diversity Spreads Out: Metropolitan Shifts in Hispanic, Asian, and Black Populations Since 2000*. Washington, DC: The Brookings Institute.

Gamboa, E. (1990). *Mexican Labor and World War II: Braceros in the Pacific Northwest, 1942–1947*. Austin: University of Texas Press.

González, G. G. (1994). *Labor and Community: Mexican Citrus Worker Villages in a Southern California County, 1900–1950*. Chicago: University of Illinois Press.

Gozdziak, E. M., & Martin, S. F. (Eds.). (2005). *Beyond the Gateway: Immigrants in a Changing America*. Lanham, MD: Lexington Books.

Gratton, B., & Gutmann, M. P. (2000). Hispanics in the U.S., 1850–1990: Estimates of Population Size and National Origin. *Historical Methods, 33*(3), 137–153.

Gratton, B., & Gutmann, M. P. (2006). Hispanic Population. In S. B. Carter, S. S. Gartner, M. R. Haines, A. L. Olmstead, R. Sutch, & G. Wright (Eds.), *Historical Statistics of the United States. Vol. One. Part A: Population*. New York: Cambridge University Press.

Gratton, B., Gutmann, M. P., & Skop, E. (2004). *The 'Textbook Case': Family Structure and Assimilation Among Mexican and Other Immigrant Children, 1880 to 1970*. Unpublished manuscript, Arizona State University.

Guerin-Gonzales, C. (1994). *Mexican Workers and American Dreams: Immigration, Repatriation and California Farm Labor, 1900–1939*. New Brunswick, NJ: Rutgers University Press.

Gutiérrez, D. G. (1995). *Walls and Mirrors: Mexican Americans, Mexican Immigrants and the Politics of Ethnicity*. Berkeley: University of California Press.

Gutmann, M. P., Frisbie, W. P., & Blanchard, K. S. (1999). A New Look at the Hispanic Population of the U.S. in 1910. *Historical Methods, 32*, 5–19.

Gutmann, M. P., McCaa, R., Gutiérrez-Montes, R., & Gratton, B. (2000). Los Efectos Demográfios de la Revolución Mexicana en Estados Unidos [The Demographic Impact of the Mexican Revolution in the United States]. *Historica Mexicana, 50* (3), 145–165.

Haverluk, T. (1997). The Changing Geography of U.S. Hispanics. *Journal of Geography, 96*(3), 134–145.

Hoffman, A. (1974). *Unwanted Mexican Americans in the Great Depression*. Tucson: University of Arizona Press.

Jones, R. (Ed.). (2007). *Immigrants Outside Megalopolis: Ethnic Transformation in the Heartland*. Lanham, MD: Lexington Books.

Krissman, F. (2005). Sin Coyote Ni Patrón: Why the "Migrant Network" Fails to Explain International Migration. *International Migration Review, 39*(1), 4–44.

Longmore, T. W., & Hitt, H. L. (1943). A demographic Analysis of First and Second Generation Mexican Population of the U.S.: 1930. *Southwestern Social Science Quarterly, 24*(3), 138–149.

Massey, D. S. (1999). Why Does Immigration Occur? A Theoretical Synthesis. In C. Hirschman, P. Kasinitz, & J. DeWind (Eds.), *The Handbook of International Migration* (pp. 34–52). New York: Russell Sage Foundation.

Massey, D. S., Alarcon, R., Durand, J., & González, H. (1987). *Return to Aztlan*: *The Social Process of International Migration from Western Mexico*. Berkeley: University of California Press.

Meinig, D. W. (1971). *Southwest: Three Peoples in Geographical Change 1600–1970*. New York: Oxford University Press.

Menjivar, C. (2000). *Fragmented Ties: Salvadoran Immigrant Networks in America*. Berkeley: University of California Press.

Moore, J., & Pinderhughes, R. (Eds.). (1993). *In the Barrios*: *Latinos and the Underclass Debate*. New York: Russell Sage Foundation.

Nostrand, R. (1970). The Hispanic-American Borderland: Delimitation of an American Culture Region. *Annals of the Association of American Geographers, 60*(4), 638–661.

Nostrand, R. (1993). *The Hispano homeland*. Norman: University of Oklahoma Press.

Oppenheimer, R. (1985). Acculturation or Assimilation: Mexican Immigrants in Kansas, 1900 to WWII. *Western Historical Quarterly, 16*(4), 429–448.

Peck, G. (2000). *Reinventing Free Labor: Padrones and Immigrant Workers in the North American West, 1880–1930*. New York: Cambridge University Press.

Rochen, R. I., Siles, M. E., & Gomez, J. (1996, August). *Latinos in Nebraska: A Socio-historical Profile* (Statistical Brief No. 9). Julian Samora Research Institute. Michigan: East Landing.

Rosales, A. (1981). Regional Origins of Mexican Immigration. In M. Meier & F. Rivera (Eds.), *A Dictionary on Mexican American History* (pp. 297–298). Westport, CT: Greenwood Press.

Ruggles, S., Sobek, M., Alexander, T., Fitch, C. A., Goeken, R., Hall, P. K., et al. (2004). *Integrated Public Use Microdata Series, Version 3.0: User's Guide*. Minneapolis: Social History Laboratory, University of Minnesota.

Ruiz, V. (1998). *From Out of the Shadows: Mexican Women in Twentieth Century America*. New York: Oxford University Press.

Singer, A., Brettell, C., & Hardwick, S. (2007). *America's Twenty-First Century Immigrant Gateways: Immigrant Incorporation in Suburbia*. Washington, DC: The Brookings Institute.

Skop, E., Gratton, B., & Gutmann, M. (2006). *La Frontera* and Beyond: Geography and Demography in Mexican American History. *The Professional Geographer, 58*(1), 78–98.

Skop, E., & Menjívar, C. (2001). Phoenix: The Newest Latino Immigrant Gateway? *Yearbook of the Association of Pacific Coast Geographers, 63*, 63–76.

Smith, J. S. (2002). Cultural Landscape Change in a Hispanic Region. In Kate A. Berry & Mary L. Henderson (Eds.), *Geographical Identities of Ethnic America: Race, Space, and Place* (pp. 174–200). Reno: University of Nevada Press.

Suro, R., & Singer, A. (2002). *Latino Growth in Metropolitan America: Changing Patterns, New Locations*. Washington, DC: The Brookings Institution.

CHAPTER 17

Entre Nosotras/os: Theorizing, Researching, and Constructing Cross-Latina/o Relations in the United States

GILDA L. OCHOA

INTRODUCTION

In 1996, thousands of people from throughout the United States walked shoulder to shoulder as part of a historic Latino March on Washington. Flags from places such as Puerto Rico, Mexico, El Salvador, Guatemala, Nicaragua, the Dominican Republic, Cuba, and the United States filled the sky. Bilingual chants echoed in the streets and salsa, rancheros, and Afro-Cuban music set the beat. Latinas/os from different states and countries highlighted specific concerns. Californian Latinas/os denounced Governor Pete Wilson, the 1994 passage of Proposition 187 that sought to deny undocumented immigrants access to critical social services, and 1996's Proposition 209 that involved the elimination of affirmative action. Whereas many Central Americans carried placards calling for amnesty, groups of Puerto Ricans advocated for independence from the United States. Nydia Velasquez, the first Puerto Rican woman elected to Congress from New York, addressed the audience by speaking first to Puerto Ricans—citizens by birth—stating that attacks against immigrants are also attacks against Puerto Ricans. Amid such heterogeneity, there was a feeling of unity. This march was a perfect display of Latina/o pan-ethnicity. The demonstrating students, union members, politicians, teachers, and families were motivated by various critical issues, but the general platform included support for educational, health care, and citizenship rights for immigrants and workers.

Ten years later in 2006 in the midst of a resurgence of nativism against Latina/o immigration, Latinas/os again took to the streets. The demonstrations were sparked by the U.S. House of Representative Bill 4437: The Border Protection, Antiterrorism, and Illegal Immigration Control Act that proposed building a 700-mile fence along the U.S.-Mexico border and making undocumented immigrants and those who assist them felons. Millions of Latinas/os responded fervently to this draconian anti-immigration bill. Along with massive demonstrations, school walkouts, and economic boycotts in long-time Latina/o areas, the growing number of Latinas/os in the U.S. South and Midwest also protested such anti-immigrant policies.

Despite these impressive displays of unity and activism, not all Latinas/os agreed with these demonstrators, and their critiques varied. For example, over 30% of California Latinas/os voting in the 1994 and 1996 elections supported Propositions 187 and 209 (Acuña, 1996, 1998). This division among Latina/o voters has persisted since the 1980s when about 40% of Latinas/os endorsed conservative national and state issues (Martínez, 1998, pp. 200–201). Some are resentful of new immigrants who they believe are not acquiring the English language and are expecting special privileges. Others, concerned that non-Latinas/os might ignore class, generation, or country of origin differences, attempt to distinguish themselves from groups perceived to be more marginalized and stigmatized (Beserra, 2003; Ochoa, 2004; Paerregaard, 2005). Most recently, there are examples of Latina/o participation in anti-immigrant groups that are patrolling the Mexico-U.S. border against undocumented immigrants and protesting day labor sites.

In spite of the range of interactions among Latinas/os in the United States—from political mobilization to outright hostility—until recently, most scholars have ignored the interethnic and intraethnic relationships among the groups included within the broad Latina/o pan-ethnic category. Following a review of some of the academic reasons for this limited scholarship, this chapter synthesizes the literature on intraethnic and interethnic Latina/o relations to argue that cross-Latina/o relationships are dynamic and contextually specific and vary from conflict to solidarity. Cross-Latina/o relationships are best understood by analyzing the interplay of macroscopic factors, dominant ideologies, institutional practices, group dynamics, and individual experiences and perspectives. Greater awareness of these multiple factors influencing Latina/o relationships is an important step in the social justice project.

ACADEMIC CONSTRAINTS ON CROSS-LATINA/O SCHOLARSHIP IN THE UNITED STATES

Traditional social science theories and research methodologies that have been inflexible, exclusionary, and essentializing have restricted scholarship on cross-Latina/o relationships. In particular, theories of assimilation, the dominant social science framework for understanding race, ethnicity, and integration through the 1960s, compared Southern and Eastern Europeans with Blacks, Latinas/os, Native Americans, and Asian Americans. Therefore, there was an overwhelming focus on whether groups such as Mexican Americans and Puerto Ricans would follow similar or different patterns of acculturation and structural integration compared to that of Southern and Eastern Europeans. Rather than understanding the experiences of Mexican Americans and Puerto Ricans on their own terms, this scholarship tended to center Euro-Americans by making their experiences the norm by which all other national origin and ethnic groups were compared. Thus, distinct histories of conquest and colonization and varied class positions were often overlooked, and little was said about how different Latin Americans interacted with each other.

Today, scholars are increasingly researching the experiences of second-generation Latinas/os. Although this is an important area of study, the framework of assimilation and processes of integration into the Euro-American mainstream still dictates much of this academic discourse.

Challenging assimilationist paradigms and expectations, early nationalist theories that emerged from the civil rights struggles of the 1960s and 1970s provided important structural and historical contexts to understanding the distinct experiences of Chicanos and Puerto Ricans. However, in the initial wave of scholarship, within-group variations were often subsumed under a framework that centered national boundaries and narrow conceptualizations of culture. Thus, differences by class, gender, and sexuality were often ignored, as were indigenous, Asian- and Afro-Latina/o identities among Chicanas/os and Puerto Ricans. Also, because the emphasis of these nationalist frameworks was on the experience of Chicanas/os *or* Puerto Ricans and because of the historical patterns of geographic concentration by Latina/o ethnic groups, research on cross-Latina/o comparisons and relationships was restricted.

Just as the early social science paradigms of assimilation continue to limit contemporary scholarship, so do two popular binaries within the fields of race and ethnicity: Black-White binaries and race-class binaries. Through the 1970s, much of the scholarship on race and ethnicity focused on the relationships between Blacks and Whites or Mexican Americans and Whites (Martínez, 1998). As well as centering the experiences of Whites, these binary constructions also disregarded the racial/ethnic heterogeneity and simultaneity among Latinas/os who might identify as Black, White, indigenous, *and/or* Asian, and they neglect the variations in skin color, hair texture, and facial features that influence life chances in a racially stratified society. Likewise, the ongoing debate regarding the salience of race *or* class in shaping life experiences has been equally as stifling. This debate ignores the intersections of race *and* class, and it tends to assume that all Latinas/os are working class. Thus, analyses of Latina/o relationships across race/ethnicity, phenotype, and class have been stunted.

What we know about Latina/o relationships has also been shaped by established research methods. Quantitative datasets that fail to distinguish between distinct nationalities of Latinas/os or different class positions and generations camouflage Latina/o heterogeneity and impede understandings of cross-Latina/o relations. In addition, attitudinal surveys are often limiting because they capture static perceptions that lack context and do not allow for the multiple and situational nature of relationships and interactions. Finally, whereas qualitative data better allows for the nuances and situated-ness of attitudes and interactions, the amount of resources required to complete and analyze in-depth interviews and participant observations often limit the range of studies by geography and nationality. Therefore, most in-depth studies on Latina/o identities, attitudes, and relationships focus on one geographic community and one to two national origin groups.

Although there are earlier studies (see Browning & de la Garza, 1986; Padilla, 1985; Rodriguez, 1986), it is only within the past 15–20 years that growing numbers of researchers have begun to systematically explore within-group relationships among Latinas/os and the factors influencing attitudes and interactions. Fortunately, this burgeoning body of scholarship has been stimulated by several simultaneous phenomena: newer social science theories on power, inequality, transnationalism, and diaspora; the critique of narrow nationalism by feminists of color; the increase in Latina/o academics, the growth in Latina/o diversity across the United States, and a rise in Latina/o pan-ethnic mobilization. Underlying this newer scholarship is an emphasis on Latina/o heterogeneity.

LATINA/O HETEROGENITY AND THE CONFLICT-SOLIDARITY CONTINUUM: CONCEPTUALIZING CROSS-LATINA/O RELATIONSHIPS

The massive public demonstrations in 1996 and 2006 and the various responses to them capture some of the heterogeneity, unity, and division among Latinas/os. After all, included among the 41 million people categorized as Latina/o in the United States are individuals who differ by national origin, race, history, immigration, class position, gender, and language. Because each of these factors influence experiences, opportunities, and political ideologies, the significance of this variation on cross-Latina/o relationships should not be ignored. Likewise, because much variation exists within each national origin group as between different groups, harmonious intragroup or intergroup relations cannot be assumed.

Statistically, this heterogeneity is apparent in national origin and racial identifications. According to the 2000 U.S. Census, nearly 60% of the U.S. residents who selected the category "Spanish/Hispanic/Latino" identified as Mexican, Mexican American, or Chicano. Ten percent identified as Puerto Rican, 4% as Cuban, 2% as Dominican, 5% as Central American (most identifying as Salvadoran and Guatemalan), 4% as South American (most identifying as Colombian and Ecuadorian), and 16% as Hispanic, Spanish, or Latino (Suárez-Orozco & Páez, 2002). Racially, Latinas/os selected various categorizations from the Census, including a third marking more than one race. Eight percent identified as Whites, 2% as Black or African American, 15% as American Indian and Alaskan Native, 11% as Asian, Native Hawaiian, and Pacific Islander, and 97% as some "other" race (Ramirez, 2004, p. 2).

Each Latina/o national origin group has a distinct history that has been shaped by U.S. power and domination in Latin America (for further discussion, see Gonzalez, 2000). These asymmetrical relationships within the Americas have influenced migration patterns and whether groups in the United States are products of conquest or colonization or are considered U.S. citizens, permanent residents, political asylees, or undocumented immigrants. Such distinct histories and categorizations, when combined with racial/ethnic discrimination and the decline in high-waged durable goods manufacturing jobs in the United States, have also shaped the class positions of Latinas/os.

Although many Latinas/os in the United States are poor or working class, there are significant differences by subgroups that stem from the context of reception upon entering the United States, skin color, and educational and class position in countries of origin. One of the manifestations of these differences is that South Americans and Cubans have median family incomes $10,000–$14,000 higher than median family incomes of Mexican, Puerto Rican, Central American, and Dominican families (Ramirez, 2004, pp. 14–16).

Given the heterogeneity within the Latina/o category, the relationships that exist between and among individuals and communities within this category are equally as diverse. To best illustrate this diversity, I draw from the conflict-solidarity continuum that I have used elsewhere to describe Mexican American and Mexican immigrant relationships (see Ochoa, 2004). This continuum includes antagonism, a shared connection, and collective political mobilization. Conceptualizing cross-Latina/o relationships on a continuum is useful for demonstrating the simultaneity, fluidity, and range of attitudes and interactions among and between Latinas/os.

Both individual and group relations might vary across time and place. Over a lifetime, people's views might shift. During waves of anti-immigrant sentiment, some Mexican Americans who have previously disassociated and even ridiculed immigrants might start to affirm their shared histories, cultural connections, and experiences of discrimination with immigrants. In particular cases, Mexican Americans have described changing their view toward immigrants after realizing that non-Latinas/os might not distinguish between Mexicans born in the United States and Mexican immigrants. Awareness of such "racial lumping" or homogenization has helped to reduce the generational boundaries dividing Mexican Americans from immigrants (Jiménez, 2005; Ochoa, 2004).

Even within a single day, people's attitudes might fluctuate depending on the situation. There are examples of Mexican Americans who in the comfort of their own homes might antagonistically claim that immigrants should speak English and "learn American customs." However, in public places, they contest similar pronouncements by non-Latinas/os (Ochoa, 2004).

At the group level, this situational character of Latina/o relationships is evident in the many examples of Latina/o collective political mobilization, including the two that began this chapter. In his seminal work, Padilla (1985) provided examples of pan-Latina/o situational identity among Puerto Ricans and Mexican Americans in 1970s Chicago. According to Padilla, these different groups maintained their own national identities, but at critical moments, they also forged pan-ethnic Latino ties because of their shared experiences of inequality and discrimination.

At the other end of the conflict-solidarity continuum, not all Latinas/os identify with other Latinas/os or believe that they have much in common with people from diverse backgrounds and regions (Oboler, 1995). They criticize the use of pan-ethnic labels because they believe that they distort these differences and fuel stereotyped perceptions.

Because the conflict-solidarity continuum captures the range of cross-Latina/o relations and how they might change over time, place, and context, it allows for the possibilities of replacing antagonist relationships among Latinas/os with ones that are characterized by solidarity and a shared awareness of systems of power and inequality. Overall, greater consciousness of the multiple factors and processes shaping experiences and relationships is important for facilitating collective identity and social action.

MACRO-MICRO PROCESSES CONSTRUCTING CROSS-LATINA/O RELATIONSHIPS

Cross-Latina/o relationships—antagonism, a shared connection, and/or collective political mobilization—are not fixed and cannot be presumed. Instead, they are constructed and negotiated within the context of several simultaneous and interacting phenomena and within various locations including the following: (1) a matrix of structural factors, ideological processes, and historical antecedents; (2) dominant institutions; (3) Latina/o organizations; and (4) individual agency. These macro and micro phenomena and locations influence one another; that is, just as the matrix of macroscopic factors influence dominant institutions that might shape cross-Latina/o relationships, cross-Latina/o relationships are experienced and lived from the bottom-up—through microscopic, everyday interactions by individuals and Latina/o organizations that might work to change institutions and macro factors.

Macroscopic Factors and Processes

Although not always apparent, structural factors, dominant ideologies, and historical antecedents frame relationships. Structural factors include capitalism and class and racial hierarchies that privilege the upper classes and whiteness over poor and working-class communities of color. They are transnational where U.S. imperialism, capitalism, and neo-liberalism have intensified hierarchies and disparities within and between countries. Such structural factors are also justified and reproduced by dominant ideologies like white supremacy—including support for the dominance of English-oriented linguistic and cultural practices, the belief that Latina/o immigrants drain the economy, and the myth of meritocracy.

Contemporary structural factors, ideologies, and cross-Latina/o relationships originate in historical processes. Among the historical precursors critical to understanding these relationships is the subordinate position of Mexicans and Puerto Ricans in the United States that stems from conquest and colonization, the asymmetrical power relationships between the United States and Latin American, and the racial, cultural, and historical distinctions that exist among Latin Americans. These distinct histories have influenced life chances, others' perceptions, and group relations. In particular, three different case studies on Peruvians, Brazilians, and Mexicans in the United States uncover both the specificity and the simultaneity of macroscopic factors and processes on cross-Latina/o relations.

PERUVIANS IN LOS ANGELES, MIAMI, AND PATERSON   One poignant example that magnifies the salience of historical precursors within the United States and in Latin America on cross-Latina/o relationships is provided in the work of Paerregaard (2005) on Peruvians in three cities: Los Angeles, Miami, and Paterson. Paerregaard found Peruvians in each of these locations who attempted to distinguish themselves from the predominant and/or stigmatized Latina/o group: Mexicans in Los Angeles, Cubans in Miami, and Puerto Ricans in Paterson, New Jersey. Hoping to avoid being lumped together with these groups, Peruvians used art, culture, and religious celebrations as forms of disassociation. Ironically, rather than foster unity among Peruvians in the United States, middle- and upper-class migrants competed with indigenous migrants in the construction of what constituted Peruvianess, thereby reinforcing preexisting class and cultural tensions from Peru. Thus, Paerregaard's study suggested that not only do historical patterns of migration and marginalization have contemporary consequences for how new immigrant groups relate to longer-established Latina/o communities, but in the U.S. context, class, culture, and ethnic inequalities from Latin America might be reproduced *within* national-origin groups.

BRAZILIANS IN LOS ANGELES   Beserra's (2003) framework for analyzing how Brazilian immigrants in Los Angeles responded to the category "Latina/o" is helpful for demonstrating the intersections of structural factors, ideologies, and historical precursors on cross-Latina/o relationships. To understand why Brazilians in Los Angeles might distance themselves from the Latina/o pan-ethnic category, Beserra (2003, p. 60) focused on five related factors: (1) the placement of different countries in the international division of labor; (2) an immigrant's social position in his/her country of origin; (3) the relational positioning of different immigrants; (4) U.S. labor market demands; and (5) imperialist ideologies that naturalize hierarchies of race, gender, and class. According to Beserra, given the placement of Brazil as a peripheral country dependent on the United States, Brazilians regardless of class position are categorized by others in the United States as "Latina/o." However, middle-class and lighter-skinned Brazilians are able to distance themselves from the "Latina/o" category, a category that some Brazilians have accepted as derogatory because of its association with working-class Mexicans and Central Americans in Los Angeles (Beserra, 2003).

MEXICAN AMERICAN–MEXICAN IMMIGRANT RELATIONS IN SANTA PAULA, CALIFORNIA   Menchaca's (1995) study of Santa Paula, California captures the significance of structural factors, ideological processes, and historical antecedents on intragroup relations. Her analysis of Mexican American–Mexican immigrant relations suggests how an unequal class structure and the ideology of white superiority has generated intragroup conflict and cooperation. Menchaca described how in the 1900s, a cultural prestige ranking system was established by Anglo-Saxon citrus growers who claimed to be biologically superior to Mexicans. Once this ideology was created, it became institutionalized as part of Santa Paula's norms, and it determined appropriate and inappropriate modes of behavior. Thus, since the 1900s, Anglos have expected Mexicans to behave like them by downplaying their ethnicity. In turn, Mexican Americans have internalized these expectations, and Mexican immigrants are only admitted into Mexican Americans' social circles after learning Anglo norms, practices, and values. Mexicans who have not acculturated are seen as culturally "backward," and those who are proficient in English are ascribed higher social prestige (Menchaca, 1995).

Despite these divisions, the relationships between Mexican Americans and Mexican immigrants are not fixed. During times of severe crises when Anglo business owners tried to impose harsher practices on Mexicans, there were important examples of Mexican cohesion across generations.

As these three qualitative studies illustrate, macro-structural factors and processes are critical for framing and understanding Latina/o relationships. However, by including the voices and experiences of different community members, these studies also remind us that analysis should not stop with these top-down frameworks. After all, these larger structures and ideologies impact institutional practices, political organizations, and individual experiences. Institutions and organizations are the spaces where cross-Latina/o relationships are constructed on a daily basis, and individuals play an active role in negotiating their identities and relationships.

Mediating Institutions Structuring Everyday Relations

As Lamphere (1992) described, "institutions shape, structure, and constrain interrelations" (p. 4). Because institutions are hierarchically structured by race/ethnicity and class, different individuals and groups possess unequal amounts of power, have clearly defined roles such as worker-employee or owner-tenet, occupy different locations within an institution, and have limited opportunities for interaction (Lamphere, 1992). The results are that Latinas/os of differing backgrounds might only interact in formal situations within the context of power differentials.

To the extent that institutional practices segregate groups by race/ethnicity, class, and immigration status, unequal and limited contact might reinforce group boundaries. So, on the one hand, working- and upper-middle-class Latinas/os might live in different communities and occupy distinct physical spaces in schools and at work. They might have different class interests and have limited interaction. Limited exchanges across disparate backgrounds might fuel prevailing stereotypes and foster conflictual relationships. However, individuals who share marginalized positions because of history, immigration, color, language, and/or class background might develop a sense of identity stemming from comparable experiences and daily exchanges in community spaces.

To illustrate how institutional practices influence cross-Latina/o attitudes and interactions, the following subsections present some of the recent scholarship on relationships within schools, work sites, communities, and religious organizations. Although these sections focus on the factors influencing conflict, to the extent that institutions are restructured in more inclusive and democratic ways, the possibilities for cross-Latina/o solidarity are enhanced.

SCHOOLS   Typically, school practices divide students by race/ethnicity, English-language skills, and class position, and these divisions have important consequence for cross-Latina/o relationships. Based on biased standardized tests and school officials' raced and classed stereotypes, students are often separated into different classes, distinct parts of the school campus, and unequal curriculum tracks (Oakes, 1985). These divisions often happen at early ages in the form of different reading groups in elementary school, and they persist in high school through course placement in vocational, college preparatory, or honors tracks. English- language learners typically experience a "cultural track" where they are steered away from their English-dominant peers into remote areas of campus (Valenzuela, 1999). These disparate tracks are reproduced in peer groups in which students often interact with peers in their classes and those who share their languages, socioeconomic positions, and generations.

Studies on Mexican American and Mexican immigrant students in the Southwest reveal how these constructed divisions, when combined with Eurocentric course curriculum and other assimilationist policies that minimize and denigrate students' cultures, foster misunderstanding, ridicule, and outright conflict (Matute-Bianchi, 1986; Ochoa, 2004; Valenzuela, 1999). Such dynamics might lead students to develop different identities and ways of negotiating school practices. Some students might establish a strong sense of being Mexicana/o, Mexican American, *or* Chicana/o as strategies of resistance against the marginalization that they face in schools and in opposition to other students (Bejarano, 2005; Matute-Bianchi, 1986). Thus, students might draw lines around and prejudge peer groups in ways that duplicate the politics of difference within schools by language abilities, citizenship, styles of dress, and skin color.

Early school experiences of Americanization and punishment for speaking Spanish have influenced the views that some older and more established generations of Latinas/os have of immigrants. For example, some Mexican Americans who were raised during the 1940s and 1950s when Mexicans were likely to be at least third generation believe that they "played by the rules" by acquiring English and "becoming American" as quickly as possible without institutional support. Now, they blame immigrants for the use of Spanish in today's schools and oppose programs such as bilingual education that they see as serving immigrants to the detriment of U.S.-born Latinas/os (Ochoa, 2004).

Just as school practices might fuel cross-Latina/o tensions and divisions, to the extent that schools implement heterogeneous and untracked classrooms and adopt curriculum that explores diverse histories and experiences, there are opportunities for greater awareness and enhanced interactions. Some elementary school teachers tout the cross-generational, class, and racial/ethnic connections that dual-language immersion programs promote because they bring together families and students of varied backgrounds into one classroom with the shared goal of bilingualism. Diaz Soto's (1997) work on bilingual education in a Puerto Rican community in Pennsylvania offered a promising example of the ways that intergenerational communication and relations are enhanced when schools focus on developing rather than subtracting students' home languages and cultures. Furthermore, at the college level, Mexican Americans who have completed Chicana/o Studies, sociology, and politics courses described an increased awareness of the shared histories and experiences of exclusion encountered by various marginalized groups in the United States. For these individuals, this awareness diminished scapegoating and, instead, nurtured a commitment for social justice (Ochoa, 2004).

WORK AND THE ECONOMY   As with schools, the physical structure and organization of work sites might also negatively structure group relations. To the extent that established Latinas/os possess higher occupations than working-class or recent immigrants, the division of labor within many occupations becomes more than just classed. It becomes nationalized, and the differential power dimensions of jobs might unequally position groups in ways that constrain interactions across occupation and solidify group relations within similar jobs. Likewise, during economic recessions, workplaces are often sites of contestation, and nativist sentiment simultaneously fuels animosity and fosters collaboration among Latinas/os.

A research team in Miami documented how workplace structure has controlled relationships between Cuban managers and Cuban, Nicaraguan, and Haitian workers in the apparel industry (see Grenier & Stepick, 1992). An extreme form of division of labor, a fast-paced and repetitive workplace, and a piece-rate system resulted in competition between workers, limited opportunities for interaction, the reinforcement of cross-group stereotypes, and the maintenance of boundaries by nationality, race/ethnicity, and language. Although employers structured the workplace that negatively influenced cross-Latina/o relationships, women employees fostered more harmonious cross-group interactions by organizing plantwide parties for U.S. holidays that united people across their differences.

As Bonacich (1972) documented with her split labor market theory on race relations, conflict that emerges from a tripartite relationship among owner, high-wage labor, and low-wage labor serves capitalists' interests. It prevents high-wage labor and low-wage labor from coalescing for higher salaries, improved working conditions, and benefits. A poignant example of the fostering of cross-Latina/o divisions by maintaining an extremely exploited class of workers is the use of temporary guest workers to fulfill labor-intensive and poorly remunerated jobs. Scholars have recounted how the Bracero Program (1942–1964) under which U.S. agribusiness recruited workers from Mexico pitted migrant workers against Mexican-Americans (Gutiérrez, 1995). Such temporary worker programs create a social and economic hierarchy among Latina/o workers that benefit business interests at the expense of worker relationships and improved working conditions.

Within the labor market, tensions across race/ethnicity, class position, and generation are exacerbated during economic downturns. During declines in the U.S. economy, debates often turn to controlling immigration and blaming the poor for draining social services, thereby making working-class communities and immigrants the scapegoats for capitalist outcomes. Today's scapegoating leads many to overlook the devastating impacts of global economic restructuring in Latin America and the United States. The results of such scapegoating is that whereas some Latinas/os unite because of their shared experiences of exclusion and inequality, others participate in the anti-immigrant backlash that ranges from negative beliefs to active involvement in campaigns to roll back social services and criminalize immigrants.

OTHER COMMUNITY SPACES   As with schools and work sites, neighborhoods are structured in ways that influence relationships. The history of exclusionary racial covenants and the class divisions within and between many cities where apartments and single-family homes are separated reduce opportunities for cross-generational, cross-class, and cross-ethnic interactions. This is the case in La Puente, California, where recent Latina/o immigrants tend to live in apartments while more financially and socially established Mexican Americans often own single-family homes. Residents in separate and unequal neighborhoods are further divided by the distinct geographical locations of their neighborhood supermarkets, schools, and parks. Such physical distance from groups seen as different from one's own offers little opportunity to dispel stereotypical beliefs. However, at times when outsiders maintain disparaging perceptions of an entire city because of its racial/ethnic or class composition, internal neighborhood divisions are overshadowed by a sense of shared identity (Ochoa, 2004).

De Genova and Ramos-Zayas (2003) also described the persistence of geographic divisions and their implications for Latina/o relationships. They recount how Chicago's enduring history of racial segregation has combined with distinct racialized constructions of Mexicans as "illegal aliens" and Puerto Ricans as "welfare dependents" to enforce spatial divisions between the two largest Latina/o groups in the area.

Whereas the structure of cities might engender separation between communities and across class positions, public facilities and the everyday uses of public spaces, especially in working-class areas, might promote neighborly exchanges among local residents. In the working class community of Corona, New York, Ricourt and Danta (2003) observed the daily interactions of Latinas from Colombia, Cuba, the Dominican Republic, Ecuador, Peru, Puerto Rico, and Uruguay in laundro-mats, hospitals, buses, subways, churches, and parks. "Experiential pan-ethnicity" emerged from these women's activities in neighborhood settings, their use of the Spanish language, and their residence in a high-density working-class community. Over time, this experiential pan-ethnicity eventually led to "categorical pan-ethnicity" where national identities were not eliminated but neighbors referred to one another collectively in pan-ethnic terms such as "hispanos" or "latinoa-mericanos." Furthermore, in Protestant and Roman Catholic churches, Ricourt and Danta (2003) detected harmonious pan-Latina/o relationships among diverse nationalities. They found that a Latina/o pan-ethnic identity was reinforced by everyday experiences of discrimination and institutional practices that fostered a shared identity within the churches.

Although this "categorical pan-ethnicity" might have existed in churches among Spanish-speaking Latinas/os in Corona, New York, when institutional practices within religious organizations are combined with differences in generation and language, harmonious pan-Latina/o relationships are not always evident. Mexican American and Mexican immigrant Catholics in La Puente, California have responded diversely to the rise in Spanish-language services and the increase in immigrant parishioners. Some embrace the use of Spanish, attend Spanish-language masses to ensure that their children maintain the language, and contest anti-Spanish language sentiment. Nevertheless, some older parishioners critique Spanish-language masses. Explaining how they have acculturated, they resent institutional practices that they believe accommodate Latina/o immigrants at the expense of long-term residents (Ochoa, 2004).

To further understand why some groups of Latinas/os might be responding negatively to the growth in immigrant parishioners and services, additional scholarship should consider how church practices and church leaders foster cross-Latina/o conflict and/or solidarity.

Political Organizations and Mobilizations

Just as dominant institutions structure cross-Latina/o relationships, the philosophies and actions of political organizations also construct group boundaries. Two Los Angeles-area mobilizations—the 1993 UCLA student movement and the 1995 Justice for Janitors union campaign—are illustrative of how group beliefs and activities influence cross-Latina/o relationships and a sense of belonging. Both of these organizing attempts were in response to institutional subordination, and the organizers employed different cultural practices as part of the organizing campaign that had varied impacts on cross-Latina/o relations.

Documenting the 1993 UCLA student movement, Soldatenko (2005) had detailed how patriarchical and Chicano nationalist practices usurped the possibilities for an inclusively defined movement for educational justice that involved a broad-based coalition that reflected Los Angeles demographics. Initially, a diverse group of students from various communities organized as Conscious Students of Color (CSC) against the academy's policies, including budget cuts to the Ethnic and Women's Studies programs and the failure to establish a Chicana/o Studies department. However, a power struggle between CSC and student organizations that focused specifically on Chicana/o Studies evolved, and the student movement began to center around several Mexican American hunger strikers that "sought a nationalist Chicano Studies department" (Soldatenko, 2005, p. 259). Accompanying this hunger strike was the invoking of specific Mexican and indigenous symbols such as the Mexican flag, the Virgin, and the burning of copal. This shift resulted in a narrowing of the student movement organizers and issues. Feminism was subordinated until after the struggle for Chicano Studies was complete, and the identity and political commitments of some non-Latinas/os, biracial/ethnic Latinas/os, and Central and South Americans were questioned. Strict Mexican nationalism reinscribed narrow boundaries that marginalized various individuals, groups, and perspectives. According to Soldatenko (2005), these narrow politics also limited the possibilities for a transformative analysis and a rethinking of traditional ethnic studies.

Just 2 years after the 1993 UCLA student movement, Service Employees International (SEIU) Local 399 Justice for Janitors (JfJ) utilized various measures to successfully organize a broad base of Los Angeles-area Latinas/os in Woodland Hills. As Gutierrez de Soldentenko (2005) described, JfJ had been exemplary in its ability to organize Latina/o workers. Key to its success had been its community-based approach, its hiring of Latina/o and non-Latina/o union organizers knowledgeable about *Latinidad*, and its ability to draw upon working-class Latinas/os' "cultural repertoire," including the Spanish language and Latin American rituals and practices. In this case where working-class Latinas/os—primarily Central American and Mexican women—share work experiences and are concentrated in janitorial positions because of gender, race/ethnicity, and class inequalities, JfJ successfully fostered pan-ethnic mobilization in their 1995 union movement. As with the 1993 UCLA student movement, cultural practices were part of the organizing campaign, but they were ones that were more broadly conceived, allowing for greater inclusion of Latinas/os from across Latin America. Likewise, in contrast to the student movement, Latinas were not pushed to the periphery of the movement. Instead, their concerns and presence were central to the union struggle (Gutierrez de Soldentenko, 2005).

The case studies of these two mid-1990s struggles capture the salience of exclusionary ideologies and actions by institutional representatives—such as college administrators and business employers—and organizers on cross-Latina/o relations. These examples also suggest how broadly constructed cultural connections can be strategically used to mobilize around shared class, racial/ethnic, and gender interests (for more examples, see Ochoa, 2004; Padilla, 1985; Ricourt & Danta, 2003; Valenzuela, 1999).

The Importance of Individual Differences and Personal Agency

In spite of the significance of macro-structural factors and institutions on cross-Latina/o relations and the activities of political organizations, Latina/o relationships are not predetermined. Individuals experience these relationships differently and have varied roles in constructing them. These differences and personal agency on cross-Latina/o relations are apparent when considering what Bozorgmehr (1992) described as "internal ethnicity." Though Bozorgmehr (1992) used this concept to describe the heterogeneity that exists among Iranians, it can also be applied to the diversity by gender, generation, language, ethnicity, and so forth within and between specific groups of Latinas/os.

Studies on cross-Latina/o relations suggest that in comparison to Latinos, Latinas' gendered obligations often result in their community-building activities. By taking children to school, participating in religious organizations, and looking out for the interests of their families and communities, women often do the "social work of neighboring" (Goode & Schneider, 1994, p. 148). According to Hardy-Fanta's (1993) work on political activism among Puerto Ricans, Dominicans, and Central and South Americans in Boston, Latinas are more likely than Latinos to focus on collaboration, community participation, and making connections with people. Focusing on Mexican Americans in East Los Angeles, Pardo (1998) also documented the critical role of women in grassroots organizing for community concerns.

As with gender, there are indications that distinct experiences in the United States based on length of time in the country might influence attitudes and interactions among and between Latinas/os. For example, in the city of La Puente, the community-builders include Mexican immigrants who came to the United States in their early teens. Several individuals have been able to draw upon their bilingual-bicultural skills and their experiences in both Mexican and U.S. institutions to understand the experiences and perspectives of Mexican Americans and immigrants. From this unique vantage point, they assist with immigrant integration into the United States and serve as brokers and unifiers between Mexican Americans and Mexican immigrants (Ochoa, 2004).

Finally, the "internal ethnicity" among Latinas/os and its significance on relationships is becoming increasingly apparent in current research on indigenous, African, and Asian Latinas/os (see DeFay, 2004; Hagan, 1994; Malpica, 2005; Thomas, 2005). As well as describing the distinct languages, styles of dress, and other cultural practices that exist within and across specific national origin groups, much of this newer scholarship also includes historical and structural understandings for the racial/ethnic and class distinctions that persist within the U.S. context. For example, DeFay's (2004) qualitative research in Los Angeles detailed the strong community and cultural connections among Garifuna immigrants from Central America, where their identities as Afro-indigenous Garifuna often take precedence over other identities—including a Belizean national identity. However, even within this close-knit community, tensions have emerged over gender, religious, class, and generational differences.

FUTURE RESEARCH

Because Latinas/os are so heterogeneous, researching cross-Latina/o relations not only expands what we know about the individuals and groups within this pan-ethnic category, but it also furthers our knowledge of how we can improve relationships across varied groups structurally, ideologically, institutionally, organizationally, and individually. Thus, additional research in this area has the potential to enhance understanding of cross-racial/ethnic relationships in general and the types of change required for social justice.

As Latinas/os form newer communities throughout the United States, future research should explore the formation of these communities. For instance, researchers might consider how institutional structures and Euro-American or African American communities in southern and midwestern cities are influencing Latina/o relationships. Comparisons between more established Latina/o communities and newer communities will help to better elucidate the contextual nuances involved in cross-Latina/o dynamics.

Just as research on newer geographical communities will capture more of the heterogeneity among Latina/os, so will research that centers the voices, experiences, and perspectives of a wider cross-section of Latinas/os. The experiences of several groups and communities remain dramatically understudied. First, there is a significant gap in research on how colorism and differing racial/ethnic identities (such as Afro-Latina/o, mestiza/o, and indigenous) influence Latina/o relationships (for exceptions, see DeFay, 2004; Thomas, 2005). Second, little research exists on Central

American and Mexican American relations, even in areas in Los Angeles and San Francisco, where these groups often reside in similar communities and share neighborhood spaces (for an exception, see Castañeda, Manz, & Davenport, 2002). Third, age remains an understudied dynamic in cross-Latina/o relationships. Although some quantitative studies on Mexican Americans suggest that older residents might possess more negative perceptions of immigrants (Binder, Polinard, & Wrinkle, 1997), qualitative researchers have not thoroughly explored the significance of age. Additionally, outside of school interactions, we know little about how younger Latinas/os experience and understand cross-Latina/o relationships (for an exception on intergenerational Salvadoran relationships within families in San Francisco, see Menjívar, 2000). Finally, although the research on newer generations of Latinas/os in the United States has tended to center the voices and perspectives of immigrants, the research on more established communities, such as Mexican Americans and Puerto Ricans, has not sufficiently documented and theorized these within-group relationships from the perspective of newer arrivals.

By listening to the attitudes and experiences of a wider section of Latinas/os, this research will add to our understanding of the factors that foster solidarity and enhance coalition-building. What recent cross-racial/ethnic tensions in schools and the immigrant rights movement have magnified is the importance of research on how working-class communities and other communities of color are interacting with Latinas/os. Some of the same historical, structural, ideological, and institutional factors that are influencing Latinas/os are shaping cross-racial/ethnic relationships and hindering other marginalized communities. Awareness of these similarities has the potential to enliven the social justice movement. The demonstrations that began this chapter capture the power of pan-ethnicity. However, the real power to dramatically transform the system of inequality that continues to divide us exists in our ability to build bridges and make connections across race/ethnicity, class, gender, generation, and so forth.

REFERENCES

Acuña, R. (1996). *Anything But Mexican: Chicanos in Contemporary Los Angeles*. London: Verso.

Acuña, R. (1998). *Sometimes There Is No Other Side: Chicanos and the Myth of Equality*. Notre Dame, IN: University of Notre Dame Press.

Bejarano, C. (2005). *Qué Onda? Urban Youth Culture and Border Identity*. Tucson: University of Arizona Press.

Beserra, B. (2003). *Brazilian Immigrants in the United States: Cultural Imperialism and Social Class*. New York: LBF Scholarly Publishing.

Binder, N. E., Polinard, J. E., & Wrinkle, R. D. (1997). Mexican American and Anglo Attitudes Toward Immigration Reform: A View from the Border. *Social Science Quarterly, 78*, 324–337.

Bonacich, E. (1972). A Theory of Ethnic Antagonism. *American Sociological Review, 37*, 547–599.

Bozorgmehr, M. (1992). *Internal Ethnicity: Armenian, Bahai, Jewish, and Muslim Iranians in Los Angeles*. Unpublished doctoral dissertation, University of California, Los Angeles.

Browning, H. L., & de la Garza, R. O. (1986). *Mexican Immigrants and Mexican Americans: An Evolving Relation*. Austin: University of Texas Press.

Castañeda, X., Manz, B., & Davenport, A. (2002). Mexicanization: A Survival Strategy for Guatemalan Mayans in the San Francisco Bay Area. *Migraciones Internacionales, 3*, 102–123.

DeFay, J. B. (2004). *Identity Matters: Immigration and the Social Construction of Identity in Garifuna Los Angeles*. Unpublished doctoral dissertation, University of California, San Diego.

De Genova, N., & Ramos-Zayas, A. Y. (2003). *Latino Crossings: Mexicans, Puerto Ricans, and the Politics of Race and Citizenship*. New York: Routledge.

Diaz Soto, Lourdes. (1997). *Language, Culture, and Power: Bilingual Families and the Struggle for Quality Education*. Albany: State University of New York Press.

Gonzalez, J. (2000). *Harvest of Empire: A History of Latinos in America*. New York: Viking Press.

Goode, J., & Schneider, J. A. (1994). *Reshaping Ethnic and Racial Relations in Philadelphia: Immigrants in a Divided City*. Philadelphia: Temple University Press.

Grenier, G. J., & Stepick, A. (with Draznin, D., LaBorwit, A., Morris, S., & Coppée, B.). (1992). On Machines and Bureaucracy: Controlling Ethnic Interaction in Miami's Apparel and Construction Industries. In L. Lamphere (Ed.), *Structuring Diversity: Ethnographic Perspectives on the New Immigration* (pp. 65–93). Chicago: University of Chicago Press.

Gutiérrez, D. G. (1995). *Walls and Mirrors: Mexican Americans, Mexican Immigrants, and the Politics of Ethnicity.* Berkeley: University of California Press.

Gutierrez de Soldatenko, M. (2005). Justice for Janitors Latinizing Los Angeles: Mobilizing Latina(o) Cultural Repertoire. In E. C. Ochoa & G. L. Ochoa (Eds.), *Latino Los Angeles: Transformations, Communities and Activism* (pp. 225–245). Tucson: University of Arizona Press.

Hagan, J. M. (1994). *Deciding to Be Legal: A Maya Community in Houston.* Philadelphia: Temple University Press.

Hardy-Fanta, C. (1993). *Latina politics, Latino Politics: Gender, Culture, and Political Participation.* Philadelphia: Temple University Press.

Jiménez, T. (2005). Immigrant Replenishment and the Continuing Significance of Ethnicity and Race: The Case of the Mexican-Origin Population (Working Paper 130). San Diego: University of California, The Center for Comparative Immigration Studies.

Lamphere, L. (1992). Introduction: The Shaping of Diversity. In L. Lamphere (Ed.), *Structuring Diversity: Ethnographic Perspectives on the New Immigration* (pp. 1–34). Chicago: University of Chicago Press.

Malpica, D. M. (2005). Indigenous Mexican Migrants in a Modern Metropolis: The Reconstruction of Zapotec Communities in Los Angeles. In E. C. Ochoa & G. L. Ochoa (Eds.), *Latino Los Angeles: Transformations, Communities and Activism* (pp. 111–136). Tucson: University of Arizona Press.

Martínez, E. (1998). *De Colores Means All Of Us: Latina Views for a Multi-colored Century.* Cambridge, MA: South End Press.

Matute-Bianchi, M. E. (1986). Ethnic Identities and Patterns of School Success and Failure Among Mexican-Descent and Japanese-American Students in a California High School: An Ethnographic Analysis. *American Journal of Education, 95,* 233–255.

Menchaca, M. (1995). *The Mexican Outsiders: A Community History of Marginalization and Discrimination in California.* Austin: University of Texas Press.

Menjívar, C. (2000). *Fragmented Ties: Salvadoran Immigrant Networks in America.* Berkeley: University of California Press.

Oakes, J. (1985). *Keeping Track: How Schools Structure Inequality.* New Haven, CT: Yale University Press.

Oboler, S. (1995). *Ethnic Labels, Latino Lives: Politics of (Re)presentation in the United States.* Minneapolis: University of Minnesota Press.

Ochoa, G. L. (2004). *Becoming Neighbors in a Mexican American Community: Power, Conflict and Solidarity.* Austin: University of Texas Press.

Padilla, F. (1985). *Latino Ethnic Consciousness: The Case of Mexican Americans and Puerto Ricans in Chicago.* Notre Dame, IN: University of Notre Dame Press.

Paerregaard, K. (2005). Inside the Hispanic Melting Pot: Negotiating National and Multicultural Identities Among Peruvians in the United States. *Latino Studies, 3,* 76–96.

Pardo. M. (1998). *Mexican American Women Activists: Identity and Resistance in Two Los Angeles Communities.* Philadelphia: Temple University Press.

Ramirez, R. R. (2004). *We the People: Hispanics in the United States* (U.S. Bureau 2000 Special Report). Washington, DC: U.S. Government Printing Office.

Ricourt, M., & Danta, R. (2003). *Hispanas de Queens: Latino Panethnicity in a New York City Neighborhood.* Ithaca, NY: Cornell University Press.

Rodriguez, N. (1986). Chicano-Indocumentado Work Relations: Findings of the Texas Indocumentado Study. In T. Mindiola Jr. & M. Martinez (Eds.), *Chicano-Mexicano Relations* (pp. 72–84). Mexican American Studies Monograph No. 4, Mexican American Studies Program. Houston: University of Houston, University Park.

Soldatenko, M. (2005). Constructing Chicana and Chicano Studies: 1993 UCLA Conscious Students of Color Protest. In E. C. Ochoa & G. L. Ochoa (Eds.), *Latino Los Angeles: Transformations, Communities and Activism* (pp. 246–277). Tucson: University of Arizona Press.

Suárez-Orozco, M. M., & Páez, M. M. (2002). The Research Agenda. In M. M. Suárez-Orozco & M. M. Páez (Eds.), *Latinos Remaking America* (pp. 1–37). Berkeley: University of California Press.

Thomas, A. (2005). Black Face, Latin Looks: Racial-Ethnic Identity Among Afro-Latinos in the Los Angeles Region. In E. C. Ochoa & G. L. Ochoa (Eds.), *Latino Los Angeles: Transformations, Communities and Activism* (pp. 197–221). Tucson: University of Arizona Press.

Valenzuela, A. (1999). *Subtractive Schooling: U.S.-Mexican Youth and the Politics of Caring.* Albany: State University of New York Press.

CHAPTER 18

Beyond Gender Dichotomies: Toward a New Century of Gendered Scholarship in the Latina/o Experience

MAURA I. TORO-MORN

INTRODUCTION[1]

> Gender is a human invention…[that] organizes human social life in culturally patterned ways.
>
> (Judith Lorber, 1994, p. 6).

Feminist scholars frequently describe gender as "like fish talking about water" (Lorber, 1994, p. 13). Indeed, gender is one those social categories we take for granted and we tend to assume it is "bred into our genes." In fact, "most people find it hard to believe that gender is constantly created and re-created out of human interaction, out of social life, and is the texture and order of that social life" (Lorber, 1994, p. 13). Today, there is scholarly consensus that gender is a human invention and that whether we recognize it or not, we are constantly "doing gender" (West & Zimmerman, 1987). This recognition represents an important contribution of the "academic feminist revolution" (Stacey & Thorne, 1985) that swept the social sciences and humanities with varying degrees of influence in the late 1980s and early 1990s.

Feminist and nonfeminist scholars have not only contributed to the theoretical grounding of gender as a unifying category of analysis (Ferre, Lorber, & Hess, 2000), but, more importantly, they have managed to produce an extraordinary body of scholarly literature across the social sciences and humanities. Feminists in the fields of Latin American, Caribbean, and

Latino studies have made impressive contributions to key theoretical debates in the study of gender and politics (Dore, 1997; Saldivar-Hull, 2000), international migration (Hondagneu-Sotelo, 1994, 2003; Menjivar, 2000; Repak, 1995; Toro-Morn, 1995), feminist thought (Acosta-Belen & Bose, 1993; Anzaldua, 1987; Anzaldua & Keating, 2002; Garcia, 1997; Morraga & Anzaldua, 1981; Mohammed, 2002; The Latina Feminist Group, 2001), feminist methodology (Sandoval, 2000); gender, work, and globalization (Beneria & Roldan, 1987; Nash & Fernandez-Kelly, 1983; Nash & Safa, 1986; Safa, 1995; Tiano, 1994), among many other areas.

For those interested in doing research about gender, today there is a battery of concepts and theories to help us describe, analyze, and explain how gender is socially constructed and (re)produced at both the individual and institutional levels (Lorber, 1994); how gender intersects with social class and race to create complex hierarchies of power and inequality (Acker, 2000; Glenn, 2000; Hill-Collins, 2000); and the consequences of gendered systems for families (Roschelle, 2000); institutions (Martin & Collinson, 2000; Scott, 2000); and the global economy (Moghadam, 2000). We know that when we describe gender roles at the individual level, we might be drawing on one's gendered identity, sexual orientation, and gendered beliefs, among other conceptual categories (Lorber, 2004). We also know that gender functions as a system of social stratification that generally privileges men and that exists with its own gender ideology, gender imagery, and gendered processes. Finally, gender is an institution that structures every aspect of our lives, most principally family life through the gender division of labor. Feminist scholar Judith Lorber (1994) connected the various levels of analysis in the following way: Through face-to-face interaction, individuals enforce gender norms and expectations, and, in the process, construct gendered systems of dominance and power.

This chapter seeks to deconstruct the stereotypical notions of how gender operates in the Latina/o community and attempts to map out a new scholarly agenda that is attentive to gender as a socially constructed category that is relational, contested, negotiated, and historically grounded. A popular idea in both the social science literature and popular media is the notion of Latin America and Caribbean societies as steeped in traditional gender roles with a rigid division of labor. The tendency is to describe Latina/o gender roles as relations between men and women frozen in time. The notion of the public/private (*calle/casa*) spheres of social life is central to this view. The mapping of gender roles into the public/private dichotomy places men in the public world of politics and women in the private, domestic, and, presumably nonpolitical world of the home.

These stereotypes rest in the pervasive distortion of Latin America and the Caribbean as societies in which Latino men are "traditional and machistas" and Latina women are submissive "marianistas." To deconstruct the gendered duality that has come to characterize the analysis and description of Latinas/os, one has to take account the socioeconomic and political realities that have historically shaped (and continue to shape) the lives of Latinos on both sides of the border. In other words, in this chapter, I attempt to move the analysis of gender in the Latina/o community away from the gender role paradigm,[2] where gender is a characteristic of individuals, to gender as a category of analysis and connection that is historical and contextual and intersects with other equally important categories such as social class, race/ethnicity, and sexuality.

This chapter is organized in the following fashion. I begin with a critical analysis of *machismo* and *marianismo,* two central, yet deeply problematic concepts used to describe Latina/o gender roles. Next, I attempt to develop a historical analysis that shows how gender identities, changes in the gender division of labor, and migration strategies have been forged in the context of larger historical forces, such as colonialism and capitalism. Then a description of the exciting new scholarship that examines how gender shapes contemporary migration processes across nationality groups and how Latino immigrants reconstruct the gendered division of labor in the process of settlement follows. The last part of the chapter examines how second- and third-generation Latinos, born and raised in the United States, are also (re)creating new gendered identities and the gender division of labor with profound consequences for the future of Latina/o families.

This chapter seeks to contribute to the (re)framing of U.S. Latina/o research from a "here and now" perspective focusing solely on today's social, economic, and political issues facing Latinos/as in the United States. Here, I propose a perspective that recognizes the historical continuities in the experiences of Latinas/os across the hemisphere and that holds in tension the connections existing between Latin America and U.S. Latino communities. This perspective represents a new stage in the scholarship about Latin America, the Caribbean, and Latino Studies (for a detailed analysis, see Escobar, 2006) that seeks a more integrated approach to understanding the hemisphere.

As a Latina feminist, I present this chapter as part of a broader effort to (re)animate the work of feminist cross-cultural analysis, an important component of feminist scholarship that has been recently subject of criticism. I am aware of the dangers of making universalist claims about gender oppression and inequality that have generated so much debate among feminists, but as a Latina feminist, I am committed to the development of a new Latina/o scholarship that challenges a-historical perspectives and theoretical exclusions. Instead, this work seeks to deepen our understanding of gendered processes in the hemisphere. Like Ruth Behar, I believe the Latina/o experience offers an exciting location to reflect about gender and for "doing gender as a form of critical practice" (Behar, 2002, p. ix).

"MACHISMO" AND "MARIANISMO": KEY CONCEPTS AND ASSUMPTIONS

Unfortunately, the language of "machismo"[3] and "marianismo"[4] has become synonymous with Latino men and women across the hemisphere. Social scientists and popular writers have endorsed and applied a duality that depicts men as strong, tough, virile "machos" and women as passive, docile, and submissive. These concepts have been deployed by social policy analysts and social scientists to make blanket assessments and evaluations of Latin American, Caribbean, and Latino men, women, and families without much empirical evidence to support them (Navarro, 2002; Vega, 1990). In fact, the apparent machismo of Latino men has become a "monocausal explanation" (Ybarra, 1982) for the lack of changes in Latino families. On the other hand, the docile mother who only leaves home to go to church or the faithful wife who endures her husband's sexual infidelity have become images used to support the ahistorical and stereotypical notion of Latinas as the ever-suffering, family-and-church-bound women.

Writing in the 1970s, anthropologist Nora Scott Kinzer (1973, p. 303) located scientists' commitment to the interpretive power of machismo to researchers—most of whom were male, U.S.-based Latin Americanists—who continuously emphasized women's passivity, overlooking how men also exhibited this characteristic. She identified a class bias that permeating research conducted about gender roles in Latin America, in that most studies were based on rural-peasant, mestizos, Indians, and slum-dwellers because upper-class Latinos refused to talk to researchers viewed as outsiders. Researchers were committed to the machismo/marianismo duality even when data cried for different interpretations. Oscar Lewis' work in Puerto Rico is a case in point (Kinzer, 1973; Toro-Morn, 2005). He was a vociferous proponent of the traditional family ideal and the machismo ethic. Lewis described the women in the Rios family as demanding, aggressive, and more violence-prone than men (Toro-Morn, 2005). It was their inability to accept the traditional role of women that made their families unstable, disorganized, and pathological: the underpinning of the culture of poverty thesis, another theoretical construct that has had profound consequences for the analysis of Latino families.

The application and endorsement of marianismo can be traced back to early efforts to theorize what came to be known as "the cult of womanhood," a concept used in the United States and Great Britain to describe women's experiences (Navarro, 2002). The lack of scholarship about women, a problem that stemmed from decades of neglect and research with a mostly male focus, gave the first generation of U.S.-based feminist scholars and some Latin American feminists *carte blanche* in describing and constructing the work and family experiences of Latinas. In that context, marianismo, like machismo, emerged as a powerful sociological explanation applied to women across social classes and nationalities. In other words, marianismo became the "security blanket which covers all women" (Stevens, 1973, p. 98). Navarro (2002) evaluated the evidence underlying this construct and established that most of this work has been based on impression-istic, personal accounts and some empirical, but limited, work done in Mexico and Puerto Rico (p. 266). Yet, 30 years later, marianismo continues to maintain an intellectual legitimacy that it does not merit.

More recently, a new generation of social scientists in both Latin America and the United States has helped "discard manly dichotomies" by producing a new body of work focusing on men, masculinities, and male identities (see, e.g., Gutmann, 2003, p. 1). Although this work builds upon important insights generated by the feminist literature about gender, it can also be seen as an unintended consequence of the wave of feminist research that appropriately privileged women's experience and voices due to their institutional exclusion, thus creat-ing a need to know more about men. Drawing on the concept of hegemonic masculinity as a way to capture both normative and practical manifestations of masculinity, this new research has transformed the way we look at Latino men and, by consequence, women. For exam-ple, through rich ethnographic research conducted in a Mexican colonia in the early 1980s, Gutmann (1996) analyzed the impact of Mexico's economic crisis on the daily lives of men and women. He, too, was critical of the machismo rhetoric and argued that no single model of Mexican masculinity can capture the complexities of how men see themselves as fathers, husbands, and men. He argued that social class matters in the (re)construction of Mexican fatherhood. He found that in working-class and poor families, men cared for small children, whereas in upper-class and wealthy families, maids and nannies cared for children. Contrary to the popular notion that working-class and poor men tend to be more rigid with respect to the gender division of labor, he found that women's involvement in paid work shaped men's involvement with housework.

Another theme found in this new body of work is the intersection of race and gender in studies of masculinity in Latin America. In Peru, Fuller (2003) found that working-class men recognize the existence of a racial hierarchy, claiming virile attitudes for themselves and feminizing men of the dominant classes. This literature has also questioned the "irksome clichés" (Guttman, 2003, p. 15) that men prove their virility by male progeny by examin-ing male sexual desires and practices with other men. An important contribution of this work is the understanding of both men and women as gendered subjects and awareness that the intersection of nationality and sexuality have produced complex gendered hierarchies between men of the same nationality and men of different sexual orientations. Yet, Guttman (2003) cautioned against using this new research to herald "the new Latino man paradigm," as romanticism tends to breed essentialism (p. 20).

In the U.S. Latina/o literature, researchers aware of the negative representations associated with machismo have "worked to correct the ethnocentric perspective of machismo" by providing an alternative view of machismo as a form of masculinity and gender ideology with positive dimensions (Torres, Solberg, & Carlstrom, 2002, p. 164). For example, Torres et al. (2002) sought to develop a typology of machismo that accounts for the "complex interaction of learned and reinforced social, cultural, and behavioral components constituting the content of male gender role identities in the socio-political context of the Latino society" (p. 167). Using a sample of 148 mostly Puerto Rican and Mexican men, many of whom were born in the United States, they found that a very small subset of the sample fell into the stereotypical view of machismo (authoritarian, controlling) and that the majority of the men tended to cluster around a measure that integrated attitudinal and behavioral gender role dimensions that included, among other characteristics, flexible male and female roles and a negotiated style to conflict management. Torres et al. (2002) concluded that we need to place less emphasis on the negative characteristics of machismo.

In the end, the constructs of *machismo* and *marianismo* do not shed much light on the reality of men and women's lived experiences partly because asymmetrical gender relations are shaped by material and historical conditions. In other words, gender inequality in the Latino community has been forged historically and has varied by race and social class, a topic that I attempt to address in the next section.

GENDER INEQUALITY: HISTORICAL OVERVIEW

It is beyond the scope of this chapter to offer an exhaustive analysis of the last 500 years of Latin American and Caribbean history, yet this historical overview offers a point of departure to historicizing the development of gender inequality in the continent and how it has been (re)produced in the context of changing historical conditions. It would represent a significant oversight if the experiences of indigenous people before and after colonization were not addressed. Gender and sexuality represent a significant dimension of pre-Colombian life that needs to be addressed here, albeit briefly.

Colonization and Gender Inequality

Recent archeological research has shown that gender relations and practices among pre-Colombian cultures were complex, varied, innovative, and open to many interpretations (Gustafson & Trevelyan, 2002). In fact, lively debates continue to take place about gender as more archeological discoveries are made about Mesoamerica and Andean cultures. Research about pre-European Mayan Indians has shown that "gender relations developed with many influences inherited from the long occupation of Mesoamerica prior to the Mayan florescence" (Gustafson, 2002, p. 56). In Mesoamerica, Gustafson (2002) observed that hierarchical gender relations developed very early, before the agricultural revolution (p. 57). Some scholars have explained the emergence of patrilineal and patriarchal social practices to the influence of social invaders, but Gustafson (2002) argued that although invaders played a role in Mayan life, the rise of a patrilineal and patriarchal political system developed gradually and might have resulted as societies became larger and more complex. In the Caribbean, the paucity of research about indigenous cultures makes interpretations and conclusions more difficult to reach.[5]

Yet, after 500 years of colonization, the notion of indigenous people as traditional and primitive persists. For example, Nelson (1999) observed that today *"la mujer maya"* has been used as an image that embodies the "feminization of the primitive," and when applied to contemporary

Mayan women in Guatemala, it reduces them to the notion that they belong to the "primitive" past and are incapable of making changes and contributions to modern societies. The notion of "la mujer maya" as the embodiment of a subordinated, feminized, and primitive other is reinforced when contrasted with the representation of ancient Maya society found in archeological accounts that tends to privilege men and represents Mayan culture using mostly male artifacts (Cohodas, 2002). The political consequence of such distortions is that indigenous women continue to be perceived as inferior and primitive, yet their political activism and resistance to over 500 years of exploitation and colonization is overlooked. Two key figures that have come to represent the spirit of resistance and activism are Guatemalan human rights activist Rigoberta Menchu, who won the Nobel Peace Prize in 1992 and Comandanta Ester, a member of EZLN (Zapatista Army of National Liberation), in Chiapas, Mexico.

Although much has been written about the new world *mestizaje* in the Americas that produced complex multiracial and multilingual societies in the aftermath of European colonization, there is still much to be done to fully analyze how colonial ideologies with respect to race, social class, and gender were imposed, resisted, and reformulated by indigenous groups, elites, and emerging social groups in both colonial and postcolonial societies.[6] The colonization of the Americas was (and continues to be) a profoundly gendered process.

It is common knowledge that indigenous men and women in the Americas bore the brunt of the colonization process as their gendered worlds were disrupted and turned upside down. The imposition of new cultural demands and their incorporation into colonial society as laborers through forced migration was disastrous for indigenous societies. For example, Spanish colonizers made every effort to eradicate sexual and gender norms that they considered "malas costumbres" (bad customs) (Sanabria, 2007). In colonial times, the institution of marriage, for example, re-created a social class structure that tended to privilege men of European descent and maintained the political and economic superiority of the colonizer over the colonized. A Spanish gender ideology organized around the notion of honor, defined as female chastity and church-sanctioned marriages, sought to eradicate indigenous sexual practices such as premarital intercourse (Sanabria, 2007). These notions did not apply to Spanish and Indian men and, consequently, a gender hierarchy was (re)created in the colonization of the Americas.

Ironically, at the turn of the 21st century, descendants of Mayan and indigenous people in the Americas continue to feel the impact of colonization and capitalist development. Radcliff, Laurie, and Andolina (2003) reported that in the Andes, the gender division of labor continues to allocate to women agricultural work that is undervalued and unacknowledged (p. 391). Internal migration continues to be a survival strategy for indigenous groups. Now, regional and international migration have become ways to resolve the structural inequality faced by indigenous communities in the midst of neoliberal and globalization policies that continue to uproot them from their land and turn them, yet again, into laborers for multinational corporations in the region or nannies for highly educated women in North America.

The Rise of Nation-States, Capitalism, and Gender Inequality

Historians agree that the wars of independence in Latin America were long, bloodied, and brutal contests (Martin & Wasserman, 2005), yet very little is known about the role that women played in such movements. Once independence was achieved, Martin and Wasserman (2005) pointed out that most Latin American and Caribbean countries confronted three significant challenges: (1) deciding who was to rule and what type of government was most appropriate; (2) rebuilding their economies; and (3) persuading people who thought about politics in very local ways to render allegiance to the newly developed nation-state (p. 263). Social class and race/ethnic divisions throughout the continent also complicated the process of nation-building. Clearly, this historical period provides yet another important location to discuss the reconstruction of gender in the Latino experience and the intersection of social class, gender, and race/ethnicity in the Americas.

Anthropologist Harry Sanabria (2007) wrote that "after independence from colonial rule, national elites went about consolidating their nation-states, and in so doing often viewed 'well-ordered' families and states as mirror images of each other" (p. 151). In the 19th century, most people earned their livelihoods from the land, namely through the *hacienda* system (Mexico, Central America, and the Caribbean), *estancias* (Argentina), or *fazendas* (Brazil). Haciendas constitute a hierarchical gendered and racialized world of their own. Life in the hacienda system was difficult, in particular for the peasantry, working class, mostly Indians, Blacks, and *mestizos*, who lived under conditions of servitude. Competition for work, low wages, and debt peonage placed hacienda workers in a vulnerable position. Men and women worked in the fields together, although researchers have reported greater gender differentiation with respect to agricultural tasks. In the large coffee plantations of Brazil, for example, women endured additional burdens imposed by planters' demand for large families (Stolcke, 1991).

Evidence from Peru also suggests that although women across social classes were economically active in a multiplicity of ways, there was also a "fairly high degree of patriarchal control over women, exercised within the household and reinforced through legal and political institutions" (Mallon, 1986, p. 153). In the end, the intersection of gender, social class, and race, led to two different forms of patriarchal household economy: (1) hacendado-based families, where women faced limited economic participation, but had access to property as vehicles of accumulation; and (2) Indian-peasant households where women contributed economically, but under men's familial control (Mallon, 1986).

The transition to capitalism (i.e., from family labor to individual wage labor) under the auspices of export agricultural production—a significant economic strategy used by many countries in the region in the early parts of the 20th century—affected men and women differently. Again, Brazil provides a case in point. As working-class men left agriculture and moved to jobs that paid better (construction industry), women found themselves becoming wage laborers in agriculture, work that continued to be undervalued and underpaid. In other words, in the transition to capitalism, the plight of rural women worsens. In the pueblos and large imperial cities—vestiges of Spanish colonialism—life was equally precarious for the largely urban Indian population.

This is also the historical juncture when the region became subject to the influence of a newly emerging colonial power, namely the United States. The U.S. government, encouraged by the business community, made considerable investments in oil-rich countries such as Mexico, Venezuela, Trinidad, and Aruba and land-rich nations such as Costa Rica, Nicaragua, Panama, and the Dominican Republic. Gender, social class, and race mattered a great deal at this point in history. In 1898, the U.S. occupation of Cuba and Puerto Rico stimulated the development of the sugar plantation economy and promoted social reforms that privileged men and women of the upper class. The sugar plantation economy was labor-intensive, thus labor recruiters roamed the Caribbean in search of mostly male workers. Male workers were preferred in labor- hungry sites throughout the hemisphere due to the transitional nature of work and gendered notions about women's proper place in the family. In addition, lessons from the turbulent past of forced labor, peonage, and indentured labor history in the United States made employers view voluntary contracted workers as more "rational" and "humanistic" and an efficient way to meet labor needs. Male immigrant workers helped build the Panama Canal and worked in the sugar fields of Cuba and Puerto Rico, the coffee plantations in Brazil, and in the banana plantations of Costa Rica and Nicaragua.

The legacy of this new form of colonialism and the newly implemented economic reforms of the new colonial power created widespread poverty and destitution among the lower and working classes, thus driving men to take work as contracted workers in order to provide for their families. At the end of the 19th century and beginning decades of the 20th century, the Caribbean islands became islands of women and children left behind due to out-migration of males. Women survived by finding wage work in their rural villages or moving to urban centers to work as domestics. Thus, we begin to see how the "myth of the male breadwinner" does not hold true for some Latino families. Working-class and poor Latin American, Caribbean, and Latina women have always worked, and these experiences have shaped the construction of gender and the gender division of labor. For women left behind, there was no public-private separation of tasks; they had to do both.

Did the increasing economic role of women at this point in time lead to a redefinition of the gender division of labor and power relations within the family? Evidence throughout the hemisphere suggests that patriarchal relations between men and women among the working and peasant classes persisted through the transition to capitalism. Mallon (1986) summarized the predicament of women as follows:

> Whether rich or poor, however, women faced subordination at the hand of their men, playing roles in the overall management and reproduction of their households already blocked out for them by existing patterns of gender hierarchy and ideology—participating in the reproduction of class relations in ways that were both dependent on and fundamentally different from the roles played by men. (p. 166)

Globalization and Gender Inequality

Feminist researchers have poured their analytic might to capture the emerging complexities of globalization in the hemisphere, the new chapter in the global division of labor. "The neoliberal regime of flexible production" (Nash, 2005, p. 149) has increased the need for female labor, solidified women's role as a source of inexpensive labor, and reinforced the use of migration as a survival strategy for men, women, and families, characteristics that make this phase of capitalism distinctive and ripe for a gendered analysis. Elegant ethnographic accounts have captured the plight of maquila workers (Fernandez-Kelly, 1983), the reconstruction of gender traits through subcontracting and industrial work (Beneria & Roldan, 1987), the uneven benefits of maquila employment (Tiano, 1994), the plight of flower workers in agroindustrial enterprises in Bogota (Talcott, 2003), the rise of the sex and tourism in Cuban and the Dominican Republic (Cabezas, 2004), and the connections between globalization and migration (Hondagneu-Sotelo & Cranford, 1999). Without doubt, the North American Free Trade Agreement (NAFTA) and the Central American Free Trade Agreement (CAFTA) have solidified the economic integration of the hemisphere and the dependence on Latinas/os as a flexible, dependable, and expendable source of inexpensive labor on both sides of the border.

Studies of maquila workers in the new international division of labor continue to deepen our analysis of production, reproduction, and the gender division of labor (Tiano, 1994). For several decades, the debate had been framed as one of integration versus exploitation (Tiano, 1994). In other words, proponents of the integration thesis proposed that women's employment in export-processing zones (EPZs) represented an improvement over the employment options available to women (i.e., mostly agriculture and informal economy); that working in EPZs increased women's social status because of the prestige associated with such jobs; and that maquila employment enabled women to challenge patriarchy in the household by giving them material resources and a new-found pride as workers. On the other hand, the exploitation thesis proposed that maquila work did not liberate women of the burdens of patriarchy, but it contributed to their dual exploitation as women and workers. Researchers found evidence of the exploitation of women in their employment experiences, wages, lack of job security and benefits, and inability to organize as workers—social problems attributed to the intersection of the patriarchy and capitalism.

At the turn of the 21st century, new scholarship about gender in Latin America has moved beyond the exploitation/integration framework to recognize that neither perspective is in itself adequate to explain women's diverse motivations for waged employment and its social consequences (Tiano, 1994). In fact, working in EPZs might give women a new location for resistance and protest and a new awareness as members of a global labor force. In the Caribbean, the pioneering work of anthropologist Helen Safa (1995) has contributed to reframing the integration-exploitation dichotomy by analyzing the differential impact of women's wage in three countries: Puerto Rico, Cuba, and the Dominican Republic. In Puerto Rico and the Dominican Republic, development strategies favored the incorporation of women as workers and as a source of inexpensive labor for export-led industrialization.

In Cuba, women's incorporation into paid employment was a result of a state-promoted policy connected to the Cuban revolution. Safa (1995) found that working-class women's experiences with wage work helped redefine their domestic roles and challenged the myth of the male breadwinner. In the Dominican Republic, and to some extent Puerto Rico, when women's wages substituted men's wages due to male unemployment, changes in the gender division of labor were not as permanent. In Cuba, state-supported employment policies for both men and women allowed more permanent changes with respect to the gender division of labor. However, gender relations between men and women have grown tenser as the ability of the state to maintain the promises of the revolution has been seriously eroded due to the fall of the Soviet block and the economic crisis that ensued (Toro-Morn, Roschelle, & Facio, 2002).

In closing, when seen from a historical perspective, it is clear that the idea of Latin American and Caribbean societies as "traditional" supported by the ideology that women belong in the home does not square with the historical reality of women's work and family experiences. Further, women's involvement in 20th century revolutionary movements in Mexico, Cuba, Nicaragua, Guatemala, El Salvador, Peru, Colombia, and Chile also challenges the notion of the assumed submission and passivity of Latinas.

GENDER AND THE MIGRATION PROCESS

One of the most significant contributions of research about Latino/a immigration has been the work that focuses on gender as a constitutive dimension of the migration process. Here again, we can see first hand the impact of the gender role paradigm when applied to Latina/o immigration studies in that research tended to privilege men as subjects of inquiry because of the assumption that they were the heads of households—providers—thus the actors in the migration process. Women left behind were not only invisible, but also was the work they performed on behalf of the supposedly "traditional family." Researchers have acknowledged the importance of migration networks, yet tended to assume that these male immigrant networks were neutral and transferable to women. Cecilia Menjivar's (2000) groundbreaking work *Fragmented Ties: Salvadorean Immigrant Networks in America* challenged such notions as she documented how immigrant men and women differed in their contributions to social networks and derived dissimilar benefits from their informal networks of assistance. Salvadorean women's networks tended to be more reliable, as women loaned each other money, shared information about housing, provided child care support, and offered tips and information about jobs, health services, and legal information, but they can also become exploitative and oppressive.

Researchers have also documented the recruitment of mostly male workers from Latin America and the Caribbean, but they have frequently failed to see the gendered and racialized dimensions of such recruitment processes. For example, the Bracero Program, a labor recruitment program designed to address the shortage of agricultural workers in the United States in the 1940s and 1950s, represents an example of a gender-specific labor recruitment that brought mostly Mexican men under temporary labor contracts. Here we need to recognize that the migration of men—a policy enforced by the U.S. government and employers in order to discourage permanent settlement—impacted Mexican families and communities of origin in profound ways. The migration of men meant that Mexicans were denied the right to form families in the United States through both law and social practice. As families were split across the border, the productive and reproductive dimensions of family life were also separated across the border. Historians have documented that in spite of such restrictions, women migrated with their children and families to work sites. Life for Mexican women in the early barrios was very hard. Mexican immigrant women took jobs in the fruit cannery industry and engaged in seasonal agricultural labor.

A gender-specific labor recruitment program brought Puerto Rican women to Chicago in the 1950s (Toro-Morn, 2001). Using a gendered ideology that perceived Puerto Rican women as inherently suited for domestic work, government officials helped in the recruitment and migration of Puerto Rican women to Chicago. In moving to Chicago as domestic workers, the productive and reproductive spheres of women's work intersected in the migration process, but, more importantly, they linked Puerto Rico and Chicago in distinctive gendered ways. Today, gender-specific labor recruitment continues to bring to the United States mostly women from Central America to do domestic work (Repak, 1995). As Hondagneu-Sotelo and Cranford (1999) put it, "gender-specific migration and recruitment does not follow from immutable gender roles" (p. 108). Instead, it flows from the gendered global economy that has historically linked Latin America, the Caribbean, and the United States.

Gender scholars in the field of migration have proposed that any formulation of the macrostructural determinants of migration must also include gender oppression and patriarchy as hidden causes for the migration of women (Parrenas, 2001). Increasingly, more Latinas are using migration as a way to escape gender oppression and domestic violence. Although newspaper accounts continue to report the increasing number of Latinas that are seeking asylum on the basis of gender oppression, very little research exists that documents their experiences. We do know that migration burdens women because they are held responsible for the transnational work that sustains families across spaces (Alicea, 1997).

Ethnographic research among Mexican immigrant communities in California has yielded fascinating and critical insights about the consequences of migration for Latino families—in particular, the impact of migration on the gender division of labor. Feminist sociologist, Pierrette Hondagneu-Sotelo (1994) broke new ground in her analysis of Mexican immigrants in California as she documented how women used women's networks to challenge their husband's opposition to migration. Women's networks assisted in the formulation of arguments to persuade husbands to let them move, helped them make the move to the U.S. destination without their husband's assistance, and most importantly, helped in the process of settlement. However, Hondagneu-Sotelo's (1994) work is most insightful in her analysis of the consequences of migration for conjugal relations and the gender division of labor. She found that a more egalitarian division of labor emerged in the context of spousal separation prompted by restrictive immigration policies. Traditional patriarchal family norms were also weakened as women became wage earners, frequently as domestic workers, and as they assumed a more public role in the process of settlement.

My own work with Puerto Rican migrants in Chicago suggested that even though men tried to impose a more traditional division of labor by taking on two jobs, thus freeing women to stay home and care for children, women found ways to work outside the home. Among working-class families, I did not find evidence of a change in the gender division of labor, as women reported being responsible for both the reproductive work that supported their families and working outside the home. In contrast, middle-class and educated Puerto Rican migrants were more flexible with respect to the gender division of labor, partly because they had already negotiated work and family arrangements from Puerto Rico. In the end, evidence seems to suggest that working outside the home gives women a measure of freedom and empowerment, but such "liberation" can be seriously eroded by racial and social class hierarchies that compound immigrant lives in postindustrial economies of destination societies.

Research with Central American immigrants has shown that, in the United States, women have become primary breadwinners for their families, but it does not produce a drastic change in gender relations. In fact, Menjivar (1999) reported that Salvadoran men turn to drinking and domestic violence as a way to deal with the frustrations of this role reversal. In contrast, indigenous Guatemalan immigrants come from more egalitarian family arrangements and thus perceive women's increased ability to procure jobs as an opportunity that benefits everyone in the family. Menjivar (1999) pointed out that the advantages of employment for women do not come necessarily from the monetary gains but from the social processes that accompany employment. For example, live-in domestics and child care workers have the opportunity to observe middle-class patterns of behavior and practices that they can selectively incorporate into their own families. However, in the end, the social position of Central American immigrants shaped by race, social class, nationality, and immigration status interacts with larger social forces to produce vastly different outcomes for men and women, thus making claims about the impact of migration on gender relations more difficult to universalize.

Research with Dominican immigrants in New York has shown that immigrant women are more likely to express a desire to settle permanently abroad as a way to protect their new-found roles and opportunities, whereas men seek to return home in order to regain the status and privileges lost as a result of migration (Pessar, 2003). Clearly, there is much more work remaining to be done to fully understand how migration reshapes gender and vice versa. Most of the research discussed here focuses on relations between married men and women, but the migration of men and women in other family arrangements deserves to be studied as well.

Researchers have also studied the gendered arrangements of Latino families once they are in the United States. Unfortunately, in two separate reviews of this vast literature, reviewers reported that *machismo* and *marianismo* ideologies continue to be deployed as explanations for gender scripts between men and women, even when there is empirical evidence of shared decision-making among Latina/o parents (Galanti, 2003; Vega, 1990). In the 1980s and 1990s, the tendency to study U.S. Latino families in a vacuum continued to produce problematic accounts. Ybarra's (1982) study of gender roles among Mexican Americans is one exception, in that she placed men and women gendered identities in a spectrum of gender roles in which practices among families could fall somewhere in between a patriarchal, role-segregated structure and an egalitarian, joint-role structure.

Interethnic comparative research among Latinos is rare, but when it is done, it reveals fascinating results with respect to gender issues. Fernandez-Kelly and Garcia (1989) found that Cuban women in Miami and Mexican immigrant women in Los Angeles experienced greater autonomy as a result of external employment, but when coupled with economic marginality, employment became a sign of family and individual vulnerability for Mexican immigrant women. Similarly, comparative research among African American, European American, and Latino families is also rare, but it has shown that African Americans and Mexicans have more liberal attitudes toward the idea of women's work roles, but they tended to endorse a view of men as providers, a notion connected to the rather fragile position that African American and Latino men face in the United States, namely subject to unemployment, underemployment, and racism (McLoyd, Cause, Takeuchi, & Wilson, 2000).

SECOND- AND THIRD GENERATION LATINAS/OS AND GENDER

Research among second- and third-generation Latinos has yielded important insights relevant to efforts to theorize the transmission of gender identities and how social class and race shapes socialization and family formation. Research has documented that, for Latina/o families, proximity to the countries of origin extends the field of gender socialization for children. Gina Perez (2004) documented that Puerto Rican parents in Chicago sent their daughters back to the Island "para que no se dañen" (so that they are not ruined). Research about the mother-daughter relationship among Mexican immigrant women in Los Angeles suggested that whereas some women promote premarital virginity as a strategy to protect their daughters from men's oppression, others replaced marriage goals with educational opportunities (Gonzalez-Lopez, 2003).

Toro-Morn and Alicea (2003) conducted interviews with second- and third-generation Puerto Ricans in Chicago and found that Puerto Rican parents worked hard to reconstruct family life in Puerto Rico, in keeping with perceived traditional cultural norms and expected their children to conform to traditional gender roles and values, processes that have been found among Puerto Rican parents in New York. Puerto Rican parents in Chicago worked hard to build home life as a space where children were socialized into traditional Puerto Rican ways of living. The authors also found that rigid socialization schemes led to the conflicts between parents and children. For example, they report that daughters admired their mothers' struggle to juggle work and family responsibilities, but they resented their parents' overprotectiveness and gendered expectations concerning their sexuality. Similarly, sons worked hard to reconcile the conflicts, ambiguities, and tensions of their masculine identities.

Toro-Morn and Alicea (2003) explained that underlying parental expectations and conflicts was a desire to (re)define a cultural space challenging definitions of Puerto Ricans as second-class citizens. Yet, Puerto Rican parents believed in the value of education for social mobility and, consequently, supported their children's educational efforts, even if it meant that they would be away from home. They concluded that as parents socialized children in the values and beliefs of Puerto Rican culture, they inadvertently presented Puerto Rican culture as fixed in time and space. The second- and third-generation Puerto Ricans they interviewed struggled with such views because it meant "their submission and conformity to rules and codes of behavior that many saw as oppressive" (Toro-Morn and Alicea, 2003, p. 210). Instead, they saw themselves as active agents in the process of (re)creating Puerto Rican culture and they wanted to decide which aspects of their culture to take and which to reject. Yet, some second- and third-generation Puerto Ricans tended to fall into a dualistic way of thinking with respect to perceiving U.S. society as being more egalitarian than their homeland and U.S. Puerto Rican communities. Toro-Morn and Alicea (2003) called this "the distortions of the borderlands" because it fails to see the exploitation and subordination that their parents and other family members encountered as workers and as immigrants.

Research with dual-earner Chicano couples has also revealed some fascinating insights. For example, Coltrane and Valdez (1997) interviewed a sample of fairly young, educated, dual-earner Chicanos in southern California to address specifically the relationship between employment and the gender division of labor. In keeping with previous studies of minority families, they found that Chicanas worked outside the home for considerable hours and their economic contributions were significant to the family's household income, but some families struggled with the notion of the spouse as a permanent coprovider. They found that families tended to fall within the following patterns: Eight out of the 20 families in the sample were labeled primary/secondary provider families because husbands made more money than wives and men viewed themselves as primary breadwinner. Wives' income was treated as secondary, extra money, and they readily accepted responsibility for managing the household. These families tended to view the traditional division of labor as "natural" and "normal." Men contributed to child care and housework, but it was constructed as "helping out." The remaining 12 families were labeled "coproviders"; these families tended to have more equal earnings and valued the wife's employment more highly.

Coprovider families equally shared housework and child care. Some families within this group were labeled ambivalent coproviders because husbands tended to show ambivalence about their wives' career. These men also saw themselves as helpers in the gender division of labor and did not let family demands intrude in their work life. Two families within this group resolved the tensions around the gender division of labor by hiring a housekeeper and a live-in baby-sitter, respectively. Interestingly, educated and middle-class Chicanos evaluated themselvesas being more egalitarian and financially successful and frequently compared themselves to Anglo and Chicano friends, whom they perceived to be even more egalitarian. Coltrane and Valdez (1997) argued that because there was no fixed standard against which they judged themselves, these families have become "post-modern" (p. 243), a concept first develop by sociologist Judith Stacey to signify "the contested, ambivalent, and undecided character of contemporary gender and kinship arrangements" (as quoted by Coltrane & Valdez, 1997, p. 243).

CONCLUSION

In this chapter, I have analyzed how the scripts of machismo and marianismo have been used by researchers to describe the gendered identities of Latino men and women resulting in the creation of distorted and stereotypical accounts of the Latina/o experience. It is clear that the machismo/marianismo sociological mantra is deeply flawed, and when applied to Latina/o men and women, it gives us very little space to be truly gendered subjects. My hope is that social scientists continue to move beyond distorted gender dichotomies and support the development of scholarship that is attentive to the complexities of the intersection of race, class, and gender in the hemisphere.

One avenue that offers current and future researchers a great deal of promise is historical and comparative work. At one level, the historical overview offered here—although limited—suggests that there is much to be done to continue to foster an understanding of colonialism, capitalism, and globalization as "inherently gendered" systems (Radcliffe, Laurie & Andolina, 2003, p. 389). The research cited here shows great promise on that front, in particular as it connects to key theoretical debates in the field of feminist theory (i.e., the relationship between women's wage work and changes in the division of labor, to name one). The work of anthropologist Helen Safa is an example of the theoretical and empirical value of comparative work.

In the current age of neoliberal policies and globalization, it is clear that future researchers will need to be attentive to the intersections of social class, gender, and sexuality given the flexibility of capital accumulation. Broadening the scope of gender to include sexuality represents an important avenue of research in this area, namely because of the increase in the number of countries involved in sex tourism and sex labor in the hemisphere. Similarly, the connection between globalization and migration is a deeply gendered one, thus the need to examine it more closely.

Although much more work remains to be done, all in all, feminist scholars in Latin America, the Caribbean, and the United States have deepened our understanding of gender in the Latina/o experience and have given us a more sophisticated and complex analysis of Latinas/os as gendered, raced, and classed subjects.

ACKNOWLEDGEMENT

I would like to thank the editors of the volume for their valuable support and suggestions. Also, a special thanks to Virginia Gill for her generous comments of earlier drafts of this manuscript.

NOTES

1. I am aware that pan-ethnic labels lend themselves to numerous interpretations; thus, in order to avoid confusion, the following is a brief explanation of the usage adopted in this chapter. Although Hispanic is a fairly recognized label to describe Latin American and Caribbean immigrants and their descendants, I prefer the label Latina/o. Because this chapter addresses gender issues in both Latin America and U.S. Latino communities, I have implicitly extended the use of the term "Latina/o: to signify yet another linguistic practice that places the concept in the broadest context as including Latin American, Caribbean, and U.S. Latino communities.

2. The gender role paradigm represents an important but now nearly obsolete way to think about gender relations. It tended to represent relations between men and women as complementary of one another. The notion of the public/private (*calle/casa*) spheres of social life was a central tenet of this early work. For example, in politics, the mapping of gender roles into the public/private dichotomy placed men in the public world of politics and women in the private, domestic, and, presumably, nonpolitical world of the home. It is clear that feminist thinking has moved beyond the gender role paradigm.

3. This term is associated with the Spanish word "macho" and is used to define a hypermasculine, aggressive, and virile male. As a gender ideology, machismo is used to describe the collective behavior of Latino men as violence-prone, domineering, and unemotional. Torres, Roschelle, & Facio (2002) pointed out that dominant models of masculinity in the United States frequently include many of the characteristics associated with machismo (i.e., men who take charge, protect and defend their women, and are tough, unafraid, and unemotional), but when applied to Latinos, they become negative.

4. Marianismo is also a gender ideology used to describe women who are submissive, passive, and self-sacrificing.

5. We know that the Caribbean Taino Indians had a matrilineal family structure and that indigenous women had access to the highest political position in Taino society as *caciques,* tribal leaders (Acosta-Belen, 1986), that their religious culture included both male and female gods, and that, as agricultural societies, a gender division of labor assigned both men and women important tasks in the production and reproduction of food, shelter, and clothing (Toro-Morn, 2005). However, within a few years of the Spanish invasion, the Taino population had been virtually wiped out by wars and disease; thus, their influence on the formation of gendered cultural practices is less well known.

6. Another area that has not been investigated is the experiences of Spanish women who accompanied the *Conquistadores* to the New World. Many questions can be raised about the role they played in the colonization process and their role as women and agents of the empire in the emerging gendered and racial hierarchy of the colonies.

REFERENCES

Acker, J. (2000). Rewriting Class, Race, and Gender: Problems in Feminist Rethinking. In M.M. Ferre, J. Lorber, & B.B. Hess (Eds.), *Revisioning Gender* (pp. 44–69).Walnut Creek, CA: Altamira Press.

Acosta-Belen, E. (1986). *The Puetro Rican Woman: Perspectives on Culture, History, and Society.* New York: Praeger.

Acosta-Belen, E., & Bose, C. (1993). *Researching Women in Latin America and the Caribbean.* Boulder, CO: Westview Press.

Alicea, M. (1997). 'A Chambered Nautilus:' The Contradictory Nature of Puerto Rican Women's Role in the Social Construction of a Transnational Community. *Gender and Society, 11*(5), 597–626.

Anzaldua, G. (1987). *Borderlands/La Frontera: The New Mestiza.* San Francisco: Aunt Lute Books.

Anzaldua, G., & Keating, A. L. (2002). *This Bridge We Call Home: Radical Visions of Transformation.* New York: Routledge.

Behar, R. (2002). Gender Que Pica un Poco. In R. Montoya, L. J. Frazier, & J. Hurtig (Eds.), *Gender's Place: Feminist Anthropologies of Latin America* (pp. ix–xii). New York: Palgrave.

Beneria, L., & Roldán, M. (1987). *The Crossroads of Class and Gender: Industrial Homework, Subcontracting, and Household Dynamics in Mexico City.* Chicago: University of Chicago Press.

Cabezas, A. (2004). Between Love and Money: Sex, Tourism, and Citizenship in Cuba and the Dominican Republic. *Signs, 29*(4), 987–1015.

Cohodas, N. (2002). Multiplicity and Discourse in Maya Gender Relations. In L. S. Gustafson & A. M. Trevelyan (Eds.), *Ancient Maya Gender Identity and Relations* (pp. 11–53). Westport, CT: Bergin and Garvey.

Coltrane S., & Valdez, E. O. (1997). Reluctant Compliance: Work-Family Allocation in Dual-Earner Chicano Families. In M. Romero, P. Hondagneu-Sotelo, & V. Ortiz (Eds.), *Challenging Fronteras: Structuring Latina and Latino Lives in the U.S.* (pp. 229–246) New York: Routledge.

Dore, E. (1997). *Gender Politics in Latin America: Debates in Theory and Practice.* New York: Monthly Review Press.

Escobar, A. (2006). Revisioning Latin American and Caribbean Studies: A Geopolitics of Knowledge Approach. *Forum, 37*(2), 11–14.

Fernandez-Kelly, M. P. (1983). *For We Are Sold: I and My People.* Albany: State University of New York Press.

Fernandez-Kelly, M. P., & Garcia, A. (1989). Power Surrendered, Power Restored: The Politics of Home and Work Among Hispanic Women in Southern California and Southern Florida. In L. Tilly & P. Guerin (Eds.), *Women and Politics in America* (pp. 130–149). New York: Russell Sage Foundation.

Ferre, M. M., Lorber, J., & Hess, B. B. (2000). *Revisioning Gender.* Walnut Creek, CA: Altamira Press.

Fuller, N. (2003). The Social Construction of Gender Identity Among Peruvian Males. In M. Guttman (Ed.), *Changing Men and Masculinities in Latin America* (pp. 134–152). Durham, NC: Duke University Press.

Galanti, G. (2003). The Hispanic Family and Male-Female Relationships: An Overview. *Journal of Transcultural Nursing, 14*(3), 180–185.

Garcia, A. (1997). *Chicana Feminist Thought: The Basic Historical Writings.* New York: Routledge.

Glenn, E. N. (2000). The Social Construction and Institutionalization of Gender and Race: An Integrative Framework. In M. M. Ferre, J. Lorber, & B. B. Hess (Eds.), *Revisioning Gender* (pp. 3–43). Walnut Creek, CA: Altamira Press.

Gonzalez-Lopez, G. (2003). De Madres a Hijas: Gendered Lessons on Virginity Across Generations. In P. Hondagneu-Sotelo (Ed.), *Gender and U.S. Immigration: Contemporary Trends* (pp. 217–240). Berkeley: University of California Press.

Gutmann, M. (1996). *The Meanings of Macho: Being a Man in Mexico City.* Berkeley: University of California Press.

Gutmann, M. (2003). *Changing Men and Masculinities in Latin America.* Durham, NC: Duke University Press.

Gustafson, L. S. (2002). Shared Gender Relations: Early Mesoamerica and the Maya. In L. S. Gustafson & A. M. Trevelyan (Eds.), *Ancient Maya Gender Identity and Relations* (pp. 55–74). Wesport, CT: Bergin and Garvey.

Gustafson, L. S., & Trevelyan, A. M. (2002). *Ancient Maya Gender Identity and Relations.* Westport, CT: Bergin and Garvey.

Hill-Collins, P. (2000). Moving Beyond Gender: Intersectionality and Scientific Knowledge. In M. M. Ferre, J. Lorber, & B. B. Hess (Eds.), *Revisioning Gender* (pp. 261–284).Walnut Creek, CA: Altamira Press.

Hondagneu-Sotelo, P. (1994). *Gendered Transitions: Mexican Experiences of Immigration.* Berkeley: University of California Press.

Hondagneu-Sotelo, P. (2003). *Gender and U.S. Immigration: Contemporary Trends.* Berkeley: University of California Press.

Hondagneu-Sotelo, P., & Cranford, C. (1999). Gender and Migration. In J. S. Chalets (Ed.), *Handbook of the Sociology of Gender* (pp. 105–126). New York: Kluwer Academic/Plenum.

Kinzer, N. S. (1973). Priests, Machos, and Babies: Or, Latin American Women and the Manichaen Heresy. *Journal of Marriage and the Family*, *35*(2), 300–312.

Lorber, J. (1994). *Paradox of Gender*. New Haven, CT: Yale University Press.

Mallon, F. E. (1986). Gender and Class in the Transition to Capitalism: Household and Mode of Production in Central Peru. *Latin American Perspectives, 13*(1), 147–174.

Martin, P. Y., & Collinson, D. L. (2000). Gender and Sexuality in Organizations. In M. M. Ferre, J. Lorber, & B. B. Hess (Eds.), *Revisioning Gender* (pp. 285–310). Walnut Creek, CA: Altamira Press.

Martin, C. E., & Wasserman, M. (2005). *Latin America and Its People*. New York: Pearson.

McLoyd, V. C., Cause, A. M., Takeuchi, D., & Wilson, L. (2000). Marital Processes and Parental Socialization in Families of Color: A Decade Review of Research. *Journal of Marriage and the Family, 62*(4), 1070–1093.

Menjivar, C. (1999). The Intersection of Work and Gender: Central American Immigrant Women and Employment in California. *American Behavioral Scientist*, *42*(4), 601–627.

Menjivar, C. (2000). *Fragmented Ties: Salvadoran Immigrant Networks in America*. Berkeley: University of California Press.

Moghadam, V. (1998). Gender and the Global Economy. In M. M. Ferre, J. Lorber, & B. B. Hess (Eds.), *Revisioning Gender* (pp. 128–160). Thousand Oaks, CA: Sage.

Mohammed, P. (2002). *Gendered Realities: Essays in Caribbean Feminist Thought*. Barbados, Jamaica: University of the West Indies Press.

Morraga, C., & Anzaldua, G. (1981). This Bridge Called My Back: Writing by Radical Women of Color. Watertown, Massachusetts: Persephone Press.

Nagel, J. (2003). *Race, Ethnicity, and Sexuality: Intimate Intersections, Forbidden Frontiers*. New York: Oxford University Press.

Nash, J. (2005). Women in Between: Globalization and the New Enlightenment. *Signs*, *31*(1), 145–167.

Nash, J., & Fernandez-Kelly, M. P. (1983). *Women, Men, and the International Division of Labor*. Albany: State University of New York Press.

Nash, J., & Safa, H. (1986). *Women and Change in Latin America*. South Hadley, Massachusetts: Bergin and Garvey.

Navarro, M. (2002). Against Marianismo. In R. Montoya, L. J. Frazier, & J. Hurtig (Eds.), *Gender's Place: Feminist Anthropologies of Latin America* (pp. 257–272). New York: Palgrave.

Nelson, D. (1999). A Finger in the Wound: Body Politics in Quincentennial Guatemala. Berkeley: University of California Press.

Parrenas, R. S. (2001). *Servants of Globalization: Women, Migration, and Domestic Work*. Stanford: Stanford University Press.

Pessar, P. (2003). Engendering Migration Studies: The Case of New Immigrants in the United States. In P. Hondagneu-Sotelo (Ed.), *Gender and U.S. Immigration: Contemporary Trends* (pp. 20–42). Berkeley: University of California Press.

Perez, G. (2004). *The Near Northwest Side Story: Migration, Displacement, and Puerto Rican Families*. Berkeley: University of California Press.

Radcliffe, S. A., Laurie, N., & Andolina, R. (2003). The Transnationalization of Gender and Reimagining Andean Indigenous Development. *Signs*, *29*(2), 387–415.

Repak, T.A. (1995). *Waiting on Washington: Central American Workers in the Nation's Capital*. Philadelphia: Temple University Press.

Roschelle, A. (2000). Gender, Family Structure, and Social Structure: Racial Ethnic Families in the United States. In M. M. Ferre, J. Lorber, & B. B. Hess (Eds.), *Revisioning Gender* (pp. 311–340). Walnut Creek, CA: Altamira Press.

Safa, H. I. (1995). *The Myth of the Male Breadwinner: Women and Industrialization in the Caribbean*. Boulder, CO: Westview Press.

Sanabria, H. (2007). *The Anthropology of Latin America and the Caribbean*. Boston: Pearson.

Salvidar-Hull, S. (2000). *Feminism on the Border: Chicana Gender Politics and Literature*. Berkeley: University of California Press.

Sandoval, C. (2000). *Methodology of the Oppressed*. Minneapolis: University of Minnesota Press.

Scott, J. W. (2000). Some Reflections on Gender and Politics. In M. M. Ferre, J. Lorber, and B. B. Hess (Eds.), *Revisioning Gender* (pp.70–96). Walnut Creek: Altamira Press.

Stacey, J., & Thorne, B. (1985). The Missing Feminist Revolution in Sociology. *Social Problems, 32*, 301–316.

Stevens, E. (1973). Marianismo: The Other Face of Machismo. In A. Pescatello (Ed.), *Female and Male in Latin America*, (pp. 89–101). Pittsburgh: Pittsburgh University Press.

Stolcke, V. (1991). The Exploitation of Family Morality: Labor Systems and Family Structure on Sao Paulo Coffee Plantations, 1850–1979. In E. Jelin (Ed.), *Family, Household, and Gender Relations in Latin America* (pp. 69–100). Paris: Kegan Paul International.

Talcott, M. (2003). Gendered Webs of Development and Resistance: Women, Children, and Flowers in Bogota. *Signs*, *29*(2), 465–489.

Tiano, S. (1994). *Patriarchy on the Line: Labor, Gender, and Ideology in the Mexican Maquila Industry*. Philadelphia: Temple University Press.

The Latina Feminist Group. (2001). *Telling to Live: Latina Feminist Testimonios*. Durham, NC: Duke University Press.

Torres, J. B., Solberg, V. S., & Carlstrom, A. H. (2002). The Myth of Sameness Among Latino Men and Their Machismo. *American Journal of Orthopsychiatry*, *72*(2), 163–181.

Toro-Morn, M. I. (1995). Gender, Class, Family, and Migration: Puerto Rican Women in Chicago. *Gender and Society, 9*(6), 706–720.

Toro-Morn, M. I. (2001). Yo era muy arriesgada: A Historical Overview of the Work Experiences of Puerto Rican Women in Chicago. *Centro: Journal of the Center for Puerto Rican Studies, 8*(2), 25–43.

Toro-Morn, M. (2005). The Family in Puerto Rico: Colonialism, Industrialization, and Migration. In B. N. Adams & J. Trost (Eds.), *Handbook of World Families* (pp. 440–463). Thousand Oaks, CA: Sage Publications.

Toro-Morn, M. I., & Alicea, M. (2003). Gendered Geographies of Home: Mapping Second and Third Generation Puerto Ricans' Sense of Home. In P. Hondagneu-Sotelo (Ed.), *Gender and U.S. Immigration: Contemporary Trends* (pp. 194–214). Berkeley: University of California Press.

Toro-Morn, M., Roschelle, A., & Facio, E. (2002). Gender, Work, and Family in Cuba: The Challenges of the Special Period. *Journal of Developing Societies, 18*(2–3), 32–58.

Vega, W. A. (1990). Hispanic Families in the 1980's: A Decade of Research. *Journal of Marriage and the Family, 52*(4), 1015–1024.

West, C., & Zimmerman, D. (1987). Doing Gender. *Gender and Society*, *1*, 125–51.

Ybarra, L. (1982). When Wives Work: The Impact on the Chicano Family. *Journal of Marriage and the Family*, *44*, 169–178.

CHAPTER 19

Adelante Mujer: Latina Activism, Feminism, and Empowerment

Denise A. Segura[1] and Elisa Facio

INTRODUCTION

Across geographic borders and historical space, Latinas have engaged in diverse forms of activism and leadership in their communities and families. This chapter examines Latina agency both in traditional organizational settings as well as in the informal or everyday spaces in their communities. Latina activism in these domains challenges "notions of leadership [that] are generally grounded on assumptions about a universal and male understanding of power and authority" (Mendez-Negrete, 1999, p. 27). Our exploration of Latinas' political work organizing workers and in secular and faith-based organizations that build strong transnational relationships and networks reveals continuity across historical space. Ultimately we argue that Latina ways of being and knowing create global and pan-ethnic connections critical for social change.

Activism and leadership occur in diverse social arenas. One strand of Latina women's activism is connected to labor movements that span U.S. history and highlights leaders such as Puerto Rican feminist and anarchist Luisa Capetillo, who organized workers during the first two decades of the 20th century, 1930s Chicana labor organizer Emma Tenayuca, Guatemala-born labor activist Luisa Moreno, and contemporary labor leaders Dolores Huerta and Maria Elena Durazo, among others. Another strand analyzes women's political activism within left, feminist, civil rights, and sanctuary movements. In addition to conventional notions of political and labor activism, feminist scholarship emphasizes building theory and knowledge based on women's agency in everyday life or what Milagros Ricort and Ruby Danta (2003) refer to as "*convivencia diaria*" (p. xi). Much of this work can be understood within the context of what Nancy Naples (1998) refers to as "activist mothering" and Teresa Carrillo (1998) describes as

294

"militant motherhood" or "feminine consciousness" (p. 395). That is, Latina agency in pursuit of quality health care, educational access, and immigration rights demonstrates political leadership that connects diverse political bases through gendered organizational strategies.

Given the length of time Chicanas/Mexican American women and Puerto Rican women have been in the United States, we draw on their experiences in our discussion of the historical antecedents of women's activism. However, the reinvigoration of Latina/o communities by intensive immigration from El Salvador, Guatemala, and Nicaragua since the 1970s gives us an opportunity to incorporate more diverse Latina voices. We argue that the growing diversification among Latinas in the United States is broadening the development of activism, leadership, and political consciousness that is both oppositional and visionary in present-day progressive politics. Increasingly, Latinas are reaching across borders to broaden coalition-building in the tradition of Luisa Moreno, who, according to historian Vicki Ruiz (2004), "remains the only transcontinental Latina union organizer" (p. 1). Latina activism today, however, goes beyond union activism and reflects agendas anchored in an intersectional analysis framed in women's everyday lives and needs.

WOMEN'S RIGHTS

In the United States, scholarship on women's activism has focused on the movement for women's rights and trade unionism. The "first wave" or women's rights movement for suffrage centered on agendas crafted by White women from middle- and upper-class origins. In 1848, the same year as the Treaty of Guadalupe Hidalgo delivered the northern half of Mexico to the United States, a group of White women led by Elizabeth Cady Stanton drafted the "Declaration of Sentiments" at Seneca Falls. The "Declaration" pressed for women's rights in a number of arenas, including full citizenship for women—in particular, the right to vote, a right not granted until passage of the 19th amendment to the Constitution in 1920. The agenda of the early women's rights movement did not include specific references to the lack of basic civil rights for women and men of color during that time. After women secured the right to vote, the women's rights movement moved in various directions, with much of its early agenda becoming institutionalized with the formation of organizations such as the League of Women Voters.

While middle-class White women actively agitated for suffrage, other women, mainly from working-class origins and racial-ethnic minorities, were fighting for decent working conditions, education, and health care. Few (if any) suffragettes articulated awareness of the dehumanizing conditions under which Mexican women and families were living in territories annexed by the United States in 1848. Similarly, the transfer of Puerto Rico from Spain to the United States in 1898 destabilized the life chances of Puerto Rican women and men, leading to their migration to the mainland in search of work (Acosta-Belén, 1986). During this time period, Mexican women publicly resisted racial inequality alongside of Latino men in *mutualistas* (mutual aid societies) and Puerto Rican women played a major role in the development of the early *colonia hispana* (Hispanic settlements) in New York City (Sánchez Korrol, 1983).

Mutualistas developed during the late 19th century in urban barrios and rural *colonias* to offer life insurance, organize cultural celebrations, and provide charitable and legal assistance to the Mexican population (Ruiz, 1998). *Mutualistas* were often connected to the local Mexican consulate. These organizations typically created a separate "ladies auxiliary" involved in such support activities as preparing food baskets and organizing dances and suppers (Orozco, 1997). They were also key sources of information and ways for women to work for the betterment of their communities. Historian Vicki Ruiz (1998) indicates that much of the work of women in the *mutualistas* "remained invisible outside the barrio" (p. 88). Similarly, the work of Puerto Rican women in informal information networks and in maintaining connections between U.S. *colonias* and the island while reaffirming ethnic identity among their children has been essential to community-building. Although much of the work women did in these networks or the *mutualistas* did not overtly challenge patriarchal privilege, it provided spaces where they could develop their own analysis of family and community needs. Arguably, these spaces enhanced the development of women's sense of self away from the male gaze and were strategies for empowerment also utilized by later Latina immigrants and activists.

Historically, women's work, when anchored in community betterment activities that do not capture a public spotlight, is not recognized as either "political" or "leadership." Yet, this work is crucial in generating community empowerment. In her study of contemporary Boston, Carol Hardy-Fanta (2002) argues that many Latinas deploy gendered forms of "community leadership" that "emphasize the relational rather than positional aspects of leadership, are less concerned with power or control of turf, and lead others into political participation through the use of personal relationships (p. 203). She observes that when leadership is defined as elected or appointed positions in government or organizations, males dominate the discourse. Moreover, ignoring the community work of Latinas as political, or as a form of leadership, bypasses critical social processes.

LABOR ACTIVISM

Historically, Latinas have demonstrated considerable leadership and activism organizing for safe and better working conditions. During the early 20th century, many trade unions did not focus much attention or devote significant resources to organizing industries in which women predominated. Despite this neglect, women rose from the ranks to demand employment opportunities, safe working conditions, and decent wages. Latinas such as Luisa Capetillo organized tobacco workers during the first two decades of the 20th century in her native Puerto Rico as well as in New York and Florida. Despite the feminist orientation of her work, Capetillo dedicated her energy to the labor movement as the better vehicle for poor working women to obtain justice and equality. Capetillo's choice to be immersed in a movement that articulated principles on behalf of the working class as opposed to exclusive attention to equal rights for women resonated with other Latinas and historicizes the historical gulf between feminist organizations and Latinas in the United States.

In the 1930s, Latinas, including Emma Tenayuca, Josefina Fierro de Bright, and Luisa Moreno, organized thousands of workers in the United States (Gutiérrez, 1995). Guatemalan immigrant Luisa Moreno drew inspiration from Luisa Capetillo in her organizing work during the Great Depression and World War II (Ruiz, 2004). She was the driving force behind *El Congreso del Pueblo de Habla Española* (The Congress of Spanish Speaking people), founded in 1938, with an agenda focused on immigration policy, workers' rights, education, and affordable housing (Mariscal, 2002; Ruiz, 2004). A feminist and a leftist, Moreno faced government harassment and red-baiting in the late 1940s. She was deported in 1950 on the grounds that she had once belonged to the Communist Party.

In contemporary times, Latinas have been at the forefront of numerous labor-organizing activities. Latina workers, immigrant and undocumented, have entered the lower echelons of the secondary and informal labor markets (Hamilton & Chinchilla, 2001; Chinchilla, Hamilton &

Loucky, 1993). Whether garment workers, janitors, domestic workers, street vendors, or day laborers, Latinas have organized boycotts of exploitative sweatshop working conditions through such organizations as the Union of Needletrades, Industrial and Textile Employees. Latinas have been equally involved in the Justice for Janitors campaign (Cranford, 1998) and in efforts to organize domestic workers under a program sponsored by the Coalition for Humane Immigrant's Rights of Los Angeles (CHIRLA). Fighting for the rights of immigrant workers, both documented and undocumented, alongside of U.S.-born workers has been the mission of women such as Maria Elena Durazo, the first Latina elected to the post of Secretary-Treasurer of the Los Angeles County Federation of Labor, the largest labor council in the nation, composed of 350 local unions with 850,000 members in May 2006.

LEADERSHIP IN SECULAR AND FAITH-BASED ORGANIZATIONS

Between 1981and 1990, almost 1 million Salvadoran, Guatemalans, and Nicaraguans fled from civil war, repression, and economic devastation at home and made the dangerous journey across Mexico, often entering the United States clandestinely. Thousands traveled undetected to major cities such as Washington, DC, Los Angeles, San Francisco, Boston, New York, and Chicago. However, thousands were also detained at or near the Mexico-U.S. border. As word of the conditions in Central America and the plight of refugees came to public attention in the early 1980s, three sectors began to work in opposition to the *de facto* "no asylum" policy: the religious sector, the legal sector, and the refugees themselves.

The network of religious congregations that became known as the Sanctuary Movement started with a Presbyterian church and a Quaker meeting in Tucson, Arizona (Gzesh, 2006). In many of these cities, Salvadoran and Guatemalan refugees formed projects such as *Casa Guatemala*, *Casa El Salvador*, and *Comité El Salvador*, which provided the community with legal advice, information about conditions back home, as well as information about health care and food assistance. These groups also worked with local lawyers' organizations and religious and antiwar activists, who assisted in decisions regarding class-action litigation and support of individual asylum applicants.

During the 1980s and 1990s, immigrants used network resources and formed grassroots organizations in the face of oppressive social and economic conditions in exile and expanded identities in the exile communities. Over 20 years later, a number of these immigrant-led projects, including *Centro Presente* in Boston, *Centro Romero* in Chicago, and *El Rescate* in Los Angeles, still exist as full-service, nonprofit legal and community centers. The role of churches and faith-based organizations in the Sanctuary movement and immigrant rights is consistent with Latina activism in these spaces. Adaptation to life in the United States often has been facilitated by women helping other women through the aegis of organizations within organized religions.

In the parishes observed by Ricourt and Danta, Latinas have played important roles as parent association officers, organizers, and, in one case, director of a youth program. However, Nancy Naples (1998) found few Latina activists involved in Catholic church-based organizations; rather, their involvement was uneven and subject to both the receptivity of the pastor and the preference of the parishioners. Mary Pardo's (1998) research on the Mothers of East Los Angeles (MELA) emphasized that although the organization developed within Resurrection Parish in 1984 with the goal of thwarting the construction of a prison in the neighborhood, the organization quickly evolved beyond the church. Mexican women of MELA deployed the ideology of motherhood to develop personal and community empowerment.

Milagros Peña's (2007) research on the work of Latina activists in faith-based and grass-roots nongovernmental organizations that articulate women-centered agendas in both the United States and Mexico examines women's agenda-setting and empowerment in both settings. The narratives she presents of women self-consciously developing a gendered sense of self—what she terms, "*fé-en-mi-mismo*" (faith in myself)—are remarkable illustrations of the ways feminism and spiritual agency interact on both sides of the border. Integral to this analysis is the distinction Peña's informants make between feminism and women's movements. Women in her study feel more comfortable describing their work in grassroots organizations as part of a "women's" movement rather than emanating from feminism. Latina activists utilize a discursive strategy of identifying their work as both woman-centered and part of a larger woman's movement, with the understanding that these needs require sustained struggle against poverty, racism, and other forms of disenfranchisement. This strategy effectively broadens the appeal of women's empowerment projects within grassroots organizations and intersects with global feminist coalition-building.

LATINA FEMINISMS

Latinas across class and national boundaries have been vocal actors in social movements dedicated to gender equality and sexuality. The relationship between White feminists and Latinas has been fraught with tension, however, given differences in their social locations. Historically, Latinas have not had equal access to education, compounding occupational segregation in low-paying jobs. Their distinctive social locations have given rise to priorities that often differ with White feminists. Latina activists typically do not prioritize agendas to dismantle the patriarchal state without equal attention to ameliorating racism and class privilege. Some of this tension is illustrated by the reluctance of many Latinas to utilize the term "feminist" to describe their political consciousness and activism, particularly by women involved in grassroots movements (Pardo, 1998; Peña, 2007). These tensions have existed historically but burst into public view during the Second Wave Women's Movement and the Civil Rights movements of the 1960s.

During the turbulent 1960s and 1970s, Chicanas and Puerto Rican women, among others, participated actively in a number of Latino/a civil rights social movements, including the Chicano and Puerto Rican social movements. These movements had gained momentum from the overwhelming protest against the Vietnam War, the Black Civil Rights Movement, and the Women's Movement; however, it is important to acknowledge the continuity that this activism represented for Latinas. As they had done within the *mutualistas* and in other community projects, Latinas performed the invisible work essential to keeping organizations functional, such as addressing mail, pamphleting, keeping records of meetings, and organizing fundraisers. When women spoke out and assumed more public leadership roles, however, conflict often arose with movement activists who, by and large, adhered to masculinist cultural nationalisms that prioritized male voices as the legitimate "heads" of the organization political "family." The two major ideological frameworks that guided the Chicano Movement and the subsequent development of Chicano Studies departments and programs, *El Plan Espiritual de Aztlán* and *El Plan de Santa Bárbara*, articulated an agenda of self-determination and empowerment that was fundamentally nationalistic and male-centered (Fregoso & Chabram, 1990).

Chicano Movement discourse relied on actualizing a series of categorical opposites: a racialized class of colonized Chicanos (men) versus a superordinate class of Anglo colonizers; Chicano (male) activists versus Mexican American assimilationists; and Chicana loyalists versus

Chicana feminists (Segura & Zavella, 2007). Chicana feminism was highly contested terrain where men challenged women activists as disloyal sell-outs if they strayed too far from the nationalist agenda (Nieto-Gomez, 1974). According to the undifferentiated nationalist text, racial oppression is primary and all Chicanos are victims of White racism and have been oppressed more or less equally by all Anglo-Americans. This principle predominated within the earliest Chicano movement-informed texts [e.g., Rodolfo Acuña's often-cited *Occupied America* 1972/1981)] that have informed generations of Chicano scholarship. Thus, the earliest blueprints for Chicano Studies did not situate women at the center of the intellectual or political paradigm (Garcia, 1989; Segura, 2001). The growth of Chicana feminism has led to a fundamental shift in the analytic male-centered core of "ChicanO" discourse to an increasingly more inclusionary "Chicana and Chicano" Studies framework (Segura, 2001). This shift also occurred within Puerto Rican and other Latino organizations. The platform of the Young Lords of New York, for example, articulated strong principles of gender equality (The Sixties Project, 1993).[2] Nevertheless, asserting Latina voices remains one of the most pressing challenges.

Often Latinas feel caught between two cultures (Scott, 1994). Many activists identify strongly with their culture and ethnic origins but do not wish to validate heterosexual gendered norms. "As Margarite Fernández Olmos observed of mainland puertorriqueñas: 'The delicate balance between defending one's culture and traditions, and analyzing it with a critical eye are difficult choices for the Latina writer who feels a sense of responsibility towards all of her people and towards herself'" (in Scott, 1994, p. 64). The writings of Latina scholars and activists illustrate the fine line many of them walk to critique the patriarchal structure of their respective societies while maintaining an oppositional stance to heteronormative racism and, more recently, color-blind racism (Bonilla-Silva, 2003). Latina lesbians, in particular, have vociferously challenged heteronormativity within Latina feminisms and organizational settings (Anzaldúa, 1987; Trujillo, 1998). Latina activists have pursued the development of agendas to undermine patriarchal privilege within their cultural spaces as well as in the larger society.

Many Latinas, particularly those with Movement experiences, have felt the need to develop spaces where they could pursue women-centered strategies for empowerment. Naples' (1998) research on community activists notes that women's expressed need to organize separately as Latinas has been more pronounced among older Latinas than in their younger sisters (p. 169). The view that Latina-centered spaces build women's empowerment grows out of a long tradition of women using their "separate" spaces (i.e., women's auxiliaries) to carry out the work they deem essential for their community and recognition that inclusion into mainstream organizations is often problematic in accomplishing their goals.

CENTRAL AMERICAN LATINA ACTIVISM AND FEMINISMS

Although much of the literature on Latina feminisms reflects the standpoints of Chicanas and Puerto Rican women, growing numbers of women from Central America are bringing their own strong traditions of activism to contemporary feminist discourse and practice. Contemporary Central American Latina activism and feminism is rooted in the context of civil war, immigration to the United States, and the processes of refugee adjustment and settlement. Given these social conditions, Latinas from El Salvador, Guatemala, and Nicaragua deploy distinct forms of activism and feminism. Graciela Freyermuth Enciso and Mariana Fernández Guerrero (1995) argue that Latin American women's activism revolves around *campo de acción*, which, citing María Luisa Tarres, "refers to the control that women develop over different areas of their everyday space, as determined objectively as well as by the definition that women themselves give to this space" (p. 972). Enciso and Guerrero's case study of Guatemalan women who joined a women's group against violence engages a methodology wherein they collectively arrive at an awareness of the growing contradictions in traditional family roles and in state-sanctioned structural violence. They found that through their struggle against violence, women change other aspects of their lives. The emphasis on change in women's everyday life resonates with Latinas in the United States.

Karen Kampwirth's (2002) research on women who joined insurrectionary movements in Nicaragua and El Salvador offers insight on the foundations of Central American women's activism and feminism transported by refugees to the United States. Kampwirth argue that after the triumph of the Cuban Revolution in 1959, women joined revolutionary activity in great numbers due to a combination of political, structural, ideological, and personal changes that had relaxed traditional gender roles. Women crossed traditional boundaries by daring to participate in national revolution, demanding a voice in their national development programs, and organizing state-integrated and autonomous women's groups. Women's survival (and that of their families), rather than national feminist identity, was the crucial factor in promoting the initial stages of Nicaraguan women's activism. Yet, the revolutionary commitment gained by valuing the traditional class roles of working and peasant women also led women to successfully challenge those roles. Thus, the traditional roles of women were transformed into fundamental catalysts for revolutionary activity.

According to Kampwirth, revolutionary activism is reflected by female combatants as well as other social movements such as student groups, radical Catholic groups, labor unions, human rights groups, and economic cooperatives, all of which include significant numbers of women. Several scholars argue that revolutionary activism is embedded in working toward expanding and defining the content of citizenship in order to achieve representation of women's rights and interests (Deere & Leon, 2001; Gonzalez & Kampwirth, 2001). More specifically, they suggest that women's relationships to the state and their substantive experiences of rights are ultimately questions of citizenship. Hence, their struggles have focused on a wide range of issues. Some women have fought for civil and political rights, including suffrage and family and labor law reform. Others have pressed for respect for human rights, often rooting their activism in their roles as wives and mothers. Poor and working-class women have demanded guarantees for socioeconomic rights like food, decent employment, education, housing, and health care, which are frequently denied to women and their families in the context of neoliberalism and structural adjustment. Although many of these agendas could be considered "feminist," they tend to be discussed as "revolutionary" or "activist."

Given that Latin America is the birth home of over half of all Latinas residing in the United States, the concept of feminism needs to be problematized in light of the distinction made in Latin America between a "woman's movement" and a "feminist movement." According to Enciso and Fernandez (1995), a woman's movement is where women predominate to form an agenda that does not necessarily center on women but often embraces improving living conditions in key arenas such as labor, education, and health. Feminist movements in Latin America, on the other hand, are mobilizations centered on gender demands (i.e., social, economic, and political equality of women with men in terms of rights and obligations). This distinction is, we argue, helpful in terms of understanding Latina activism in the United States. In this sense, what has been termed "activist mothering" is related to the women's movement paradigm, and what have been termed "Chicana/Latina feminisms" closely mirror the feminist movements in Latin America. Both Latina activism and feminisms, however, seek global connections. Latina activism in the United

States often becomes "feminist" and institutionalized within nonprofit organizations both secular and faith based. Latina activism is historical, with connections to Latin American paradigms, and unique in its challenge to coalesce across myriad Latina ethnicities.

COMMUNITY ACTIVISM AND LEADERSHIP

National organizations are not the only site for Latina activism. Securing quality education for their children has mobilized countless Latinas at the grassroots level. In New York City, Puerto Rican female teachers and mothers led the fight for bilingual education. Virginia Sánchez Korrol's (1996) research on Spanish-speaking Substitute Auxiliary Teachers (SATs), who taught in New York City during 1947–1967 and challenged the effectiveness of the prevailing English-only "immersion-method" of teaching Puerto Rican migrant children, is one example of Latinas making connections across class boundaries.

During the late 1960s and early 1970s, Latinas mobilized the community for educational access and quality in local organizations such as the People's Board of Education, United Bronx Parents, and ASPIRA (Matos Rodriguez, 1998, p. 25). In Los Angeles, young Chicanas assumed leadership in the 1968 walkouts to protest educational inequality. Increasingly, parents, mainly Latinas, have become involved in local school sites and community organizations to advocate for their children. Latina feminists in university settings (e.g., "Hermanas Unidas," "Mujer") and community organizations have committed themselves to strengthen the pipeline to higher education for young women, resulting in higher levels of high school and college graduation for Latinas. However, at the same time, the graduation and college-going rates for Latino men has been declining. In 2002, 11.1% of Latinos had secured college degrees or higher compared to 29.% of non-Hispanic Whites (U.S. Bureau of the Census, 2002). One of the most urgent needs across Latino communities is to maintain pressure on schools to deliver quality education to all children in the K-12 systems and beyond.

Much of the work to empower self and community occurs at the grassroots level. Research on Latina community activism and leadership demonstrates the multiple ways women assert agency and voice. Hardy-Fanta's (2002) research on Boston illustrates how Latinas play important leadership roles in both the traditional electoral arena and at the community level. She notes that the literature on Latino politics "virtually ignores the political participation of Latina women" but, rather, assumes "that Latina women are passive, submissive, and uninvolved in politics," which is, however, "belied by reality" in that nationally they comprise "a larger proportion of Latino elected officials than women in general as a percentage of all elected officials" (Hardy-Fanta, 2002, p. 197).

Hardy-Fanta (2002) does not privilege the political activism of Latina elected officials; rather, she views this work as one strand of Latina leadership. Her interviews with *la gente del pueblo,* "common folk" individuals (her translation), reveals that they conceptualize politics as "making connections at the community level" (Hardy-Fanta, 2002, p. 201). Latina leadership focuses on developing relationships between people to develop a collective, shared vision to solve community problems. Hardy-Fanta argue that Latina leadership is an important pathway to Latino community empowerment; that is, their leadership, based on community members seeing themselves "in charge," empowers the community in ways that top-down dominance styles of leadership do not (2002, p. 204). Hardy-Fanta observed that women were less interested in titles and positions and more concerned with developing community connectedness. This type of leadership empowers hitherto voiceless subjects to speak at meetings and claim space for their political viewpoints. This might be particularly important in multiethnic settings like Boston comprised of multiple Latino groups.

Ricourt and Danta's (2003) case study of Queens in New York City (NYC) analyzes women's leadership, finding changes alongside of neighborhood demographics. Once overwhelmingly Puerto Rican, by 2000 Dominicans comprised 27% of the population in NYC, behind Puerto Ricans (38%), with smaller proportions of other Latinos (14%), Mexicans (9%), and Colombians and Ecuadorians (6% each). They found that many women had begun their activism in "single-nationality immigrant associations" but moved to "panethnic social service, cultural and political organizations" (p. 97). Reminiscent of the first Puerto Rican public librarian, Pura Belpré, "who steered her professional activities to create and nurture ties between Puerto Rico and New York City" (Matos Rodriguez, 1998, p. 25), Queens' Latinas maintain transnational family and community networks. However, as women become more involved in bettering their community, the search for necessary resources leads them to connect with broader, panethnic bases of support through everyday activities, or *convivencia diaria*. This involvement in Latino pan-ethnic organizations and neighbors differs significantly from the actions of Latino men in the same community.

Central American immigrant women have relied extensively on the establishment of myriad informal social networks and grassroots organizations in negotiating adjustment, settlement, and general survival as refugees in the United States (Hagan, 1998; Menjivar, 2000). Cecilia Menjivar (2002) defines social networks as "the web of family, friends, neighbors....who can provide material, financial, informational, and emotional assistance on a regular basis" (p. 2). In her study of Salvadoran immigrants in San Francisco, Menjivar deploys the concept of "gendered networks" to refer to the ways that gender shapes informal exchanges for women and men. In general, women have fewer financial and material resources, thus placing them at a disadvantage in exchanges of financial or material help. However, women are heavily involved in the exchange of in-kind resources. Latina mobilization of familial and social networks provides valuable assistance and information from job-related matters to health advice to housing availability. Also, it is women who frequently seek out assistance from community organizations and other local institutions to meet the needs of their family's general survival. Women actively seek out resources in community organizations that can provide assistance for their family's needs. She further notes that women are drawn to organizations and social interactions because of their families and become pivotal members in different forms of community-building.

This form of activism increases their opportunities for expanding their networks and creating more personal relationships with community organization directors, workers, and volunteers. Furthermore, in the process of procuring assistance for themselves and their families and actively building community, immigrant women acquire knowledge about their rights as women, refugees, and potential citizens. Much of this knowledge is gained through their involvement with community organizations and observing a relatively more egalitarian behavior of their mostly middle-class employers.

Women's participation in "gendered networks" might have important implications in the development of feminist consciousness. Zentgraf (2002) argues that immigration's impact on gender relations often provides Latinas with greater autonomy, independence, confidence, and a stronger sense of self (p. 626). However, women do not necessarily have to overtly challenge traditional patriarchal roles after migration or employment in the United States. Zentgraf's (2002) study of Salvadoran women in Los Angeles found that their sense of freedom reflected "a breaking down of gender-related cultural and social roles that kept them tightly regulated and watched" in El Salvador (p. 637) as they participated in activities outside the home. Women were "not only wage laborers and family members but community members who are involved in churches, schools, labor unions, or immigrant organizations, all of which may be affected by (and in turn, affect) their productive and reproductive roles" (Zentgraf, 2002, p. 628). Latinas' greater flexibility in accessing public space in the United States "may serve as catalysts for important transformations in gender relations as a result of migration" (Menjivar, 2000, p. 197).

RESEARCH AND POLICY: FUTURE DIRECTIONS

Acknowledging the broad base upon which gender is being negotiated within families has consequences for women's activism and leadership. Broadening our understanding of the nature of activism is an important contribution to scholarship and social policy. Recognizing that many Latinas are in different stages in social change processes strengthens possibilities for empowerment. Given persistent social inequalities in Latino communities, Latina leadership on these issues constitutes a "best practice" that should be supported and extended. One of the most important changes to emerge from Latina activism and their diverse feminisms are changes in women's subjectivity—newly empowered ways in which women have come to see themselves in relation to society. The processes whereby Latina voices increasingly inform policy and praxis are important subjects for future research. Although Latinas are making inroads in traditional activist forums, such as the labor movement, their involvement in emerging transnational campaigns for workers' rights is not well examined. Do Latinas who are involved in such activities utilize alternative leadership models or does the structure of transnational discourse require new forms of leadership?

Related to labor concerns for Latinas is immigration policy. Latinas in general are faced with a national discourse profiling undocumented workers as fueling terrorism and being economic burdens to (White) North Americans. Today, the Bush administration is using immigration enforcement as a "magic bullet" for national security. The United States finds itself in a congressional stalemate over such issues as guest worker plans, temporary visa programs, citizenship, and the "legitimate" dissemination of federal and state services—policies that affect the immigrant community's access to employment, education, and health care. Aggressive anti-immigrant legislation regarding proof of citizenship and the enforcement of penalties against employers who hire people not "authorized" to work in the United States are directed at immigrant communities.

In addition, more and more immigrant women are single heads of households. A growing number of single heads of households in Latina/o immigrant communities are women in their late teens and early twenties who risk their lives to reach the United States and have children who are born as U.S. citizens. Congress, however, is seriously considering revising the U.S. Constitution to deny automatic citizenship to babies born to undocumented mothers. Also, there are thousands of youth in middle and high schools in need of legal status in the United States to be able to access higher education with the ease granted to previous generations of (largely European) immigrant youth and adults. In order to better develop and implement a comprehensive immigration policy, more research is needed in the areas of settlement and adjustment issues for families with differential citizenship statuses and labor issues regarding immigrant workers.

Another issue in Latino families that rarely receives adequate critical scrutiny or public attention is domestic violence. According to the National Coalition Against Domestic

Violence, one in four women will experience domestic violence in her lifetime. There are cultural factors that assist Latinas who experience domestic violence and others that hinder dealing with the issue. In general, many Latinas turn to extended family members rather than community organizations for assistance in dealing with domestic violence and partners. The fear of one's culture being stereotyped and the lack of cultural competency in the availability of social services are some of the reasons why Latinas in general do not seek assistance outside the family. Immigrant women often remain silent about domestic violence in their families for fear of deportation, removal of their children, and overall lack of knowledge regarding community assistance and services.

With respect to elected office, Hardy-Fanta (1993, 2002) argues that Latinas are involved in both electoral and community politics. How does Latina involvement in both political spheres affect the political consciousness of Latina/o youth? If role-modeling principles are correct, the growing numbers of Latinas involved in both community-based organizations and electoral politics might encourage young Latinas/os to engage in similar involvement, which could have a positive effect on educational attainment. Future research in this area might provide insight into this process that is so critical given the current crisis in Latina/o education.

One of the most pressing policy issues in the nation is Latina/o education. Much educational research and policy focuses on ways to develop Latina/o parental involvement in their children's education. This research and policy, however, tends to be anchored in what schools perceive is important (i.e., having parents read at night to their children, check homework, monitor attendance, and attend school meetings). Schools tend not to consider that many Latina/o parents cannot do most of these things if they do not speak English well and/or work in jobs that do not provide personal time off or even a regular work schedule. The perspectives of Latina/o parents—in particular, Latinas who tend to be the parent in charge of monitoring children's education—are rarely integrated into school policy. We suggest that educational policy integrate findings on Latina leadership that demonstrates their high interest in their children's education and expertise in developing connections with others, to build on mothers' "funds of knowledge" rather than assume deficiency. Such partnerships could draw on the parent empowerment workshop models developed by MALDEF (Mexican American Legal and Defense Educational Fund) and other community-based organizations that give parents information on their rights as well as responsibilities in the schools. Research indicates that mothers are the key players in schools; thus school policy needs to focus on hearing what they do with their children and not necessarily expect them to do the job of a teacher assistant. Rather, women teach their children core values of honor and respect. Mothers seek to build self-respect in their children and a sense of their connectedness to others. Considering the values of their Latina/o constituents as assets to build on rather than as liabilities to fix is essential for policy makers. This principle transcends the educational sphere and is part of a counterhegemonic project for social change.

The implications of unique forms of Latina activism are more likely to impact policy now than before, given the increasing numbers of Latinas involved in electoral as well as community-based leadership. Ricourt and Danta (2003) argues that growing Latina/o pan-ethnicity is facilitating transnational cultural diffusion across different Latino nationalities in the United States and Latin America. As transnational cultural diffusion affects expectations regarding education, employment, and political rights across national borders and within local communities, additional research questions will unfold that are integral to social change policy and initiatives.

CONCLUSION

This chapter has discussed the multiple forms of Latina activism and leadership in the contemporary United States. We have argued that women's diverse forms of agency are connected to the past and transnational present. Daily life struggles both in the United States and Latin America serve as the context wherein women demand respect in the arenas of labor, education, and family. Although more and more Latinas are securing elected office, it is women in local community agencies and neighborhoods whose collective work strikes chords that resonate across borders. Some Latina voices claim feminism; others do not. Understanding that many Latinas bring to the United States traditions of activism that do not necessarily operate under a feminist banner might be helpful to analysts wondering how to account for Latinas' woman-centered agendas that are not always gender-specific.

Women, the collective "other," have been reclaiming their own subjectivities in interaction with one another and through action anchored in a shared vision of community. They recognize that gender equality and the idea of strong, healthy, and creative feminine identities must be deployed in conjunction with all women. The vision of Latina activists must have triple lenses that focus on colonial histories, ideological differences that often divide the community, and the appropriateness of legal and economic policies for women.

Since the annexations of northern Mexico and Puerto Rico and the intervention of the United States into the economic lives of Latin America, Latinas coming to the United States have brought with them ways of being and knowing that assert self in the new society. They have developed informal informational networks to ease adaptation while seeking to maintain varying levels of Latino culture. Because they work in social and reproductive labor, their activism rarely has been recognized, given its departure from traditional understandings of power and authority. The participation of Latinas in broad-based grassroots coalitions suggest a significant change in women's political consciousness as they decide to move beyond women's projects and help create feminist organizations; that is, many have made a transition from a "female consciousness," which places human nurturing above all other social and political requirements (Kaplan, 1982) and from actions based on "practical interests" (Molyneux, 1986) centered around family survival, to a "feminist" and "strategic consciousness" (Pessar, 2001). We are not implying that a rigid dichotomy exists between pragmatic/female interests and strategic/feminist ones. Rather, women's consciousness is dynamic and fluctuates along a continuum spanning these two positions. Our challenge becomes one of determining how women's consciousness develops and how fluctuations in consciousness are explained by such factors as life-cycle phasing, social location, and the gendering of specific social localities where women reside.

Across borders, "New Women" are voicing new values. More specifically, more global and pan-ethnic feminisms are emerging from the grassroots realities of many nations and communities that disseminate the wisdom and strength of women's diverse voices, their political methods, and their distinct social realities. Latinas are expanding the meanings of "womanhood" and "feminist" by dismantling essentialist stereotypes of Eurocentric, first-world feminist discourses that have historically excluded cross-cultural and multiclass analysis. Latina women's organizations contribute to the dignity of their members when they express community concerns at local, national, and international levels simultaneously. Our analysis points to Latina women's ways of knowing and being as strengthening transnational activism. Increasingly, the voices of immigrant and Indigenous women will become even stronger, not only in providing *testimonios*, which has been the tradition among international human rights groups, but in analysis and policy formulation for the future.

NOTES

1. Authors names are arranged in reverse alphabetical order.
2. Items 10 and 11 of the "Young Lords Party 13-Point Program and Platform" reads: 10. "We want equality for women. Machismo must be revolutionary … not oppressive" (The Sixties Project, 1993, p. 4).

REFERENCES

Acosta-Belén, Edna. (1986). Puerto Rican Women in Culture, History and Society. In Edna Acosta-Belen (Ed.), *The Puerto Rican Woman, Perspectives on Culture, History and Society* (2nd ed.) (pp. 1-29). New York: Praeger.

Acuña, Rodolfo. (1981). *Occupied America: A History of Chicanos.* New York: Harper and Row. (Original work published 1972)

Anzaldúa, Gloria. (1987). *Borderlands/La Frontiera: The New Mestiza.* San Francisco: Spinsters/Aunt Lute.

Bonilla-Silva, Eduardo. (2003). *Racism Without Racists: Color-Blind Racism and the Persistence of Racial Inequality in the United States.* Lanham, MD: Rowman and Littlefield Publishers.

Carrillo, Teresa. (1998). Cross-Border Talk: Transnational Perspectives on Labor, Race and Sexuality. In Ella Shohat (Ed.), *Talking Visions* (pp. 391–411). New York: New Museum of Contemporary Art.

Chinchilla, Norma Stoltz, Hamilton, Nora, & Loucky, James. (1993). Central Americans in Los Angeles: The Central American Community. In Joan Moore & Raquel Pinderhughes (Eds.), *In the Barrios: Latinos and the Underclass Debate* (pp. 51–78). New York: Russell Sage Foundation.

Cranford, Cynthia. (1998). Gender and Citizenship in the Restructuring of Janitorial Work in Los Angeles. *Gender Issues, 16*(4), 25–51.

Deere, Carmen Diana, & Leon, Magdalena. (2001). *Empowering Women: Land and Property Rights in Latin America.* Pittsburgh: University of Pittsburgh Press.

Enciso, Graciela Freyermuth, & Guerrero, Mariana Fernández. (1995). Migration, Organization, and Identity: The Case of a Woman's Group from San Cristóbal de las Casas. *SIGNS, 20*(4), 970–995.

Fregoso, Rosa Linda, & Chabram, Angie. (1990). Chicana/o Cultural Representations: Reframing Alternative Critical Discourses. *Cultural Studies, 4*(3), 203–212.

Garcia, Alma M. (1989). The Development of Chicana Feminist Discourse, 1970–1980. *Gender & Society, 3*(2), 217–237.

Gonzalez, Victoria, & Kampwirth, Karen. (2001). *Radical Women in America: Left and Right.* University Park: Pennsylvania State University Press.

Gutiérrez, David. (1995). *Walls and Mirrors, Mexican Americans, Mexican Immigrants, and the Politics of Ethnicity.* Berkeley: University of California Press.

Gzesh, Susan. (2006). Central Americans and Asylum Policy in the Reagan Era. Retrieved December 8, 2006, from http: www.migrationinformation.org/Feature/ display.cfm?id=384.

Hagan, Jacqueline Maria. (1998). Social Networks, Gender and Immigrant Incorporation: Resources and Constraints. *American Sociological Review, 63,* 55–67.

Hamilton, Nora, & Chinchilla, Norma Stoltz. (2001). *Seeking Community in a Global City: Guatemalans and Salvadorans in Los Angeles.* Philadelphia: Temple University Press.

Hardy-Fanta, Carol. (1993). *Latina Politics, Latino Politics: Gender, Culture, and Political Participation in Boston.* Philadelphia: Temple University Press.

Hardy-Fanta, Carol. (2002). Latina Women and Political Leadership: Implications for Latino Community Empowerment. In C. Hardy-Fanta & J. N. Gerson (Eds.), *Latino Politics in Massachusetts: Struggles, Strategies, and Prospects* (pp. 192–212). New York: Routledge.

Kampwirth, Karen. (2002). *Women and Guerrilla Movements: Nicaragua, El Salvador, Chiapas and Cuba.* University Park: Pennsylvania State University Press.

Kaplan, Temma. (1982). Female Consciousness and Collective Action: The Case of Barcelona, 1910–1918. *SIGNS: Journal of Women in Culture and Society, 7*(3), 545–566.

Mariscal, Jorge. (2002, July–August). Left Turns in the Chicano Movement, 1965–1975. *Monthly Review, 54,* 59–68.

Matos Rodriguez, Felix A. (1998). Women's History in Puerto Rican Historiography: The Last Thirty Years. In F. V. Matos Rodriquez & L. C. Degaldo (Eds.), *Puerto Rican Women's History, New Perspectives* (pp. 9–37). New York: M. E. Sharpe.

Mendez-Negrete, Josephine. (1999). Awareness, Consciousness and Resistance: Raced, Classed, and Gendered Leadership Interactions in Milagro County, California. *Frontiers: A Journal of Women Studies, 20*(1), 25–44.

Menjivar, Cecilia. (2000). *Fragmented Ties: Salvadoran Immigrant Networks in America.* Berkeley: University of California Press.

Molyneux, Maxine. (1986). Mobilization Without Emancipation? Women's Interests, State and Revolution in Nicaragua. In Richard R. Fagen, Carmen Diana Deere & Jose Luis Goraggio (Eds.), *Transition and Development: Problems of Third World Socialism (pp. 280–302).* New York: Monthly Review Press and Center for the Study of the Americas.

Naples, Nancy A. (1998). *Grassroots Warriors: Activist Mothering, Community Work, and the War on Poverty.* New York: Routledge.

Nieto-Gomez, Anna. (1974). La Femenista. *Encuentro Femenil, 1*(2), 34–47.

Orozco, Cynthia E. (1997). Beyond Machismo, La Familia, and Ladies Auxiliaries: A Historiography of Mexican-Origin Women's Participation in Voluntary Associations and Politics in the United States, 1870–1990. *Renato Rosaldo Lecture Series Monograph, 10,* 37–77.

Pardo, Mary. (1998). *Mexican American Women Activists: Identity and Resistance in Two Los Angeles Communities.* Philadelphia: Temple University Press.

Peña, Milagros. (2007). *Latina Activists Across Borders: Women's Grassroots Organizing in Mexico and Texas.* Durham, NC: Duke University Press.

Pessar, Patricia R. (2001). Women's Political Consciousness and Empowerment in Local, National, and Transnational Contexts; Guatemalan Refugees and Returnees. *Identities, 7*(4), 461–500.

Ricourt, Milagros, & Danta, Ruby. (2003). *Hispanas de Queens, Latino Panethnicity in a New York City Neighborhood.* Ithaca: Cornell University Press.

Ruiz, Vicki. (1998). *From Out of the Shadows: Mexican Women in Twentieth Century America.* New York: Oxford University Press.

Ruiz, Vicki. (2004). Una Mujer Sin Fronteras: Luisa Moreno and Latina Labor Activism. *Pacific Historical Review, 73*(1), 1–20.

Sánchez Korrol, Virginia. (1983). *From Colonia to Community: The History of Puerto Ricans in New York City.* Westport, CT: Greenwood Press.

Sánchez Korrol, Virginia. (1996). Toward Bilingual Education: Puerto Rican Women Teachers in New York City Schools 1947–1967. In Altagracia Ortiz (Ed.), *Puerto Rican Women and Work* (pp. 82–104). Philadelphia: Temple University Press.

Scott, Nina M. (1994). The Politics of Language: Latina Writers in United States Literature and Curricula. *MELUS, 19*(1), 57–71.

Segura, Denise A. (2001). Challenging the ChicanO Text: Towards a More Inclusive Contemporary 'Causa.' *Signs, 26*(2), 541–550.

Segura, Denise A., & Zavella, Patricia. (2007). *Women and Migration in the U.S. Mexico Borderlands: A Reader.* Durham, NC: Duke University Press.

The Sixties Project. (1993). *Young Lords Party 13 Point Program and Platform.* University of Virginia at Charlottesville: Viet Nam Generation, Inc. and the Institute of Advanced Technology in the Humanities. Retrieved December 8, 2006, from http://www3.iath.virgihia.edu/sites/HTML_docs/Resources/Primary/Manifestos/Young_Lords_platform.html.

Trujillo, Carla (Ed.). (1998). *Living Chicana Theory.* Berkeley, CA: Third Woman Press.

U.S. Bureau of the Census. (2002, March). *U.S. Hispanic Population* (Current Population Survey, PC-P5). Washington, DC: U. S. Government Printing Office.

Zentgraf, Kristine M. (2002). Immigration and Women's Empowerment: Salvadorans in Los Angeles. *Gender & Society, 16*(5), 625–646.

CHAPTER 20

Latinas and Latinos, Sexuality, and Society: A Critical Sociological Perspective

GLORIA GONZÁLEZ-LÓPEZ
SALVADOR VIDAL-ORTIZ

INTRODUCTION

What happens when we put Latinas, Latinos, and sexuality together? What if we add "society" to this complex interaction? As we inquire about Latinas, Latinos, sexuality, and society as mutually connected, what kind of processes emerge as we unpack them?[1] This chapter examines the issues and concerns that surface as we explore some sociological answers to these questions. We offer (1) a critical analysis of the limited yet gradually flourishing area of theorizing and research on Latina/o sexuality in sociology, (2) a sociological examination of the state of the art of sexuality research with U.S. Latina and Latino populations[2] across disciplines, and (3) our reflections with regard to some of the implications for future research in sociology of sexualities with these social groups.

Our own personal histories and subjectivities are both diverse and unique; yet, they are unrepresentative of the populations commonly identified as Latinas and Latinos in the social sciences. The first author was born and raised in northern Mexico and migrated to the U.S. Southwest in her mid-twenties; the second author was born and raised in Puerto Rico and has lived in the United States since 1994.

Thus, we are well aware of the heterogeneity that exists among the Latino groups and how these groups differ from one another. A specific challenge in using terms like "Latina" and "Latino" is that their use inherently signals the impossibility of accurately representing the communities often included in it. For instance, historical, regional, political, and economic forces that have shaped each one of the Latino groups have influenced their sex lives, sexual moralities, views of relationships, marriage, family life, and so forth in very unique ways. For example, a Mexican American woman from Santa Fé, New Mexico is going to be vulnerable to a very unique history and politics of the U.S. Southwest that has shaped the lives of Mexican Americans. A Puerto Rican couple from the Bronx is going to be influenced by similar forces that have shaped Puerto Rican communities within the context of the Northeast and the very unique relationship between this part of the United States and a history of colonization of the Island. A third scenario could be represented by a lesbian couple: one Cuban and the other one from El Salvador. Each one of them is going to be affected in more nuanced ways by the specific politics in their places of origin and in the United States. However, sociological scholarship on this topic is too modest, and the lack of research looking at all of the complexities that emerge when we look at the countless scenarios of Latinas/os in the United States represents a challenge in discussing this heterogeneity. Sociology of sexualities scholarship has not been able to catch up and reflect the fast pace with which U.S. Latino communities are growing and changing. In the last section of this chapter, we discuss our final reflections with regard to some of these and other issues and concerns.

What is sexuality? Based on the first author's research with Mexican immigrants, we define sexuality as "the attitudes and behaviors, beliefs and practices, emotions and feelings, and fantasies and acts they (Latinas and Latinos) engage as they experience the erotic" (González-López, 2005, p. 19).[3] We understand sexuality as both an individual and collective process in deep connection with social forces and as a socially constructed phenomenon that becomes alive by, through, and within multiple erotic desires, expressions, identities, and communities. We use the concept of "sexualities" to refer to the latter. Accordingly, we selectively use both sexuality and sexualities in this chapter.

MÁS ALLÁ DE LAS SÁBANAS: WHAT DO WE KNOW ABOUT LATINAS, LATINOS, SEXUALITY, AND SOCIETY?

Sociological research and theorizing on the sex lives of U.S. Latino populations is relatively recent. Tomás Almaguer (1991) was the first sociologist to study Latino sexuality by offering a theoretical analysis of sexual desire, practices, and identities of gay men of Mexican origin living the United States. Indeed, his work has been characterized as "a paradigmatic shift in the anthropological study of Latino homosexualities" for its "Latino-centricity" (Guzmán, 2006, p. 83). Maxine Baca Zinn (1982) did not conduct sexuality research per se but offered some of the first sociological reflections on gender and both women and men of Mexican origin and alerted us to some misconceptions and stereotypes with regard to this population and sexuality.[4] More recently, other sociologists have examined Latina and Latino sexualities with regard to immigration (Cantú, 2000, 2002; González-López, 2005; Luibhéid, 2002; Luibhéid & Cantú, 2005; Peña, 2005), the family (Cantú, 2001), adolescent sexuality (García, 2006), reproductive health (Silliman, Fried, Ross, & Gutiérrez, 2004), religion and spirituality (González-López, 2007; Vidal-Ortiz, 2005), HIV/AIDS (Mutchler, 2000), and feminist examinations on gender and sexuality (Baca Zinn, 1982, 2001).

At the same time, recent edited volumes on sociology and sexuality have addressed many of the sociological complexities and concerns examined in cutting-edge research on sex, the erotic, and society. Interestingly, even though they might include chapters that examine the experiences of Latino groups (and African American or Asian American populations), race, ethnicity, and culture are not identified as themes to organize the tables of content in these relevant publications.[5]

As these studies have emerged in sociology, writing and research across many disciplines has informed our understanding of these groups and sexuality within social and cultural contexts. Sociological research with Latinas and Latinos and sexuality has not (and could have not) evolved in academic isolation. Relevant research has been conducted in anthropology (Argüelles & Rivero, 1993; Ascencio, 2002; Erickson, 2001; Hirsch, 2003; Juárez & Kerl, 2003; Zavella, 1997), the humanities (Alarcón, Castillo, & Moraga, 1993; Anzaldúa, 1987; Moraga, 1983), history (Gutiérrez, 1991), psychology (Espín, 1999), and public health and HIV/AIDS (Alonso & Koreck, 1993; Carballo-Dieguez, 1989; Carrillo, 2002; Díaz, 1998; Díaz & Ayala, 1999). These publications have selectively informed and inspired sociological research on Latinas, Latinos, and sexuality.

All of the sociological research has relied on theorizing and publications across disciplines and within *Las Américas*. For instance, the humanities, anthropology, public health, and epidemiology have established bridges to inform these projects. As a case in point, Chicana lesbians (e.g., Moraga and Anzaldúa relying on their own life experiences) have helped us understand the sex lives of this particular population; paradoxically, although these literatures have flourished within these other fields, there is no major sociological research on U.S. Latina lesbians. Because of the centrality of such work, we proceed to analyze the most important paradigms, concepts, and contributions examined in these disciplines, as well as the ways in which they have reproduced stereotypes and misconceptions that have damaged our sociological understanding of Latina and Latino populations and sexuality. The areas we (un)cover in this section are studies focusing on (1) gay male sexuality, (2) madonna/whore, machismo and marianismo, sexual silence, and love and relationships, and (3) HIV/AIDS. We aim to discuss how issues of cultural analysis (cultural differentiation)[6] are privileged in many of these accounts and propose additional ways to frame arguments and analyze Latinas' and Latinos' sexuality in this country. All of the research that addressed culture was needed at some point. However, we are concerned about the need to update these frameworks, especially in sociology. Put differently, we offer an alternative that takes care of contradictions in these literatures and reconciles both cultural and structural arguments without privileging one over the other.

Gay Men Studies, *Activo-Pasivo*

Díaz (1998), Carrier (1995), and Lancaster (1992) are, among others, some of the scholars outside sociology who wrote about the cultural differences between men who have sex with men from Latin America and those in the United States. From their various angles, they have looked at the behavioral practices and general patterns of Latin American men having sex with men in relation to HIV/AIDS, sexual stigma, identity formation, and relationship to gay communities. Although significant when written, an unfortunate result of many of these writings was the emphasis in cultural differentiation to justify the "*activo-pasivo*" model (which we discuss in brief).

Citing some of these literatures, as well as autobiographical writings by Moraga, sociologist Tomás Almaguer (1991) argued that unlike Western countries, where sexuality and gender were distinct aspects of self, enacted through different vectors, in Mexico and other Latin American countries the distinction of gender and sexuality has been notoriously marked by an understanding of the (male) actors' positioning in sexual activity. Almaguer noted how a heterosexual man is still considered such in the event of having sex with another man if he is the *activo*, relegating the homosexual stigma to the penetrated, or *pasivo* person (see also Carrier, 1995; Lancaster, 1992; Murray, 1995); that is, the social organization of the penetrative male, the *activo*, remains heterosexual within his communities, and the mark of deviance is placed upon the (feminized) penetrated male. Further sociological writings expanded and contested Almaguer's work, noting how his location of this complexity in Mexican/Latin American contexts implies that models of sexuality and gender in Western contexts are simpler (Cantú, 2000), that this typology ignores the mutual influence of migration (Carrier, 1995), and that an oversimplification is made when assuming a gender expression to be linear with sexual behavior and social stigma (a feminine man is supposed to be the penetrated and chastised in his community; a masculine man is not presumed to be penetrated and it is not stigmatized).

Two main strands of sociology have emerged in response to this *activo-pasivo* paradigm (stuck with Latino and Latin American sexuality studies) that move beyond the cultural while still recognizing it. First, Cantú (1999, 2000, 2001, 2002) argued for a political economy of migration—a queer political economy—that addressed materialist aspects in relation to the lives of Mexican men who have sex with men. His work critiqued the culturalist argument privileged in previous literatures and forced us to acknowledge how issues of globalization, economics, and politics frame much of the structural component (often minimized in these discussions). Cantú (2002) asked: "If the literature on the social construction of a Western gay identity is correct in linking sexual identities to capitalist development, then why should our understanding of sexual identities in the developing world give primacy to culture and divorce it from political economy?" (p. 141). His answer was that among U.S. scholars, "culture became the mechanism that reified difference and reproduced the imagined distance of 'the others' in academic discourse itself" (p. 141). In this way, Cantú's queer materialist analysis highlighted the ways in which different traditions of academic research perpetuate ethnocentric and cultural determinist views of sexual difference.

Second, Guzmán (2006) utilized a psychoanalytical, Queer Theory-based framework that merges race and sexuality discussions. In evaluating Almaguer's work, Guzmán argued that it was not a cultural distinction that Almaguer was posing but one based on structural arrangements occupied by Mexican and Chicano families in the U.S. social/racial/economic landscape. Guzmán (2006) stated: "What could very well be understood as an economically structured ethno-racial commitment that reinforces a patriarchal regime is construed, instead, as a culturally based commitment to traditional patriarchal values simply because that is what Chicano family life is about" (p. 83). "The Chicano family's" location and the same-gender loving individuals living within an already liminal location (class and race based) are what framed Almaguer's groundbreaking work but were often missed for its oppositional sexuality discussions.

However different these might be from each other, these two strands continue to critique the capitalist/gay identity argument put forth by historians and anthropologists (D'Emilio, 1983; Rubin, 1984/1993) and, in doing so, challenge the identity-based restrictions of gay and lesbian communities. Noteworthy of mention is how lesbian women in *Latinoamérica*, especially in cities such as Mexico City and Monterrey, are casually beginning to assume the "*activa*" and "*pasiva*" categories when looking for sexual partners in lesbian and gay settings, as observed by the first author in her ongoing research. Finally, Latino gay and bisexual men in academic and activist settings seem to be fighting the cultural-based arguments of difference set up by anthropologists and other social scientists. While this takes place, it is fascinating to observe how these terms are being used by some of the U.S. Latino and Latin American populations in their everyday interactions. We hope that Latina lesbian and bisexual activists incorporate our reflections and observations in their conversations. We also hope that the emergent "*activa-pasiva*" paradigm stimulates future research on Latina women's sexuality, desire, behaviors, identities, and romantic relationships in both the United States and Latin America.

Finally, sexuality research that attempts to blur the socially constructed borders of hetero-sexuality with working-class men such as day laborers or *jornaleros* exposes the ways in which the latter are vulnerable to sexual harassment on the part of (and engagement in commercial sex with) their employers (frequently White gay men), as part of processes that reflect the paradoxi-cal nature of heterosexuality within these migration-related contexts and new capitalist relations that globalize and commodify the bodies of self-identified heterosexual Latin American immi-grant men (González-López, 2006).

Madonna/Whore, Marianismo, Machismo, and Sexual Silences: Love, Relationships, and Sex "the Latino Way"

Madonnas, putas, marianas, and *machos* have created an intellectual culture of their own in aca-demic and popular culture literature examining the sexual experiences and romantic relationships of U.S. Latina and Latino populations across disciplines.[7] Although becoming theoretically ficti-tious and empirically problematic, the madonna/whore, marianismo, and machismo paradigms have not only promoted stereotypes and further stigmatized these groups, but they have also misinformed and misled students and academics who have become interested in studying the sex lives of these populations—ironically—from "culturally sensitive" perspectives.[8]

Some of the most damaging aspects that these concepts and paradigms have promoted include the cultural essentialism, racism, and classism that they have reproduced in their attempt to explain gender inequality and its consequences on different aspects of the love and sex lives of Latina women and Latino men. Research studies on White middle-class populations rarely use those paradigms to explain, for example, sexual violence. In contrast, with Mexican and other Latino groups, the machismo and marianismo paradigms have become uncritically accepted—they have become shorthand to explain gender inequality from a culture-blaming perspective. In that regard, González-López & Gutmann (2005) reflected: "As theoretical categories, therefore, machismo and *marianismo* are not only culturally chauvinist but elitist as well" (p. 1329). This pattern in academic discussions also represents the intellectual colonization prevalent in academic circles or, more bluntly, the colonized mind that, paradoxically, some Latina and Latino scholars still embrace.

The above reflections have followed or preceded other critical examinations that have simi-larly challenged simplistic and problematic ways to study diverse aspects of U.S. Latinas' and Latinos' sex lives in anthropology (see Hirsch, 2003; Juárez & Kerl, 2003; Zavella, 1997) and sociology (see Baca Zinn, 1982, 2001; González-López, 2005). Interestingly, in the midst of these emerging attempts to challenge "culturally specific" ways of being romantic or sexual, other relevant concepts have emerged in the literature, such as that of "sexual silence."

In the prolific research on HIV/AIDS and U.S. Latino populations, "sexual silence" has become an emblematic construct to identify the difficulties that women and men encounter to talk openly about sexuality-related issues (see Carrillo, 2002; Díaz, 1998; Marín & Gómez, 1997). Although this concept might potentially identify the "cultural" ways in which U.S. Lati-nas and Latinos might be sexually silenced, this concept represents some challenges. As with the problematic concepts and paradigms previously discussed, "sexual silence" has the risk to be interpreted as a cultural trait exclusive of Latinas and Latinos—as if White middle-class families and communities, for example, were open and articulate when it comes to talking about sexuality-related matters.

The concept of sexual silence attempts to address the cultural specificity with regard to U.S. Latina women's and Latino men's difficulty in talking about sexuality. Paradoxically, the concept overlooks the nuanced and more sophisticated ways in which popular culture avenues have allowed these groups to talk openly (and at times crudely) about sexuality. For example, *radiopornografía* has emerged as a genre to identify the increasing presence of U.S.-based and U.S.-aired Spanish-language radio shows discussing sexualized jokes and commentary in highly Latino populated cities, such as Los Angeles, Houston, and Chicago.[9] Similarly, Univisión and Telemundo (the largest U.S.-based Spanish-language broadcasting companies) have capitalized on sexualized themes, which are openly discussed in (1) talk shows such as *El Show de Cristina*, (2) comedy shows, sitcoms, and movies celebrating *la picardía* (linguistic wit; wicked; playful, sexualized sense of humor), and (3) *Sábado Gigante,* which is hosted by Don Francisco, who openly harasses and flirts with the statuesque Latina models who have become emblematic in his popular and highly celebrated 20-year-old weekend variety show.

Thus, we argue that the sexual repression and control responsible for "sexual silence" in U.S. Latino families and communities might, paradoxically, enhance pleasure. Mexican immigrant women and men, in fact, might use their social networks while becoming creative enough to enjoy the conversations they engage in with one another in order to discuss and resolve their sensitive sexual concerns within their groups of immigrant relatives and friends (see González-López, 2005, pp. 161—186). The same social system that at some level tells U.S. Latina women and Latino men that sexuality cannot be discussed openly in a given social context or society is the same system that creates the social spaces for them so that they can selectively talk about it (see Foucault, 1978/1990).

There is sexual silence in many cultures, and U.S. Latino groups are not the exception. Additionally, we do not deny the difficulties that some U.S. Latinas and Latinos might encounter in comfortably discussing important aspects of their sex lives and that culture might shape the ways in which they reproduce these processes. We argue, however, that sexual silence is not absolute but highly selective and that selectivity is not shaped by a so-called "Latino culture" but by multiple forms of social inequality affecting other cultural groups as well.

Both U.S. Latinas and U.S. Latinos are silenced with regard to sexuality because of homophobia,[10] gender inequality, and the dehumanization of children. A lesbian woman, a gay man, or a bisexual person might not talk about her or his romantic relationships within her/his family circles because of homophobia; a woman might not talk about being raped because of gender inequality; and a little girl or a little boy might not talk about the sexual abuse her or his uncle is exercising against her/him because children (like lesbians, gays, and women) are unprotected and highly vulnerable in patriarchal societies. These cases of sexual silence are about power, control, inequality, and vulnerability—their sexual silence is not about culture per se. In short, we argue that U.S Latinas and Latinos are sexually silenced because of deeper sociological forces similarly affecting other Western and Westernized societies.

Finally, placing culture at the center of sociological examinations only erases what some social and community psychologists have argued (in more recent writings) are institutional and structural concerns such as racism (Díaz et al., 2001). A move beyond culture is to acknowledge how discrimination, racism, and socioeconomic marginality affect Latinas/os in U.S. society. For Latino gay men in particular, their experiences with discrimination, racism, and socioeconomic marginality often come from within gay communities and this is also recognized as part of the problem in HIV prevention in men of color. This is the topic we turn our attention to next.

El SIDA: HIV/AIDS

There continues to be a disproportionate rate of HIV infection among U.S. Latinas and Latinos. In 2004 alone, Latinas/os comprised 20% of all newly diagnosed HIV cases, but they represent only 13–14% of the total U.S. population.[11] Cumulative numbers of Latinas/os living with AIDS have reached 19% of the *total* AIDS cases, showing the overrepresentation of Latinas/os in the epidemic. Not only are the numbers increasing, but the proportion of newer infections is higher (33%) when compared to Whites (22%).[12] This has forced New York City community leaders to call for a state of emergency on HIV/AIDS' impact in the Latino community. Latino gay men and heterosexual-identified Latina women are among[13] the hardest hit.[14] A substantial part of the literatures emergent in the 1980s critiqued the unison prevention approach of dealing with HIV risk, which was based on White gay men's identities (see, for instance, Patton, 1990). Early in the epidemic, Carballo-Dieguez (1989), Marín (1990), and others (Morales, 1990) framed "AIDS prevention" in culturally distinctive terms that would later require tailoring to Latinas and Latinos specifically; the same was true of members of groups such as the Latino Caucus of *Act-up!* (AIDS Coalition to Unleash Power) that organized around the late 1980s to early 1990s. Charging cultural difference with culturally distinctive patterns that require specific methods or tactics began a process that has allowed for Latino gay identity formation in the United States and, given the current trends of globalization, all over Latin America. This is partly why HIV/AIDS research is the most prolific (and funded) sexuality-related area of research with U.S. Latino populations.

The predominant paradigm in this work in the early years was framed directly by public health; this work was epidemiology based and behavioral science oriented, and it has been dominated by causality based on the individual behavior and little on institutional barriers (see, for instance, Carballo-Dieguez & Dolezal, 1995). A second focus of this work has been the psychological needs of those perceived to be most "at risk," or those infected with HIV, instead of on the structural circumstances that place them in such risky position. The work that succeeded such frameworks was later developed by Díaz (1998), who established a psycho-cultural model as a central aspect of how to deal with HIV prevention (among Latino gay men). His work followed medical anthropological research that reified the cultural difference assumptions we discussed earlier. Thus, we moved from science, to psychology, to the uses of culture in the development of strategies to analyze AIDS' impact in U.S. Latina and Latino communities (mostly Latino gay men). This is another place where homophobia, machismo, marianismo, religion, and the family coincide. Today, much of HIV prevention research depends on several disciplines, although sociology is not particularly central in this field of study.[15]

FUTURE DIRECTIONS AND FINAL REFLECTIONS IN LATINA AND LATINO SOCIOLOGY AND SEXUALITIES

Within sociology, this is what we think are the future directions. We want to acknowledge that our peers and the two authors are literally shaping the field and that although there are a handful of sociologists, more scholars are continuing to pursue Ph.D.s and are publishing their work in this field of study. The speed in which such scholars complete their degrees and publish their work will (hopefully) make this chapter outdated, but in the meantime, the following are some of the emergent scholars we see developing the field.[16]

Sociologists Susana Peña (2005), Manolo Guzmán (2006), Elena Gutiérrez (forthcoming) and Lorena García (2006) are currently engaged with a vast scope of work on Latino homosexualities, gender identity/sexual orientation and the U.S. nation-state discourse on immigrants, and Latina adolescent sexuality and their sense of agency in sexual behavior decision-making. Both González-López (2005, 2006) and Vidal-Ortiz (2005, 2006) owe much of their development and scholarship as sexuality scholars focusing on Latino immigrant communities to the late Lionel Cantú Jr. (1999, 2000, 2001, 2002). Senior scholar Tomás Almaguer has also been of priceless support to both authors. There are also a handful of non-Latina/o sociologists whose sexuality work incorporates Latinas and Latinos (Mutchler, 2000). We hope that we are not missing or overlooking the *compañeras* y *compañeros* who are doing sexuality research among Latino populations in the United States, and we recognize that future directions in thinking about Latina/o sexuality studies within sociology will emerge and be sustained through the initial network of the already named scholars.[17] We provide six areas as examples of the kinds of question in need of empirical answers in the continuous development of the field, and we conclude with some reflections on how these and other areas of sociological study of Latina/o sexualities will be addressed.

Examples of Future Directions in Latino Sociology and Sexuality

In the following scenarios, a culturalist framework is often put forth. Yet sociology could make groundbreaking contributions by examining critical discussion on migration and the economy, institutional and structural forces, and militarization, globalization, and colonization. As we hope to illustrate with our few examples on future research, there is a political economy hidden underneath those cultural differences marked in recent literature. A basic question we ask in each of these scenarios is: How can we conduct sexuality research on these specific areas from a sociological perspective?

Jornaleros, their Sex Lives, and Globalized Economies

The limited sexuality research on jornaleros (daily laborers) frames them in cultural opposition to people from the United States. Could sociologists think of jornaleros as different within contexts of inequality or within a political economy that is local and global and simultaneously alive in Los Angeles, Habana, and Monterrey? Because of the United States' centrality in globalization, world economic restructuring, and the emergence of "global cities" (see Sassen-Koob, 1984), jornaleros engage in a wide variety of highly needed and underpaid labor. Rarely, however, is the work of jornaleros linked to the possibility of sexual harassment by their employers or these men's engagement in sex as a way to survive in the margins of society. As we begin to look at aspects of sexual harassment at work for those jornaleros (González-López, 2006) or at the mere possibility that some jornaleros might consider engaging in opposite- or same-sex sexual behavior with an employer (for pay and/or driven by desire), sociologists could begin to look at the interlocking political economic forces that mediate in regulating or expanding jornaleros' sexualities, beyond overused cultural frameworks to explain these men's sexual experiences. Furthermore, instead of immediately responding with traditional public health worries that might pathologize this behavior based on culture-blaming perspectives, sociologists could look deeper into the complex and nuanced dynamics shaping the decision to engage in commercial sex within constrained choice and in contexts of extreme inequality and injustice.

Our Parents and Grandparents, and Their Sex Lives

The elderly (as well as children and people with disabilities) are frequently desexualized. Because of stigma and sexuality being linked to the notion of reproductive functions, elderly sexuality is often unspoken. Yet illnesses such as AIDS have greatly affected the elderly, given the lack of attention doctors give to elders' own sexuality. For instance, the second author, in his political activism with health professionals in Puerto Rico, learned about an interesting case involving the "Social Security escapades of seniors." Immediately after people on Social Security received their monthly checks, elderly men and women would come to sexually trans-mitted infection (STI) clinics with symptoms of STIs. As this information was shared by clinic staff with the second author, elders' access to paid sexual favors at that time of the month hap-pened in great part due to their access to income. For example, a sociologist could explore the "political economy of risk" that seems to be, in part, responsible for this pattern (see Rapp in González-López, 2005, p. 149).

As some of our fellow scholars, parents, and friends (of all sexual orientations) approach their maturing sexuality, what are the sociological issues to address? Some include (but are not limited to) gendered expectations across generations, dating, views on access to health care, migration and family/friends networks, the impact of everyday institutions potentially involved in their lives (e.g., church, sports, social/health clubs), bodily restrictions and self-sustenance, and the individual choices elders might make when confronted with any given everyday life experiences and interactions.

Women, Fantasies, and Pleasure

Sociological examinations of complex and nuanced aspects of what is erotically pleasurable in Latinas women's sex lives are almost at a "virginal" state. Reclaiming our bodies and voices and exploring feminist possibilities in order to lose our academic virginity are necessary in the process. How can Latina sexuality (the array of the erotic, desire, sexual acts, sexual his-tory, and emotional links to it) be untangled from a masculinist approach (or a male gaze)? As sociologists, we could study women's personal erotic and/or emotionally intimate stories that transcend the biographical and describe and analyze the social through "traditional" empirical work. Can we conduct sociological quantitative and qualitative studies that foreground Latinas' experiences with sexuality that move beyond the usual topics (e.g., bearing of children, eco-nomic hardship linked to the former, health concerns, sexual victimization) while not erasing them altogether and further develop others (e.g., sexual pleasure, identity and sexuality among Latina women of all sexual orientations, sexuality and racialization) (González-López, 2005)? Can Latina sexuality research focus on the levels of agency and informed decision-making throughout the life span (García, 2006)?

Las Olvidadas, Los Olvidados: Transgender Latina/o Groups

Transgender and transsexual people are often the target of prejudice and stereotypes by mainstream society.[18] Because of this poor understanding and lack of research on these particular populations, transgender people pay a high price in their sexual health. Various HIV research studies have illustrated how both Black and Latina/o transgender people (mostly male-to-female transsexuals, or "trans" people on the male-to-female continuum) are disproportionately exposed to HIV in their line of work.[19] Instead of using a culturalist framework that blames these transgender sex workers, we propose to turn the eye back into societal structural forces: (1) immigration status; (2) limitations of skills in conducting other jobs; (3) social stigmatization and rejection of transsexuality (sometimes employment and school discrimination is based on issues of "passing" as the gender the person wishes to present as); (4) the challenge of finding jobs that can produce high pay (which sometimes occurs in this kind of sex work); (5) basic housing needs, and completion of high school or college education, among others. The above are all issues that go beyond simplistic cultural or antiassimilationist paradigms and that directly affect the lives of Latina and Latino transgender and transsexual people (Vidal-Ortiz, 2005).

Familias Gay and Latino Communities

Instead of posing a question about whether gay marriage—"Latino style"—is beneficial or detrimental to U.S. Latino communities, we wish to proceed with less opinion-based and more sociologically oriented inquiries. What are the potential challenges of gay marriage in the Latina/o communities? What alternative forms of "marriage" (or other like-type arrangements) already exist in Latino communities? Is gay marriage going to change, or further stabilize, the institution of marriage as we know it? (a question that presumes *any* marriage could be damaging to gender equality or each partner's individual aspirations). Is the same idea of homosexuality in Latino communities the gayness of non-Latino ones (Guzmán, 2006)? What are the gender differences of acceptance of same-sex committed relationships among U.S. Latinos? Does migration back and forth to/from Latin American nations influence having different views on "gay marriage" versus other familiar arrangements and, if so, in which ways? Moreover, is the figure of heterosexual marriage being utilized by Latina/o gays to receive U.S. citizenship and can that be further explored (Cantú, 1999)?

Más Allá de la Culpa: Spirituality, Religion, and Sex

Vergüenza y culpa (shame and guilt) have been at the core of traditional academic and popular culture publications exploring the intersections between religion and the sex lives of Latino groups. However, societies are changing their religious practices, and their sexual moralities and practices cannot escape change. For instance, with an increasing migration of protestant, Creole/Afro-Latino religions (Vidal-Ortiz, 2005, 2006) and overall non-Catholic Latinas and Latinos, we wonder: Can we continue to pursue the cultural oppositional framework (i.e., White-Anglo as Protestant vs. Latin American as Catholic) that sustains Latino as based on "traditional" notions of family? Our proposed movement to sociological topics in this area of scholarship would entail asking: What are the social and network consequences of Latinas' and Latinos' involvement with protestant religiosity in the United States? How do these groups define both concepts (religion and spirituality) and how does this understanding shape their sexual moralities and actual sex lives? What is the influence of such involvement on their sexual beliefs and practices? What about the racial undertones of Afro-Latino religions (Santería, Espiritismo, even Curaderismo, Candomble, and Umbanda) in reshaping Latina/o spirituality and sexual moralities? How do transnational religiosities and spiritualities shape their sex lives? How do families with diverse and nondominant religious and spiritual practices (e.g., Buddhism) perceive sexuality and the sex education of their family members?[20]

When we think about the diversity within the diversity of Latino groups, the aforementioned examples would become even more informative and detailed, particularly if we were to explore these research questions for each of the Latino subgroups. This is especially the case for the most recent immigrants. For example, it would be interesting to examine marriage and intragroup relationships between the children of a woman from Honduras and a man from Bolivia. It is imperative that we address these questions and other issues taking into account the heterogeneity of U.S. Latinas/os.

FINAL REFLECTIONS

In this chapter, we have not particularly addressed crucial themes such as sex tourism, lesbian women (in the same degree that we have focused on Latino gay men), gay families, bisexual desire, behaviors and identities, cyber sex and cyber dating/romance, sexual trafficking of children, immigration and sexual violence against women, pornography, religion and Latino feminist writings in sexuality and society, Latino sexualities and disability, reproductive health, teenage pregnancy, social movements and women's rights, and Latina/o sexual harassment and employment. As this list shows, we recognize that sociology of sexuality encompasses a vast land that in the case of Latino groups is still yet to be explored. We hope that our reflections invite others to also engage in examinations of methodologies and epistemologies on sociological research of Latinas/os and their sex lives.

In our own research, we have learned that sex is not private or personal, and it is often deceivingly intimate. Sex and the erotic frame much in the lives of Latinas/Latinos in this country in more than one way—for example, in terms of the absence or presence of sexuality in their social institutions, the management of the state, the ways in which Latinas and Latinos are seen as hypersexual, and how gender and sexuality are interconnected and distinctive simultaneously in their everyday lives, interactions, and relationships. Indeed, these groups make use of many social spaces to negotiate and discuss sexuality in ways that clearly challenge the preconceived notion of coming from a "sexual silence"-driven culture.[21]

Whereas sociologists have only focused on Latina/o sexuality scholarship for less than 20 years, the promise of such scholarship is evident. Reflections for future sociological research include the challenges of (1) incorporating innovative critical discussions on short- and long-term implications of policy issues with regard to each and every one of the issues we discussed in this chapter, (2) supporting Latina and Latino sociologists while not chastising non-Latinas/os who are also interested in pursuing Latina/o sexuality scholarship, (3) promoting the creation of forums for publications and presentations on sociological studies of sexualities among Latinas/os, and (4) developing funding and mentoring to support the cadre of professionals involved in this scholarship. As authors, we hope that our contribution in this volume will facilitate the scholarship in research, teaching, and service to continue the work of interrogating the scope of Latinas, Latinos, and sexuality within critically informed sociological frameworks.

NOTES

1. Both authors are currently involved in a "Latina/o Sexualities" initiative funded by the Ford Foundation; our work here is thus informed, even if partially, by conversations with other board members about the direction of this initiative. (The Latino Sexualities initiative is not solely focused on social scientific or sociological literatures and thus differs from our work here.) Anthropologist Marysol Asencio (Puerto Rican and Latino Studies, University of Connecticut), is publishing a set of commissioned articles on the state of Latina/o Sexuality scholarship in the United States and a monograph or some other document focusing on the various topics discussed there will be prepared and available in the upcoming few years.

2. For an elaboration on the uses of the "Latino" term, see the introduction to the book.

3. The relationship among sex, gender, and sexuality as analytical and interrelated concepts is extremely undertheorized; much less research depicting these relationships is available within the context of the lives of Latinas and Latinos. We view the study of sexualities in its own light but concur with other sociologists who have looked at the gendered dimensions of sexuality (Gagné & Tewksbury, 2002; Ingraham 1994, 2005; Schwartz & Rutter, 1998) as well as how gender and sexuality are often intertwined in popular (and sometimes academic) discourse.

4. Norma Williams' (1990) work on the Mexican American family and double morality sexuality is also important, although sexuality per se was not the focus of her work.

5. See, for example, *Sexuality and Gender* by Christine L. Williams and Arlene Stein (2002) and *Sexualities: Identities, Behaviors, and Society* by Michael S. Kimmel and Rebecca F. Plante (2004).

6. Conceptual examinations of "culture" have become relevant in long-standing anthropological and sociological theorizing and research, and such an ambitious endeavor goes beyond the scope of this chapter. However, as sociologists (and for purposes of this chapter), we define "culture" as a socially constructed system of values, beliefs, practices, and behaviors *associated* with a specific social group—U.S. Latino populations in this particular case. Moreover, the concept of "cultural arguments" helps identify an analytical pattern in the literature on U.S. Latinas and Latinos that is based on distinctive (sometimes oppositional) notions of culture: the United States vis-à-vis the other Latin American countries (see Cantú, 2000, p. 225). Thus, because "culture" is often used as shorthand for difference and it is interpreted in many different ways, we tackle the use of the term "culture" in order to address political economic and structural issues in our examples throughout the chapter.

7. Popular culture and traditional publications on gender frequently identify machismo as an exaggerated expression of masculinity in men of Latin American origin—a behavior that usually leads to sexist beliefs and practices. Interestingly, the concept of marianismo seems to be less frequently used (and at times unknown) in Latin American academic groups concerned about women's lives. As a concept, marianismo was coined by Evelyn Stevens in the early 1970s and argues that women of Latin American origin socially learn to emulate the Virgin Mary. Accordingly, they learn to endure self-sacrifice, pain, and suffering and to tolerate sexism in the process. For a critique of both machismo and marianismo as theoretical categories and paradigms, see González-López & Gutmann (2005) and González-López (2005). See also, Ehlers (1991).

8. For an in-depth critique of the madonna/whore paradigm see González-López (2005, pp. 76–81).

9. For a discussion of radiopornografía, see "Group Assails Spanish Stations for Obscenities," *San Francisco Chronicle*, August 16, 2001, p. D2.

10. As Guzmán (2006) has argued, that Latino families are homophobic (like families of any social or ethno-racial group might be), should not be construed as these families being more homophobic than any other group.

11. Retrieved August 31, 2006, from http://www.cdc.gov/hiv/spanish/resources/factsheets/hispanic.htm

12. CDC HIV/AIDS Surveillance Report, Volume 16, 2005. Retrieved August 31, 2006, from cdc.gov

13. Retrieved August 31, 2006, from http://www.kaisernetwork.org/daily_reports/rep_index.cfm?hint=1&DR_ID=1599. Of course, the numbers provided tend to underreport these cases. As well, it is important to note how "Latino" or "Hispanic" might be terms that do not always encompass a person's identity, especially among Latinos in accessing U.S. health care. Afro-Latinos, for instance, could be easily classified among Blacks by Department of Health staffers, especially when living in a still-dichotomized Black/White racial system that reads phenotype as identity.

14. For the reader interested in HIV testing and/or services, refer to Internet pages from organizations such as the Latino Commission on AIDS, the Hispanic AIDS Forum, the National Minority AIDS Council, and the Centers for Disease Control and Prevention.

15. As sociologists, we identify two central issues. First, Latino populations had to get infected in order for scholars to do this kind of research. We think that they felt validated by White researchers who legitimized this kind of epidemiological research. Second, research on HIV/AIDS in Latino groups has informed us about a serious problem; however, this prolific body of literature has promoted stereotypes previously discussed in this chapter, including an overemphasis on acculturation paradigms and culture-blaming perspectives.

16. If we extend the scope of the Latino sexualities work to encompass work on race and the sociology of gender (including feminist writings), sociologists such as Ginetta Candelario and Nancy López will offer great insights into the migration patterns, gender, and sexuality complexities of Caribbean immigrants to the United States (particularly in the Northeast).

17. We are aware that non-Latino scholars are beginning to focus on Latina and/or Latino sexuality for their dissertation research and other projects.

18. Male-to-female transgenders in particular experience social forces/factors that seem to be responsible for their disproportionate engagement in sex work.

19. See the San Francisco Transgender Health Project at http://hivinsite.ucsf.edu/ InSite.jsp?doc=2098.473e

20. For a sociological exploration of Mexican immigrant women, Catholic religion, and sexual morality, see González-López (2007) *Confesiones de mujer:* The Catholic Church and Sacred Morality in the Sex Lives of Mexican Immigrant Women. In Niels F. Teunis (Ed.), *Sexuality Inequalities: Case Studies from the Field.* Berkeley: University of California Press. Also see, González-López (2005, pp. 242–247) for examinations of Catholic religion in contemporary Mexican society.

21. For an in-depth discussion of immigrants' everyday life engagement in sex-related conversations, see the chapter entitled "Sexual Discourses and Cultures in the Barrio" in González-López (2005, pp. 161–187).

REFERENCES

Almaguer, Tomás. (1991). Chicano Men: A Cartography of Homosexual Identity and Behavior. *Differences: A Journal of Feminist Cultural Studies, 3*(2), 75–100.

Alarcón, Norma, Castillo, Ana, & Moraga, Cherríe (Eds.). (1993). *The Sexuality of Latinas.* Berkeley: Third Woman Press.

Alonso, Ana María, & Koreck, María Teresa. (1993). Silences: "Hispanics," AIDS, and Sexual Practices. In Henry Abelove, Michele A. Barale, & David M. Halperin (Eds.), *The Lesbian and Gay Studies Reader* (pp. 110–126). New York: Routledge.

Anzaldúa, Gloria. (1987). *Borderlands/La Frontera: The New Mestiza.* San Francisco: Aunt Lute.

Argüelles, Lourdes, & Rivero, Anne M. (1993). Gender/Sexual Orientation Violence and Transnational Migration: Conversations with Some Latinas We Think We Know. *Urban Anthropology, 22*(3–4), 259–275.

Asencio, Marysol. (2002). *Sex and Sexuality Among New York's Puerto Rican Youth.* Boulder, CO: Lynne Rienner Publishers.

Baca Zinn, Maxine. (1982). Mexican American Women in the Social Sciences. *Signs 8*(2), 259–72.

Baca Zinn, Maxine. (2001). Chicano Men and Masculinity. In Michael S. Kimmel & Michael A. Messner (Eds.), *Men's Lives* (5th ed., pp. 24–32). Boston: Allyn & Bacon.

Cantú, Lionel. (1999). *Border Crossings: Mexican Men and the Sexuality of Migration.* Unpublished doctoral dissertation, University of California, Irvine.

Cantú, Lionel. (2000). Entre Hombres/Between Men: Latino Masculinities and Homosexualities. In Peter Nardi (Ed.), *Gay Masculinities* (pp. 224–246). Thousand Oaks, CA: Sage Press.

Cantú, Lionel. (2001). A Place Called Home: A Queer Political Economy of Mexican Immigrant Men's Family Experiences. In Mary Bernstein & Renate Reimann (Eds.), *Queer Families, Queer Politics: Challenging Culture and the State* (pp. 112–136). New York: Columbia University Press.

Cantú, Lionel. (2002). *De Ambiente*: Queer Tourism and the Shifting Boundaries of Mexican Male Sexualities. *GLQ: A Journal of Lesbian and Gay Studies, 8*(1), 139–166.

Carballo-Dieguez, Alex. (1989). Hispanic Culture, Gay Male Culture, and AIDS: Counseling Implications. *Journal of Counseling and Development, 68*(1), 26–30.

Carballo-Dieguez, Alex, & Dolezal, Curtis. (1995). Association Between History of Childhood Sexual Abuse and Adult HIV risk sexual behavior in Puerto Rican Men Who Have Sex with Men. *Child Abuse & Neglect, 19*(5), 595–605.

Carrier, Joseph. (1995). *De Los Otros: Intimacy and Homosexuality Among Mexican Men.* New York: Columbia University Press.

Carrillo, Hector. (2002). *The Night Is Young: Sexuality in Mexico in the Time of AIDS.* Chicago: University of Chicago Press.

D'Emilio, John. (1983). *Sexual Politics, Sexual Communities: The Making of a Modern Minority.* Chicago: University of Chicago Press.

Díaz, Rafael. (1998). *Latino Gay Men and HIV: Culture, Sexuality, and Risk Behavior.* New York: Routledge.

Díaz, Rafael, & Ayala, George. (1999). Love, Passion and Rebellion: Ideologies of HIV Risk Among Latino Gay Men in the USA. *Culture, Health & Sexuality, 1*(3), 277–293.

Díaz, Rafael M., Ayala, George, Bein, E., Henne, J., & Marin, Barbara V. (2001). The Impact of Homophobia, Poverty, and Racism on the Mental Health of Gay and Bisexual Latino Men: Findings from 3 US Cities. *American Journal of Public Health, 91,* 927–932.

Ehlers, Tracy Bachrach (1991). Debunking Marianismo: Economic Vulnerability and Survival Strategies Among Guatemalan Wives. *Ethnology, 30*(1), 1–16.

Erickson, Pamela I. (2001). Negotiation of First Sexual Intercourse Among Latina Adolescent Mothers. In J. Kenneth Davidson, Jr. & Nelwyn B. Moore (Eds.), *Speaking of Sexuality: Interdisciplinary Readings* (pp. 97–107). Los Angeles: Roxbury Publishing.

Espín, Olivia M. (1999). *Women Crossing Boundaries: A Psychology of Immigration and Transformations of Sexuality.* New York: Routledge.

Foucault, Michel. (1990). *The History of Sexuality, An Introduction: Volume 1.* New York: Vintage Books. (Original work published 1978).

Gagné, Patricia, & Tewksbury, Richard. (2002). *Gendered Sexualities* (Advances in Gender Research 6). New York: Elsevier Press.

García, Lorena. (2006). *Beyond the Latina Virgin/Whore Dichotomy: Investigating Latina Adolescent Sexual Subjectivity.* Unpublished doctoral dissertation, University of California, Santa Barbara.

González-López, Gloria. (2005). *Erotic Journeys: Mexican Immigrants and Their Sex Lives.* Berkeley: University of California Press.

González-López, Gloria. (2006). Heterosexual Fronteras: Immigrant Mexicanos, Sexual Vulnerabilities, and Survival. *Sexuality Research & Social Policy, 3*(3), 67–81.

González-López, Gloria. (2007). Confesiones de Mujer: The Catholic Church and Sacred Morality in the sex Lives of Mexican Immigrant Women. In N. Teunis & G. Herdt (Eds.), *Sexual Inequalities and Social Justice* (pp. 148–173). Berkeley: University of California Press.

González-López, Gloria, & Gutmann, Matthew C. (2005). Machismo. In the *New Dictionary of the History of Ideas: Volume 4* (pp. 1328–1330). New York: Charles Scribner's Sons.

Gutiérrez, Elena. (forthcoming). *Fertile Matters: The Politics of Mexican Origin Women's Reproduction.* Austin: University of Texas Press.

Gutiérrez, Ramón A. (1991). *When Jesus Came, the Corn Mothers Went Away.* Stanford, CA: Stanford University Press.

Guzmán, Manolo. (2006). *Gay Hegemony/Latino Homosexualies.* New York: Routledge.

Hirsch, Jennifer S. (2003). *A Courtship After Marriage: Sexuality and Love in Mexican Transnational Families.* Berkeley: University of California Press.

Ingraham, Chrys. (1994). The Heterosexual Imaginary: Feminist Sociology and Theories of Gender. *Sociological Theory, 12,* 203–219.

Ingraham, Chrys. (2005). *Thinking Straight: The Promise, the Power and Paradox of Heterosexuality.* New York: Routledge.

Juárez, Ana María, & Kerl, Stella Beatriz. (2003). What Is the Right (White) Way to be Sexual? Reconceptualizing Latina Sexuality. *Aztlán, 28*(1), 7–37.

Lancaster, Roger N. (1992). *Life Is Hard: Machismo, Danger, and the Intimacy of Power in Nicaragua.* Berkeley: University of California Press.

Luibhéid, Eithne. (2002). *Entry Denied: Controlling Sexuality at the Border.* Minneapolis: University of Minnesota Press.

Luibhéid, Eithne, & Cantú, Lionel (Eds.). (2005). *Queer Migrations: Sexuality, U.S. Citizenship, and Border Crossings.* Minneapolis: University of Minnesota Press.

Marín, Barbara V. (1990). AIDS Prevention for Non-Puerto Rican Hispanics (National Institute on Drug Abuse Research Monograph). In Z. Amsel, R. Battjes, & Z. Leukefeld (Eds.), *AIDS and Intravenous Drug Use: Future Directions for Community Based Prevention Research* (pp. 35–52). Washington, DC: US Government Printing Office.

Marín, Barbara V., & Gómez, Cynthia A. (1997). Latino Culture and Sex: Implications for HIV Prevention. In Jorge G. García & María Cecilia Zea (Eds.), *Psychological Interventions and Research with Latino Populations* (pp. 73–93). Boston: Allyn and Bacon.

Moraga, Cherríe. (1983). *Loving in the War Years: Lo Que Nunca Pasó Por Sus Labios.* Boston: South End Press Collective.

Morales, Edward. (1990). HIV Infection and Hispanic Gay and Bisexual Men. *Hispanic Journal of Behavioral Sciences, 12*(2), 212–222.

Murray, Steven O. (1995). *Latin American Male Homosexualities.* Albuquerque: University of New Mexico Press.

Mutchler, Matt G. (2000). Young Gay Men's Stories in the States: Scripts, Sex, and Safety in the Time of AIDS. *Sexualities, 3*, 31–54.

Patton, Cindy. (1990). *Inventing AIDS*. New York: Routledge.

Peña, Susana. (2005). Visibility and Silence: Mariel and Cuban American Gay Male Experience and Representation. In E. Luibhéid & L. Cantú, Jr. (Eds.), *Queer Migrations: Sexuality, U.S. Citizenship, and Border Crossings* (pp. 125–145). Minneapolis: University of Minnesota Press.

Rubin, Gayle. (1984). Thinking Sex: Notes for a Radical Theory of the Politics of Sexuality. In Carole Vance (Ed.), *Pleasure and Danger: Exploring Female Sexuality* (pp. 267–319). (Reprinted and expanded in Henry Abelove, Michèle Aina Barale, & David M. Halperin (Eds.), *The Gay and Lesbian Studies Reader* (pp. 3–44). New York: Routledge, 1993)

Sassen-Koob, Saskia. (1984). The New Labor Demand in Global Cities. In Michael Peter Smith (Ed.), *Cities in Transformation: Class, Capital and the State* (pp. 139–171). Beverly Hills, CA: Sage.

Schwartz, Pepper, & Rutter, Virginia. (1998). *The Gender of Sexuality*. Thousand Oaks, CA: Pine Forge Press.

Silliman, Jael, Fried, Marlene Gerber, Ross, Loretta, & Gutiérrez, Elena. (2004). *Undivided Rights: Women of Color Organize for Reproductive Justice*. Boston: South End Press.

Vidal-Ortiz, Salvador. (2005). Sexuality and Gender in Santería: LGBT Identities at the Crossroads of Religious Practices and Beliefs. In Scott Thumma & Edward R. Gray (Eds.), *Gay Religion* (pp. 115–137). Walnut Creek, CA: Altamira Press.

Vidal-Ortiz, Salvador. (2006). Sexuality Discussions in Santería: A Case Study of Religion and Sexuality. *Sexuality Research and Social Policy, 3*(3), 52–66.

Williams, Norma. (1990). *The Mexican American Family: Tradition and Change*. Dix Hills, NY: General Hall.

Zavella, Patricia. (1997). Playing with Fire: The Gendered Construction of Chicana/Mexicana Sexuality. In Roger N. Lancaster and Micaela di Leonardo (Eds.), *The Gender Sexuality Reader: Culture, History, Political Economy* (pp. 392–408). New York: Routledge.

POLITICAL MOBILIZATION AND PARTICIPATION AMONG LATINAS/OS

CHAPTER 21

Latino Partisanship, Political Activity and Vote Choice

Kim Geron

Melissa R. Michelson

INTRODUCTION

The increasing size and potential political power of Latinos in the United States has spawned a host of recent scholarly work on various aspects of Latino political attitudes and behavior. Although Latinos have yet to live up to their billing as the "sleeping giant" of American politics, their presence and influence is increasingly recognized by researchers interested in political attitudes and behavior. This chapter explores the contemporary contours of Latino political participation, including available research on Latinos in general and on specific Latino national-origin groups. Although much still remains to be learned, particularly about Latinos not in the "big three" national-origin groups (Mexicans, Puerto Ricans, and Cubans), as detailed below there is already a considerable amount of scholarship available on how Latinos think and act in the political arena. Although, as is detailed below, there are areas in which scholars disagree, there are some findings about Latino politics that are consistent and increasingly viewed as "truths."

In recent decades, minorities in the United States have preferred the Democratic Party, and the degree to which this is true for various Latino national-origin groups, and why, has been examined by many scholars. In addition, researchers have examined the acquisition of partisanship by those new to the American political system (e.g., Latino immigrants) and the degree to which the Republican Party might or might not be able to increase its share of partisan identifiers. Although there are continuing debates in the literature on these topics, most research indicates that Latinos (with the notable exception of Cubans) tend to prefer the Democratic Party and that there is little indication that the Republican Party is increasing its share of partisan identifiers to any significant degree. However, some caveats to this overarching finding are noted below. Although Latino political participation lags behind that of other groups in most areas, they are more likely to attend local political meetings, and their political power is growing.

Scholars have also examined how Latinos make vote choice decisions. How important is partisanship and how does this compare to the role of partisanship among non-Latinos? How strong is the tendency to vote for coethnics (fellow Latinos), and is this tendency stronger or weaker than the power of shared partisanship? How important are candidate issue positions and symbolic outreach, such as speaking Spanish while campaigning? Again, debates continue. However, most research indicates that Latinos are willing to cross party and ethnic lines for a candidate they support, either for partisan, ethnic, or other reasons such as ideology and issue positions. Whereas low-education/low-information Latino voters are more likely to use non-policy cues (such as speaking Spanish), high-education/high-information Latino voters are more likely to consider ideology and issue positions.

LATINO PARTISANSHIP

Latinos tend to affiliate with the Democratic Party, with the notable exception of Cuban-descent Latinos, who generally prefer the Republican Party. The Latino National Political Survey (LNPS), conducted in 1989–1990, found that more than two-thirds of Mexican and Puerto Rican respondents identified with or leaned toward the Democratic Party, whereas more than two-thirds of Cubans identified with or leaned toward the Republican Party. Among Anglos (non-Latino Whites), by comparison, about half were Democrats and 40% were Republicans (de la Garza et al., 1992).[1] This pattern of partisan affiliations is generally attributed to the perception among Latinos that the Democratic Party and its policies are more favorably inclined toward minorities, in general, and Latinos, in particular, and to the Republican Party's traditional hard-line stance on Communism, which is more salient to Cubans than to other Latinos. However, how do Latinos, particularly Latino immigrants, acquire partisanship, and is there any evidence that the Republican Party has or could make inroads into this large and growing segment of the population?

To some extent, the answer depends on what evidence is examined. Alvarez and García Bedolla (2003) argued that Latino partisanship is more explicitly political than that of Anglos, who tend to be socialized into their political affiliations. Using a nationally representative sample of Latinos identified as likely voters in the 2000 elections, they tested a variety of factors as predictors of professed partisanship, including social and demographic questions, political and issue questions, and economic status questions. Overall, they found that 56.6% of likely Latino voters identified as Democrats, 24.5% identified as Republicans, and 13.2% identified as independents. Compared to the LNPS, the partisanship of Mexican-descent Latinos has remained stable (67% Democrat, 13% Republican), Cubans have become more Republican (increasing from 66.7% to 70%), and Puerto Ricans have become slightly less Democratic (decreasing from 69.3% to 64.4%).

Central Americans were not included in the LNPS, but the 2000 survey indicates that 57% are Democrats. Alvarez and García Bedolla (1992) found that Latinos with more education were more likely to be Republicans than Democrats, whereas Latinos with liberal opinions on abortion, affirmative action, school vouchers and government-funded health insurance were more likely to be Democrats. Those with more positive economic perceptions were more likely to be Democrats, but income did not affect partisanship. Some commentators have argued that Latino social conservatism (such as positions on abortion and homosexuality) and socioeconomic mobility will move them toward the Republican Party; Alvarez and García Bedolla (1992) claimed that this is unlikely. Although newly-arrived Latino immigrants might not learn partisanship through intergenerational transmission as do Anglos, they learn the preferred partisanship of their national-origin group (Democratic for Mexicans and Puerto Ricans, Republican for Cubans) over time.

Hajnal and Lee (2006) noted that newly-arrived immigrants tended to not associate with either major political party. They cited the 1993–1994 Multi-City Study of Urban Inequality (MCSUI), conducted in large metropolitan areas more likely to be populated by low-income immigrants, which found that more than 45% of Latinos surveyed did not choose to identify as Democratic, Republican, or independent. So how and when do Latino immigrants acquire partisanship? Wong (2000), using the 1993–1994 Los Angeles Survey of Urban Inequality (LASUI) and the LNPS (both large-sample face-to-face studies), found a strong relationship between the number of years an immigrant has been in the United States and the acquisition of partisanship. She found that "a process of reinforcement through exposure to the political system underlies the development of political attitudes" (Wong, 2000, p. 343). Other significant variables included naturalization, gains in English skills, and media use.

Cain, Kiewiet, and Uhlaner (1991), using a 1984 survey of Californians, found that Latino immigrants were more likely to be Democrats and to have strong party preferences as their time in the United States increases. Subsequent generations of Latinos also become more likely to be Democrats and strong partisans. Given that the Democratic Party for preceding decades had the image of being more supportive of policies favoring minorities, Cain, Kiewiet, and Uhlaner (1991) argued that immigrants become more likely to identify as Democrats the longer they have lived in the United States (and thus the more likely they are to have experienced discrimination and identified as a member of a minority group). Given that children tend to inherit the partisanship of their parents, subsequent generations are even more strongly Democratic. Partisanship also increases with education, citizenship, and abandonment of plans to return to the country of origin. They also found that as Latino immigrants advance economically, they become more favorable toward the Republican Party.

Wong (2000) noted that Cain, Kiewiet, and Uhlaner (1991) did not include age in their models, which is often used as a proxy for exposure to the political system and is therefore a determinant of partisanship. Arvizu and Garcia (1996) included both length of residence and age in their study of Latinos in the 1988 election and found that both variables contributed to turnout. Uhlaner and Garcia (1998) found that length of residence and age both contribute to partisan identification among Mexican immigrants but that only age affects partisanship among Puerto Ricans and Cubans. Wong (2000) found that partisanship (identification with either the Democratic Party or Republican Party) was predicted by length of residence, but not by age, for all LASUI Latinos and LNPS Mexicans and Puerto Ricans, whereas the opposite was true for LNPS Cubans. She concluded that length of residence, not maturity, was key to the development of partisanship among most Latino immigrants. Adding citizenship to the model eliminated the statistically significant effect for LNPS Mexicans, but the effect persisted among LASUI Latinos. English proficiency was also found to be a significant predictor of partisan identification among LASUI Latinos, as was exposure to newspapers among LNPS Mexicans and Puerto Ricans. Her major point was that it was length of residence, not age, that led to acquisition of partisanship, and this was mostly explained by citizenship and also somewhat by English proficiency. Cubans were the big exception: Their acquisition of partisanship was predicted by age, citizenship, and economic resources. Wong concluded that, "consistent with the political exposure model (Claggett, 1981; Converse, 1969, 1976), a process of reinforcement through exposure underlies the development of political attitudes" (2000, p. 356).

Some researchers have found evidence to suggest that the Republican Party is making or has the potential to make significant inroads among Latino voters. Hajnal and Lee (2006), examining pooled biennial National Election Studies, found that there has been a marked shift toward the Republican Party. From 1978 to 2002, Republican identification increased from 15% to almost 38% while Democratic identification declined from 68% to 53%. Hajnal and Lee noted, however, that the American National Election Studies (ANES) data are biased toward assimilated and acculturated Latinos. Kelly and Kelly (2005), again using pooled ANES data, found that a declining proportion of Latinos are Catholic and that Latinos of other religious denominations are less likely to be Democrats than are Catholic Latinos, particularly evangelicals and mainline Protestants. In addition, they found that mainline Protestants were much more likely to vote than other Latinos. They concluded that trends in religious affiliation among Latinos benefited the Republican Party. Kosmin and Keysar (1995), using a 1990 national survey on religion, also found that religion matters, in that Latinos who identified as Protestants were more likely to be Republicans than were Latino Catholics, and that this difference persists when controlling for other variables such as socioeconomic status, age, and gender. However, García Bedolla, Alvarez, and Nagler (2006), using a national survey of likely Latino voters conducted in July 2004, found that religious affiliation and attendance were not significant predictors of partisanship once variables were introduced to control for political predispositions and issue preferences.

García Bedolla, Alvarez, and Nagler (2006), using national surveys conducted in July 2004, argued that Latino partisanship, compared to Anglo partisanship, was more likely to be influenced by short-term factors like economic and issue preferences. Their multivariate analysis found that ideology, family income, education, gender, national origin, and language use are all significant predictors of Latino partisanship. Compared to Anglos, Latino partisanship was more influenced by issues [gay marriage, the Iraq War, the North American Free Trade Agreement (NAFTA), affordable health care, the war on terrorism, and moral values]. They also found that Latinos were influenced by a larger set of issues than were Anglos.

A final note on partisanship among Latinos relates to the gender gap. As with Anglos and other groups, women (Latinas) are more strongly Democratic than their male counterparts. Using a series of exit polls from 1980, 1984, and 1988, Welch and Sigelman (1992) found that women were consistently more liberal and Democratic than men in all racial-ethnic groups, but Latinos had the widest gap in partisan identification. Latino-Latina differences in political ideology, however, were small, although Latinas were slightly more liberal.

LATINO POLITICAL PARTICIPATION

Latino participation in politics takes place in the electoral arena, including voting and working for a candidate's election and nonelectoral political activities such as attending meetings, joining community organizations, and participating in protests. In the electoral arena, where participation is limited to citizens, Latino participation, not surprisingly, lags behind that of Anglos and African Americans. However, registration and turnout rates still lag among Latinos even when looking only at citizens. Early models of political participation established that socioeconomic variables such as age, education, and income were closely linked to propensity to vote in elections (Verba & Nie, 1972; Wolfinger & Rosenstone, 1980). Many Latinos who have low socioeconomic status (SES) are relatively young; electoral participation is thus depressed compared to other groups (U.S. Census, November 2006).

Looking within the Latino population, the 1989–1990 LNPS found that there is significant internal variation within the three largest Latino communities: Mexicans, Cubans, and Puerto Ricans, which collectively made up 80% of all Latinos in the United States at the time of the survey. Cuban Americans had the highest voting rates among the three groups, but they were no more likely and in most cases less likely to participate in other forms of political participation than Mexican Americans and Puerto Ricans. U.S. Latino citizens were, on average, more likely to participate in political activities than were non-citizens (de la Garza et al., 1992). Uhlaner (2002), using LNPS data, found that the factors that explain higher rates of political participation in the population (e.g., socioeconomic status, age) also explain higher levels of activity among Latino citizens and that participation increased with length of time spent in the United States. However, studies that control for sociodemographic factors found that Latino turnout still lagged behind that of other groups (DeSipio, 1996; Hero & Campbell, 1996).

Rodolfo O. de la Garza has been arguing for some time that mobilization is critical to Latino voter turnout, and recent research has borne this out. Latinos have largely been excluded from get-out-the-vote efforts conducted by the major political parties (Hero, Garcia, Garcia, & Pachon, 2000; Verba, Schlozman, & Brady, 1995). Shaw, de la Garza, and Lee (2000), using a survey of Latino citizens in California, Florida, and Texas, found that individuals who reported being encouraged to participate by a non-Latino individual or group were no more likely to have voted, but those who reported being encouraged to register or vote by a Latino candidate or political organization were more likely to have participated.

Further investigations of the power of voter mobilization have moved from survey research to field experiments. Michelson (2003), using Latino door-to-door canvassers to encourage participation in the nonpartisan 2001 Dos Palos-Oro Loma, California (CA) Unified School Board election, found that Latino citizens were more likely to vote if targeted by a door-to-door get-out-the-vote effort, whereas non-Latino citizens targeted by Latino canvassers were not. Another nonpartisan effort, this time in Fresno, California for the 2002 gubernatorial election, found that non-Latino canvassers were just as effective as Latino canvassers in encouraging Latino voters to participate, but Latino canvassers were better able to make contact with targeted voters (Michelson, 2006a). Door-to-door Latino voter mobilization has also been proven effective in partisan efforts: The Association of Community Organizations for Reform Now (ACORN) urged Latinos in Maricopa County, Arizona to vote in favor of a proposition on the November 2003 ballot to help keep open a local hospital. Turnout doubled in targeted one-voter households and tripled in two-voter households (Michelson, 2006b). Efforts by the National Association of Latino Elected Officials (NALEO) have demonstrated that Latino voter turnout can also be increased with telephone and direct-mail canvassing: A telephone effort in California in 2002 increased Latino turnout by 4.6 percentage points, and direct-mail efforts in Colorado and Texas also increased participation slightly (Ramírez, 2005).

Others have found that issues and events occurring in the political environment can potentially increase Latino turnout. Pantoja, Ramirez, and Segura (2001), using a three-state survey, found that the political context at the state level explained higher levels of political participation among Latinos. In the early 1990s in California when the anti-immigrant ballot Proposition 187 was placed on the ballot in 1994, there were higher participation rates by Latinos than in Texas or Florida at the same time. Michelson and Pallares (2001) found that Latinos in Chicago reacted to the national anti-immigrant, anti-Latino atmosphere of the mid-1990s by naturalizing and voting. Another key factor in mobilizing Latino turnout is where one resides. Barreto, Segura, and Woods (2004), looking at turnout in Southern California, found that Latinos living in majority-Latino districts were more likely to vote. Bishin, Kaufman, and Stevens (2005) found the Miami-Dade

County local context influenced the political socialization of non-Cuban Latinos and their vote choice for national, state, and local offices in the 2004 elections.

In the area of nonelectoral participation, Latinos also participate at lower levels than non-Latinos in most typical categories. Verba, Schlozman, and Brady (1995) found that Latinos had a lower likelihood for civic skills, civic engagement, and recruitment into civic activities. There was also a big gap between U.S.-born and foreign-born Latinos. U.S.-born Latinos behaved comparably to Anglos and Blacks, whereas foreign-born Latinos had lower rates of civil engagement, were the least recruited, and had a low level of civic skills (Verba, Schlozman, & Brady, 1995, p. 234). These findings were supported by DeSipio (1996), who found that naturalized Latinos were less likely to register and vote than were U.S.-born Latino citizens.

Other scholars found that foreign-born newly naturalized Latinos participated at a higher rate than did U.S.-born Latino citizens in California in the hostile anti-immigrant environment of the early 1990s (Pantoja, Ramirez, & Segura, 2001). Leal (2002), using the LNPS data, found that Latino noncitizens participated to a lesser degree than did Latino U.S. citizens. Although Latino noncitizens did participate in various political activities, their participation was significantly less than for Latino citizens. However, Barreto and Munoz (2003), using the 1999 Washington Post/ Henry J. Kaiser Family Foundation/Harvard University Survey, found that there were no substantive differences among Mexican immigrants (whether they were citizens or noncitizens) and that length of residency and language fluency increased the likelihood of political participation.

As mentioned previously, the Latino population in the United States is extremely diverse and not homogeneous. Although there is a common language, there is wide variation in the thinking and actions of Latinos who arrived from distinct political environments throughout Latin America and others who grew up in the social/political context of U.S. local and regional politics. DeSipio, Pachon, de la Garza, and Lee (2003) studied the participation of four of the five largest Latino immigrant groups: Mexicans, Puerto Ricans, Salvadorans, and Dominicans. They found that Dominicans and Puerto Ricans, compared to Mexicans and Salvadorans, were more likely to engage in transnational electoral or partisan activities, such as voting in nation of origin elections, contributing money to a candidate running for office or a political party in the nation of origin, or attending a rally in the United States in which a home nation candidate or representative of a home-country political party spoke. They were also more likely to report having been contacted by a home nation representative to become involved in home nation political or cultural affairs. About two-thirds of Mexicans, Puerto Ricans, and Dominicans followed the politics of their nation of origin in Spanish-language media, compared to fewer than half of Salvadorans. Puerto Ricans and Dominicans (again compared to Mexicans and Salvadorans) were also more likely to report participation in country of origin-focused political activities, such as attending a meeting to discuss home-country politics. DeSipio et al. (2003) also found that Latino immigrant involvement in U.S. politics was quite low, but comparing the four national-origin groups, there were some notable differences. Puerto Ricans and Dominicans (compared to Mexicans and Salvadorans) were more likely to have worn a campaign button for a candidate running for U.S. office, to have written a letter to a U.S. government official, to have distributed literature for a U.S. candidate for office, to have canvassed or marched in the United States, and to have contributed money to a U.S. political candidate or political party. Among citizen respondents to the survey, Puerto Ricans and Dominicans were more likely to have helped people to register or to vote in U.S. elections, but Salvadorans and Dominicans were more likely to report voting. On average, Latino immigrants were more involved in U.S. politics than in their respective home-country politics. Respondents who were involved in home-country electoral activities were most likely to be involved in U.S. electoral activities. On average, 81% of the respondents from each of the four immigrant groups followed U.S. politics, including nearly 89% of Dominican immigrants. Also, higher levels of education and the experience of discrimination in the United States were strong predictors of participation in U.S. electoral activities. In terms of other forms of civic engagement, Latino immigrants generally had low levels of engagement in U.S. civic activities such as attending parent-teacher association meetings and participation in labor unions and hometown associations. The study did note that Puerto Ricans were slightly more likely than Mexican respondents to be members of U.S. organizations.

Bueker (2005) studied the political incorporation of immigrants from 10 countries and found that immigrants from Cuba showed the highest levels of voter turnout and a high propensity to naturalize. Immigrants from Mexico were among those least likely to naturalize but were among the most likely to vote.

Among the newest immigrants, Dominicans have the highest citizenship rate (57%) compared to Salvadorans and Colombians. The 2003 Tomás Rivera Policy Institute survey also indicated that Dominicans in the United States have a higher level of political participation on average compared to Mexicans, Puerto Ricans, and Salvadorans. This survey also demonstrated that a higher percentage of Dominicans followed U.S. politics in the news, wore campaign buttons, distributed fliers for candidates running for office in the United States, and registered people to vote, compared to the other Latino groups that were surveyed. As of 2004, this political activism and engagement resulted in the election of 25 Dominicans in the United States (Tavres, 2004). By 2010, their population numbers should propel them into becoming the third largest Latino subgroup, with growing political clout in New York and other East Coast states.

Cuban Americans have a unique migration and settlement pattern, compared to other Latinos in the United States, which has resulted in their close affiliation with the Republican Party historically (Moreno, 1997). However, polls done in 2000 of Florida residents of Cuban descent indicated that a more nuanced picture of Cuban American political beliefs is required. Political beliefs vary according to the timing and cohort of immigration and the generation of U.S. born Cuban-Americans. Although opposition to Cuban leader Fidel Castro is still the majority opinion, there is a definite trend toward a more conciliatory approach to dealing with the Cuban government (Chun & Grenier, 2004).

Puerto Ricans, both in the LNPS and in a more recent New York City Participation Survey in 1997, were found to have lower levels of voting and contacting elected officials than others; yet they had high levels of other forms of participation including participating in protests and attending meetings. Although Puerto Ricans were found to participate less than other groups in the New York survey, their membership in associations was found to boost the overall participation of Latinos (Vargas-Ramos, 2003).

Another avenue of research in the field of participation is the role of group consciousness among Latinos whereby through group affinity and identification a collective group orientation is forged to become more politically active. Stokes (2003) found that group consciousness increased Latino political participation; however, it was not uniform across all of the major Latino groups, with different aspects of group consciousness, including power, systemic blame, and group identification, having a distinct impact on each of the three main Latino subgroups. Sanchez (2006) used the 1999 Kaiser/Post National Survey of Latinos to identify the role of group consciousness for Latino political behavior. Sanchez found that group consciousness was positively correlated with political participation. In particular, "commonality," a measure used to capture the cohesive cultural affinity among Latinos, and "perceived discrimination" had the most significant impacts on political participation.

LATINO VOTE CHOICE

Although partisanship is a known and strong predictor of vote choice, the two concepts are not identical. Individuals might cross party lines to vote for a candidate not of their shared partisanship and must often make voting decisions in nonpartisan elections, using, instead, cues of ethnicity, issue positions, or other information gleaned from the campaign. The lack of strong feelings of partisan identification among many Latinos, particularly newer immigrants, suggests that, even in partisan races, their vote choice decision might be significantly impacted by other factors. However, for most Latinos, as with most non-Latinos, partisanship is a clear and strong predictor of vote choice. García Bedolla, Alvarez, and Nagler (2006) examined partisan and voting attitudes of Anglo and Latino likely voters in the months before the 2004 presidential election, using two July 2004 surveys. They found that partisanship is a strong predictor for both groups: 91% of Latino Democrats (and 91% of Anglo Democrats) said that they planned to vote for Kerry, whereas 87% of Latino Republicans (and 95% of Anglo Republicans) supported Bush. Latino Republicans were almost twice as likely (13% vs. 8%) to report plans to defect than were Anglo Republicans, but the strength of partisanship was clearly dominant.

On the other hand, Arteaga (2000), using a February 2000 telephone survey of California Latinos, found that although partisanship is the most dominant predictor of Latino vote choice, shared ethnicity can cause Latino voters to cross party lines. When asked whether they would vote for a Democratic or a Republican candidate "if the election were held today," only 6% of Democratic respondents said they probably or definitely would vote for a Republican, compared to 34% of Republican respondents. However, 29% of Democratic respondents said that they would cross party lines to support a Latino Republican candidate. Survey respondents were also given a hypothetical choice between "Smith" and "Hernandez," where Smith was given a traditional Democratic platform and Hernandez was given a typical Republican platform. Asked to choose between the two candidates, 46% of Democrats chose Hernandez (as did 51% of Republicans). In sum, Arteaga found that California Latino voters were willing to cross party lines, either to support a coethnic or to support a candidate with whom they share issue positions, particularly in a nonpartisan setting.

Other, less hypothetical research has found that shared ethnicity is a strong predictor of vote choice among Latinos. Kaufmann (2003) examined Latino vote choice in the Denver mayoral races of 1983 and 1987, which saw the election and reelection of the city's first Latino mayor, Federico Peña. Using a variety of public opinion polls, Kaufmann found that 96% of Latinos voted for Peña in 1983 and 92% voted for Peña in 1987.

As Bullock noted, "voting for a candidate of one's own race may be a product of racism, or it may be the result of reliance on a simple, readily available cue" (1984, p. 240); in other words, Latinos might support Latino candidates based on the assumption that their coethnic shares their basic political views.

In most elections, the partisanship of the Latino candidate matches the partisanship of most Latino voters (i.e., Mexican or Puerto Rican Democrats and Cuban Republicans). In these cases, it can be difficult to determine whether ethnicity or partisanship is driving vote choice. However, given that there is often more than one contest being decided in an election, some elections do offer the opportunity to study the relative power of both ethnicity and partisanship. In addition, some natural experiments have emerged in which the partisanship and ethnicity of candidates present Latino voters with competing cues (i.e., Cuban Democrats and Mexican Republicans), which researchers have used to further investigate the power of each to predict vote choice.

Abrajano, Nagler, and Alvarez (2005) examined the Los Angeles city elections of 2001, including the mayoral and city attorney contests. This provided a natural experiment in vote choice, in that the nonpartisan election included two competitive races for open seats in which one candidate in each race was Latino and one was Anglo. Furthermore, the Latino mayoral candidate (Antonio Villaraigosa) was more liberal than the Anglo mayoral candidate (Jim Hahn), whereas the Latino city attorney candidate (Rocky Delgadillo) was more moderate than the Anglo city attorney candidate (Mike Feuer). Abrajano, Nagler, and Alvarez found that whereas 82% of Latinos voted for Villaraigosa and 79% for Delgadillo, only 66.2% voted for both Latino candidates. In other words, a third of Latino voters chose one Anglo candidate over a coethnic. They concluded that ethnicity was not solely responsible for vote choice, but that ideology, issues, economic evaluation, and education were also important. Conservatives were more likely to choose Hahn and Delgadillo; more educated Latinos were more likely to vote for an Anglo candidate.

The same election was examined, with markedly different conclusions, by Barreto, Villareal, and Woods (2005). Whereas Abrajano, Nagler, & Alvarez (2005) claimed that ethnicity was not the overriding factor mobilizing Latino voters in the 2001 Los Angeles mayoral election, Barreto, Villareal, and Woods disagreed. They noted that several factors were present in the LA context that make ethnic-based voting more likely: enhanced Latino cohesiveness and politicization in the wake of a series of anti-immigrant and anti-Latino initiatives and rhetoric in the 1990s, the presence of a viable Latino candidate, and mobilization drives conducted by Latino organizations [in this case, by the Southwest Voter Registration and Education Project (SVREP) and NALEO]. Registered Latinos voted at higher rates than non-Latinos and tended to support their coethnic (85% chose Villaraigosa). Abrajano, Nagler, and Alvarez claimed that vote choice in the election was driven by ideology, not ethnicity. However, Barreto, Villareal, and Woods showed, using a comparison to the 2000 presidential election, that turnout in 2001 was linked to the percentage of Latinos registered in a precinct. In addition, they found that precincts with higher percentages of Latinos greatly favored Villaraigosa; in other words, vote choice was influenced by ethnicity.[2]

Graves and Lee (2000) employed a survey conducted just before a 1996 U.S. Senate race in Texas, where a Democratic Mexican American challenged an Anglo incumbent, to examine the pathways by which ethnicity influences vote choice. Using a statewide survey of 500 Texas Latinos and 206 Anglos, conducted in mid-October 1996, they found that ethnicity plays a key role in vote choice, but it does so indirectly through partisanship, ethnic-related issue positions, and candidate evaluations. Ethnicity predicts partisanship and issue positions, partisanship predicts issue positions, partisanship and issue positions affect candidate evaluations, and partisanship and candidate evaluations directly affect vote choice. Graves and Lee concluded that "ethnicity exerts a substantial *indirect* influence on voting preference" (2000, p. 234).

Spatial models of voting predict that voters will choose the candidate who is closest to them in space, but which arena of space is more salient to voters: ethnicity, or partisanship? Two elections have provided researchers with the opportunity to test competing vote cues of partisanship and ethnicity on vote choice, with conflicting results. Hill, Moreno, and Cue (2001) analyzed the 1996 Dade County, Florida mayoral election of September 1996, which presented a unique natural experiment on the power of ethnicity to influence vote choice. The four major candidates included a Black Republican, a Puerto Rican Democrat, a Cuban American Democrat, and a Cuban American Independent. The run-off included the Black Republican (Art Teele) and the Cuban American Democrat (Alex Penelas). Over 80% of Black voters in the county were registered as Democrats, whereas over 60% of registered Latinos were Republicans. In other words, ethnicity and partisanship were not aligned, as is the case in most elections. Hill, Moreno, and Cue (2001) found that ethnicity was an overwhelmingly more powerful predictor of vote choice than was partisanship. This study supported Wolfinger's (1965) claim for the persistence of ethnicity as an influence on vote choice, and it argued that ethnicity is a more powerful predictor than partisanship. In a poll conducted a week before the election, 97% of Latino respondents supported one of the three Latino candidates, whereas 83% of African American respondents supported Teele. Most Democrats supported the only Republican, whereas 79% of Republicans supported one of the Democrats. Partisanship was completely overwhelmed by ethnicity as a predictor of vote choice.

Michelson (2005) examined yet another natural experiment in how Latino voters react to competing vote cues—this time in California, where an Anglo Democrat incumbent was challenged by a Mexican American Republican in a heavily Latino district (55%) in the Central Valley. Contrary to the findings of Hill, Moreno, and Cue (2001), Michelson found that Latino voters chose to vote in this election for their copartisan, rather than for their coethnic. Not only did the incumbent, Cal Dooley, easily beat Richard Rodriguez in his bid for a sixth term, taking 52.4% of the vote to Rodriguez's 45.5%, but a poll of Latino voters just before the election showed that 60% of respondents planned to vote for the Anglo Democrat. These conflicting results suggested a third variable that must be considered: context. In California in 2000, the memory of Proposition 187 and its proponent, former Republican Governor Pete Wilson, made partisanship more salient for California Latinos. In Miami-Dade County, on the other hand, ethnicity was more salient. The mayoral race was officially nonpartisan, and although Hill, Moreno, and Cue claimed that most voters were aware of the candidates' partisanship, often due to efforts on the part of the candidates themselves, it is possible that this contributed to the reduced salience of partisanship on vote choice.

Partisanship and ethnicity are clearly the dominant influences on Latino vote choice, but other factors such as issue positions and symbolic cues also play a role. Abrajano (2005), using a national survey conducted in 2000, found that low-education Latinos are more likely than high-education Latinos to use nonpolicy cues when evaluating a candidate. For example, if a candidate speaks Spanish or is Latino or if the candidate promises to appoint Latino officials, uses Spanish-language advertisements, or campaigns in Latino neighborhoods, then low-income Latinos are more likely to evaluate the candidate favorably. However, high-education Latinos are more likely to use policy and ideology cues, as predicted by the classic spatial model.

Nicholson, Pantoja, and Segura (2006) examined the use of heuristics and symbols by Latinos in making their vote choices in the 2000 presidential election, using a preelection poll. They found that candidate characteristics and behavior, such as likeability or speaking Spanish, were much more important determinants of vote choice among low-information Latinos. High-information Latinos, in contrast, were more likely to use issue-based information. The survey asked voters for their opinions on school vouchers, gun control, and abortion. They found that voters who incorrectly matched issue positions to candidates did so in such a way as to attribute their own opinions to the candidate they preferred, indicating that to some degree "voters are swayed by preferences that precede issue-based information" (Nicholson, Pantoja, and Segura, 2006, p. 10). Their analysis revealed that a favorable opinion of candidate George W. Bush was a strong predictor of incorrect issue position attributions to the candidates, but opinion about candidate Al Gore was not. Latinos with a preference between the two candidates tended to hold issue positions consistent with those of their preferred candidate, especially when looking only at better informed voters. All voters and well-informed voters had more issue positions in common with Gore than with Bush. In the full model, partisanship and likeability were the strongest predictors of vote choice for low-information voters, as was the salience of Spanish speaking (by the candidate), but issue positions were not important. For high-information respondents, partisanship was the most important predictor, whereas likeability was weaker and Spanish speaking was not important; the issue position variables were small, but statistically significant.

HOPE FOR THE GOP?

Hajnal and Lee (2006), examining pooled exit polls, found a trend toward support of Republican candidates among Latino voters. In 1976, 82% of Latinos voted Democrat (Jimmy Carter) and 18% voted Republican (Gerald Ford), whereas in 2000, 62% voted Democrat (Al Gore) and 35% voted Republican (George W. Bush). Leal, Barreto, Lee, and de la Garza (2005) examined Latino vote choice in the 2004 presidential election. Not only did Latino participation surge in 2004, increasing from 5.9 million in 2000 to at least 7 million, some exit polls suggested that 44% of Latino voters supported the Republican presidential candidate, George W. Bush, a record level of support for a Republican presidential candidate. Given traditional preference for the Democratic Party (except among Cubans), this figure was greeted with some little skepticism. Later analysis revealed these initial estimates of Latino support for Bush to be overstated. This is not that surprising, given that the 44% conflicted with almost all of the major preelection surveys of Latino likely voters, which found a consistent level of support for Bush of about 35%. Summing up the preelection polls, Leal et al. noted: "In sum, with regard to education, income, age, and immigrant status, every subsection of the Latino electorate stated a vote preference lower than 35% for President Bush" (2005, p. 44).

One notable exception to this, based on a 2004 Washington Post/Univision/TRPI National Survey of Latino Voters, is non-Catholic Latino likely voters, who favored Bush over Gore by almost 13 percentage points (51.1% vs. 38.3%). The same poll found, however, that even non-Catholics rated Democrats as having more concern than Republicans for Latinos, by nearly 25 percentage points. The poll also found that 66% of respondents identified as Democrats, 24% as Republicans, and 10% as Independents. Even among high-SES Latinos, the Democratic Party was preferred by well over a 2-to-1 ratio. Religion seemed to have played a significant role in vote-choice decisions, regardless of professed partisanship. Latino evangelicals favored Bush over Kerry by 25 percentage points (58% vs. 33%), and Bush also won 49% of the vote from other Latino Christians. Leal et al. concluded: "This indicates there was a religion gap within the Latino electorate… For the Republicans, appealing to Latino evangelicals and other non-Catholic Christians may be the key to making (small) inroads to the Latino electorate" (2005, p. 46). Leal et al. concluded by noting that Bush's likely 39% of the vote in 2004 closely parallels the 37% estimated Latino support for Reagan in 1984: "In this light, Bush's numbers may represent not the beginning of a Latino realignment but the electoral ceiling for Republican presidential candidates with appealing personalities" (2005, p. 48). Four years after Reagan's strong showing among Latino voters, George H. W. Bush received only 32% of the Latino vote, and in 1996, Bob Dole received only 21% of the Latino vote. Progress by the GOP in attracting votes might be limited to the appeal of the candidate George W. Bush and is not necessarily a sign that Latinos will vote Republican in 2008 or beyond.

CONCLUSION

As Latino political participation and clout continue to increase, researchers are learning more about how Latinos think and act in the political arena. Historically, most Latinos have preferred the Democratic Party, with the notable exception of Cuban loyalty to the GOP. Despite little to no knowledge of United States partisan politics on their arrival, Latino immigrants quickly learn the "preferred" partisanship of their national-origin group, and there is little evidence that Republicans are making inroads into the non-Cuban Latino population. More research is needed on the political attitudes and behaviors of Latinos not from the "big three" national-origin groups (Mexicans,

Puerto Ricans, and Cubans). This is particularly relevant, as the populations of these "other" Latinos are growing; Dominicans are expected to soon surpass Cubans as the third largest national-origin group. However, because this population growth is relatively recent, little research has been focused on "other" Latinos. Some of this will need to take into account the dominance of the big three, particularly in certain geographic areas. For example, in South Florida, how much does the Cuban American dominance of South Florida politics influence the political behavior of other Latinos such as Nicaraguans and Colombians? Are similarities in political attitudes, to the extent that they exist, the result of this Cuban-dominant context, or are they a result of a shared class outlook by wealthy and influential immigrants who have left Latin America for political and economic reasons? Future research on Latino political participation should also include subnationality groups, such as the large influx of indigenous language migrants from southern Mexico and Guatemala. Further investigation is also needed on the political behavior and interconnectivity of multiple national origin groups that reside in the same cities and regions such as the Puerto Ricans, Dominicans, Peruvians, Brazilians, Salvadorans, Mexicans, and other Latino groups in the Northeast.

In summary, although Latino participation lags behind that of other groups, with the notable exception of attendance at local meetings, their participation is steadily increasing, in both electoral and nonelectoral settings. When targeted by mail, telephone, or door-to-door campaigns, Latino turnout increases significantly. Latino participation is also influenced by political context, including anti-Latino legislation, Latino representatives, and the presence of viable Latino candidates. Other research indicates that Latinos are willing to cross party and ethnic lines for a candidate they support, either for partisan, ethnic, or other reasons such as ideology and issue positions. When deciding how to vote, low-education/low-information Latino voters are more likely to use nonpolicy cues (such as speaking Spanish), whereas high-education/high-information Latino voters are more likely to consider ideology and issue positions.

Although recent research has significantly expanded how much we know and understand about Latino political attitudes and behavior, much remains to be explored. What more can we learn from the massive Latino demonstrations witnessed in the spring of 2006, as the U.S. Congress debated various approaches to immigration reform? Will those street protests lead to increased Latino voter participation and naturalization rates? And if so, what will be the reaction by the American political system and elected officials? Future research is needed to address these and other important questions. As de la Garza commented, "Hispanic political clout rides the crest of the immigrant wave. Immigrants are the core around which new Latino districts have been constructed at every level of elected office. They know it and the officials know it, and that shared knowledge is the basis of their growing influence" (2004, p. 108).

NOTES

1. Traditionally, partisan identification is measured with a two-part question. The first asks respondents if they consider themselves Democrats, Republicans, independents, or something else. Those who do not initially identify with one of the two major parties are then asked if they think of themselves as closer to either, and are often considered "covert" partisans, as they exhibit much of the same political behaviors as those naming a major party in response to the first question. The LNPS figures here and the figures from Alvarez and García Bedolla (2003) treat leaners as partisans.
2. A similar election, albeit a partisan one, is examined by Cain and Kiewiet (1984). In 1982, the Latino Democratic incumbent for California's heavily Latino 30th congressional district, Marty Martinez, was challenged by Anglo Republican John Rousselot. The ballot also included the race for governor between George Deukmejian (Anglo Republican) and Tom Bradley (Black Democrat) and the U.S. Senate race between Pete Wilson (Anglo Republican)

and Jerry Brown (Anglo Democrat). Looking at data from a telephone survey in the third week of October and an exit poll, Cain and Kiewiet found that some Latinos, including some Latino Democrats, defected from Martinez to vote for his Anglo Republican opponent. Rousselot took 14% of the Latino Democratic vote, as well as two-thirds of the vote from Latino Republicans. More notable are the 7% of Latino respondents who voted for Rousselot but also for the Democratic candidates for governor and U.S. Senate, Bradley and Brown. Although 78% of Latinos voted a straight Democratic ballot, some voters did defect: 36% of Latino Republicans and 19% of Anglo Republicans defected to vote for Martinez. Cain and Kiewiet concluded that the support of Latino voters for Latino candidates "is by no means automatic" (1984, p. 317). On the other hand, controlling for a variety of variables, they found that Latino voters were more likely than Anglo voters to vote a straight ticket and that when they did so, it was most likely to vote for Martinez (when also voting for GOP candidates Deukmejian and Wilson).

REFERENCES

Abrajano, M. A. (2005). Who Evaluates a Presidential Candidate by Using Non-Policy Campaign Messages? *Political Research Quarterly*, 58(1), 55–67.

Abrajano, M. A., Nagler, J., & Alvarez, R. M. (2005). A Natural Experiment of Race-Based and Issue Voting: The 2001 City of Los Angeles Elections. *Political Research Quarterly*, 58(2), 203–218.

Alvarez, R. M., & García Bedolla, L. (2003). The Foundations of Latino Voter Partisanship: Evidence from the 2000 Election. *Journal of Politics*, 65(1), 31–49.

Arteaga, L. (2000). The Latino Vote 2000: Are Latinos Pro-Democrat or Anti-Republican? An Examination of Party Registration and Allegiance in the 2000 Election And Beyond. *Latino Issues Forum report*. Retrieved July 19, 2006, from http://www.lif.org/civic/vote_2000.html

Arvizu, J. R., & Garcia, F. C. (1996). Latino Voting Participation: Explaining and Differentiating Latino Voter Turnout. *Hispanic Journal of Behavioral Sciences, 18*(2), 104–128.

Barreto, M. A., & Munoz, J. A. (2003). Reexamining the "Politics of In-Between": Political Participation Among Mexican Immigrants in the United States. *Hispanic Journal of Behavioral Sciences, 25*(4), 427–447.

Barreto, M. A., Segura, G., & Woods, N. (2004). The Effects of Overlapping Majority-Minority Districts on Latino Turnout. *American Political Science Review, 98*(1), 65–75.

Barreto, M. A., Villarreal, M., & Woods, N. D. (2005). Metropolitan Latino Political Behavior: Voter Turnout and Candidate Preference in Los Angeles. *Journal of Urban Affairs*, 27(1), 71–97.

Bishin, B. G., Kaufmann, K. M., & Stevens, D. P. (2005, September). Turf Wars: How Local Power Struggles Influence Latino Political Socialization and Voting Behavior. Paper presented at the annual meeting of the American Politics Workshop, Department of Government and Politics, University of Maryland. Retrieved July 7, 2006, www.bsos. umd.edu/gvpt/apworkshop/kaufmann05f.pdf

Bueker, C. S. (2005, Spring). Political Incorporation Among Immigrants from Ten Areas of Origin: The Persistence of Source Country Effects. *International Migration Review, 39*(1), 103–140.

Bullock, C. S., III. (1984). Racial Crossover Voting and the Election of Black Officials. *Journal of Politics, 46*(1), 238–251.

Cain, B. E., & Kiewiet, D. R. (1984). Ethnicity and Electoral Choice: Mexican American Voting Behavior in the California 30th Congressional District. *Social Science Quarterly, 65*, 315–327.

Cain, B. E., Kiewiet, D.R., & Uhlaner, C. J. (1991, May). The Acquisition of Partisanship by Latinos and Asian Americans. *American Journal of Political Science*, 35(2), 390–422.

Chun, S., & Grenier, G. J. (2004, November). Anti-Castro Political Ideology Among Cuban Americans in the Miami Area: Cohort and Generational Differences. *Latino Research @ ND.* 2(1), 1–3. Retrieved July 7, 2006, from http://www.nd.edu/~latino/research/pubs/Grenchun.pdf#4.pdf

Claggett, W. (1981). Partisan Acquisition Versus Partisan Intensity: Life-cycle, Generation, and Period Effects 1952–1976. *American Journal of Political Science, 25*(2), 193–214.

Converse, P. E. (1969). Of Time and Partisan Stability. *Comparative Political Studies*, 2, 139–171.

Converse, P. E. (1976). *The Dynamics of Party Support: Cohort-Analyzing Party Identification*. Beverly Hills, CA: Sage Publications.

Day, J., Jamieson, A., & Shin, H. B. (2002, February). *Voting and Registration in the Election of November 2000* (U.S. Census Bureau). Washington, DC: U.S. Government Printing Office, 1.

de la Garza, R. O. (2004). Latino Politics. *Annual Review of Political Science*, 7, 91–123.

de la Garza, R. O., DeSipio, L., Garcia, F. C., Garcia, J., & Falcón, A. (1992). *Latino Voices: Mexican, Puerto Rican, and Cuban Perspectives on American Politics*. Boulder, CO: Westview Press.

DeSipio, L. (1996). *Counting on the Latino Vote: Latinos as a New Electorate*. Charlottesville, VA: University Press of Virginia.

DeSipio, L., Pachon, H., de la Garza, R.O., & Lee, J. (2003, March). *Immigrant Politics at Home and Abroad: How Latino Immigrants Engage the Politics of their Home Communities and the United States*, Tomás Rivera Policy Institute Report, Los Angeles.

García Bedolla, L., Alvarez, M. A., & Nagler, J. (2006, March). Anglo and Latino Vote Choice in the 2004 Election. Paper presented at the annual meeting of the Western Political Science Association, Albuquerque, NM.

Graves, S., & Lee, J. (2000). Ethnic Underpinnings of Voting Preference: Latinos and the 1996 U.S. Senate Election in Texas. *Social Science Quarterly, 81*(1), 226–236.

Hajnal, Z., & Lee, T. (2006). Out of Line: Immigration and Party Identification Among Asian Americans and Latinos. In Taeku Lee, Kathrick Ramakrishnan, & Ricardo Ramírez (Eds.), *Transforming Politics, Transforming America: The Political and Civic Incorporation of Immigrants in the United States* (pp. 129–150). Charlottesville, VA: University of Virginia Press.

Hero, R. E., & Campbell, A. G. (1996). Understanding Latino Political Participation: Exploring the Evidence from the Latino National Political Survey. *Hispanic Journal of Behavioral Sciences, 18*(2), 129–141.

Hero, R., Garcia, F. C., Garcia, J., & Pachon, H. (2000). Latino Participation, Partisanship, and Office Holding. *PS: Political Science and Politics, 33*(3), 529–534.

Hill, K. A, Moreno, D., & Cue, L. (2001). Racial and Partisan Voting in a Tri-Ethnic City: The 1996 Dade County Mayoral Election. *Journal of Urban Affairs, 23*(3–4), 291–307.

Kaufmann, K. (2003). Black and Latino Voters in Denver: Responses to Each Other's Political Leadership. *Political Science Quarterly, 118*(1), 107–126.

Kelly, N. J., & Kelly, J. M. (2005). Religion and Latino Partisanship in the United States. *Political Research Quarterly, 58*(1), 87–95.

Kosmin, B. A., & Keysar, A. (1995). Political Party Preferences of U.S. Hispanics: The Varying Impact of Religion, Social Class and Demographic Factors. *Ethnic and Racial Studies, 18*(2), 336–347.

Leal, D. L. (2002, April). Political Participation by Latino Non-Citizens in the United States. *British Journal of Political Science, 32*(2), 353–370.

Leal, D. L., Barreto, M. A., Lee, J., & de la Garza, R. O. (2005). The Latino Vote in the 2004 Election. *PS: Political Science and Politics, 38*(1), 41–49.

Lopez, M. H. (2003, December). *Electoral Engagement Among Latinos*. Report prepared for the Institute of Latino Studies at University of Notre Dame. Retrieved July 7, 2006, from www.nd.edu/~latino/research/pubs/

Michelson, M. R. (2003). Getting out the Latino Vote: How Door-to-Door Canvassing Influences Voter Turnout in Rural Central California. *Political Behavior, 25*(3), 247–263.

Michelson, M. R. (2005). Does Ethnicity Trump Party? Competing Vote Cues and Latino Voting Behavior. *Journal of Political Marketing, 4*(4), 1–25.

Michelson, M. R. (2006a, December). Mobilizing the Latino Youth Vote: Some Experimental Results. *Social Science Quarterly, 87*(5), 1188–1206.

Michelson, M. R. (2006b). Mobilizing Latino Voters for a Ballot Proposition. *Latino(a) Research Review 6*(1–2), 33–49.

Michelson, M. R., & Pallares, A. (2001). The Politicization of Chicago Mexican Americans: Naturalization, the Vote, and Perceptions of Discrimination. *Aztlan, 26*(2), 63–85.

Moreno, D. (1997). The Cuban Model: Political Empowerment in Miami. In F. C. García (Ed.), *Pursuing Power: Latinos and the U.S. Political System* (pp. 208–226). Notre Dame, IN: University of Notre Dame Press.

Nicholson, S. P., Pantoja, A. D., & Segura, G. M. (2006). Explaining the Latino Vote: Issue Voting Among Latinos in the 2000 Presidential Election. *Political Research Quarterly, 59*(2), 259–271.

Pachon, H., & DeSipio, L. (1994). *New Americans by Choice: Political Perspectives of Latino Immigrants*. Boulder, CO: Westview Press.

Pantoja, A. D., Ramírez, R., & Segura, G. M. (2001). Citizens by Choice, Voters by Necessity: Patterns in Political Mobilization by Naturalized Latinos. *Political Research Quarterly, 54*(4), 729–750.

Ramírez, R. (2005, September). Giving Voice to Latino Voters: A Field Experiment on the Effectiveness of a National Nonpartisan Mobilization Effort. *Annals of the American Academy of Political and Social Science, 601*, 66–84.

Sanchez, G. R. (2006). The Role of Group Consciousness in Political Participation Among Latinos in the United States. *American Politics Research, 34*, 427–450.

Shaw, D., de la Garza, R. O., & Lee, J. (2000). Examining Latino Turnout in 1996: A Three-State, Validated Survey Approach. *American Journal of Political Science, 44*(2), 332–340.

Stokes, A. K. (2003). Latino Group Consciousness and Political Participation. *American Politics Research, 31*(4), 361–378.

Tavres, D. (2004). *A Study of Dominican-American Voter Capacity*. Report for the Dominican American National Round-table. Retrieved July 7, 2006, from dr1.com/business/dominican_american/

Uhlaner, C. J. (2002, July). *The Impact of Perceived Representation on Latino Political Participation. Center for the Study of Democracy 02–06*, University of California, Irvine.

Uhlaner, C. J., & Garcia, F. C. (1998, June). *Foundations of Latino Party Identification: Learning, Ethnicity and Demographic Factors Among Mexicans, Puerto Ricans, Cubans and Anglos in the United States*. Center for the Study of Democracy 98–06, University of California, Irvine.

U.S. Census Bureau. (2006). *Current Population Survey, November 2004* (P20-556). Washington, DC: U.S. Government Printing Office.

U.S. Census Bureau. (2006). *Voting and Registration in the Election of November 2004*. Current Population Reports P20–556. March.

Vargas-Ramos, C. (2003). The Political Participation of Puerto Ricans in New York City. *Centro: Journal of the Center for Puerto Rican Studies, 15*(1), 41–71.

Verba, S., & Nie, N. H. (1972). *Participation in America: Political Democracy and Social Equality*. Chicago: University of Chicago Press.

Verba, S., Schlozman, K. H., & Brady, H. E. (1995). *Voice and Equality: Civic Voluntarism in American Politics*. Cambridge, MA: Harvard University Press.

Welch, S., & Sigelman, L. (1992). A Gender Gap Among Hispanics? A Comparison with Blacks and Anglos. *Western Political Quarterly, 45*(1), 181–199.

Wolfinger, R. E. (1965). The Development and Persistence of Ethnic Voting. *American Political Science Review, 59*(4), 896–908.

Wolfinger, R. E., & Rosenstone, S. J. (1980). *Who Votes?* New Haven, CT: Yale University Press.

Wong, J. S. (2000). The Effects of Age and Political Exposure on the Development of Party Identification Among Asian American and Latino Immigrants in the United States. *Political Behavior, 22*(4), 341–371.

CHAPTER 22

Political Orientations and Latino Immigrant Incorporation

Sarah Allen Gershon
Adrian D. Pantoja

INTRODUCTION

Latino immigrant incorporation into the American political structure is vital for the political future of the Latino community in the United States, a group marked by considerable numbers of noncitizens as well as relatively low voter turnout among citizens. To gain a more significant political voice for the American Latino population, immigrants must become politically incorporated through naturalization and political activism. The term *political incorporation* has been used by scholars to refer to many things, including naturalization, formal participation in politics, group representation in elected office and policy outcomes, as well as participation in nonelectoral activities and organizations (Barreto & Muñoz, 2003; DeSipio, 1996a; Jones-Correa, 1998; Ramakrishnan & Espenshade, 2001). Although political incorporation might include a number of activities, in this chapter we measure immigrant incorporation into the American political system through two basic behavioral indicators: naturalization and nonelectoral political participation.

The acquisition of U.S. citizenship is a critical first step toward the political incorporation of immigrants, as it confers upon them the right to vote and hold elective office. For politically underrepresented groups like Latinos, the presence of a large segment of noncitizens is particularly troubling, significantly limiting their electoral strength. The 2000 U.S. Census reports that out of 23 million adult Latinos, only 13.2 million, or 57%, are U.S. citizens. In other words, close to half of the voting-age Latino population is ineligible to vote because they are noncitizens. Having a large noncitizen population in itself is not significant if naturalization is undertaken rather quickly. Yet, naturalization rates among Latinos, with the exception of Cuban Americans, have tended to be among the lowest, approximately half the naturalization rate of non-Latino immigrant groups. The length of time that it takes for Latinos to naturalize has important political implications for the Latino community in the United States. Should naturalization rates change, Latinos stand to gain significant political power due to the increasing size of the Latino electorate. It is of little wonder that scholars of Latino politics have long considered lack of citizenship to be the single most important obstacle to Latino political empowerment.

Like naturalization, participation in politics, among both naturalized and non-naturalized immigrants, leads to greater political incorporation into the American political structure. Unfortunately, the length of time associated with completing the process of naturalization results in many Latino immigrants spending several years in the United States before acquiring citizenship and the right to formally express their policy concerns to elected officials at the polls. Although a significant portion of the Latino immigrant population remain noncitizens and are therefore unable to vote, they are still subject to changes in U.S. law, giving them significant motivation to try to impact political outcomes through nonelectoral participation (Leal, 2002). Given the recent and ongoing national debate over immigration reform, Latino immigrants (including noncitizens) have arguably more reasons than ever before to try to shape policy through participation in demonstrations, meetings, and campaigns.

Although unable to participate formally in politics by voting, several recent studies suggest that Latino noncitizens might actually participate in some political activities at higher rates than Latino citizens, indicating that among Latino immigrants, citizenship status might not significantly impact nonelectoral participation (Barreto & Muñoz, 2003; Leal, 2002). If political incorporation through nonelectoral participation among Latino immigrants increases in the future, the political voice of this growing population will magnify, perhaps resulting in greater policy responsiveness toward Latinos and immigrants as a whole.

POLITICAL ORIENTATIONS AND INCORPORATION

In this study of Latino immigrant political incorporation, we focus on the impact of political orientations on the choice to naturalize and participate in nonelectoral political activities.[1] By political orientations, we mean citizens' subjective feelings about the political system: whether they know and care about politics, desire to participate in politics, and feel capable of affecting change in the political system (Burns, Schlozman, & Verba, 2001). We expect these orientations (including attitudes toward voting and interest in politics) to significantly effect naturalization and participation among Latino immigrants.

The absence of political orientations in naturalization studies might be driven by the assumption that citizenship is primarily pursued for economic benefits, not out of a desire to participate in politics. As Borjas (2001) noted, "Many immigrants will become citizens not because they want to fully participate in the U.S. political and social systems, but because naturalization is required to receive welfare benefits" (p. 383). This assumption is reinforced by early studies on Latino political behavior demonstrating that foreign-born Latino citizens participate in electoral politics at rates lower than their native-born counterparts (DeSipio, 1996b). Ironically, when the National Latino Immigrant Survey (NLIS), a nationally drawn survey of 1,635 Latino immigrants carried out in 1989, asked respondents to state the reason why they sought naturalization, the most common answer given was that "naturalization allows the right to vote." When asked to identify the single most important reason for naturalizing, a majority of respondents stated "to participate in politics." Hence, a major finding of the NLIS was that Latino immigrants sought

U.S. citizenship out of a desire to participate in American politics, rather than obtaining welfare or other economic benefits (Pachon & DeSipio, 1994). Most recently, in the mass protests on behalf of immigrant rights in the spring of 2006, many migrants held signs that read "Today We March, Tomorrow We Vote" (McFadden, 2006), suggesting a sustained link between naturalization and a desire to participate in politics for Latino immigrants.

As noted in the introduction, recent studies on Latino political behavior have shown that newly naturalized Latino immigrants are as engaged, if not more politically engaged, than native-born Latinos (Barreto & Muñoz, 2003; Barreto, 2005; Leal, 2002; Pantoja, Ramirez, & Segura, 2001). Leal's (2002) study on Latino noncitizens found that respondents who planned on becoming U.S. citizens participated in nonelectoral activities at rates higher than those who had no plans to become citizens. If these works find that naturalized Latino immigrants are equally or more politically engaged than native-born Latinos and that political participation is contingent on having positive political orientations, it follows that these orientations among immigrants will foster naturalization. In other words, political orientations are pivotal resources for electoral participation among citizens and might therefore be pivotal in explaining naturalization among noncitizens.

Like the naturalization literature, studies on political orientations and Latino immigrant nonelectoral participation are fairly limited. Although the literature on Latino electoral participation is quite developed, studies of nonelectoral participation, particularly among noncitizens, are far less prominent (Barreto & Muñoz, 2003). Previous research has demonstrated that possessing positive political orientations is critical for both electoral and nonelectoral participation among citizens generally (Verba, Schlozman, & Brady, 1995). Additionally, some Latino-specific literature has also demonstrated that political orientations might significantly impact electoral participation among Latino citizens (Pantoja, Ramirez, & Segura, 2001) and nonelectoral participation among Latinos as a whole (Leal, 2002). We expect that if these orientations matter in encouraging Latino participation generally, they will also affect nonelectoral participation among Latino immigrants, including those who have yet to be naturalized.

Within the fairly limited body of literature concerning noncitizen participation, there is some disagreement over the role of political orientations in prompting participation. Some scholars have found positive orientations, such as political interest, to significantly impact nonelectoral participation among Latino immigrants (Leal, 2002), whereas others have found orientations, such as political efficacy, to have little impact on participation in these activities (Barreto & Muñoz, 2003). At this point, the impact (or lack thereof) of political orientations on political participation among noncitizen Latinos is somewhat unclear.

In order to offer a systematic analysis of the role that political orientations play in political incorporation through naturalization and nonelectoral participation by contemporary Latino immigrants, this chapter draws on survey data from the 1999 Harvard/Kaiser/Washington Post "Latino Political Survey."[2] We rely on the 1999 Latino Political Survey for several reasons. First, the survey includes a plethora of political attitudes and other questions relevant to our study and is preferable to U.S. Census or Immigration and Naturalization Service data, which lack many relevant individual-level measures. Second, as one of the most recent national surveys of Latinos, the data offer a contemporary portrait of Latino immigrants beyond that offered by the Latino National Political Survey and National Latino Immigrant Survey over 15 years ago. Finally, as a national survey, the 1999 Latino Political Survey is preferable to more parochial surveys because the conclusions drawn are far-reaching rather than regional in scope (Barreto & Muñoz, 2003). Before undertaking our first analysis, we provide a brief overview of the previous literature concerning our indicators of political incorporation: immigration naturalization and nonelectoral political participation.

AN OVERVIEW OF IMMIGRANT NATURALIZATION

The rise in immigration from Latin America, along with findings that their naturalization rates lag significantly behind other immigrant groups, has generated intense attention from policy makers and researchers. According to the naturalization literature, the relative slowness in Mexican and Latin American naturalization is attributed to a host of sociodemographic, cultural, contextual, and transnational factors. To varying degrees, multivariate studies on Latino naturalization empha-size the primacy of factors falling into one or more of the four categories previously listed. One of the earliest quantitative studies on Mexican naturalization was carried out by Grebler (1966). Using Immigration and Nationalization Service (INS) data, Grebler found that Mexican natu-ralization rates were driven by a combination of sociodemographic (length of residency in the United States, age, and gender) and contextual factors (area of residence).

A significant contribution to the study of Mexican naturalization was made by Garcia (1981), whose study was based on the 1979 Chicano survey, one of the first national political and social surveys of the Mexican population. Garcia found that naturalization is tied to cultural (family and personal ties to Mexico, English language proficiency) rather than sociodemographic (age, educa-tional attainment, length of residence in the United States) or sociopolitical factors (evaluation of U.S. social agents, identification with being an American, and a preference for interacting with other Mexicans). Although Garcia was the first to consider the interplay between political orientations and naturalization, the proxies used in his study failed to measure attitudes toward participation in U.S. politics—orientations that we believe are critical for understanding immigrant naturalization.

Some scholars contend that the decision to naturalize is largely influenced by forces outside of the United States, in the country of origin. Research by Portes and Mozo (1985) and Aguirre and Saenz (2002) indicated that immigrants who left for political reasons (e.g., Cubans) have significantly higher rates of naturalization than immigrants who migrated for economic reasons. Other contextual factors in the country of origin have also been found to influence the pursuit of U.S. citizenship, including an immigrant's proximity to the nation of origin, the per capita Gross National Product, literacy rates, level of urbanization, and regime type (Portes & Curtis, 1987; Portes & Mozo, 1985; Yang, 1994). Also debated is the impact of contextual factors in the United States, the so-called "destination characteristics" (DeSipio, 1996a; Portes & Curtis, 1987).

The latest scholarship on immigrant naturalization has turned to examining the impact of transnational ties (Jones-Correa, 1998, 2001; Pantoja, 2005; Yang, 1994). Transnational ties, as applied to immigration, are typically defined as "the process by which immigrants forge and sustain simultaneous multi-stranded social relations that link together their societies of origin and settlement" (Basch, Schiller, & Blanc, 1994, p. 7). Some consider transnational networks to be incompatible with U.S. political incorporation because they create a "transient mentality" among immigrants, leading them to devalue naturalization and/or political participation in the United States (Huntington, 2004). Others claim that immigrants from nations that are supportive of transnational ties, such as those recognizing dual nationality, are more likely to seek out U.S. citizenship (Escobar, 2004; Jones-Correa, 1998).

OVERVIEW OF IMMIGRANT NONELECTORAL
POLITICAL PARTICIPATION

Much of the scholarship in Latino politics focuses on the voting behavior of naturalized and native-born citizens (DeSipio, 1996a, 1996b; Johnson, Stein, & Wrinkle, 2003; Pantoja, Ramakrishnan & Espenshade, 2001; Ramirez, & Segura, 2001). Few examine the political behavior of noncitizens, which comprise a significant portion of our sample. Because noncitizens cannot participate in electoral politics, we review scholarship on Latino nonelectoral behavior. A number of variables are associated with participation in nonelectoral politics. Demographic variables, including education, age, gender, length of residency, nation of origin, and generational differences have all been found to significantly impact nonelectoral participation (DeSipio, 1996a; Hill & Moreno, 1996; Jones-Correa & Leal, 2001; Wrinkle, et al., 1996). Other attitudinal and behavioral variables, such as attitudes toward one's own ethnic group, experiences with discrimination, mobilization (Wrinkle et al., 1996), and attending religious services (Jones-Correa & Leal, 2001), have also been found to significantly impact nonelectoral participation. Although these studies greatly expand our knowledge of the forces influencing Latino nonelectoral participation, like the Latino voting literature many ignore noncitizens in their analyses.

The most recent work on noncitizen participation by Leal (2002) and Barreto and Muñoz (2003) identified several socioeconomic and political forces impacting nonelectoral participation. Leal (2002) found, using data from the 1989 Latino National Political Survey, that citizenship increases the likelihood of participating in nonelectoral activities among Latinos. He further found that beyond citizenship, nonelectoral participation was also impacted positively by political interest, socioeconomic status, political awareness, positive attitudes toward the United States, and nation of origin. In addition, Leal also found that, among noncitizens, plans to become a U.S. citizen were positively related to their participation in nonelectoral activities.

Barreto and Muñoz (2003) challenged some of Leal's (2002) core findings using a sample of Mexican immigrants from the same dataset employed by this study. Barreto and Muñoz found that gender, education, party affiliation, attitudes toward life in the United States, and transnational economic ties all significantly effect participation in nonelectoral political activities among Mexican immigrants. However, citizenship status and political efficacy had no significant impact on the choice to participate in these activities.

DATA AND METHODS

The 1999 Latino Political Survey includes a nationally drawn sample of 2,417 Latinos. Our analysis is limited to foreign-born Latinos who are either naturalized citizens or eligible for naturalization. Thus, respondents who are Puerto Rican, born in the United States, and have resided in the United States for less than 5 years were eliminated. Also dropped from the present analysis are individuals who are ineligible for citizenship because they are likely undocumented immigrants.[3] Fifty-five respondents fell into that category. The final sample used in our analysis consists of a sample of 1,042 immigrant Latinos. Among our respondents, 496 (47.6%) were U.S. citizens; 167 (16%) were currently applying for U.S. citizenship; 268 (25.7%) were planning to apply, and 92 (8.8%) had no plans to apply for citizenship. These responses are combined to create a four-point ordinal scale, ranging from 0 "no plans to apply for citizenship" to 3 for "U.S. citizens" (Aguirre & Saenz, 2002). This measure will serve as our first dependent variable.

Although less than half of Latino immigrants who are eligible for U.S. citizenship have become naturalized citizens, there is a high degree of variation among Mexicans, Cubans, and Salvadorans (the three largest groups in the survey). Cubans had the highest rates of citizenship acquisition among the three groups, with 75% being U.S. citizens. Salvadorans, on the other hand, had the lowest rates of naturalization: 22% were U.S. citizens. Mexican respondents, at 36% being U.S. citizens, fell between these two extremes. Finally, among the "other Latinos," composed of non-Salvadoran Central Americans and South Americans, 48% were U.S. citizens.

Because we are concerned with an immigrant population, many of whom remain ineligible to vote due to lack of citizenship, our second dependent variable is based on three questions capturing nonelectoral political participation. These questions are as follows: (1) Have you worked as a volunteer or for pay for a Latino political candidate? (2) Have you attended a public meeting or demonstration regarding Latino concerns? (3) Have you contributed money to a Latino candidate or Latino political organization? These questions are combined to form a nonelectoral participation variable ranging from 0 to 3, 0 indicating participation in none of these activities and 3 indicating participation in all three. The differences in nonelectoral participation among Mexicans, Cubans and Salvadorans are negligible. Among Mexicans, 21.4% had participated in at least one of the three political activities noted earlier. Participation in one of these activities was at 23.6% for Cubans, 27.4% for Salvadorans, and 19.2% for the other Latino national-origin groups.

From the 1999 survey, we are able to construct 18 predictors for our multivariate analyses. Our primary interest is in assessing the relative impact of immigrant political orientations on our two indicators of incorporation, naturalization, and nonelectoral political participation. Two measures of political orientations are included. The first is based on a question asking the degree to which an individual agrees or disagrees with the statement "voting is a waste of time." The variable, *Voting is a Waste,* is based on a four-point scale, ranging from 0 "disagree strongly" to 3 "agree strongly." The second variable is a measure of political interest. Respondents are asked "How much attention would you say you pay to politics and government?" The variable is based on a four-point scale ranging from 0 "none at all" to 3 "a lot." We hypothesize that having positive political orientations will lead immigrants to pursue U.S. citizenship at higher rates and participate in nonelectoral political activities, *ceteris paribus.*

Seven predictors fall under the category of individual demographic characteristics. Most of these control variables, including age, education, income,[4] gender, marital status, length of residency, and English language proficiency, are traditional predictors of naturalization and participation and do not require much explanation.

In addition to these six control variables, which are standard in naturalization and participation studies, we use dummies to separate *Mexican*, *Cuban*, and *Salvadoran* respondents from the "other Latinos" to isolate the effects of ethnic ancestry on the pursuit of U.S. citizenship. A dichotomous variable measuring personal experience with discrimination is included, as experience with discrimination has been found to foster naturalization, civic engagement, and participation among Latinos (DeSipio, 1996a; Wrinkle et al., 1996).

Some scholars have examined the reasons why people migrate and whether this has an impact on incorporation. The survey asks respondents if they emigrated to the United States (1) "to join family members," (2) "to escape political oppression or dictatorship," (3) "to find a better job or for other economic reasons," or (4) for some other reason. Dummies are used to isolate the first three responses to create the following variables: *Family Migration, Political Migration,* and *Economic Migration.* Some contend that migrants fleeing political repression, such as Cubans, are more likely to acquire U.S. citizenship because of an appreciation for new-found political freedoms or because returning to the country of origin is a forgone option (Aguirre & Saenz, 2002; Yang, 1994). On the other hand, fleeing politically repressive regimes might lead individuals to be distrustful of government, leading them to avoid interacting with coercive, often hostile, U.S. government institutions such as the INS.

There is a burgeoning scholarship on immigrant transnational ties that examines their impact on immigrants' social, economic, and political incorporation. Some scholars suggest that transnational ties might hamper incorporation by decreasing naturalization and participation

(Huntington, 2004), whereas others indicate that ties with one's country of origin might be positive for political incorporation, as they impact participation levels (Jones-Correa, 1998; Pantoja, 2005). We include two dichotomous variables capturing transnational political and economic ties. The variable *Transnational Political Ties* is measured by a question asking if the respondent has voted in the country of origin since he or she moved to the United States. The variable *Transnational Economic Ties* is measured by a question asking if the migrant regularly sends money back to the country of origin.

RESULTS: INCORPORATION VIA NATURALIZATION

Because the naturalization variable is based on a four-point ordinal scale ranging from 0 for "no plans to apply for citizenship" to 3 for "U.S. citizens," we use ordered logistic regression analysis. Table 1 presents two sets of results: (1) the ordered logistic coefficients with the standard errors and (2) the *average unit change* in the dependent variable, given a fixed change in the independent variable from its minimum value to its maximum value, holding all others constant at their mean (Long, 1997).

In the model, many of the traditional sociodemographic predictors of naturalization stand out as having a significant impact on Latino rates of naturalization. Beyond the significance of many of these predictors, the results demonstrate that having a negative orientation toward voting decreased

TABLE 1. **The Determinants of Latino Naturalization**

	b (SE)	Average change
Voting is a Waste	−.124 (.061)*	.0464
Political Interest	.134 (.075)†	.0503
Age	.010 (.006)	.0997
Education	.091 (.045)*	.0676
Credit Card	.510 (.139)***	.0635
Female	.229 (.136)†	.0286
Married	.059 (.137)	.0074
Length of Residency	.093 (.010)***	.3820
English Language	.155 (.043)***	.1147
Mexican	−.436 (.169)**	.0543
Cuban	.664 (.267)**	.0810
Salvadoran	−.507 (.221)*	.0627
Discrimination	−.102 (.135)	.0127
Family Migration	.624 (.282)*	.0768
Political Migration	.389 (.319)	.0483
Economic Migration	.643 (.280)*	.0795
Transnational Political Ties	−.198 (.159)	.0248
Transnational Economic Ties	.005 (.140)	.0006
Cut Point 1	.800 (.465)	
Cut Point 2	2.948 (.470)	
Cut Point 3	3.912 (.477)	
Chi-square	407.42	
Significance	.000	
Sample Size	997	

Significance levels: †$p \leq .10$, *$p \leq .05$, **$p \leq .01$, ***$p \leq .001$, two-tailed.

the probability of becoming a U.S. citizen, whereas having an interest in politics increased the probability of becoming a U.S. citizen, *ceteris paribus*. These findings are significant because they demonstrate a connection between having positive political orientations and the acquisition of U.S. citizenship—a connection established over a decade ago by immigrants interviewed in the NLIS and, until now, ignored by researchers.

In addition to the impact of political orientations, the results also show that immigrants who are women are more likely to pursue naturalization than men, even after controlling for a host of factors, suggesting that the incentive for naturalization is greater for Latina immigrants than it is for Latino immigrants. Our finding is consistent with gendered approaches to immigration, which note a stronger orientation toward permanent settlement in the United States among women, often driven by their greater access to economic, social, and political resources, as well as an increase in personal autonomy and status within the family and community (Hondagneu-Sotelo, 1994, 2003).

The strongest predictor was *Length of Residency*. The impact of the variables *English Language* and *Age* is also substantial. Not surprisingly, as English proficiency, age, education, and income increase, so does the likelihood of becoming a naturalized U.S. citizen. Counter to Yang (1994), we find no relationship between being married and naturalization. Also, we find no evidence that experience with discrimination influences the naturalization decision.

Turning to the variables isolating *Mexican, Cuban, and Salvadoran* respondents, we find that immigrants who are Mexican or Salvadoran are less likely to naturalize than other Latinos. Cubans, on the other hand, are more likely to seek out naturalization. The difference between Cubans and other Latin Americans has been assumed to be driven by their motives for emigrating; they were fleeing for political rather than economic reasons (Portes & Mozo, 1985). Counter to this belief, we show that Latin American immigrants who migrated for political reasons are no more likely to pursue naturalization than those leaving for nonpolitical reasons. In fact, migrating for family or economic reasons had a positive and statistically significant effect, whereas fleeing for political reasons has no impact on the likelihood of becoming a naturalized citizen.

Having found political orientations to significantly impact our first indicator of political incorporation, naturalization, we now turn to an examination of their impact on our second measure, participation in nonelectoral activities.

RESULTS: INCORPORATION VIA NONELECTORAL POLITICAL PARTICIPATION

In our second model, we include the same 18 predictors used in the naturalization model. As in Table 1, we present two sets of results in Table 2: (1) the ordered logistic coefficients with the standard errors and (2) the average unit change in the dependent variable, given a fixed change in the independent variable from its minimum value to its maximum value, holding all other variables constant at their means (Long, 1997).

The model demonstrates that political orientations do indeed significantly impact nonelectoral political participation among Latino immigrants. In other words, the more Latino immigrants disagree with the statement "voting is a waste of time" and the more interested in politics they are, the greater their likelihood of participating in nonelectoral activities is. This result falls in line with previous work by Leal (2002) and Burns, Schlozman, and Verba (2001), which suggests that positive political orientations are critical for participation in politics. Although not entirely unexpected, this result is significant in that it indicates that, like the choice to naturalize, participation in nonelectoral activities might be spurred by attitudes that Latino immigrants have toward U.S. politics, in addition

TABLE 2. The Determinants of Latino Immigrant Nonelectoral Participation

	b (SE)	Average change
Voting is a Waste	−.131 (.071)*	.0386
Political Interest	.319 (.082)***	.0966
U.S. Citizenship	.077 (.168)	.0080
Age	.001 (.006)	.0154
Education	.074 (.048)	.0470
Credit Card	.128 (.162)	.0131
Female	−.223 (.146)	.0231
Married	−.132 (.149)	.0137
Length of Residency	.007 (.008)	.0665
English Language	.093 (.047)*	.0559
Mexican	.436 (.194)*	.0463
Cuban	.602 (.248)**	.0662
Salvadoran	.698 (.255)**	.0788
Discrimination	.659 (.146)***	.0698
Family Migration	.239 (.302)	.0251
Political Migration	.206 (.328)	.0251
Economic Migration	.164 (.304)	.0171
Transnational Political Ties	.500 (.161)	.0300
Transnational Economic Ties	.282 (.184)***	.0527
Cut Point 1	2.99 (.498)	
Cut Point 2	4.66 (.512)	
Cut Point 3	6.40 (.560)	
Chi-square	100.79	
Significance	.000	
Sample Size	997	

Significance levels: *$p \le .05$, **$p \le .01$, ***$p \le .001$, two-tailed.

to the sociodemographic, cultural, transnational, and contextual variables found in prior studies to impact participation. Additionally, the impact of political orientations has the strongest relative effect on Latino immigrants in moving them to participate in one of the three nonelectoral activities from not participating at all.

Beyond the impact of political orientations on Latino immigrant participation, several of the remaining variables are significant. In contrast to findings by Leal (2002), our model suggests that citizenship has no significant effect on Latino immigrants' choice to participate in nonelectoral activities. Our results support those of Barreto and Muñoz (2003) in their study of the Mexican population. We believe that many Latino immigrants who are not yet citizens, might be as engaged (if not more so) in nonelectoral activities as naturalized Latino immigrants, particularly because they are limited to these activities to express their political needs and opinions.

Predictably, English language proficiency significantly and positively impacts immigrants' participation. Nation of origin significantly and positively impacts participation among all of the groups included in our analysis, indicating that Cuban, Mexican, and Salvadoran immigrants are more likely to participate in nonelectoral political activities than other Latinos. We further found that experiences with discrimination increase the likelihood of participation among Latino immigrants. Counter to Huntington's thesis, we find that transnational economic ties significantly increased the likelihood of participation, indicating that those who send money back to their country of origin are more likely to participate in nonelectoral activities than those who do not.

Somewhat surprisingly, many sociodemographic variables often associated with participation among Latinos and immigrants (such as education, age, length of residency, and income) were found to have no significant impact on participation in nonelectoral activities. These findings suggest that Latino immigrants might not require significant periods of time in the United States before becoming politically active and that the traditional predictors of political activity in native-born Americans (such as age, education, and income) might not exert the same influence over participation among Latino immigrants. Finally, the reason for migration to the United States appears to bear no relationship to participation in politics, indicating that immigrants migrating for political reasons are no more likely to participate in nonelectoral political activities than those who migrate for economic or family reasons.

CONCLUSIONS

The degree to which Latino political power is proportional to their demographic size is largely dependent on whether its foreign-born segment becomes politically incorporated by acquiring U.S. citizenship in a timely manner and participating in political activities of all kinds. An ongoing theme in Latino political development is that for a significant portion of Latino immigrants, the acquisition of U.S. citizenship often takes decades, leaving them adrift in a state of political limbo. Our findings are instructive for Latino and non-Latino interest groups seeking to incorporate immigrants. The pursuit of U.S. citizenship and participation in politics are not merely the result of possessing greater socioeconomic resources. Immigrants must also possess political resources—in particular, positive political orientations. Hence, political incorporation can be induced by stressing the importance of voting, civic engagement, and being politically informed.

We do find evidence that economic motives matter in naturalization. However, our findings also support an alternative discourse: During this period, Latino immigrants were also driven by a desire to participate in politics. More specifically, immigrants with positive political orientation were naturalizing at high rates. We also found that many socioeconomic and demographic variables did not significantly impact participation, indicating that immigrants, who might be hampered in their ability to participate formally by voting, are not limited in their nonelectoral participation by factors such as the length of time associated with naturalization or possibly limited financial and educational resources.

The subjective feelings that Latino immigrants have toward the American political system significantly impacts their acquisition of U.S. citizenship and participation in nonelectoral politics. Political orientations are likely to have a significant impact on other forms of political expressions such as voting, supporting political candidates, and pursuing political office. As such, future studies should further examine the role of positive political orientations (including, but not limited to those orientations examined here) in encouraging Latino immigrants' legal and political incorporation in the United States.

Additionally, we believe that future research should not only seek to understand the consequences of political orientations for Latino immigrants but also their origins. Are political orientations the result of early childhood political socialization developed prior to migration in Latin America, or are they forged within enclaves and social networks developed in the United States? It has long been argued that the development of political identities begins at an early age through parental influences (Jennings & Markus, 1984). However, among immigrants, children play an important role in the settlement process. Children of immigrants typically master the English language quickly and are frequently used as translators and mediators by parents. Although immigrant parents influence their children, children might also serve as important sources of political socialization for their parents by explaining U.S. politics and translating political materials (Wong & Tseng, 2007). Although this research is in its infancy, we believe that bidirectional approaches to political socialization and the formation of political orientations offer a promising avenue for understanding immigrant political incorporation in the United States.

As Congress now considers the fate of nearly 11 million undocumented immigrants, should a path toward citizenship become a reality, then the Latino population stands to make significant political gains as these immigrants become citizens and expand their participation in politics to include voting as well as other political activities. We suspect that Latino immigrants, long portrayed as politically insignificant, will be at the forefront of Latino political empowerment in the near future.

NOTES

1. Although we examine naturalization in this chapter in terms of a "choice" on the part of immigrants, we recognize that there are numerous bureaucratic and political variables outside of the immigrants' control that might slow or quicken the naturalization process, thus constraining the immigrants' ability to acquire citizenship (see Pachon, 1987). We attempt to control for these influences in our analysis by including nation of origin and reason for migration in our multivariate model; however, a complete analysis of the impact of these factors on the naturalization process is beyond the scope of this chapter.
2. This study was conducted by telephone June 30 to August 30, 1999 among a nationally representative sample of 4,614 adults 18 years and older, including 2,417 Latinos. The study included interviews with a representative number of Latinos in four ethnic groups, based on country of origin: Mexican (818), Puerto Rican (318), Cuban (312), and Central and South American (593).
3. The survey asked respondents if one of the reasons why they were not pursuing naturalization was because they were not legal residents. We surmised that the 55 respondents who answered "yes" were undocumented immigrants.
4. Because a large percentage of Latinos generally, and immigrants in particular, refuse to answer questions pertaining to personal or household earnings, scholars often rely on alternative proxies such as homeownership. Because the survey did not include a question tapping whether a respondent was a homeowner, we use the variable *Credit Card* as a proxy for income. The variable is dichotomous: 1 for persons who have a credit card(s) and 0 for those without credit cards. Having a credit card could also be used as a measure of acculturation, economic incorporation, and the development of social networks. Hondagneu-Sotelo (1994) noted: "Credit also marks one's financial establishment in the U.S. The purchase of services and consumer goods on credit is an important achievement, one that reflects the accumulation of employment stability, references, and experience with institutions in the United States" (p. 169).

REFERENCES

Aguirre, B. E., & Saenz, R. (2002). Testing the Effects of Collectively Expected Durations of Migration: The Naturalization of Mexicans and Cubans. *International Migration Review, 36*, 103–124.
Barreto, M. A. (2005). Latino Immigrants at the Polls: Foreign-Born Voter Turnout in the 2002 Election. *Political Research Quarterly, 58*, 79–95.
Barreto, M. A., & Muñoz, J. A. (2003). Reexamining the 'Politics of In-Between': Political Participation Among Mexican Immigrants in the United States. *Hispanic Journal of Behavioral Sciences, 25*, 427–447.
Basch, L., Schiller, N. G., & Blanc, C. S. (1994). *Nations Unbound: Transnational Projects, Postcolonial Predicaments, and the Deterritorialized Nation-State*. Amsterdam: Gordon and Breach.
Borjas, G. (2001). Welfare Reform and Immigration. In R. Blank & R. Haskins (Eds.), *The New World of Welfare* (pp. 369–390). Washington, DC: Brookings Institution.
Burns, N., Schlozman, K. L., & Verba, S. (2001). *The Private Roots of Public Action: Gender, Equality, and Political Participation*. Cambridge, MA: Harvard University Press.

DeSipio, L. (1996a). *Counting on the Latino Vote: Latinos as A New Electorate*. Charlottesville, VA: University of Virginia Press.

DeSipio, L. (1996b). Making Citizens or Good Citizens? Naturalization as a Predictor of Organizational and Electoral Behavior Among Latino Immigrants. *Hispanic Journal of Behavioral Sciences, 18*, 194–213.

Escobar, C. (2004). Dual Citizenship and Political Participation: Migrants in the Interplay of United States and Colombian Politics. *Latino Studies, 2*, 45–69.

Garcia, J. (1981). Political Integration of Mexican Immigrants: Explorations into the Naturalization Process. *International Migration Review, 15*, 608–625.

Grebler, L. (1966). The Naturalization of Mexican Immigrants in the United States. *International Migration Review, 1*, 17–32.

Hill, K. A., & Moreno, D. (1996). Second Generation Cubans. *Hispanic Journal of Behavioral Sciences, 18*, 175–193.

Hondagneu-Sotelo, P. (1994). *Gendered Transitions, Mexican Experiences of Immigration*. Los Angeles: University of California Press.

Hondagneu-Sotelo, P. (2003). Gender and Immigration, a Retrospective and Introduction. In P. Hondagneu-Sotelo (Ed.), *Gender and U.S. Immigration, Contemporary Trends* (pp. 3–19). Berkeley: University of California Press.

Huntington, S. P. (2004). *Who Are We? The Challenges to American National Identity*. New York: Simon and Schuster.

Jennings, M. K., & Markus, G. S. (1984). Partisan Orientations over the Long Haul: Results from the Three-Wave Political Socialization Panel Study. *American Political Science Review, 78*, 1000–1018.

Johnson, M., Stein, R. M., & Wrinkle, R. (2003). Language Choice, Residential Stability, and Voting Among Latino Americans. *Social Science Quarterly, 84*, 412–424.

Jones-Correa, M. (1998). *Between Two Nations: THE POLITICAL PREDICAMENT of Latinos in New York City*. Ithaca, NY: Cornell University Press.

Jones-Correa, M. (2001). Under Two Flags: Dual Nationality in Latin America and Its Consequences for Naturalization in the United States. *International Migration Review, 35*, 997–1029.

Jones-Correa, M., & Leal, D. (2001). Political Participation: Does Religion Matter? *Political Research Quarterly, 54*, 751–770.

Leal, D. L. (2002). Political Participation by Latino Non-citizens in the United States. *British Journal of Political Science, 32*, 353–370.

Long, J. S. (1997). Regression Models for Categorical and Limited Dependent Variables. *Advanced Quantitative Techniques in the Social Sciences*. (Vol. 7). Thousand Oaks, CA: Sage Publications.

McFadden, R. (2006, April 10). Protests Staged for Immigrants Across the U.S. *The New York Times*. p. A1.

Pachon, H. (1987). An Overview of Citizenship in the Hispanic Community. *International Migration Review, 21*, 299–310.

Pachon, H., & DeSipio, L. (1994). *New Americans by Choice: Political Perspectives of Latino Immigrants*. Boulder, CO: Westview Press.

Pantoja, A. D. (2005). Transnational Ties and Immigrant Political Incorporation: The Case of Dominicans in Washington Heights, New York. *International Migration, 43*, 123–146.

Pantoja, A. D., Ramirez, R., & Segura, G. M. (2001). Citizens by Choice, Voters by Necessity: Patterns in Political Mobilization by Naturalized Latinos. *Political Research Quarterly, 54*, 729–750.

Portes, A., & Curtis, J. W. (1987). Changing Flags: Naturalization and Its Determinants Among Mexican Immigrants. *International Migration Review, 21*, 352–371.

Portes, A., & Mozo, R. (1985). The Political Adaptation Process of Cubans and Other Ethnic Minorities in the United States: A Preliminary Analysis. *International Migration Review, 19*, 35–63.

Ramakrishnan, K., & Espenshade, T. (2001). Immigrant Incorporation and Political Participation in the United States. *International Migration Review, 35*, 870–909.

Verba, S., Schlozman, K. L., & Brady, H. (1995). *Voice and Equality: Civic Voluntarism in American Politics*. Cambridge, MA: Harvard University Press.

Wong, Janelle, & Tseng, Vivian (2007). Political Socialisation Within Immigrant Families: Challenging Parental Socialisation Models. *Journal of Ethnic and Migration Studies*.

Wrinkle, R. D., Stewart, J., Jr., Polinard, J. L., Meier, K. J., & Arvizu, J. R. (1996). Ethnicity and Nonelectoral Political Participation. *Hispanic Journal of Behavioral Sciences, 18*, 142–153.

Yang, P. Q. (1994). Explaining Immigrant Naturalization. *International Migration Review, 28*, 449–477.

CHAPTER 23

Political Mobilization and Activism Among Latinos/as in the United States

Christian Zlolniski

INTRODUCTION

It is a sunny Sunday on April 9, 2006 in Dallas when we arrive downtown to attend a massive rally in favor of immigrants' rights. Organized by the League of United Latin American Citizens (LULAC) and many other Latino organizations, the march has attracted around 500,000 people, the largest march in the city's history. The rally, like many others organized across the country, came at a moment of fierce political struggle in Washington and against a House proposal to further criminalize undocumented immigrants and people who assist them. The demonstrations represent the largest effort by immigrants in recent memory to influence public policy, and many immigrant advocates have described them as the beginning of a new, largely Hispanic civil rights movement. While we wait in front of the Cathedral Santuario de Guadalupe, a major symbol for Mexicans and other Latinos, the crowd chants and waves U.S. flags in response to a call by LULAC and other organizations to display symbols of patriotism and avoid the use of Mexican flags that could antagonize their opponents. Under the heat of the sun, dozens of ice cream and other street vendors also wait for the march to start, carrying their own banners and selling their merchandise in the meantime. Security agents can be seen on top of the downtown skyscrapers watching the marchers, many of whom, following the recommendations of the organizers, wear white T-shirts to symbolize the peaceful tone of the rally.

After a long wait and when Mass at the Guadalupe church ends, people finally start marching amid a happy explosion of chants and the waving of flags and banners. "Si se puede" (Yes we can),

"Latinos unidos jamás serán vencidos" (Latinos united will never be defeated), "Hoy marchamos mañana no compramos" (Today we march, tomorrow we won't buy) are some of the most common slogans people enthusiastically chant. Although well planned and organized, the march does not have a central or charismatic leader and, instead, has a bottom-up, grassroots quality that surprises organizers and opponents alike, it is clearly a march in which working-class people are the main protagonists taking over the streets, bringing their children and families along, and chanting to make their feelings and demands heard in a peaceful but resolute manner. Indeed, the march is marked by a rather festive tone, with many families pushing baby strollers and walking with their relatives and friends. Many people carry banners distributed by LULAC that read "Justicia y dignidad para todos los inmigrantes" (Justice and dignity for all immigrants), whereas others have brought their own home-made signs to express their own feelings and messages.

A young woman wearing shorts and a white hat carries a sign that reads "We are not delinquents! We are only here to work! We only ask for legal status," whereas a large banner carried out by several people declares "We don't want to be separated from our family. We support the economy in this country so don't kick us out." The mix of creativity and humor shows up in a huge, two-sided banner that says "Immigrants work 2 hard 2 serve you!" with pictures in the corners of "Burro Bueno," "Taco Bells," "Wendys," and so forth, and the opposite side depicts a landscaper and a construction worker asks "Who will mow your lawns and build homes?" Some banners use classic Latino religious symbols, including several that portray the Virgin of Guadalupe; others that are carried by pastors of Protestant congregations depict brief passages from the Bible urging people to be compassionate toward immigrants: "If being an immigrant is a crime may God forgive US all." Showing that the march is not just about parents mobilizing on behalf of their families but also about children and teenagers mobilizing on behalf of their undocumented immigrant parents, a boy in his early teens walks alongside his parents with a white T-shirt that exclaims "We do pay taxes. Don't mess with my dad!!" We also see several groups of teenagers in the rally speaking and chanting in English and Spanish and often using their cell phones to call and coordinate with relatives and friends, revealing the creative use of this modern technology for political purposes.

What explains this march? What caused such an unprecedented crowd to take to the streets of downtown Dallas, a city known for its conservative political environment? What does this and other political demonstrations organized around the country on behalf of immigrants' rights say about Latino grassroots social movements and protest politics today? And how does this movement fit with the history and tradition of Latino political mobilization in the past? This chapter seeks to address these questions and provide an explanation of the main issues that have driven activism among Latinos in the United States over the past few decades. Rather than focusing on the history of Latino grassroots groups, which is well examined in other places, I will focus on the building of a pan-Latino grassroots movement in the past 15 years. My purpose is to examine pan-Latino grassroots community politics since the 1980s, the themes that have ignited such movements, and the concepts and theoretical frameworks that have been used to study protest politics among Latinos in the United States. I also seek to discuss the emergence of the new movement for immigrants' rights and outline the continuities and differences with earlier civil and political struggles on behalf of Chicanos and other Latino groups in the 1960s and 1970s.

I argue that we cannot understand this movement solely as a progression of the civil rights movement and demographic growth of Latinos per se. Instead, economic globalization and the emergence of a transnational immigrant labor are crucial to understanding the timing, demands, political strategies, and nature of this movement. Thus, we might be witnessing the infancy of a new movement at the turn of the 21st century to redefine the very nature of citizenship in which immigrants claim rights as legitimate members of society and polity, similar to the struggle for civil rights for "minority" populations in the 1960s.

The chapter is divided into five sections. First, I provide a brief sketch to situate Latino protest politics in historical perspective. Then I discuss the similarities and differences that characterize political activism by different Latino subgroups. In the third section, I focus on the role of women in grassroots community organizing and the gendered theoretical perspective that has been used to study Latinas' grassroots politics. The fourth section discusses the role of religion and the Catholic Church in the history of Latino social movements, and in the fifth section, I examine the contemporary movement for immigrants' rights and the emergence of transnational forms of immigrants' political mobilization. In the conclusion, I outline new directions in the study of Latino social and political activism and a few key issues for future research.

HISTORICAL ANTECEDENTS

Grassroots political mobilization refers to the different forms of nonelectoral political activism by which both citizens and people officially excluded from a polity seek to express their concerns and demands by shaping the decision-making process on issues that are of central importance to them. Often recognized under a variety of names such as protest politics, community organizing, community-level politics, and others, it is considered a key dimension of the way by which minority and low-income groups participate in the political arena as well as a central political resource for these groups (Magana & Mejia, 2004, p. 58). In the case of Latinos, community politics often takes different forms, including the formation of political organizations to seek goods and services, loosely organized groups formed around a shared sense of religious, cultural, and national origin identities, and community organizations that bring people together around common demands (DeSipio, 2004, pp. 439–440). Moreover, grassroots mobilizations can also take place at different levels. In the case of Latino immigrants in the United States, Gustavo Cano distinguished three levels of political action: local-neighborhood, dealing with issues like housing, education, health, and others; local-community, dealing with city and state issues; and national-community, dealing with broader issues of immigrants' legalization, immigration policy, and others (Cano, 2002, p. 23). However, although there is a common agreement that community politics is a central avenue through which Latinos/as channel their demands and concerns, especially in the case of immigrants excluded from participating in electoral politics, the study of grassroots politics has received considerably less academic attention and scrutiny compared to Latino socialization and behavior in electoral politics. As a result, the concepts and theoretical tools to interpret the different forms of protest politics are still loosely developed, often borrowing from the literature on social movements by political sociologists.[1]

If theoretization of Latinos grassroots politics has not been extensively developed, the discussion of the periodization of Latino protest politics has attracted considerably greater attention. The history of Latino grassroots organizations in the United States is both long and dynamic, as these organizations date back to the 19th century and are found in many communities where Latinos reside (García, 2003, p. 160). Lisa Magana and Armando Mejia (2004) provided a historical framework that, despite small differences with those proposed by other authors, identifies five major stages in the history of Latino grassroots politics. The first "era" started in 1848 in response to the Anglo takeover of Hispanic lands by force and the subsequent experience of and reaction to the processes of economic, social, and political subordination and discrimination. Rampant poverty and open discrimination, along with the difficulty of developing a well-organized resistance movement, explain the emergence of social-banditry, a loosely organized and individualistic form of armed resistance characteristic of times of great economic and social change and illustrated by iconic figures of Mexican American history such as Gregorio Cortez, Tiburcio Vazquez, and Joaquin Murieta (Magana & Mejia, 2004, p. 63). The second period of Latino protest politics covers the first three decades of the 20th century, an epoch characterized by the proliferation of mutual aid societies among Mexicans and Puerto Ricans and the effervescence of labor activism. During this time, immigrants from Mexico, Cuba, and Puerto Rico began to settle throughout the United States, forming large communities in many U.S. cities (Magana & Mejia, 2004, p. 60). For example, Mexicans in the Southwest started forming mutual aid societies such as the Alianza Hispano Americana, the Sociedad Progresista Mexicana, and others that provided help in times of need to laborers and their families, including death benefits, financial assistance during sickness, and help for important family events like baptisms and weddings, whereas Puerto Ricans also formed their own mutual aid societies in New York, Philadelphia, and Chicago to provide health care assistance, legal aid, and social services for their fellow immigrants (Magana & Mejia, 2004, p. 65). The third stage in Latino grassroots politics started with the post-World War II generation from the 1940s to the early 1960s led by groups like LULAC and the American GI Forum, organizations that were made up of war veterans claiming equality and struggling against discrimination in education, housing, and employment. In addition to using the court system, Mexican American war veterans also engaged in grassroots organized movements to protest racial discrimination, labor exploitation, police abuse, and housing segregation, using newspapers such as *La Opinion* and *El Espectador* to vent their demands and organizations like the Asociación Nacional Mexico-Americana (ANMA) to protest unfair labor practices (Magana & Mejia, 2004, p. 70).

In the context of the history of Latino protest politics, most scholars agree that the civil rights era of the 1960s and 1970s represents a watershed in both the nature and magnitude of mass mobilizations among Latinos. In contrast to the more moderate approach of the former generation of war veterans, this stage was characterized by more militant efforts that challenged the status quo to bring immediate and tangible change. Charismatic leaders like Cesar Chavez—who along with Dolores Huerta led the first successful large-scale union organization of farm workers in California and founded the National Farm Workers of America (NFWA)—were pioneers in the use of innovative and effective political tactics such as boycotts, pilgrimages, hunger strikes, and others that not only mobilized thousands of Mexican workers but also galvanized the attention of the media and Anglo sympathizers beyond the Latino community, tactics that would dramatically change the approach to Latino protest politics for decades to come. Chicano students participated in massive school "blowouts" to demand quality education, the end of discrimination in public schools, the right to speak Spanish, and the establishment of a Mexican American curriculum in high schools and colleges throughout the Southwest (Acuña, 1972), whereas Puerto Ricans engaged in different forms of political activism and founded groups like the Young Lords to protest police oppression and to demand better education, employment opportunities, and independence of their homeland from the United States (Magana & Mejia, 2004, pp. 70–71).

The final period of political mobilization among Latinos covers the 1980s to the present. Discussed in further detail below, this period is characterized by three trends: the large growth of immigrants as part of the Latino population and the formation of local and transnational grassroots groups in which they play a central activist role; the consolidation of a pan-ethnic Latino political movement that brings together increasingly heterogeneous Latino subgroups; and the reemergence of street politics and activism that was in decline since the end of the civil rights era. In addition to the traditional big three Latino groups (Mexican- Americans, Puerto Ricans, and Cubans), the new period has witnessed a growing diversity of Latino subgroups, including

Central Americans, Dominicans, Colombians, as well as smaller groups of South Americans (Magana & Mejia, 2004, p. 76). Authors like Armando Navarro (2005) interpreted the resurgence of Latino political activism since the mid-1990s as a response to an anti-immigrant political climate and the revival of White nativism in the United States along with a pan-Latinoism predicated on Latin American immigrants' shared cultural and historical experience.

DIVERSITY AMONG LATINO SUBGROUPS' PROTEST POLITICS

Whereas in the recent past community-based activism among Latinos has evolved as a pan-ethnic political phenomenon predicated under a single ethnic identity label, it is important to differentiate the types of concern addressed by each of the Latino groups. Thus, Mexican Americans have a long history of grassroots activism. Their social activism started with mutual aid societies that became vehicles to mobilize the community around basic working-class issues while serving to promote ethnic solidarity and pride (Navarro, 2004, pp. 94–95). In the history of Mexican American grassroots activism, community-based organizations have played a central role, especially since the movement for civil rights in the 1970s. Community organizations were modeled after the famous Industrial Areas Foundation (IAF) founded by the legendary urban activist Saul Alinsky in Chicago, an organization that developed an exemplary and effective model of grassroots mobilizing based on direct action and confrontation tactics, concrete and multipurpose goals, coalition- building, leadership development, and close cooperation with religious congregations (García, 2003, pp. 161–162). IAF served as a model for numerous Mexican American groups for years to come, including Community Services Organization (CSO) in Southern California, Communities Organized for Public Service (COPS) in San Antonio (1974), United Neighborhood Organization (UNO) in Los Angeles (1976), and Valley Interfaith and El Paso Inter-Faith Service Organization in Texas (García, 2003, p. 162). Using local parishes to build a large membership, these organizations mobilized thousands of Latino parents and families around concerns such as housing, social services, police brutality, use of redevelopment funds in large cities, and others, and they benefited from strong leadership by Catholic priests who provided moral and political legitimacy in the public arena.

If Mexican Americans' political activism has been critically shaped by their experience of economic, social, and political subordination and discrimination since the mid-19th century, what Gutiérrez (2004) called the "legacy of conquest," the political mobilization by Puerto Ricans is largely the result of the historical experience of colonization of their homeland by Spain and the United States and racial discrimination of Puerto Ricans in the United States. Particularly in the Northeast and Midwest, Puerto Ricans have historically supported a struggle for independence (Navarro, 2004, p. 105), whereas in California there is also evidence of organized movement toward independence despite its smaller Puerto Rican population (Rodriguez, 1999). The Puerto Rican movement for independence picked up in the 1970s and was led by a group of organizations such as the Young Lords Party, The Puerto Rican Socialist Party (PSP), El Comité-Puerto Rican National Left Movement, and others (Navarro, 2004, p. 106). At the time, young Puerto Ricans also formed organizations like the Puerto Rican Community Development Project and other community-based groups to play a role in civic politics in New York, New Jersey, Chicago, Philadelphia and other U.S. cities (Santiago-Valles & Jiménez-Muñóz, 2004, p. 99).

In the late 1970s, Puerto Ricans started to mobilize in Chicago alongside Mexican Americans under the pan-ethnic "Latino" label to gain political muscle and push for improvements in their community. As Padilla has shown (1985), this watershed moment in the history of Latino grassroots struggles played a key role in the construction of a unified Latino political consciousness and front. After this era of radical politics, Puerto Rican protest politics has centered on other issues, most recently the struggle for the demilitarization of the island of Vieques by the U.S. Navy and the improvement of the employment and living conditions of working-class Puerto Ricans living in inner cities like New York (Navarro, 2004, pp. 108–109). An example is ASPIRA, a long-standing Puerto Rican organization that focuses on educational issues, usually in the Northeast (García, 2003, p. 163). Young Puerto Rican students have also organized to protest the dismantling of bilingual education and push for Puerto Rican and Latino studies college programs (Santiago-Valles & Jiménez-Muñóz, 2004, p. 110). These protests take place in the context of economic restructuring that has led to economic and social polarization between lighter-complexioned middle-class Puerto Rican *blanquitos* and the majority of working-poor black Puerto Ricans (Santiago-Valles & Jiménez-Muñóz, 2004, p. 123).

Dominicans are one of the Latino immigrant groups that are more invested in mobilizing in home-country affairs. They have traditionally mobilized in both the United States and the home country over issues that affect Dominicans in both countries, particularly migration, law enforcement, and local problems affecting the urban communities where they live (Navarro, 2004, p. 110). Political activism among Dominicans developed especially since the 1980s and its success is largely due to their organizational skills that have led them to become key players in civic affairs in cities like New York, with a large concentration of first- and second-generation Dominican immigrants (Navarro, 2004, p. 110). From an analytical perspective, Dominican activists have been characterized as truly transnational political actors, those who are active in civic and nonelectoral political affairs both in their home and host countries by belonging to hometown associations that support community improvement projects in the island and by participating in civic politics under pan-Latino organizations in cities like New York (Levitt, 2004).

Contrary to general wisdom, Cubans' political activism is far from monolithic and depends on both ethno-cultural identity (belonging to a specific generation of Cuban Americans) and socioeconomic status. Cuban immigrant politics has traditionally been controlled by Cuban exiles of the post-1959 migration to the United States focused on undermining and eventually overthrowing the Castro regime in their homeland (Garcia, 2004). Yet, since the 1970s an immigrant-focused group has developed that is more concerned with improving life in the United States, especially for young and second-generation Cuban immigrants (Navarro, 2004, p. 100). For example, in Miami, organizations such as the Spanish American League Against Discrimination (SALAD) focused on fighting discrimination against Cubans and other Latinos, a controversial topic for older, first-wave Cuban exiles (Navarro, 2004, p. 100). The first generation—the exile generation—more clearly identifies with the homeland and organizes its political efforts to destabilize the Castro regime, whereas the 1.5 generation—those born in Cuba but who came of age in the United States—regard themselves as both Cuban and American and are therefore more active in civic affairs in their host communities. The latter group often holds less conservative political values than their parents and are more likely to identify with a pan-ethnic label such as "Hispanic" or "Latino" (García, 2004, pp. 174–175).[2] In the late 1990s, Cuban Americans mobilized around the so-called Elian Gonzalez case when the U.S. Cost Guard rescued a 6-year-old Cuban boy whose mother had perished while trying to reach U.S. soil, after which a controversy erupted about whether the boy should be returned to his father in Cuba or given refuge in the United States (Navarro, 2004, p. 104).

Whereas the political activism led by Mexican Americans, Puerto Ricans, and, to a lesser extent, Cubans and Dominicans have attracted considerable attention, activism by Central Americans is more recent and novel, has received comparatively less attention, and yet provides an important example of a relatively new but politically engaged Latino immigrant group. Indeed, Central Americans have emerged as central political actors since the 1980s as the result of the surge of immigration from the region fueled by political and economic displacement and violence. Salvadoran and Guatemalan activist immigrants with previous experience in grassroots activism in peasant and labor movements, Christian-based communities, and human rights organizations, among others, started arriving in California and, capitalizing on such political experience, they provided valuable leadership to Latino political causes (Chinchilla & Hamilton, 2004). In addition to pressing for changes in U.S. foreign policies toward Central America, they formed numerous organizations and social service agencies to help fellow immigrants find emergency food, medical care, and jobs, and they raised funds to send help to their home countries, often with the help of local churches that provided a safe haven for them (Chinchilla & Hamilton, 2004). With support from religious-sector allies, academics, and others, Salvadoran activists also formed solidarity organizations such as CISPES (Committee in Solidarity with the People of El Salvador) and social service institutions such as the Central American Resource Center (CARECEN) in Los Angeles, Washington, and New York, and they participated in multifunctional mixed organizations and communities made up of Central American countries (Chinchilla & Hamilton, 2004, pp. 206–207). Salvadoran and Guatemalan immigrant activists were later joined by Hondurans and Nicaraguans in the 1980s to protest the inhumane conditions and violation of immigrant rights by the Immigration and Naturalization Service (INS), a political groundwork that paved the way for important victories such as the approval of the TPS (temporary protected status) for Salvadorans and Nicaraguans and asylum cases for Central Americans in the early 1990s. Later in the 1990s, Central American activists refocused their efforts to address the needs of established immigrants as well as new undocumented immigrants (Chinchilla & Hamilton, 2004).

An arena in which Central American activists have provided valuable leadership is labor union mobilizations, particularly in California. Thus, along with Mexican immigrants, Central Americans played a central role in the union drive to organize hotel workers in San Francisco, where Salvadoran workers were especially valued by union representatives because of their loyalty and militant attitude (Wells, 2000). Central American workers were also at the forefront of the movement to unionize garment workers in Los Angeles, capitalizing on their previous experience in political resistance and struggle in their home countries (Bonacich, 2000). Also, like other Latino immigrants, many Central Americans actively participate in hometown associations to provide help and assistance to their home communities, many of which are rural areas that have become highly dependent on both family remittances and help channeled through hometown associations to develop public projects (Chinchilla & Hamilton, 2004, p. 211). Over the past 15 years or so, Central American and immigrant-rights organizations have engaged in extensive advocacy around immigrant-focused initiatives at the local, state, and national levels. In short, since the 1980s, Central American immigrants have provided renewed energy and leadership to both labor unions and community-based organizations in the United States, helping to transform them and achieving leadership positions that in the past used to be in the hands of Mexican Americans and Mexican immigrants, especially in the Southwest.

Nonelectoral politics among South American Latinos is perhaps the most recent and therefore least studied case among all Latino subgroups. Yet, as the size of communities of South American Latinos, like Colombians and Ecuadorians, has grown, there has been a rise in grassroots organizations among them. Colombian organizations in the United States tend to mobilize primarily over domestic issues such as immigrant legalization, employment, and social services, and in 1995, several of these organizations created a political action committee named Coalición

Colombo Americana to lobby Congress, particularly the Hispanic Congressional Caucus (Navarro, 2004, p. 111). Colombians are also active in transnational organizations and practices that keep them closely tied to their home communities, which shape the agenda of the civic organizations they form in the United States, as the latter are often used to organize campaigns for political candidates in Colombia and to encourage immigrants to vote at their consulates in the United States (Espitia, 2004). The study of the political participation of Colombians, Peruvians, and Ecuadorians—the three largest South American groups—in civic and community organizations in the United States still remains largely uncharted territory.

In sum, it is important to distinguish the variety of issues that have attracted the attention of political organizations and mobilizations among different Latino subgroups. The particular historical experience of each group—particularly in terms of their colonized experience at the hands of the United States, the timing and conditions under which migration to the United States took place, as well as the groups' class and ethnic background—largely shapes the issues they address, their political tactics and ideologies, and their alliances with other groups. Despite these important differences, which clearly demonstrate that grassroots politics among Latinos is far from a monolithic field, two trends have gained strength since the late 1980s. First, there is a growing trend among these groups to unite under a single, inclusive pan-ethnic Latino umbrella to push their demands. As I will explain later, the consolidation of a single pan-Latino political identity label has been crucial for the organizational victories of Latino immigrants in both labor unions and community politics in the recent past and has, to a large extent, emerged as a response to the anti-immigrant political environment and neo-nativist movements on the rise since the 1990s. The second trend is the development of transnational forms of political activism among several Latino groups, particularly among Mexican, Central American, Dominican, and Colombian immigrants, many of whom are politically invested in pushing for change in their homelands through hometown associations and other organizations. As Navarro (2004, p. 99) argued, with globalization has come a new form of grassroots organization, one that transcends national boundaries by involving Latino immigrants in the social and political affairs of both their homelands and host country of residence.

LATINA WOMEN IN COMMUNITY POLITICS

Without a doubt, Latina women have been at the forefront of grassroots social and political activism in most Latino subgroups. They have provided the glue that keeps community organizing together, playing a key leadership role in many local grassroots organizations, recruiting members through their kin and social networks, and serving as the bridge between local parishes, where community organizing often takes place, and the local community at large. The role of Latina women in defining the goals, strategies, and recruitment tools for community politics thus should not be underestimated. Yet, it was not until the early 1990s that a body of literature led by feminist Latina scholars started to challenge the male bias that traditionally had prevailed in the field of Latino politics, which both traditionally disregarded locally based community activism in favor of more formal, institutionalized electoral politics, and ignored the role of Latinas in grassroots organizing (Hardy-Fanta, 1993; Pardo, 1998).

The concept of triple oppression according to which Latina women are subordinated because of their race, gender, and the patriarchal nature of Latino culture is at the heart of feminist studies on Latina political activism. Whereas in the past, common wisdom used the notion of women's segregation as a key factor to explain the low level of participation of Latina women in electoral politics, a theoretical position that served to reinforce their image as passive and apolitical actors and to legitimate the lack of attention to the study of Latina politics, over the past 15 years Latina feminist scholars have turned this idea upside down, showing that sexism, racial, and gender subordination often push working-class Latinas to actively participate in community and political activism to challenge those very forces of their oppression. Most studies show that ethnicity and gender mutually interact in a dynamic fashion to foster a sense of political consciousness, which later translates into active and committed involvement in local civic and political activism.

Latina's style of community activism and political engagement is illustrated by Mothers of East Los Angeles (MELA) studied by Pardo (2000, 1998). In this case, women acted as neighborhood activists to avoid the construction of a prison in their neighborhood in Eastside Los Angeles, framing their civic activism as an extension of their familial responsibilities. Pardo (2000) viewed women's political activism as an "extra job" they take in addition to wage work and household caretaking, one in which politics is deeply shaped by their sense of motherhood as well as class and ethnic consciousness (p. 111). Hardy-Fanta's (1993) study of Latina political activism in Boston arrived at similar conclusions, showing that Puerto Rican, Dominican, and Central American Latina activities that traditionally have been interpreted as social are indeed political. For Latina women in Boston, community politics means building bridges between their private concerns and public issues, and, as in the case of Mexican American women studied by Pardo, politics is deeply embedded in their everyday lives and is an interpersonal phenomenon. Like Pardo, Hardy-Fanta challenged the narrow view that reduces (Latina) politics to electoral participation—an approach that tends to portray women as passive and submissive.

Other studies have also documented women's activism in community-based organizations in different Latino subgroups. Norma Chinchilla and Nora Hamilton (2004), for example, have shown the leadership role played by Salvadoran women in Los Angeles in both labor unions and community organizations. Gabrielle Kohpahl (1998) has demonstrated that political activism not only included U.S. native-born Latinas and first-generation Latina immigrant mestizas but also indigenous Guatemala Maya immigrant women who actively participated in community organizations in Los Angeles. These, like other similar studies, showed that Latinas use their kin and social networks as basic recruiting tools for community organization and activism. An example is COPS, which has traditionally cultivated the leadership of women to address issues of family and neighborhood services that are of paramount importance to them (Ruiz, 2000). Many other organizations modeled after COPS, such as UNO in Los Angeles and People Acting in Community Together (PACT) in San Jose, also heavily depend on women both as leaders and recruiting agents to build a large and dense community base that can be mobilized at any time at the local level (Zlolniski, 2006). Despite the insights of all these recent studies, it would be a mistake, as Vicki Ruiz reminded us, to think that Latina political activism is a recent phenomenon, as indeed it goes back historically to earlier periods in Chicana history with *mutualista* associations such as La Asociación Hispano Americana, the Hijas de Maria, as well as labor unions like UCAPAWA (Ruiz, 2000, p. 27).

The close integration of family, work, and social and political activism in women's everyday lives is a key feature that characterizes Latina participation in community politics. Rather than an independent realm on its own, as is often the case of Latino participation in more institutionalized forms of politics, community politics for Latinas is so deeply interwoven with their work and family activities that it is difficult to identify the boundaries between all of these activities— a phenomenon called political familism by Maxine Baca Zinn (Ruiz, 2000, p. 21). According to this concept, women transform traditional social networks and resources into political weapons to improve living conditions in their local communities, showing a different and broader view of political participation than their male counterparts. By translating personal problems into social concerns to be resolved in the political arena, Latina women challenge established and narrow views of citizenship centered on participation in formal political institutions and electoral politics (Ruiz, 2000).

Women's political activism, however, should not be romanticized. Latina activists often have to overcome the resistance of their husbands and/or male relatives to become involved in political activities in the public arena, something that often produces family tensions. Not surprisingly, Latinas often do not frame their civic and community activism as political; instead, they tend to portray such community-oriented activities as a projection of their concern for their children and families. Rather than interpreting this as lack of political consciousness, it is often an indication of how women might use the public arena to challenge the very basis that keeps assigning them to the household sphere and to try to carve a space in the public domain to politicize their private, gender-based concerns (Hardy-Fanta, 1993; Pardo, 2000; Zlolniski, 2006).[3]

In view of the central role played by Latinas in community-based organizations, some authors argued there are clear gender differences in how Latina women and Latino men address and become involved in political participation. According to Hardy-Fanta, whereas Latina women's involvement in politics is characterized by a focus on building social connections, developing a sense of collectivity, and building links between the private and public spheres, Latino men tend to focus on formal positions and status, hierarchies, and formal structures in established and formal political organizations (1993, p. 36). Likewise, Jones-Correa's study of a Latino neighborhood in Queens, New York mostly inhabited by Dominicans and South American immigrants, finds clear gender patterns that distinguish the political involvement of Latina women versus Latino men. Jones-Correa (1998) argued that when Latino immigrant men lose social status as they incorporate in the job market, they seek to counteract this trend by joining ethnic-based organizations in which they retain positions of power and leadership and where their social status is upheld. In contrast, rather than joining traditional immigrant organizations where men maintain a monopoly over positions of power, Latina immigrant women prefer to join community-based organizations that seek to address the needs of their families and communities and where they gain political experience, participate in the decision-making process, and become intermediaries between state and government agencies and their families and communities. These and other studies further show the importance of a gender perspective in studying the political socialization and behavior of Latinas and Latinos in the United States.

RELIGION AND CHURCH-BASED ACTIVISM

As should be evident by now, Latino grassroots activism cannot be fully understood without taking into account the important historical role played by the Catholic Church. Stevens-Arroyo traced the history of the social and political involvement of the church to the 1950s with the emergence of the *cursillo*, a forum in which lay people working under the supervision of local priests discussed Catholic beliefs to bridge the gap between the clergy and the people (2004, pp. 313–315). He used the concept of "cultural religion" to refer to the close interrelationship between religion and culture within Latino communities that, among other results, fosters the involvement of the Catholic Church into community-related issues and activism (Stevens-Arroyo, 2004, pp. 305–306). Through the *cursillos*, many members become engaged in the cause for social justice during the Chicano Movement, and the Catholic Church also closely supported Puerto Rican groups like Young Lords in Philadelphia, mentoring them in political activism (Stevens-Arroyo, 2004, p. 315).

In a similar vein, Roberto Treviño (2006) has used the term "Ethno-Catholicism" to refer to Mexican Americans' own brand of Catholicism in which sacred and secular practices were deeply interwoven in their everyday lives in 20th-century Houston, helping to promote a sense of community, ethnic pride, and social solidarity while also fostering social and political activism at the local community level. For example, while enhancing spiritual life, parish societies—organizations formed by lay people in local churches such as the Society of Our Lady of Guadalupe, the *Socias del Altar*, and the *Socias del Sagrado Corazón*—also served to foment a sense of community and solidarity and a sense of social obligation to the needs of Mexican *colonias* by raising money in times of hardship and providing diverse community services (Treviño, 2006, pp. 66–70).

Key to the involvement of the Catholic Church in issues of social justice within the Latino community was the Campaign for Human Development that set up of a fund of several million dollars to support faith-based action groups at the grassroots level (Stevens-Arroyo, 2004, p. 318). The grant required petitioners to belong to grassroots groups and address social issues by direct community involvement (Stevens-Arroyo, 2004, p. 318). The reforms promoted by the Second Vatican Council helped to foster the direct involvement of the Catholic Church in social and political issues that concerned Mexican Americans, Puerto Ricans, and other Latino groups. An example are the "encuentros"—meetings that first started in 1972 under the leadership of Latino activist priests to provide a forum for the leaders of Spanish-speaking communities to present their grievances and needs (Treviño, 2006). The strength and density of church-based Latino groups has been such that, according to authors like Stevens-Arroyo, interfaith organizations have been more effective, stable, and resilient than many major Latino secular political groups such as La Raza Unida Party, Mecha, or the Young Lords, most of which were in clear decline in the post-civil rights era. Many of the Latino community-based organizations rooted in the activism of the 1960s and 1970s that drew extensive membership by building bridges with Catholic parishes, such as COPS and PICO, are still active, promoting political involvement to address the needs and demands of Latinos living in large urban communities (Stevens-Arroyo, 2004; Treviño, 2006, pp. 214–215). According to Stevens-Arroyo (2004, p. 334), today many Latino community organizations are more likely to be linked to churches than to political or labor associations, which is largely due to the church's ability to unite different ideologies under a single umbrella.[4]

An important change in the relation between religion and community activism in Latino communities is the rapid growth of evangelical Protestantism among Latinos since the 1980s. This growth has brought more heterogeneity in the religious practices of Mexican Americans and other Latinos who historically were mostly Catholic. The expansion of several evangelical Protestant denominations within the Latino community has important implications for the future involvement of Latinos in social and political activism, as evangelical Protestantism is generally less inclined toward grassroots community action. Yet, some preliminary evidence seems to indicate that, contrary to common wisdom, the rise of Latino evangelical Protestantism is fostering a collective social consciousness and seeks to combat certain social problems that affect urban Mexican Americans and Puerto Ricans, such as alcoholism, drug abuse, and domestic violence (Díaz-Stevens & Stevens-Arroyo, cited by Treviño, 2006, p. 215). It remains to be seen, however, whether the expansion of evangelical Protestantism among Latinos will foster a renewed sense of community involvement and activism or, instead, as one could argue, foster a less political approach by narrowly focusing on individuals and families as the vehicles to address social problems—an approach more in consonance with today's neo-liberal political ideology.

TOWARD A NEW MOVEMENT FOR LATINO IMMIGRANTS' RIGHTS?

Whereas grassroots political activism has a long history among Latinos, the social movement for human and civil rights of Latino immigrants is more recent. Indeed, we can trace the development of a new movement for immigrants' rights to the 1980s. This movement is the result of the mutual interaction of several factors, including the demographic growth of the Latino immigrant population, anti-immigrant political climate and legislation, the resurgence of nativist groups and organizations around the country, and the political maturation of numerous Latino organizations that, along with new transnational immigrant organizations, seek to redefine notions of immigrants' labor, civil, and political rights.

Whereas White nativism has a long history in the United States, anti-Latino immigrant nativist feelings go back to the mid-1970s (Navarro, 2005), a trend that has continued into the 2000s. Yet, as Wayne Cornelius (2002) has shown, unlike in the past when anti-immigrant political climate oscillated in consonance with the broader economic environment and was most vitreous during harsh economic times, in the recent past White nativism has become decoupled from the economic climate and, instead of being expressed in racial terms, is more often cast in ethno-cultural terms, a form of cultural racism. Indeed, a series of U.S. immigration legislation measures along with both federal- and state-level initiatives to deter further (Latino) immigration reveal the growing anti-immigrant political climate. For example, since the mid-1990s, there has been an increasing militarization of the U.S.-Mexico border with Operations Gatekeeper, Safeguard, and Rio Grande. This trend, which sociologist Timothy Dunn has termed "low-intensity conflict," is characterized by a dramatic increase of military technology and human resources deployed at the U.S.-Mexico border and is directly connected to the sharp rise in deaths along the border over the past decade, especially in the Arizona desert. At the federal level, the escalation of anti-immigrant legislation is illustrated by the Illegal Immigrant Reform and Immigrant Responsibility Act (IIRIRA), approved in 1996, which further penalized undocumented immigrants, diminished the rights of legal immigrants and called for tighter control of the border with Mexico. At the state level, White nativism has also escalated, especially in California, where, since the mid-1990s, several anti-Latino immigrant propositions have been approved. Proposition 187, for example, sought to deny public education, health, and other services to undocumented immigrants. Meanwhile, in an effort to make the lives of undocumented immigrants as harsh as possible, many states with large Latino immigrant populations started changing their laws to deny driver's licenses to undocumented immigrants. And at the local level, several cities have passed ordinances to fine landlords who rent their properties to undocumented immigrants. White nativism was also evident in the rise of vigilante groups such as the Minuteman Project founded in 2005 that sent thousands of civilians to patrol the U.S.-Mexico border (Navarro, 2005). Furthermore, since the attacks of September 11, the issue of immigration has become increasingly interwoven with issues of national security in the national political discourse, leading to renewed calls by nativists to seal the border and further criminalize undocumented immigrants.

The anti-immigrant political climate and legislation, along with the resurgence of ethno-cultural nativism, has increasingly prompted the reactions among Latino grassroots organizations active since the late 1990s. The issue of immigration has indeed become the heart of the agenda of Latino political activism and mobilization since the 2000s because of the perception that Latino immigrants are used as scapegoats of many economic and social problems in the United States. This is what Louis DeSipio (2004) called the "primordial tie," referring to the mobilizing effects that immigration as a political issue has on most Latinos today (p. 454). For example, Proposition 187 prompted Latino mobilization in 1994, including several rallies in Los Angeles and Southern

California that involved several thousand people, students' walkouts, and one of the largest demonstrations to date in San Diego. Another issue that prompted massive protest was the veto of Senate Bill 60 (SB60) in California that would have allowed undocumented immigrants to obtain driver's licenses. Introduced by Gil Cedillo and passed in 2002 but vetoed by California Governor Davis, the veto led to the California One-Day Latino boycott in December 12, 2003 that used Latino economic power as a weapon for social change (Navarro, 2005).

The current movement for immigrants' rights has contributed to the consolidation of a pan-ethnic Latino identity and coalition to a degree never before seen. According to Armando Navarro (2005), the strength of the contemporary pan-Latino identity reflects a generational change in which the Hispanic generation (1975–1999) that followed the Chicano generation and was individual oriented, anti-immigrant, and politically conservative has been replaced by a new Mexican generation that has a large component of young foreign-born immigrants and tends to be more militant, cultural pluralist, and politically progressive than its predecessor. However, the strength and effervescency of the contemporary movement for Latino immigrants' rights is also the result of the political symbiosis between experienced leaders and organizations of the Mexican American generation and the Chicano era, and a new cadre of young Latino immigrant activists and organizations that have infused the movement with new blood and members. Just as the rejuvenation of labor unions in the service sector is largely due to the growth of Latino immigrant workers among the rank and file, the reinvigoration of community organizations and grassroots protest politics centered on immigration policy has benefited from the active role by thousands of Latino immigrants across the country (Zlolniski, 2006).

There are other important features that characterize the current movement for immigrants' rights, some of which are novel and seem to distinguish it from earlier forms of Latino protest politics. The first is the central role played by transnational immigrant organizations to mobilize immigrants at the grassroots. Unlike traditional Latino ethnic organizations centered on combating racial discrimination and enhancing civic rights for the Latino population as a whole, transnational immigrant organizations, such as hometown associations, are most often founded by first-generation immigrants to address needs and concerns in their home countries. Transnational immigrants—those who actively engage into social and political practices across national borders—are at the forefront of these organizations. Through hometown and home-state associations, transnational immigrants raise money to finance public projects in their home communities. Hometown groups and Latino organizations often pursue different political agendas, and whereas the latter emphasize civil rights and electoral politics in the United States, immigrant transnational organizations seek to address needs and concerns in the home communities of their members (Goldring, 2002). Yet, increasingly, hometown associations have become involved in political issues concerning the civil rights of immigrants in the United States, such as workers' rights, education, and getting driver's licenses for undocumented immigrants (Cano, 2002). They also serve as vehicles for claiming what Luin Goldring (2002) calls "substantive membership and citizenship"—that is, *de facto* forms of participation and membership claims not limited to the traditional notion of citizenship in their country of origin.

Second, the current movement lacks a clear and central leadership and, instead, consists of a loose coalition of dozens of Latino and immigrant organizations trying to respond to the demands for action by a mobilized base, a sign of a truly grassroots movement. The movement has not yet produced highly visible leaders as those of the Chicano era, but their emergence in the future could help to give it further unity and strength. Also, unlike the Chicano movement characterized by strident nationalism and even separatist notions, the current pan-Latino movement is much more inclusive, with a strong undertone of patriotism, which might reflect the shift to a conservative political climate in the country.

Third, the mobilization for immigrants' rights cannot be fully understood without the Spanish-speaking media, which since the 1990s has become a central player in orchestrating and mobilizing grassroots protests. Local Hispanic television news (Telemundo and Univisión) as well as Spanish radio stations in large cities like Los Angeles, San Diego, Dallas, and others play a central role in familiarizing the immigrant community with itself, making them aware of the problems they share in common, energizing them to mobilize, and disseminating important information on plans for street demonstrations. Another novel element found in the movement for immigrants' rights is the use of modern communication technologies like cell phones to coordinate mobilizations quickly and efficiently. Young Latinos in particular, a central constituency of the current movement, are making a savvy use of these technologies as tools to recruit people through their kin and social networks as well as to plan and coordinate, in a precise manner, rallies and other demonstrations. The use of these technologies enhances the grassroots potential of this movement and builds upon a long tradition of Latino grassroots mobilizations of using family, social networks, and word of mouth to recruit people.

In sum, the new Latino immigrants' rights movement signals the consolidation of a pan-Latino solidarity that includes traditional groups from the civil rights era, immigrant-based organizations and hometown associations, and interfaith groups with a political strategy that combines rallies and mass demonstrations with boycotts and sporadic strikes that use a nonconfrontational approach and a symbolic display of American patriotism. If the strategies are not as radical as those used during the Chicano generation, the political agenda is indeed ambitious, challenging the social and political exclusion of Latino immigrants and redefining the very notions of membership and citizenship by claiming immigrants' rights as basic universal and human rights. If the 1960s is generally recognized as the watershed for gaining basic civic and political rights for Mexican American and other minority groups, the early 21st century could be the next stage for basic human and civil rights for immigrants as legitimate members of U.S. society as well as other industrialized countries with substantive immigrant populations, thus significantly redefining the legal and political meanings of membership in a nation-states.

CONCLUSION

Latino grassroots politics has a long history that goes back to the mid-19th century and is a central vehicle through which Latinos, especially the working class, have traditionally channeled their political demands and concerns. Yet, the study of Latino political mobilization has focused on the empirical description of the organizations, factors, causes, goals, and strategies used by the different groups involved at the expense of a theoretical framework through which to analyze the historical diversity of Latino social movements and protest politics. As a result and compared to electoral politics, Latino grassroots politics is still an underdeveloped field in which theoretical work has not kept pace with the changes in the goals, issues, leadership style, political strategies, and symbols used in Latino mobilization, particularly in the change to a pan-ethnic Latino political movement. In light of the current movement for immigrants' rights, there is a renewed need to address these shortcomings and further develop this field of study. Two lines of inquiry could help advance the theoretical work of Latino protest politics. First, there is an urgent need to move beyond the often parochial flavor that characterizes the study of Latino grassroots politics and situate it in the larger picture of social movements that emerge in the context and as a response to globalization. The analysis of the emergent movement for immigrants' rights particularly needs to develop a structural approach that highlights the political opportunities and limitations that Latino immigrants face today in the context of economic globalization and transnational migration. A promising lead in this regard can be found in the work by Rodolfo Torres and George Katsiaficas (1999), who rightly argue for the need to study Latino social movements in relation to changes in the U.S. political economy and the international division of labor rather than solely emphasizing cultural and identity issues. As globalization and transnational migration give impetus to new forms of social movements, we also need to develop a comparative approach between Latino nonelectoral politics in the United States and similar protest movements in Europe and elsewhere.

Second, there is the need to better connect the study of Latino protest politics with the academic literature on the concepts of membership and citizenship. The notion of "cultural citizenship" originally proposed by Renato Rosaldo—which seeks to expand the narrow view of citizenship as a legal issue to include a large array of civic, political, and cultural manifestations though which Latinos try to redefine the very notion of citizenship by claiming new spaces, voices, and rights in public arenas from which they are often excluded—can be quite fruitful in this regard (Flores & Benmayor, 1997). From this perspective, political activism and contestation cannot be reduced solely to the manifestation of social movements but also should include more subtle cultural practices that play an important role in creating social and cultural identity.[5] In a similar fashion Hondagneu-Sotelo, Gaudinez, Lara, & Ortz (2004, p. 137) have used the concept of postnational citizenship to interpret Latino immigrants' claims to work and residency rights by reference to wider notions of universal human rights and personhood rooted in religious beliefs. The notions of political and cultural citizenship can also serve to bridge the literature on Latino political activism developed from a social science perspective with the study of Latino cultural manifestations of identity and citizenship, a connection often lost in many studies that reduce Latino activism to the realm of either of these two analytical perspectives.

There are other research issues that the study of Latino protest politics should take into account. First, there is the need to pay further attention to the growing class polarization both within the Latino population as a whole and within each of the diverse Latino subgroups and to how such a process shapes the contours of grassroots politics. Just as we cannot take Latinos as a monolithic group but need to consider the important ethnic and cultural differences that distinguish them, so we need to develop a class-based analysis that allows us to better understand how class interests shape the goals, demands, political strategies, and symbols pursued and used by the large array of Latino groups and organizations active in grassroots politics. Second, we need to better understand the structural barriers that keep Latinos from participating in different forms of community and grassroots politics. The current optimistic view of the ability of Latinos to engage into massive political demonstrations should not obscure the fact that tremendous barriers still prevent many working-class Latinos/as from taking a more active role in protest politics, especially undocumented immigrants, whose potential deportability makes them extremely cautious in engaging in public activities that could strip them of their invisibility (Cano, 2002). Finally, there is also the need to further study the connection between Latino community politics and religion. As explained earlier, whereas the role of the Catholic Church in the history of Latino community politics has been well documented, the position of evangelical Protestant congregations with respect to Latino protest politics has received scant attention. In view of the rapid growth of Latinos, including many immigrants, who are joining evangelical congregations, we need to move beyond the stereotypical image of the Latinos as a monolithic Catholic population. Indeed, how the increasing heterogeneity of the religious affiliation of Latinos shapes their involvement in both electoral and nonelectoral politics should be a central issue for future research.

NOTES

1. For example, in a recent study of Latino protest politics, Sharon Navarro argued that the new social movements literature espoused by authors like Melucci is the most appropriate to interpret the goals and strategies of political activism by Latinos. According to this model, collective action by disenfranchised groups focuses on cultural and symbolic issues such as environmental, civil rights, sexual rights, and others related to ethnic identity rather than economic concerns alone (Navarro, 2004, p. 91).
2. For example, 1.5- and second-generation Cuban Americans are more likely to participate in pan-Latino organizations such as LULAC or create others on their own such as the Cuban National Planning Council, the Spanish American League Against Discrimination, and the National Coalition of Cuban Americans, which are focused on issues such as voting rights, employment, housing, education, and health (García, 2004, p. 178).
3. Hardy-Fanta (1993), for example, argued that motherhood is not a constraint for Latina involvement into community politics but, rather, a motivating factor that fuels them to seek solutions to their private concerns in the public arena using their socialization in political participation to promote their own self-development.
4. Despite the involvement of Catholic parishes in the struggle for racial equality and social justice in the Mexican American and the Latino community at large, the Catholic Church has been traditionally divided in two camps: the pastoralists and the liberationists. Pastoralists are interested in reforming church institutions, whereas the liberationists want the church to address the social needs of the community through social services and community agencies (Stevens-Arroyo, 2004, p. 334). Historically, the Latino Catholic Church has oscillated between these two positions, reflecting the political environment in the society at large. Whereas in the 1960s and 1970s the liberationist approach encountered a good reception among Latinos, in general, and Chicanos, in particular, the shift to a conservative political climate in the United States that started in the 1980s led to a decline of the church involvement in social causes and involvement (Treviño, 2006, p. 212). More recently, the Catholic Church is playing a central supportive role in the current movement, demanding a reform of U.S. immigration policy. For example, a national campaign called Justice for Immigrants was recently launched by the U.S. Conference of Catholic Bishops and other church organizations to fast, pray, and press for humane immigration reform (Watanabe, 2006).
5. William Flores, for example, interpreted the battle to extend the right to vote to undocumented immigrants as evidence of how immigrants are claiming legitimacy in a system in which they contribute economically and pay taxes but do not have political representation (Flores, 1997, p. 260).

REFERENCES

Acuña, Rodolfo. (1972). *Occupied America: The Chicano's Struggle Toward Liberation*. New York: Harper and Row.

Bonacich, Edna. (2000). Intense Challenges, Tentative Possibilities: Organizing Immigrant Garment Workers in Los Angeles. In Ruth Milkman (Ed.), *Organizing Immigrants: The Challenge for Unions in Contemporary California* (pp. 130–149). Ithaca, NY: Cornell University Press.

Cano, Gustavo. (2002, October). The Chicago-Houston Report: Political Mobilization of Mexican Immigrants in American Cities. Paper presented at the Research Seminar on Mexico and US-Mexican Relations, Center for U.S.-Mexican Studies, University of California, San Diego.

Chinchilla, Norma Stoltz, & Hamilton, Nora. (2004). Central American Immigrants: Diverse Populations, Changing Communities. In David G. Gutiérrez (Ed.), *The Columbia History of Latinos in the United States Since 1960* (pp. 187–228). New York: Columbia University Press.

Cornelius, Wayne A. (2002). Ambivalent Reception: Mass Public Responses to the 'New' Latino Immigration to the United States. In Marcelo Suárez-Orozco (Ed.), *Latinos: A Research Agenda for the 21st Century* (pp. 165–189). Berkeley: University of California Press.

Desipio, Louis. (2004). The Pressures of Perpetual Promise: Latinos and Politics, 1960–2003. In David G. Gutiérrez (Ed.), *The Columbia History of Latinos in the United States Since 1960* (pp. 421–465). New York: Columbia University Press.

Espitia, Marilyn. (2004). The Other "Other Hispanics": South American-Origin Latinos in the United States. In David G. Gutiérrez (Ed.), *The Columbia History of Latinos in the United States Since 1960* (pp. 257–280). New York: Columbia University Press.

Flores, William. (1997). Citizens vs. Citizenry: Undocumented Immigrants and Latino Cultural Citizenship. In William Flores & Rina Benmayor (Eds.), *Latino Cultural Citizenship: Claiming Identity, Space, and Rights* (pp. 255–278). Boston: Massachusetts.

Flores, William, & Benmayor, Rina. (1997). Introduction: Constructing Cultural Citizenship. In William Flores & Rina Benmayor (Eds.), *Latino Cultural Citizenship: Claiming Identity, Space, and Rights* (pp. 1–25). Boston: Massachusetts.

García, John A. (2003). *Latino Politics in America: Community, Culture, and Interests*. Oxford: Rowman & Littlefield.

García, María Cristina. (2004). Exiles, Immigrants, and Transnationals: The Cuban Communities of the United States. In David G. Gutiérrez (Ed.), *The Columbia History of Latinos in the United States Since 1960* (pp. 146–186). New York: Columbia University Press.

Goldring, Luin. (2002). The Mexican State and Transmigrant Organizations: Negotiating the Boundaries of Membership and Participation. *Latin American Research Review, 37*(3), 55–99.

Gutiérrez, David G. (2004). Globalization, Labor Migration, and the Demographic Revolution: Ethnic Mexicans in the Late Twentieth Century. In David G. Gutiérrez (Ed.), *The Columbia History of Latinos in the United States Since 1960* (pp. 43–86). New York: Columbia University Press.

Hardy-Fanta, Carol. (1993). *Latina Politics, Latino Politics: Gender, Culture and Political Participation in Boston*. Philadelphia: Temple University Press.

Hondagneu-Sotelo, P., Gaudinez, G., Lara, H., & Ortiz, B. (2004). "There's a Spirit that Transcends the Border": Faith, Ritual, and Postnational Protest at the U.S.-Mexico Border. *Sociological Perspectives, 47*(2), 133–159.

Jones-Correa, Michael. (1998). Different Paths: Gender, Immigration and Political Participation. *Immigration Research Review, 32*(2), 326–349.

Kohpahl, Gabrielle. (1998). *Voices of Guatemalan Women in Los Angeles: Understanding Their Immigration*. New York: Garland.

Levitt, Peggy. (2004). Transnational Ties and Incorporation: The Case of Dominicans in the United States. In David G. Gutiérrez (Ed.), *The Columbia History of Latinos in the United States Since 1960* (pp. 229–256). New York: Columbia University Press.

Magana, Lisa, & Mejia, Armando. (2004). Protest Politics. In Sharon Ann Navarro & Armando Xavier Mejia (Eds.), *Latino Americans and Political Participation: A Reference Handbook* (pp. 57–87). Santa Barbara, CA: ABC-CLIO.

Navarro, Armando. (2005). *Mexicano Political Experience in Occupied Aztlán: Struggles and Change*. Walnut Creek, CA: AltaMira Press.

Navarro, Sharon Ann. (2004). Interest Groups and Social Movements. In Sharon Ann Navarro & Armando Xavier Mejia (Eds.), *Latino Americans and Political Participation: A Reference Handbook* (pp. 89–119). Santa Barbara, CA: ABC-CLIO.

Padilla, Felix M. (1985). *Latino Ethnic Consciousness: The Case of Mexican Americans and Puerto Ricans in Chicago*. Notre Dame, IN: University of Notre Dame Press.

Pardo, Mary S. (1998). *Mexican American Women Activists: Identity and Resistance in Two Los Angeles Communities*. Philadelphia: Temple University Press.

Pardo, Mary S. (2000). Creating Community: Mexican American Women in Eastside Los Angeles. In Vicki L. Ruiz (Ed.), *Las Obreras: Chicana Politics of Work and Family* (pp. 107–135). Los Angeles: UCLA Chicano Studies Research Center.

Rodriguez, Victor M. (1999). Boricuas, African Americans, and Chicanos in the "Far West": Notes on the Puerto Rican Pro-Independence Movement in California, 1960s–1980s. In Rodolfo D. Torres & George Katsiaficas (Eds.), *Latino Social Movements: Historical and Theoretical Perspectives* (pp. 79–110). New York: Routledge.

Ruiz, Vicki L. (2000). Claiming Public Space at Work, Church, and Neighborhood. In Vicki L. Ruiz (Ed.), *Las Obreras: Chicana Politics of Work and Family* (pp. 13–39). Los Angeles: UCLA Chicano Studies Research Center.

Santiago-Valles, Kelvin, & Jiménez-Muñóz, Gladys M. (2004). Social Polarization and Colonized Labor: Puerto Ricans in the United States, 1945–2000. In David G. Gutiérrez (Ed.), *The Columbia History of Latinos in the United States Since 1960* (pp. 87–145). New York: Columbia University Press.

Stevens-Arroyo, Anthony. (2004). From Barrios to Barricades: Religion and Religiosity in Latino Life. In David G. Gutiérrez (Ed.) *The Columbia History of Latinos in the United States Since 1960* (pp. 303–354). New York: Columbia University Press.

Torres, Rodolfo D., & Katsiaficas, George. (1999). Introduction. In Rodolfo D. Torres & George Katsiaficas (Eds.), *Latino Social Movements: Historical and Theoretical Perspectives* (pp. 1–10). New York: Routledge.

Treviño, Roberto R. (2006). *The Church in the Barrio: Mexican American Ethno-Catholicism in Houston*. Chapel Hill: University of North Carolina Press.

Watanabe, Teresa. (2006, March 1). Immigrants Gain the Pulpit. *Los Angeles Times, pp.* A1.

Wells, Miriam J. (2000). Immigration and Unionization in the San Francisco Hotel Industry. In Ruth Milkman (Ed.), *Organizing Immigrants: The Challenge for Unions in Contemporary California* (pp. 109–129). Ithaca, NY: Cornell University Press.

Zlolniski, Christian. (2006). *Janitors, Street Vendors, and Activists: The Lives of Mexican Immigrants in Silicon Valley*. Berkeley: University of California Press.

CHAPTER 24

Unions and the Unionization of Latinas/os in the United States

Héctor L. Delgado

INTRODUCTION

For nearly a century, Latina/o workers knocked on organized labor's door only to be ignored. The first to be ignored were Latina/o farm workers repeatedly seeking organized labor's help to fight against unscrupulous employers and to improve working conditions even more severe than those revealed to the nation in *Harvest of Shame*, a 1960 exposé on migrant workers by Edward R. Murrow. The labor movement's neglect of these and nonagricultural Latina/o workers continued well into the second half of the 20th century; but today, after decades of decline, the labor movement is in trouble and, ironically, its hopes for revitalization hinge substantially on its ability to organize Latinas/os, the fastest growing segment of the U.S. workforce and population. Meanwhile, Latina/o workers' hope for a better future rests substantially on their ability to organize.

The literature on the labor movement is voluminous, but the history of Latina/o workers and unionization and accounts of organized labor's hostility toward these workers occupy relatively few pages in these volumes. The literature on Latinas/os and unionization, however, has grown considerably in the last 25 years, principally because of the expansion and strategic location of Latina/o workers in the population and workforce, their participation in union drives, and unions' growing reliance on these workers for their survival. This research has enhanced substantially our knowledge of a population neglected for too long by union organizers and scholars. With its emphasis on the organization of Mexican workers, however, this new literature has failed to capture adequately the heterogeneity and geographical dispersion of the Latina/o population and the participation of Central American and other Latinas/os in the labor force and the labor movement.

This chapter will focus on the participation of Latina/o workers in past and contemporary labor struggles and the role that Latina/o workers can, should, and are likely to play in the labor movement in the 21st century. The emphasis, because it is the emphasis in the literature, will be on Mexican workers in the West and Southwest and, to a lesser degree, Puerto Rican workers on the East Coast. However, one of the aims of this chapter is to call attention to other Latina/o groups in the labor movement and to underscore the need for future research on these groups and other regions of the country, including the South, long a part of the country with very low levels of unionization. This chapter will provide a review of important labor campaigns in which Latina/o workers, often immigrant workers, played a critical role. Latina/o workers' militancy revealed in this review belies stereotypes of the passive Latina/o and calls into question the claim by some in the labor movement that these workers were (and are) "unorganizable." The chapter also offers contemporary evidence of Latina/o workers' receptivity to unionization and the benefits of unionization for workers, including Latina/o workers, the group likely to benefit the most from a revitalized labor movement. Organized labor's woes are discussed, as is its future and the future of Latina/o workers. Finally, this chapter prescribes what organized labor needs to do to organize Latina/o workers, including recognizing the heterogeneity of this population and the implications of this heterogeneity for organization, and what scholars can do to enhance our understanding of the evolving relationship between organized labor and Latinas/os.

LATINA/O GROWTH, UNION DECLINE

Between 1990 and 2000, the Latina/o population in the United States grew by 61%, from 21.9 million to 35.2 million. During the same period, the total population of the United States grew by 13%. Labor force projections reveal that Latinas/os will make up 13.3% of the civilian labor force in 2010, compared to 5.7% in 1980, 8.5% in 1990, and 10.9% in 2000. During the same period of time, Whites' share of the labor force dropped from 81.9% to 73.1%, and by 2010 it will drop even further to 69.2% (Fullerton & Toosi, 2001). In some states, the numbers are especially striking. Latinas/os make up 17% of California's workforce, but 36% of service workers, 42% of factory operatives, and virtually half of laborers (Lichtenstein, 2002). Latinas/os are concentrated in jobs characterized by low wages, poor working conditions, and few health and other benefits and protections. Consequently, Latinas/os have been especially hurt by the growing inequality in the United States. In 2004, 2.5 million new jobs were created and Latinas/os accounted for more than 1 million of these jobs, but they were the only major group of workers to have experienced a 2-year decline in wages. Eighty-one percent of new jobs for foreign-born Latinas/os and 76% of new jobs for native-born Latinas/os required minimal formal education Pew Hispanic Center, 2006). Meanwhile, at the most inopportune time for Latina/o workers, unions have been hit hard by deindustrialization, globalization, and a sharp ideological turn to the right in the country.

The decline in union membership is well documented. In 2005, only 12.5% of wage and salary workers were members of a union. In the private sector, only 7.8% of the workforce was unionized, compared to 39% in 1958 (Bureau of Labor Statistics, 2006a). The membership doldrums continued despite the economic expansion of the 1990s and an administration in Washington DC friendly to labor. Another measure of organized labor's weakness is work stoppages, historically labor's most formidable weapon. Between 1947 and 1979 there was only 1 year with fewer than 200 work stoppages and only on 7 occasions was the number of workers involved lower than 1 million. Since 1995, the number of work stoppages has never exceeded 40 and the number of workers involved has not risen above 394,000. In 2005, there were 22 work stoppages involving 100,000 workers (Bureau of Labor Statistics, 2006b). Virtually disarmed, organized labor must now organize workers at a torrid pace. Despite a recent increase in the unionization rate of Latina/o workers, they are the ethnic group with the lowest rate at 10.4%, compared to 15.1%, 12.2%, and 11.2% for Blacks, Whites, and Asians, respectively (Bureau of Labor Statistics, 2006a). Their underrepresentation reflects principally unions' failure in the past to target them and their location in difficult-to-organize sectors of the economy. For most of the previous century, when unions attempted to organize them, they were receptive, but even when they did not, Latina/o workers formed their own organizations to demand higher wages and better working conditions. Nowhere was this more evident than in the Southwest.

MEXICAN WORKERS AND UNIONS IN THE SOUTHWEST

The enormous contribution of Mexican workers to the economic development of the Southwest in the first half of the 20th century, especially in agriculture, is indisputable. By 1929, the Southwest was supplying 40% of the nation's produce. McWilliams (1968) attributed much of this phenomenal increase to Mexican labor, writing, "In the growth of commercial fruit and vegetable production in the Southwest between 1900 and 1940, there is not a single crop in the production and harvesting of which Mexicans have not played a major role" (pp. 176–177). Their contributions in construction, the railroad industry, and other areas were equally impressive, especially when the conditions under which they labored are taken into account. One reason that they were attractive to employers was because they were believed to be passive and not likely to challenge the authority of their *patrones*. However, as employers soon learned, there were limits to what they were willing to endure.

Mexican workers organized, despite employers' efforts to prevent them from organizing and organized labor's failure to assist them. The American Federation of Labor (AFL) became increasingly concerned with Mexican immigrants' entry into nonagricultural industries and voted in their 1919 convention to lobby for more restrictive immigration legislation. Organized labor's concerns were not completely unfounded, because employers used immigrant workers to undercut native workers. However, instead of organizing them, unions shunned them. For a short time a decade earlier, the AFL had toyed with a strategy to organize migrant workers, partly in response to the Industrial Workers of the World's (IWW) interest in organizing migrant workers. By the 1919 convention, however, the AFL was out of the migrant-worker organizing business. Prompted principally by a desire to protect native White workers, the AFL considered organizing Mexican workers in the mid-to-late 1920s, but, again, with little zeal and success. The IWW was more successful, but it, too, never established itself as an effective and lasting organizational vehicle for agricultural workers.

Among the earliest examples of Mexican labor activism were joint activities by the Knights of Labor and *Las Gorras Blancas* (White Hats) in the 1880s and 1890s in New Mexico. *Las Gorras Blancas* was formed to protect communal lands against land companies and large landowners, but some of its members joined the Knights to protect workers' rights (Gómez-Quiñones, 1979, pp. 497–499). Another early example occurred in Oxnard in 1903, when 1200 Mexican and Japanese workers waged a successful strike to improve their wages and working conditions and to eliminate the contractor or middleman. When the AFL offered the union, the Sugar Beet and Farm Laborer's Union of Oxnard, a charter with the condition that the Japanese workers be excluded, the Mexican workers declined and unsuccessfully implored the AFL to grant the union a charter "under which we can unite all sugar beet and field laborers of Oxnard without regard to their color or race" (Foner, 1964, p. 277). That same year, Mexican lemon pickers and graders walked off the job in Santa Barbara, paralyzed production, and eventually won a 9-hour day and overtime from the Johnston Fruit Company (Acuña, 1988). In 1917, a strike of cantaloupe workers in Turlock, California resulted in the loss of carloads of fruit. In 1919, citrus workers went on strike in San Dimas, San Gabriel, Azusa, Monrovia, Duarte, Pomona, La Verne, and Ventura. Most of these strikes were broken easily by employers who enjoyed almost unbridled power and who often were assisted by local police serving as their private police force. Meanwhile, the AFL stood on the sidelines, forcing Mexican workers to form their own unions, usually small in size and with few resources.

One of the earliest "stable" organizations uniting Mexican farm workers was formed with the assistance of mutual aid societies and benefit associations. Local unions formed the *Confederación de Uniones Obreras Mexicanas* (CUOM), which at its zenith in 1928 enjoyed a membership of nearly 3,000 workers. However, by 1929, the number had dropped to only 300. One of its locals, *La Union de Trabajadores del Valle Imperial*, with the help of the Mexican consulate in Calexico, waged a strike against cantaloupe growers in the Imperial Valley in 1928. Local police broke the strike, but workers were still able to extract concessions from the growers (Jamieson, 1976, pp. 76–77). That same year, pea pickers in Monterey County and cotton pickers in Merced County went on strike. These and other worker actions did not escape the notice of Governor C. C. Young's Mexican Fact-Finding Committee in 1930. "That the Mexican immigrants are beginning to orient themselves in California is evidenced by the fact that they have begun to organize into unions for the purpose of improving living and working conditions in the land of their adoption" (Mexicans in California, 1930, p. 13).

Mexican railway workers in Los Angeles formed the *Union Federal Mexicana* and went on strike against the Pacific Electric Railway and the Los Angeles Railway in 1903, but the strike was broken when the company fired 68 union supporters and hired Japanese and Black replacement workers and when White railway workers reneged on their promise to walk out. Other labor actions followed in the ensuing years, but most failed as well. That same year, however, Los Angeles gas works workers, overwhelmingly Mexican, won concessions from their employer with the help of the IWW (Gómez-Quiñones, 1973, p. 28). Clearly, Mexican workers were willing to engage in militant labor actions, as evidenced by cement workers in Colton, California, who, in 1917, waged a strike against the Portland Cement Company, formed the *Trabajadores Unidos* union, and eventually won wage concessions, union recognition, and the reinstatement of workers fired during the campaign (Gómez-Quiñones, 1973, p. 35).

In southeastern Arizona, approximately 5,000 miners, two-thirds or more of them Mexican, walked out on the Arizona Copper Company, Shannon Copper Company, and Detroit Copper Company in 1915 and endured extreme hardships, including hunger, to secure federally mediated concessions from the mining companies (Foner, 1982; Kluger, 1970). A strike against Phelps-Dodge 2 years later proved less successful, despite the involvement of the International Union of Mine, Mill, and Smelter Workers (UMMSW) and the IWW. Mass deportations were employed to break the strike (Maciel, 1981, p. 135). Mexican workers' militancy was on display as well in the famous Ludlow strike against the Rockefeller-owned Colorado Fuel and Iron Company. The strike lasted nearly a year and cost the lives of 18 miners, at least half of them Mexican, when vigilantes set fire to the workers' makeshift camp. In some respects, these and other strikes set the stage for the agricultural strikes of the 1930s.

WORKER MILITANCY IN THE THIRTIES AND SIXTIES

Agricultural strikes in California during the 1930s seemed unlikely. There was an oversupply of labor, employer resistance was very strong, and the AFL demonstrated virtually no interest in organizing agricultural workers. Yet, during the thirties, agricultural workers launched some 180 strikes. In January 1930, Mexican and Filipino lettuce workers walked off their jobs in the Brawley area. because most of the workers were Mexican, the Mexican Mutual Aid Society of the Imperial Valley assumed leadership of the action, but quickly needed and received the help of Trade Union Unity League (TUUL). TUUL organizers formed a branch of the Agricultural Workers Industrial League (AWIL) and quietly began to organize. Growers played the "communist card" and deported strikers to end the strike. Mexican consuls, in fact, worked on more than one occasion with U.S. employers and authorities to undermine the militant unions and actions by Mexican workers (González, 1999). Nonetheless, Mexican workers were forcing growers to reconsider old assumptions regarding their tractability and docility. A relatively quiet period followed, but, in 1933, nearly 48,000 agricultural workers engaged in a series of strikes against growers.

The Cannery and Agricultural Workers Industrial Union (CAWIU) led most of the strikes during 1933. Twenty-one of the strikes resulted in gains for workers (Jamieson, 1976). One of the largest strikes was a berry pickers' strike in El Monte. Predominantly Mexican, workers were organized initially by the CAWIU, but the Mexican consulate intervened against the union, union organizers were arrested, and the sheriff prevented more CAWIU organizers from entering El Monte, rendering the union ineffective and forcing workers to form their own union, the *Confederación de Uniones Obreras Mexicanas* (CUOM). The strike, directed principally at Japanese growers, eventually involved over 5,000 workers, not only in the berry fields but also in onion and celery fields in Santa Monica and Culver City (Lopez, 1970). An agreement was reached a little over a month later among the strike committee, growers, Mexican and Japanese consuls, and representatives of the State Division of Labor Statistics and Law Enforcement. An even larger and more dramatic labor action took place in the San Joaquin Valley by cotton pickers.

The San Joaquin Valley's Cotton Pickers Strike began in the southern counties of Kern, King, and Tulare and threatened to spread to the northern San Joaquin Valley as the number of strikers, 75% or higher Mexican, rose to 12,000. The CAWIU trained workers with prior union experience as organizers. Employer resistance was intense. Vigilantism, the arrest of union leaders and organizers, the failure of relief agencies to provide relief to strikers, deportations, replacement workers, and evictions were employed to break the strike, but strikers held firm. A fact-finding committee appointed by the governor intervened and pressured growers and workers to accept a settlement. Many of the union activists were blacklisted, but the most intransigent of the growers had problems recruiting pickers (Jamieson, 1976). Hailed by the CAWIU as "the most important victory of workers that [had] ever taken place in the history of agricultural struggle," Daniel (1981, p. 219) observed that the claim was not without merit. The number of workers involved, the size of the wage increase, and the steadfastness of the strikers in the face of stiff employer resistance was significant. Formal recognition by employers and the establishment of hiring halls, however, were not achieved, and by the end of 1933, the CAWIU was all but dead. In the end, employers' repressive tactics and superior resources and the complicity of the state were too much for the workers and the CAWIU.

After the demise of the CAWIU, the *Confederación de Uniones de Campesinos y Obreros Mexicano del Estado de California* (CUCOM) became the most active farm workers' labor organization in California. Between 1935 and 1937, CUCOM organized several successful labor actions and succeeded in working with other ethnic groups. In January 1936, the Federation of Agricultural Workers Union of America (FAWUA), a federation of Mexican, Filipino, and other independent organizations, was formed, with the assistance of CUCOM. CUCOM's leadership and the leadership of other organizations recognized that they were too small to make major gains and decided to affiliate with a larger body. In July 1937, CUCOM affiliated with the United Cannery, Agricultural, Packing, and Allied Workers of America (UCAPAWA), a CIO affiliate. The UCAPAWA concentrated on cannery and pack-shed workers because they were not migratory, could "afford" a union, and were protected by the National Labor Relations Act (NLRA). Their support of agricultural workers was weak, and by 1940, they were no longer organizing in the fields.

In Los Angeles, Mexican garment workers, overwhelmingly women, began to organize themselves in the late 1920s. Emboldened by the National Industrial Act (NIRA) in 1933, legislation that protected a worker's right to unionize, the International Ladies' Garment Workers' Union (ILGWU) from its base in New York sent organizers to Los Angeles and was joined by the Needle Trades Industrial Workers' Union (NTIWU). Seven thousand workers walked off their jobs and, in the face of stiff employer resistance, persisted in their demands (Gómez-Quiñones, 1994). In the end, they failed, but their activism prompted ILGWU organizer Rose Pesotta (1944) to write in her book, *Bread Upon the Water*, that despite the fear of deportation among the Mexican strikers, "The spirit of the strikers was excellent. The Mexican girls and women, who were by far the majority, acted almost like seasoned unionists" (p. 40). The ILGWU took their campaigns to Texas, recording minor victories but ultimately changing working conditions in sweatshops.

Women's labor militancy was not confined to the garment industry. Women were active in the agricultural strikes of the 1930s, and in San Antonio, Texas, between 1933 and 1938, pecan shellers, many of them women, almost all Mexican, demonstrated their militancy by forming their own union, striking, and winning concessions from their bosses. Emma Tenayuca, a *Mexicana*, headed the strike committee. The UCAPAWA intervened in the campaign and brought in Luisa Moreno, Guatemalan by birth, to organize the workers. An effective labor organizer for many years, Moreno is perhaps best known for her role in the creation of *El Congreso del Pueblo de Habla Española*. A victim of the McCarthy era, she was deported in 1950, but not before (and probably because of) organizing cannery workers, principally Mexican women, in southern California, including food-processing workers in Los Angeles during World War II. Workers formed Local 3, the UCAPAWA's second largest affiliate in the country. According to the historian Vicki L. Ruiz (1998), Moreno encouraged alliances between plants and women to assume leadership positions (pp. 79–82). In 1943, Mexican women filled more than half of the 15 elected positions of the local. World War II was a watershed event for many subordinate groups in the country, and Latina/o workers were not the exception.

During World War II, the demand for immigrant labor increased dramatically and the Emergency Labor or Bracero Program was fashioned to meet the demand. A bilateral agreement between the executive branches of the Mexican and U.S. governments, the Bracero Program issued 4.6 million contracts between 1942 and 1964 to Mexican workers to work in the fields. The program undermined the unionization of agricultural workers, as *braceros* were used to break up organized work crews and strikes. The program virtually crippled the National Farm Labor Union (NFLU) and the Agricultural Workers Organizing Committee (AWOC). In October 1947, for example, the NFLU called for a strike against a DiGiorgio Fruit Corporation camp in Arvin and *braceros* walked out in support of the strike. However, under pressure by the sheriff and a representative of the U.S. Department of Agriculture, they retuned to work and eventually broke the strikers' backs (Galarza, 1964). The political climate in the 1930s, 1940s, and 1950s; the migratory nature of agricultural workers; determined and well-financed employer resistance; and the failure of organized labor to target the fields were not conducive to the organization of these workers. However, this started to change in the 1960s and 1970s.

In 1964, the Bracero Program finally ended, and in 1965, the Agricultural Workers Organizing Committee (AWOC) called for a strike against grape growers in the Delano area and was joined 8 days later by the National Farm Workers Association (NFWA). This time, farm workers were more successful. Farm workers received support from civil rights and other organizations, prominent politicians and activists, and unions. Led ably by Cesar Chavez and Dolores Huerta, they launched a grape boycott campaign that received wide media coverage and public support and forced growers to negotiate collective bargaining agreements with them. The political impact of the farm workers' victories was not limited to the fields. The impact was felt on college campuses where Chicana/o students demanded an increase in Chicana/o faculty and students and the creation of Chicano Studies programs. Communities demanded greater accountability from their elected officials and more Chicanos entered the political arena and even created their own parties and organizations. However, labor actions by Latina/o workers were not confined to the Southwest.

PUERTO RICAN WORKERS ON THE EAST COAST

On the other side of the country, Puerto Rican workers were organizing as well. Shortly following the colonization of Puerto Rico by the United States in 1898, Puerto Rican needle workers began to arrive in New York City. By 1920, Puerto Rican women were an important component of the needle trades, principally performing piecework out of their homes. However, by the 1950s, many of them had entered shops and consequently became members of the ILGWU, despite some early reluctance by the union to organize them. Although the women benefited from unionization, they encountered resistance within the union when they and their male counterparts attempted to get higher-paying jobs and to assume leadership positions in the union. In the late 1950s, Puerto Rican workers began to agitate within the union, accusing the leadership of negotiating sweetheart deals with employers. Unfortunately, the garment industry in New York had entered a period of decline during the late 1950s and 1960s, which, in turn, drove down wages and weakened the union (Ortiz, 1990).

Puerto Rican and Cuban migrants had been involved in unions since the turn of the century in other industries. Cigar makers organized in Florida and New York and formed the International Cigar Workers "*La Resistencia*" caucus. Puerto Ricans formed a number of organizations in New York City at the turn of the century to address a wide range of issues. Many of these organizations were social and cultural, but some were formed explicitly to address workplace issues, such as the *Union International de Tabaqueros* and *La Resistencia*, tobacco worker organizations. *La Alianza Obrera* was formed to promote syndicalist ideas (Sanchez Korrol, 1983). In his memoirs as an immigrant in New York City at the turn of the century, Bernardo Vega (1984) recalled the support "foreign" workers received from the Socialist Party, the Cigarmaker's Union, and the Seaman's Union. Other unions showed no interest or were too weak to do anything. Vega recalled "readings" in tobacco factories while *tabaqueros* (tobacco workers) worked. The readings ranged from current events to works of philosophical, political, or scientific interest to novels by writers such as Zola, Dumas, Hugo, and Tolstoy. Debates often ensued. "The institution of factory readings," Vega (1984) believed, "made the *tabaqueros* into the most enlightened sector of the working class" (p. 22). Labor migration to the United States from Puerto Rico trickled prior to World War II, but after the war, it became a strong and steady stream.

Operation Bootstrap, a program designed to industrialize the island, was introduced in Puerto Rico in the 1950s. The program accelerated the decline of agriculture on the island but never produced the number of jobs promised, principally because of the capital-intensive nature of the investment. The program and other factors contributed to increased labor migration to the fields and factories of the continental United States. Then, as today, Puerto Rican migrant workers performed the lowest-paying, least desirable work. During and subsequent to World War II, Puerto Ricans were active in labor unions, including the National Maritime and the Bakery and Confectionery Workers unions. Figueroa (1996) reported that in the post-WWII period, half of all Puerto Rican workers in the United States, concentrated principally in New York, were members of a union.

Puerto Ricans remained active in unions during the 1960s in New York, but a severe economic downturn during the 1970s depleted the number of manufacturing jobs in the city. Puerto Rican workers and unions were hit hard. Many of these jobs never returned, replaced by service sector jobs characterized by even lower wages and lower levels of unionization. During this time, the Young Lords Party, the Puerto Rican Socialist Party, and other leftist organizations began to train militant trade unionists and unions. These unions had short lives, but they managed to tie Puerto Rican workers more closely to other workers, including Black workers, principally in New York, and to the labor and liberation struggle on the island (Figueroa, 1996). Increasingly, Puerto Rican and other Latino workers entered the service sector as health care workers and, according to some estimates, comprised 25% of New York's health care workers by 2000 (Trumpbour & Bernard, 2002). Many became members of Local 1199 of the Service Employees International Union (SEIU). Led by Dennis Rivera, the local is one of the most active and strongest locals in the Northeast. Other unions have not fared as well. The Union of Needletrades, Industrial, and Textile Employees (UNITE) is a case in point.

Once garment workers were a force to be reckoned with, but garment unions have lost members steadily for decades. Bonacich and Appelbaum's (2000) succinct explanation for UNITE's decline applies as well to other unions in disrepair: "The dismantling of the welfare state, the rise of anti-labor conservative thinking (especially in the Republican Party, but also among centrist Democrats), the restructuring of the global economy, the hegemony of neo-liberalism, and a right-wing assault on the labor movement have taken their toll" (p. 264). Despite these impediments to unionization, organized labor shares some of the blame for failing to respond creatively and forcefully to a rapidly changing global work environment. In the late 1960s, the two major garment workers' unions combined had 800,000 members, but then they experienced a precipitous decline in membership. In an attempt to consolidate their power and stem the loss of members, the two unions merged as UNITE in 1995. In 1997, they reported a combined membership of only 300,000. Increasingly, UNITE began targeting nongarment industries to make up for lost membership in the garment industry. The organization of garment workers on either coast is virtually nonexistent today, but unions have enjoyed victories in other industries.

LATINA/O WORKERS IN THE SOUTH

For the past 20 years the organization of Latina/o workers has been taking place in the usual places such as Los Angeles and New York, but also in unlikely places. Latina/o workers are being organized as far north as Puget Sound, where the Carpenters' union organized hundreds of Latino construction workers. Even in cold climes, unions recognize that these workers are a permanent fixture in the labor force and have to be organized. As Eric Franklin, the organizing director of the Pacific Northwest District Council of Carpenters, observed, "There's no alternative but to organize them. It's a fact of life" (Carpenters Union, 1999). In North Carolina, chicken-processing plant workers, most of them Guatemalan immigrants, voted 238 to 183 to unionize, but they encountered both employer resistance and resentment by White and Black workers. The latter believed Guatemalan workers were receiving preferential treatment from the union and feared the influx of even more immigrant workers in the area. Consequently, the union received little support from these workers. North Carolina is also a right-to-work state. The employer, Case Farms, pulled out of the negotiations in April 1999 and shut down the plant (Fink & Dunn, 2000). The Case Farm campaign nonetheless illustrated Latina/o immigrant workers' determination to unionize, even under extremely adverse conditions, and it underscored the diversity and diffusion of the Latina/o workforce.

The Latina/o population in the South is growing rapidly; between 1990 and 2000, it grew by 200% on the low end and 400% on the high end, compared to a 58% increase in the country overall. The uneven increase of the Latina/o population in the South should not come as a surprise because the South added jobs at a faster rate than the rest of the country during the 1990s. Latino workers in the South tend to be predominantly male and foreign born, to have arrived recently, and to be single and young. Compared to other regions of the country, the number of Latinas/os in the South is relatively low, but the rate at which the Latina/o population is growing and jobs are being added, relative to the rest of the country, makes it a region organized labor has to target, despite unionization rates markedly below the national average. For example, in 2005, Arkansas sported a rate of 4.8%, Florida 5.4%, Georgia 5%, Mississippi 7.1%, North Carolina 2.9%, South Carolina 2.3%, Tennessee 5.4%, Virginia 4.8%, Louisiana 6.4%, and Alabama 10.2%, compared to 26.1% in New York (Bureau of Labor Statistics, 2006a). It is not likely that an increase in the Latina/o population in the South will change unionization prospects appreciably. Even under the best of circumstances, the South proved a tough nut for labor to crack; but unions, again, were partly to blame, for not targeting with sufficient zeal Black workers, despite the fact that they have the highest unionization rate of any group. Unfortunately, as the Case Farm campaign illustrates, there is now distrust of Latina/o immigrant workers among Black workers—a problem the labor movement has to address and to which I will return in the conclusion to this chapter. However, there is another issue confronting organizers: the heterogeneity of the Latina/o population.

LATINAS/OS: HETEROGENEOUS AND DISPERSED

Although Puerto Rican workers tend to be concentrated in the Northeast and Chicana/o and Mexican workers in the Southwest, these populations are much more dispersed nationally than at any other time in the country's history. The growing Latina/o population in the South reflects this phenomenon. In the Northeast, organizers are organizing not only Puerto Rican workers but, increasingly Cuban, Dominican, Mexican, and South American workers. In the textile mills of Passaic and Paterson, New Jersey, Edgar de Jesus, an organizer for UNITE, reported an increase in Colombian and Peruvian workers, who have brought with them a more militant style honed in their countries of origin (Ocasio, 1996). Latinas/os are not a homogenous group and differences in culture, including language, history, immigration experience, integration in the labor market, and geography, sometimes reveal themselves in organizing campaigns and internecine fights. Unions have to adjust to this heterogeneity and the adjustment sometimes means ameliorating ethnic tensions between Latina/o groups. There are labor advocacy groups like the Labor Council for Latin American Advancement (LCLAA), Latina/o caucuses in several AFL-CIO affiliates and Central Labor Councils, and Latina/o and immigrant workers associations and centers trying to reconcile differences among groups in order to forge a common labor agenda. Mexican/Mexican American workers constitute the largest segment of the Latina/o workforce, but since the early 1980s, the number of Central and South Americans in the workforce has been growing at the fastest pace. They and Cubans have the highest rate of participation in the labor force, followed by Mexicans. Puerto Ricans have the lowest rate and are more likely than other Latinas/os to be unemployed. Central and South Americans and Mexicans are much more likely than Cubans to work in low-skill occupations. Cubans are much more likely to be managers and professionals and, consequently, enjoy a higher standard of living. All of these and other factors bear on each group's response to unionization.

Mexican and Central and South American workers tend to be concentrated in high-growth areas like the West and Southeast and it is in these areas that unions have been most successful. Central American immigrants have proven to be especially strong union members and activists. The older industrial regions in the Northeast and Midwest are struggling economically and it is in these areas that Puerto Rican and Dominican workers are concentrated (Figueroa, 1996). Meanwhile, local unions blackballed Cuban workers in Miami's construction industry in the 1960s and 1970s. Some persisted and eventually made it into a union, but others simply formed their own companies by securing "character" loans. By 1979, Cubans owned over 50% of the major construction companies in Dade County and slowly displaced older, unionized firms. Between 1960 and 1980, unionized new construction dropped from 90% to 10%. A Carpenter's Union's organizer put it succinctly: "We paid dearly for not letting the Cubans in" (Portes & Stepick, 1993, p. 134).

RECENT CAMPAIGNS

Despite a litany of labor woes and defeats, organized labor has not thrown in the towel and it has been Latina/o workers who, time and time again, have kept it in the fight. Many, if not most, of labor's largest drives have involved Latina/o workers. SEIU has organized predominantly Mexican, Central American, and other Latina/o janitors in Los Angeles, San Francisco, Silicon Valley, Washington, DC, Hartford, Detroit, Chicago, and Milwaukee. The Laborers International Union of North America (LIUNA) organized asbestos workers, mostly Latinas/os and recent Polish immigrants, in New York City. UNITE has been organizing in light manufacturing, industrial laundries, and retail trades in numerous cities, including Fort Worth, where they organized over 1,000 workers, mostly Latina/o immigrant workers, in a window manufacturing plant. UNITE has established Garment Workers' Justice Centers in New York and Los Angeles to help immigrant and other workers with immigration and workplace issues. The United Farm Workers Union (UFW) won several victories in the 1990s, even if they have yet to recapture the glory of the 1960s and 1970s. The UFCW and Laborers have targeted poultry workers, mainly Guatemalan and Mexican immigrants, in the South, with some success.

Meanwhile, worker centers have been sprouting up in different parts of the country. These centers, typically easily accessible geographically to workers, provide nonunion workers with information on a wide range of labor and civil rights issues, help workers with grievances, tie workers into a broader social movement, and try to get workers to become more active politically. In some communities, worker centers serve as hiring halls for day laborers and thus cater principally to low-income and immigrant workers. The National Day Laborer Organizing

Network has linked many of these centers to one another. This is an alternative form of organizing and, clearly, these centers provide a valuable service to immigrant workers. Their impact on organized labor, however, is less clear, but they provide organized labor with an opportunity to explore new and creative ways of organizing workers.

In the southern California–Los Angeles area, where many of these workers' centers have sprouted, unions have enjoyed more success than in most other parts of the country. A strong county federation of labor, led ably by Miguel Contreras for 12 years before he passed away unexpectedly in May 2005, can take substantial credit for an increase in union membership and political influence in Los Angeles County. However, even prior to Contreras's stint as Executive Secretary-Treasurer of the federation, workers had been organizing. Examples include the Justice for Janitors campaign in 1990, the American Racing Equipment campaign in 1991, and a strike by drywall construction workers in 1992. Although these campaigns and others offered a measure of hope for a beleaguered movement, the amount of support that these campaigns required was sobering. This was Delgado's (1993) observation in his study of a successful union campaign by Mexican and Central American workers in a Los Angeles waterbed factory in the early 1980s. The union invested heavily in the campaign and won, but if every campaign requires the type of investment these campaigns required, unions will have to divert an even larger chunk of their funds to organizing. The one-third promised by Sweeney when he assumed the helm of the AFL-CIO in 1995 will not be enough. As an important postscript, the waterbed factory eventually moved to the South and the Carpenter's Union has seen its share of the residential drywall industry erode since 1992. Winning campaigns is insufficient. Unions must hold onto new members: a difficult task if organized labor's survival requires more of an emphasis on organizing and less on servicing existing members. However, unions and workers have little choice but to continue organizing. The benefits of unionization are too important, not only for union members but for the larger society as well.

THE BENEFITS OF UNIONIZATION

What are the benefits of unionization for workers and for the rest of society? Unionized workers are entitled to due process. If they are terminated or disciplined, they, as a rule, have the right, under their collective bargaining agreement or contract, to force their employer to show "just cause." They can negotiate their benefits and working conditions. Unionized workers enjoy higher wages, better health care and other benefits, and better working conditions than nonunion workers. The benefits are quantifiable and were summarized in a 2003 briefing paper by the Economic Policy Institute (Mishel & Walters, 2003). The data show that unions raise the wages of their members relative to nonunion members by 20%, and when benefits are added, the wages are raised by 28%. Union members are more likely to have paid leave, 18–28% more likely to have health insurance provided by the employer, and much more likely to have employer-provided pension plans. Furthermore, union members pay lower deductibles and retired union members are 24% more likely to have employer-paid health insurance. Unionized workers receive more vacation time and paid leave.

A revitalization of the labor movement, in which Latina/o workers must play a prominent role, will strengthen the position of workers across the board and especially low- and middle-wage workers. Unions have had another effect on the lives of workers and their families: their impact on public policy in the labor market and workplace. During the last century, a myriad of laws and regulations have been passed to protect workers. The labor movement played a critical role not only in the enactment of these laws and regulations but in their enforcement as well. Organized labor can take substantial credit for the enactment of the National Labor Relations, Social Security, Occupational Safety and Health, and Family Medical Leave acts and has been a strong advocate for the minimum wage, overtime pay, and health coverage for working people. "The research evidence clearly shows that the labor protections enjoyed by the entire U.S. workforce can be attributed in large part to unions" (Mishel & Walters, 2003). Furthermore, workers are more knowledgeable about their rights and, not coincidentally, these laws and regulations are much more likely to be enforced in unionized firms. Issues of concern to workers and the people who depend on them must be expressed and addressed for a democratic society to be truly democratic. If both major political parties continue to represent principally, if not exclusively, the interests of employers and corporations, the gap between the "haves" and "have nots" will continue to widen. A strong labor movement, preferably as part of a broader social movement, is essential and Latinas/os can contribute to and gain abundantly from such a movement.

THE FUTURE OF THE LABOR MOVEMENT AND LATINA/O WORKERS

However, the future of the labor movement does not rest solely on the ability of organized labor to organize Latina/o workers. Why has organized labor failed to turn the tide? Kate Bronfenbrenner (2001) distinguished between "building capacity for organizing," which the AFL-CIO has committed itself to do (with varying degrees of success), and "changing the structure, culture and strategy of the large, entrenched, democratic institutions that American unions have become," which organized labor has been slow to do. Impediments to organizing include stiff employer resistance; an employer-friendly political climate, packaged with weak and poorly enforced labor laws, and a global economy that pits workers against one another across regional and international borders. However, none of these factors are likely to disappear. What organized labor has failed to do is to consistently and aggressively mount comprehensive campaigns, infused with the necessary resources, for the long haul. Bronfenbrenner cautioned organized labor against focusing its efforts solely where its chances of success are greatest, namely in the hotel and health care sectors, to the exclusion of manufacturing, where, currently, it wins only a third of its campaigns. "If manufacturing is not organized, there will be nothing to stop the race to the bottom in wages, benefits and working conditions for all organized and unorganized workers in all industries" (Bronfenbrenner, 2001). The AFL-CIO's and labor movement's future, however, became more uncertain in 2005, with a major defection of unions from the federation.

In 2005, five unions, among them three of the largest, "seceded" from the federation. The SEIU, International Brotherhood of the Teamsters (IBT), and UFCW, alone, took over 5 million members with them in an attempt to revitalize the labor movement. The United Brotherhood of Carpenters and Joiners of America (UBC) had disaffiliated in 2001, and in January 2006 UFW joined these four unions, LIUNA, and the Union of Needle and Industrial Textile Employees–Hotel Employees and Restaurant Employees (UNITE-HERE) to form a new coalition: Change to Win (CTW) (Reddy, 2005). The SEIU, especially, had become frustrated with the AFL-CIO leadership and other union affiliate's inability, if not reluctance, to organize new workers. The break was not simply from the AFL-CIO but also from the old industrial models of the past. The impact of this new federation on the health of organized labor is uncertain, but what *is* certain is that the road to recovery for the labor movement will be a long and difficult one.

The prognosis for organized labor's recovery and the economic health of working-class people, and workers of color in particular, is not good. Inequality and the power of multinationals (and the two are not unrelated) continue to grow. Consequently, many union and community activists are calling more loudly than ever for the creation of a broader social justice movement that challenges corporate power head on, with organized labor and workers playing an integral part. This will require unions to work with community groups to address not only workplace issues but other issues as well. It will require difficult collaboration between labor groups across borders. However, first it will require unions in the United States to collaborate (i.e., to act, collectively, as a movement). Collaboration is possible. A case in point is the Stamford Organizing Project, in which several unions came together to organize collectively in a relatively rare multiunion, community-based campaign involving several racial and ethnic groups. From conversations with workers, the project identified housing as the most pressing issue in workers' lives outside of the workplace. The project worked with the workers, clergy, and local and state politicians to resolve some of these issues. This facilitated organizing and placed organized labor in the middle of where it needs to be if it ever hopes to recapture lost ground: workers' communities. Workplace and community issues are not separate sets of issues, because, invariably, one bears on the other. Whether Stamford can be replicated in other cities is an open question, but to the chagrin of some labor activists, it is one that few individuals in the labor movement are attempting to answer.

In a number of cities, Los Angeles among them, a growing number of workers, immigrant workers mainly, live in working-class communities near where they work. This is an advantage labor once had, but lost, and now it has it again in a number of cities. The Los Angeles Manufacturing Action Program (LAMAP) attempted to build a community-based, multiunion campaign to organize workers in the largest manufacturing sector in the country, but it folded when it failed to get the support of the AFL-CIO and several unions (Delgado, 2000). The project failed as well to target Black workers as vigorously as it did Latina/o workers. In Boston in the early 1990s, curtain factory workers walked out and received considerable support from a number of unions and organizations. In this case and several others, including the drywaller's and Justice for Janitor campaigns, Clawson (2003) observed that ethnic and community solidarity was essential. In Los Angeles, for example, several unions worked with the Los Angeles Alliance for a New Economy (LAANE), clergy, academics, and community organizations on a number of issues, including a living-wage ordinance. There are other examples in other cities, including community support. Local 2 of the Hotel Employees and Restaurant Employees union (HERE) solicited and received in its protracted Park 55 Hotel campaign in San Francisco (Wells, 2000). What organized labor must avoid are one-night stands. Instead, it needs to establish long-term relationships with the communities in which people work and live. However, this takes resources that labor might not possess. Meanwhile, Latina/o labor activists, both within and outside of organized labor, are not interested in simply repairing the house of labor. They want to rebuild it and they want to play an integral part in the design of a new structure responsive to the needs of people of color and women. What this means is that power in the movement must be shared. The leadership of the AFL-CIO, CTW, and unions must reflect the ethnic and gender makeup of the workforce and member unions. This will not solve labor's problems, but it is a necessary first step.

CONCLUSION

A number of economic, political, and social factors for over a century have affected the "organizability" of Latina/o workers. The first of these factors is unions' commitment to organize these workers, immigrant or native, women as well as men. For much of the 20th century, organized labor demonstrated more reluctance than commitment. For the past 25 years, however, unions have had to open their doors to Latina/o workers. Now they have to be given access to the entire house of labor, including the rooms where important decisions are made. Most unions have already recognized the importance of hiring Latina/o organizers and slowly are recognizing the heterogeneity of Latina/o workers and the need to hire not only Mexican and Puerto Rican organizers but Central and South American organizers as well. Women, Latina and non-Latinas, have had to fight against the sexist practices and attitudes not only of union officials but of their male counterparts in the rank and file as well. Women have proven time and time again that their commitment to unionism is equal to that of the men and some have become important leaders in the movement in their own right, among them Maria Elena Durazo, now the Executive Secretary-Treasurer of the L.A. County Federation of Labor, and Linda Chavez Thompson, AFL-CIO Executive Vice-President.

A second factor is the stability of these workers' communities—a factor that made the organization of migrant agricultural workers difficult. Today, only a very small percentage of Latinas/os are agricultural workers and most are rooted in stable communities. A third variable is the location of Latina/o workers in the labor market. They tend to be located in sectors of the economy where organization historically has not been easy, yet, a disproportionate number of the victories enjoyed by organized labor in the past 20 years have involved Latina/o, principally immigrant, workers. A fourth factor is globalization. The ability of manufacturing forms to exploit less expensive labor in other markets explains in part why unions in the United States have been more successful organizing in the service sector than in manufacturing in the last 10–20 years.

Today, in fact, manufacturing workers, the lifeblood of the labor movement historically, are no more likely to be unionized than the average worker. Organized labor and other progressive organizations have the political task of stemming and eventually reversing the power of corporations. This requires a broader social movement, of which organized labor can and should be an integral part. Environmental organizations and labor unions (and other groups) came together in Seattle to protest against the World Trade Organization (WTO). This type of collaboration has to be nurtured and sustained.

A fifth variable is the role of the state. Immigration and labor laws and the enforcement (or nonenforcement) of these laws have had and will continue to have an impact not only on the unionization of Latina/o workers but workers generally. This continues to be a headache for the labor movement and a major source of its problems. However, again, organized labor has to work with other organizations and to organize *all* workers if it hopes to win. A sixth and related variable is employer resistance. Weak laws protecting workers, lax enforcement, and a political climate hostile to workers and unionization all invite stronger employer resistance. However, although employer resistance is an important variable, so is workers' determination to organize, and Latina/o workers in the United States have exhibited this determination for over a century.

Whereas the prognosis for organized labor and working people in the United States generally tend to be poor to fair, Latina/o workers have little choice but to organize and organized labor has little choice but to organize them and, of equal importance, to allow them to sit at the table where the future of the labor movement is planned. As alluded to earlier, making the task more difficult is a measure of distrust between Black and Latina/o immigrant workers and, on occasion, even between different Latina/o groups. Many Blacks, in places like Los Angeles, accuse Latina/o immigrants of taking their jobs by depressing wages and working conditions. There was a time in Los Angeles, for example, when African Americans held many of the janitorial jobs. The jury is still out on the question, but in her recent book on labor in Los Angeles, Ruth

Milkman (2006) argued that "deunionization" and, consequently, a decline in wages, benefits, and job security in janitorial and other services predated the heavy influx of immigrant workers. Whatever the answer is, it is a problem that labor and Black and Latina/o leaders have to solve. Milkman is also one of several leading labor scholars who believe that labor's demise is exaggerated. In *L.A. Story: Immigrant Workers and the Future of the U.S. Labor Movement*, Milkman (2006) provides a superb analysis of labor's revitalization in southern California and suggests that it portends good things for the rest of the country. Clawson (2003) is equally hopeful and both he and Milkman underscore the pivotal role Latina/o immigrant workers have played in some of the most important campaigns in the last 20 years and the role they must play for labor to recapture lost ground in the future.

Labor and Latina/o Studies scholars have their work cut out for them as well, because, despite the great deal of work that has been done in the last 20–25 years, there is a great deal left to be done. The Latina/o or Hispanic population is indeed a heterogeneous one by almost any measure. It is a population made up of different groups, each with its own history, immigrant experiences, and customs. Within each group, there are generational, class, gender, and ideological differences. Each of these has implications for unionization. The pan-ethnic designation "Latina/o" is useful, but at the same time it conceals too much and it is the task of scholars to reveal what is unique about Mexicans, Puerto Ricans, Cubans, Salvadorans, Guatemalans, Dominicans, Colombians, and other Latina/o groups—in this case, each group's unique response to and participation in the labor movement and labor market. As these groups grow in size and heterogeneity, as they become more dispersed geographically, and as the movement of labor and capital across borders continues relatively unabated, the task of making sense of all this becomes increasingly harder *and*, for both theoretical and practical reasons, necessary.

REFERENCES

Acuña, Rodolfo. (1988). *Occupied America: A History of Chicanos*. New York: Harper and Row.

Bonacich, Edna, & Appelbaum, Richard. (2000). *Behind the Label: Inequality in the Los Angeles Apparel Industry*. Berkeley: University of California Press.

Bronfenbrenner, Kate. (2001, September 3). Changing to Organize. *The Nation*. Retrieved October 15, 2006, from http://www.thenation.com/doc/ 20010903/bronfenbrenner

Bureau of Labor Statistics, U.S. Department of Labor. (2006a). *Union Membership (Annual)*. Retrieved October 15, 2006, from http://stats.bls. gov/news.release/ union2.toc.htm

Bureau of Labor Statistics, U.S. Department of Labor. (2006b). *Work Stoppages Involving 1,000 or More Workers, 1947–2005*. Retrieved October 15, 2006, from http://www.bls.gov/news. release/wkstp.t01.htm

Carpenters Union Organizes Hispanic Workers. (1999, July 15). *Seattle Daily Journal*, pp.? Retrieved October 14, 2006, from http://www.djc.com/news/ const/10055761.html

Clawson, Dan. (2003). *The Next Upsurge: Labor and the New Social Movements*. Ithaca, NY: Cornell University Press.

Daniel, Cletus E. (1981). *Bitter Harvest: A History of California Farmworkers, 1870–1941*. Ithaca, NY: Cornell University Press.

Delgado, Hector L. (1993). *New Immigrants, Old Unions: Organizing Undocumented Workers in Los Angeles*. Philadelphia: Temple University Press.

Delgado, Hector L. (2000). The Los Angeles Manufacturing Action Project: An Opportunity Squandered? In Ruth Milkman (Ed.), *Organizing Immigrants: The Challenge for Unions in Contemporary California* (pp. 225–238). Ithaca, NY: Cornell University Press.

Figueroa, Hector. (1996, November/December). *Puerto Rican Workers: A Profile*. (NACLA Report on the Americas). New York: NACLA.

Fink, Leon, & Dunn, Alvis. (2000). The Maya of Morganton: Exploring Worker Identity. In James Loucky & Marilyn M. Moors (Eds.), *The Maya Diaspora: Guatemalan Roots, New American Lives* (pp. 175–196). Philadelphia: Temple University Press.

Foner, Philip S. (1964). *History of the Labor Movement in the United States. Vol. III. The Policies and Practices of the Mexican Federation of Labor, 1900–1909*. New York: International Publishers.

Foner, Philip S. (1982). *History of the Labor Movement in the United States. Vol. VI. On the Eve of America's Entrance into World War I, 1915–1916*. New York: International Publishers.

Fullerton, Howard N., Jr., & Toosi, Mitra. (2001, November). Labor Force Projections to 2010: Steady Growth and Changing Composition. *Monthly Review Press, 124*, 21–38.

Galarza, Ernesto. (1964). *Merchants of Labor: The Mexican Bracero Story*. San Jose, CA: Rosicrucian Press.

Gómez-Quiñones, Juan. (1973). The First Steps: Chicano Labor Conflict and Organizing 1900–1920. *Aztlan, 3*(1), 13–49.

Gómez-Quiñones, Juan. (1994). *Mexican American Labor: 1790–1990*. Albuquerque: University of New Mexico Press.

González, Gilbert G. (1999). *Mexican Consuls and Labor Organizing: Imperial Politics in the American Southwest*. Austin: University of Texas Press.

Jamieson, Stuart. (1976). *Labor Unionism in American Agriculture*. New York: Arno Press.

Kluger, James R. (1970). *The Clifton-Morenci Strike: Labor Difficulty in Arizona, 1915–1916*. Tucson: The University of Arizona Press.

Lichtenstein, Nelson. (2002). *State of the Union: A Century of American Labor*. Princeton: Princeton University Press.

Lopez, Ronald W. (1970). El Monte Berry Strike of 1933. *Aztlan, 1*(1), 101–114.

Maciel, David. (1981). Luchas Laborales y Conflictos de Clase de los Trabajadores Mexicanos en los Estados Unidos, 1900–1930. In Juan Gómez-Quiñones & David Maciel (Eds.), *La Clase Obrera en la Historia de México: Al Norte del Río Bravo (pasado lejano) (1600–1930)* (pp. 89–217). México, D.F.: Siglo Veintiuno Editores.

McWilliams, Carey. (1968). *North from Mexico: The Spanish-speaking People of the United Sates*. New York: Greenwood Press.

Mexicans in California. (1930, October). Report of Governor C.C. Young's Mexican Fact-Finding Committee, San Francisco.

Milkman, Ruth. (2006). *L.A. Story: Immigrant Workers and the Future of the U.S. Labor Movement*. New York: Russell Sage Foundation.

Mishel, Lawrence, & Walters, Matthew. (2003, August). *How Unions Help All Workers* (Briefing Paper 143). Washington, D.C.: Economic Policy Institute. Retrieved October 7, 2006, from http://www.epi.org

Ocasio, Linda. (1996, November/December). Portrait of an Organizer: Edgar de Jesus. *NACLA Report on the Americas, 30*(3). Retrieved May 29. 2006, from http:www.nacla.org/art_display_printable.php?art=1805

Ortiz, Altagracia. (1990). Puerto Rican Workers in the Garment Industry of New York City, 1920–1960. In Robert Asher & Charles Stephenson (Eds.), *Labor Divided: Race and Ethnicity in United States Labor Struggles 1835–1960* (pp. 105–125). Albany: State University of New York Press.

Pesotta, Rose. (1944). *Bread Upon the Waters*. New York: Dodd, Mead & Company.

Pew Hispanic Center. (2006, May 2). Hispanics Gaining Jobs But Suffering Worse Wage Losses in U.S. Labor Force.. (Press release).. Pew Hispanic Center, Washington, DC.

Portes, Alejandro, & Stepick, Alex. (1993). *City on the Edge: The Transformation of Miami*. Berkeley: University of California Press.

Reddy, Raahi. (2005, Winter). Labor Pains. *Colorlines Magazine: Race, Action, Culture*. Retrieved October 8, 2006, from http:// findarticles.com/p/articles/mi_m0KAY/is 48/ai_n1596941

Ruiz, Vicki L. (1998). *From out of the Shadows: Mexican Women in Twentieth-Century America*. New York: Oxford University Press.

Sánchez Korrol, Virginia E. (1983). *From Colonia to Community: The History of Puerto Ricans in New York City, 1917–1948*. Westport, CT: Greenwood Press.

Trumpbour, John, & Bernard, Elaine. (2002). Unions and Latinos: Mutual Transformation. In Marcelo M. Suarez-Orozco & Mariela M. Paez (Eds.), *Latinos: Remaking America* (pp. 126–145). Berkeley: University of California Press.

Vega, Barnardo. (1984). *Memoirs of Bernardo Vega: A Contribution to the History of the Puerto Rican Community in New York*. (Edited by César Andreu Iglesias). New York: Monthly Review Press.

Wells, Miriam J. (2000). Immigration and Unionization in the San Francisco Hotel Industry. In Ruth Milkman (Ed.), *Organizing Immigrants: The Challenge for Unions in Contemporary California* (pp. 109–129). Ithaca, NY: Cornell University Press.

Index

Printed in the United States of America.